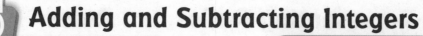

**MODULE 5** Adding and Subtracting Integers

**TEKS**

**MODULE 6** Multiplying and Dividing Integers

**TEKS**

# UNIT 3 Proportionality: Ratios and Rates

## MODULE 7 Representing Ratios and Rates

**TEKS**

## MODULE 8 Applying Ratios and Rates

**TEKS**

# MODULE 9 Percents

Real-World Video . . . . . . . 231
Are You Ready? . . . . . . . . 232
Reading Start-Up . . . . . . . 233
Unpacking the TEKS . . . . . . 234

## MODULE 10   Generating Equivalent Numerical Expressions

TEKS

## MODULE 11   Generating Equivalent Algebraic Expressions

TEKS

# MODULE 12 Equations and Relationships

**TEKS**

# MODULE 13 Inequalities and Relationships

**TEKS**

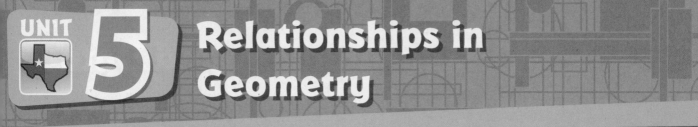

# UNIT 5 Relationships in Geometry

## MODULE 15 Angles, Triangles, and Equations

## MODULE 16 Area and Volume Equations

# UNIT 6 Measurement and Data

## MODULE 17 Displaying, Analyzing, and Summarizing Data

**TEKS**

# UNIT 7  Personal Financial Literacy

## MODULE 18  Becoming a Knowledgeable Consumer and Investor

TEKS

# Texas Essential Knowledge and Skills for Mathematics

## Correlation for HMH Texas Go Math Grade 6

| Standard | Descriptor | Citations |
|---|---|---|
| 6.1 Mathematical process standards. The student uses mathematical processes to acquire and demonstrate mathematical understanding. The student is expected to: | | *The process standards are integrated throughout the book. See, for example, the citations below.* |
| 6.1.A | apply mathematics to problems arising in everyday life, society, and the workplace; | SE: 20–21, 69–72, 81–84, 159–162, 181–184, 224–226 |
| 6.1.B | use a problem-solving model that incorporates analyzing given information, formulating a plan or strategy, determining a solution, justifying the solution, and evaluating the problem-solving process and the reasonableness of the solution; | SE: 105–108, 136, 363–364, 395–396, 437–438, 461–462 |
| 6.1.C | select tools, including real objects, manipulatives, paper and pencil, and technology as appropriate, and techniques, including mental math, estimation, and number sense as appropriate, to solve problems; | SE: 13–16, 63–66, 93–94, 117–120, 281–284, 335, 424, 427 |
| 6.1.D | communicate mathematical ideas, reasoning, and their implications using multiple representations, including symbols, diagrams, graphs, and language as appropriate; | SE: 7–10, 37–38, 75, 193–196, 211–214, 241–244 |
| 6.1.E | create and use representations to organize, record, and communicate mathematical ideas; | SE: 99–102, 129–132, 147–151, 205–208, 235–238, 275–278 |
| 6.1.F | analyze mathematical relationships to connect and communicate mathematical ideas; and | SE: 153–154, 217–220, 367, 423–425 |
| 6.1.G | display, explain, and justify mathematical ideas and arguments using precise mathematical language in written or oral communication. | SE: 31–34, 187–190, 302, 429, 447, 465 |

| Standard | Descriptor | Taught | Reinforced |
|---|---|---|---|
| 6.2 Number and operations. The student applies mathematical process standards to represent and use rational numbers in a variety of forms. The student is expected to: | | | |
| 6.2.A | classify whole numbers, integers, and rational numbers using a visual representation such as a Venn diagram to describe relationships between sets of numbers; | SE: 32–34 | SE: 35–36, 49–50, 52–53, 55–56 |
| 6.2.B | identify a number, its opposite, and its absolute value; | SE: 7–10, 19–22, 37–40 | SE: 11–12, 23–24, 25–26, 41–42, 49–50, 51–52, 53–54, 55–56, 173 |
| 6.2.C | locate, compare, and order integers and rational numbers using a number line; | SE: 13–16 | SE: 17–18, 25–26, 51–52, 55–56 |

| Standard | Descriptor | Taught | Reinforced |
|---|---|---|---|
| 6.2.D | order a set of rational numbers arising from mathematical and real-world contexts; and | SE: 43–46 | SE: 47–48, 49–50, 53, 55–56 |
| 6.2.E | extend representations for division to include fraction notation such as $\frac{a}{b}$ represents the same number as $a \div b$ where $b \neq 0$. | SE: 31–32, 34 | SE: 35–36, 49–50, 55–56 |

**6.3 Number and operations. The student applies mathematical process standards to represent addition, subtraction, multiplication, and division while solving problems and justifying solutions. The student is expected to:**

| Standard | Descriptor | Taught | Reinforced |
|---|---|---|---|
| 6.3.A | recognize that dividing by a rational number and multiplying by its reciprocal result in equivalent values; | SE: 76–78, 82–84 | SE: 79–80, 85–86, 87–88, 167–168, 173–174 |
| 6.3.B | determine, with and without computation, whether a quantity is increased or decreased when multiplied by a fraction, including values greater than or less than one; | SE: 63–66, 69, 71–72 | SE: 73, 88, 173 |
| 6.3.C | represent integer operations with concrete models and connect the actions with the models to standardized algorithms; | SE: 117–118, 120, 123–126, 129–132, 135, 147–148, 153 | SE: 121, 142, 151 |
| 6.3.D | add, subtract, multiply, and divide integers fluently; and | SE: 119–120, 125–126, 131–132, 135–138, 149–150, 154–156, 159–162 | SE: 121–122, 127–128, 133–134, 139–142, 151–152, 157–158, 163–166, 169–171, 173–174 |
| 6.3.E | multiply and divide positive rational numbers fluently. | SE: 63–66, 69–72, 75–78, 81–84, 93–96, 99–102, 105–108 | SE: 67–68, 73–74, 79–80, 85–86, 87–88, 97–98, 103–104, 109–110, 111–112, 167–169, 173–174 |

**6.4 Proportionality. The student applies mathematical process standards to develop an understanding of proportional relationships in problem situations. The student is expected to:**

| Standard | Descriptor | Taught | Reinforced |
|---|---|---|---|
| 6.4.A | compare two rules verbally, numerically, graphically, and symbolically in the form of $y = ax$ or $y = x + a$ in order to differentiate between additive and multiplicative relationships; | SE: 205–208 | SE: 209–210, 229–230 |
| 6.4.B | apply qualitative and quantitative reasoning to solve prediction and comparison of real-world problems involving ratios and rates; | SE: 193–196 | SE: 197, 199–200, 257 |
| 6.4.C | give examples of ratios as multiplicative comparisons of two quantities describing the same attribute; | SE: 181–184 | SE: 185–186, 199–200, 261 |

| Standard | Descriptor | Taught | Reinforced |
|---|---|---|---|
| 6.4.D | give examples of rates as the comparison by division of two quantities having different attributes, including rates as quotients; | SE: 187–190 | SE: 191–192, 199–200 |
| 6.4.E | represent ratios and percents with concrete models, fractions, and decimals; | SE: 181, 184, 235–238, 242, 244 | SE: 239–240, 255–256, 259, 261 |
| 6.4.F | represent benchmark fractions and percents such as 1%, 10%, 25%, 33 1/3%, and multiples of these values using 10 by 10 grids, strip diagrams, number lines, and numbers; | SE: 236–238, 242, 244 | SE: 239–240, 255–256 |
| 6.4.G | generate equivalent forms of fractions, decimals, and percents using real-world problems, including problems that involve money; and | SE: 241–244, 249 | SE: 245–246, 253–254, 255–256, 259–260 |
| 6.4.H | convert units within a measurement system, including the use of proportions and unit rates. | SE: 223–226 | SE: 227–228, 229–230, 261 |

**6.5 Proportionality. The student applies mathematical process standards to solve problems involving proportional relationships. The student is expected to:**

| Standard | Descriptor | Taught | Reinforced |
|---|---|---|---|
| 6.5.A | represent mathematical and real-world problems involving ratios and rates using scale factors, tables, graphs, and proportions; | SE: 211–214, 217–220 | SE: 215–216, 221–222, 229–230, 257–259, 261 |
| 6.5.B | solve real-world problems to find the whole given a part and the percent, to find the part given the whole and the percent, and to find the percent given the part and the whole, including the use of concrete and pictorial models; and | SE: 247–252 | SE: 252, 253–254, 255–256 |
| 6.5.C | use equivalent fractions, decimals, and percents to show equal parts of the same whole. | SE: 241–244 | SE: 245–246, 255–256, 259 |

**6.6 Expressions, equations, and relationships. The student applies mathematical process standards to use multiple representations to describe algebraic relationships. The student is expected to:**

| Standard | Descriptor | Taught | Reinforced |
|---|---|---|---|
| 6.6.A | identify independent and dependent quantities from tables and graphs; | SE: 385–390, 399–400 | SE: 391–392, 403–404, 405, 414–415, 418 |
| 6.6.B | write an equation that represents the relationship between independent and dependent quantities from a table; and | SE: 393–396, 400 | SE: 397–398, 405–406, 415 |
| 6.6.C | represent a given situation using verbal descriptions, tables, graphs, and equations in the form $y = kx$ or $y = x + b$. | SE: 385–390, 393–396, 399–402 | SE: 391–392, 397–398, 403–404, 405–406, 414–415, 417 |

**6.7 Expressions, equations, and relationships. The student applies mathematical process standards to develop concepts of expressions and equations. The student is expected to:**

| Standard | Descriptor | Taught | Reinforced |
|---|---|---|---|
| 6.7.A | generate equivalent numerical expressions using order of operations, including whole number exponents and prime factorization; | SE: 269–272, 275–278, 281–284, 301–304 | SE: 273–274, 279–280, 285–288, 305–306, 315–316, 409–411, 417 |

| Standard | Descriptor | Taught | Reinforced |
|----------|-----------|--------|------------|
| 6.7.B | distinguish between expressions and equations verbally, numerically, and algebraically; | SE: 321–323 | SE: 325–326, 344 |
| 6.7.C | determine if two expressions are equivalent using concrete models, pictorial models, and algebraic representations; and | SE: 293–297, 307–308, 310, 312 | SE: 298–300, 313–314, 315–316, 409–411, 417 |
| 6.7.D | generate equivalent expressions using the properties of operations: inverse, identity, commutative, associative, and distributive properties. | SE: 309–312 | SE: 313–314, 315–316, 409–411, 417 |

**6.8  Expressions, equations, and relationships. The student applies mathematical process standards to use geometry to represent relationships and solve problems. The student is expected to:**

| Standard | Descriptor | Taught | Reinforced |
|----------|-----------|--------|------------|
| 6.8.A | extend previous knowledge of triangles and their properties to include the sum of angles of a triangle, the relationship between the lengths of sides and measures of angles in a triangle, and determining when three lengths form a triangle; | SE: 423–426, 429–432, 435–438 | SE: 427–429, 433–434, 439–440, 441–442, 475–476, 479–480 |
| 6.8.B | model area formulas for parallelograms, trapezoids, and triangles by decomposing and rearranging parts of these shapes; | SE: 447–449, 453–454 | SE: 451–452, 456, 457–458 |
| 6.8.C | write equations that represent problems related to the area of rectangles, parallelograms, trapezoids, and triangles and volume of right rectangular prisms where dimensions are positive rational numbers; and | SE: 459–462 | SE: 463–464, 471–472, 476–477, 479–480 |
| 6.8.D | determine solutions for problems involving the area of rectangles, parallelograms, trapezoids, and triangles and volume of right rectangular prisms where dimensions are positive rational numbers. | SE: 448–450, 454–456, 459–462 | SE: 451–452, 457–458, 463–464, 471–472, 476–477, 479–480 |

**6.9  Expressions, equations, and relationships. The student applies mathematical process standards to use equations and inequalities to represent situations. The student is expected to:**

| Standard | Descriptor | Taught | Reinforced |
|----------|-----------|--------|------------|
| 6.9.A | write one-variable, one-step equations and inequalities to represent constraints or conditions within problems; | SE: 322–324, 349, 351–352 | SE: 325–326, 343–344, 353–354, 373–374, 412,417 |
| 6.9.B | represent solutions for one-variable, one-step equations and inequalities on number lines; and | SE: 328–329, 332, 336–337, 340, 349–352, 355–358, 361–364, 368–370 | SE: 344, 353–354, 359, 365, 371, 413, 417 |
| 6.9.C | write corresponding real-world problems given one-variable, one-step equations or inequalities. | SE: 331–332, 339, 357–358, 361, 364 | SE: 333, 341–342, 366, 414 |

| Standard | Descriptor | Taught | Reinforced |
|---|---|---|---|
| **6.10 Expressions, equations, and relationships. The student applies mathematical process standards to use equations and inequalities to solve problems. The student is expected to:** | | | |
| 6.10.A | model and solve one-variable, one-step equations and inequalities that represent problems, including geometric concepts; and | SE: 327–332, 335–340, 355, 357–358, 361, 363–364, 367, 369–370 | SE: 333–334, 341–344, 359–360, 365–366, 371–372, 373–374, 412–414, 417 |
| 6.10.B | determine if the given value(s) make(s) one-variable, one-step equations or inequalities true. | SE: 321–324, 350–352, 355–358, 362–363, 368–369 | SE: 325–326, 343–344, 353, 359–360, 365–366, 372, 373–374, 411–412, 417 |
| **6.11 Measurement and data. The student applies mathematical process standards to use coordinate geometry to identify locations on a plane. The student is expected to:** | | | |
| 6.11 | graph points in all four quadrants using ordered pairs of rational numbers. | SE: 379–382 | SE: 383–384, 405–406, 414–415, 418 |
| **6.12 Measurement and data. The student applies mathematical process standards to use numerical or graphical representations to analyze problems. The student is expected to:** | | | |
| 6.12.A | represent numeric data graphically, including dot plots, stem-and-leaf plots, histograms, and box plots; | SE: 491–494, 498–501, 505–508 | SE: 495–496, 502–504, 509–510, 517–518, 521–524 |
| 6.12.B | use the graphical representation of numeric data to describe the center, spread, and shape of the data distribution; | SE: 492–494, 500–501, 505–508 | SE: 495–496, 502–504, 509–510, 517–518, 521–524 |
| 6.12.C | summarize numeric data with numerical summaries, including the mean and median (measures of center) and the range and interquartile range (IQR) (measures of spread), and use these summaries to describe the center, spread, and shape of the data distribution; and | SE: 485–488, 491–494 | SE: 489–490, 495–496, 517–518, 521–524 |
| 6.12.D | summarize categorical data with numerical and graphical summaries, including the mode, the percent of values in each category (relative frequency table), and the percent bar graph, and use these summaries to describe the data distribution. | SE: 511–514 | SE: 515–516, 517–518, 521–524 |

| Standard | Descriptor | Taught | Reinforced |
|---|---|---|---|
| **6.13** | **Measurement and data. The student applies mathematical process standards to use numerical or graphical representations to solve problems. The student is expected to:** | | |
| 6.13.A | interpret numeric data summarized in dot plots, stem-and-leaf plots, histograms, and box plots; and | SE: 493, 498, 501, 505–508 | SE: 495, 502–504, 509–510, 517–518, 521–522 |
| 6.13.B | distinguish between situations that yield data with and without variability. | SE: 497, 501 | SE: 502–503 |
| **6.14** | **Personal financial literacy. The student applies mathematical process standards to develop an economic way of thinking and problem solving useful in one's life as a knowledgeable consumer and investor. The student is expected to:** | | |
| 6.14.A | compare the features and costs of a checking account and a debit card offered by different local financial institutions; | SE: 529, 532 | SE: 533–534, 553–554, 557–558 |
| 6.14.B | distinguish between debit cards and credit cards; | SE: 530–531, 532 | SE: 533–534, 553–554, 558, 561 |
| 6.14.C | balance a check register that includes deposits, withdrawals, and transfers; | SE: 531–532 | SE: 533–534, 553–554 |
| 6.14.D | explain why it is important to establish a positive credit history; | SE: 535, 538 | SE: 538, 539–540, 553–554, 557, 561 |
| 6.14.E | describe the information in a credit report and how long it is retained; | SE: 536, 538 | SE: 539–540, 553–554, 561 |
| 6.14.F | describe the value of credit reports to borrowers and to lenders; | SE: 537–538 | SE: 539–540, 553–554, 561 |
| 6.14.G | explain various methods to pay for college, including through savings, grants, scholarships, student loans, and work-study; and | SE: 541–544 | SE: 545–546, 553–554, 561–562 |
| 6.14.H | compare the annual salary of several occupations requiring various levels of post-secondary education or vocational training and calculate the effects of the different annual salaries on lifetime income. | SE: 547–550 | SE: 551–552, 553–554, 557–558, 561–562 |

# Texas English Language Proficiency Standards (ELPS)

HMH Texas Go Math supports English language learners at all proficiency levels. The HMH Texas Go Math Student Edition provides integrated resources to assist all levels of learners, as shown in the correlation tables provided below.

In addition, students at various levels may benefit from additional program support:

**Beginning** - Students at a Beginning level are supported by *Spanish Student Edition, Spanish Assessment Resources*, Success for Every Learner and Leveled Practice A worksheets in *Differentiated Instruction, Math On the Spot* videos with Spanish closed captioning, and the *Multilingual Glossary*.

**Intermediate** - Students at the Intermediate level may use any of the resources above, and may also use Reading Strategies in *Differentiated Instruction*.

**Advanced and Advanced High** - Students at these levels will be successful as the *Student Edition* promotes vocabulary development through visual and context clues. The Multilingual Glossary may also be helpful.

| ELPS | Student Edition Citations |
|---|---|
| c.1.A use prior knowledge and experiences to understand meanings in English | This standard is met in:<br>Reading Startup in each module—Examples: 5, 29, 61, 91<br>Unpacking the TEKS in each module—Examples: 6, 92, 116, 146 |
| c.1.D speak using learning strategies such as requesting assistance, employing non-verbal cues, and using synonyms and circumlocution (conveying ideas by defining or describing when exact English words are not known) | This standard is met in Math Talk in most lessons—Examples: 10, 15, 20, 39 |
| c.2.C **learn** new language structures, expressions, **and basic and academic vocabulary heard during classroom instruction and interactions** | This standard is met in:<br>Math Talk in most lessons—Examples: 45, 65, 70, 83<br>Reflect questions in most lessons—Examples: 13, 20, 32, 37 |
| c.2.D monitor understanding of spoken language during classroom instruction and interactions and **seek clarification [of spoken language] as needed** | This standard is met in:<br>Math Talk in most lessons—Examples: 100, 105, 119, 125<br>Reflect questions in most lessons—Examples: 43, 65, 76, 81 |
| c.2.E **use** visual, contextual, and **linguistic support to enhance and confirm understanding of increasingly complex and elaborated spoken language** | This standard is met in Visualize Vocabulary in each module—Examples: 115, 145, 179, 203 |
| c.2.I **demonstrate listening comprehension of increasingly complex spoken English by** following directions, retelling or summarizing spoken messages, **responding to questions and requests,** collaborating with peers, **and taking notes commensurate with content and grade-level needs** | This standard is met in:<br>Active Reading in each module—Examples: 29, 61<br>Math Talk in most lessons—Examples: 131, 137, 194, 207<br>My Notes in many lessons— Examples: 9, 33, 39, 64 |
| c.3.B **expand and internalize initial English vocabulary by learning and using** high-frequency English words necessary for identifying and describing people, places, and objects, by retelling simple stories and basic information represented or supported by pictures, and by learning and using **routine language needed for classroom communication** | This standard is met in:<br>Vocabulary Puzzle in each unit—Examples: 2, 58, 176, 264<br>Active Reading in each module—Examples: 29, 61, 91, 115<br>Unpacking the TEKS in each module—Examples: 30, 62, 180, 204<br>Active Reading in each module—Examples: 145, 179, 203, 233<br>Reflect questions in most lessons—Examples: 8, 69, 93, 99<br>Math Talk in most lessons—Examples: 207, 211, 217, 225<br>Explore Activities in many lessons—Examples: 7, 13, 19, 31 |

| ELPS | Student Edition Citations |
|---|---|
| **c.3.C speak using a variety of** grammatical structures, sentence lengths, sentence types, and **connecting words with increasing accuracy and ease as more English is acquired** | This standard is met in Math Talk in most lessons—Examples: 218, 237, 241, 248 |
| **c.3.D** speak using grade-level content area vocabulary in context to internalize new English words and build academic language proficiency | This standard is met in:<br>Vocabulary Puzzle in each unit—Examples: 2, 420, 482, 526<br>Active Reading in each module—Examples: 267, 291, 319, 347<br>Math Talk in most lessons—Examples: 251, 270, 275, 295 |
| **c.3.E** share information in cooperative learning interactions | This standard is met in:<br>Math Talk in most lessons—Examples: 271, 302, 310, 322<br>Explore Activities in many lessons—Examples: 37, 43, 63, 69 |
| **c.3.F** ask [for] and give information ranging from using a very limited bank of high-frequency, high-need, concrete vocabulary, including key words and expressions needed for basic communication in academic and social contexts, to using abstract and content-based vocabulary during extended speaking assignments | This standard is met in:<br>Math Talk in most lessons—Examples: 311, 327, 331, 335<br>Explore Activities in many lessons—Examples: 75, 81, 93, 99 |
| **c.3.H** narrate, describe, and **explain with increasing specificity and detail as more English is acquired** | This standard is met in:<br>Reflect questions in most lessons—Examples: 118, 123, 130, 136<br>Math Talk in most lessons—Examples: 337, 350, 355, 356<br>Independent Practice exercises in each lesson—Examples: 12, 18, 23, 36 |
| **C.4.C** develop basic sight vocabulary, derive meaning of environmental print, and comprehend English vocabulary and language structures used routinely in written classroom materials | This standard is met in:<br>Vocabulary Puzzle in each unit—Examples: 58, 176, 264, 420<br>Active Reading in each module—Examples: 5, 377, 423, 447<br>Unpacking the TEKS in each module—Examples: 234, 268, 292, 320<br>Highlighted vocabulary at point of use in instruction—Examples: 8, 15, 19, 33 |
| **c.4.D** use prereading supports such as graphic organizers, illustrations, and pretaught topic-related vocabulary and other prereading activities to enhance comprehension of written text | This standard is met in Active Reading in each module—Examples: 61, 91, 485, 529 |
| **c.4.F** use visual and contextual support and support from peers and teachers to read grade-appropriate content area text, enhance and confirm understanding, and develop vocabulary, grasp of language structures, and background knowledge needed to comprehend increasingly challenging language | This standard is met through photographs, illustrations, and diagrams throughout instruction—Examples: 7, 13, 20, 31 |
| **c.4.G demonstrate comprehension of increasingly complex English by** participating in shared reading, **retelling or summarizing material, responding to questions, and taking notes commensurate with content area and grade level needs** | This standard is met in:<br>Math Talk in most lessons—Examples: 149, 155, 160, 182<br>Reflect questions in most lessons—Examples: 147, 153, 160, 181<br>Essential Question Check In exercises in each lesson—Examples: 10, 14, 22, 34<br>H.O.T.S. exercises in each lesson—Examples: 24, 42, 48, 68 |

# Succeeding with HMH Texas Go Math

Actively participate in your learning with your write-in Student Edition. Explore concepts, take notes, answer questions, and complete your homework right in your textbook!

**YOUR TURN**

Your Turn exercises check your understanding of new concepts.

**EXPLORE ACTIVITY**

Explore Activities help you develop a deeper understanding of math concepts.

**Math On the Spot**

my.hrw.com

Scan QR codes with your smart phone to watch Math On the Spot tutorial videos for every example in the book!

**UNIT 2 MIXED REVIEW**

**Texas Test Prep**

Check your mastery of concepts through review and practice for the Texas test.

# Enhance Your Learning!

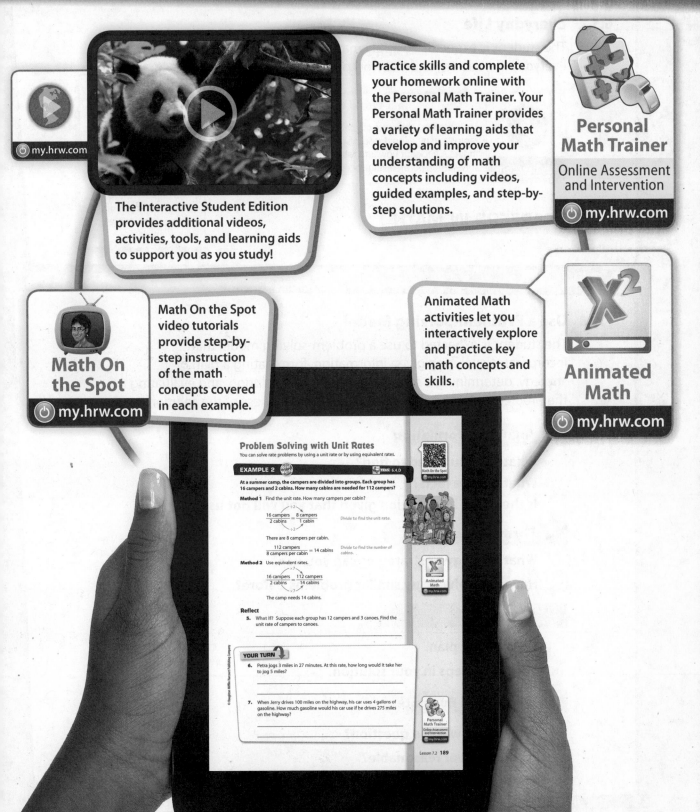

my.hrw.com

**The Interactive Student Edition** provides additional videos, activities, tools, and learning aids to support you as you study!

Practice skills and complete your homework online with the Personal Math Trainer. Your Personal Math Trainer provides a variety of learning aids that develop and improve your understanding of math concepts including videos, guided examples, and step-by-step solutions.

**Personal Math Trainer**
Online Assessment and Intervention
my.hrw.com

**Math On the Spot**
my.hrw.com

**Math On the Spot** video tutorials provide step-by-step instruction of the math concepts covered in each example.

**Animated Math** activities let you interactively explore and practice key math concepts and skills.

**Animated Math**
my.hrw.com

## Problem Solving with Unit Rates
You can solve rate problems by using a unit rate or by using equivalent rates.

**EXAMPLE 2**  TEKS 6.4.D

At a summer camp, the campers are divided into groups. Each group has 16 campers and 2 cabins. How many cabins are needed for 112 campers?

**Method 1**  Find the unit rate. How many campers per cabin?

$$\frac{16 \text{ campers}}{2 \text{ cabins}} = \frac{8 \text{ campers}}{1 \text{ cabin}}$$   Divide to find the unit rate.

There are 8 campers per cabin.

$$\frac{112 \text{ campers}}{8 \text{ campers per cabin}} = 14 \text{ cabins}$$   Divide to find the number of cabins.

**Method 2**  Use equivalent rates.

$$\frac{16 \text{ campers}}{2 \text{ cabins}} = \frac{112 \text{ campers}}{14 \text{ cabins}}$$

The camp needs 14 cabins.

**Reflect**

5. **What If?** Suppose each group has 12 campers and 3 canoes. Find the unit rate of campers to canoes.

**YOUR TURN**

6. Petra jogs 3 miles in 27 minutes. At this rate, how long would it take her to jog 5 miles?

7. When Jerry drives 100 miles on the highway, his car uses 4 gallons of gasoline. How much gasoline would his car use if he drives 275 miles on the highway?

Lesson 7.2 **189**

© Houghton Mifflin Harcourt Publishing Company

# Mathematical Process Standards

**6.1** **Mathematical process standards.** The student uses mathematical processes to acquire and demonstrate mathematical understanding.

**6.1.A** **Everyday Life**

The student is expected to apply mathematics to problems arising in everyday life, society, and the workplace.

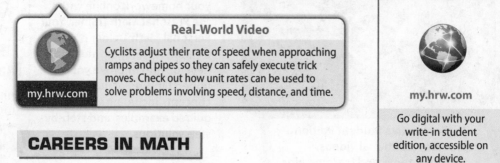

**Real-World Video**

Cyclists adjust their rate of speed when approaching ramps and pipes so they can safely execute trick moves. Check out how unit rates can be used to solve problems involving speed, distance, and time.

my.hrw.com

**CAREERS IN MATH**

my.hrw.com

Go digital with your write-in student edition, accessible on any device.

**6.1.B** **Use a Problem-Solving Model**

The student is expected to use a problem-solving model that incorporates analyzing given information, formulating a plan or strategy, determining a solution, justifying the solution, and evaluating the problem-solving process and the reasonableness of the solution.

**Analyze Information**

What are you asked to find?

What are the facts?

Is there any information given that you will not use?

**Formulate a Plan**

What strategy or strategies can you use?

Have you solved any similar problems before?

**Solve**

Follow your plan.

Show the steps in your solution.

**Justify and Evaluate**

Did you answer the question?

Is your answer reasonable?

Are there other strategies that you could use?

## 6.1.C  Select Tools

The student is expected to select tools, including real objects, manipulatives, paper and pencil, and technology as appropriate, and techniques, including mental math, estimation, and number sense as appropriate, to solve problems.

**EXPLORE ACTIVITY** *Real World*

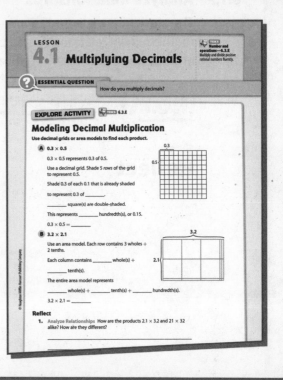

## 6.1.D  Multiple Representations

The student is expected to communicate mathematical ideas, reasoning, and their implications, using multiple representations, including symbols, diagrams, graphs, and language as appropriate.

## 6.1.E  Use Representations

The student is expected to create and use representations to organize, record, and communicate mathematical ideas.

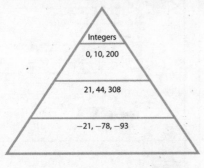

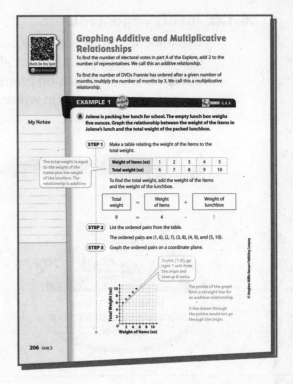

## 6.1.F  Analyze Relationships

The student is expected to analyze mathematical relationships to connect and communicate mathematical ideas.

**H.O.T.** FOCUS ON HIGHER ORDER THINKING

# Reflect

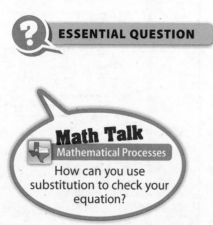

### Multiplying Mixed Numbers

Multiplying a mixed number by another mixed number is the same as multiplying a fraction by a mixed number. Rewrite each mixed number as a fraction. Then multiply the numerators and multiply the denominators.

**EXAMPLE 2** Real World                                TEKS 6.3.E

Grace is making $2\frac{1}{2}$ batches of muffins for her school's annual bake sale. If one batch of muffins requires $1\frac{1}{4}$ cups of flour, how many cups of flour does Grace need to make $2\frac{1}{2}$ batches of muffins?

**STEP 1** Estimate the product. Round each mixed number to the nearest whole number.

$2\frac{1}{2}$ is close to 3 and $1\frac{1}{4}$ is close to 1, so multiply 3 by 1.

$3 \times 1 = 3$

**STEP 2** Multiply. Write the product in simplest form.

$2\frac{1}{2} \times 1\frac{1}{4}$

$2\frac{1}{2} \times 1\frac{1}{4} = \frac{5}{2} \times \frac{5}{4}$   Rewrite each mixed number as a fraction greater than 1.

$= \frac{5 \times 5}{2 \times 4}$   Multiply numerators. Multiply denominators.

$= \frac{25}{8},\ or\ 3\frac{1}{8}$   Write the fraction greater than 1 as a mixed number.

Grace will need $3\frac{1}{8}$ cups of flour.

**Reflect**

8. **Analyze Relationships** When you multiply two mixed numbers, will the product be less than or greater than the factors? Use an example to explain.

_____

_____

**YOUR TURN**

Multiply. Write each product in simplest form.

9. $2\frac{2}{3} \times 1\frac{1}{2}$ _____    10. $2\frac{3}{8} \times 1\frac{1}{5}$ _____

11. $4\frac{1}{2} \times 3\frac{3}{7}$ _____    12. $5\frac{1}{4} \times 4\frac{2}{3}$ _____

Lesson 3.2  71

---

## 6.1.G  Justify Arguments

The student is expected to display, explain, and justify mathematical ideas and arguments using precise mathematical language in written or oral communication.

**?** ESSENTIAL QUESTION

**Math Talk**
Mathematical Processes

How can you use substitution to check your equation?

### Dividing Decimals by Whole Numbers

Dividing decimals is similar to dividing whole numbers. When you divide a decimal by a whole number, the placement of the decimal point in the quotient is determined by the placement of the decimal in the dividend.

**EXAMPLE 1** Real World                                TEKS 6.3.E

**A** A high school track is 9.76 meters wide. It is divided into 8 lanes of equal width for track and field events. How wide is each lane?

Divide using long division as with whole numbers.

Place a decimal point in the quotient directly above the decimal point in the dividend.

Each lane is 1.22 meters wide.

$$\begin{array}{r} 1.22 \\ 8\overline{)9.76} \\ -8\phantom{.00} \\ \hline 17 \\ -16 \\ \hline 16 \\ -16 \\ \hline 0 \end{array}$$

**B** Aerobics classes cost $153.86 for 14 sessions. What is the fee for one session?

Divide using long division as with whole numbers.

Place a decimal point in the quotient directly above the decimal point in the dividend.

The fee for one aerobics class is $10.99.

$$\begin{array}{r} 10.99 \\ 14\overline{)153.86} \\ -14\phantom{.000} \\ \hline 13 \\ -0 \\ \hline 138 \\ -126 \\ \hline 126 \\ -126 \\ \hline 0 \end{array}$$

**Reflect**

2. **Check for Reasonableness** How can you estimate to check that your quotient in **A** is reasonable?

_____

_____

**My Notes**

**Math Talk**
Mathematical Processes
How can you check to see that the answer is correct?

**YOUR TURN**

Divide.

3. $5\overline{)9.75}$    4. $7\overline{)6.44}$

100  Unit 2

GRADE 5 PART 1

# Review Test

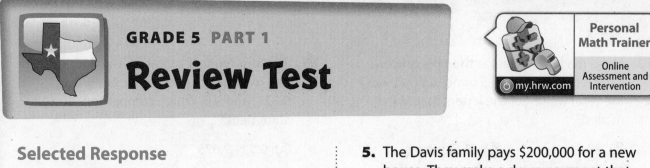

Personal
Math Trainer

Online
Assessment and
Intervention

my.hrw.com

## Selected Response

**1.** Amanda used the expression $8 + 25 \times 2 - 45$ to find how many beads she has. How many beads does she have?

Ⓐ 3     Ⓒ 21

Ⓑ 13     Ⓓ 103

**2.** In which decimal place is the digit 8 In the number 325.1786?

Ⓐ thousandths

Ⓑ hundredths

Ⓒ tenths

Ⓓ hundreds

**3.** Jamie baked 24 cupcakes. Her sister Mia ate 3 cupcakes, and her brother David ate 2 cupcakes. Which expression can Jamie use to find how many cupcakes are left?

Ⓐ $24 + (3 + 2)$

Ⓑ $24 - (3 + 2)$

Ⓒ $(24 - 3) + 2$

Ⓓ $24 - (3 - 2)$

**4.** What is the unknown number in sequence 2 in the chart?

| Sequence Number | 1 | 2 | 3 | 5 | 7 |
|---|---|---|---|---|---|
| Sequence 1 | 3 | 6 | 9 | 15 | 21 |
| Sequence 2 | 15 | 30 | 45 | 75 | ? |

Ⓐ 63     Ⓒ 105

Ⓑ 90     Ⓓ 150

**5.** The Davis family pays $200,000 for a new house. They make a down payment that is $\frac{1}{10}$ of the price of the house. How much is the down payment?

Ⓐ $20     Ⓒ $2,000

Ⓑ $200     Ⓓ $20,000

**6.** What is the quotient of 43.8 and 12?

Ⓐ 3.65

Ⓑ 3.92

Ⓒ 27.39

Ⓓ 36.5

**7.** Jackie found a rock that has a mass of 78.852 grams. What is the mass of the rock rounded to the nearest tenth?

Ⓐ 78.85 grams

Ⓑ 78.9 grams

Ⓒ 79 grams

Ⓓ 80 grams

**8.** A company manufactures 295 toy cars each day. How many toy cars do they manufacture in 34 days?

Ⓐ 3,065     Ⓒ 10,030

Ⓑ 7,610     Ⓓ 10,065

**9.** There are 6 buses transporting students to a baseball game with 32 students on each bus. Each row at the baseball stadium seats 8 students. If the students fill rows completely, how many rows of seats will the students need altogether?

Ⓐ 22     Ⓒ 24

Ⓑ 23     Ⓓ 1,536

**10.** Marci mailed 9 letters at the post office. Each letter weighed 3.5 ounces. What was the total weight of the letters that Marci mailed?

Ⓐ 33.5 ounces    Ⓒ 31.5 ounces

Ⓑ 32.5 ounces    Ⓓ 27.5 ounces

**11.** Denise, Keith, and Tim live in the same neighborhood. Denise lives 0.3 mile from Keith. The distance that Tim and Keith live from each other is 0.2 times longer than the distance between Denise and Keith. How far from each other do Tim and Keith live?

Ⓐ 0.6 mile    Ⓒ 0.1 mile

Ⓑ 0.5 mile    Ⓓ 0.06 mile

**12.** Madison needs to buy enough meat to make 1,000 hamburgers for the company picnic. Each hamburger will weigh 0.25 pound. How many pounds of hamburger meat should Madison buy?

Ⓐ 2.5 pounds    Ⓒ 250 pounds

Ⓑ 25 pounds    Ⓓ 2,500 pounds

**13.** There are 12 apartments on each floor of a building. All but 3 apartments on each floor have only one bedroom. The building has 4 floors. Which expression does *not* represent the number of one-bedroom apartments in the building?

Ⓐ 4(12 − 3)    Ⓒ 48 − 12

Ⓑ 4(12) − 3    Ⓓ 4(12) − 4(3)

**14.** Rayna correctly wrote the population of her city as $(9 \times 100) + (6 \times 10,000) + (2 \times 100,000) + (8 \times 10)$. What is the population written as a whole number?

Ⓐ 2,698 people

Ⓑ 9,628 people

Ⓒ 260,980 people

Ⓓ 900,602,008 people

**15.** The four highest scores on the floor exercise at a gymnastics meet were 9.675, 9.25, 9.325, and 9.5. Which comparison is a true statement?

Ⓐ 9.5 > 9.675

Ⓑ 9.325 < 9.25

Ⓒ 9.675 < 9.325

Ⓓ 9.25 < 9.325

**16.** Allison and Justin's father donated $3 for every lap they swam in a swim-a-thon. Allison swam 21 laps and Justin swam 15 laps. How much money did their father donate?

Ⓐ $108    Ⓒ $39

Ⓑ $78    Ⓓ $18

## Gridded Response

**17.** Jennifer has $12 to spend on lunch and the roller rink. Admission to the roller rink is $5.75. Jennifer wants to buy a large drink and a turkey sandwich. How much more money does Jennifer need in dollars?

| Sandwiches | Drinks |
| --- | --- |
| Tuna $3.95 | Small $1.29 |
| Turkey $4.85 | Medium $1.59 |
| Grilled Cheese $3.25 | Large $1.79 |

## Selected Response

**1.** Charles bought $\frac{7}{8}$ foot of electrical wire and $\frac{5}{6}$ foot of copper wire for his science project. What is the least common denominator of the fractions?

Ⓐ 14　　　　　Ⓒ 24

Ⓑ 18　　　　　Ⓓ 48

**2.** Tom jogged $\frac{3}{5}$ mile on Monday and $\frac{2}{6}$ mile on Tuesday. How much farther did Tom jog on Monday than on Tuesday?

Ⓐ $\frac{1}{30}$ mile　　　Ⓒ $\frac{8}{30}$ mile

Ⓑ $\frac{3}{15}$ mile　　　Ⓓ $\frac{14}{15}$ mile

**3.** Three fences on a ranch measure $\frac{15}{16}$ mile, $\frac{7}{8}$ mile, and $\frac{7}{16}$ mile. Which is the best estimate of the total length of all three fences?

Ⓐ $1\frac{1}{2}$ miles　　Ⓒ $2\frac{1}{2}$ miles

Ⓑ $1\frac{3}{4}$ miles　　Ⓓ 3 miles

**4.** Lawrence bought $\frac{3}{4}$ pound of roast beef. He used $\frac{1}{4}$ pound to make a sandwich. How much roast beef remained after Lawrence made his sandwich?

Ⓐ $\frac{1}{4}$ pound

Ⓑ $\frac{1}{3}$ pound

Ⓒ $\frac{1}{2}$ pound

Ⓓ 3 pounds

**5.** A pizza box measures 16 inches by 16 inches by 2 inches. What is the volume of the box?

Ⓐ 128 cubic inches

Ⓑ 256 cubic inches

Ⓒ 512 cubic inches

Ⓓ 640 cubic inches

**6.** Vanessa made 6 sandwiches for a party and cut them all into fourths. How many $\frac{1}{4}$-sandwich pieces did she have?

Ⓐ $1\frac{1}{2}$　　　　Ⓒ 4

Ⓑ $2\frac{1}{4}$　　　　Ⓓ 24

**7.** Dr. Watson combines 400 mL of detergent, 800 mL of alcohol, and 1,500 mL of water. How many liters of solution does he have?

Ⓐ 2.7 liters　　Ⓒ 270 liters

Ⓑ 27 liters　　Ⓓ 2,700 liters

**8.** Give the most descriptive name for the figure.

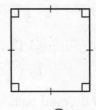

Ⓐ square　　　Ⓒ parallelogram

Ⓑ rectangle　　Ⓓ rhombus

**9.** Find the volume of the rectangular prism.

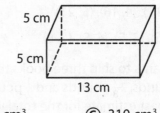

5 cm

5 cm

13 cm

Ⓐ 23 cm³　　　Ⓒ 310 cm³

Ⓑ 184 cm³　　Ⓓ 325 cm³

**10.** Which ordered pair describes the location of Point A?

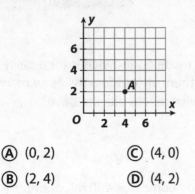

Ⓐ (0, 2)　　Ⓒ (4, 0)

Ⓑ (2, 4)　　Ⓓ (4, 2)

**11.** Which ordered pair describes the location of Point B?

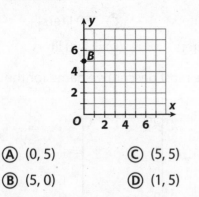

Ⓐ (0, 5)　　Ⓒ (5, 5)

Ⓑ (5, 0)　　Ⓓ (1, 5)

**12.** Which set of ordered pairs was generated by the equation $y = x + 5$?

Ⓐ (1, 5), (2, 10), (3, 15), (4, 20)

Ⓑ (3, 8), (4, 9), (6, 11), (8, 13)

Ⓒ (2, 11), (4, 16), (5, 21)

Ⓓ (1, 5), (3, 5), (4, 5), (7, 5)

**13.** Gina wants to ship three books that weigh $2\frac{7}{16}$ pounds, $1\frac{7}{8}$ pounds and $\frac{1}{2}$ pound. Which is the best estimate for the total weight of the three books?

Ⓐ $3\frac{1}{2}$ pounds　　Ⓒ 5 pounds

Ⓑ 4 pounds　　Ⓓ 6 pounds

**14.** How much trail mix will each person get if 5 people share $\frac{1}{2}$ pound of trail mix?

Ⓐ $\frac{1}{10}$ pound　　Ⓒ $2\frac{1}{2}$ pounds

Ⓑ $\frac{1}{5}$ pound　　Ⓓ 10 pounds

**15.** Each cube in the solid figure represents one cubic centimeter. What is the volume in cubic centimeters of the solid?

Ⓐ 24 cubic centimeters

Ⓑ 48 cubic centimeters

Ⓒ 72 cubic centimeters

Ⓓ 96 cubic centimeters

## Gridded Response

**16.** It took Ray 0.45 hour to rake the leaves and $\frac{3}{4}$ hour to mow the lawn. How many minutes did it take him to do both tasks?

| ⊕ | ⓪ | ⓪ | ⓪ | ⓪ | • | ⓪ | ⓪ |
|---|---|---|---|---|---|---|---|
| ⊖ | ① | ① | ① | ① |   | ① | ① |
|   | ② | ② | ② | ② |   | ② | ② |
|   | ③ | ③ | ③ | ③ |   | ③ | ③ |
|   | ④ | ④ | ④ | ④ |   | ④ | ④ |
|   | ⑤ | ⑤ | ⑤ | ⑤ |   | ⑤ | ⑤ |
|   | ⑥ | ⑥ | ⑥ | ⑥ |   | ⑥ | ⑥ |
|   | ⑦ | ⑦ | ⑦ | ⑦ |   | ⑦ | ⑦ |
|   | ⑧ | ⑧ | ⑧ | ⑧ |   | ⑧ | ⑧ |
|   | ⑨ | ⑨ | ⑨ | ⑨ |   | ⑨ | ⑨ |

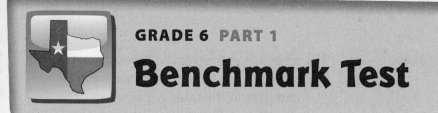
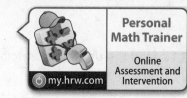
## Selected Response

**1.** Which temperature is coldest?

Ⓐ −13°F     Ⓒ −20°F

Ⓑ 20°F     Ⓓ 13°F

**2.** Which group of numbers is in order from least to greatest?

Ⓐ 2.58, $2\frac{5}{8}$, 2.6, $2\frac{2}{3}$

Ⓑ $2\frac{2}{3}$, $2\frac{5}{8}$, 2.6, 2.58

Ⓒ $2\frac{5}{8}$, $2\frac{2}{3}$, 2.6, 2.58

Ⓓ 2.58, 2.6, $2\frac{5}{8}$, $2\frac{2}{3}$

**3.** Evaluate $a + b$ for $a = -46$ and $b = 34$.

Ⓐ −12     Ⓒ −80

Ⓑ 80     Ⓓ 12

**4.** One winter day, the temperature ranged from a high of 40°F to a low of −5°F. By how many degrees did the temperature change?

Ⓐ 45°F     Ⓒ 25°F

Ⓑ 35°F     Ⓓ 55°F

**5.** Find the quotient. $9\frac{3}{5} \div \frac{8}{15}$

Ⓐ 2     Ⓒ $16\frac{7}{8}$

Ⓑ 18     Ⓓ $18\frac{3}{4}$

**6.** Juan purchased 3.4 pounds of nails at a cost of $4.51 per pound. What was the cost of the nails?

Ⓐ $153.34     Ⓒ $7.91

Ⓑ $1.53     Ⓓ $15.33

**7.** You are working as an assistant to a chef. The chef has 6 cups of berries and will use $\frac{2}{3}$ cup of berries for each dessert he makes. How many desserts can he make?

Ⓐ 4 desserts     Ⓒ 9 desserts

Ⓑ $6\frac{2}{3}$ desserts     Ⓓ 12 desserts

**8.** Jorge is building a table out of boards that are 3.75 inches wide. He wants the table to be at least 36 inches wide. How many boards does he need?

Ⓐ 9     Ⓒ 10

Ⓑ 9.6     Ⓓ 135

**9.** The fuel for a chainsaw is a mix of oil and gasoline. The label says to mix 6 ounces of oil with 16 gallons of gasoline. How much oil would you use if you had 24 gallons of gasoline?

Ⓐ 3 ounces     Ⓒ 12 ounces

Ⓑ 9 ounces     Ⓓ 85.3 ounces

**10.** A grocery store sells the brands of yogurt shown in the table.

| Brand | Size (ounces) | Price ($) |
|-------|---------------|-----------|
| Sunny | 12 | 2.00 |
| Fruity | 14 | 2.34 |
| Smooth | 18 | 2.60 |
| Yummy | 16 | 2.24 |

Which brand of yogurt has the lowest unit price?

Ⓐ Sunny     Ⓒ Smooth

Ⓑ Fruity     Ⓓ Yummy

**11.** Find the unit rate. Patricia paid $385 for 5 nights at a hotel.

Ⓐ $\frac{\$77}{1\text{ night}}$     Ⓒ $\frac{\$385}{1\text{ night}}$

Ⓑ $\frac{\$154}{1\text{ night}}$     Ⓓ $\frac{\$39}{1\text{ night}}$

**12.** Which of the following does NOT show a pair of equivalent ratios?

Ⓐ $\frac{3}{7}, \frac{9}{21}$     Ⓒ $\frac{3}{7}, \frac{9}{28}$

Ⓑ $\frac{24}{56}, \frac{3}{7}$     Ⓓ $\frac{3}{7}, \frac{12}{28}$

**13.** Gina paid $129 for a bicycle that was on sale for 75% of its original price. What was the original price of the bicycle?

Ⓐ $54.00     Ⓒ $172

Ⓑ $96.75     Ⓓ $204

**14.** Write the fraction $\frac{9}{50}$ as a percent. If necessary, round your answer to the nearest hundredth.

Ⓐ 0.18%     Ⓒ 18%

Ⓑ 0.45%     Ⓓ 45%

**15.** Write an equation you can use to find the missing value in the table.

| Tom's Age (t) | Kim's Age (a) |
|---|---|
| 10 | 13 |
| 11 | 14 |
| 12 | 15 |
| a | ? |

Ⓐ $t = a + 1$     Ⓒ $t = a + 3$

Ⓑ $t = a + 15$     Ⓓ $t = a + 10$

**16.** Which expression is NOT equivalent to the expression $38 - 14$?

Ⓐ $2(19 - 7)$     Ⓒ $(19 - 7)2$

Ⓑ $2(19) - 2(7)$     Ⓓ $2(36 - 12)$

**17.** Suppose you have developed a scale that indicates the brightness of sunlight. Each category in the table is 9 times brighter than the next category. For example, a day that is dazzling is 9 times brighter than a day that is radiant. How many times brighter is a dazzling day than an illuminated day?

| Sunlight Intensity | |
|---|---|
| **Category** | **Brightness** |
| Dim | 2 |
| Illuminated | 3 |
| Radiant | 4 |
| Dazzling | 5 |

Ⓐ 2 times brighter    Ⓒ 81 times brighter

Ⓑ 9 times brighter    Ⓓ 729 times brighter

**18.** Evaluate the expression.
$(28 \div 4) \cdot 5 - 6 + 4^2$

Ⓐ 9     Ⓒ 37

Ⓑ 13     Ⓓ 45

## Gridded Response

**19.** Shari bought $2\frac{1}{2}$ yards of fabric for $7.99 per yard. She used $\frac{3}{4}$ of the fabric to make decorative pillows. How much money could Shari have saved by only buying the amount of fabric that she used? Write your answer in dollars and round to the nearest tenth.

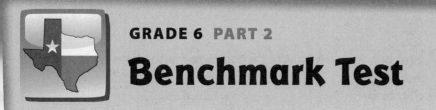

## Selected Response

**1.** What is the prime factorization of 300?

Ⓐ $2 \times 3 \times 5$    Ⓒ $3 \times 10$

Ⓑ $3 \times 4 \times 5^2$    Ⓓ $2^2 \times 3 \times 5^2$

**2.** Wilson bought gift cards for some lawyers and their assistants. Each lawyer got a gift card worth \$$\ell$. Each assistant got a gift card worth \$$a$. There are 12 lawyers. Each lawyer has two assistants. The expression for the total cost of the gift cards is $12\ell + 24a$. Write an expression that is equivalent to the given expression.

Ⓐ $12(\ell + 2a)$    Ⓒ $12(\ell + 24a)$

Ⓑ $12(\ell + 3a)$    Ⓓ $24(\ell + 2a)$

**3.** A triangle has sides with lengths of $2x - 7$, $5x - 3$, and $2x - 2$. What is the perimeter of the triangle?

Ⓐ $9x - 12$    Ⓒ $-x - 6$

Ⓑ $5x - 12$    Ⓓ $-3x$

**4.** Brian is ordering tickets online for a concert. The price of each ticket for the concert is \$$t$. For online orders, there is an additional charge of \$11 per ticket and a service charge of \$14 for the entire order. The cost for 7 tickets purchased online can be represented by the expression $7(t + 11) + 14$. Which expression is equivalent to the cost expression?

Ⓐ $18t + 14$    Ⓒ $32t$

Ⓑ $7t + 91$    Ⓓ $7t + 25$

**5.** A driveway is 81 feet long, 12 feet wide, and 6 inches deep. How many cubic feet of concrete will be required for the driveway?

Ⓐ 423 cubic feet    Ⓒ 486 cubic feet

Ⓑ 458 cubic feet    Ⓓ 5,832 cubic feet

**6.** What is the area of the polygon?

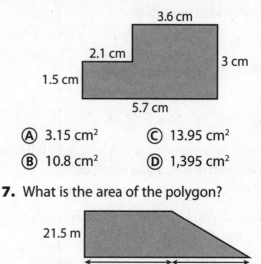

Ⓐ 3.15 cm²    Ⓒ 13.95 cm²

Ⓑ 10.8 cm²    Ⓓ 1,395 cm²

**7.** What is the area of the polygon?

Ⓐ 861.075 m²    Ⓒ 1,722.15 m²

Ⓑ 1,317.95 m²    Ⓓ 2,635.9 m²

**8.** Kahlil is recording a rhythm track for a new song that he is working on. He wants the track to be more than 10 seconds long. His friend tells him the track needs to be at least 5 seconds longer than that to match the lyrics he has written. Write an inequality to represent the track's length in seconds.

Ⓐ $t > 5$

Ⓑ $t > 15$

Ⓒ $t < 5$

Ⓓ $t < 10$

**9.** In a fish tank, $\frac{8}{11}$ of the fish have a red stripe on them. If 16 of the fish have red stripes, how many total fish are in the tank?

Ⓐ 21 fish    Ⓒ 20 fish

Ⓑ 22 fish    Ⓓ 26 fish

**10.** Solve the equation $u \times 5.6 = 6.16$.

Ⓐ $u = 34.5$    Ⓒ $u = 1.1$

Ⓑ $u = 1$    Ⓓ $u = 0.77$

**11.** It will be Lindsay's birthday soon, and her friends Chris, Mikhail, Wolfgang, and Adrian have contributed equal amounts of money to buy her a present. They have a total of $27.00 to spend. Write an equation that models the situation and find the amount each friend contributed.

- (A) $4x = $27.00$; $x = $7.75$
- (B) $5x = $27.00$; $x = $5.40$
- (C) $4x = $27.00$; $x = $108.00$
- (D) $4x = $27.00$; $x = $6.75$

**12.** Write an equation for the function. Tell what each variable you use represents.
A plant's height is 1.4 times its age.

- (A) $x$ = plant's height; $y$ = plant's age; $x = 1.4y$
- (B) $x$ = plant's age; $y$ = plant's height; $x = 1.4y$
- (C) $x$ = plant's height; $y$ = plant's age; $y = 1.4x$
- (D) $x$ = plant's height; $y$ = plant's age; $1.4 = xy$

**13.** Jared is redoing his bathroom floor with tiles measuring 6 in. by 14 in. The floor has an area of 8,900 in². What is the least number of tiles he will need?

- (A) 105 tiles
- (C) 106 tiles
- (B) 105.95 tiles
- (D) 445 tiles

**14.** Mrs. Rissoto filled her daughter's plastic swimming pool with water. The water level in the pool changed by −8 gallons each hour due to a small hole in the bottom of the pool. After 6 hours, the pool contained 132 gallons of water. How much water was in the pool originally?

- (A) 180 gallons
- (C) 124 gallons
- (B) 140 gallons
- (D) 84 gallons

**15.** What is the range of the data represented by the box-and-whisker plot?

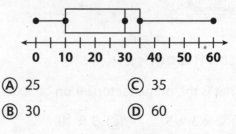

- (A) 25
- (C) 35
- (B) 30
- (D) 60

**16.** In a box-and-whisker plot, the interquartile range is a measure of the spread of the middle half of the data. Find the interquartile range for the data set 10, 3, 7, 5, 9, 12, 15.

- (A) 12
- (C) 7
- (B) 8
- (D) 6

**17.** What is the area of the base of a rectangular prism with a height of 10 centimeters and a volume of 400 cubic centimeters?

- (A) 4 square centimeters
- (B) 40 square centimeters
- (C) 400 square centimeters
- (D) 4,000 square centimeters

## Gridded Response

**18.** To find the mileage, or how many miles a car can travel per gallon of gasoline, you can use the expression $\frac{m}{g}$, where $m$ is the distance in miles and $g$ is the number of gallons of gas used. Find the gas mileage in miles per gallon for a car that travels 212 miles on 8 gallons of gas.

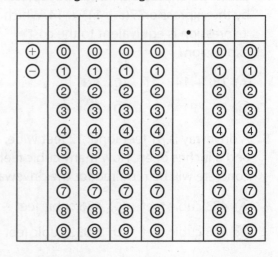

## CAREERS IN MATH

**Climatologist** A climatologist is a scientist who studies long-term trends in climate conditions. These scientists collect, evaluate, and interpret data and use mathematical models to study the dynamics of weather patterns and to understand and predict Earth's climate.

If you are interested in a career in climatology, you should study these mathematical subjects:
- Algebra
- Trigonometry
- Probability and Statistics
- Calculus

Research other careers that require the analysis of data and use of mathematical models.

**Unit 1 Performance Task**

At the end of the unit, check out how **climatologists** use math.

# Vocabulary Preview

Use the puzzle to preview key vocabulary from this unit. Unscramble the circled letters within found words to answer the riddle at the bottom of the page.

```
E R I N E Q U A L I T Y I L N
U S E R O J U J P Z Y M B E M
L U E B P P H K R J A L G R Z
A M G Z M Y P G I R Y A R A D
V K B E D U G O G C T K W G X
E D M F S L N A S I J J H Z C
T B K H V M I L V I Q E L D R
U R I M R D I E A Y T Z G K P
L V N T N H N D Y N L E F T H
O X T N K U K Q F X O A S T E
S R E B M U N E V I T I S O P
B V G B D Z A F E A X Y T Y A
A D E P X N V I U B V S T A A
O R R V R R X I R G L V B U R
S X S M I Q V Y N L N P S S I
```

- Any number that can be written as a ratio of two integers. (Lesson 2-1)
- Numbers greater than zero. (Lesson 1-1)
- A diagram used to show the relationship between two sets or groups. (Lesson 2-1)
- A mathematical statement that shows two quantities are not equal. (Lesson 1-2)
- The set of all whole numbers and their opposites. (Lesson 1-1)
- The distance of a number from zero on the number line. (Lesson 1-3)
- Numbers less than zero. (Lesson 1-1)

**Q:** Why did the integer get a bad evaluation at work?

**A:** He had a __ __ __ __ __ __ __ __ __ __
__ __ __ __ __ __ __ __!

# Integers

## ESSENTIAL QUESTION

How can you use integers to solve real-world problems?

### Real-World Video

Integers can be used to describe the value of many things in the real world. The height of a mountain in feet may be a very great integer while the temperature in degrees Celsius at the top of that mountain may be a negative integer.

⏻ my.hrw.com

# GO DIGITAL
my.hrw.com

|  |  | X² |  |
|---|---|---|---|
| **my.hrw.com** | **Math On the Spot** | **Animated Math** | **Personal Math Trainer** |
| Go digital with your write-in student edition, accessible on any device. | Scan with your smart phone to jump directly to the online edition, video tutor, and more. | Interactively explore key concepts to see how math works. | Get immediate feedback and help as you work through practice sets. |

# Are YOU Ready?

Complete these exercises to review skills you will need for this chapter.

## Compare Whole Numbers

> **EXAMPLE**
>
> 3,564 ● 3,528     Compare digits in the thousands place: $3 = 3$
>
> 3,564 ● 3,528     Compare digits in the hundreds place: $5 = 5$
>
> $3,564 > 3,528$     Compare digits in the tens place: $6 > 2$

**Compare. Write $<$, $>$, or $=$.**

1. 471 ◯ 468     **2.** 5,005 ◯ 5,050     **3.** 398 ◯ 389

4. 10,973 ◯ 10,999     **5.** 8,471 ◯ 9,001     **6.** 108 ◯ 95

## Order Whole Numbers

> **EXAMPLE**
>
> 356, 348, 59, **416**     Compare digits. Find the greatest number.
>
> **356**, 348, 59, 416     Find the next greatest number.
>
> 356, **348**, 59, 416     Find the next greatest number.
>
> 356, 348, **59**, 416     Find the least number.
>
> $416 > 356 > 348 > 59$     Order the numbers.

**Order the numbers from greatest to least.**

7. 156; 87; 177; 99          **8.** 591; 589; 603; 600

 

9. 2,650; 2,605; 3,056; 2,088     **10.** 1,037; 995; 10,415; 1,029

 

## Locate Numbers on a Number Line

> **EXAMPLE**
>
>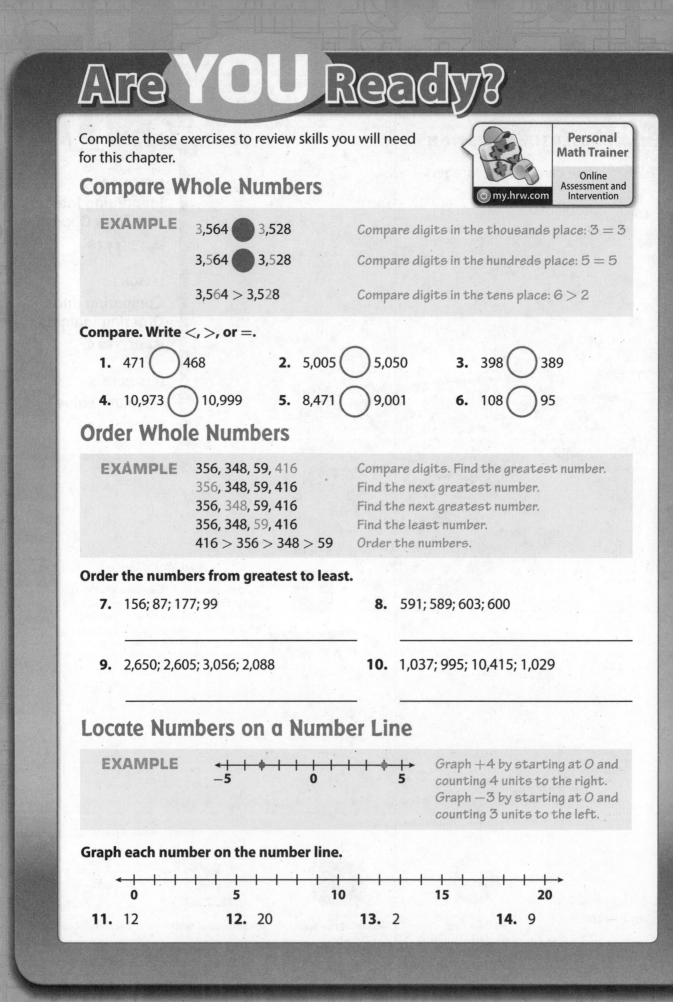
>
> Graph $+4$ by starting at 0 and counting 4 units to the right.
> Graph $-3$ by starting at 0 and counting 3 units to the left.

**Graph each number on the number line.**

11. 12     **12.** 20     **13.** 2     **14.** 9

# Reading Start-Up

## Visualize Vocabulary

**Use the ✔ words to complete the chart. Write the correct vocabulary word next to the symbol.**

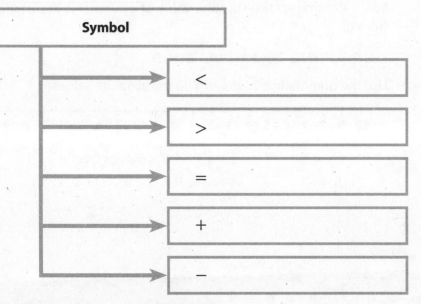

| Symbol |
|---|
| < |
| > |
| = |
| + |
| − |

## Understand Vocabulary

**Complete the sentences using the preview words.**

1. An _____ is a statement that two quantities are not equal.

2. The set of all whole numbers and their opposites are _____.

3. Numbers greater than 0 are _____. Numbers less

   than 0 are _____.

## Vocabulary

**Review Words**

✔ equal *(igual)*
✔ greater than *(más que)*
✔ less than *(menos que)*
✔ negative sign *(signo negativo)*
  number line *(recta numérica)*
✔ plus sign *(signo más)*
  symbol *(símbolo)*
  whole number *(número entero)*

**Preview Words**

  absolute value *(valor absoluto)*
  inequality *(desigualdad)*
  integers *(enteros)*
  negative numbers *(números negativos)*
  opposites *(opuestos)*
  positive numbers *(números positivos)*

## Active Reading

**Key-Term Fold** Before beginning the module, create a key-term fold to help you learn the vocabulary in this module. Write the highlighted vocabulary words on one side of the flap. Write the definition for each word on the other side of the flap. Use the key-term fold to quiz yourself on the definitions in this module.

# Unpacking the TEKS

Understanding the TEKS and the vocabulary terms in the TEKS will help you know exactly what you are expected to learn in this module.

---

**TEKS 6.2.B**

Identify a number, its opposite, and its absolute value.

**Key Vocabulary**

**integers** *(enteros)*
The set of all whole numbers and their opposites.

**opposites** *(opuestos)*
Two numbers that are equal distance from zero on a number line.

**absolute value** *(valor absoluto)*
A number's distance from 0 on the number line.

## What It Means to You

You will learn that the absolute value of a number is its distance from 0.

**UNPACKING EXAMPLE 6.2.B**

Use the number line to determine the absolute values.

$$\begin{array}{cccccccccccccccccccccc} & & & & & \bullet & & & & & & & & & & & \bullet & & & & & \\ -10 & -9 & -8 & -7 & -6 & -5 & -4 & -3 & -2 & -1 & 0 & 1 & 2 & 3 & 4 & 5 & 6 & 7 & 8 & 9 & 10 \end{array}$$

$|-5| = 5$      because −5 is 5 units from 0

$|5| = 5$      because 5 is 5 units from 0

---

**TEKS 6.2.C**

Locate, compare, and order integers and rational numbers using a number line.

**Key Vocabulary**

**rational number**
*(número racional)*
Any number that can be expressed as a ratio of two integers.

## What It Means to You

You can use a number line to order rational numbers.

**UNPACKING EXAMPLE 6.2.C**

At a golf tournament, David scored +6, Celia scored −16, and Xavier scored −4. One of these three players was the winner of the tournament. Who won the tournament?

The winner will be the player with the lowest score. Draw a number line and graph each player's score.

$$\begin{array}{ccccccccccccc} & \bullet & & & & & & \bullet & & & & & \bullet \\ -18 & -16 & -14 & -12 & -10 & -8 & -6 & -4 & -2 & 0 & 2 & 4 & 6 & 8 \end{array}$$

Celia's score, −16, is the farthest to the left, so it is the lowest score. Celia won the tournament.

---

Visit **my.hrw.com** to see all the **TEKS** unpacked.

my.hrw.com

# LESSON 1.1 Identifying Integers and Their Opposites

**TEKS**
**Number and operations—6.2.B**
Identify a number, its opposite, and its absolute value.

## ? ESSENTIAL QUESTION

How do you identify an integer and its opposite?

**EXPLORE ACTIVITY 1** Real World **TEKS** 6.2.B

# Positive and Negative Numbers

**Positive numbers** are numbers greater than 0. Positive numbers can be written with or without a plus sign; for example, 3 is the same as +3. **Negative numbers** are numbers less than 0. Negative numbers must always be written with a negative sign.

> The number 0 is neither positive nor negative.

−5 −4 −3 −2 −1 0 1 2 3 4 5

Negative integers          Positive integers

The elevation of a location describes its height above or below sea level, which has elevation 0. Elevations below sea level are represented by negative numbers, and elevations above sea level are represented by positive numbers.

**A** The table shows the elevations of several locations in a state park. Graph the locations on the number line according to their elevations.

| Location | Little Butte *A* | Cradle Creek *B* | Dinosaur Valley *C* | Mesa Ridge *D* | Juniper Trail *E* |
|---|---|---|---|---|---|
| **Elevation (ft)** | 5 | −5 | −9 | 8 | −3 |

−10 −9 −8 −7 −6 −5 −4 −3 −2 −1 0 1 2 3 4 5 6 7 8 9 10

**B** What point on the number line represents sea level? _____

**C** Which location is closest to sea level? How do you know?

_____

**D** Which two locations are the same distance from sea level? Are these locations above or below sea level?

_____

**E** Which location has the least elevation? How do you know?

_____

## Reflect

**1.** **Analyze Relationships** Morning Glory Stream is 7 feet below sea level. What number represents the elevation of Morning Glory Stream?

_____

**2.** **Multiple Representations** Explain how to graph the elevation of Morning Glory Stream on a number line.

_____

EXPLORE ACTIVITY 2    TEKS 6.2.B

# Opposites

Two numbers are **opposites** if, on a number line, they are the same distance from 0 but on different sides of 0. For example, 5 and −5 are opposites. 0 is its own opposite.

$$-6\ -5\ -4\ -3\ -2\ -1\quad 0\quad 1\quad 2\quad 3\quad 4\quad 5\quad 6$$

**Integers** are the set of all whole numbers and their opposites.

> Remember, the set of whole numbers is 0, 1, 2, 3, 4, 5, 6, …

**On graph paper, use a ruler or straightedge to draw a number line. Label the number line with each integer from −10 to 10. Fold your number line in half so that the crease goes through 0. Numbers that line up after folding the number line are opposites.**

**A** Use your number line to find the opposites of 7, −6, 1, and 9. _____

**B** How does your number line show that 0 is its own opposite?

_____

**C** What is the opposite of the opposite of 3? _____

## Reflect

**3.** **Justify Reasoning** Explain how your number line shows that 8 and −8 are opposites.

_____

**4.** **Multiple Representations** Explain how to use your number line to find the opposite of the opposite of −6.

_____

_____

_____

# Integers and Opposites on a Number Line

Positive and negative numbers can be used to represent real-world quantities. For example, 3 can represent a temperature that is 3 °F above 0. −3 can represent a temperature that is 3 °F below 0. Both 3 and −3 are 3 units from 0.

Math On the Spot
my.hrw.com

## EXAMPLE 1  Real World

TEKS 6.2.B

Sandy kept track of the weekly low temperature in her town for several weeks. The table shows the low temperature in °F for each week.

| Week | Week 1 | Week 2 | Week 3 | Week 4 |
|------|--------|--------|--------|--------|
| Temperature (°F) | −1 | 3 | −4 | 2 |

**A**  Graph the temperature from Week 3 and its opposite on a number line. What do the numbers represent?

**STEP 1**  Graph the value from Week 3 on the number line.

The value from Week 3 is −4.
Graph a point 4 units below 0.

**STEP 2**  Graph the opposite of −4.

Graph a point 4 units above 0.

The opposite of −4 is 4.

−4 represents a temperature that is 4 °F below 0 and 4 represents a temperature that is 4 °F above 0.

**B**  The value for Week 5 is the opposite of the opposite of the value from Week 1. What was the low temperature in Week 5?

**STEP 1**  Graph the value from Week 1 on the number line.

The value from Week 1 is −1.

**STEP 2**  Graph the opposite of −1.

The opposite of −1 is 1.

**STEP 3**  Graph the opposite of 1.

The opposite of 1 is −1.

```
←+——+——+——+——+——+——+——+——+——+——+——+——+→
 −6 −5 −4 −3 −2 −1  0  1  2  3  4  5  6
```

The opposite of the opposite of −1 is −1.
The low temperature in Week 5 was −1 °F.

## Reflect

5.  **Analyze Relationships**  Explain how you can find the opposite of the opposite of any number without using a number line.

_____

My Notes

Use this space to take notes as you listen in class.

**YOUR TURN**

**Graph the opposite of the number shown on each number line.**

6.

```
←┼──┼──┼──┼──┼──┼──┼──┼──┼──┼──◆──┼──┼──┼──┼──┼──┼──┼──┼──┼──┼→
 −10 −9 −8 −7 −6 −5 −4 −3 −2 −1  0  1  2  3  4  5  6  7  8  9 10
```

7.

```
←┼──┼──┼──┼──┼──┼──┼──┼──┼──┼──┼──┼──┼──┼──┼──┼──┼──◆──┼──┼──┼→
 −10 −9 −8 −7 −6 −5 −4 −3 −2 −1  0  1  2  3  4  5  6  7  8  9 10
```

**Write the opposite of each number.**

8. 10 _____    9. −5 _____    10. 0 _____

11. What is the opposite of the opposite of 6? _____

**Math Talk**
Mathematical Processes

Explain how you could use a number line to find the opposite of 8.

## Guided Practice

1. Graph and label the following points on the number line.
   (Explore Activity 1)

   a. −2     b. 9     c. −8     d. −9     e. 5     f. 8

```
←┼──┼──┼──┼──┼──┼──┼──┼──┼──┼──┼──┼──┼──┼──┼──┼──┼──┼──┼──┼──┼→
 −10 −9 −8 −7 −6 −5 −4 −3 −2 −1  0  1  2  3  4  5  6  7  8  9 10
```

**Graph the opposite of the number shown on each number line.**
(Explore Activity 2 and Example 1)

2.

```
←┼──┼──┼──┼──┼──┼──┼──┼──┼──┼──◆──┼──┼──┼──┼──┼──┼──┼──┼──┼──┼→
 −10 −9 −8 −7 −6 −5 −4 −3 −2 −1  0  1  2  3  4  5  6  7  8  9 10
```

3.

```
←┼──┼──◆──┼──┼──┼──┼──┼──┼──┼──┼──┼──┼──┼──┼──┼──┼──┼──┼──┼──┼→
 −10 −9 −8 −7 −6 −5 −4 −3 −2 −1  0  1  2  3  4  5  6  7  8  9 10
```

4.

```
←┼──┼──┼──┼──┼──┼──┼──┼──┼──┼──┼──◆──┼──┼──┼──┼──┼──┼──┼──┼──┼→
 −10 −9 −8 −7 −6 −5 −4 −3 −2 −1  0  1  2  3  4  5  6  7  8  9 10
```

**Write the opposite of each number.** (Explore Activity 2 and Example 1)

5. 4 _____      6. −11 _____      7. 3 _____

8. −3 _____      9. 0 _____      10. 22 _____

**? ESSENTIAL QUESTION CHECK-IN**

11. Given an integer, how do you find its opposite?

_____

_____

# 1.1 Independent Practice

TEKS 6.2.B

**Personal Math Trainer**

Online Assessment and Intervention

my.hrw.com

**12. Chemistry** Atoms normally have an electric charge of 0. Certain conditions, such as static, can cause atoms to have a positive or a negative charge. Atoms with a positive or negative charge are called *ions*.

| Ion | A | B | C | D | E |
|---|---|---|---|---|---|
| Charge | −3 | +1 | −2 | +3 | −1 |

**a.** Which ions have a negative charge?

_____

**b.** Which ions have charges that are opposites?

_____

**c.** Which ion's charge is not the opposite of another ion's charge?

_____

**Name the integer that meets the given description.**

**13.** the opposite of −17 _____

**14.** 4 units left of 0 _____

**15.** the opposite of the opposite of 2 _____

**16.** 15 units right of 0 _____

**17.** 12 units right of 0 _____

**18.** the opposite of −19 _____

**19. Analyze Relationships** Several wrestlers are trying to lose weight for a competition. Their change in weight since last week is shown in the chart.

| Wrestler | Tino | Victor | Ramsey | Baxter | Luis |
|---|---|---|---|---|---|
| Weight Change (in pounds) | −2 | 6 | 2 | 5 | −5 |

**a.** Did Victor lose or gain weight since last week? _____

**b.** Which wrestler's weight change is the opposite of Ramsey's? _____

**c.** Which wrestlers have lost weight since last week? _____

**d.** Frankie's weight change since last week was the opposite of Victor's.

What was Frankie's weight change? _____

**e.** Frankie's goal last week was to gain weight. Did he meet his goal? Explain.

_____

**Find the distance between the given number and its opposite on a number line.**

**20.** 6 _____

**21.** −2 _____

**22.** 0 _____

**23.** −7 _____

**24.** **What If?** Three contestants are competing on a trivia game show. The table shows their scores before the final question.

| Contestant | Score Before Final Question |
|---|---|
| Timothy | −25 |
| Shawna | 18 |
| Kaylynn | −14 |

   **a.** How many points must Shawna earn for her score to be the opposite of Timothy's score before the final question? _____

   **b.** Which person's score is closest to 0? _____

   **c.** Who do you think is winning the game before the final question? Explain.

   _____

**H.O.T.** FOCUS ON HIGHER ORDER THINKING

**Work Area**

**25.** **Communicate Mathematical Ideas** Which number is farther from 0 on a number line: −9 or 6? Explain your reasoning.

   _____

   _____

**26.** **Analyze Relationships** A number is $k$ units to the left of 0 on the number line. Describe the location of its opposite.

   _____

**27.** **Critique Reasoning** Roberto says that the opposite of a certain integer is −5. Cindy concludes that the opposite of an integer is always negative. Explain Cindy's error.

   _____

   _____

**28.** **Multiple Representations** Explain how to use a number line to find the opposites of the integers 3 units away from −7.

   _____

   _____

   _____

TEKS
Number and operations—
6.2.C Locate, compare, and order integers ... using a number line.

### ? ESSENTIAL QUESTION

How do you compare and order integers?

EXPLORE ACTIVITY  TEKS 6.2.C

## Comparing Positive and Negative Integers

The Westfield soccer league ranks its teams using a number called the "win/loss combined record." A team with more wins than losses will have a positive combined record, and a team with fewer wins than losses will have a negative combined record. The table shows the total win/loss combined record for each team at the end of the season.

| Team | Sharks A | Jaguars B | Badgers C | Tigers D | Cougars E | Hawks F | Wolves G |
|---|---|---|---|---|---|---|---|
| Win/Loss Combined Record | 0 | 4 | −4 | −6 | 2 | −2 | 6 |

**A** Graph the win/loss combined record for each team on the number line.

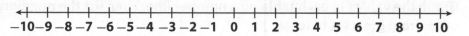

−10 −9 −8 −7 −6 −5 −4 −3 −2 −1 0 1 2 3 4 5 6 7 8 9 10

**B** Which team had the best record in the league? How do you know?

_____

**C** Which team had the worst record? How do you know?

_____

### Reflect

1. **Analyze Relationships** Explain what the data tell you about the win/loss records of the teams in the league.

_____

_____

_____

_____

# Ordering Positive and Negative Integers

When you read a number line from left to right, the numbers are in order from least to greatest.

## EXAMPLE 1 Real World

TEKS 6.2.C

Fred recorded the following golf scores during his first week at the golf academy. In golf, the player with the lowest score wins the game.

| Day | Mon | Tues | Wed | Thurs | Fri | Sat | Sun |
|-----|-----|------|-----|-------|-----|-----|-----|
| Score | 4 | −2 | 3 | −5 | −1 | 0 | −3 |

Graph Fred's scores on the number line, and then list the numbers in order from least to greatest.

**STEP 1** Graph the scores on the number line.

$$-10\ -9\ -8\ -7\ -6\ -5\ -4\ -3\ -2\ -1\ 0\ 1\ 2\ 3\ 4\ 5\ 6\ 7\ 8\ 9\ 10$$

**STEP 2** Read from left to right to list the scores in order from least to greatest.

The scores listed from least to greatest are −5, −3, −2, −1, 0, 3, 4.

### Math Talk
**Mathematical Processes**

What day did Fred have his best golf score? How do you know?

## YOUR TURN

Graph the values in each table on a number line. Then list the numbers in order from greatest to least.

2.

| Change in Stock Price ($) | | | | | |
|------|------|------|------|------|------|
| −5 | 4 | 0 | −3 | −6 | 2 |

$$-10\ -9\ -8\ -7\ -6\ -5\ -4\ -3\ -2\ -1\ 0\ 1\ 2\ 3\ 4\ 5\ 6\ 7\ 8\ 9\ 10$$

_____

3.

| Elevation (meters) | | | | | | | |
|---|----|----|---|-----|---|---|---|
| 9 | −1 | −6 | 2 | −10 | 0 | 5 | 8 |

$$-10\ -9\ -8\ -7\ -6\ -5\ -4\ -3\ -2\ -1\ 0\ 1\ 2\ 3\ 4\ 5\ 6\ 7\ 8\ 9\ 10$$

_____

# Writing Inequalities

An **inequality** is a statement that two quantities are not equal. The symbols < and > are used to write inequalities.

- The symbol > means "is greater than."
- The symbol < means "is less than."

You can use a number line to help write an inequality.

**Math On the Spot**

⊙ my.hrw.com

## EXAMPLE 2  Real World

TEKS 6.2.C

**A** In 2005, Austin, Texas, received 51 inches in annual precipitation. In 2009, the city received 36 inches in annual precipitation. In which year was there more precipitation?

Graph 51 and 36 on the number line.

```
20 24 28 32 36 40 44 48 52 56 60
```

- 51 is to the *right* of 36 on the number line.

  This means that 51 is **greater than** 36.

  Write the inequality as 51 > 36.

- 36 is to the *left* of 51 on the number line.

  This means that 36 is **less than** 51.

  Write the inequality as 36 < 51.

  There was more precipitation in 2005.

**B** Write two inequalities to compare −6 and 7.
−6 < 7; 7 > −6

**C** Write two inequalities to compare −9 and −4.
−4 > −9; −9 < −4

**Math Talk**
**Mathematical Processes**

Is there a greatest integer? Is there a greatest negative integer? Explain.

## YOUR TURN

Compare. Write > or <. Use the number line to help you.

**4.** −10 ◯ −2    **5.** −6 ◯ 6    **6.** −7 ◯ −8

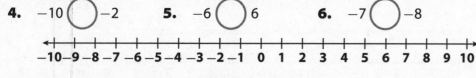

```
−10−9 −8 −7 −6 −5 −4 −3 −2 −1  0  1  2  3  4  5  6  7  8  9  10
```

**7.** Write two inequalities to compare −2 and −18. _____

**8.** Write two inequalities to compare 39 and −39. _____

**Personal Math Trainer**

Online Assessment and Intervention

⊙ my.hrw.com

**1a.** Graph the temperature for each city on the number line. (Explore Activity)

| City | A | B | C | D | E |
|------|-----|-----|-----|-----|-----|
| Temperature (°F) | −9 | 10 | −2 | 0 | 4 |

**b.** Which city was coldest? _____

**c.** Which city was warmest? _____

**List the numbers in order from least to greatest.** (Example 1)

**2.** 4, −6, 0, 8, −9, 1, −3

_____

**3.** −65, 34, 7, −13, 55, 62, −7

_____

**4.** Write two inequalities to compare −17 and −22. _____

**Compare. Write < or >.** (Example 2)

**5.** −9 ◯ 2

**6.** 0 ◯ 6

**7.** 3 ◯ −7

**8.** 5 ◯ −10

**9.** −1 ◯ −3

**10.** −8 ◯ −4

**11.** −4 ◯ 1

**12.** −2 ◯ −6

**13.** Compare the temperatures for the following cities. Write < or >. (Example 2)

| City | Alexandria | Redwood Falls | Grand Marais | Winona | International Falls |
|------|-----|-----|-----|-----|-----|
| Average Temperature in March (°C) | −3 | 0 | −2 | 2 | −4 |

**a.** Alexandria and Winona _____

**b.** Redwood Falls and International Falls _____

**? ESSENTIAL QUESTION CHECK-IN**

**14.** How can you use a number line to compare and order numbers?

_____

_____

_____

Name_____ Class_____ Date_____

## 1.2 Independent Practice

Personal
Math Trainer

Online
Assessment and
Intervention

my.hrw.com

**15. Multiple Representations** A hockey league tracks the plus-minus records for each player. A plus-minus record is the difference in even strength goals for and against the team when a player is on the ice. The following table lists the plus-minus values for several hockey players.

| Player | A. Jones | B. Sutter | E. Simpson | L. Mays | R. Tomas | S. Klatt |
|---|---|---|---|---|---|---|
| Plus-minus | −8 | 4 | 9 | −3 | −4 | 3 |

**a.** Graph the values on the number line.

```
-10-9 -8 -7 -6 -5 -4 -3 -2 -1  0  1  2  3  4  5  6  7  8  9 10
```

**b.** Which player has the best plus-minus record? _____

**Astronomy** The table lists the average surface temperature of some planets. Write an inequality to compare the temperatures of each pair of planets.

**16.** Uranus and Jupiter _____

**17.** Mercury and Mars _____

**18.** Arrange the planets in order of average surface temperature

from greatest to least. _____

_____

| Planet | Average Surface Temperature (°C) |
|---|---|
| Mercury | 167 |
| Uranus | −197 |
| Neptune | −200 |
| Earth | 15 |
| Mars | −65 |
| Jupiter | −110 |

**19. Represent Real-World Problems** For a stock market project, five students each invested pretend money in one stock. They tracked gains and losses in the value of that stock for one week. In the following table, a gain is represented by a positive number and a loss is represented by a negative number.

| Students | Andre | Bria | Carla | Daniel | Ethan |
|---|---|---|---|---|---|
| Gains and Losses ($) | 7 | −2 | −5 | 2 | 4 |

Graph the students' results on the number line. Then list them in order from least to greatest.

**a.** Graph the values on the number line.

```
-10-9 -8 -7 -6 -5 -4 -3 -2 -1  0  1  2  3  4  5  6  7  8  9 10
```

**b.** The results listed from least to greatest are _____.

**Geography** The table lists the lowest elevation for several countries. A negative number means the elevation is below sea level, and a positive number means the elevation is above sea level. Compare the lowest elevation for each pair of countries. Write < or >.

| Country | Lowest Elevation (feet) |
|---|---|
| Argentina | −344 |
| Australia | −49 |
| Czech Republic | 377 |
| Hungary | 249 |
| United States | −281 |

20. Argentina and the United States _____

21. Czech Republic and Hungary _____

22. Hungary and Argentina _____

23. Which country in the table has the lowest elevation? _____

24. **Analyze Relationships** There are three numbers a, b, and c, where $a > b$ and $b > c$. Describe the positions of the numbers on a number line.

_____

_____

_____

_____

**H.O.T.** FOCUS ON HIGHER ORDER THINKING

Work Area

25. **Critique Reasoning** At 9 A.M. the outside temperature was −3°F. By noon, the temperature was −12°F. Jorge said that it was getting warmer outside. Is he correct? Explain.

_____

26. **Problem Solving** Golf scores represent the number of strokes above or below par. A negative score means that you hit a number below par while a positive score means that you hit a number above par. The winner in golf has the lowest score. During a round of golf, Angela's score was −5 and Lisa's score was −8. Who won the game? Explain.

_____

27. **Look for a Pattern** Order −3, 5, 16, and −10 from least to greatest. Then order the same numbers from closest to zero to farthest from zero. Describe how your lists are similar. Would this be true if the numbers were −3, 5, −16 and −10?

_____

_____

_____

_____

# 1.3 Absolute Value

TEKS
Number and operations—
6.2.B Identify a number, its opposite, and its absolute value.

## ? ESSENTIAL QUESTION

How do you find and use absolute value?

### EXPLORE ACTIVITY 1 | TEKS 6.2.B

## Finding Absolute Value

The **absolute value** of a number is the number's distance from 0 on a number line. For example, the absolute value of −3 is 3 because −3 is 3 units from 0. The absolute value of −3 is written |−3|.

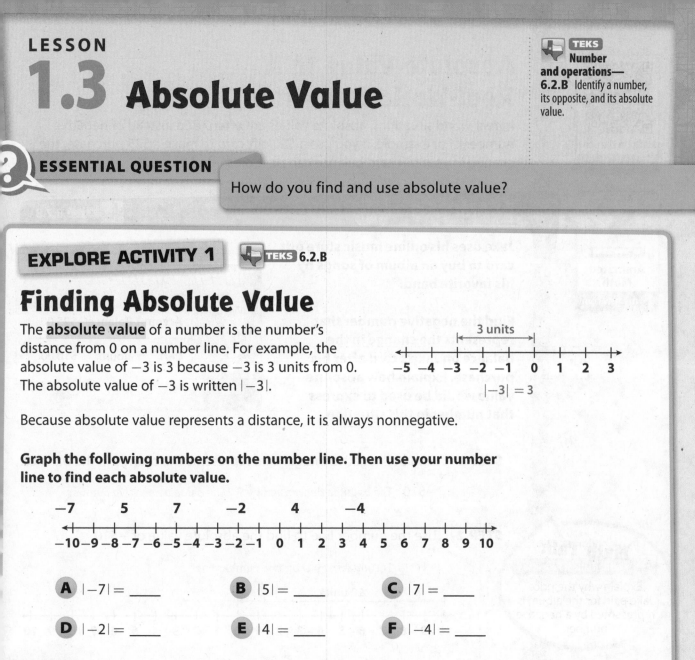

Because absolute value represents a distance, it is always nonnegative.

**Graph the following numbers on the number line. Then use your number line to find each absolute value.**

−7    5    7    −2    4    −4

**A** |−7| = _____    **B** |5| = _____    **C** |7| = _____

**D** |−2| = _____    **E** |4| = _____    **F** |−4| = _____

## Reflect

1. **Analyze Relationships** Which pairs of numbers have the same absolute value? How are these numbers related?

   _____

   _____

2. **Justify Reasoning** Negative numbers are less than positive numbers. Does this mean that the absolute value of a negative number must be less than the absolute value of a positive number? Explain.

   _____

   _____

   _____

   _____

# Absolute Value In A Real-World Situation

In real-world situations, absolute values are often used instead of negative numbers. For example, if you use a $50 gift card to make a $25 purchase, the change in your gift card balance can be represented by −$25.

**EXAMPLE 1** Real World · · · · · · · · · · · · · · · · · · TEKS 6.2.B

Jake uses his online music store gift card to buy an album of songs by his favorite band.

Find the negative number that represents the change in the balance on Jake's card after his purchase. Explain how absolute value would be used to express that number in this situation.

**Music Online**

| Account Balance | $25.00 |
| Cart    1 album | $10.00 |

**STEP 1** Find the negative integer that represents the change in the balance.

−$10   *The balance decreased by $10, so use a negative number.*

**Math Talk**
Mathematical Processes
Explain why the price Jake paid for the album is represented by a negative number.

**STEP 2** Use the number line to find the absolute value of −$10.

*−10 is 10 units from 0 on the number line.*

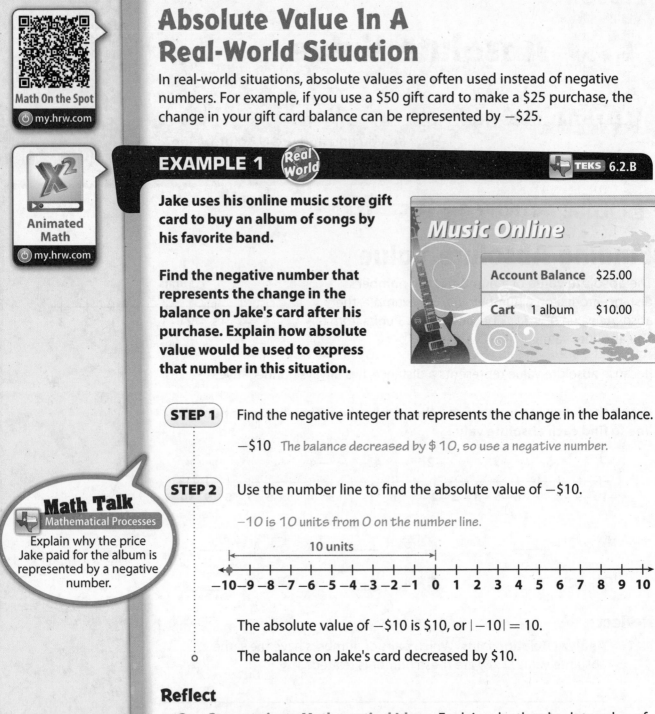

10 units

−10 −9 −8 −7 −6 −5 −4 −3 −2 −1  0  1  2  3  4  5  6  7  8  9  10

The absolute value of −$10 is $10, or |−10| = 10.

The balance on Jake's card decreased by $10.

## Reflect

3. **Communicate Mathematical Ideas** Explain why the absolute value of a number will never be negative.

_____

_____

_____

4. The temperature at night reached −13°F. Write an equivalent statement about the temperature using the absolute value of the number.

_____

**Find each absolute value.**

5. |−12| _____  6. |91| _____  7. |−55| _____

8. |0| _____  9. |88| _____  10. |1| _____

**EXPLORE ACTIVITY 2**  Real World  🔲 TEKS 6.2.B

# Comparing Absolute Values

You can use absolute values to compare negative numbers in real-world situations.

**Maria, Susan, George, and Antonio checked their credit card balances on their smartphones. The amounts owed are shown.**

You owe: $20    You owe: $25    You owe: $30    You owe: $45

_____  _____  _____  _____

**Answer the following questions. When you have finished, you will have enough clues to match each statement with the correct person.**

Remember: When someone owes a positive amount of money, this means that he or she has a *negative* balance.

**A** Maria's credit card balance is less than −$30. Does Maria owe more than $30 or less than $30? _____

**B** Susan's credit card balance is greater than −$25. Does Susan owe more than $25 or less than $25? _____

**C** George's credit card balance is $5 less than Susan's balance. Does George owe more than Susan or less than Susan? _____

**D** Antonio owes $15 less than Maria owes. This means that Antonio's balance is _____ than Maria's balance.

**E** Write each person's name underneath his or her smartphone.

**Reflect**

11. **Analyze Relationships** Use absolute value to describe the relationship between a negative credit card balance and the amount owed.

_____

## Guided Practice

1. **Vocabulary** If a number is _____, then the number is less than its absolute value. (Explore Activity 1)

2. If Ryan pays his car insurance for the year in full, he will get a credit of $28. If he chooses to pay a monthly premium, he will pay a $10 late fee for any month that the payment is late. (Explore Activity 1, Example 1)

   a. Which of these values could be represented with a negative number? Explain.

   _____

   _____

   b. Use the number line to find the absolute value of the amount from

   part a. _____

   ```
   ←+—+—+—+—+—+—+—+—+—+—+—+—+—+—+—+—+—+—+—+—+→
    -10 -9 -8 -7 -6 -5 -4 -3 -2 -1  0  1  2  3  4  5  6  7  8  9  10
   ```

3. Leo, Gabrielle, Sinea, and Tomas are playing a video game. Their scores are described in the table below. (Explore Activity 2)

   | Name | Leo | Gabrielle | Sinea |
   |------|-----|-----------|-------|
   | Score | less than −100 points | 20 more points than Leo | 50 points less than Leo |

   a. Leo wants to earn enough points to have a positive score. Does he need to earn more than 100 points or less than 100 points? _____

   b. Gabrielle wants to earn enough points to not have a negative score. Does she need to earn more points than Leo or less points than Leo? _____

   c. Sinea wants to earn enough points to have a higher score than Leo. Does she need to earn more than 50 points or less than 50 points? _____

**? ESSENTIAL QUESTION CHECK-IN**

4. When is the absolute value of a number equal to the number?

_____

# 1.3 Independent Practice

TEKS 6.2.B

Personal Math Trainer

Online Assessment and Intervention

my.hrw.com

**5. Financial Literacy** Jacob earned $80 babysitting and deposited the money into his savings account. The next week he spent $85 on video games. Use integers to describe the weekly changes in Jacob's savings account balance.

_____

_____

**6. Financial Literacy** Sara's savings account balance changed by $34 one week and by −$67 the next week. Which amount represents the greatest

change? _____

**7. Analyze Relationships** Bertrand collects movie posters. The number of movie posters in his collection changes each month as he buys and sells posters. The table shows how many posters he bought or sold in the given months.

| Month | January | February | March | April |
|-------|---------|----------|-------|-------|
| Posters | Sold 20 | Bought 12 | Bought 22 | Sold 28 |

**a.** Which months have changes that can be represented by positive numbers? Which months have changes that can be represented by negative numbers? Explain.

_____

_____

_____

_____

**b.** According to the table, in which month did the size of Bertrand's poster collection change the most? Use absolute value to explain your answer.

_____

_____

_____

**8. Earth Science** Death Valley has an elevation of −282 feet relative to sea level. Explain how to use absolute value to describe the elevation of Death Valley as a positive integer.

_____

_____

9. **Communicate Mathematical Ideas** Lisa and Alice are playing a game. Each player either receives or has to pay play money based on the result of their spin. The table lists how much a player receives or pays for various spins.

| Red | Pay $5 |
|-----|--------|
| Blue | Receive $4 |
| Yellow | Pay $1 |
| Green | Receive $3 |
| Orange | Pay $2 |

a. Express the amounts in the table as positive and negative numbers.

_____

b. Describe the change to Lisa's amount of money when the spinner lands on red.

_____

_____

10. **Financial Literacy** Sam's credit card balance is less than −$36. Does Sam owe more or less than $36? _____

11. **Financial Literacy** Emily spent $55 from her savings on a new dress. Explain how to describe the change in Emily's savings balance in two different ways.

_____

_____

_____

**FOCUS ON HIGHER ORDER THINKING**

**Work Area**

12. **Make a Conjecture** Can two different numbers have the same absolute value? If yes, give an example. If no, explain why not.

_____

13. **Communicate Mathematical Ideas** Does $-|-4| = |-(-4)|$? Justify your answer.

_____

14. **Critique Reasoning** Angelique says that finding the absolute value of a number is the same as finding the opposite of the number. For example, $|-5| = 5$. Explain her error.

_____

_____

_____

# Ready to Go On?

Personal
Math Trainer

Online Assessment
and Intervention

my.hrw.com

## 1.1 Identifying Integers and Their Opposites

1. The table shows the elevations in feet of several locations around a coastal town. Graph and label the locations on the number line according to their elevations.

| Location | Post Office A | Library B | Town Hall C | Laundromat D | Pet Store E |
|---|---|---|---|---|---|
| Elevation (feet) | 8 | −3 | −9 | 3 | 1 |

−10 −9 −8 −7 −6 −5 −4 −3 −2 −1 0 1 2 3 4 5 6 7 8 9 10

**Write the opposite of each number.**

2. −22 _____

3. 0 _____

## 1.2 Comparing and Ordering Integers

**List the numbers in order from least to greatest.**

4. −2, 8, −15, −5, 3, 1 _____

**Compare. Write < or >.**

5. −3 ◯ −15

6. 9 ◯ −10

## 1.3 Absolute Value

**Graph each number on the number line. Then use your number line to find the absolute value of each number.**

−10 −9 −8 −7 −6 −5 −4 −3 −2 −1 0 1 2 3 4 5 6 7 8 9 10

7. 2 _____

8. −8 _____

9. −5 _____

### ? ESSENTIAL QUESTION

10. How can you use absolute value to represent a negative number in a real-world situation?

_____

_____

MODULE 1 MIXED REVIEW

# Texas Test Prep

Personal
Math Trainer

Online
Assessment and
Intervention

my.hrw.com

## Selected Response

1. Which number line shows 2, 3, and −3?

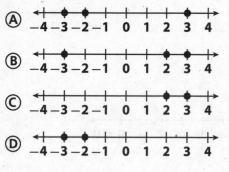

2. What is the opposite of −3?

   (A) 3

   (B) 0

   (C) −$\frac{1}{3}$

   (D) $\frac{1}{3}$

3. Darrel is currently 20 feet below sea level. Which correctly describes the opposite of Darrel's elevation?

   (A) 20 feet below sea level

   (B) 20 feet above sea level

   (C) 2 feet below sea level

   (D) At sea level

4. Which has the same absolute value as −55?

   (A) 0

   (B) −1

   (C) 1

   (D) 55

5. In Bangor it is −3°F, in Fairbanks it is −12°F, in Fargo it is −8°F, and in Calgary it is −15°F. In which city is it the coldest?

   (A) Bangor

   (B) Fairbanks

   (C) Fargo

   (D) Calgary

6. Which shows the integers in order from least to greatest?

   (A) 20, 6, −2, −13

   (B) −2, 6, −13, 20

   (C) −13, −2, 6, 20

   (D) 20, −13, 6, −2

7. How would you use a number line to put integers in order from greatest to least?

   (A) Graph the integers, then read them from left to right.

   (B) Graph the integers, then read them from right to left.

   (C) Graph the absolute values of the integers, then read them from left to right.

   (D) Graph the absolute values of the integers, then read them from right to left.

## Gridded Response

8. The table shows the change in several savings accounts over the past month. Which value represents the least change?

| Account | Change |
|---------|--------|
| A | $25 |
| B | −$45 |
| C | −$302 |
| D | $108 |

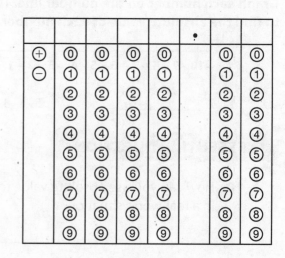

# Rational Numbers

**ESSENTIAL QUESTION**

How can you use rational numbers to solve real-world problems?

**Real-World Video**

my.hrw.com

In sports like baseball, coaches, analysts, and fans keep track of players' statistics such as batting averages, earned run averages, and runs batted in. These values are reported using rational numbers.

**GO DIGITAL**

my.hrw.com

**my.hrw.com**

Go digital with your write-in student edition, accessible on any device.

**Math On the Spot**

Scan with your smart phone to jump directly to the online edition, video tutor, and more.

**Animated Math**

Interactively explore key concepts to see how math works.

**Personal Math Trainer**

Get immediate feedback and help as you work through practice sets.

Complete these exercises to review skills you will need for this chapter.

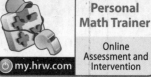

**Personal Math Trainer**

Online Assessment and Intervention

my.hrw.com

## Write an Improper Fraction as a Mixed Number

**EXAMPLE**

$\frac{11}{3} = \frac{3}{3} + \frac{3}{3} + \frac{3}{3} + \frac{2}{3}$    Write as a sum using names for one plus a proper fraction.

$= 1 + 1 + 1 + \frac{2}{3}$    Write each name for one as one.

$= 3 + \frac{2}{3}$    Add the ones.

$= 3\frac{2}{3}$    Write the mixed number.

**Write each improper fraction as a mixed number.**

**1.** $\frac{7}{2}$ _____    **2.** $\frac{12}{5}$ _____    **3.** $\frac{11}{7}$ _____    **4.** $\frac{15}{4}$ _____

## Write a Mixed Number as an Improper Fraction

**EXAMPLE**

$3\frac{3}{4} = 1 + 1 + 1 + \frac{3}{4}$    Write the whole number as a sum of ones.

$= \frac{4}{4} + \frac{4}{4} + \frac{4}{4} + \frac{3}{4}$    Use the denominator of the fraction to write equivalent fractions for the ones.

$= \frac{15}{4}$    Add the numerators.

**Write each mixed number as an improper fraction.**

**5.** $2\frac{1}{2}$ _____    **6.** $4\frac{3}{5}$ _____    **7.** $3\frac{4}{9}$ _____    **8.** $2\frac{5}{7}$ _____

## Find Common Denominators

**EXAMPLE**    Find a common denominator for $\frac{3}{10}$ and $\frac{7}{8}$.

10: 10, 20, 30, ⓐ40, 50, 60, 70, ⓐ80    List multiples of each denominator.

8: 8, 16, 24, 32, ⓐ40, 48, 56, 64, 72, ⓐ80    Circle common multiples.

Least common denominator: 40

**Find the least common denominator.**

**9.** $\frac{1}{2}$ and $\frac{3}{5}$ _____    **10.** $\frac{1}{6}$ and $\frac{3}{8}$ _____    **11.** $\frac{9}{10}$ and $\frac{7}{12}$ ___    **12.** $\frac{4}{9}$ and $\frac{5}{12}$ _____

# Reading Start-Up

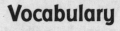

## Visualize Vocabulary

**Use the ✔ words to complete the web. You may put more than one word in each box.**

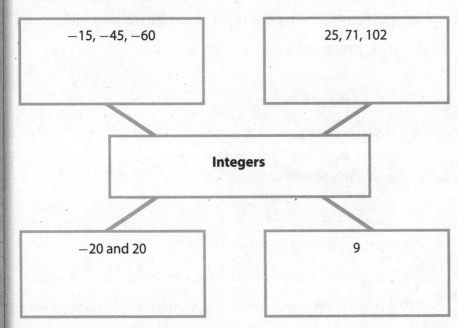

| −15, −45, −60 | | 25, 71, 102 |
| :---: | :---: | :---: |
| | **Integers** | |
| −20 and 20 | | 9 |

## Understand Vocabulary

**Fill in each blank with the correct term from the preview words.**

1. A _____ is any number that can be written as a ratio of two integers.

2. A _____ is used to show the relationships between groups.

## Active Reading

**Tri-Fold** Before beginning the module, create a tri-fold to help you learn the concepts and vocabulary in this module. Fold the paper into three sections. Label the columns "What I Know," "What I Need to Know," and "What I Learned." Complete the first two columns before you read. Use the third column to take notes on important concepts and vocabulary terms as you listen in class. Then complete the third column after studying the module.

## Vocabulary

**Review Words**

absolute value *(valor absoluto)*

decimal *(decimal)*

dividend *(dividendo)*

divisor *(divisor)*

fraction *(fracción)*

integers *(enteros)*

✔ negative numbers *(números negativos)*

✔ opposites *(opuestos)*

✔ positive numbers *(números positivos)*

✔ whole number *(número entero)*

**Preview Words**

rational number *(número racional)*

Venn diagram *(diagrama de Venn)*

**MODULE 2**

# Unpacking the TEKS

Understanding the TEKS and the vocabulary terms in the TEKS will help you know exactly what you are expected to learn in this module.

---

**TEKS 6.2.A**

Classify whole numbers, integers, and rational numbers using a visual representation such as a Venn diagram to describe relationships between sets of numbers.

### Key Vocabulary

**integer** *(entero)*
A member of the set of whole numbers and their opposites.

**Venn diagram**
*(diagrama de Venn)*
A diagram used to show the relationship between groups of numbers.

## What It Means to You

You can identify the type of number you are working with.

**UNPACKING EXAMPLE 6.2.A**

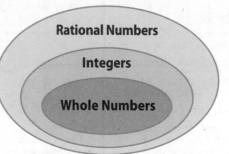

Classify the following numbers.

−3    *an integer, which also makes it a rational number*

130    *a whole number, which also makes it an integer and a rational number*

---

**TEKS 6.2.D**

Order a set of rational numbers arising from mathematical and real-world contexts.

### Key Vocabulary

**rational number**
*(número racional)*
Any number that can be expressed as a ratio of two integers.

## What It Means to You

You can order rational numbers to understand relationships between values in the real world.

**UNPACKING EXAMPLE 6.2.D**

The table shows the fraction of crude oil produced in the United States in 2011.

| CA | $\frac{1}{100}$ | TX | $\frac{9}{50}$ |
|----|----|----|----|
| ND | $\frac{3}{50}$ | AL | $\frac{3}{25}$ |

Which state produced the least oil?

$CA = \frac{1}{100}$        $TX = \frac{9}{50} = \frac{18}{100}$

$ND = \frac{3}{50} = \frac{6}{100}$        $AL = \frac{3}{25} = \frac{12}{100}$

California (CA) produced the least crude oil in 2011.

Visit **my.hrw.com** to see all the **TEKS** unpacked.

my.hrw.com

# Classifying Rational Numbers

TEKS
Number and operations—6.2.A
Classify whole numbers, integers, and rational numbers using a visual representation such as a Venn diagram to describe relationships between sets of numbers. *Also 6.2.E.*

**ESSENTIAL QUESTION**

How can you classify rational numbers?

**EXPLORE ACTIVITY** Real World TEKS 6.2.E

## Representing Division as a Fraction

Alicia and her friends Brittany, Kenji, and Ellis are taking a pottery class. The four friends have to share 3 blocks of clay. How much clay will each of them receive if they divide the 3 blocks evenly?

**A** The top faces of the 3 blocks of clay can be represented by squares. Use the model to show the part of each block that each friend will receive. Explain.

_____

_____

**B** Each piece of one square is equal to what fraction of a block of clay?

_____

**C** Explain how to arrange the pieces to model the amount of clay each person gets. Sketch the model.

A
A   A
A

Alicia   Brittany   Kenji   Ellis

_____

**D** What fraction of a square does each person's pieces cover? Explain.

_____

_____

**E** How much clay will each person receive?

_____

**F** **Multiple Representations** How does this situation represent division?

_____

_____

Alamy

### Reflect

1. **Communicate Mathematical Ideas** $3 \div 4$ can be written $\frac{3}{4}$. How are the dividend and divisor of a division expression related to the parts of a fraction?

_____

_____

2. **Analyze Relationships** How could you represent the division as a fraction if 5 people shared 2 blocks? if 6 people shared 5 blocks?

_____

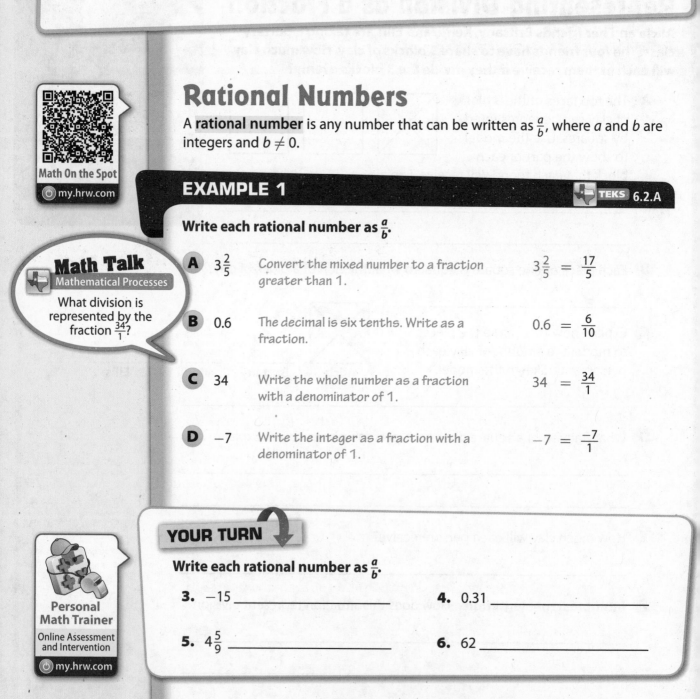

**Math On the Spot**

my.hrw.com

# Rational Numbers

A **rational number** is any number that can be written as $\frac{a}{b}$, where $a$ and $b$ are integers and $b \neq 0$.

## EXAMPLE 1

TEKS 6.2.A

Write each rational number as $\frac{a}{b}$.

**Math Talk**
Mathematical Processes

What division is represented by the fraction $\frac{34}{1}$?

**A** $3\frac{2}{5}$    Convert the mixed number to a fraction greater than 1.    $3\frac{2}{5} = \frac{17}{5}$

**B** $0.6$    The decimal is six tenths. Write as a fraction.    $0.6 = \frac{6}{10}$

**C** $34$    Write the whole number as a fraction with a denominator of 1.    $34 = \frac{34}{1}$

**D** $-7$    Write the integer as a fraction with a denominator of 1.    $-7 = \frac{-7}{1}$

### YOUR TURN

Write each rational number as $\frac{a}{b}$.

3. $-15$ _____

4. $0.31$ _____

5. $4\frac{5}{9}$ _____

6. $62$ _____

**Personal Math Trainer**

Online Assessment and Intervention

my.hrw.com

# Classifying Rational Numbers

A **Venn diagram** is a visual representation used to show the relationships between groups. The Venn diagram below shows how rational numbers, integers, and whole numbers are related.

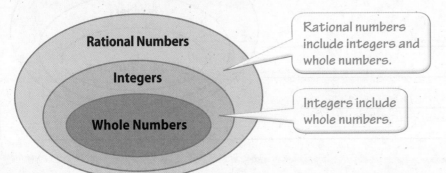

Rational numbers include integers and whole numbers.

Integers include whole numbers.

---

## EXAMPLE 2

TEKS 6.2.A

**Place each number in the Venn diagram. Then classify each number by indicating in which set or sets each number belongs.**

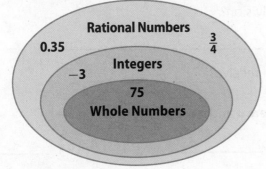

**A** 75    The number 75 belongs in the sets of whole numbers, integers, and rational numbers.

**B** −3    The number −3 belongs in the sets of integers and rational numbers.

**C** $\frac{3}{4}$    The number $\frac{3}{4}$ belongs in the set of rational numbers.

**D** 0.35    The number 0.35 belongs in the set of rational numbers.

## Reflect

**7. Analyze Relationships** Name two integers that are not also whole numbers.

_____

**8. Analyze Relationships** Describe how the Venn diagram models the relationship between rational numbers, integers, and whole numbers.

_____

_____

**My Notes**

Use this space to take notes as you listen in class.

## YOUR TURN

Place each number in the Venn diagram. Then classify each number by indicating in which set or sets it belongs.

9. 14.1 _____

10. $7\frac{1}{5}$ _____

11. −8 _____

12. 101 _____

**Rational Numbers**

**Integers**

**Whole Numbers**

# Guided Practice

1. Sarah and four friends are decorating picture frames with ribbon. They have 4 rolls of ribbon to share evenly. (Explore Activity)

   a. How does this situation represent division?

   _____

   b. How much ribbon does each person receive? _____

Write each rational number in the form $\frac{a}{b}$, where $a$ and $b$ are integers. (Example 1)

2. 0.7 _____

3. −29 _____

4. $8\frac{1}{3}$ _____

Place each number in the Venn diagram. Then classify each number by indicating in which set or sets each number belongs. (Example 2)

5. −15 _____

6. $5\frac{10}{11}$ _____

**Rational Numbers**

**Integers**

**Whole Numbers**

### ? ESSENTIAL QUESTION CHECK-IN

7. How is a rational number that is not an integer different from a rational number that is an integer?

_____

_____

_____

# 2.1 Independent Practice

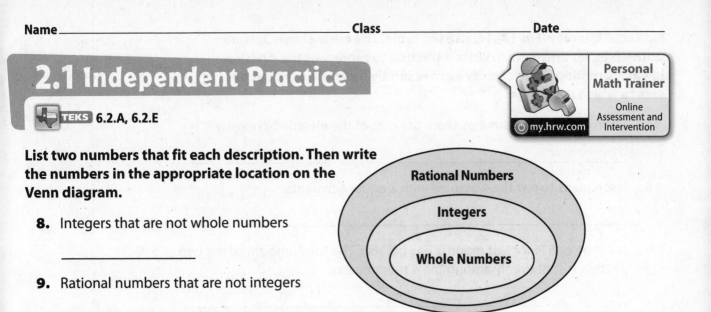

**TEKS** 6.2.A, 6.2.E

Personal
Math Trainer

Online
Assessment and
Intervention

my.hrw.com

**List two numbers that fit each description. Then write the numbers in the appropriate location on the Venn diagram.**

Rational Numbers

Integers

Whole Numbers

8. Integers that are not whole numbers

   _____

9. Rational numbers that are not integers

   _____

10. **Multistep**  A nature club is having its weekly hike. The table shows how many pieces of fruit and bottles of water each member of the club brought to share.

| Member | Pieces of Fruit | Bottles of Water |
|--------|-----------------|------------------|
| Baxter | 3 | 5 |
| Hendrick | 2 | 2 |
| Mary | 4 | 3 |
| Kendra | 5 | 7 |

   a. If the hikers want to share the fruit evenly, how many pieces should each person receive?

   _____

   b. Which hikers received more fruit than they brought on the hike?

   _____

   c. The hikers want to share their water evenly so that each member has the same amount. How much water does each hiker receive?

   _____

11. Sherman has 3 cats and 2 dogs. He wants to buy a toy for each of his pets. Sherman has $22 to spend on pet toys. How much can he spend on each pet? Write your answer as a fraction and as an amount in dollars and cents.

   _____

12. A group of 5 friends is sharing 2 pounds of trail mix. Write a division problem and a fraction to represent this situation.

   _____

13. **Vocabulary**  A _____ diagram can represent set relationships visually.

**Financial Literacy** For 14–16, use the table. The table shows Jason's utility bills for one month. Write a fraction to represent the division in each situation. Then classify each result by indicating the set or sets to which it belongs.

| March Bills | |
|---|---|
| Water | $35 |
| Gas | $14 |
| Electric | $108 |

**14.** Jason and his 3 roommates share the cost of the electric bill evenly.

_____

**15.** Jason plans to pay the water bill with 2 equal payments.

_____

**16.** Jason owes $15 for last month's gas bill also. The total amount of the two gas bills is split evenly among the 4 roommates.

_____

**17.** Lynn has a watering can that holds 16 cups of water, and she fills it half full. Then she waters her 15 plants so that each plant gets the same amount of water. How many cups of water will each plant get?

_____

## H.O.T. FOCUS ON HIGHER ORDER THINKING

Work Area

**18. Critique Reasoning** DaMarcus says the number $\frac{24}{6}$ belongs only to the set of rational numbers. Explain his error.

_____

_____

_____

_____

**19. Analyze Relationships** Explain how the Venn diagrams in this lesson show that all integers and all whole numbers are rational numbers.

_____

_____

_____

_____

**20. Critical Thinking** Is it possible for a number to be a rational number that is not an integer but is a whole number? Explain.

_____

_____

# Identifying Opposites and Absolute Value of Rational Numbers

TEKS
Number and operations—6.2.B
Identify a number, its opposite, and its absolute value.

## ? ESSENTIAL QUESTION

How do you identify opposites and absolute value of rational numbers?

---

**EXPLORE ACTIVITY** Real World   TEKS 6.2.B

## Positive and Negative Rational Numbers

Recall that positive numbers are greater than 0. They are located to the right of 0 on a number line. Negative numbers are less than 0. They are located to the left of 0 on a number line.

**Water levels with respect to sea level, which has elevation 0, may be measured at beach tidal basins. Water levels below sea level are represented by negative numbers.**

**A** The table shows the water level at a tidal basin at different times during a day. Graph the level for each time on the number line.

| Time | 4 A.M. A | 8 A.M. B | Noon C | 4 P.M. D | 8 P.M. E |
|------|----------|----------|--------|----------|----------|
| Level (ft) | 3.5 | 2.5 | −0.5 | −2.5 | 0.5 |

```
<-+--+--+--+--+--+--+--+--+--+--+->
 -5 -4 -3 -2 -1  0  1  2  3  4  5
```

**B** How did you know where to graph −0.5? _____

**C** At what time or times is the level closest to sea level? How do you know?

_____

**D** Which point is located halfway between −3 and −2? _____

**E** Which point is the same distance from 0 as *D*? _____

## Reflect

1. **Communicate Mathematical Ideas** How would you graph −2.25? Would it be left or right of point *D*?

_____

# Rational Numbers and Opposites on a Number Line

You can find the opposites of rational numbers the same way you found the opposites of integers. Two rational numbers are opposites if they are the same distance from 0 but on different sides of 0.

$2\frac{3}{4}$ and $-2\frac{3}{4}$ are opposites.

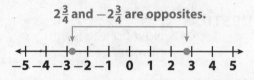

## EXAMPLE 1  Real World

TEKS 6.2.B

Until June 24, 1997, the New York Stock Exchange priced the value of a share of stock in eighths, such as $27\frac{1}{8}$ or at $41\frac{3}{4}$. The change in value of a share of stock from day to day was also represented in eighths as a positive or negative number.

The table shows the change in value of a stock over two days. Graph the change in stock value for Wednesday and its opposite on a number line.

| Day | Tuesday | Wednesday |
|---|---|---|
| Change in value ($) | $1\frac{5}{8}$ | $-4\frac{1}{4}$ |

**STEP 1** Graph the change in stock value for Wednesday on the number line.

The change in value for Wednesday is $-4\frac{1}{4}$

Graph a point $4\frac{1}{4}$ units below 0.

**STEP 2** Graph the opposite of $-4\frac{1}{4}$.

The opposite of $-4\frac{1}{4}$ is the same distance from 0 but on the other side of 0.

The opposite of $-4\frac{1}{4}$ is $4\frac{1}{4}$.

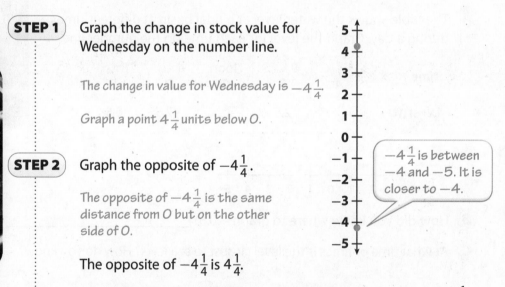

$-4\frac{1}{4}$ is between $-4$ and $-5$. It is closer to $-4$.

The opposite of the change in stock value for Wednesday is $4\frac{1}{4}$.

## YOUR TURN

**2.** What are the opposites of 7, −3.5, 2.25, and $9\frac{1}{3}$?

_____

# Absolute Values of Rational Numbers

You can also find the absolute value of a rational number the same way you found the absolute value of an integer. The absolute value of a rational number is the number's distance from 0 on the number line.

Math On the Spot
my.hrw.com

## EXAMPLE 2 · Real World

TEKS 6.2.B

The table shows the average low temperatures in January in one location during a five-year span. Find the absolute value of the average January low temperature in 2009.

| Year | 2008 | 2009 | 2010 | 2011 | 2012 |
|------|------|------|------|------|------|
| Temperature (°C) | −3.2 | −5.4 | −0.8 | 3.8 | −2 |

**STEP 1** Graph the 2009 average January low temperature.

The 2009 average January low is −5.4 °C.
Graph a point 5.4 units below 0.

**STEP 2** Find the absolute value of −5.4.

−5.4 is 5.4 units from 0.

$|{-5.4}| = 5.4$

## Reflect

3. **Communicate Mathematical Ideas** What is the absolute value of the average January low temperature in 2011? How do you know?

_____

_____

**Math Talk**
Mathematical Processes

How do you know where to graph −5.4?

### My Notes

## YOUR TURN

Graph each number on the number line. Then use your number line to find each absolute value.

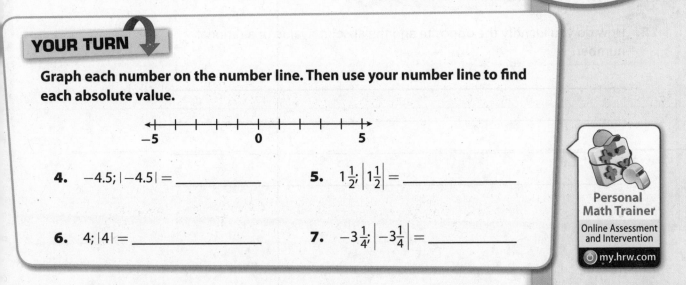

4. −4.5; $|{-4.5}|$ = _____

5. $1\frac{1}{2}$; $\left|1\frac{1}{2}\right|$ = _____

6. 4; $|4|$ = _____

7. $-3\frac{1}{4}$; $\left|-3\frac{1}{4}\right|$ = _____

**Personal Math Trainer**

Online Assessment and Intervention

my.hrw.com

**Graph each number and its opposite on a number line.** (Explore Activity and Example 1)

**1.** −2.8

$$\overset{\longleftrightarrow}{\underset{-5 \qquad\qquad\qquad 0 \qquad\qquad\qquad 5}{\rule{0pt}{0pt}}}$$

**2.** 4.3

$$\overset{\longleftrightarrow}{\underset{-5 \qquad\qquad\qquad 0 \qquad\qquad\qquad 5}{\rule{0pt}{0pt}}}$$

**3.** $-3\frac{4}{5}$

$$\overset{\longleftrightarrow}{\underset{-5 \qquad\qquad\qquad 0 \qquad\qquad\qquad 5}{\rule{0pt}{0pt}}}$$

**4.** $1\frac{1}{3}$

$$\overset{\longleftrightarrow}{\underset{-5 \qquad\qquad\qquad 0 \qquad\qquad\qquad 5}{\rule{0pt}{0pt}}}$$

**Find the opposite of each number.** (Example 1)

**5.** 3.78 _____

**6.** $-7\frac{5}{12}$ _____

**7.** 0 _____

**8.** 4.2 _____

**9.** 12.1 _____

**10.** 2.6 _____

**11.** **Vocabulary** Explain why 2.15 and −2.15 are opposites. (Example 1)

_____

_____

**Find the absolute value of each number.** (Example 2)

**12.** 5.23 _____

**13.** $-4\frac{2}{11}$ _____

**14.** 0 _____

**15.** $-6\frac{3}{5}$ _____

**16.** −2.12 _____

**17.** 8.2 _____

**? ESSENTIAL QUESTION CHECK-IN**

**18.** How do you identify the opposite and the absolute value of a rational number?

_____

_____

_____

_____

# 2.2 Independent Practice

TEKS 6.2.B

**Personal Math Trainer**

Online Assessment and Intervention

my.hrw.com

**19. Financial Literacy** A store's balance sheet represents the amounts customers owe as negative numbers and credits to customers as positive numbers.

| Customer | Girardi | Lewis | Stein | Yuan | Wenner |
|----------|---------|-------|-------|------|--------|
| Balance ($) | −85.23 | 20.44 | −116.33 | 13.50 | −9.85 |

**a.** Write the opposite of each customer's balance.

_____

_____

**b.** Mr. Yuan wants to use his credit to pay off the full amount that another customer owes. Which customer's balance does Mr. Yuan

have enough money to pay off? _____

**c.** Which customer's balance would be farthest from 0 on a number line? Explain.

_____

_____

**20. Multistep** Trina and Jessie went on a vacation to Hawaii. Trina went scuba diving and reached an elevation of −85.6 meters, which is below sea level. Jessie went hang-gliding and reached an altitude of 87.9 meters, which is above sea level.

**a.** Who is closer to the surface of the ocean? Explain.

_____

_____

**b.** Trina wants to hang-glide at the same number of meters above sea level as she scuba-dived below sea level. Will she fly higher than Jessie did? Explain.

_____

_____

**21. Critical Thinking** Carlos finds the absolute value of −5.3, and then finds the opposite of his answer. Jason finds the opposite of −5.3, and then finds the absolute value of his answer. Whose final value is greater? Explain.

_____

_____

_____

**22. Explain the Error** Two students are playing a math game. The object of the game is to make the least possible number by arranging the given digits inside absolute value bars on a card. In the first round, each player will use the digits 3, 5, and 7 to fill in the card.

    **a.** One student arranges the numbers on the card as shown. What was this student's mistake?

    _____

    _____

    _____

    **b.** What is the least possible number the card can show? _____

**H.O.T.** FOCUS ON HIGHER ORDER THINKING

                                                                      Work Area

**23. Analyze Relationships** If you plot the point −8.85 on a number line, would you place it to the left or right of −8.8? Explain.

_____

_____

**24. Make a Conjecture** If the absolute value of a negative number is 2.78, what is the distance on the number line between the number and its absolute value? Explain your answer.

_____

_____

**25. Multiple Representations** The deepest point in the Indian Ocean is the Java Trench, which is 25,344 feet below sea level. Elevations below sea level are represented by negative numbers.

    **a.** Write the elevation of the Java Trench. _____

    **b.** A mile is 5,280 feet. Between which two integers is the elevation

    in miles? _____

    **c.** Graph the elevation of the Java Trench in miles.

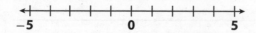

**26. Draw Conclusions** A number and its absolute value are equal. If you subtract 2 from the number, the new number and its absolute value are <u>not</u> equal. What do you know about the number? What is a possible number that satisfies these conditions?

_____

_____

# Comparing and Ordering Rational Numbers

TEKS
Number and operations—6.2.D Order a set of rational numbers arising from mathematical and real-world contexts.

**? ESSENTIAL QUESTION**

How do you compare and order rational numbers?

---

**EXPLORE ACTIVITY** TEKS 6.2.D

## Equivalent Fractions and Decimals

Fractions and decimals that represent the same value are *equivalent*. The number line shows equivalent fractions and decimals from 0 to 1.

**A** Complete the number line by writing the missing decimals or fractions.

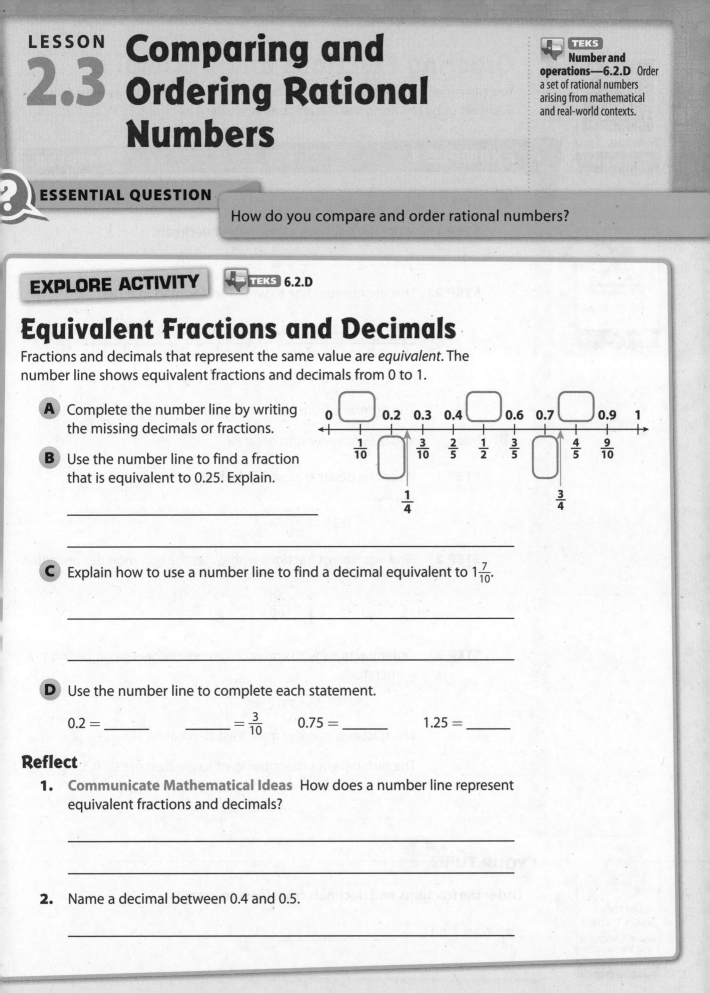

**B** Use the number line to find a fraction that is equivalent to 0.25. Explain.

_____

_____

**C** Explain how to use a number line to find a decimal equivalent to $1\frac{7}{10}$.

_____

_____

_____

**D** Use the number line to complete each statement.

$0.2 =$ _____     _____ $= \frac{3}{10}$     $0.75 =$ _____     $1.25 =$ _____

## Reflect

**1. Communicate Mathematical Ideas** How does a number line represent equivalent fractions and decimals?

_____

_____

**2.** Name a decimal between 0.4 and 0.5.

_____

# Ordering Fractions and Decimals

You can order fractions and decimals by rewriting the fractions as equivalent decimals or by rewriting the decimals as equivalent fractions.

## EXAMPLE 1

TEKS 6.2.D

**A** Order 0.2, $\frac{3}{4}$, 0.8, $\frac{1}{2}$, $\frac{1}{4}$, and 0.4 from least to greatest.

**STEP 1** Write the fractions as equivalent decimals.

$$\frac{1}{4} = 0.25 \qquad \frac{1}{2} = 0.5 \qquad \frac{3}{4} = 0.75$$

**STEP 2** Use the number line to write the decimals in order.

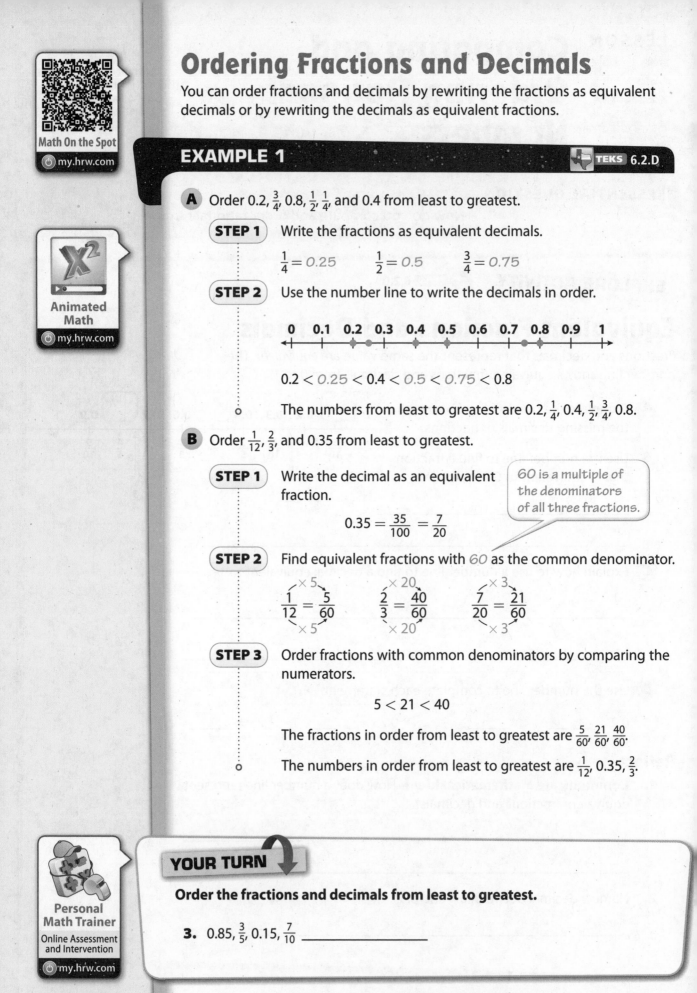

| 0 | 0.1 | 0.2 | 0.3 | 0.4 | 0.5 | 0.6 | 0.7 | 0.8 | 0.9 | 1 |

$$0.2 < 0.25 < 0.4 < 0.5 < 0.75 < 0.8$$

The numbers from least to greatest are 0.2, $\frac{1}{4}$, 0.4, $\frac{1}{2}$, $\frac{3}{4}$, 0.8.

**B** Order $\frac{1}{12}$, $\frac{2}{3}$, and 0.35 from least to greatest.

**STEP 1** Write the decimal as an equivalent fraction.

> 60 is a multiple of the denominators of all three fractions.

$$0.35 = \frac{35}{100} = \frac{7}{20}$$

**STEP 2** Find equivalent fractions with 60 as the common denominator.

$$\overset{\times 5}{\frac{1}{12} = \frac{5}{60}}\underset{\times 5}{} \qquad \overset{\times 20}{\frac{2}{3} = \frac{40}{60}}\underset{\times 20}{} \qquad \overset{\times 3}{\frac{7}{20} = \frac{21}{60}}\underset{\times 3}{}$$

**STEP 3** Order fractions with common denominators by comparing the numerators.

$$5 < 21 < 40$$

The fractions in order from least to greatest are $\frac{5}{60}$, $\frac{21}{60}$, $\frac{40}{60}$.

The numbers in order from least to greatest are $\frac{1}{12}$, 0.35, $\frac{2}{3}$.

## YOUR TURN

**Order the fractions and decimals from least to greatest.**

**3.** 0.85, $\frac{3}{5}$, 0.15, $\frac{7}{10}$ _____

# Ordering Rational Numbers

You can use a number line to order positive and negative rational numbers.

**Math On the Spot**

my.hrw.com

## EXAMPLE 2 · Real World

**TEKS** 6.2.D

Five friends completed a triathlon that included a 3-mile run, a 12-mile bike ride, and a $\frac{1}{2}$-mile swim. To compare their running times they created a table that shows the difference between each person's time and the average time, with negative numbers representing times less than the average.

| Runner | John | Sue | Anna | Mike | Tom |
|---|---|---|---|---|---|
| Time above or below average (minutes) | $\frac{1}{2}$ | 1.4 | $-1\frac{1}{4}$ | $-2.0$ | 1.95 |

**Order the numbers from greatest to least.**

**STEP 1** Write the fractions as equivalent decimals.

$$\frac{1}{2} = 0.5 \qquad -1\frac{1}{4} = -1.25$$

**STEP 2** Use the number line to write the decimals in order.

```
    −2.0  −1.5  −1.0  −0.5   0.0   0.5   1.0   1.5   2.0
    <+--+--+--+--+--+--+--+--+--+--+--+--+--+--+--+--+-->
```

★ Average Time

$$1.95 > 1.4 > 0.5 > -1.25 > -2.0$$

The numbers in order from greatest to least are 1.95, 1.4, $\frac{1}{2}$, $-1\frac{1}{4}$, $-2.0$.

### Math Talk
**Mathematical Processes**

Who was the fastest runner? Explain.

## Reflect

4. **Communicate Mathematical Ideas** Describe a different way to order the numbers.

_____

_____

_____

## YOUR TURN

5. To compare their bike times, the friends created a table that shows the difference between each person's time and the average bike time. Order the bike times from least to greatest.

| Biker | John | Sue | Anna | Mike | Tom |
|---|---|---|---|---|---|
| Time above or below average (minutes) | $-1.8$ | 1 | $1\frac{2}{5}$ | $1\frac{9}{10}$ | $-1.25$ |

**Personal Math Trainer**

Online Assessment and Intervention

my.hrw.com

_____

**Find the equivalent fraction or decimal for each number.**
(Explore Activity)

1. $0.6 =$ _____

2. $\frac{1}{4} =$ _____

3. $0.9 =$ _____

4. $0.1 =$ _____

5. $\frac{3}{10} =$ _____

6. $1.4 =$ _____

7. $\frac{4}{5} =$ _____

8. $0.4 =$ _____

9. $\frac{6}{8} =$ _____

**Use the number line to order the fractions and decimals from least to greatest.** (Example 1)

10. $0.75, \frac{1}{2}, 0.4$, and $\frac{1}{5}$

0   0.1   0.2   0.3   0.4   0.5   0.6   0.7   0.8   0.9   1

_____

11. The table shows the lengths of fish caught by three friends at the lake last weekend. Write the lengths in order from greatest to least. (Example 1)

_____

| Lengths of Fish (cm) | | |
|---|---|---|
| **Emma** | **Anne** | **Emily** |
| 12.7 | $12\frac{3}{5}$ | $12\frac{3}{4}$ |

**List the fractions and decimals in order from least to greatest.**
(Example 1, Example 2)

12. $2.3, 2\frac{4}{5}, 2.6$

13. $0.5, \frac{3}{16}, 0.75, \frac{5}{48}$

14. $0.5, \frac{1}{5}, 0.35, \frac{12}{25}, \frac{4}{5}$

_____   _____   _____

15. $\frac{3}{4}, -\frac{7}{10}, -\frac{3}{4}, \frac{8}{10}$

16. $-\frac{3}{8}, \frac{5}{16}, -0.65, \frac{2}{4}$

17. $-2.3, -2\frac{4}{5}, -2.6$

_____   _____   _____

18. $-0.6, -\frac{5}{8}, -\frac{7}{12}, -0.72$

19. $1.45, 1\frac{1}{2}, 1\frac{1}{3}, 1.2$

20. $-0.3, 0.5, 0.55, -0.35$

_____   _____   _____

**? ESSENTIAL QUESTION CHECK-IN**

21. Explain how to compare 0.7 and $\frac{5}{8}$.

_____

_____

_____

# 2.3 Independent Practice

TEKS 6.2.D

**Personal Math Trainer**

Online Assessment and Intervention

my.hrw.com

**22.** Rosa and Albert receive the same amount of allowance each week. The table shows what part of their allowance they each spent on video games and pizza. Use a number line to help you compare.

| | Video games | Pizza |
|---|---|---|
| **Rosa** | 0.4 | $\frac{2}{5}$ |
| **Albert** | $\frac{1}{2}$ | 0.25 |

**a.** Who spent more of their allowance on video games? Write an inequality to compare the portion spent on video games.

_____

**b.** Who spent more of their allowance on pizza? Write an inequality to compare the portion spent on pizza.

_____

**c.** Draw Conclusions  Who spent the greater part of their total allowance? How do you know?

_____

_____

**23.** A group of friends is collecting aluminum for a recycling drive. Each person who donates at least 4.25 pounds of aluminum receives a free movie coupon. The weight of each person's donation is shown in the table.

| | Brenda | Claire | Jim | Micah | Peter |
|---|---|---|---|---|---|
| **Weight (lb)** | 4.3 | 5.5 | $6\frac{1}{6}$ | $\frac{15}{4}$ | $4\frac{3}{8}$ |

**a.** Order the weights of the donations from greatest to least.

_____

**b.** Which of the friends will receive a free movie coupon? Which will not?

_____

**c.** What If?  Would the person with the smallest donation win a movie coupon if he or she had collected $\frac{1}{2}$ pound more of aluminum? Explain.

_____

_____

_____

**24.** Last week, several gas stations in a neighborhood all charged the same price for a gallon of gas. The table below shows how much gas prices have changed from last week to this week.

| Gas Station | Gas and Go | Samson Gas | Star Gas | Corner Store | Tip Top Shop |
|---|---|---|---|---|---|
| Change from last week (in cents) | −6.6 | 5.8 | $-6\frac{3}{4}$ | $\frac{27}{5}$ | $-5\frac{5}{8}$ |

**a.** Order the numbers in the table from least to greatest.

_____

**b.** Which gas station has the cheapest gas this week? _____

**c.** **Critical Thinking** Which gas station changed their price the least this week?

_____

## H.O.T. — FOCUS ON HIGHER ORDER THINKING

Work Area

**25.** **Analyze Relationships** Explain how you would order from least to greatest three numbers that include a positive number, a negative number, and zero.

_____

_____

_____

**26.** **Critique Reasoning** Luke is making pancakes. The recipe calls for 0.5 quart of milk and 2.5 cups of flour. He has $\frac{3}{8}$ quart of milk and $\frac{18}{8}$ cups of flour. Luke makes the recipe with the milk and flour that he has. Explain his error.

_____

_____

_____

**27.** **Communicate Mathematical Ideas** If you know the order from least to greatest of 5 negative rational numbers, how can you use that information to order the absolute values of those numbers from least to greatest? Explain.

_____

_____

_____

_____

_____

# Ready to Go On?

## 2.1 Classifying Rational Numbers

1. Five friends divide three bags of apples equally between them. Write the division represented in this situation as a fraction.

_____

Write each rational number as $\frac{a}{b}$.

2. $5\frac{1}{6}$ _____

3. $-12$ _____

Determine if each number is a whole number, integer, or rational number. Include all sets to which each number belongs.

4. $-12$ _____

5. $\frac{7}{8}$ _____

## 2.2 Identifying Opposites and Absolute Value of Rational Numbers

6. Graph $-3$, $1\frac{3}{4}$, $-0.5$, and $3$ on the number line.

$$\xleftarrow{\hspace{0.3em}}\overset{\displaystyle -4\ -3\ -2\ -1\ \ \ 0\ \ \ 1\ \ \ 2\ \ \ 3\ \ \ 4}{\mid\ \mid\ \mid\ \mid\ \mid\ \mid\ \mid\ \mid\ \mid}\xrightarrow{\hspace{0.3em}}$$

7. Find the opposite of $\frac{1}{3}$ and $-\frac{7}{12}$ _____

8. Find the absolute value of 9.8 and $-\frac{10}{3}$ _____

## 2.3 Comparing and Ordering Rational Numbers

9. Over the last week, the daily low temperatures in degrees Fahrenheit have been $-4$, 6.2, $18\frac{1}{2}$, $-5.9$, 21, $-\frac{1}{4}$, and 1.75. List these numbers in order from greatest to least.

_____

### ? ESSENTIAL QUESTION

10. How can you solve problems by ordering rational numbers from least to greatest?

_____

_____

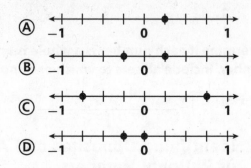

Personal
Math Trainer

Online
Assessment and
Intervention

my.hrw.com

## Selected Response

**1.** Suki split five dog treats equally among her six dogs. Which fraction represents this division?

(A) $\frac{6}{5}$ of a treat       (C) $\frac{1}{5}$ of a treat

(B) $\frac{5}{6}$ of a treat       (D) $\frac{1}{6}$ of a treat

**2.** Which set or sets does the number 15 belong to?

(A) whole numbers only

(B) rational numbers only

(C) integers and rational numbers only

(D) whole numbers, integers, and rational numbers

**3.** Which of the following statements about rational numbers is correct?

(A) All rational numbers are also whole numbers.

(B) All rational numbers are also integers.

(C) All rational numbers can be written in the form $\frac{a}{b}$.

(D) Rational numbers cannot be negative.

**4.** Which of the following shows the numbers in order from least to greatest?

(A) $-\frac{1}{5}, -\frac{2}{3}, 2, 0.4$

(B) $2, -\frac{2}{3}, 0.4, -\frac{1}{5}$

(C) $-\frac{2}{3}, 0.4, -\frac{1}{5}, 2$

(D) $-\frac{2}{3}, -\frac{1}{5}, 0.4, 2$

**5.** What is the absolute value of $-12.5$?

(A) 12.5       (C) $-1$

(B) 1       (D) $-12.5$

**6.** Which number line shows $-\frac{1}{4}$ and its opposite?

(A) ![number line from -1 to 1 with a point between 0 and 1]

(B) ![number line from -1 to 1 with two points]

(C) ![number line from -1 to 1 with two points]

(D) ![number line from -1 to 1 with two points near 0]

**7.** Horatio climbed to the top of a ladder that is 10 feet high. What is the opposite of Horatio's height on the ladder?

(A) $-10$ feet       (C) 0 feet

(B) 10 feet       (D) $\frac{1}{10}$ foot

## Gridded Response

**8.** The heights of four students in Mrs. Patel's class are $5\frac{1}{2}$ feet, 5.35 feet, $5\frac{4}{10}$ feet, and 5.5 feet. What is the height in feet of the shortest student written as a decimal?

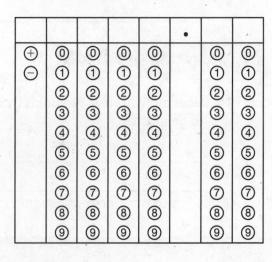

### MODULE 1 ▶ Integers

**ESSENTIAL QUESTION**

How can you use integers to solve real-world problems?

### EXAMPLE 1

**James recorded the temperature at noon in Fairbanks, Alaska, over a week in January.**

| Day | Mon | Tues | Wed | Thurs | Fri |
|---|---|---|---|---|---|
| Temperature | 3 | 2 | 7 | −3 | −1 |

**Graph the temperatures on the number line, and then list the numbers in order from least to greatest.**

Graph the temperatures on the number line.

Read from left to right to list the temperatures in order from least to greatest.

The temperatures listed from least to greatest are −3, −1, 2, 3, 7.

### EXAMPLE 2

**Graph the following numbers on the number line. Then use the number line to find each absolute value.**

−4    0    2    −1

|−4| = _____     |0| = _____

|2| = _____     |−1| = _____

### EXERCISES

1. Graph each number on the number line. (Lesson 1.1)
   7, −2, 5, 1, −1

**Write the opposite of each number .** (Lesson 1.1)

**2.** 8 _____     **3.** −3 _____

**List the numbers from least to greatest.** (Lesson 1.2)

**4.** 4, 0, −2, 3     **5.** −3, −5, 2, −2

_____     _____

**Use a number line to help you compare the numbers. Use < or >.** (Lesson 1.2)

**6.** 4 ◯ 1     **7.** −2 ◯ 2

**8.** −3 ◯ −5     **9.** −7 ◯ 2

**Find each absolute value.** (Lesson 1.3)

**10.** |6| _____     **11.** |−2| _____

---

**MODULE 2** **Rational Numbers**

**?** **ESSENTIAL QUESTION**

How can you use rational numbers to solve real-world problems?

**Key Vocabulary**

rational number (*número racional*)

Venn digram (*diagrama de Venn*)

### EXAMPLE 1

**Use the Venn diagram to determine in which set or sets each number belongs.**

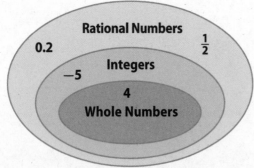

**A.** $\frac{1}{2}$  The number $\frac{1}{2}$ belongs in the set of rational numbers.

**B.** −5  The number −5 belongs in the sets of integers and rational numbers.

**C.** 4  The number 4 belongs in the sets of whole numbers, integers, and rational numbers.

**D.** 0.2  The number 0.2 belongs in the set of rational numbers.

## EXAMPLE 2

**A.** Order $\frac{1}{10}$, 0.9, 0.2, $\frac{3}{5}$, and 0.35 from least to greatest.

Write the fractions as equivalent decimals. $\frac{1}{10} = 0.1$    $\frac{3}{5} = 0.6$

Use the number line to write the decimals in order.

$0.1 < 0.2 < 0.35 < 0.6 < 0.9$

The numbers in order from least to greatest are $\frac{1}{10}$, 0.2, 0.35, $\frac{3}{5}$, 0.9.

**B.** Order $\frac{2}{5}$, 0.2, and $\frac{4}{15}$ from greatest to least.

Write the decimal as an equivalent fraction. $0.2 = \frac{2}{10} = \frac{1}{5}$

Find equivalent fractions with 15 as the common denominator.

$\frac{2 \times 3}{5 \times 3} = \frac{6}{15}$        $\frac{1 \times 3}{5 \times 3} = \frac{3}{15}$        $\frac{4}{15} = \frac{4}{15}$

Order fractions with common denominators by comparing the numerators.

$6 > 4 > 3$        $\frac{6}{15} > \frac{4}{15} > \frac{3}{15}$

The numbers in order from greatest to least are $\frac{2}{5}$, $\frac{4}{15}$, 0.2.

## EXERCISES

**Classify each number by indicating in which set or sets it belongs.**
(Lesson 2.1)

**1.** 8 _____

**2.** 0.25 _____

**Find the absolute value of each rational number.** (Lesson 2.2)

**3.** $|3.7|$ _____    **4.** $\left|-\frac{2}{3}\right|$ _____

**Graph each set of numbers on the number line and order the numbers from greatest to least.** (Lesson 2.1, 2.3)

**5.** $-0.5, -1, -\frac{1}{4}, 0$

_____

# Unit 1 Performance Tasks

1. **CAREERS IN MATH** | Climatologist Each year a tree is alive, it adds a layer of growth, called a tree ring, between its core and its bark. A climatologist measures the width of tree rings of a particular tree for different years:

| Year | 1900 | 1910 | 1920 | 1930 | 1940 |
|---|---|---|---|---|---|
| Width of ring (in mm) | $\frac{14}{25}$ | $\frac{29}{50}$ | $\frac{53}{100}$ | $\frac{13}{20}$ | $\frac{3}{5}$ |

The average temperature during the growing season is directly related to the width of the ring, with a greater width corresponding to a higher average temperature.

**a.** List the years in order of increasing ring width.

_____

**b.** Which year was hottest? How do you know?

_____

**c.** Which year was coldest? How do you know?

_____

2. A parking garage has floors above and below ground level. For a scavenger hunt, Gaia's friends are given a list of objects they need to find on the third and fourth level below ground, the first and fourth level above ground, and ground level.

**a.** If ground level is 0 and the first level above ground is 1, which integers can you use to represent the other levels where objects are hidden? Explain your reasoning.

_____

_____

**b.** Graph the set of numbers on the number line. 

$$\underset{-5\ -4\ -3\ -2\ -1\ \ 0\ \ 1\ \ 2\ \ 3\ \ 4\ \ 5}{\longleftrightarrow}$$

**c.** Gaia wants to start at the lowest level and work her way up. List the levels in the order that Gaia will search them.

_____

**d.** If she takes the stairs, how many flights of stairs will she have to climb? How do you know?

_____

_____

## Selected Response

**1.** What is the opposite of −9?

Ⓐ 9

Ⓑ $-\frac{1}{9}$

Ⓒ 0

Ⓓ $\frac{1}{9}$

**2.** Kyle is currently 60 feet above sea level. Which correctly describes the opposite of Kyle's elevation?

Ⓐ 60 feet below sea level

Ⓑ 60 feet above sea level

Ⓒ 6 feet below sea level

Ⓓ At sea level

**3.** What is the absolute value of 27?

Ⓐ −27

Ⓑ 0

Ⓒ 3

Ⓓ 27

**4.** In Albany it is −4°F, in Chicago it is −14°F, in Minneapolis it is −11°F, and in Toronto it is −13°F. In which city is it the coldest?

Ⓐ Albany

Ⓑ Chicago

Ⓒ Minneapolis

Ⓓ Toronto

**5.** Which shows the integers in order from greatest to least?

Ⓐ 18, 4, 3, −2, −15

Ⓑ −2, 3, 4, −15, 18

Ⓒ −15, −2, 3, 4, 18

Ⓓ 18, −15, 4, 3, −2

**6.** Joanna split three pitchers of water equally among her eight plants. What fraction of a pitcher did each plant get?

Ⓐ $\frac{1}{8}$ of a pitcher

Ⓑ $\frac{1}{3}$ of a pitcher

Ⓒ $\frac{3}{8}$ of a pitcher

Ⓓ $\frac{8}{3}$ of a pitcher

**7.** Which set or sets does the number −22 belong to?

Ⓐ Whole numbers only

Ⓑ Rational numbers only

Ⓒ Integers and rational numbers only

Ⓓ Whole numbers, integers, and rational numbers

**8.** Carlos swam to the bottom of a pool that is 12 feet deep. What is the opposite of Carlos's elevation relative to the surface?

Ⓐ −12 feet

Ⓑ 0 feet

Ⓒ 12 feet

Ⓓ $\frac{1}{12}$ foot

**9.** Which number line shows $\frac{1}{3}$ and its opposite?

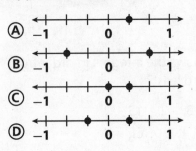

**10.** Which of the following shows the numbers in order from least to greatest?

Ⓐ $-\frac{2}{3}, -\frac{3}{4}, 0.7, 0$

Ⓑ $0.7, 0, -\frac{2}{3}, -\frac{3}{4},$

Ⓒ $-\frac{2}{3}, -\frac{3}{4}, 0, 0.7$

Ⓓ $-\frac{3}{4}, -\frac{2}{3}, 0, 0.7$

**11.** Which number line shows an integer and its opposite?

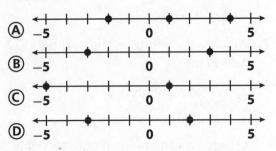

## Gridded Response

**12.** Which is the greatest out of $\frac{1}{3}, -1.2, 0.45,$ and $-\frac{4}{5}$?

**13.** As part of a research team, Ryanne climbed into a cavern to an elevation of $-117.6$ feet. What is the absolute value of Ryanne's elevation, in feet?

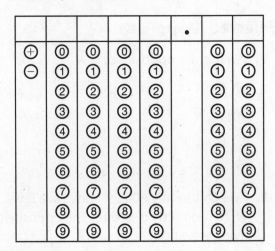

**Hot Tip!** Correct answers in gridded problems can be positive or negative. Enter the negative sign in the first column when it is appropriate. Check your work!

**14.** Melvin has a certain number of files on his computer. The opposite of this number is $-653$. How many files are on Melvin's computer?

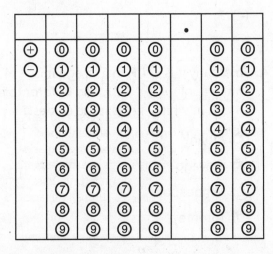

# Number Operations

## CAREERS IN MATH

**Chef** The role of a chef is diverse and can include planning menus, overseeing food preparation, training staff, and ordering and purchasing food items. Chefs use mathematics when scaling recipes and converting units of measure, as well as in budgeting and financial planning.

If you are interested in a career as a chef, you should study these mathematical subjects:
- Basic Math
- Business Math

Research other careers that require the use of scaling, converting units, and financial planning.

**Unit 2 Performance Task**

At the end of the unit, check out how **chefs** use math.

# Vocabulary Preview

Use the puzzle to preview key vocabulary from this unit. Unscramble the circled letters to answer the riddle at the bottom of the page.

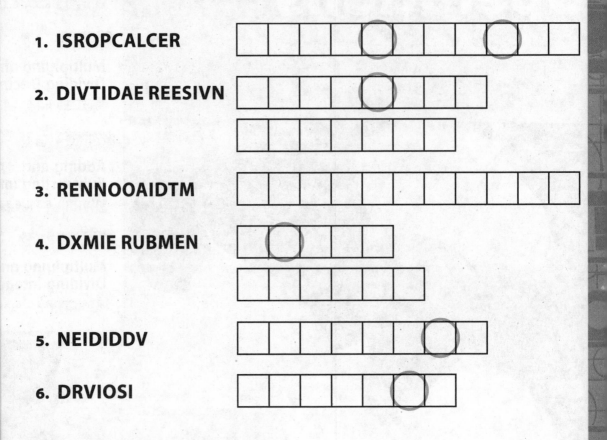

1. **ISROPCALCER**

2. **DIVTIDAE REESIVN**

3. **RENNOOAIDTM**

4. **DXMIE RUBMEN**

5. **NEIDIDDV**

6. **DRVIOSI**

1. Two numbers whose product is one. (Lesson 3-3)
2. The opposite of a number. (Lesson 5-2)
3. The part of a fraction that represents how many parts the whole is divided into. (Lesson 3-1)
4. A number that is a combination of a whole number and a fraction. (Lesson 3-2)
5. The amount that you want to divide in a division problem. (Lesson 4-2)
6. The number you divide by in a division problem. (Lesson 4-2)

**Q:** Decimals always win in arguments with fractions. What do decimals have that fractions don't?

**A:** __ __ __ __ __ __!

# Multiplying and Dividing Fractions

**? ESSENTIAL QUESTION**

How can you use products and quotients of fractions to solve real-world problems?

### Real-World Video

To find your average rate of speed, divide the distance you traveled by the time you traveled. If you ride in a taxi and drive $\frac{1}{2}$ mile in $\frac{1}{4}$ hour, your rate was 2 mi/h which may mean you were in heavy traffic.

my.hrw.com

## GO DIGITAL
my.hrw.com

**my.hrw.com**

Go digital with your write-in student edition, accessible on any device.

**Math On the Spot**

Scan with your smart phone to jump directly to the online edition, video tutor, and more.

**Animated Math**

Interactively explore key concepts to see how math works.

**Personal Math Trainer**

Get immediate feedback and help as you work through practice sets.

# Are YOU Ready?

Complete these exercises to review skills you will need for this chapter.

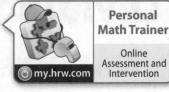

**Personal Math Trainer**

Online Assessment and Intervention

my.hrw.com

## Write an Improper Fraction as a Mixed Number

**EXAMPLE**

$\frac{13}{5} = \frac{5}{5} + \frac{5}{5} + \frac{3}{5}$  Write as a sum using names for one plus a proper fraction.

$= 1 + 1 + \frac{3}{5}$  Write each name for one as one.

$= 2 + \frac{3}{5}$  Add the ones.

$= 2\frac{3}{5}$  Write the mixed number.

**Write each improper fraction as a mixed number.**

**1.** $\frac{9}{4}$ _____  **2.** $\frac{8}{3}$ _____  **3.** $\frac{23}{6}$ _____  **4.** $\frac{11}{2}$ _____

**5.** $\frac{17}{5}$ _____  **6.** $\frac{15}{8}$ _____  **7.** $\frac{33}{10}$ _____  **8.** $\frac{29}{12}$ _____

## Multiplication Facts

**EXAMPLE**

$7 \times 6 = \blacksquare$

$7 \times 6 = 42$

Use a related fact you know.
$6 \times 6 = 36$
Think:  $7 \times 6 = (6 \times 6) + 6$
$= 36 + 6$
$= 42$

**Multiply.**

**9.** $6 \times 5$ _____  **10.** $8 \times 9$ _____  **11.** $10 \times 11$ _____  **12.** $7 \times 8$ _____

**13.** $9 \times 7$ _____  **14.** $8 \times 6$ _____  **15.** $9 \times 11$ _____  **16.** $11 \times 12$ _____

## Division Facts

**EXAMPLE**

$63 \div 7 = \blacksquare$

$63 \div 7 = 9$

Think:  7 times what number equals 63?
$7 \times 9 = 63$

So, $63 \div 7 = 9$.

**Divide.**

**17.** $35 \div 7$ _____  **18.** $56 \div 8$ _____  **19.** $28 \div 7$ _____  **20.** $48 \div 8$ _____

**21.** $36 \div 4$ _____  **22.** $45 \div 9$ _____  **23.** $72 \div 8$ _____  **24.** $40 \div 5$ _____

# Reading Start-Up

## Vocabulary

**Review Words**
  area (*área*)
✔ denominator (*denominador*)
  factor (*factor*)
✔ fraction (*fracción*)
  length (*longitud*)
✔ mixed number (*número mixto*)
✔ numerator (*numerador*)
  product (*producto*)
  width (*ancho*)

**Preview Words**
  reciprocals (*recíprocos*)
  model (*modelo*)
  whole number (*número entero*)

## Visualize Vocabulary

**Use the ✔ words to complete the triangle. Write the review word that fits the description in each section of the triangle.**

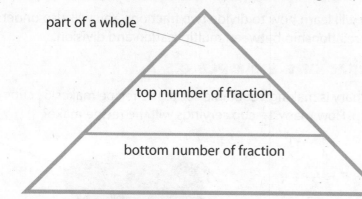

part of a whole

top number of fraction

bottom number of fraction

## Understand Vocabulary

**In each grouping, select the choice that is described by the given vocabulary word.**

1. reciprocals    Ⓐ 1:15    Ⓑ $\frac{3}{4} \div \frac{1}{6}$    Ⓒ $\frac{3}{5}$ and $\frac{5}{3}$

2. mixed number    Ⓐ $\frac{1}{3} - \frac{1}{5}$    Ⓑ $3\frac{1}{2}$    Ⓒ $-5$

3. whole number    Ⓐ $-1$    Ⓑ 7    Ⓒ $\frac{2}{5}$

## Active Reading

**Layered Book** Before beginning the module, create a layered book to help you learn the concepts in this module. Label each flap with lesson titles. As you study each lesson, listen and take notes on important ideas, such as vocabulary and formulas, under the appropriate flap. Refer to your finished layered book as you work on exercises from this module.

# Unpacking the TEKS

Understanding the TEKS and the vocabulary terms in the TEKS will help you know exactly what you are expected to learn in this module.

---

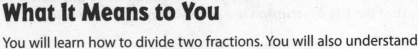

**TEKS 6.3.A**

Recognize that dividing by a rational number and multiplying by its reciprocal result in equivalent values.

### Key Vocabulary

**quotient** *(cociente)*
The result when one number is divided by another.

**fraction** *(fracción)*
A number in the form $\frac{a}{b}$, where $b \neq 0$.

## What It Means to You

You will learn how to divide two fractions. You will also understand the relationship between multiplication and division.

**UNPACKING EXAMPLE 6.3.A**

Zachary is making vegetable soup. The recipe makes $6\frac{3}{4}$ cups of soup. How many $1\frac{1}{2}$-cup servings will the recipe make?

$$6\frac{3}{4} \div 1\frac{1}{2}$$
$$= \frac{27}{4} \div \frac{3}{2}$$
$$= \frac{27}{4} \cdot \frac{2}{3}$$
$$= \frac{9}{2}$$
$$= 4\frac{1}{2}$$

The recipe will make $4\frac{1}{2}$ servings.

---

**TEKS 6.3.B**

Determine, with and without computation, whether a quantity is increased or decreased when multiplied by a fraction, including values greater than or less than one.

## What It Means to You

You will learn how to determine whether the product of a number and a fraction will be greater than or less than the number.

**UNPACKING EXAMPLE 6.3.B**

Will the product of $\frac{6}{10} \times 6$ be less than 6 or greater than 6?

The product will be less than 6 because $\frac{6}{10}$ is less than 1.

$$\frac{6}{10} \times 6 = \frac{36}{10} = 3\frac{6}{10}$$

---

Visit **my.hrw.com** to see all the **TEKS** unpacked.

my.hrw.com

## TEKS
**Number and operations—6.3.E**
Multiply and divide positive rational numbers fluently. *Also 6.3.B.*

# LESSON
# 3.1 Multiplying Fractions

## ? ESSENTIAL QUESTION

How do you multiply fractions?

---

### EXPLORE ACTIVITY (Real World) TEKS 6.3.B

# Modeling Fraction Multiplication

Sam and Pete had a party. After the party, they discovered that $\frac{3}{4}$ of a casserole was left over. Sam and Pete ate $\frac{1}{2}$ of the leftover casserole. What fraction of the original casserole did Sam and Pete eat?

Shade the model to show $\frac{1}{2} \times \boxed{\phantom{x}}$.

**A** Shade the rectangle to represent the $\frac{3}{4}$ of the casserole that was left over after the party.

**B** Double shade $\frac{1}{2}$ of $\frac{3}{4}$. Divide the remaining fourth into two parts so that all of the parts are equal.

**C** Sam and Pete ate _____ of the original casserole.

**D** Did the amount of casserole increase or decrease when multiplied by $\frac{1}{2}$? How does the model show this? Explain.

_____

_____

_____

**E** Write the multiplication shown by the model. $\frac{1}{2} \times \frac{3}{4} = \boxed{\phantom{x}}$

## Reflect

1. **Communicate Mathematical Ideas** Will the product of $\frac{1}{2}$ and $\frac{2}{3}$ be greater or less than $\frac{2}{3}$? Explain.

_____

_____

# Multiplying Fractions

To multiply two fractions you first multiply the numerators and then multiply the denominators. Write the product in simplest form.

$$\frac{\text{numerator} \times \text{numerator}}{\text{denominator} \times \text{denominator}} = \frac{\text{numerator}}{\text{denominator}}$$

**EXAMPLE 1**  🌟 **TEKS** 6.3.E

**My Notes**

**Multiply. Write the product in simplest form.**

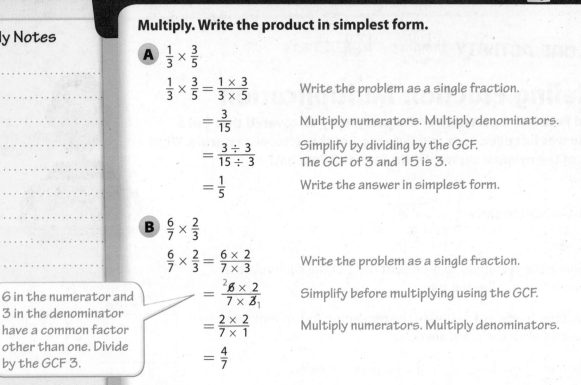

**A** $\frac{1}{3} \times \frac{3}{5}$

$\frac{1}{3} \times \frac{3}{5} = \frac{1 \times 3}{3 \times 5}$     Write the problem as a single fraction.

$= \frac{3}{15}$     Multiply numerators. Multiply denominators.

$= \frac{3 \div 3}{15 \div 3}$     Simplify by dividing by the GCF.
The GCF of 3 and 15 is 3.

$= \frac{1}{5}$     Write the answer in simplest form.

**B** $\frac{6}{7} \times \frac{2}{3}$

$\frac{6}{7} \times \frac{2}{3} = \frac{6 \times 2}{7 \times 3}$     Write the problem as a single fraction.

$= \frac{{}^2\cancel{6} \times 2}{7 \times \cancel{3}_1}$     Simplify before multiplying using the GCF.

$= \frac{2 \times 2}{7 \times 1}$     Multiply numerators. Multiply denominators.

$= \frac{4}{7}$

> 6 in the numerator and 3 in the denominator have a common factor other than one. Divide by the GCF 3.

## Reflect

**2.** **Communicate Mathematical Ideas**  Is the product less than or greater than the factors? Explain.

_____

_____

_____

_____

**3.** **Analyze Relationships**  How can you determine when to simplify using the GCF before multiplying?

_____

_____

_____

_____

Multiply. Write each product in simplest form.

4. $\frac{1}{6} \times \frac{3}{5}$ _____

5. $\frac{3}{4} \times \frac{7}{9}$ _____

6. $\frac{3}{7} \times \frac{2}{3}$ _____

7. $\frac{4}{5} \times \frac{2}{7}$ _____

**Personal Math Trainer**

Online Assessment and Intervention

my.hrw.com

# Multiplying Fractions and Whole Numbers

To multiply a fraction by a whole number, you rewrite the whole number as a fraction and multiply the two fractions.

**Math On the Spot**

my.hrw.com

## EXAMPLE 2 · Real World

TEKS 6.3.E

A class has 18 students. The teacher asks how many students in the class have pets and finds $\frac{5}{9}$ of the students have pets. How many students have pets?

**STEP 1** Estimate the product. Multiply the whole number by the nearest benchmark fraction.

$\frac{5}{9}$ is close to $\frac{1}{2}$, so multiply $\frac{1}{2}$ times 18.

$\frac{1}{2} \times 18 = 9$

**STEP 2** Multiply. Write the product in simplest form.

You can write $\frac{5}{9}$ times 18 three ways.

$\frac{5}{9} \times 18 \quad \frac{5}{9} \cdot 18 \quad \frac{5}{9}(18)$

$\frac{5}{9} \times 18$

$\frac{5}{9} \times 18 = \frac{5}{9} \times \frac{18}{1}$  Rewrite 18 as a fraction.

$= \frac{5 \times \cancel{18}^2}{\cancel{9}_1 \times 1}$  Simplify before multiplying using the GCF.

$= \frac{5 \times 2}{1 \times 1}$  Multiply numerators. Multiply denominators.

$= \frac{10}{1} = 10$  Simplify by writing as a whole number.

10 students have pets.

**Math Talk**
Mathematical Processes

How can you check to see if the answer is correct?

### Reflect

8. **Analyze Relationships** Is the product of a fraction and a whole number greater than or less than the whole number? Explain.

_____

_____

_____

## YOUR TURN

**Multiply. Write each product in simplest form.**

**9.** $\frac{5}{8} \times 24$ _____

**10.** $\frac{3}{5} \times 20$ _____

**11.** $\frac{1}{3} \times 8$ _____

**12.** $\frac{1}{4} \times 14$ _____

**13.** $\frac{7}{10} \times 7$ _____

**14.** $\frac{7}{10} \times 10$ _____

# Guided Practice

**1.** Lisa, Taryn, and Catherine go to a store to buy party supplies. The store has a sale on the supplies they want for $\frac{3}{4}$ the original price. The girls agree to each pay $\frac{1}{3}$ of the cost. (Explore Activity)

**a.** Draw a model to show what fraction of the original price they will each pay.

**b.** What fraction of the original price did each girl pay? _____

**c.** Write the multiplication shown by the model. _____

**d.** Did the fraction representing the sale price increase or decrease when multiplied by $\frac{1}{3}$? Explain.

_____

_____

**Multiply. Write each product in simplest form.** (Example 1)

**2.** $\frac{1}{2} \times \frac{5}{8}$ _____

**3.** $\frac{3}{5} \times \frac{5}{9}$ _____

**4.** $\frac{3}{8} \times \frac{2}{5}$ _____

**Find each amount.** (Example 2)

**5.** $\frac{1}{4}$ of 12 bottles of water = _____ bottles

**6.** $\frac{2}{3}$ of 24 bananas = _____ bananas

**7.** $\frac{3}{5}$ of $40 restaurant bill = $ _____

**8.** $\frac{5}{6}$ of 18 pencils = _____ pencils

**? ESSENTIAL QUESTION CHECK-IN**

**9.** How can you multiply two fractions?

_____

_____

# 3.1 Independent Practice

**TEKS** 6.3.E

**Solve. Write each answer in simplest form.**

**10.** Erin buys a bag of peanuts that weighs $\frac{3}{4}$ of a pound. Later that week, the bag is $\frac{2}{3}$ full. How much does the bag of peanuts weigh now? Show your work.

_____

**11.** **Multistep** Marianne buys 16 bags of potting soil that comes in $\frac{5}{8}$-pound bags.

**a.** How many pounds of potting does Marianne buy?

_____

_____

**b.** If Marianne's father calls and says he needs 13 pounds of potting soil, will 4 more bags be enough to cover the extra soil needed?

_____

_____

**12.** **Analyze Relationships** Name three different pairs of fractions that have the same product when multiplied. Explain how you found them.

_____

_____

_____

_____

_____

_____

---

**Fruit Salad**

$3\frac{1}{2}$ cups thinly sliced rhubarb

15 seedless grapes, halved

$\frac{1}{2}$ orange, sectioned

10 fresh strawberries, halved

$\frac{3}{5}$ apple, cored and diced

$\frac{2}{3}$ peach, sliced

1 plum, pitted and sliced

$\frac{1}{4}$ cup fresh blueberries

---

**13.** Marcial found a recipe for fruit salad that he wanted to try to make for his birthday party. He decided to triple the recipe.

**a.** What is the new amount for the oranges, apples, blueberries, and peaches?

_____

_____

_____

**b.** **Communicate Mathematical Ideas** The amount of rhubarb in the original recipe is $3\frac{1}{2}$ cups. Using what you know of whole numbers and what you know of fractions, explain how you could triple that mixed number.

_____

_____

_____

_____

**14. Music** Two-fifths of the instruments in the marching band are brass. One-eighth of the brass instruments are tubas.

**a.** What fraction of the band is tubas? _____

**b.** If there are 240 band instruments total, how many are tubas?

_____

**15.** Compare simplifying before multiplying fractions with simplifying after multiplying the fractions.

_____

_____

_____

**16. Sports** Kevin is a quarterback on the football team. He completed 36 passes during the season. His second-string replacement, Mark, completed $\frac{2}{9}$ as many passes as Kevin. How many passes did Mark complete?

_____

 **FOCUS ON HIGHER ORDER THINKING**

**17. Represent Real-World Problems** Kate wants to buy a new bicycle from a sporting goods store. The bicycle she wants normally sells for $360. The store has a sale where all bicycles cost $\frac{5}{6}$ of the regular price. What is the sale price of the bicycle?

_____

**18. Error Analysis** To find the product $\frac{3}{7} \times \frac{4}{9}$, Cameron simplified $\frac{3}{7}$ to $\frac{1}{7}$ and then multiplied the fractions $\frac{1}{7}$ and $\frac{4}{9}$ to find the product $\frac{4}{63}$. What is Cameron's error?

**Work Area**

_____

_____

_____

_____

**19. Justify Reasoning** When multiplying a whole number by a fraction, the whole number is written as a fraction by placing the value of the whole number in the numerator and 1 in the denominator. Does this change the final answer? Explain why or why not.

_____

_____

# Multiplying Mixed Numbers

**TEKS**
**Number and operations—**
**6.3.E** Multiply and divide positive rational numbers fluently. *Also 6.3.B*

## ESSENTIAL QUESTION

How do you multiply mixed numbers?

**EXPLORE ACTIVITY** *Real World* **TEKS 6.3.B**

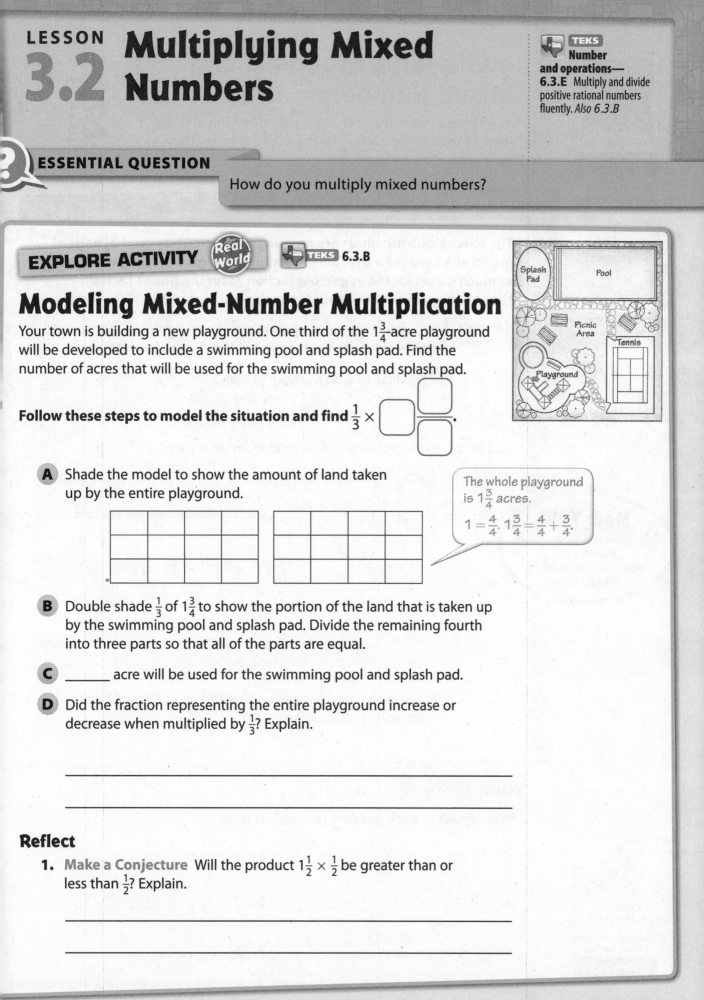

## Modeling Mixed-Number Multiplication

Your town is building a new playground. One third of the $1\frac{3}{4}$-acre playground will be developed to include a swimming pool and splash pad. Find the number of acres that will be used for the swimming pool and splash pad.

**Follow these steps to model the situation and find $\frac{1}{3} \times \boxed{\phantom{x}} \frac{\boxed{\phantom{x}}}{\boxed{\phantom{x}}}$.**

**A** Shade the model to show the amount of land taken up by the entire playground.

> The whole playground is $1\frac{3}{4}$ acres.
> $1 = \frac{4}{4}$. $1\frac{3}{4} = \frac{4}{4} + \frac{3}{4}$.

**B** Double shade $\frac{1}{3}$ of $1\frac{3}{4}$ to show the portion of the land that is taken up by the swimming pool and splash pad. Divide the remaining fourth into three parts so that all of the parts are equal.

**C** _____ acre will be used for the swimming pool and splash pad.

**D** Did the fraction representing the entire playground increase or decrease when multiplied by $\frac{1}{3}$? Explain.

_____

_____

## Reflect

1. **Make a Conjecture** Will the product $1\frac{1}{2} \times \frac{1}{2}$ be greater than or less than $\frac{1}{2}$? Explain.

_____

_____

# Multiplying Fractions and Mixed Numbers

To rename a mixed number as a fraction, first multiply the denominator of the fraction by the whole number. Then add the product to the numerator.

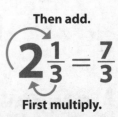
## EXAMPLE 1

**My Notes**

The science club members are planting a garden. They used $2\frac{1}{4}$ bags of gravel as a border for the flower section of the garden. They will need $\frac{1}{3}$ as much gravel for the vegetable section as for the flower section. How much gravel will they use in the vegetable section?

**STEP 1**  Estimate the product. Round the mixed number to the nearest whole number. Find the nearest benchmark for the fraction.

$2\frac{1}{4}$ is close to 2, so multiply $\frac{1}{3}$ times 2.

$\frac{1}{3} \times 2 = \frac{2}{3}$

**STEP 2**  Multiply. Write the product in simplest form.

$\frac{1}{3} \times 2\frac{1}{4}$

$\frac{1}{3} \times 2\frac{1}{4} = \frac{1}{3} \times \frac{9}{4}$  — Rewrite the mixed number as a fraction greater than 1.

$= \frac{1 \times \cancel{9}^{3}}{\cancel{3} \times 4}$  — Simplify before multiplying using the GCF.

$= \frac{1 \times 3}{1 \times 4}$  — Rewrite fraction.

$= \frac{3}{4}$  — Multiply numerators. Multiply denominators.

The science club members will need $\frac{3}{4}$ bag of gravel for the vegetable section of the garden.

**Math Talk**
Mathematical Processes

How can you determine if the answer is reasonable?

## YOUR TURN

**Multiply. Write each product in simplest form.**

**2.** $3\frac{1}{3} \times \frac{3}{4}$ _____

**3.** $1\frac{4}{5} \times \frac{1}{2}$ _____

**4.** $\frac{5}{6} \times 2\frac{3}{4}$ _____

**5.** $\frac{3}{5} \times 2\frac{1}{5}$ _____

**6.** $\frac{9}{10} \times 4\frac{1}{3}$ _____

**7.** $5\frac{1}{6} \times \frac{1}{8}$ _____

# Multiplying Mixed Numbers

Multiplying a mixed number by another mixed number is the same as multiplying a fraction by a mixed number. Rewrite each mixed number as a fraction. Then multiply the numerators and multiply the denominators.

## EXAMPLE 2  Real World

TEKS 6.3.E

Grace is making $2\frac{1}{2}$ batches of muffins for her school's annual bake sale. If one batch of muffins requires $1\frac{1}{4}$ cups of flour, how many cups of flour does Grace need to make $2\frac{1}{2}$ batches of muffins?

**STEP 1**  Estimate the product. Round each mixed number to the nearest whole number.

$2\frac{1}{2}$ is close to 3 and $1\frac{1}{4}$ is close to 1, so multiply 3 by 1.

$3 \times 1 = 3$

**STEP 2**  Multiply. Write the product in simplest form.

$2\frac{1}{2} \times 1\frac{1}{4}$

$2\frac{1}{2} \times 1\frac{1}{4} = \frac{5}{2} \times \frac{5}{4}$   Rewrite each mixed number as a fraction greater than 1.

$= \frac{5 \times 5}{2 \times 4}$   Multiply numerators. Multiply denominators.

$= \frac{25}{8}$, or $3\frac{1}{8}$   Write the fraction greater than 1 as a mixed number.

Grace will need $3\frac{1}{8}$ cups of flour.

Muffins
1¼ cups all purpose flour
3/4 cup white sugar
½ teaspoon salt
2 teaspoons baking powder
⅓ cup vegetable oil
1 egg
⅓ cup milk
1 cup fresh blueberries

## Reflect

8. **Analyze Relationships** When you multiply two mixed numbers, will the product be less than or greater than the factors? Use an example to explain.

_____

_____

_____

## YOUR TURN

**Multiply. Write each product in simplest form.**

9.  $2\frac{2}{3} \times 1\frac{1}{7}$ _____

10. $2\frac{3}{8} \times 1\frac{3}{5}$ _____

11. $4\frac{1}{2} \times 3\frac{3}{7}$ _____

12. $5\frac{1}{4} \times 4\frac{2}{3}$ _____

**1.** Mr. Martin's yard is $1\frac{1}{3}$ acres. He wants to plant grass on $\frac{1}{6}$ of his yard.
(Explore Activity)

   **a.** Draw a model to show how many acres will be covered by grass.

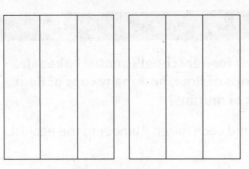

   **b.** How many acres will be covered by grass? _____

   **c.** Write the multiplication shown by the model. _____

   **d.** Will the mixed number that represents the original size of
Mr. Martin's yard increase or decrease when multiplied by $\frac{1}{6}$? Explain.

   _____

   _____

**Multiply. Write each product in simplest form.** (Example 1 and Example 2)

**2.** $1\frac{1}{5} \times \frac{3}{5}$ _____

**3.** $1\frac{3}{4} \times \frac{4}{7}$ _____

**4.** $1\frac{5}{6} \times \frac{2}{5}$ _____

**5.** $1\frac{7}{10} \times \frac{4}{5}$ _____

**6.** $\frac{5}{9} \times 3\frac{9}{10}$ _____

**7.** $\frac{7}{8} \times 3\frac{1}{3}$ _____

**8.** $2\frac{1}{5} \times 2\frac{3}{5}$ _____

**9.** $4\frac{3}{4} \times 3\frac{4}{5}$ _____

**? ) ESSENTIAL QUESTION CHECK-IN**

**10.** How can you multiply two mixed numbers?

_____

_____

_____

_____

# 3.2 Independent Practice

TEKS 6.3.B, 6.3.E

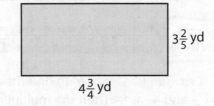

Personal Math Trainer

Online Assessment and Intervention

my.hrw.com

**Estimate. Then solve.**

**11.** Carly is making $3\frac{1}{2}$ batches of biscuits. If one batch calls for $2\frac{1}{3}$ cups of flour, how much flour will she need?

_____

_____

**12.** Bashir collected $4\frac{1}{3}$ baskets of peaches at an orchard. If each basket holds 21 peaches, how many peaches did he collect in all?

_____

_____

**13.** Jared used $1\frac{2}{5}$ bags of soil for his garden. He is digging another garden that will need $\frac{1}{5}$ as much soil as the original. How much will he use total?

_____

_____

**14.** **Critical Thinking** Is the product of two mixed numbers less than, between, or greater than the two factors? Explain.

_____

_____

_____

_____

**15.** There are approximately $402\frac{1}{4}$ meters around a typical running track. Sandra has challenged herself to run 10 laps a day for 5 days. How many meters will Sandra run if she meets her challenge?

_____

**16.** Ron wants to make a rectangular basketball court. What is the area of Ron's court?

$3\frac{2}{5}$ yd

$4\frac{3}{4}$ yd

_____

**17.** Each of 15 students will give a $1\frac{1}{2}$-minute speech in English class.

**a.** How long will it take to give the speeches?

_____

**b.** If the teacher begins recording on a digital camera with an hour available, is there enough time to record everyone if she gives a 15-minute introduction at the beginning of class and every student takes a minute to get ready? Explain.

_____

_____

_____

_____

_____

**c.** How much time is left on the digital camera?

_____

18. **Communicate Mathematical Ideas** How is multiplying a whole number by a mixed number the same as multiplying two mixed numbers?

_____

_____

_____

_____

**H.O.T.** FOCUS ON HIGHER ORDER THINKING

19. **Critique Reasoning** To find the product $3\frac{3}{8} \times 4\frac{1}{9}$, Tara rewrote $3\frac{3}{8}$ as $\frac{17}{8}$ and $4\frac{1}{9}$ as $\frac{13}{9}$. Then she multiplied the fractions to find the product $\frac{221}{72}$. What were her errors?

_____

_____

_____

_____

_____

_____

20. **Represent Real-World Problems** Ian is making his special barbecue sauce for a party. His recipe makes $3\frac{1}{2}$ cups of barbecue sauce and uses $2\frac{1}{4}$ tablespoons of soy sauce. He wants to increase his recipe to make five times as much barbecue sauce. He checks his refrigerator and finds that he has 8 tablespoons of soy sauce. Will he have enough soy sauce? Explain.

_____

_____

21. **Analyze Relationships** Is it possible to find the product of two mixed numbers by multiplying the whole number parts together, then multiplying the two fractional parts together, and finally adding the two products? Use an example to support your answer.

_____

_____

_____

_____

# 3.3 Dividing Fractions

**TEKS**
**Number and operations—6.3.E**
Multiply and divide positive rational numbers fluently.
*Also 6.3.A*

**? ESSENTIAL QUESTION**

How do you divide fractions?

**EXPLORE ACTIVITY 1** Real World **TEKS** 6.3.E

## Modeling Fraction Division

In some division problems, you may know a number of groups and need to find how many or how much are in each group. In other division problems, you may know how many there are in each group, and need to find the number of groups.

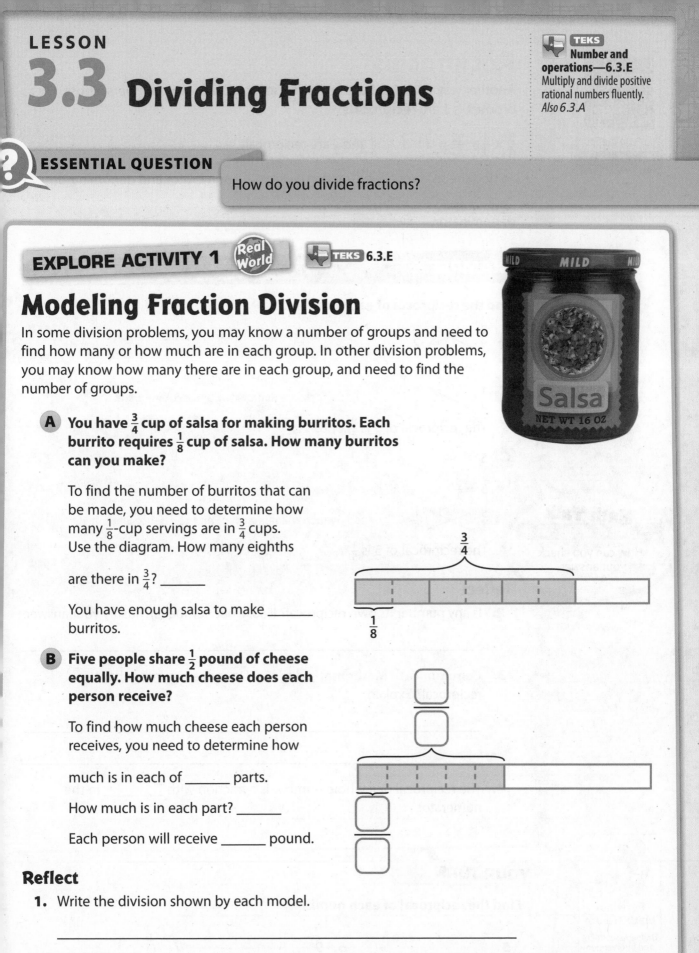

**A** You have $\frac{3}{4}$ cup of salsa for making burritos. Each burrito requires $\frac{1}{8}$ cup of salsa. How many burritos can you make?

To find the number of burritos that can be made, you need to determine how many $\frac{1}{8}$-cup servings are in $\frac{3}{4}$ cups. Use the diagram. How many eighths

are there in $\frac{3}{4}$? _____

You have enough salsa to make _____ burritos.

**B** Five people share $\frac{1}{2}$ pound of cheese equally. How much cheese does each person receive?

To find how much cheese each person receives, you need to determine how

much is in each of _____ parts.

How much is in each part? _____

Each person will receive _____ pound.

## Reflect

1. Write the division shown by each model.

_____

# Reciprocals

Another way to divide fractions is to use *reciprocals*. Two numbers whose product is 1 are **reciprocals**.

$$\frac{3}{4} \times \frac{4}{3} = \frac{12}{12} = 1 \qquad \frac{3}{4} \text{ and } \frac{4}{3} \text{ are reciprocals.}$$

To find the reciprocal of a fraction, switch the numerator and denominator.

$$\frac{\text{numerator}}{\text{denominator}} \cdot \frac{\text{denominator}}{\text{numerator}} = 1$$

## EXAMPLE 1      TEKS 6.3.A

**Find the reciprocal of each number.**

**A**   $\frac{2}{9}$ ⤬ $\frac{9}{2}$      Switch the numerator and denominator.

The reciprocal of $\frac{2}{9}$ is $\frac{9}{2}$.

**B**   $\frac{1}{8}$ ⤬ $\frac{8}{1}$      Switch the numerator and denominator.

The reciprocal of $\frac{1}{8}$ is $\frac{8}{1}$, or 8.

**C**   5

$5 = \frac{5}{1}$      Rewrite as a fraction.

$\frac{5}{1}$ ⤬ $\frac{1}{5}$      Switch the numerator and the denominator.

The reciprocal of 5 is $\frac{1}{5}$.

> **Math Talk**
> Mathematical Processes
>
> How can you check your answer?

### Reflect

**2.** Is any number its own reciprocal? If so, what number(s)? Justify your answer.

_____

**3.** **Communicate Mathematical Ideas** Does every number have a reciprocal? Explain.

_____

_____

**4.** The reciprocal of a whole number is a fraction with _____ in the numerator.

**YOUR TURN**

**Find the reciprocal of each number.**

**5.** $\frac{7}{8}$ _____     **6.** 9 _____     **7.** $\frac{1}{11}$ _____

# Using Reciprocals to Find Equivalent Values

**A** Complete the table below.

| Division | Multiplication |
|---|---|
| $\frac{6}{7} \div \frac{2}{7} = 3$ | $\frac{6}{7} \times \frac{7}{2} =$ |
| $\frac{5}{8} \div \frac{3}{8} = \frac{5}{3}$ | $\frac{5}{8} \times \frac{8}{3} =$ |
| $\frac{1}{6} \div \frac{5}{6} = \frac{1}{5}$ | $\frac{1}{6} \times \frac{6}{5} =$ |
| $\frac{1}{4} \div \frac{1}{3} = \frac{3}{4}$ | $\frac{1}{4} \times \frac{3}{1} =$ |

**B** How does each multiplication problem compare to its corresponding division problem?

_____

_____

_____

**C** How does the answer to each multiplication problem compare to the answer to its corresponding division problem?

_____

_____

## Reflect

**8. Make a Conjecture** Use the pattern in the table to make a conjecture about how you can use multiplication to divide one fraction by another.

_____

_____

**9.** Write a division problem and a corresponding multiplication problem like those in the table. Assuming your conjecture in **8** is correct, what is the answer to your division problem?

_____

_____

# Using Reciprocals to Divide Fractions

Dividing by a fraction is equivalent to multiplying by its reciprocal. So, to divide by a fraction, multiply by its reciprocal.

$$\frac{1}{5} \div \frac{1}{4} = \frac{4}{5} \qquad \frac{1}{5} \times \frac{4}{1} = \frac{4}{5}$$

## EXAMPLE 2

TEKS 6.3.A

**Divide $\frac{5}{9} \div \frac{2}{3}$. Write the quotient in simplest form.**

**STEP 1** Rewrite as multiplication, using the reciprocal of the divisor.

$$\frac{5}{9} \div \frac{2}{3} = \frac{5}{9} \times \frac{3}{2} \qquad \text{The reciprocal of } \frac{2}{3} \text{ is } \frac{3}{2}.$$

**STEP 2** Multiply and simplify.

$$\frac{5}{9} \times \frac{3}{2} = \frac{15}{18} \qquad \text{Multiply the numerators. Multiply the denominators.}$$

$$\frac{5}{6} \qquad \text{Write the answer in simplest form.}$$

$$\frac{5}{9} \div \frac{2}{3} = \frac{5}{6} \qquad \boxed{\frac{15 \div 3}{18 \div 3} = \frac{5}{6}}$$

## YOUR TURN

**Divide.**

**10.** $\frac{9}{10} \div \frac{2}{5} =$ _____

**11.** $\frac{9}{10} \div \frac{3}{5} =$ _____

## Guided Practice

**Find the reciprocal of each fraction.** (Example 1)

**1.** $\frac{2}{5}$ _____

**2.** $\frac{1}{9}$ _____

**3.** $\frac{10}{3}$ _____

**Divide.** (Explore 1, Explore 2, and Example 2)

**4.** $\frac{4}{3} \div \frac{5}{3} =$ _____

**5.** $\frac{3}{10} \div \frac{4}{5} =$ _____

**6.** $\frac{1}{2} \div \frac{2}{5} =$ _____

**? ESSENTIAL QUESTION CHECK-IN**

**7.** How do you divide fractions?

_____

# 3.3 Independent Practice

Personal Math Trainer

Online Assessment and Intervention

my.hrw.com

**TEKS** 6.3.A, 6.3.E

**8.** Alison has $\frac{1}{2}$ cup of yogurt for making fruit parfaits. Each parfait requires $\frac{1}{8}$ cup of yogurt. How many parfaits can she make?

_____

**9.** A team of runners is needed to run a $\frac{1}{4}$-mile relay race. If each runner must run $\frac{1}{16}$ mile, how many runners will be needed?

_____

**10.** Trevor paints $\frac{1}{6}$ of the fence surrounding his farm each day. How many days will it take him to paint $\frac{3}{4}$ of the fence?

_____

**11.** Six people share $\frac{3}{5}$ pound of peanuts equally. What fraction of a pound of peanuts does each person receive?

_____

**12. Biology** If one honeybee makes $\frac{1}{12}$ teaspoon of honey during its lifetime, how many honeybees are needed to make $\frac{1}{2}$ teaspoon of honey?

**13.** Jackson wants to divide a $\frac{3}{4}$-pound box of trail mix into small bags. Each of the bags will hold $\frac{1}{12}$ pound of trail mix. How many bags of trail mix can Jackson fill?

_____

**14.** A pitcher contains $\frac{2}{3}$ quart of lemonade. If an equal amount of lemonade is poured into each of 6 glasses, how much lemonade will each glass contain?

_____

**15.** How many tenths are there in $\frac{4}{5}$?

_____

**16.** You make a large bowl of salad to share with your friends. Your brother eats $\frac{1}{3}$ of it before they come over.

   **a.** You want to divide the leftover salad evenly among six friends. What expression describes the situation? Explain.

_____

_____

_____

_____

   **b.** What fractional portion of the original bowl of salad does each friend receive?

_____

_____

_____

Fotolia

**17. Interpret the Answer** The length of a ribbon is $\frac{3}{4}$ meter. Sun Yi needs pieces measuring $\frac{1}{3}$ meter for an art project. What is the greatest number of pieces measuring $\frac{1}{3}$ meter that can be cut from the ribbon? How much ribbon will be left after Sun Yi cuts the ribbon? Explain your reasoning.

_____

_____

_____

**18. Represent Real-World Problems** Liam has $\frac{9}{10}$ gallon of paint for painting the birdhouses he sells at the craft fair. Each birdhouse requires $\frac{1}{20}$ gallon of paint. How many birdhouses can Liam paint? Show your work.

_____

_____

**19. Justify Reasoning** When Kaitlin divided a fraction by $\frac{1}{2}$, the result was a mixed number. Was the original fraction less than or greater than $\frac{1}{2}$? Explain your reasoning.

_____

_____

_____

**20. Communicate Mathematical Ideas** The reciprocal of a fraction less than 1 is always a fraction greater than 1. Why is this?

_____

_____

_____

_____

**21. Make a Prediction** Susan divides the fraction $\frac{5}{8}$ by $\frac{1}{16}$. Her friend Robyn divides $\frac{5}{8}$ by $\frac{1}{32}$. Predict which person will get the greater quotient. Explain and check your prediction.

_____

_____

_____

# Dividing Mixed Numbers

**TEKS**
Number and
operations—6.3.E
Multiply and divide positive
rational numbers fluently.
*Also 6.3.A*

**?** **ESSENTIAL QUESTION**

How do you divide mixed numbers?

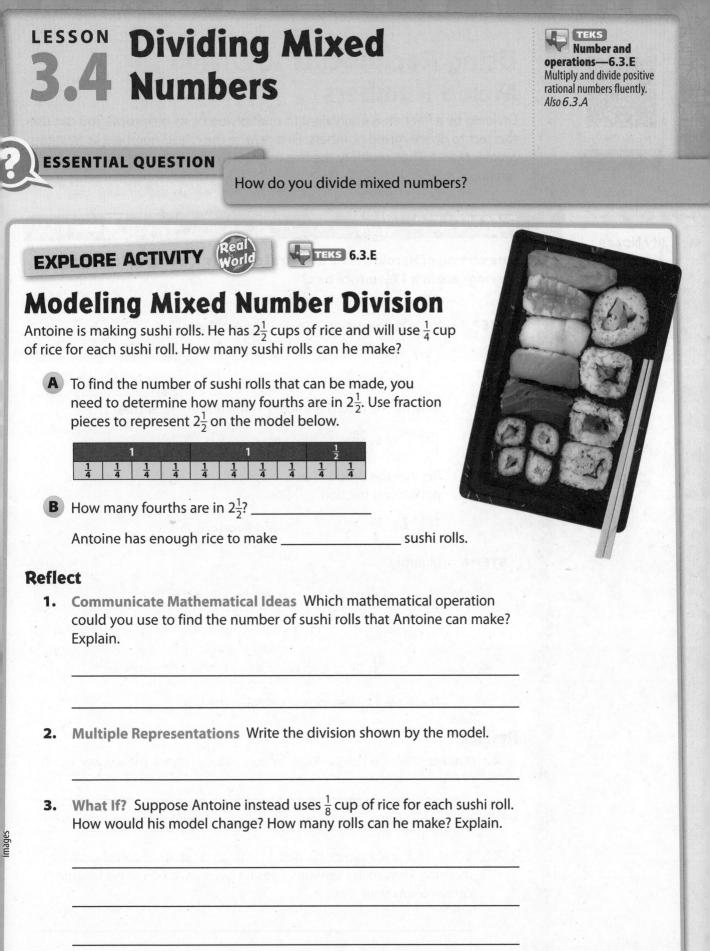

**EXPLORE ACTIVITY** (Real World) **TEKS** 6.3.E

## Modeling Mixed Number Division

Antoine is making sushi rolls. He has $2\frac{1}{2}$ cups of rice and will use $\frac{1}{4}$ cup of rice for each sushi roll. How many sushi rolls can he make?

**A** To find the number of sushi rolls that can be made, you need to determine how many fourths are in $2\frac{1}{2}$. Use fraction pieces to represent $2\frac{1}{2}$ on the model below.

| 1 | | | | 1 | | | | $\frac{1}{2}$ | |
|---|---|---|---|---|---|---|---|---|---|
| $\frac{1}{4}$ | $\frac{1}{4}$ | $\frac{1}{4}$ | $\frac{1}{4}$ | $\frac{1}{4}$ | $\frac{1}{4}$ | $\frac{1}{4}$ | $\frac{1}{4}$ | $\frac{1}{4}$ | $\frac{1}{4}$ |

**B** How many fourths are in $2\frac{1}{2}$? _____

Antoine has enough rice to make _____ sushi rolls.

### Reflect

1. **Communicate Mathematical Ideas** Which mathematical operation could you use to find the number of sushi rolls that Antoine can make? Explain.

   _____

   _____

2. **Multiple Representations** Write the division shown by the model.

   _____

3. **What If?** Suppose Antoine instead uses $\frac{1}{8}$ cup of rice for each sushi roll. How would his model change? How many rolls can he make? Explain.

   _____

   _____

   _____

My Notes

# Using Reciprocals to Divide Mixed Numbers

Dividing by a fraction is equivalent to multiplying by its reciprocal. You can use this fact to divide mixed numbers. First rewrite the mixed numbers as fractions greater than 1. Then multiply the first fraction by the reciprocal of the second fraction.

## EXAMPLE 1  Real World                    TEKS 6.3.A

One serving of Harold's favorite cereal contains $1\frac{2}{5}$ ounces. How many servings are in a $17\frac{1}{2}$-ounce box?

**STEP 1**  Write the situation as a division problem.

$$17\frac{1}{2} \div 1\frac{2}{5}$$

> You need to find how many groups of $1\frac{2}{5}$ are in $17\frac{1}{2}$.

**STEP 2**  Rewrite the mixed numbers as fractions greater than 1.

$$17\frac{1}{2} \div 1\frac{2}{5} = \frac{35}{2} \div \frac{7}{5}$$

**STEP 3**  Rewrite the problem as multiplication using the reciprocal of the second fraction.

$$\frac{35}{2} \div \frac{7}{5} = \frac{35}{2} \times \frac{5}{7} \qquad \text{The reciprocal of } \frac{7}{5} \text{ is } \frac{5}{7}.$$

**STEP 4**  Multiply.

$$\frac{35}{2} \times \frac{5}{7} = \frac{\overset{5}{\cancel{35}}}{2} \times \frac{5}{\underset{1}{\cancel{7}}} \qquad \text{Simplify first using the GCF.}$$

$$= \frac{5 \times 5}{2 \times 1} \qquad \text{Multiply numerators. Multiply denominators.}$$

$$= \frac{25}{2}, \text{ or } 12\frac{1}{2} \qquad \text{Write the result as a mixed number.}$$

There are $12\frac{1}{2}$ servings of cereal in the box.

## Reflect

**4.  Analyze Relationships**  Explain how you can check the answer.

_____

_____

**5.  What If?**  Harold serves himself $1\frac{1}{2}$-ounce servings of cereal each morning. How many servings does he get from a box of his favorite cereal? Show your work.

_____

6. Sheila has $10\frac{1}{2}$ pounds of potato salad. She wants to divide the potato salad into containers, each of which holds $1\frac{1}{4}$ pounds. How many containers does she need? Explain.

_____

**Personal Math Trainer**

Online Assessment and Intervention

⏺ my.hrw.com

# Solving Problems Involving Area

Recall that to find the area of a rectangle, you multiply length × width. If you know the area and only one dimension, you can divide the area by the known dimension to find the other dimension.

**Math On the Spot**

⏺ my.hrw.com

## EXAMPLE 2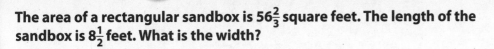

TEKS 6.3.E

The area of a rectangular sandbox is $56\frac{2}{3}$ square feet. The length of the sandbox is $8\frac{1}{2}$ feet. What is the width?

**STEP 1** Write the situation as a division problem.

$$56\frac{2}{3} \div 8\frac{1}{2}$$

**STEP 2** Rewrite the mixed numbers as fractions greater than 1.

$$56\frac{2}{3} \div 8\frac{1}{2} = \frac{170}{3} \div \frac{17}{2}$$

**STEP 3** Rewrite the problem as multiplication using the reciprocal of the second fraction.

$$\frac{170}{3} \div \frac{17}{2} = \frac{170}{3} \times \frac{2}{17}$$

**STEP 4** Multiply.

$$\frac{170}{3} \times \frac{2}{17} = \frac{{}^{10}\cancel{170} \times 2}{3 \times \cancel{17}_{1}}$$   Multiply numerators. Multiply denominators.

$$= \frac{20}{3}, \text{ or } 6\frac{2}{3}$$   Simplify and write as a mixed number.

The width of the sandbox is $6\frac{2}{3}$ feet.

> **Math Talk**
> Mathematical Processes
>
> Explain how to find the length of a rectangle when you know the area and the width.

## Reflect

7. **Check for Reasonableness** How can you determine if your answer is reasonable?

_____

_____

_____

_____

**YOUR TURN**

8. The area of a rectangular patio is $12\frac{3}{8}$ square meters. The width of the patio is $2\frac{3}{4}$ meters. What is the length? _____

9. The area of a rectangular rug is $14\frac{1}{12}$ square yards. The length of the rug is $4\frac{1}{3}$ yards. What is the width? _____

## Guided Practice

**Divide. Write each answer in simplest form.** (Explore Activity and Example 1)

1. $4\frac{1}{4} \div \frac{3}{4}$

$$\frac{\boxed{\phantom{0}}}{4} \div \frac{3}{4} =$$

$$\frac{\boxed{\phantom{0}}}{4} \times \frac{\boxed{\phantom{0}}}{\boxed{\phantom{0}}} =$$

_____

2. $1\frac{1}{2} \div 2\frac{1}{4}$

$$\frac{\boxed{\phantom{0}}}{2} \div \frac{\boxed{\phantom{0}}}{4} =$$

$$\frac{\boxed{\phantom{0}}}{2} \times \frac{\boxed{\phantom{0}}}{\boxed{\phantom{0}}} =$$

_____

3. $4 \div 1\frac{1}{8} =$ _____

4. $3\frac{1}{5} \div 1\frac{1}{7} =$ _____

5. $8\frac{1}{3} \div 2\frac{1}{2} =$ _____

6. $15\frac{1}{3} \div 3\frac{5}{6} =$ _____

**Write each situation as a division problem. Then solve.** (Example 2)

7. A sandbox has an area of 26 square feet, and the length is $5\frac{1}{2}$ feet. What is the width of the sandbox? _____

8. Mr. Webster is buying carpet for an exercise room in his basement. The room will have an area of 230 square feet. The width of the room is $12\frac{1}{2}$ feet. What is the length? _____

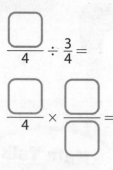 **ESSENTIAL QUESTION CHECK-IN**

9. How does dividing mixed numbers compare with dividing fractions?

_____

_____

# 3.4 Independent Practice

TEKS 6.3.E

**10.** Jeremy has $4\frac{1}{2}$ cups of iced tea. He wants to divide the tea into $\frac{3}{4}$-cup servings. Use the model to find the number of servings he can make.

| 1 | 1 | 1 | 1 | 1 |
|---|---|---|---|---|
| $\frac{1}{4}$ $\frac{1}{4}$ $\frac{1}{4}$ $\frac{1}{4}$ | $\frac{1}{4}$ $\frac{1}{4}$ $\frac{1}{4}$ $\frac{1}{4}$ | $\frac{1}{4}$ $\frac{1}{4}$ $\frac{1}{4}$ $\frac{1}{4}$ | $\frac{1}{4}$ $\frac{1}{4}$ $\frac{1}{4}$ $\frac{1}{4}$ | $\frac{1}{4}$ $\frac{1}{4}$ $\frac{1}{4}$ $\frac{1}{4}$ |

_____

**11.** A ribbon is $3\frac{2}{3}$ yards long. Mae needs to cut the ribbon into pieces that are $\frac{2}{3}$ yard long. Use the model to find the number of pieces she can cut.

| 1 | 1 | 1 | 1 |
|---|---|---|---|
| $\frac{1}{3}$ $\frac{1}{3}$ $\frac{1}{3}$ | $\frac{1}{3}$ $\frac{1}{3}$ $\frac{1}{3}$ | $\frac{1}{3}$ $\frac{1}{3}$ $\frac{1}{3}$ | $\frac{1}{3}$ $\frac{1}{3}$ |

_____

**12.** Dao has $2\frac{3}{8}$ pounds of hamburger meat. He is making $\frac{1}{4}$-pound hamburgers. Does Dao have enough meat to make 10 hamburgers? Explain.

_____

_____

**13.** **Multistep** Zoey made $5\frac{1}{2}$ cups of trail mix for a camping trip. She wants to divide the trail mix into $\frac{3}{4}$-cup servings.

**a.** Ten people are going on the camping trip. Can Zoey make enough $\frac{3}{4}$-cup servings so that each person on the trip has one serving?

_____

**b.** What size would the servings need to be for everyone to have a serving? Explain.

_____

**c.** If Zoey decides to use the $\frac{3}{4}$-cup servings, how much more trail mix will she need? Explain.

_____

_____

**14.** The area of a rectangular picture frame is $30\frac{1}{3}$ square inches. The length of the frame is $6\frac{1}{2}$ inches. Find the width of the frame.

_____

**15.** The area of a rectangular mirror is $11\frac{11}{16}$ square feet. The width of the mirror is $2\frac{3}{4}$ feet. If there is a 5 foot tall space on the wall to hang the mirror, will it fit? Explain.

_____

**16.** Ramon has a rope that is $25\frac{1}{2}$ feet long. He wants to cut it into 6 pieces that are equal in length. How long will each piece be?

_____

**17.** Eleanor and Max used two rectangular wooden boards to make a set for the school play. One board was 6 feet long, and the other was $5\frac{1}{2}$ feet long. The two boards had equal widths. The total area of the set was $60\frac{3}{8}$ square feet. What was the width?

_____

**H.O.T.** FOCUS ON HIGHER ORDER THINKING

Work Area

**18. Draw Conclusions** Micah divided $11\frac{2}{3}$ by $2\frac{5}{6}$ and got $4\frac{2}{17}$ for an answer. Does his answer seem reasonable? Explain your thinking. Then check Micah's answer.

_____

_____

_____

_____

_____

**19. Explain the Error** To divide $14\frac{2}{3} \div 2\frac{3}{4}$, Erik multiplied $14\frac{2}{3} \times \frac{4}{3}$. Explain Erik's error.

_____

_____

_____

**20. Analyze Relationships** Explain how you can find the missing number in $3\frac{4}{5} \div \blacksquare = 2\frac{5}{7}$. Then find the missing number.

_____

_____

_____

# Ready to Go On?

Personal
Math Trainer

Online Assessment
and Intervention

my.hrw.com

## 3.1 Multiplying Fractions

**Multiply.**

**1.** $\frac{4}{5} \times \frac{3}{4}$ _____

**2.** $\frac{5}{7} \times \frac{9}{10}$ _____

**3.** Fred had 264 books in his personal library. He donated $\frac{2}{11}$ of these books to the public library. How many books did he donate? _____

## 3.2 Multiplying Mixed Numbers

**Multiply.**

**4.** $\frac{3}{8} \times 2\frac{1}{2}$ _____

**5.** $3\frac{3}{5} \times \frac{5}{6}$ _____

**6.** Jamal and Dorothy were hiking and had a choice between two trails. One was $5\frac{1}{3}$ miles long, and the other was $1\frac{3}{4}$ times as long. How long was the longer trail? _____

## 3.3 Dividing Fractions

**Divide.**

**7.** $\frac{7}{8} \div \frac{3}{4}$ _____

**8.** $\frac{4}{5} \div \frac{6}{7}$ _____

**9.** $\frac{1}{3} \div \frac{7}{9}$ _____

**10.** $\frac{1}{3} \div \frac{5}{8}$ _____

## 3.4 Dividing Mixed Numbers

**Divide.**

**11.** $3\frac{1}{3} \div \frac{2}{3}$ _____

**12.** $1\frac{7}{8} \div 2\frac{2}{5}$ _____

**13.** $4\frac{1}{4} \div 4\frac{1}{2}$ _____

**14.** $8\frac{1}{3} \div 4\frac{2}{7}$ _____

## ? ESSENTIAL QUESTION

**15.** Describe a real-world situation that is modeled by multiplying two fractions or mixed numbers.

_____

MODULE 3 MIXED REVIEW

# Texas Test Prep

Personal
Math Trainer

Online
Assessment and
Intervention

my.hrw.com

## Selected Response

**1.** Which of the following statements is correct?

Ⓐ The product of $\frac{3}{4}$ and $\frac{7}{8}$ is less than $\frac{7}{8}$.

Ⓑ The product of $1\frac{1}{3}$ and $\frac{9}{10}$ is less than $\frac{9}{10}$.

Ⓒ The product of $\frac{3}{4}$ and $\frac{7}{8}$ is greater than $\frac{7}{8}$.

Ⓓ The product of $\frac{7}{8}$ and $\frac{9}{10}$ is greater than $\frac{9}{10}$.

**2.** Which shows the GCF of 18 and 24 with $\frac{18}{24}$ in simplest form?

Ⓐ GCF: 3; $\frac{3}{4}$

Ⓑ GCF: 3; $\frac{6}{8}$

Ⓒ GCF: 6; $\frac{3}{4}$

Ⓓ GCF: 6; $\frac{6}{8}$

**3.** A jar contains 133 pennies. A bigger jar contains $1\frac{2}{7}$ times as many pennies. What is the value of the pennies in the bigger jar?

Ⓐ $1.49

Ⓑ $1.52

Ⓒ $1.68

Ⓓ $1.71

**4.** Which of these is the same as $\frac{3}{5} \div \frac{4}{7}$?

Ⓐ $\frac{3}{5} \div \frac{7}{4}$

Ⓑ $\frac{4}{7} \div \frac{3}{5}$

Ⓒ $\frac{3}{5} \times \frac{4}{7}$

Ⓓ $\frac{3}{5} \times \frac{7}{4}$

**5.** What is the reciprocal of $3\frac{3}{7}$?

Ⓐ $\frac{7}{24}$

Ⓑ $\frac{3}{7}$

Ⓒ $\frac{7}{3}$

Ⓓ $\frac{24}{7}$

**6.** A rectangular patio has a length of $12\frac{1}{2}$ feet and an area of $103\frac{1}{8}$ square feet. What is the width of the patio?

Ⓐ $4\frac{1}{8}$ feet

Ⓑ $8\frac{1}{4}$ feet

Ⓒ $16\frac{1}{2}$ feet

Ⓓ 33 feet

## Gridded Response

**7.** Jodi is cutting out pieces of paper that measure $8\frac{1}{2}$ inches by 11 inches from a large sheet that has an area of 1,000 square inches. What is the area of each piece of paper that Jodi is cutting out written as a decimal?

# Multiplying and Dividing Decimals

## ? ESSENTIAL QUESTION

How can you use products and quotients of decimals to solve real-world problems?

### Real-World Video

The gravitational force on Earth's moon is less than the gravitational force on Earth. You can calculate your weight on the moon by multiplying your weight on Earth by a decimal.

my.hrw.com

## GO DIGITAL

my.hrw.com

**my.hrw.com**
Go digital with your write-in student edition, accessible on any device.

**Math On the Spot**
Scan with your smart phone to jump directly to the online edition, video tutor, and more.

**Animated Math**
Interactively explore key concepts to see how math works.

**Personal Math Trainer**
Get immediate feedback and help as you work through practice sets.

# Are YOU Ready?

Complete these exercises to review skills you will need for this chapter.

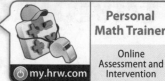

**Personal Math Trainer**

Online Assessment and Intervention

my.hrw.com

## Represent Decimals

**EXAMPLE**

Think: 1 square = 1 of 100 equal parts
$= \frac{1}{100}$, or 0.01

10 squares = 10 of 100 equal parts
$= \frac{1}{10}$, or 0.1

So, 20 squares represent $2 \times 0.1$, or 0.2.

**Write the decimal represented by the shaded square.**

1. _____   2. _____   3. _____   4. _____

## Multiply Decimals by Powers of 10

**EXAMPLE**   $6.574 \times 100$          Count the zeros in 100: 2 zeros.

$6.574 \times 100 = 657.4$          Move the decimal point 2 places to the right.

**Find the product.**

**5.**  $0.49 \times 10$ _____   **6.**  $25.34 \times 1{,}000$ _____   **7.**  $87 \times 100$ _____

## Words for Operations

**EXAMPLE**   Write a numerical expression for the product of 5 and 9.          Think: *Product* means "to multiply."

$5 \times 9$          Write 5 times 9.

**Write a numerical expression for the word expression.**

**8.**  20 decreased by 8 _____   **9.**  the quotient of 14 and 7 _____

**10.**  the difference between 72 and 16 _____   **11.**  the sum of 19 and 3 _____

# Reading Start-Up

## Visualize Vocabulary

Use the ✔ words to complete the chart. You may put more than one word in each section.

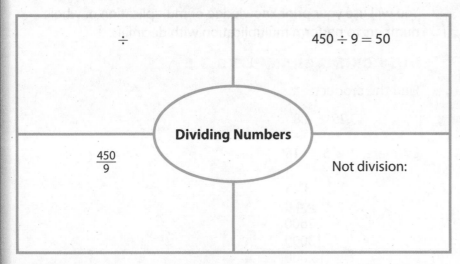

| | |
|---|---|
| ÷ | 450 ÷ 9 = 50 |
| $\frac{450}{9}$ | Not division: |

*(center: **Dividing Numbers**)*

## Vocabulary

**Review Words**

  decimal *(decimal)*

✔ denominator *(denominador)*

  divide *(dividir)*

✔ dividend *(dividendo)*

✔ divisor *(divisor)*

✔ fraction bar *(barra de fracciones)*

✔ multiply *(multiplicar)*

✔ numerator *(numerador)*

✔ operation *(operación)*

✔ product *(producto)*

✔ quotient *(cociente)*

✔ rational number *(número racional)*

✔ symbol *(símbolo)*

  whole number *(número entero)*

## Understand Vocabulary

Match the term on the left to the definition on the right.

**1.** divide              **A.** The bottom number in a fraction.

**2.** denominator     **B.** The top number in a fraction.

**3.** quotient           **C.** To split into equal groups.

**4.** numerator        **D.** The answer in a division problem.

## Active Reading

**Double-Door Fold** Create a double-door fold to help you understand the concepts in this module. Label one flap "Multiplying Decimals" and the other flap "Dividing Decimals." As you study each lesson, write important ideas under the appropriate flap. Include information about unit examples that will help you remember the concepts later when you look back at your notes.

## MODULE 4

# Unpacking the TEKS

Understanding the TEKS and the vocabulary terms in the TEKS will help you know exactly what you are expected to learn in this module.

---

**TEKS 6.3.E**

**Multiply** and divide positive rational numbers fluently.

**Key Vocabulary**

**algorithm** *(algoritmo)*
A set of rules or a procedure for solving a mathematical problem in a finite number of steps.

## What It Means to You

You will use your prior knowledge of multiplication of whole numbers to perform multiplication with decimals.

**UNPACKING EXAMPLE 6.3.E**

Find the product:

$$3.25 \times 4.8$$

Estimate: $3 \times 5 = 15$

$$
\begin{array}{r}
3.25 \\
\times\,4.8 \\
\hline
2600 \\
13000 \\
\hline
15.600
\end{array}
$$

---

**TEKS 6.3.E**

Multiply and **divide** positive rational numbers fluently.

**Key Vocabulary**

**quotient** *(cociente)*
The result when one number is divided by another.

## What It Means to You

You will use your prior knowledge of division of whole numbers to perform division with decimals.

**UNPACKING EXAMPLE 6.3.E**

Eugenia and her friends bought frozen yogurt for 45 cents per ounce. Their total was $11.25. How many ounces did they buy?

Divide 11.25 by 0.45.

$$
\begin{array}{r}
25 \\
0.45)\overline{11.25} \\
90 \\
\hline
225 \\
225 \\
\hline
0
\end{array}
$$

They bought 25 ounces of frozen yogurt.

Visit **my.hrw.com** to see all the **TEKS** unpacked.

my.hrw.com

**TEKS**
**Number and operations—6.3.E**
Multiply and divide positive rational numbers fluently.

**ESSENTIAL QUESTION**

How do you multiply decimals?

**EXPLORE ACTIVITY** | **TEKS** 6.3.E

## Modeling Decimal Multiplication

Use decimal grids or area models to find each product.

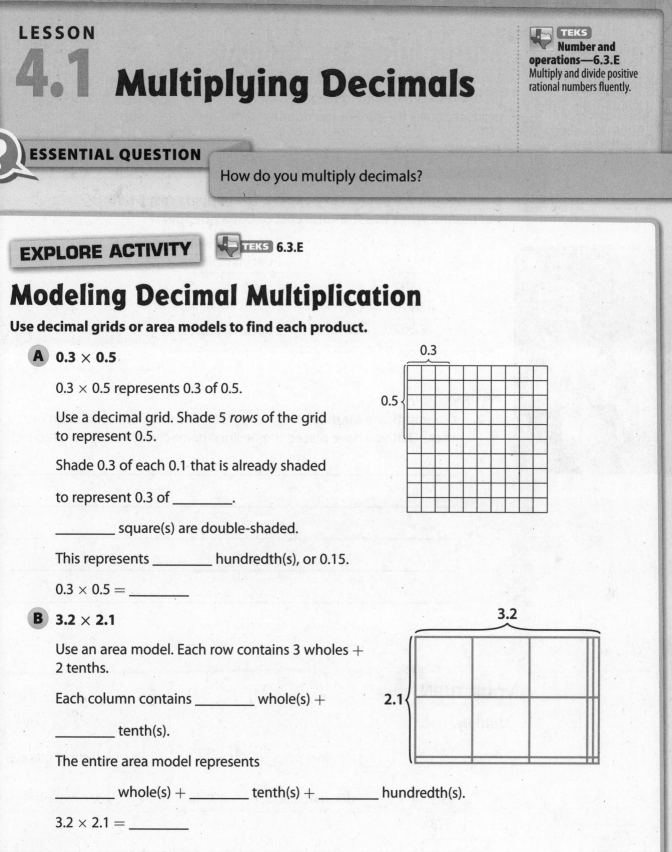

**A** **0.3 × 0.5**

0.3 × 0.5 represents 0.3 of 0.5.

Use a decimal grid. Shade 5 *rows* of the grid to represent 0.5.

Shade 0.3 of each 0.1 that is already shaded

to represent 0.3 of _____.

_____ square(s) are double-shaded.

This represents _____ hundredth(s), or 0.15.

0.3 × 0.5 = _____

**B** **3.2 × 2.1**

Use an area model. Each row contains 3 wholes + 2 tenths.

Each column contains _____ whole(s) +

_____ tenth(s).

The entire area model represents

_____ whole(s) + _____ tenth(s) + _____ hundredth(s).

3.2 × 2.1 = _____

## Reflect

1. **Analyze Relationships** How are the products 2.1 × 3.2 and 21 × 32 alike? How are they different?

_____

_____

# Multiplying Decimals

To multiply decimals, first multiply as you would with whole numbers. Then place the decimal point in the product. The number of decimal places in the product equals the sum of the number of decimal places in the factors.

## EXAMPLE 1 Real World

Delia bought 3.8 pounds of peppers. The peppers cost $1.99 per pound. What was the total cost of Delia's peppers?

$$
\begin{array}{r}
1.99 \quad \leftarrow \quad 2 \text{ decimal places} \\
\times \; 3.8 \quad \leftarrow + \; 1 \text{ decimal place} \\
\hline
1592 \\
+ \; 5970 \\
\hline
7.562 \quad \leftarrow \quad 3 \text{ decimal places}
\end{array}
$$

The peppers cost $7.56.

Round the answer to hundre to show a dollar amount.

### Reflect

**2. Communicate Mathematical Ideas** How can you use estimation to check that you have placed the decimal point correctly in your product?

_____

_____

_____

_____

_____

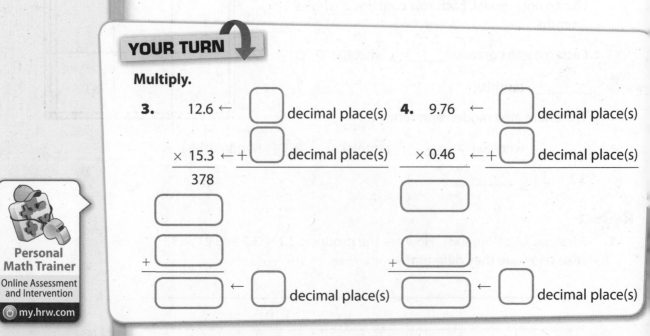

## YOUR TURN

**Multiply.**

**3.**   12.6 ← ⬜ decimal place(s)

   × 15.3 ← + ⬜ decimal place(s)

   378

   ⬜

   + ⬜

   ⬜ ← ⬜ decimal place(s)

**4.**   9.76 ← ⬜ decimal place(s)

   × 0.46 ← + ⬜ decimal place(s)

   ⬜

   + ⬜

   ⬜ ← ⬜ decimal place(s)

# Estimating to Check Reasonableness

In Example 1, you used estimation to check whether the decimal point was placed correctly in the product. You can also use estimation to check that your answer is reasonable.

## EXAMPLE 2 | Real World

**TEKS** 6.3.E

**Blades of grass grow 3.75 inches per month. If the grass continues to grow at this rate, how much will the grass grow in 6.25 months?**

$$
\begin{array}{r}
3.75 \quad \leftarrow \quad \text{2 decimal places} \\
\times \, 6.25 \quad \leftarrow + \, \text{2 decimal places} \\
\hline
1875 \\
7500 \\
+ \, 225000 \\
\hline
23.4375 \quad \leftarrow \quad \text{4 decimal places}
\end{array}
$$

The grass will grow 23.4375 inches in 6.25 months.

Estimate to check whether your answer is reasonable.

Round 3.75 to the nearest whole number. _____

Round 6.25 to the nearest whole number. _____

Multiply the whole numbers. _____ × _____ = 24

The answer is reasonable because 24 is close to 23.4375.

---

## YOUR TURN

**Multiply.**

5.
$$
\begin{array}{r}
7.14 \\
\times \, 6.78 \\
\hline
5712 \\
\end{array}
$$

6.
$$
\begin{array}{r}
11.49 \\
\times \, 8.27 \\
\hline
\end{array}
$$

7. Rico bicycles at an average speed of 15.5 miles per hour.

   What distance will Rico bicycle in 2.5 hours? _____ miles

8. Use estimation to show that your answer to **7** is reasonable.

   _____

## Guided Practice

**1.** Use the grid to multiply 0.4 × 0.7.
(Explore Activity)

0.4 × 0.7 = _____

**2.** Draw an area model to multiply 1.1 × 2.4.
(Explore Activity)

1.1 × 2.4 = _____

**Multiply.** (Example 1 and Example 2)

**3.** 0.18 × 0.06 = _____

**4.** 35.15 × 3.7 = _____

**5.** 0.96 × 0.12 = _____

**6.** 62.19 × 32.5 = _____

**7.** 3.4 × 4.37 = _____

**8.** 3.762 × 0.66 = _____

**9.** Chan Hee bought 3.4 pounds of coffee that cost $6.95 per pound.

How much did he spend on coffee? $_____

**10.** Adita earns $9.40 per hour working at an animal shelter.

How much money will she earn for 18.5 hours of work? $_____

**Catherine tracked her gas purchases for one month.**

**11.** How much did Catherine spend on gas in week 2?

$_____

**12.** How much more did she spend in week 4 than

in week 1? $_____

| Week | Gallons | Cost per gallon ($) |
|---|---|---|
| 1 | 10.4 | 2.65 |
| 2 | 11.5 | 2.54 |
| 3 | 9.72 | 2.75 |
| 4 | 10.6 | 2.70 |

**? ESSENTIAL QUESTION CHECK-IN**

**13.** How can you check the answer to a decimal multiplication problem?

_____

_____

# 4.1 Independent Practice

TEKS 6.3.E

**Personal Math Trainer**

Online Assessment and Intervention

my.hrw.com

## Make a reasonable estimate for each situation.

**14.** A gallon of water weighs 8.354 pounds. Simon uses 11.81 gallons of water while taking a shower. About how many pounds of water did Simon use?

_____

**15.** A snail moves at a speed of 2.394 inches per minute. If the snail keeps moving at this rate, about how many inches will it travel in 7.489 minutes?

_____

**16.** Tricia's garden is 9.87 meters long and 1.09 meters wide. What is the area of her garden?

_____

**Kaylynn and Amanda both work at the same store. The table shows how much each person earns, and the number of hours each person works in a week.**

|          | Wage            | Hours worked per week |
|----------|-----------------|-----------------------|
| Kaylynn  | $8.75 per hour  | 37.5                  |
| Amanda   | $10.25 per hour | 30.5                  |

**17.** Estimate how much Kaylynn earns in a week.

_____

**18.** Estimate how much Amanda earns in a week.

_____

**19.** Calculate the exact difference between Kaylynn and Amanda's weekly salaries.

_____

**20.** Victoria's printer can print 8.804 pages in one minute. If Victoria prints pages for 0.903 minutes, about how many pages will she have?

_____

## A taxi charges a flat fee of $4.00 plus $2.25 per mile.

**21.** How much will it cost to travel 8.7 miles? _____

**22.** **Multistep** How much will the taxi driver earn if he takes one passenger 4.8 miles and another passenger 7.3 miles? Explain your process.

_____

_____

_____

**Kay goes for several bike rides one week. The table shows her speed and the number of hours spent per ride.**

|  | Speed (in miles per hour) | Hours Spent on Bike |
|---|---|---|
| **Monday** | 8.2 | 4.25 |
| **Tuesday** | 9.6 | 3.1 |
| **Wednesday** | 11.1 | 2.8 |
| **Thursday** | 10.75 | 1.9 |
| **Friday** | 8.8 | 3.75 |

**23.** How many miles did Kay bike on Thursday? _____

**24.** On which day did Kay bike a whole number of miles? _____

**25.** What is the difference in miles between Kay's longest bike ride and her shortest bike ride? _____

**26.** **Check for Reasonableness** Kay estimates that Wednesday's ride was about 3 miles longer than Tuesday's ride. Is her estimate reasonable? Explain.

_____

_____

_____

_____

# H.O.T. FOCUS ON HIGHER ORDER THINKING

**Work Area**

**27.** **Explain the Error** To estimate the product 3.48 × 7.33, Marisa multiplied 4 × 8 to get 32. Explain how she can make a closer estimate.

_____

_____

**28.** **Represent Real-World Problems** A jeweler buys gold jewelry and resells the gold to a refinery. The jeweler buys gold for $1,235.55 per ounce, and then resells it for $1,376.44 per ounce. How much profit does the jeweler make from buying and reselling 73.5 ounces of gold?

_____

**29.** **Problem Solving** To find the weight of the gold in a 22 karat gold object, multiply the object's weight by 0.916. To find the weight of gold in a 14 karat gold object, multiply the object's weight by 0.585. Which contains more gold, a 22 karat gold object or a 14 karat gold object that each weigh 73.5 ounces? How much more gold does it contain?

_____

LESSON
# 4.2 Dividing Decimals

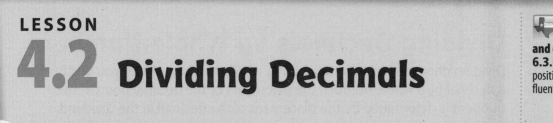

TEKS
**Number and operations—**
6.3.E Multiply and divide positive rational numbers fluently.

## ESSENTIAL QUESTION

How do you divide decimals?

**EXPLORE ACTIVITY**  TEKS 6.3.E

# Modeling Decimal Division

**Use decimal grids to find each quotient.**

**A** **6.39 ÷ 3**

Shade grids to model 6.39. Separate the model into 3 equal groups.

How many are in each group? _____

$6.39 \div 3 =$ _____

**B** **6.39 ÷ 2.13**

Shade grids to model 6.39. Separate the model into groups of 2.13.

How many groups do you have? _____

$6.39 \div 2.13 =$ _____

## Reflect

1. **Multiple Representations** When using models to divide decimals, when might you want to use grids divided into tenths instead of hundredths?

_____

_____

# Dividing Decimals by Whole Numbers

Dividing decimals is similar to dividing whole numbers. When you divide a decimal by a whole number, the placement of the decimal point in the quotient is determined by the placement of the decimal in the dividend.

**My Notes**

.................
.................
.................
.................
.................
.................
.................

## EXAMPLE 1

TEKS 6.3.E

**A** A high school track is 9.76 meters wide. It is divided into 8 lanes of equal width for track and field events. How wide is each lane?

$$\begin{array}{r} 1.22 \\ 8\overline{)9.76} \\ -8\phantom{.00} \\ \hline 17 \\ -16 \\ \hline 16 \\ -16 \\ \hline 0 \end{array}$$

Divide using long division as with whole numbers.

Place a decimal point in the quotient directly above the decimal point in the dividend.

Each lane is 1.22 meters wide.

**B** Aerobics classes cost $153.86 for 14 sessions. What is the fee for one session?

$$\begin{array}{r} 10.99 \\ 14\overline{)153.86} \\ -14\phantom{.000} \\ \hline 13 \\ -0\phantom{0} \\ \hline 138 \\ -126 \\ \hline 126 \\ -126 \\ \hline 0 \end{array}$$

Divide using long division as with whole numbers.

Place a decimal point in the quotient directly above the decimal point in the dividend.

The fee for one aerobics class is $10.99.

**Math Talk**

Mathematical Processes

How can you check to see that the answer is correct?

### Reflect

2. **Check for Reasonableness** How can you estimate to check that your quotient in **A** is reasonable?

_____

_____

_____

_____

**YOUR TURN**

**Divide.**

**3.** $5\overline{)9.75}$          **4.** $7\overline{)6.44}$

# Dividing a Decimal by a Decimal

When dividing a decimal by a decimal, first change the divisor to a whole number by multiplying by a power of 10. Then multiply the dividend by the same power of 10.

**Math On the Spot**
my.hrw.com

## EXAMPLE 2 · Real World

TEKS 6.3.E

**A** Ella uses 0.5 pound of raspberries in each raspberry cake that she makes. How many cakes can Ella make with 3.25 pounds of raspberries?

**STEP 1** The divisor has one decimal place, so multiply both the dividend and the divisor by 10 so that the divisor is a whole number.

$0.5\overline{)3.25}$     $0.5\overline{)3.25}$

$0.5 \times 10 = 5$

$3.25 \times 10 = 32.5$

Ella can make 6 cakes.

**STEP 2** Divide.

$$\begin{array}{r} 6.5 \\ 5\overline{)32.5} \\ -30 \phantom{.5} \\ \hline 2\,5 \\ -2\,5 \\ \hline 0 \end{array}$$

**Math Talk**
Mathematical Processes

The number of cakes Ella can make is not equal to the quotient. Why not?

**B** Anthony spent $11.52 for some pens that were on sale for $0.72 each. How many pens did Anthony buy?

**STEP 1** The divisor has two decimal places, so multiply both the dividend and the divisor by 100 so that the divisor is a whole number.

$0.72\overline{)11.52}$     $0.72\overline{)11.52}$

$0.72 \times 100 = 72$

$11.52 \times 100 = 1152$

Anthony bought 16 pens.

**STEP 2** Divide.

$$\begin{array}{r} 16 \\ 72\overline{)1152} \\ -72 \phantom{2} \\ \hline 432 \\ -432 \\ \hline 0 \end{array}$$

## YOUR TURN

Divide.

**5.** $0.5\overline{)4.25}$

**6.** $0.84\overline{)15.12}$

**Personal Math Trainer**

Online Assessment and Intervention

my.hrw.com

## Guided Practice

**Divide.** (Explore Activity, Examples 1 and 2)

**1.** $4\overline{)29.6}$ _____

**2.** $3.1\overline{)10.261}$ _____

**3.** $2.4\overline{)16.8}$ _____

**4.** $0.96\overline{)0.144}$ _____

**5.** $38.5 \div 0.5 =$ _____

**6.** $23.85 \div 9 =$ _____

**7.** $5.6372 \div 0.17 =$ _____

**8.** $8.19 \div 4.2 =$ _____

**9.** $66.5 \div 3.5 =$ _____

**10.** $0.234 \div 0.78 =$ _____

**11.** $78.74 \div 12.7 =$ _____

**12.** $36.45 \div 0.09 =$ _____

**13.** $90 \div 0.36 =$ _____

**14.** $18.88 \div 1.6 =$ _____

**15.** Corrine has 9.6 pounds of trail mix to divide into 12 bags. How many pounds of trail mix will go in each bag? _____

**16.** Michael paid $11.48 for sliced cheese at the deli counter. The cheese cost $3.28 per pound. How much cheese did Michael buy? _____

**17.** A four-person relay team completed a race in 72.4 seconds. On average, what was each runner's time? _____

**18.** Elizabeth has a piece of ribbon that is 4.5 meters long. She wants to cut it into pieces that are 0.25 meter long. How many pieces of ribbon will she have? _____

**19.** Lisa paid $43.95 for 16.1 gallons of gasoline. What was the cost per gallon, rounded to the nearest hundredth? _____

**20.** One inch is equivalent to 2.54 centimeters. How many inches are there in 50.8 centimeters? _____

**? ESSENTIAL QUESTION CHECK-IN**

**21.** How can you determine if you divided the numbers correctly?

_____

_____

_____

_____

# 4.2 Independent Practice

TEKS 6.3.E

**Use the table for 22 and 23.**

| Custom Printing Costs | | | | |
|---|---|---|---|---|
| **Quantity** | 25 | 50 | 75 | 100 |
| **Mugs** | $107.25 | $195.51 | $261.75 | $329.00 |
| **T-shirts** | $237.50 | $441.00 | $637.50 | $829.00 |

**22.** What is the price per mug for 25 coffee mugs? _____

**23.** Find the price per T-shirt for 75 T-shirts. _____

**A movie rental website charges $5.00 per month for membership and $1.25 per movie.**

**24.** How many movies did Andrew rent this month if this month's bill was $16.25? _____

**25.** Marissa has $18.50 this month to spend on movie rentals.

   **a.** How many movies can she view this month? _____

   **b.** **Critique Reasoning** Marisa thinks she can afford 11 movies in one month. What mistake could she be making?

   _____

   _____

**Victoria went shopping for ingredients to make a stew. The table shows the weight and the cost of each of the ingredients that she bought.**

| Ingredient | Weight (in pounds) | Cost |
|---|---|---|
| Potatoes | 6.3 | $7.56 |
| Carrots | 8.5 | $15.30 |
| Beef | 4 | $9.56 |
| Bell peppers | 2.50 | $1.25 |

**26.** What is the price for one pound of bell peppers? _____

**27.** Which ingredient costs the most per pound? _____

**28.** **What If?** If carrots were $0.50 less per pound, how much would Victoria have paid for 8.5 pounds of carrots? _____

**29.** Brenda is planning her birthday party. She wants to have 10.92 liters of punch, 6.5 gallons of ice cream, 3.9 pounds of fudge, and 25 guests at the birthday party.

   **a.** Brenda and each guest drink the same amount of punch. How many liters of punch will each person drink? _____

   **b.** Brenda and each guest eat the same amount of ice cream. How many gallons of ice cream will each person eat? _____

   **c.** Brenda and each guest eat the same amount of fudge. How many pounds of fudge will each person eat? _____

**To make costumes for a play, Cassidy needs yellow and white fabric that she will cut into strips. The table shows how many yards of each fabric she needs, and how much she will pay for those yards.**

| Fabric | Yards | Cost |
|--------|-------|------|
| Yellow | 12.8 | $86.40 |
| White | 9.5 | $45.60 |

**30.** Which costs more per yard, the yellow fabric or the white fabric? _____

**31.** Cassidy wants to cut the yellow fabric into strips that are 0.3 yards wide. How many whole strips of yellow fabric can Cassidy make? _____

 **FOCUS ON HIGHER ORDER THINKING**

**32. Problem Solving** Eight friends purchase various supplies for a camping trip and agree to share the total cost equally. They spend $85.43 on food, $32.75 on water, and $239.66 on other items. How much does each person owe? _____

**33. Analyze Relationships** Constance is saving money to buy a new bicycle that costs $195.75. She already has $40 saved and plans to save $8 each week. How many weeks will it take her to save enough money to purchase the bicycle? _____

**34. Represent Real-World Problems** A grocery store sells twelve bottles of water for $13.80. A convenience store sells ten bottles of water for $11.80. Which store has the better buy? Explain.

_____

_____

# LESSON 4.3 Applying Multiplication and Division of Rational Numbers

**TEKS**
**Number and operations—6.3.E**
Multiply and divide positive rational numbers fluently.

## ESSENTIAL QUESTION

How can you solve problems involving multiplication and division of fractions and decimals?

## Converting Fractions and Decimals to Solve Problems

Recall that you can use a number line to find equivalent fractions and decimals. If a fraction and a decimal are equivalent, they are represented by the same point on a number line.

### EXAMPLE 1 Real World

**TEKS** 6.3.E

Each part of a multipart question on a social studies test is worth the same number of points. The whole question is worth 37.5 points. Roz got $\frac{1}{2}$ of the parts of the question correct. How many points did Roz receive? Solve the problem in two different ways.

**Solution 1**

**STEP 1** Convert the decimal to a fraction.

$$\frac{1}{2} \times 37.5 = \frac{1}{2} \times \frac{75}{2}$$

**STEP 2** Multiply. Write the product in simplest form.

$$\frac{1}{2} \times \frac{75}{2} = \frac{75}{4} = 18\frac{3}{4}$$

Roz received $18\frac{3}{4}$ points.

**Solution 2**

**STEP 1** Convert the fraction to a decimal.

$$\frac{1}{2} \times 37.5 = 0.5 \times 37.5$$

**STEP 2** Multiply.

$$0.5 \times 37.5 = 18.75$$

Roz received 18.75 points.

$18\frac{3}{4} = 18.75$, so the answer is the same whether you convert both numbers to fractions or convert both numbers to decimals.

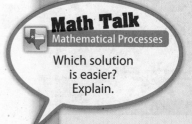

**Math Talk**
Mathematical Processes

Which solution is easier? Explain.

Math On the Spot
my.hrw.com

**Personal Math Trainer**

Online Assessment and Intervention

⏻ my.hrw.com

**Math On the Spot**

⏻ my.hrw.com

1. Some friends went out to dinner. The bill was $14.50. Charles paid for $\frac{3}{5}$ of the entire bill. How much did Charles pay? Show how to solve the problem two different ways.

   _____

   _____

2. Shaneeka is saving up to buy a camera that costs $65.60. She has already saved $\frac{3}{4}$ of the amount she needs for the camera. How much has Shaneeka saved so far? Explain your solution.

   _____

   _____

   _____

   _____

# Solving Problems with Rational Numbers

Sometimes more than one operation will be needed to solve a multistep problem. You can use parentheses to group different operations. Recall that according to the **order of operations,** you perform operations in parentheses first.

**EXAMPLE 2** *Problem Solving*                                    TEKS 6.3.E

Jon is cooking enough lentils for lentil barley soup and lentil salad. The lentil barley soup recipe calls for $\frac{3}{4}$ cup of dried lentils. The lentil salad recipe calls for $1\frac{1}{2}$ cups of dried lentils. Jon has a $\frac{1}{8}$-cup scoop. How many scoops of dried lentils will Jon need to have enough for the soup and the salad?

**Analyze Information**

Identify the important information.

- Jon needs $\frac{3}{4}$ cup of dried lentils for soup and $1\frac{1}{2}$ cups for salad.

- Jon has a $\frac{1}{8}$-cup scoop.

- You need to find the total number of scoops of lentils he needs.

## Formulate a Plan

You can use the expression $\left(\frac{3}{4} + 1\frac{1}{2}\right) \div \frac{1}{8}$ to find the number of scoops of dried lentils Jon will need for the soup and the salad.

## Solve

Follow the order of operations. Perform the operations in parentheses first.

First add to find the total amount of dried lentils Jon will need.

$$\frac{3}{4} + 1\frac{1}{2}$$

$$= \frac{3}{4} + \frac{3}{2}$$

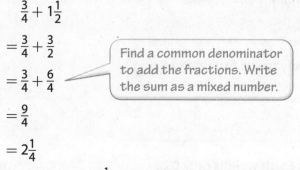 Find a common denominator to add the fractions. Write the sum as a mixed number.

$$= \frac{3}{4} + \frac{6}{4}$$

$$= \frac{9}{4}$$

$$= 2\frac{1}{4}$$

So, Jon needs $2\frac{1}{4}$ cups of dried lentils for both the soup and the salad.

Then divide the total amount of dried lentils into groups of $\frac{1}{8}$.

$$2\frac{1}{4} \div \frac{1}{8}$$

$$= \frac{9}{4} \div \frac{1}{8}$$

$$= \frac{9}{4} \times \frac{8}{1}$$

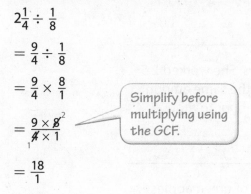 Simplify before multiplying using the GCF.

$$= \frac{9 \times \overset{2}{\cancel{8}}}{\underset{1}{\cancel{4}} \times 1}$$

$$= \frac{18}{1}$$

$$= 18$$

Jon will need 18 scoops of dried lentils to have enough for both the lentil barley soup and the lentil salad.

## Justify and Evaluate

You added $\frac{3}{4}$ and $1\frac{1}{2}$ first to find the total number of cups of lentils. Then you divided the sum by $\frac{1}{8}$ to find the number of $\frac{1}{8}$-cup scoops.

### YOUR TURN

3. Serena charges $6.50 an hour to walk dogs. She worked 5 hours last week and 9.5 hours this week. How much did she make altogether in the last two weeks? Show your work.

**Personal Math Trainer**

Online Assessment and Intervention

my.hrw.com

My Notes

**Solve. Show your work.**

**1.** Chanasia has 8.75 gallons of paint. She wants to use $\frac{2}{5}$ of the paint to paint her living room. How many gallons of paint will Chanasia use? (Example 1)

_____

**2.** Bob and Cheryl are taking a road trip that is 188.3 miles. Bob drove $\frac{5}{7}$ of the total distance. How many miles did Bob drive? (Example 1)

_____

**3.** The winner of a raffle will receive $\frac{3}{4}$ of the money raised from raffle ticket sales. The raffle raised $530.40. How much money will the winner of the raffle get? (Example 1)

_____

**4. Multistep** An object that weighs 1 pound on Earth weighs only 0.17 pound on the Moon. Zach's dog weighs $17\frac{1}{2}$ pounds on Earth. How much more does his dog weigh on Earth than on the Moon? (Examples 1 and 2)

_____

**5.** Naomi has earned $54 mowing lawns the past two days. She worked 2.5 hours yesterday and 4.25 hours today. If Naomi is paid the same amount for every hour she works, how much does she earn per hour to mow lawns? (Example 2)

_____

**6.** Harold bought 3 pounds of red apples and 4.2 pounds of green apples from Blue Star Grocery, where both kinds of apples are $1.75 a pound. How much did Harold spend on apples? (Example 2)

_____

**? ESSENTIAL QUESTION CHECK-IN**

**7.** How can you solve a problem that involves multiplying or dividing a fraction by a decimal?

_____

_____

_____

## 4.3 Independent Practice

TEKS 6.3.E

Samuel and Jason are brothers. They sell cans to a recycling center that pays $0.40 per pound of cans. The table shows the number of pounds of cans that Samuel and Jason sold for several days.

| Day | Samuel's cans (pounds) | Jason's cans (pounds) |
|---|---|---|
| Monday | 16.2 | 11.5 |
| Tuesday | 11.8 | 10.7 |
| Wednesday | 12.5 | 7.1 |

8. Samuel wants to use his earnings from Monday and Tuesday to buy new batteries for his video game device. The batteries cost $5.60 each. How many batteries can Samuel buy? Show your work.

_____

9. Jason wants to use his earnings from Monday and Tuesday for online movie rentals. The movies cost $2.96 each to rent. How many movies can Jason rent? Show your work.

_____

10. **Multistep** Samuel and Jason combine their earnings from Wednesday to buy their mother a gift. They spend $\frac{3}{4}$ of their shared earnings on the gift. How much do they spend? Use a problem solving model to determine if there is enough left over from Wednesday's earnings to buy a greeting card that costs $3.25. Explain.

_____

_____

_____

11. Eva wants to make two pieces of pottery. She needs $\frac{3}{5}$ pound of clay for one piece and $\frac{7}{10}$ pound of clay for the other piece. She has three bags of clay that weigh $\frac{4}{5}$ pound each. How many bags of clay will Eva need to make both pieces of pottery? How many pounds of clay will she have left over?

_____

12. **Multiple Representations** Give an example of a problem that could be solved using the expression $9.5 \times (8 + 12.5)$.

_____

_____

_____

Tony and Alice are trying to reduce the amount of television they watch. For every hour they watch television, they have to put $2.50 into savings. The table shows how many hours of television Tony and Alice have watched in the past two months.

| | Hours watched in February | Hours watched in March |
|---|---|---|
| Tony | 35.4 | 18.2 |
| Alice | 21.8 | 26.6 |

13. Tony wants to use his savings at the end of March to buy video games. The games cost $35.75 each. How many games can Tony buy?  _____

14. Alice wants to use her savings at the end of March to buy fabric for a crafts project. The fabric costs $17.50 a yard. How many full yards of fabric can Alice buy?  _____

 **FOCUS ON HIGHER ORDER THINKING**

**Work Area**

15. **Multiple Representations** You are measuring walnuts for banana-walnut oatmeal and a spinach and walnut salad. You need $\frac{3}{8}$ cup of walnuts for the oatmeal and $\frac{3}{4}$ cup of walnuts for the salad. You have a $\frac{1}{4}$-cup scoop. Describe two different ways to find how many scoops of walnuts you will need.

_____

_____

_____

_____

**Nadia charges $7.50 an hour for babysitting. She babysits 18.5 hours the first week of the month and 20 hours the second week of the month.**

16. **Explain the Error** To find her total earnings for those two weeks, Nadia writes $7.5 \times 18.5 + 20 = \$158.75$. Explain her error. Show the correct solution.

_____

_____

_____

17. **What If?** Suppose Nadia raises her rate by $0.75 an hour. How many hours would she need to work to earn the same amount of money she made in the first two weeks of the month? Explain.

_____

_____

_____

# Ready to Go On?

Personal Math Trainer

Online Assessment and Intervention

⏻ my.hrw.com

## 4.1 Multiplying Decimals

**1.** Marta walked at 3.9 miles per hour for 0.72 hours. How far did she walk? _____

**Multiply.**

**2.** $0.07 \times 1.22$ _____

**3.** $4.7 \times 2.65$ _____

**4.** $11.3 \times 4.16$ _____

**5.** $53.2 \times 17.6$ _____

## 4.2 Dividing Decimals

**6.** Bryan paid $19.95 for 2.5 pounds of turkey. What was the price per pound? _____

**Divide.**

**7.** $64 \div 0.4$ _____

**8.** $4.7398 \div 0.26$ _____

**9.** $26.73 \div 9$ _____

**10.** $4 \div 3.2$ _____

## 4.3 Applying Multiplication and Division of Rational Numbers

**11.** Ramiro is $\frac{3}{10}$ as tall as the flagpole. The flagpole is $\frac{5}{9}$ as tall as a nearby tree. The tree is $32\frac{2}{5}$ feet tall. How tall is Ramiro? _____

**12.** Doors for the small cabinets are 11.5 inches long. Doors for the large cabinets are 2.3 times as long as the doors for the small cabinets. How many large doors can be cut from a board that is 10 feet long? _____

**13.** Tanisha ran $\frac{3}{5}$ of a 26-mile race in 3.2 hours. If she ran at a constant rate, what was her speed in miles per hour? _____

### ? ESSENTIAL QUESTION

**14.** Describe a real-world situation that could be modeled by dividing two rational numbers.

_____

## Selected Response

**1.** Javier reads 40 pages every hour. How many pages does Javier read in 2.25 hours?

Ⓐ 80 pages    Ⓒ 90 pages

Ⓑ 85 pages    Ⓓ 100 pages

**2.** Sumeet uses 0.4 gallon of gasoline each hour mowing lawns. How much gas does he use in 4.2 hours?

Ⓐ 1.68 gallons

Ⓑ 3.8 gallons

Ⓒ 13 gallons

Ⓓ 16 gallons

**3.** Sharon spent $3.45 on sunflower seeds. The price of sunflower seeds is $0.89 per pound. How many pounds of sunflower seeds did Sharon buy?

Ⓐ 3.07 pounds

Ⓑ 3.88 pounds

Ⓒ 4.15 pounds

Ⓓ 4.34 pounds

**4.** How many 0.4-liter glasses of water does it take to fill up a 3.4-liter pitcher?

Ⓐ 1.36 glasses    Ⓒ 8.2 glasses

Ⓑ 3.8 glasses    Ⓓ 8.5 glasses

**5.** Michelle's family drove 272.48 miles. Michelle calculated that they drove 26.2 miles per gallon of gas. How many gallons of gas did the car use?

Ⓐ 10 gallons

Ⓑ 10.4 gallons

Ⓒ 11.4 gallons

Ⓓ 14 gallons

**6.** Each paper clip is $\frac{3}{4}$ of an inch long and costs $0.02. Exactly enough paper clips are laid end to end to have a total length of 36 inches. What is the total cost of these paper clips?

Ⓐ $0.36    Ⓒ $0.96

Ⓑ $0.54    Ⓓ $1.20

**7.** Keri walks her dog every morning. The length of the walk is 0.55 kilometer on each weekday. On each weekend day, the walk is 1.4 times as long as a walk on a weekday. How many kilometers does Keri walk in one week?

Ⓐ 2.75 kilometers

Ⓑ 3.85 kilometers

Ⓒ 4.29 kilometers

Ⓓ 5.39 kilometers

## Gridded Response

**8.** In preparation for a wedding, Aiden bought 60 candles. He paid $0.37 for each candle. His sister bought 170 candles at the same price. How much more money, in dollars, did Aiden's sister spend?

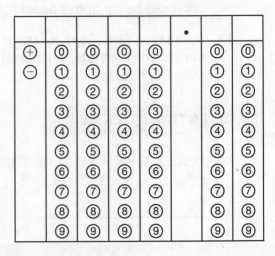

# Adding and Subtracting Integers

## ? ESSENTIAL QUESTION

How can you use addition and subtraction of integers to solve real-world problems?

### Real-World Video

Death Valley contains the lowest point in North America, elevation −282 feet. The top of Mt. McKinley, elevation 20,320 feet, is the highest point in North America. To find the difference between these elevations, you can subtract integers.

⏻ my.hrw.com

## GO DIGITAL

my.hrw.com

**my.hrw.com**

Go digital with your write-in student edition, accessible on any device.

**Math On the Spot**

Scan with your smart phone to jump directly to the online edition, video tutor, and more.

**Animated Math**

Interactively explore key concepts to see how math works.

**Personal Math Trainer**

Get immediate feedback and help as you work through practice sets.

# Are YOU Ready?

Complete these exercises to review skills you will need for this chapter.

**Personal Math Trainer**

Online Assessment and Intervention

my.hrw.com

## Understand Integers

**EXAMPLE**   A diver descended 20 meters.

$$-20$$

Decide whether the integer is positive or negative:

descended → negative

Write the integer.

**Write an integer to represent each situation.**

**1.** an elevator ride down 27 stories

**2.** a $700 profit

**3.** 46 degrees below zero

**4.** a gain of 12 yards

## Whole Number Operations

**EXAMPLE**   $245 - 28$

$$\begin{array}{r} \overset{3\ 15}{2\cancel{45}} \\ -\ 2\,8 \\ \hline 2\,1\,7 \end{array}$$

$245 - 28 = 217$

Think:
$8 > 5$
Regroup 1 ten as 10 ones.
1 ten + 5 ones = 15 ones
Subtract: $15 - 8 = 7$

**Find the sum or difference.**

**5.**
$$\begin{array}{r} 183 \\ +\ 78 \\ \hline \end{array}$$

**6.**
$$\begin{array}{r} 677 \\ -288 \\ \hline \end{array}$$

**7.**
$$\begin{array}{r} 1{,}188 \\ +\ 902 \\ \hline \end{array}$$

**8.**
$$\begin{array}{r} 2{,}647 \\ -1{,}885 \\ \hline \end{array}$$

## Locate Points on a Number Line

**EXAMPLE**

Graph $+2$ by starting at 0 and counting 2 units to the right.
Graph $-5$ by starting at 0 and counting 5 units to the left.

**Graph each number on the number line.**

**9.** 7        **10.** −4        **11.** −9        **12.** 4

# Reading Start-Up

## Visualize Vocabulary

Use the ✔ words to fill in the ovals on the graphic. You may put more than one word in each oval.

**Understanding Integers**

50

−50

−50, 50

**Vocabulary**

**Review Words**
difference *(diferencia)*
integers *(enteros)*
✔ negative number *(número negativo)*
✔ opposites *(opuestos)*
✔ positive number *(número positivo)*
sum *(suma)*
✔ whole number *(número entero)*

**Preview Words**
absolute value *(valor absoluto)*
additive inverse *(inverso aditivo)*
expression *(expresión)*
model *(modelo)*

## Understand Vocabulary

Complete the sentences using the preview words.

1. The _____ of a number gives its distance from zero.

2. The sum of a number and its _____ is zero.

## Active Reading

**Booklet** Before beginning the module, create a booklet to help you learn the concepts in this module. Write the main idea of each lesson on each page of the booklet. As you study each lesson, write important details that support the main idea, such as vocabulary and formulas. Refer to your finished booklet as you work on assignments and study for tests.

# Unpacking the TEKS

Understanding the TEKS and the vocabulary terms in the TEKS will help you know exactly what you are expected to learn in this module.

## TEKS 6.3.C

Represent integer operations with concrete models and connect the actions with the models to standardized algorithms.

### Key Vocabulary

**additive inverse** *(inverso aditivo)*
The opposite of a number.

## What It Means to You

You will learn how to use models to add and subtract integers with the same sign and with different signs.

### UNPACKING EXAMPLE 6.3.C

You will learn how to use models to add and subtract integers with the same sign and with different signs.

$4 + (-7)$

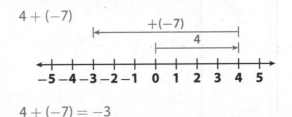

Start at 0. Move right 4 units. Then move left 7 units.

$4 + (-7) = -3$

## TEKS 6.3.D

Add, subtract, multiply, and divide integers fluently.

### Key Vocabulary

**integer** *(entero)*
A member of the set of whole numbers and their opposites.

## What It Means to You

You will learn that subtracting an integer is the same as adding its additive inverse.

### UNPACKING EXAMPLE 6.3.D

Find the difference between 3,000 °F and −250 °F, the temperatures the space shuttle must endure.

$3,000 - (-250)$

$3,000 + 250 = 3,250$

The difference in temperatures the shuttle must endure is 3,250 °F.

Visit **my.hrw.com** to see all the **TEKS** unpacked.

my.hrw.com

# Adding Integers with the Same Sign

TEKS
Number and operations—
6.3.C Represent integer operations with concrete models and connect the actions with the models to standardized algorithms. *Also 6.3.D.*

**? ESSENTIAL QUESTION**

How do you add integers with the same sign?

**EXPLORE ACTIVITY 1**    TEKS 6.3.C

## Modeling Sums of Integers with the Same Sign

You can use colored counters to add positive integers and to add negative integers.

○ = 1

● = −1

**Model with two-color counters.**

**A** $3 + 4$

3 positive counters ○ ○ ○ ⎫
⎬ total number of counters
4 positive counters ○ ○ ○ ○ ⎭

How many counters are there in total? _____

What is the sum and how do you find it?

_____

_____

**B** $-5 + (-3)$

5 negative counters ● ● ● ● ● ⎫
⎬ total number of counters
3 negative counters ● ● ● ⎭

How many counters are there in total? _____

Since the counters are negative integers, what is the sum? _____

**Math Talk**
Mathematical Processes

What does the color of each row of counters represent?

## Reflect

1. **Communicate Mathematical Ideas** When adding two numbers with the same sign, what sign do you use for the sum?

_____

# Adding on a Number Line

Just as you can add positive integers on a number line, you can add negative integers.

**The temperature was 2 °F below zero. The temperature drops by 5 °F. What is the temperature now?**

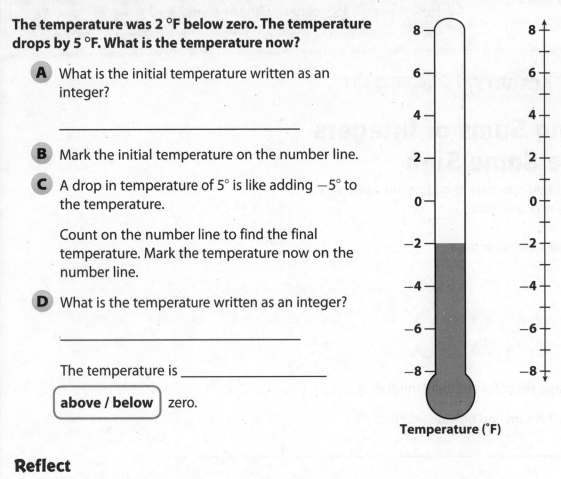

**A** What is the initial temperature written as an integer?

_____

**B** Mark the initial temperature on the number line.

**C** A drop in temperature of 5° is like adding −5° to the temperature.

Count on the number line to find the final temperature. Mark the temperature now on the number line.

**D** What is the temperature written as an integer?

_____

The temperature is _____

⟦ **above / below** ⟧ zero.

**Temperature (°F)**

## Reflect

2. **What If?** Suppose the temperature is −1 °F and drops by 3 °F. Explain how to use the number line to find the new temperature.

_____

_____

3. **Communicate Mathematical Ideas** How would using a number line to find the sum 2 + 5 be different from using a number line to find the sum − 2 + (− 5)?

_____

_____

4. **Analyze Relationships** What are two other negative integers that have the same sum as − 2 and − 5?

_____

# Adding Integers with a Common Sign

To add integers with the same sign, add the absolute values of the integers and use the sign of the integers for the sum.

## EXAMPLE 1

TEKS 6.3.D

Add $-7 + (-6)$.     The signs of both integers are the same.

**STEP 1**  Find the absolute values.

$|-7| = 7$   $|-6| = 6$     The absolute value is always positive or zero.

**STEP 2**  Find the sum of the absolute values: $7 + 6 = 13$

**STEP 3**  Use the sign of the integers to write the sum.

$-7 + (-6) = -13$     The sign of each integer is negative.

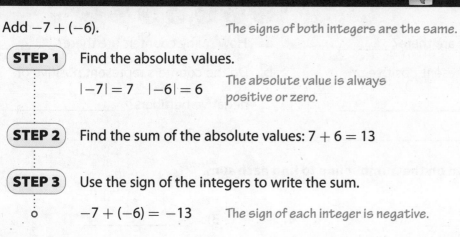

**Math Talk**
Mathematical Processes

Can you use the same procedure you use to find the sum of two negative integers to find the sum of two *positive* numbers? Explain.

## Reflect

5. **Communicate Mathematical Ideas**  Does the Commutative Property of Addition apply when you add two negative integers? Explain.

_____

_____

6. **Critical Thinking**  Choose any two negative integers. Is the sum of the integers less than or greater than the value of either of the integers? Will this be true no matter which integers you choose? Explain.

_____

_____

_____

_____

## YOUR TURN

**Find each sum.**

7.  $-8 + (-1) = $ _____

8.  $-3 + (-7) = $ _____

9.  $-48 + (-12) = $ _____

10.  $-32 + (-38) = $ _____

11.  $109 + 191 = $ _____

12.  $-40 + (-105) = $ _____

13.  $-150 + (-1,500) = $ _____

14.  $-200 + (-800) = $ _____

## Guided Practice

**Find each sum.** (Explore Activity 1)

**1.** $-5 + (-1)$

   **a.** How many counters are there? _____

   **b.** Do the counters represent positive or

      negative numbers? _____

   **c.** $-5 + (-1) =$ _____

**2.** $-2 + (-7)$

   **a.** How many counters are there? _____

   **b.** Do the counters represent positive or

      negative numbers? _____

   **c.** $-2 + (-7) =$ _____

**Model each addition problem on the number line to find each sum.**
(Explore Activity 2)

**3.** $-5 + (-2) =$ _____

**5.** $-3 + (-7) =$ _____

**7.** $-2 + (-2) =$ _____

**4.** $-1 + (-3) =$ _____

**6.** $-4 + (-1) =$ _____

**8.** $-6 + (-8) =$ _____

**Find each sum.** (Example 1)

**9.** $-5 + (-4) =$ _____

**11.** $-9 + (-1) =$ _____

**13.** $-52 + (-48) =$ _____

**15.** $-4 + (-5) + (-6) =$ _____

**10.** $-1 + (-10) =$ _____

**12.** $-90 + (-20) =$ _____

**14.** $5 + 198 =$ _____

**16.** $-50 + (-175) + (-345) =$ _____

**? ESSENTIAL QUESTION CHECK-IN**

**17.** How do you add integers with the same sign?

_____

_____

# 5.1 Independent Practice

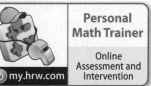

Personal Math Trainer

Online Assessment and Intervention

my.hrw.com

**TEKS** 6.3.C, 6.3.D

**18. Represent Real-World Problems** Jane and Sarah both dive down from the surface of a pool. Jane first dives down 5 feet, and then dives down 3 more feet. Sarah first dives down 3 feet, and then dives down 5 more feet.

**a. Multiple Representations** Use the number line to model the equation $-5 + (-3) = -3 + (-5)$.

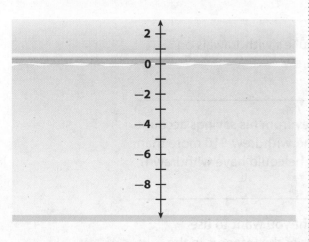

**b.** Does the order in which you add two integers with the same sign affect the sum? Explain.

_____

_____

**19.** A golfer has the following scores for a 4-day tournament.

| Day | 1 | 2 | 3 | 4 |
|-----|-----|-----|-----|-----|
| Score | −3 | −1 | −5 | −2 |

What was the golfer's total score for the tournament?

_____

**20.** A football team loses 3 yards on one play and 6 yards on another play. Write a sum of negative integers to represent this situation. Find the sum and explain how it is related to the problem.

_____

_____

**21.** When the quarterback is sacked, the team loses yards. In one game, the quarterback was sacked four times. What was the total sack yardage?

| Sack | 1 | 2 | 3 | 4 |
|------|-----|-----|-----|-----|
| Sack yardage | −14 | −5 | −12 | −23 |

_____

**22. Multistep** The temperature in Jonestown and Cooperville was the same at 1:00. By 2:00, the temperature in Jonestown dropped 10 degrees, and the temperature in Cooperville dropped 6 degrees. By 3:00, the temperature in Jonestown dropped 8 more degrees, and the temperature in Cooperville dropped 2 more degrees.

**a.** Write an equation that models the change to the temperature in Jonestown since 1:00.

_____

**b.** Write an equation that models the change to the temperature in Cooperville since 1:00.

_____

**c.** Where is it colder at 3:00, Jonestown or Cooperville?

_____

**23.** **Represent Real-World Problems** Julio is playing a trivia game. On his first turn, he lost 100 points. On his second turn, he lost 75 points. On his third turn, he lost 85 points. Write a sum of three negative integers that models the change to Julio's score after his first three turns.

_____

**24.** **Multistep** On Monday, Jan made withdrawals of $25, $45, and $75 from her savings account. On the same day, her twin sister Julie made withdrawals of $35, $55, and $65 from _her_ savings account.

a. Write a sum of negative integers to show Jan's withdrawals on Monday. Find the total amount Jan withdrew.

_____

b. Write a sum of negative integers to show Julie's withdrawals on Monday. Find the total amount Julie withdrew.

_____

c. Julie and Jan's brother also withdrew money from his savings account on Monday. He made three withdrawals and withdrew $10 more than Julie did. What are three possible amounts he could have withdrawn?

_____

**25.** **Communicate Mathematical Ideas** Why might you want to use the Commutative Property to change the order of the integers in the following sum before adding?

$$-80 + (-173) + (-20)$$

_____

_____

**26.** **Critique Reasoning** The absolute value of the sum of two different integers with the same sign is 8. Pat says there are three pairs of integers that match this description. Do you agree? Explain.

_____

_____

_____

_____

_____

# Adding Integers with Different Signs

TEKS
Number and operations—6.3.D
Add ...integers fluently.
Also 6.3.C.

## ? ESSENTIAL QUESTION

How do you add integers with different signs?

---

**EXPLORE ACTIVITY 1** | **TEKS 6.3.C**

# Adding on a Number Line

To find the sum of integers with the same sign, such as 3 + 2, you can start at 3 and move |2| = 2 units in the positive direction.

To find the sum of integers with different signs, such as 3 + (−2), you can start at 3 and move |−2| = 2 units in the negative direction.

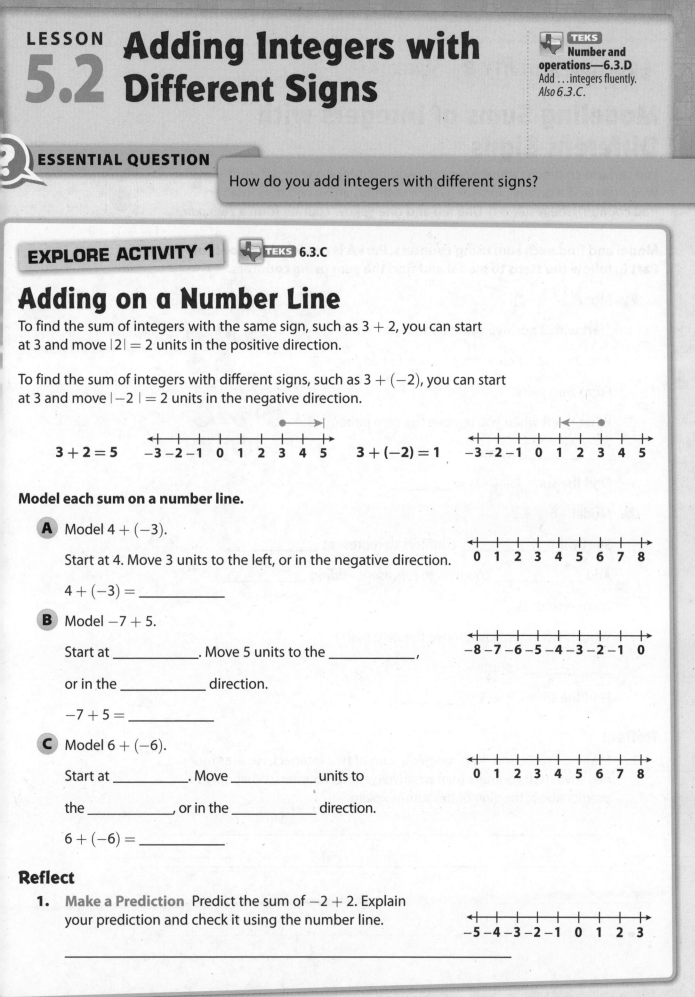

3 + 2 = 5    −3 −2 −1  0  1  2  3  4  5       3 + (−2) = 1    −3 −2 −1  0  1  2  3  4  5

**Model each sum on a number line.**

**A**  Model 4 + (−3).

Start at 4. Move 3 units to the left, or in the negative direction.

0  1  2  3  4  5  6  7  8

4 + (−3) = _____

**B**  Model −7 + 5.

Start at _____. Move 5 units to the _____,

−8 −7 −6 −5 −4 −3 −2 −1  0

or in the _____ direction.

−7 + 5 = _____

**C**  Model 6 + (−6).

Start at _____. Move _____ units to

0  1  2  3  4  5  6  7  8

the _____, or in the _____ direction.

6 + (−6) = _____

## Reflect

1.  **Make a Prediction**  Predict the sum of −2 + 2. Explain your prediction and check it using the number line.

−5 −4 −3 −2 −1  0  1  2  3

_____

# Modeling Sums of Integers with Different Signs

You can use colored counters to model adding integers with different signs. When you add a positive integer (yellow counter) and a negative integer (red counter), the result is 0. One red and one yellow counter form a *zero pair*.

$1 + (-1) = 0$

**Model and find each sum using counters. Part A is modeled for you. For Part B, follow the steps to model and find the sum using counters.**

**A** Model $3 + (-2)$.

Start with 3 positive counters to represent 3.

Add 2 negative counters to represent adding $-2$.

Form zero pairs.

What is left when you remove the zero pairs?

_____ counter

Find the sum: $3 + (-2) =$ _____

> The value of a zero pair is 0. Adding or subtracting 0 to any number does not change its value.

**B** Model $-6 + 3$.

Start with _____ counters to represent _____.

Add _____ counters to represent adding _____.

Form zero pairs.

What is left when you remove the zero pairs?

_____ counters

Find the sum: $-6 + 3 =$ _____

## Reflect

**2.** **Make a Prediction** Kyle models a sum of two integers. He uses more negative (red) counters than positive (yellow) counters. What do you predict about the sign of the sum? Explain.

_____

_____

## YOUR TURN

**Model and find each sum using counters.**

**3.** $5 + (-1)$ _____

**4.** $4 + (-6)$ _____

**5.** $1 + (-7)$ _____

**6.** $3 + (-4)$ _____

# Adding Integers

You have learned how to add integers with the same signs and how to add integers with different signs. The table below summarizes the rules for adding integers.

| Adding Integers | | Examples |
|---|---|---|
| **Same signs** | Add the absolute values of the integers. Use the common sign for the sum. | $3 + 5 = 8$ <br> $-2 + (-7) = -9$ |
| **Different signs** | Subtract the lesser absolute value from the greater absolute value. Use the sign of the integer with the greater absolute value for the sum. | $3 + (-5) = -2$ <br> $-10 + 1 = -9$ |
| **A number and its opposite** | The sum is 0. The opposite of any number is called its **additive inverse.** | $4 + (-4) = 0$ <br> $-11 + 11 = 0$ |

---

## EXAMPLE 1 　　　　　　　　　　🔲 TEKS 6.3.C, 6.3.D

**Find each sum.**

**A** $-11 + 6$

　$|-11| - |6| = 5$ 　　Subtract the lesser absolute value from the greater.

　$-11 + 6 = -5$ 　　Use the sign of the number with the greater absolute value.

**B** $(-37) + 37$

　$(-37) + 37 = 0$ 　　The sum of a number and its additive inverse is 0.

> This is also called the Inverse Property of Addition.

---

## YOUR TURN

**Find each sum.**

**7.** $-51 + 23 =$ _____

**8.** $10 + (-18) =$ _____

**9.** $13 + (-13) =$ _____

**10.** $25 + (-26) =$ _____

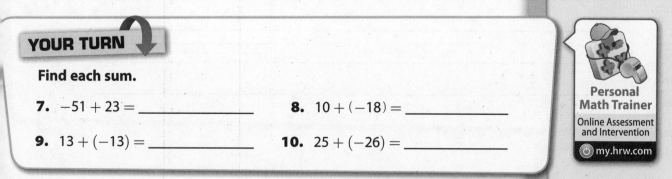

## Guided Practice

**Use a number line to find each sum.** (Explore Activity 1)

**1.** $9 + (-3) =$ _____

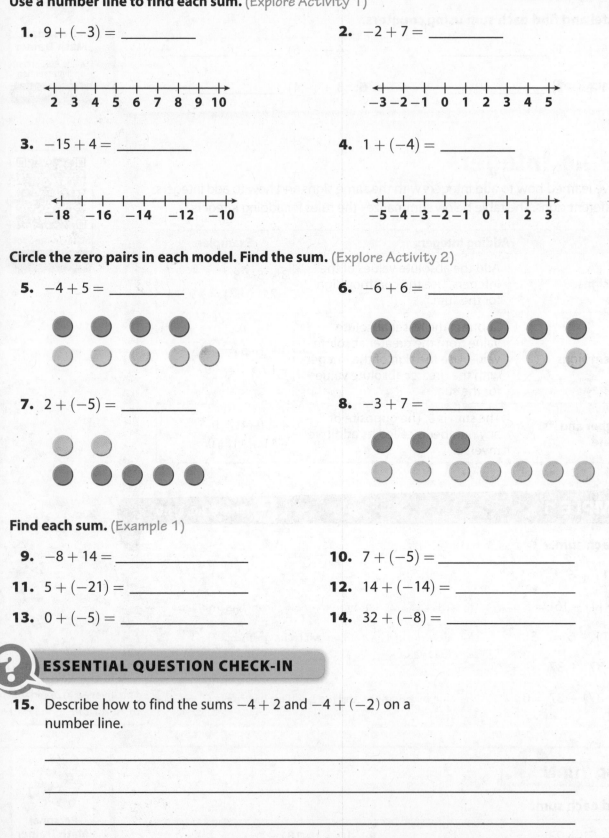

**2.** $-2 + 7 =$ _____

**3.** $-15 + 4 =$ _____

**4.** $1 + (-4) =$ _____

**Circle the zero pairs in each model. Find the sum.** (Explore Activity 2)

**5.** $-4 + 5 =$ _____

**6.** $-6 + 6 =$ _____

**7.** $2 + (-5) =$ _____

**8.** $-3 + 7 =$ _____

**Find each sum.** (Example 1)

**9.** $-8 + 14 =$ _____

**10.** $7 + (-5) =$ _____

**11.** $5 + (-21) =$ _____

**12.** $14 + (-14) =$ _____

**13.** $0 + (-5) =$ _____

**14.** $32 + (-8) =$ _____

**? ESSENTIAL QUESTION CHECK-IN**

**15.** Describe how to find the sums $-4 + 2$ and $-4 + (-2)$ on a number line.

_____

_____

_____

# 5.2 Independent Practice

**Find each sum.**

**16.** $-15 + 71 =$ _____

**17.** $-53 + 45 =$ _____

**18.** $-79 + 79 =$ _____

**19.** $-25 + 50 =$ _____

**20.** $18 + (-32) =$ _____

**21.** $5 + (-100) =$ _____

**22.** $-12 + 8 + 7 =$ _____

**23.** $-8 + (-2) + 3 =$ _____

**24.** $15 + (-15) + 200 =$ _____

**25.** $-500 + (-600) + 1200 =$ _____

**26.** A football team gained 9 yards on one play and then lost 22 yards on the next. Write a sum of integers to find the overall change in field position. Explain your answer.

_____

**27.** A soccer team is having a car wash. The team spent $55 on supplies. They earned $275, including tips. The team's profit is the amount the team made after paying for supplies. Write a sum of integers that represents the team's profit.

_____

**28.** As shown in the illustration, Alexa had a negative balance in her checking account before depositing a $47.00 check. What is the new balance of Alexa's checking account? What property did you use to find the sum?

_____

Accounts    Regular Checking    Sign Out

Search transactions

Available Balance
−$47.00

**29.** The sum of two integers with different signs is 8. Give two possible integers that fit this description.

_____

**30. Multistep** Bart and Sam played a game in which each player earns or loses points in each turn. A player's total score after two turns is the sum of his points earned or lost. The player with the greater score after two turns wins. Bart earned 123 points and lost 180 points. Sam earned 185 points and lost 255 points. Use a problem-solving model to find which person won the game. Explain.

_____

_____

_____

**31. Critical Thinking** Explain how you could use a number line to show that $-4 + 3$ and $3 + (-4)$ have the same value. Which property of addition states that these sums are equivalent?

_____

_____

_____

_____

**32. Represent Real-World Problems** Jim is standing beside a pool. He drops a weight from 4 feet above the surface of the water in the pool. The weight travels a total distance of 12 feet down before landing on the bottom of the pool. Explain how you can write a sum of integers to find the depth of the water.

_____

_____

_____

_____

**33. Communicate Mathematical Ideas** Use counters to model two integers with different signs whose sum is positive. Explain how you know the sum is positive.

_____

_____

_____

_____

**34. Analyze Relationships** You know that the sum of $-5$ and another integer is a positive integer. What can you conclude about the sign of the other integer? What can you conclude about the value of the other integer? Explain.

_____

_____

_____

_____

# 5.3 Subtracting Integers

**TEKS**
**Number and operations—**
**6.3.C** Represent integer operations with concrete models and connect the actions with the models to standardized algorithms.
*Also 6.3.D.*

## ? ESSENTIAL QUESTION

How do you subtract integers?

---

### EXPLORE ACTIVITY 1  **TEKS** 6.3.C

## Modeling Integer Subtraction

You can use counters to find the difference of two integers. In some cases, you may need to add zero pairs.

$1 + (-1) = 0$

**Model and find each difference using counters.**

**A** Model $-4 - (-3)$.

Start with 4 negative counters to represent $-4$.

Take away 3 negative counters to represent subtracting $-3$.

What is left? _____

Find the difference: $-4 - (-3) =$ _____

**B** Model $6 - (-3)$.

Start with 6 positive counters to represent 6.

You need to take away 3 negative counters, so add 3 zero pairs.

Take away 3 negative counters to represent subtracting $-3$.

What is left? _____

Find the difference: $6 - (-3) =$ _____

**C** Model $-2 - (-5)$.

Start with _____ counters.

You need to take away _____ counters, so add _____ zero pairs.

Take away _____ counters.

What is left? _____

Find the difference: $-2 - (-5) =$ _____

## Reflect

1. **Communicate Mathematical Ideas** Suppose you want to model the difference $-4 - 7$. Do you need to add zero pairs? If so, why? How many should you add? What is the difference?

_____

_____

_____

**EXPLORE ACTIVITY 2**  **TEKS** 6.3.C

# Subtracting on a Number Line

To model the difference $5 - 3$ on a number line, you start at 5 and move 3 units to the left. Notice that you model the sum $5 + (-3)$ in the same way. Subtracting 3 is the same as adding its opposite, $-3$.

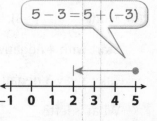

You can use the fact that subtracting a number is the same as adding its opposite to find a difference of two integers.

**Find each difference on a number line.**

**A** Find $-1 - 5$ on a number line.

Rewrite subtraction as addition of the opposite.

$-1 - 5 = -1 +$ _____

Start at _____ and move _____ units to the left.

The difference is _____

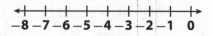

**B** Find $-7 - (-3)$.

Rewrite subtraction as addition of the opposite.

$-7 - (-3) = -7 +$ _____

Start at _____ and move _____ units to the _____.

The difference is _____

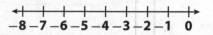

## Reflect

**2. Communicate Mathematical Ideas** Describe how to find $5 - (-8)$ on a number line. If you found the difference using counters, would you get the same result? Explain.

_____

_____

_____

_____

_____

# Subtracting Integers by Adding the Opposite

You can use the fact that subtracting an integer is the same as adding its opposite to solve problems.

### EXAMPLE 1 Real World

TEKS 6.3.C, 6.3.D

**The temperature on Monday was −5 °C. By Tuesday the temperature rose to −2 °C. Find the change in temperature.**

**STEP 1** Write a subtraction expression.

final temperature − Monday's temperature = change in temperature

$-2\,°C - (-5\,°C)$

**STEP 2** Find the difference.

$-2 - (-5) = -2 + 5$   To subtract −5, add its opposite, 5.

$-2 + 5 = 3$   Use the rule for adding integers.

The temperature increased by 3 °C.

**Math Talk**
Mathematical Processes

Why does it make sense that the change in temperature is a positive number?

**Math On the Spot**
my.hrw.com

**Animated Math**
my.hrw.com

## Reflect

**3. What If?** In Example 1, the temperature rose by 3 °C. Suppose it fell from −2 °C to −10 °C. Predict whether the change in temperature would be positive or negative. Then subtract to find the change.

_____

_____

**YOUR TURN**

**Find each difference.**

4. $-7 - 2 =$ _____

5. $-1 - (-3) =$ _____

6. $3 - 5 =$ _____

7. $-8 - (-4) =$ _____

## Guided Practice

**Explain how to find each difference using counters.** (Explore Activity 1)

1. $5 - 8 =$ _____

_____

_____

_____

2. $-5 - (-3) =$ _____

_____

_____

_____

**Use a number line to find each difference.** (Explore Activity 2)

3. $-4 - 5 = -4 +$ _____ $=$ _____

$$\overset{\longleftarrow \quad \quad \quad \quad \quad \quad \quad \quad \quad \quad \longrightarrow}{-9 \ -8 \ -7 \ -6 \ -5 \ -4 \ -3 \ -2 \ -1 \quad 0}$$

4. $1 - 4 = 1 +$ _____ $=$ _____

$$\overset{\longleftarrow \quad \quad \quad \quad \quad \quad \quad \quad \quad \quad \longrightarrow}{-4 \ -3 \ -2 \ -1 \quad 0 \quad 1 \quad 2 \quad 3 \quad 4}$$

**Solve.** (Example 1)

5. $8 - 11 =$ _____

6. $-3 - (-5) =$ _____

7. $15 - 21 =$ _____

8. $-17 - 1 =$ _____

9. $0 - (-5) =$ _____

10. $1 - (-18) =$ _____

11. $15 - 1 =$ _____

12. $-3 - (-45) =$ _____

13. $19 - (-19) =$ _____

14. $-87 - (-87) =$ _____

## ? ESSENTIAL QUESTION CHECK-IN

15. How do you subtract an integer from another integer without using a number line or counters? Give an example.

_____

_____

# 5.3 Independent Practice

**TEKS** 6.3.C, 6.3.D

Personal Math Trainer

my.hrw.com

Online Assessment and Intervention

**16.** Theo had a balance of −$4 in his savings account. After making a deposit, he has $25 in his account. What is the overall change to his account?

_____

**17.** As shown, Suzi starts her hike at an elevation below sea level. When she reaches the end of the hike, she is still below sea level at −127 feet. What was the change in elevation from the beginning of Suzi's hike to the end of the hike?

Current Elevation: −225 feet

_____

**18.** The record high January temperature in Austin, Texas, is 90 °F. The record low January temperature is −2 °F. Find the difference between the high and low temperatures.

_____

**19.** Cheyenne is playing a board game. Her score was −275 at the start of her turn, and at the end of her turn her score was −425. What was the change in Cheyenne's score from the start of her turn to the end of her turn?

_____

**20.** A scientist conducts three experiments in which she records the temperature of some gases that are being heated. The table shows the initial temperature and the final temperature for each gas.

| Gas | Initial Temperature | Final Temperature |
|-----|--------------------|--------------------|
| A | −21 °C | −8 °C |
| B | −12 °C | 12 °C |
| C | −19 °C | −15 °C |

**a.** Write a difference of integers to find the overall temperature change for each gas.

Gas A: _____

_____

Gas B: _____

_____

Gas C: _____

_____

**b.** **What If?** Suppose the scientist performs an experiment in which she cools the three gases. Will the changes in temperature be positive or negative for this experiment? Why?

_____

_____

_____

_____

_____

**21. Analyze Relationships** For two months, Nell feeds her cat Diet Chow brand cat food. Then for the next two months, she feeds her cat Kitty Diet brand cat food. The table shows the cat's change in weight over 4 months.

|  | Cat's Weight Change (oz) |
|---|---|
| **Diet Chow, Month 1** | −8 |
| **Diet Chow, Month 2** | −18 |
| **Kitty Diet, Month 3** | 3 |
| **Kitty Diet, Month 4** | −19 |

Which brand of cat food resulted in the greatest weight loss for Nell's cat? Explain.

_____

_____

**H.O.T.** FOCUS ON HIGHER ORDER THINKING

**Work Area**

**22. Represent Real-World Problems** Write and solve a word problem that can be modeled by the difference −4 − 10.

_____

_____

_____

**23. Explain the Error** When Tom found the difference −11 − (−4), he got −15. What might Tom have done wrong?

_____

_____

**24. Draw Conclusions** When you subtract one negative integer from another, will your answer be greater than or less than the integer you started with? Explain your reasoning and give an example.

_____

_____

_____

**25. Look for a Pattern** Find the next three terms in the pattern 9, 4, −1, −6, −11, … . Then describe the pattern.

_____

# Applying Addition and Subtraction of Integers

**TEKS**
Number and operations—6.3.D
Add, subtract, multiply, and divide integers fluently.

## ? ESSENTIAL QUESTION

How do you solve multistep problems involving addition and subtraction of integers?

## Solving a Multistep Problem

You can use what you know about adding and subtracting integers to solve a multistep problem.

**Math On the Spot**
my.hrw.com

### EXAMPLE 1 Real World

**TEKS** 6.3.D

A seal is swimming in the ocean 5 feet below sea level. It dives down 12 feet to catch some fish. Then, the seal swims 8 feet up towards the surface with its catch. What is the seal's final elevation relative to sea level?

**STEP 1** Write an expression.

- The seal starts at 5 feet below the surface, so its initial position is −5 ft.

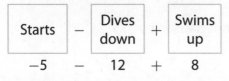

| Starts | − | Dives down | + | Swims up |
|--------|---|------------|---|----------|
| −5 | − | 12 | + | 8 |

**STEP 2** Add or subtract from left to right to find the value of the expression.

$$-5 - 12 + 8 = -17 + 8$$

$$= -9$$

This is reasonable because the seal swam farther down than up.

The seal's final elevation is 9 feet below sea level.

### YOUR TURN

1. Anna is in a cave 40 feet below the cave entrance. She descends 13 feet, then ascends 18 feet. Find her new position relative to the cave entrance.

_____

**Personal Math Trainer**

Online Assessment and Intervention

my.hrw.com

# Applying Properties to Solve Problems

You can use properties of addition to solve problems involving integers.

**EXAMPLE 2** *Problem Solving*                    TEKS 6.3.D

Irene has a checking account. On Monday she writes a $160 check for groceries. Then she deposits $125. Finally she writes another check for $40. What was the total change in the amount in Irene's account?

### Analyze Information

When Irene deposits money, she adds that amount to the account. When she writes a check, that money is deducted from the account.

### Formulate a Plan

Use a positive integer for the amount Irene added to the account. Use negative integers for the checks she wrote. Find the sum.

$$-160 + 125 + (-40)$$

### Solve

Add the amounts to find the total change in the account. Use properties of addition to simplify calculations.

$$-160 + 125 + (-40) = -160 + (-40) + 125 \qquad \text{Commutative Property}$$

$$= -200 + 125 \qquad \text{Associative Property}$$

$$= -75$$

The amount in the account decreased by $75.

### Justify and Evaluate

Irene's account has $75 less than it did before Monday. This is reasonable because she wrote checks for $200 but only deposited $125.

## Reflect

2. **Communicate Mathematical Ideas** Describe a different way to find the change in Irene's account.

_____

_____

**YOUR TURN**

3. Alex wrote checks on Tuesday for $35 and $45. He also made a deposit in his checking account of $180. Find the overall change in the amount in his checking account.

_____

# Comparing Values of Expressions

Sometimes you may want to compare values obtained by adding and subtracting integers.

**EXAMPLE 3** *Problem Solving*

TEKS 6.3.C

The Tigers, a football team, must gain 10 yards in the next four plays to keep possession of the ball. The Tigers lose 12 yards, gain 5 yards, lose 8 yards, and gain 14 yards. Do the Tigers maintain possession of the ball?

### Analyze Information

When the team gains yards, add that distance.

When the team loses yards, subtract that distance.

If the total change in yards is greater than or equal to 10, the team keeps possession of the ball.

### Formulate a Plan

$-12 + 5 - 8 + 14$

### Solve

| | |
|---|---|
| $-12 + 5 - 8 + 14$ | |
| $-12 + 5 + (-8) + 14$ | *To subtract, add the opposite.* |
| $-12 + (-8) + 5 + 14$ | *Commutative Property* |
| $(-12 + (-8)) + (5 + 14)$ | *Associative Property* |
| $-20 + 19 = -1$ | |
| $-1 < 10$ | *Compare to 10 yards.* |

The Tigers gained less than 10 yards, so they do not maintain possession.

**Math Talk**
Mathematical Processes

What does it mean that the football team had a total of −1 yard over four plays?

### Justify and Evaluate

The football team gained 19 yards and lost 20 yards for a total of −1 yard.

## YOUR TURN

4. Jim and Carla are scuba diving. Jim started out 10 feet below the surface. He descended 18 feet, rose 5 feet, and descended 12 more feet. Then he rested. Carla started out at the surface. She descended 20 feet, rose 5 feet, and descended another 18 feet. Then she rested. Which person rested at a greater depth? Explain.

_____

_____

**Personal Math Trainer**

Online Assessment and Intervention

my.hrw.com

## Guided Practice

**Write an expression. Then find the value of the expression.**
(Examples 1, 2, 3)

1. Tomas works as an underwater photographer. He starts at a position that is 15 feet below sea level. He rises 9 feet, then descends 12 feet to take a photo of a coral reef. Write and evaluate an expression to find his position relative to sea level when he took the photo.

   _____

2. The temperature on a winter night was −23 °F. The temperature rose by 5 °F when the sun came up. When the sun set again, the temperature dropped by 7 °F. Write and evaluate an expression to find the temperature after the sun set.

   _____

3. Jose earned 50 points in a video game. He lost 40 points, earned 87 points, then lost 30 more points. Write and evaluate an expression to find his final score in the video game.

   _____

**Find the value of each expression.** (Example 2)

4. $-6 + 15 + 15 =$ _____

5. $9 - 4 - 17 =$ _____

6. $50 - 42 + 10 =$ _____

7. $6 + 13 + 7 - 5 =$ _____

8. $65 + 43 - 11 =$ _____

9. $-35 - 14 + 45 + 31 =$ _____

**Determine which expression has a greater value.** (Example 3)

10. $-12 + 6 - 4$ or $-34 - 3 + 39$

    _____

11. $21 - 3 + 8$ or $-14 + 31 - 6$

    _____

### ? ESSENTIAL QUESTION CHECK-IN

12. Explain how you can find the value of the expression $-5 + 12 + 10 - 7$.

    _____

    _____

# 5.4 Independent Practice

TEKS 6.3.D

**13. Sports** Cameron is playing 9 holes of golf. He needs to score a total of at most 15 over par on the last four holes to beat his best golf score. On the last four holes, he scores 5 over par, 1 under par, 6 over par, and 1 under par.

   **a.** Write and find the value of an expression that gives Cameron's score for 4 holes of golf.

_____

   **b.** Is Cameron's score on the last four holes over or under par?

_____

   **c.** Did Cameron beat his best golf score?

_____

**14.** Herman is standing on a ladder that is partly in a hole. He starts out on a rung that is 6 feet under ground, climbs up 14 feet, then climbs down 11 feet. What is Herman's final position, relative to ground level?

_____

**15. Explain the Error** Jerome tries to find the value of the expression $3 - 6 + 5$ by first applying the Commutative Property. He rewrites the expression as $3 - 5 + 6$. Explain what is wrong with Jerome's approach.

_____

_____

_____

_____

**16.** Lee and Barry play a trivia game in which questions are worth different numbers of points. If a question is answered correctly, a player earns points. If a question is answered incorrectly, the player loses points. Lee currently has −350 points.

   **a.** Before the game ends, Lee answers a 275-point question correctly, a 70-point question correctly, and a 50-point question incorrectly. Write and find the value of an expression to find Lee's final score.

_____

   **b.** Barry's final score is 45. Which player had the greater final score?

_____

**17. Multistep** Rob collects data about how many customers enter and leave a store every hour. He records a positive number for customers entering the store each hour and a negative number for customers leaving the store each hour.

| | Entering | Leaving |
|---|---|---|
| **1:00 to 2:00** | 30 | −12 |
| **2:00 to 3:00** | 14 | −8 |
| **3:00 to 4:00** | 18 | −30 |

   **a.** During which hour did more customers leave than arrive?

_____

   **b.** There were 75 customers in the store at 1:00. The store must be emptied of customers when it closes at 5:00. How many customers must leave the store between 4:00 and 5:00?

_____

**The table shows the changes in the values of two friends' savings accounts since the previous month.**

|       | June | July | August |
|-------|------|------|--------|
| Carla | −18  | 22   | −53    |
| Leta  | −17  | −22  | 18     |

18. Carla had $100 in her account in May. How much money does she have in her account in August? _____

19. Leta had $45 in her account in May. How much money does she have in her account in August? _____

20. **Analyze Relationships** Whose account had the greatest decrease in value from May to August? _____

 **FOCUS ON HIGHER ORDER THINKING**

Work Area

21. **Represent Real-World Problems** Write and solve a word problem that matches the diagram shown.

```
    ←――――――――――――――●
      |――――――→|
  ←+――+――+――+――+――+――+――+――+――+→
   −9 −8 −7 −6 −5 −4 −3 −2 −1  0
```

_____

_____

_____

22. **Critical Thinking** Mary has $10 in savings. She owes her parents $50. She does some chores and her parents pay her $12. She also gets $25 for her birthday from her grandmother. Does Mary have enough money to pay her parents what she owes them? If not, how much more money does she need? Explain.

_____

_____

23. **Draw Conclusions** An expression involves subtracting two numbers from a given first number. Under what circumstances will the value of the expression be negative? Give an example.

_____

_____

_____

_____

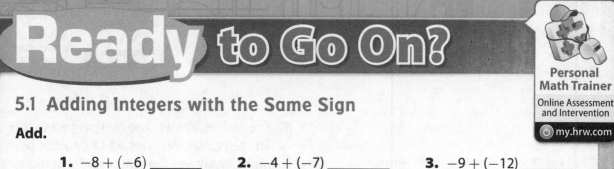

# Ready to Go On?

## 5.1 Adding Integers with the Same Sign

**Add.**

**1.** $-8 + (-6)$ _____

**2.** $-4 + (-7)$ _____

**3.** $-9 + (-12)$ _____

## 5.2 Adding Integers with Different Signs

**Add.**

**4.** $5 + (-2)$ _____

**5.** $-8 + 4$ _____

**6.** $15 + (-8)$ _____

## 5.3 Subtracting Integers

**Subtract.**

**7.** $2 - 9$ _____

**8.** $-3 - (-4)$ _____

**9.** $11 - (-12)$ _____

## 5.4 Applying Addition and Subtraction of Integers

**10.** A bus makes a stop at 2:30, letting off 15 people and letting on 9. The bus makes another stop ten minutes later to let off 4 more people. How does the number of people on the bus after the second stop compare to the number of people on the bus before the 2:30 stop?

_____

**11.** Cate and Elena were playing a card game. The stack of cards in the middle had 24 cards in it to begin with. Cate added 8 cards to the stack. Elena then took 12 cards from the stack. Finally, Cate took 9 cards from the stack. How many cards were left in the stack? _____

### ? ESSENTIAL QUESTION

**12.** Write and solve a word problem that can be modeled by addition of two negative integers.

_____

_____

_____

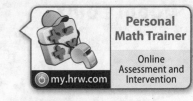
## Selected Response

**1.** Which expression has the same value as $-3 + (-5)$?

Ⓐ $-3 - (-5)$

Ⓑ $-3 + 5$

Ⓒ $-5 + (-3)$

Ⓓ $-5 - (-3)$

**2.** A diver's elevation is $-30$ feet relative to sea level. She dives down 12 feet. What is her elevation after the dive?

Ⓐ 12 feet

Ⓑ 18 feet

Ⓒ $-30$ feet

Ⓓ $-42$ feet

**3.** Which number line models the expression $-3 + 5$?

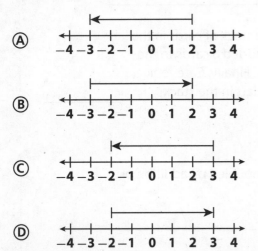

**4.** Which number can you add to 5 to get a sum of 0?

Ⓐ $-10$

Ⓑ $-5$

Ⓒ 0

Ⓓ 5

**5.** The temperature in the morning was $-3\,°F$. The temperature dropped 11 degrees by night. What was the temperature at night?

Ⓐ $-14\,°F$

Ⓑ $-8\,°F$

Ⓒ $8\,°F$

Ⓓ $14\,°F$

**6.** Which of the following expressions has the greatest value?

Ⓐ $3 - 7 + (-10)$

Ⓑ $3 + 7 - (-10)$

Ⓒ $3 - 7 - (-10)$

Ⓓ $3 + 7 + (-10)$

## Gridded Response

**7.** Mr. Renato had $150 in his bank account. He deposited $50. A couple of days later, he withdrew $20. A week later, he deposited $75. The next week he withdrew $100. What is Mr. Ranato's balance after all the transactions?

| ⊕ | ⓪ | ⓪ | ⓪ | ⓪ | • | ⓪ | ⓪ |
|---|---|---|---|---|---|---|---|
| ⊖ | ① | ① | ① | ① | | ① | ① |
| | ② | ② | ② | ② | | ② | ② |
| | ③ | ③ | ③ | ③ | | ③ | ③ |
| | ④ | ④ | ④ | ④ | | ④ | ④ |
| | ⑤ | ⑤ | ⑤ | ⑤ | | ⑤ | ⑤ |
| | ⑥ | ⑥ | ⑥ | ⑥ | | ⑥ | ⑥ |
| | ⑦ | ⑦ | ⑦ | ⑦ | | ⑦ | ⑦ |
| | ⑧ | ⑧ | ⑧ | ⑧ | | ⑧ | ⑧ |
| | ⑨ | ⑨ | ⑨ | ⑨ | | ⑨ | ⑨ |

# Multiplying and Dividing Integers

## ? ESSENTIAL QUESTION

How can you use multiplication and division of integers to solve real-world problems?

**Real-World Video**

The giant panda is an endangered animal. For some endangered species, the population has made a steady decline. This can be represented by multiplying integers with different signs.

⏻ my.hrw.com

## GO DIGITAL

my.hrw.com

**my.hrw.com**

Go digital with your write-in student edition, accessible on any device.

**Math On the Spot**

Scan with your smart phone to jump directly to the online edition, video tutor, and more.

**Animated Math**

Interactively explore key concepts to see how math works.

**Personal Math Trainer**

Get immediate feedback and help as you work through practice sets.

# Are YOU Ready?

Complete these exercises to review skills you will need for this chapter.

## Multiplication Facts

**EXAMPLES**

$7 \times 9 = $ ■

$7 \times 9 = 63$

$12 \times 10 = $ ■

$12 \times 10 = 120$

Use patterns. When you multiply 9 by a number 1 through 9, the digits of the product add up to 9.
$6 + 3 = 9$

Products of 10 end in 0.

**Multiply.**

**1.** $9 \times 3$ _____

**2.** $7 \times 10$ _____

**3.** $9 \times 8$ _____

**4.** $15 \times 10$ _____

**5.** $6 \times 9$ _____

**6.** $10 \times 23$ _____

**7.** $9 \times 9$ _____

**8.** $10 \times 20$ _____

## Division Facts

**EXAMPLE**

$48 \div 6 = $ ■

$48 \div 6 = 8$

Think: 6 times what number equals 48?
$6 \times 8 = 48$
So, $48 \div 6 = 8$

**Divide.**

**9.** $54 \div 9$ _____

**10.** $42 \div 6$ _____

**11.** $24 \div 3$ _____

**12.** $64 \div 8$ _____

**13.** $90 \div 10$ _____

**14.** $56 \div 7$ _____

**15.** $81 \div 9$ _____

**16.** $110 \div 11$ _____

## Order of Operations

**EXAMPLE**

$32 - 2(10 - 7)$

$32 - 2(3)$

$32 - 6$

$26$

To evaluate, first operate within parentheses.

Then multiply and divide from left to right.

Finally add and subtract from left to right.

**Evaluate each expression.**

**17.** $12 + 8 \div 2$ _____

**18.** $15 - (4 + 3) \times 2$ _____

**19.** $18 - (8 - 5)^2$ _____

**20.** $6 + 7 \times 3 - 5$ _____

**21.** $9 + (2^2 + 3)^2 \times 2$ _____

**22.** $6 + 5 - 4 \times 3 \div 2$ _____

# Reading Start-Up

## Visualize Vocabulary

Use the ✔ words to complete the chart. You may put more than one word in each box.

| ÷, or put into equal groups | ×, or repeated addition |
|---|---|

**Multiplying and Dividing Integers**

| 32, −32 | 32 ÷ 4 = 8 |
|---|---|

## Understand Vocabulary

**Complete the sentences using the review words.**

1. A _____ is a number that is less than 0. A _____ is a number that is greater than 0.

2. Division problems have three parts. The part you want to divide into groups is called the _____. The number that is divided into another number is called the _____. The answer to a division problem is called the _____.

3. _____ are all whole numbers and their opposites.

## Active Reading

**Double-Door Fold** Create a double-door fold to help you understand the concepts in this module. Label one flap "Multiplying Integers" and the other flap "Dividing Integers." As you study each lesson, write important ideas under the appropriate flap. Include information that will help you remember the concepts later when you look back at your notes.

# Unpacking the TEKS

Understanding the TEKS and the vocabulary terms in the TEKS will help you know exactly what you are expected to learn in this module.

---

**TEKS 6.3.D**

Add, subtract, **multiply**, and divide integers fluently.

**Key Vocabulary**

**integer** *(entero)*
A member of the set of whole numbers and their opposites.

## What It Means to You

You will use your knowledge of multiplication of whole numbers and addition of negative numbers to multiply integers.

**UNPACKING EXAMPLE 6.3.D**

Multiply $4 \times (-5)$.

$$4 \times (-5) = -5 + (-5) + (-5) + (-5)$$

*Multiplication is repeated addition.*

$$= -20$$

The product of 4 and $-5$ is the same as the negative product of 4 and 5.

A positive number times a negative number is negative.

---

**TEKS 6.3.D**

Add, subtract, multiply, and **divide** integers fluently.

**Key Vocabulary**

**integer** *(entero)*
A member of the set of whole numbers and their opposites.

## What It Means to You

You will use your knowledge of division of whole numbers and multiplication of integers to divide integers.

**UNPACKING EXAMPLE 6.3.D**

The temperature in Fairbanks, Alaska, dropped over four consecutive hours from 0° F to −44 °F. If the temperature dropped the same amount each hour, how much did the temperature change each hour?

$$\frac{-44}{4} = -11$$

The quotient of −44 and 4 is the same as the negative quotient of 44 and 4.

A negative number divided by a positive number is negative.

---

Visit **my.hrw.com** to see all the **TEKS** unpacked.

my.hrw.com

# LESSON
# 6.1 Multiplying Integers

**TEKS**
**Number and operations— 6.3.D** Add, subtract, multiply, and divide integers fluently. *Also 6.3.C.*

**? ESSENTIAL QUESTION**

How do you multiply integers?

**EXPLORE ACTIVITY 1** Real World  **TEKS** 6.3.C

## Multiplying Integers Using a Number Line

You can use a number line to see what happens when you multiply a positive number by a negative number.

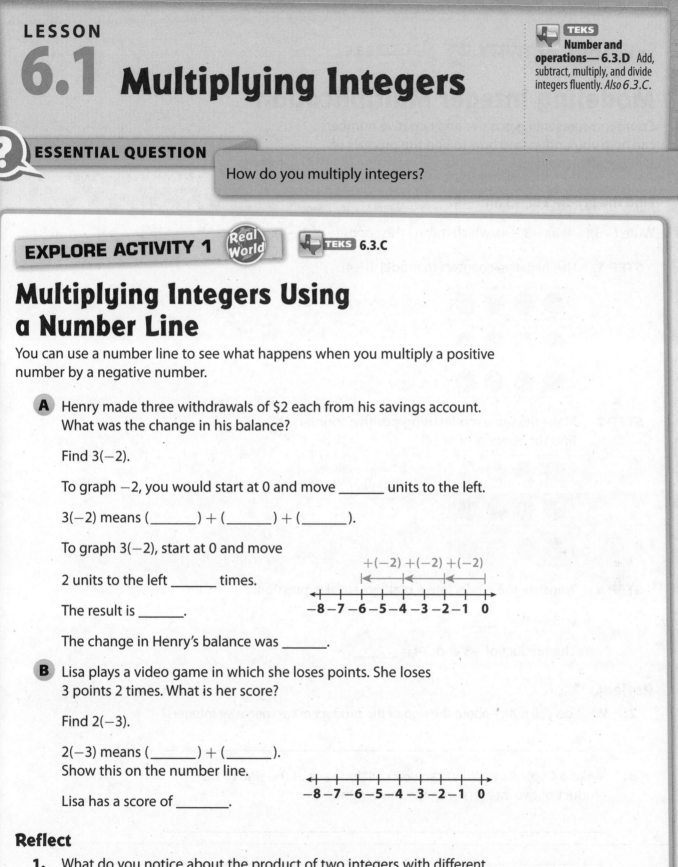

**A** Henry made three withdrawals of $2 each from his savings account. What was the change in his balance?

Find 3(−2).

To graph −2, you would start at 0 and move _____ units to the left.

3(−2) means (_____) + (_____) + (_____).

To graph 3(−2), start at 0 and move

2 units to the left _____ times.

The result is _____.

The change in Henry's balance was _____.

**B** Lisa plays a video game in which she loses points. She loses 3 points 2 times. What is her score?

Find 2(−3).

2(−3) means (_____) + (_____).
Show this on the number line.

Lisa has a score of _____.

## Reflect

**1.** What do you notice about the product of two integers with different signs?

_____

_____

# EXPLORE ACTIVITY 2 — TEKS 6.3.C

## Modeling Integer Multiplication

Counters representing positive and negative numbers can help you understand how to find the product of two negative integers.

⬤ = +1
⬤ = −1

**Find the product of −3 and −4.**

Write $(-3)(-4)$ as $-3(-4)$, which means the *opposite* of $3(-4)$.

**STEP 1** Use negative counters to model $3(-4)$.

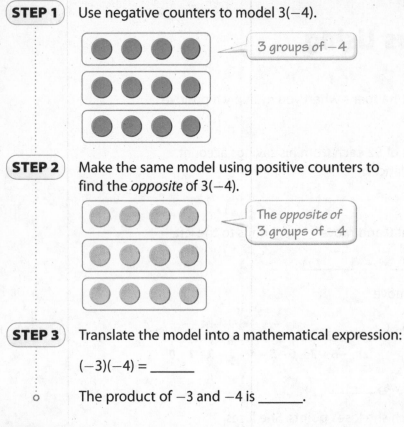

3 groups of −4

**STEP 2** Make the same model using positive counters to find the *opposite* of $3(-4)$.

The *opposite* of 3 groups of −4

**STEP 3** Translate the model into a mathematical expression:

$(-3)(-4) = $ _____

The product of −3 and −4 is _____.

### Reflect

**2.** What do you notice about the sign of the product of two negative integers?

_____

**3.** **Make a Conjecture** What can you conclude about the sign of the product of two integers with the same sign?

_____

_____

_____

_____

# Multiplying Integers

The product of two integers with opposite signs is negative. The product of two integers with the same sign is positive. The product of 0 and any other integer is 0.

## EXAMPLE 1

TEKS 6.3.D

**A** Multiply: (13)(−3).

> **STEP 1** Determine the sign of the product.
>
> > 13 is positive and −3 is negative. Since the numbers have opposite signs, the product will be negative.
>
> **STEP 2** Find the absolute values of the numbers and multiply them.
>
> > $|13| = 13$      $|−3| = 3$
> >
> > $13 \times 3 = 39$
>
> **STEP 3** Assign the correct sign to the product.
>
> > $13(−3) = −39$      *The product is −39.*

**B** Multiply: (−5)(−8).

> **STEP 1** Determine the sign of the product.
>
> > −5 is negative and −8 is negative. Since the numbers have the same sign, the product will be positive.
>
> **STEP 2** Find the absolute values of the numbers and multiply them.
>
> > $|−5| = 5$      $|−8| = 8$
> >
> > $5 \times 8 = 40$
>
> **STEP 3** Assign the correct sign to the product.
>
> > $(−5)(−8) = 40$      *The product is 40.*

**C** Multiply: (−10)(0).

> $(−10)(0) = 0$      *One of the factors is 0, so the product is 0.*

**Math Talk**
Mathematical Processes

Compare the rules for finding the product of a number and zero and finding the sum of a number and 0.

## YOUR TURN

**Find each product.**

**4.** −3(5) _____

**5.** (−10)(−2) _____

**6.** 7(−6) _____

**7.** 0(−22) _____

**8.** (−15)(−3) _____

**9.** 8(4) _____

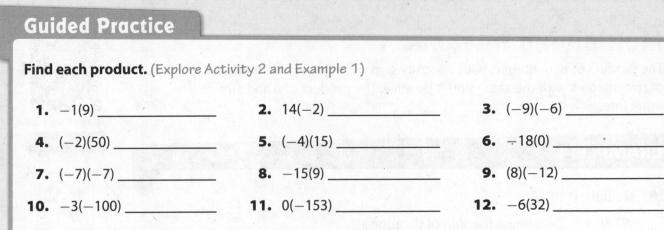

**Find each product.** (Explore Activity 2 and Example 1)

1. −1(9) _____

2. 14(−2) _____

3. (−9)(−6) _____

4. (−2)(50) _____

5. (−4)(15) _____

6. −18(0) _____

7. (−7)(−7) _____

8. −15(9) _____

9. (8)(−12) _____

10. −3(−100) _____

11. 0(−153) _____

12. −6(32) _____

13. Flora made 7 withdrawals of $75 each from her bank account. What was the overall change in her account? (Example 1)

_____

14. A football team lost 5 yards on each of 3 plays. Explain how you could use a number line to find the team's change in field position after the 3 plays. (Explore Activity 1)

_____

_____

15. The temperature dropped 2 °F every hour for 6 hours. What was the total number of degrees the temperature changed in the 6 hours? (Explore Activity 1)

_____

16. The price of one share of Acme Company declined $5 per day for 4 days in a row. How much did the price of one share change in total after the 4 days? (Explore Activity 1)

_____

17. A mountain climber climbed down a cliff 50 feet at a time. He did this 5 times in one day. What was the overall change in his elevation? (Explore Activity 1)

_____

**? ESSENTIAL QUESTION CHECK-IN**

18. Explain the process for finding the product of two integers.

_____

_____

_____

_____

# 6.1 Independent Practice

TEKS 6.3.D

**Personal Math Trainer**

Online Assessment and Intervention

my.hrw.com

**19. Critique Reasoning** Lisa used a number line to model −2(3). Does her number line make sense? Explain why or why not.

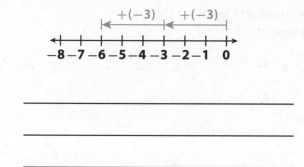

$+(−3)$   $+(−3)$

−8 −7 −6 −5 −4 −3 −2 −1  0

_____

_____

_____

**20. Represent Real-World Problems** Mike got on an elevator and went down 3 floors. He meant to go to a lower level, so he stayed on the elevator and went down 3 more floors. How many floors did Mike go down altogether?

_____

**Solve. Show your work.**

**21.** When Brooke buys lunch at the cafeteria, money is withdrawn from a lunch account. The table shows amounts withdrawn in one week. By how much did the amount in Brooke's lunch account change by the end of that week?

| Lunch Account | | | |
|---|---|---|---|
| Week 1 | Lunch | Cost | Balance |
|  |  |  | $28 |
| Monday | Pizza | $4 |  |
| Tuesday | Fish Tacos | $4 |  |
| Wednesday | Spaghetti | $4 |  |
| Thursday | Sandwich | $4 |  |
| Friday | Chicken | $4 |  |

_____

**22.** Adam is scuba diving. He descends 5 feet below sea level. He descends the same distance 4 more times. What is Adam's final elevation?

_____

_____

**23.** The price of jeans was reduced $6 per week for 7 weeks. By how much did the price of the jeans change over the 7 weeks?

_____

_____

_____

**24.** Casey uses some of his savings on batting practice. The cost of renting a batting cage for 1 hour is $6. He rents a cage for 9 hours in each of two months. What is the change in Casey's savings after two months?

_____

_____

_____

**25.** Volunteers at Sam's school use some of the student council's savings for a special project. They buy 7 backpacks for $8 each and fill each backpack with paper and pens that cost $5. By how much did the student council's savings change because of this project?

_____

_____

_____

**26. Communicate Mathematical Ideas** Describe a real-world situation that can be represented by the product 8(−20). Then find the product and explain what the product means in terms of the real-world situation.

_____

_____

_____

**27. What If?** The rules for multiplying two integers can be extended to a product of 3 or more integers. Find the following products by using the Associative Property to multiply 2 numbers at a time.

**a.** 3(3)(−3) _____  **b.** 3(−3)(−3) _____  **c.** −3(−3)(−3) _____

**d.** 3(3)(3)(−3) _____  **e.** 3(3)(−3)(−3) _____  **f.** 3(−3)(−3)(−3) _____

**g. Make a Conjecture** Based on your results, complete the following statements:

When a product of integers has an odd number of negative factors,

then the sign of the product is _____ .

When a product of integers has an even number of negative factors,

then the sign of the product is _____ .

 **FOCUS ON HIGHER ORDER THINKING**

Work Area

**28. Multiple Representations** The product of three integers is −3. Determine all of the possible values for the three factors.

_____

**29. Analyze Relationships** When is the product of two nonzero integers less than or equal to both of the two factors?

_____

_____

**30. Justify Reasoning** The sign of the product of two integers with the same sign is positive. What is the sign of the product of three integers with the same sign? Explain your thinking.

_____

_____

_____

_____

LESSON

# 6.2 Dividing Integers

TEKS **Number and operations—6.3.D** Add, subtract, multiply, and divide integers fluently. *Also 6.3.C.*

## ESSENTIAL QUESTION

How do you divide integers?

## EXPLORE ACTIVITY Real World

TEKS 6.3.C

**A diver needs to descend to a depth of 100 feet. She wants to do it in 5 equal descents. How far should she travel in each descent?**

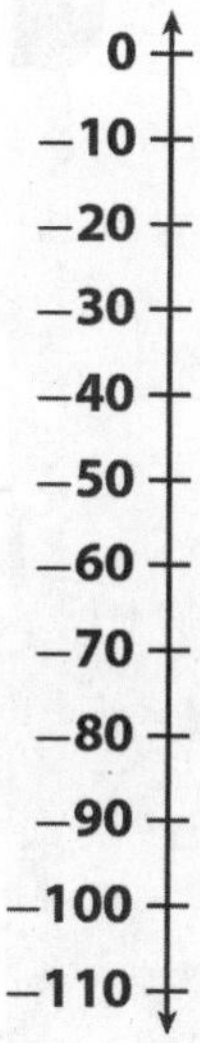

0
−10
−20
−30
−40
−50
−60
−70
−80
−90
−100
−110


**A** Use the number line at the right to find how far the diver should travel in each of the 5 descents.

________________________________________

**B** To solve this problem, you can set up a division problem: $\frac{-100}{\square} = ?$

**C** Rewrite the division problem as a multiplication problem. Think: Some number multiplied by 5 equals $-100$.

________ $\times\ ? = -100$

**D** Remember the rules for integer multiplication. If the product is negative, one of the factors must be negative. Since ________ is positive, the unknown factor must be **positive / negative.**

**E** You know that $5 \times$ ______ $= 100$. So, using the rules for integer multiplication you can say that $5 \times$ ________ $= -100$.

The diver should descend ________ feet in each descent.

**F** Use the process you just learned to find each of the quotients below.

$\frac{14}{-7} =$ ______ $\frac{-36}{-9} =$ ______ $\frac{-55}{11} =$ ______ $\frac{-45}{-5} =$ ______

### Reflect

1. **Make a Conjecture** Make a conjecture about the quotient of two integers with different signs. Make a conjecture about the quotient of two integers with the same sign.

________________________________________

________________________________________

# Dividing Integers

You used the relationship between multiplication and division to make conjectures about the signs of quotients of integers. You can use multiplication to understand why division by zero is not possible.

Think about the division problem below and its related multiplication problem.

$$5 \div 0 = ? \qquad 0 \times ? = 5$$

The multiplication sentence says that there is some number times 0 that equals 5. You already know that 0 times any number equals 0. This means division by 0 is not possible, so we say that division by 0 is undefined.

**My Notes**

## EXAMPLE 1

TEKS 6.3.D

**A** Divide: $24 \div (-3)$

**STEP 1** Determine the sign of the quotient.

24 is positive and −3 is negative. Since the numbers have opposite signs, the quotient will be negative.

**STEP 2** Divide.

$$24 \div (-3) = -8$$

**B** Divide: $-6 \div (-2)$

**STEP 1** Determine the sign of the quotient.

−6 is negative and −2 is negative. Since the numbers have the same sign, the quotient will be positive.

**STEP 2** Divide: $-6 \div (-2) = 3$

**C** Divide: $0 \div (-9)$

**STEP 1** Determine the sign of the quotient.

The dividend is 0 and the divisor is not 0. So, the quotient is 0.

**STEP 2** Divide: $0 \div (-9) = 0$

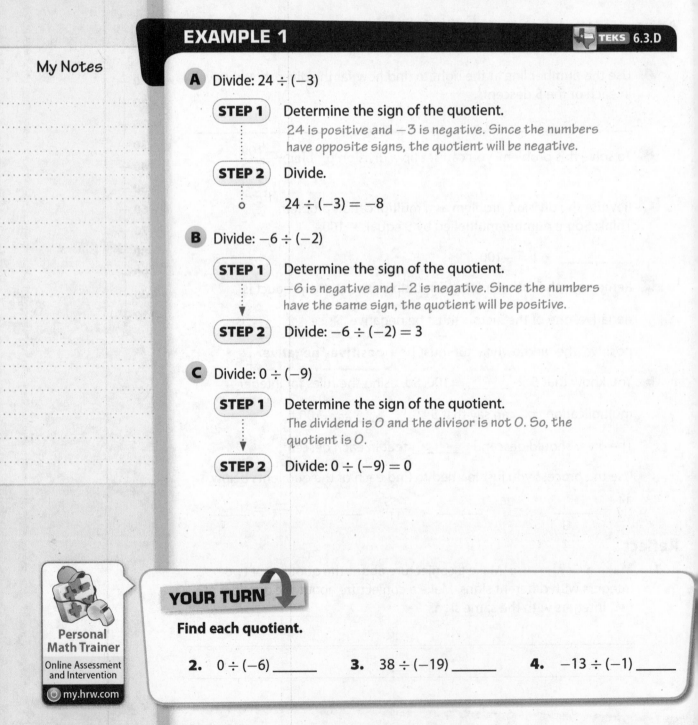

Personal
Math Trainer

Online Assessment
and Intervention

my.hrw.com

**YOUR TURN**

**Find each quotient.**

**2.** $0 \div (-6)$ _____

**3.** $38 \div (-19)$ _____

**4.** $-13 \div (-1)$ _____

# Using Integer Division to Solve Problems

You can use integer division to solve real-world problems. For some problems, you may need to perform more than one step. Be sure to check that the sign of the quotient makes sense for the situation.

**Math On the Spot**

ⓗ my.hrw.com

## EXAMPLE 2 · Real World

TEKS 6.3.D

Jake answers questions in two different online Olympic trivia quizzes. In each quiz, he loses points when he gives an incorrect answer. The table shows the points lost for each wrong answer in each quiz and Jake's total points lost in each quiz. In which quiz did he have more wrong answers?

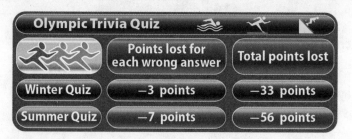

| Olympic Trivia Quiz | Points lost for each wrong answer | Total points lost |
|---|---|---|
| Winter Quiz | −3 points | −33 points |
| Summer Quiz | −7 points | −56 points |

**STEP 1** Find the number of incorrect answers in the winter quiz.

$-33 \div (-3) = 11$  Divide the total points lost by the number of points lost per wrong answer.

**STEP 2** Find the number of incorrect answers Jake gave in the summer quiz.

$-56 \div (-7) = 8$  Divide the total points lost by the number of points lost per wrong answer.

**STEP 3** Compare the numbers of wrong answers.

$11 > 8$, so Jake had more wrong answers in the winter quiz.

**Math Talk**
Mathematical Processes

What is the sign of each quotient in Steps 1 and 2? Why does this make sense for the situation?

## YOUR TURN

5. A penalty in Meteor-Mania is −5 seconds. A penalty in Cosmic Calamity is −7 seconds. Yolanda had penalties totaling −25 seconds in a game of Meteor-Mania and −35 seconds in a game of Cosmic Calamity. In which game did Yolanda receive more penalties? Justify your answer.

_____

_____

_____

**Personal Math Trainer**

Online Assessment and Intervention

ⓗ my.hrw.com

**Find each quotient.** (Example 1)

1. $\frac{-14}{2}$ _____

2. $21 \div (-3)$ _____

3. $\frac{26}{-13}$ _____

4. $0 \div (-4)$ _____

5. $\frac{-45}{-5}$ _____

6. $-30 \div (10)$ _____

7. $\frac{-11}{-1}$ _____

8. $-31 \div (-31)$ _____

9. $\frac{0}{-7}$ _____

10. $\frac{-121}{-11}$ _____

11. $84 \div (-7)$ _____

12. $\frac{500}{-25}$ _____

13. $-6 \div (0)$ _____

14. $\frac{-63}{-21}$ _____

**Write a division expression for each problem. Then find the value of the expression.** (Example 2)

15. Clark made four of his truck payments late and was fined four late fees. The total change to his savings from late fees was −$40. How much was one late fee?

_____

16. Jan received −22 points on her exam. She got 11 questions wrong out of 50 questions. How much was Jan penalized for each wrong answer?

_____

17. Allen's score in a video game was changed by −75 points because he missed some targets. He got −15 points for each missed target. How many targets did he miss?

_____

18. Louisa's savings change by −$9 each time she goes bowling. In all, it changed by −$99 during the summer. How many times did she go bowling in the summer?

_____

**? ESSENTIAL QUESTION CHECK-IN**

19. How is the process of dividing integers similar to the process of multiplying integers?

_____

_____

_____

# 6.2 Independent Practice

**TEKS** 6.3.D

Personal
Math Trainer

Online
Assessment and
Intervention

my.hrw.com

**20.** Walter buys a bus pass for $30. Every time he rides the bus,
money is deducted from the value of the pass. He rode
12 times and $24 was deducted from the value of the pass.
How much does each bus ride cost? _____

**21.** **Analyze Relationships** Elisa withdrew $20 at a time from her bank
account and withdrew a total of $140. Francis withdrew $45 at a time from
his bank account and withdrew a total of $270. Who made the greater
number of withdrawals? Justify your answer.

_____

_____

_____

**22.** **Multistep** At 7 p.m. last night, the temperature was 10 °F. At 7 a.m. the
next morning, the temperature was −2 °F.

**a.** By how much did the temperature change from 7 p.m. to 7 a.m.?

_____

**b.** The temperature changed by a steady amount overnight. By how
much did it change each hour?

_____

_____

**23.** **Analyze Relationships** Nola hiked down a trail at a steady rate for
10 minutes. Her change in elevation was −200 feet. Then she continued
to hike down for another 20 minutes at a different rate. Her change in
elevation for this part of the hike was −300 feet. During which portion of
the hike did she walk down at a faster rate? Explain your reasoning.

_____

_____

_____

**24.** Write a real world description to fit the expression −50 ÷ 5.

_____

_____

_____

**25. Communicate Mathematical Ideas** Two integers, *a* and *b*, have different signs. The absolute value of integer *a* is divisible by the absolute value of integer *b*. Find two integers that fit this description. Then decide if the product of the integers is greater than or less than the quotient of the integers. Show your work.

_____

_____

_____

**Determine if each statement is true or false. Justify your answer.**

**26.** For any two nonzero integers, the product and quotient have the same sign.

_____

_____

_____

**27.** Any nonzero integer divided by 0 equals 0.

_____

_____

Work Area

**28. Multi-step** A perfect score on a test with 25 questions is 100. Each question is worth the same number of points.

**a.** How many points is each question on the test worth? _____

**b.** Fred got a score of 84 on the test. Write a division sentence using negative numbers where the quotient represents the number of questions Fred answered incorrectly. _____

**29. Persevere in Problem Solving** Colleen divided integer *a* by −3 and got 8. Then she divided 8 by integer *b* and got −4. Find the quotient of integer *a* and integer *b*. _____

**30. Justify Reasoning** The quotient of two negative integers results in an integer. How does the value of the quotient compare to the value of the original two integers? Explain.

_____

_____

_____

# LESSON
# 6.3 Applying Integer Operations

TEKS
**Number and operations—6.3.D** Add, subtract, multiply, and divide integers fluently.

## ESSENTIAL QUESTION

How can you use integer operations to solve real-world problems?

## Using the Order of Operations with Integers

The order of operations applies to integer operations as well as positive number operations. Perform multiplication and division first, and then addition and subtraction. Work from left to right in the expression.

Math On the Spot
my.hrw.com

### EXAMPLE 1    Problem Solving                                    TEKS 6.3.D

Hannah made four withdrawals of $20 from her checking account. She also wrote a check for $215. By how much did the amount in her checking account change?

**Analyze Information**

You need to find the total *change* in Hannah's account. Since withdrawals and writing a check represent a decrease in her account, use negative numbers to represent these amounts.

**Formulate a Plan**

Write a product to represent the four withdrawals.

$$-20 + (-20) + (-20) + (-20) = 4(-20)$$

Add $-215$ to represent the check that Hannah wrote.

$$4(-20) + (-215)$$

**Solve**

Evaluate the expression to find by how much the amount in the account changed.

$4(-20) - 215 = -80 - 215$      Multiply first.

$\qquad\qquad\quad = -295$      Then subtract.

The amount in the account decreased by $295.

**Justify and Evaluate**

The value $-295$ represents a decrease of 295 dollars. This makes sense, since withdrawals and writing checks remove money from the checking account.

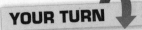
1. Reggie lost 3 spaceships in level 3 of a video game. He lost 30 points for each spaceship. When he completed level 3, he earned a bonus of 200 points. By how much did his score change?

_____

_____

2. Simplify: $-6(13) - 21$ _____

# Using Negative Integers to Represent Quantities

You can use positive and negative integers to solve problems involving amounts that increase or decrease. Sometimes you may need to use more than one operation.

**EXAMPLE 2**                      🔲 **TEKS** 6.3.C

**Three brothers each have their own savings. They borrow $72 from their parents for concert tickets. Each brother must pay back an equal share of this amount. Also, the youngest brother owes his parents $15. By how much will the youngest brother's savings change after he pays his parents?**

**STEP 1** Determine the signs of the values and the operations you will use. Write an expression.

Since the money is being paid back, it will *decrease* the amount in each brother's savings. Use $-72$ and $-15$.

Since an *equal share* of the $72 will be paid back, use division to determine 3 equal parts of $-72$. Then add $-15$ to one of these equal parts.

Change to youngest brother's savings $= (-72) \div 3 + (-15)$

**STEP 2** Evaluate the expression.

$$(-72) \div 3 + (-15) = -24 + (-15) \qquad \text{Divide}$$
$$= -39 \qquad \text{Add.}$$

The youngest brother's savings will decrease by $39.

### Math Talk
**Mathematical Processes**

Suppose the youngest brother has $60 in savings. How much will he have left after he pays his parents what he owes?

**Reflect**

3. **What If?** Suppose there were four brothers in Example 2. How much would the youngest brother need to pay?

_____

## YOUR TURN

**Simplify each expression.**

4. $(-12) \div 6 + 2$ _____

5. $-87 \div (-3) - 9$ _____

6. $40 \div (-5) + 30$ _____

7. $-39 \div 3 - 15$ _____

# Comparing Values of Expressions

Often, problem situations require making comparisons between two values. Use integer operations to calculate values. Then compare the values.

## EXAMPLE 3  Real World                    TEKS 6.3.C

Jill and Tony play a board game in which they move counters along a board. Jill moves her counter back 3 spaces four times, and then moves her counter forward 6 spaces. Tony moves his counter back 2 spaces three times, and then moves his player forward 3 spaces one time. Find each player's overall change in position. Who moved farther?

**STEP 1**  Find each player's overall change in position.

Jill: $4(-3) + 6 = -12 + 6 = -6$  *Jill moves back 6 spaces.*

Tony: $3(-2) + 3 = -6 + 3 = -3$  *Tony moves back 3 spaces.*

**STEP 2**  Compare the numbers of spaces moved by the players.

$|-6| > |-3|$  *Compare absolute values.*

Jill moves farther back than Tony.

**Math Talk**
Mathematical Processes

Why do you compare absolute values in Step 2?

## YOUR TURN

8. Amber and Will are in line together to buy tickets. Amber moves back by 3 places three times to talk to friends. She then is invited to move 5 places up in line. Will moved back by 4 places twice, and then moved up in line by 3 places. Overall, who moved farther back in line?

_____

**Evaluate each expression. Circle the expression with the greater value.**

9. $(-10) \div 2 - 2 =$ _____

10. $42 \div (-3) + 9 =$ _____

   $(-28) \div 4 + 1 =$ _____

   $(-36) \div 9 - 2 =$ _____

Personal
Math Trainer

Online Assessment
and Intervention

my.hrw.com

**Evaluate each expression.** (Example 1)

1. $-6(-5) + 12$ _____

2. $3(-6) - 3$ _____

3. $-2(8) + 7$ _____

4. $4(-13) + 20$ _____

5. $(-4)(0) - 4$ _____

6. $-3(-5) - 16$ _____

**Write an expression to represent the situation. Evaluate the expression and answer the question.** (Example 2)

7. Bella pays 7 payments of $5 each to a game store. She returns one game and receives $20 back. What is the change to the amount of money she has?

   _____

8. Ron lost 10 points seven times playing a video game. He then lost an additional 100 points for going over the time limit. What was the total change in his score?

   _____

9. Ned took a test with 25 questions. He lost 4 points for each of the 6 questions he got wrong and earned an additional 10 points for answering a bonus question correctly. How many points did Ned receive or lose overall?

   _____

10. Mr. Harris has some money in his wallet. He pays the babysitter $12 an hour for 4 hours of babysitting. His wife gives him $10, and he puts the money in his wallet. By how much does the amount in his wallet change?

    _____

**Compare the values of the two expressions using $<$, $=$, or $>$.** (Example 3)

11. $-3(-2) + 3$ _____ $3(-4) + 9$

12. $-8(-2) - 20$ _____ $3(-2) + 2$

13. $-7(5) - 9$ _____ $-3(20) + 10$

14. $-16(0) - 3$ _____ $-8(-2) - 3$

**? ESSENTIAL QUESTION CHECK-IN**

15. When you solve a problem involving money, what can a negative answer represent?

    _____

    _____

    _____

# 6.3 Independent Practice

**TEKS** 6.3.D

**Evaluate each expression.**

**16.** $-12(-3) + 7$ _____

**17.** $-42 \div (-6) + 5 - 8$ _____

**18.** $10(-60) - 18$ _____

**19.** $(-11)(-7) + 5 - 82$ _____

**20.** $35 \div (-7) + 6$ _____

**21.** $-13(-2) - 16 - 8$ _____

**22. Multistep** Lily and Rose are playing a game. In the game, each player starts with 0 points and the player with the most points at the end wins. Lily gains 5 points two times, loses 12 points, and then gains 3 points. Rose loses 3 points two times, loses 1 point, gains 6 points, and then gains 7 points.

   **a.** Write and evaluate an expression to find Lily's score.

   _____

   **b.** Write and evaluate an expression to find Rose's score.

   _____

   **c.** Who won the game?

   _____

**Write an expression from the description. Then evaluate the expression.**

**23.** 8 less than the product of 5 and $-4$

_____

**24.** 9 more than the quotient of $-36$ and $-4$.

_____

**25. Multistep** Arleen has a gift card for a local lawn and garden store. She uses the gift card to rent a tiller for 4 days. It costs $35 per day to rent the tiller. She also buys a rake for $9.

   **a.** Find the change to the value on her gift card.

   _____

   **b.** The original amount on the gift card was $200. Does Arleen have enough left on the card to buy a wheelbarrow for $50? Explain.

   _____

   _____

**26.** Carlos made up a game where, in a deck of cards, the red cards (hearts and diamonds) are negative and the black cards (spades and clubs) are positive. All face cards are worth 10 points, and number cards are worth their value.

    **a.** Samantha has a king of hearts, a jack of diamonds, and a 3 of spades. Write an expression to find the value of her cards.

    _____

    **b.** Warren has a 7 of clubs, a 2 of spades, and a 7 of hearts. Write an expression to find the value of his cards.

    _____

    **c.** If the greater score wins, who won?

    _____

    **d.** If a player always gets three cards, describe two different ways to receive a score of 7.

    _____

    _____

 **FOCUS ON HIGHER ORDER THINKING**

**Work Area**

**27. Represent Real-World Problems** Write a problem that the expression $3(-7) - 10 + 25 = -6$ could represent.

_____

_____

_____

**28. Critique Reasoning** Jim found the quotient of two integers and got a positive integer. He added another integer to the quotient and got a positive integer. His sister Kim says that all the integers Jim used to get this result must be positive. Do you agree? Explain.

_____

_____

_____

**29. Persevere in Problem Solving** Lisa is standing on a dock beside a lake. She drops a rock from her hand into the lake. After the rock hits the surface of the lake, the rock's distance from the lake's surface changes at a rate of $-5$ inches per second. If Lisa holds her hand 5 feet above the lake's surface, how far from Lisa's hand is the rock 4 seconds after it hits the surface?

_____

# Ready to Go On?

**Personal Math Trainer**

Online Assessment and Intervention

⊙ my.hrw.com

## 6.1 Multiplying Integers

**Find each product.**

**1.** $(-2)(3)$ _____

**2.** $(-5)(-7)$ _____

**3.** $(8)(-11)$ _____

**4.** $(-3)(2)(-2)$ _____

**5.** The temperature dropped 3 °C every hour for 5 hours.
Write an integer that represents the change in temperature. _____

## 6.2 Dividing Integers

**Find each quotient.**

**6.** $\dfrac{-63}{7}$ _____

**7.** $\dfrac{-15}{-3}$ _____

**8.** $\dfrac{0}{-15}$ _____

**9.** $\dfrac{96}{-12}$ _____

**10.** An elephant at the zoo lost 24 pounds over 6 months.
The elephant lost the same amount of weight each month.
Write an integer that represents the change in the elephant's
weight each month. _____

## 6.3 Applying Integer Operations

**Evaluate each expression.**

**11.** $(-4)(5) + 8$ _____

**12.** $(-3)(-6) - 7$ _____

**13.** $\dfrac{-27}{9} - 11$ _____

**14.** $\dfrac{-24}{-3} - (-2)$ _____

**? ESSENTIAL QUESTION**

**15.** Write and solve a real-world problem that can be represented by the
expression $(-3)(5) + 10$.

_____

_____

_____

_____

MODULE 6 MIXED REVIEW

# Texas Test Prep

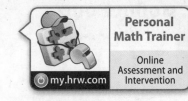

Personal
Math Trainer

Online
Assessment and
Intervention

my.hrw.com

## Selected Response

**1.** A diver is at an elevation of $-18$ feet relative to sea level. The diver descends to an undersea cave that is 4 times as far from the surface. What is the elevation of the cave?

(A) $-72$ feet

(B) $-22$ feet

(C) $-18$ feet

(D) $-14$ feet

**2.** The football team lost 4 yards on 2 plays in a row. Which of the following could represent the change in field position?

(A) $-12$ yards

(B) $-8$ yards

(C) $-6$ yards

(D) $-2$ yards

**3.** Clayton climbed down 50 meters. He climbed down in 10-meter intervals. In how many intervals did Clayton make his climb?

(A) 5

(B) 10

(C) 40

(D) 500

**4.** Which expression results in a negative answer?

(A) a negative number divided by a negative number

(B) a positive number divided by a negative number

(C) a negative number multiplied by a negative number

(D) a positive number multiplied by a positive number

**5.** Clara played a video game before she left the house to go on a walk. She started with 0 points, lost 6 points 3 times, won 4 points, and then lost 2 points. How many points did she have when she left the house to go on the walk?

(A) $-20$     (C) 12

(B) $-16$     (D) 20

**6.** Which expression is equal to 0?

(A) $\frac{-24}{6} - 4$

(B) $\frac{-24}{-6} + 4$

(C) $\frac{24}{6} + 4$

(D) $\frac{-24}{-6} - 4$

## Gridded Response

**7.** Rochelle made three $25 withdrawals and then wrote a check for $100. If she started with $200 in her account, find the total amount she has left in her account in dollars.

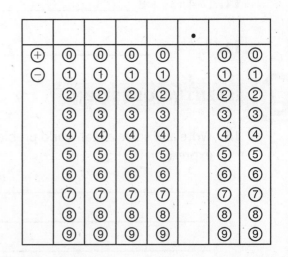

# Study Guide Review

**MODULE 3** | **Multiplying and Dividing Fractions**

**Key Vocabulary**
reciprocals (*recíprocos*)

## ? ESSENTIAL QUESTION

How can you use products and quotients of fractions to solve real-world problems?

### EXAMPLE 1

**Multiply.**

**A.** $\frac{4}{5} \times \frac{1}{8}$

$\frac{4 \times 1}{5 \times 8} = \frac{4}{40}$    Multiply numerators. Multiply denominators.

$\frac{4 \div 4}{40 \div 4} = \frac{1}{10}$    Simplify by dividing by the GCF.

**B.** $2\frac{1}{4} \times \frac{1}{5}$

$\frac{9}{4} \times \frac{1}{5}$    Rewrite the mixed number as a fraction greater than 1.

$\frac{9 \times 1}{4 \times 5} = \frac{9}{20}$    Multiply numerators. Multiply denominators.

### EXAMPLE 2

**Divide.**

**A.** $\frac{2}{7} \div \frac{1}{2}$

$\frac{2}{7} \times \frac{2}{1}$    Rewrite the problem as multiplication using the reciprocal of the second fraction.

$\frac{2 \times 2}{7 \times 1} = \frac{4}{7}$    Multiply numerators. Multiply denominators.

**B.** $2\frac{1}{3} \div 1\frac{3}{4}$

$\frac{7}{3} \div \frac{7}{4}$    Write both mixed numbers as improper fractions.

$\frac{{}^1\cancel{7} \times 4}{3 \times \cancel{7}_1} = \frac{4}{3}$    Multiply by the reciprocal of the second fraction.

$1\frac{1}{3}$    Simplify: $\frac{4}{3} = 1\frac{1}{3}$

### EXERCISES

**Multiply. Write the answer in simplest form.** (Lessons 3.1, 3.2)

**1.** $\frac{1}{7} \times \frac{4}{5}$ _____

**2.** $\frac{5}{6} \times \frac{2}{3}$ _____

**3.** $\frac{3}{7} \times \frac{14}{15}$ _____

**4.** $1\frac{1}{3} \times \frac{5}{8}$ _____

**5.** $1\frac{2}{9} \times 1\frac{1}{2}$ _____

**6.** $2\frac{1}{7} \times 3\frac{2}{3}$ _____

**Divide. Write answer in simplest form.** (Lessons 3.3, 3.4)

**7.** $\frac{3}{7} \div \frac{2}{3}$ _____

**8.** $\frac{1}{8} \div \frac{3}{4}$ _____

**9.** $1\frac{1}{5} \div \frac{1}{4}$ _____

**10.** Ron had 20 apples. He used $\frac{2}{5}$ of the apples to make pies. How many apples did Ron use for pies? (Lesson 3.4)

_____

**11.** The area of a rectangular garden is $38\frac{1}{4}$ square meters. The width of the garden is $4\frac{1}{2}$ meters. Find the length of the garden. (Lesson 3.4)

_____

**MODULE 4** # Multiplying and Dividing Decimals

### ? ESSENTIAL QUESTION

How can you use products and quotients of decimals to solve real-world problems?

## EXAMPLE 1

**Rebecca bought 2.5 pounds of red apples. The apples cost $0.98 per pound. What was the total cost of Rebecca's apples?**

$$
\begin{array}{r}
2.5 \quad \leftarrow \quad 1 \text{ decimal places} \\
\times\, .98 \quad \leftarrow\, +2 \text{ decimal places} \\
\hline
200 \\
+\, 2250 \\
\hline
2.450 \quad \leftarrow \quad 3 \text{ decimal places}
\end{array}
$$

The apples cost $2.45.

## EXAMPLE 2

**Rashid spent $37.29 on gas for his car. Gas was $3.39 per gallon. How many gallons did Rashid purchase?**

**Step 1** The divisor has two decimal places, so multiply both the dividend and the divisor by 100 so that the divisor is a whole number:

$$3.39\overline{)37.29} \qquad 339\overline{)3729}$$

**Step 2** Divide:

$$
\begin{array}{r}
11 \\
339\overline{)3729} \\
-339\phantom{0} \\
\hline
339 \\
-339 \\
\hline
0
\end{array}
$$

Rashid purchased 11 gallons of gas.

## EXERCISES

**Multiply.** (Lesson 4.1)

**1.**  12
     ×0.4  _____

**2.**  0.15
     × 9.1  _____

**3.**  3.12
     ×0.25  _____

**Divide.** (Lesson 4.2)

**4.** 5)64.5 _____

**5.** 0.6)25.2 _____

**6.** 2.1)36.75 _____

**7.** Olga worked 37.5 hours last week at the library and earned $12.50 an hour. If she gets a $2.50 per hour raise, how many hours will she have to work to make the same amount of money as she did last week? (Lesson 4.3)

_____

**8.** A pound of rice crackers costs $2.88. Matthew purchased $\frac{1}{4}$ pound of crackers. How much did he pay for the crackers? (Lesson 4.3)

_____

**MODULE 5**

# Adding and Subtracting Integers

**Key Vocabulary**
additive inverse (inverso aditivo)

## ? ESSENTIAL QUESTION

How can you use addition and subtraction of integers to solve real-world problems?

## EXAMPLE 1

**Add.**

**A.**  $-8 + (-7)$                    The signs of both integers are the same.

    $8 + 7 = 15$                    Find the sum of the absolute values.

    $-8 + (-7) = -15$                Use the sign of the integers to write the sum.

**B.**  $-5 + 11$                    The signs of the integers are different.

    $|11| - |-5| = 6$                Greater absolute value – lesser absolute value.

    $-5 + 11 = 6$                    11 has the greater absolute value, so the sum is positive.

## EXAMPLE 2

The temperature Tuesday afternoon was 3 °C. Tuesday night, the temperature was −6 °C. Find the change in temperature.

Solve −6 − 3.

Rewrite as −6 + (−3).          *−3 is the opposite of 3.*

−6 + (−3) = −9

The temperature decreased 9 °C.

## EXERCISES

**Add.** (Lessons 5.1, 5.2)

**1.** −10 + (−5) _____     **2.** 9 + (−20) _____     **3.** −13 + 32 _____

**Subtract.** (Lesson 5.3)

**4.** −12 − 5 _____     **5.** 25 − (−4) _____     **6.** −3 − (−40) _____

**7.** Antoine has $13 in his savings account. He buys some school supplies and ends up with $5 in his account. What was the overall change in Antoine's account? (Lesson 5.4)

_____

**8.** Steve finds the value of −12 + 18. Marion finds the value of −10 − (−15). Whose expression has the greater value? (Lesson 5.4)

_____

## MODULE 6  Multiplying and Dividing Integers

**? ESSENTIAL QUESTION**

How can you use multiplication and division of integers to solve real-world problems?

## EXAMPLE 1

**Multiply.**

**A.** (13)(−3)

Find the sign of the product. The numbers have different signs, so the product will be negative. Multiply the absolute values. Assign the correct sign to the product.

13(−3) = −39

**B.** $(-5)(-8)$

Find the sign of the product. The numbers have the same sign, so the product will be positive. Multiply the absolute values. Assign the correct sign to the product.

$(-5)(-8) = 40$

## EXAMPLE 2

Christine received $-25$ points on her exam. She got 5 questions wrong. How many points did Christine receive for each wrong answer?

Divide $-25$ by 5.

$-25 \div 5 = -5$     The numbers have different signs.
The quotient will be negative.

Christine received $-5$ points for each wrong answer.

## EXAMPLE 3

**Simplify: $15 + (-3) \times 8$**

$15 + (-24)$         Multiply first.

$-9$             Add.

## EXERCISES

**Multiply or divide.** (Lessons 6.1, 6.2)

**1.** $-9 \times (-5)$ _____

**2.** $0 \times (-10)$ _____

**3.** $12 \times (-4)$ _____

**4.** $-32 \div 8$ _____

**5.** $-9 \div (-1)$ _____

**6.** $-56 \div 8$ _____

**Simplify.** (Lesson 6.3)

**7.** $-14 \div 2 - 3$ _____

**8.** $8 + (-20) \times 3$ _____

**9.** $36 \div (-6) - 15$ _____

**Write an expression to represent the situation. Evaluate the expression and answer the question.**

**10.** Steve spent $24 on dog grooming supplies. He washed 6 dogs and charged the owners $12 per dog wash. How much money did Steve earn? (Lesson 6.3)

_____

**11.** Tony and Mario went to the store to buy school supplies. Tony bought 3 packs of pencils for $4 each and a pencil box for $7. Mario bought 4 binders for $6 each and used a coupon for $6 off. Who spent more money? (Lesson 6.3)

_____

**1.** **CAREERS IN MATH** Chef Chef Alonso is creating a recipe called Spicy Italian Chicken with the following ingredients: $\frac{3}{4}$ pound chicken, $2\frac{1}{2}$ cups tomato sauce, 1 teaspoon oregano, and $\frac{1}{2}$ teaspoon of his special hot sauce.

**a.** Chef Alonso wants each serving of the dish to include $\frac{1}{2}$ pound of chicken. How many $\frac{1}{2}$ pound servings does this recipe make?

_____

**b.** What is the number Chef Alonso should multiply the amount of chicken by so that the recipe will make 2 full servings, each with $\frac{1}{2}$ pound of chicken?

_____

**c.** Use the multiplier you found in part **b** to find the amount of all the ingredients in the new recipe.

_____

**d.** Chef Alonso only has three measuring spoons: 1 teaspoon, $\frac{1}{2}$ teaspoon, and $\frac{1}{4}$ teaspoon. Can he measure the new amounts of oregano and hot sauce exactly? Explain why or why not.

_____

**2.** Amira is painting a rectangular banner $2\frac{1}{4}$ yards wide on a wall in the cafeteria. The banner will have a blue background. Amira has enough blue paint to cover $1\frac{1}{2}$ square yards of wall.

**a.** Find the height of the banner If Amira uses all of the blue paint. Show your work.

_____

**b.** The school colors are blue and yellow, so Amira wants to add yellow rectangles on the left and right sides of the blue rectangle. The yellow rectangles will each be $\frac{3}{4}$ yard wide and the same height as the blue rectangle. What will be the total area of the two yellow rectangles? Explain how you found your answer.

_____

_____

**c.** What are the dimensions of the banner plus yellow rectangles? What is the total area? Show your work.

_____

_____

## Selected Response

**1.** Which of the following statements is correct?

Ⓐ The product of $\frac{5}{6}$ and $\frac{9}{10}$ is greater than $\frac{9}{10}$.

Ⓑ The product of $1\frac{1}{5}$ and $\frac{6}{7}$ is less than $1\frac{1}{5}$.

Ⓒ The product of $\frac{6}{7}$ and $\frac{5}{6}$ is greater than $\frac{5}{6}$.

Ⓓ The product of $1\frac{3}{4}$ and $\frac{2}{5}$ is less than $\frac{2}{5}$.

**2.** Which of these is the same as $\frac{8}{9} \div \frac{2}{3}$?

Ⓐ $\frac{8}{9} \div \frac{3}{2}$     Ⓒ $\frac{8}{9} \times \frac{2}{3}$

Ⓑ $\frac{2}{3} \div \frac{8}{9}$     Ⓓ $\frac{8}{9} \times \frac{3}{2}$

**3.** A rectangular tabletop has a length of $4\frac{3}{4}$ feet and an area of $11\frac{7}{8}$ square feet. What is the width of the tabletop?

Ⓐ $1\frac{1}{16}$ feet

Ⓑ $2\frac{1}{2}$ feet

Ⓒ $4\frac{1}{4}$ feet

Ⓓ $8\frac{1}{2}$ feet

**4.** Dorothy types 120 words per minute. How many words does Dorothy type in 1.75 minutes?

Ⓐ 150 words

Ⓑ 180 words

Ⓒ 200 words

Ⓓ 210 words

**5.** What is the opposite of 17?

Ⓐ $-17$

Ⓑ $-\frac{1}{17}$

Ⓒ $\frac{1}{17}$

Ⓓ 17

**6.** Each paper clip is $\frac{7}{8}$ of an inch long and costs $0.03. Exactly enough paper clips are laid end to end to have a total length of 56 inches. What is the total cost of these paper clips?

Ⓐ $0.49     Ⓒ $1.47

Ⓑ $0.64     Ⓓ $1.92

**7.** Which expression simplifies to 5?

Ⓐ $\frac{27}{3} - 14$

Ⓑ $\frac{27}{3} + 4$

Ⓒ $\frac{-27}{3} - 4$

Ⓓ $\frac{-27}{3} + 14$

**8.** What is the absolute value of $-36$?

Ⓐ $-36$

Ⓑ 0

Ⓒ 6

Ⓓ 36

**9.** Which number can you add to 13 to get a sum of 0?

Ⓐ $-26$     Ⓒ 0

Ⓑ $-13$     Ⓓ 13

**10.** Joseph owes his older brother $15, so he has a balance of $-$15 with his brother. Joseph borrows some more money from his brother, bringing his balance to 5 times the previous amount. What is Joseph's new balance with his brother?

Ⓐ $-$90

Ⓑ $-$75

Ⓒ $-$10

Ⓓ $60

**11.** Which expression simplifies to a positive answer?

Ⓐ a negative number divided by a positive number

Ⓑ a positive number divided by a negative number

Ⓒ a negative number multiplied by a negative number

Ⓓ a positive number multiplied by a negative number

**12.** Which expression has the least value?

Ⓐ $(-9) \div 3 - 2$

Ⓑ $(-24) \div 6 + 2$

Ⓒ $36 \div (-4) + 7$

Ⓓ $(-32) \div 8 - 4$

## Gridded Response

Make sure that your answer makes sense before marking it as your response. Reread the question and determine whether your answer is reasonable.

**13.** A fish is 73 feet below sea level. It then swims 14 feet toward the surface. How many feet below sea level is the fish now?

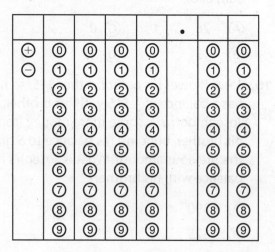

**14.** A box contained 162 matches. A bigger box contained $1\frac{4}{9}$ times as many matches. How many matches did the bigger box contain?

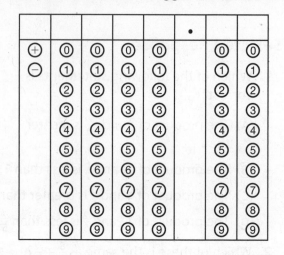

**15.** Colby and his 3 friends buy lunch. The total is $30.60. If they share the cost equally, how much, in dollars, should each person pay?

# Proportionality: Ratios and Rates

## CAREERS IN MATH

**Residential Builder** A residential builder, also called a homebuilder, specializes in the construction of residences that range from single-family custom homes to buildings that contain multiple housing units, such as apartments and condominiums. Residential builders use math in numerous ways, such as blueprint reading, measuring and scaling, using ratios and rates to calculate the amounts of different building materials needed, and estimating costs for jobs.

If you are interested in a career as a residential builder, you should study these mathematical subjects:

- Algebra
- Geometry
- Business Math
- Technical Math

Research other careers that require using ratios and rates, and measuring and scaling.

### Unit 3 Performance Task

At the end of the unit, check out how **residential builders** use math.

# Vocabulary Preview

Use the puzzle to preview key vocabulary from this unit. Unscramble the circled letters within found words to answer the riddle at the bottom of the page.

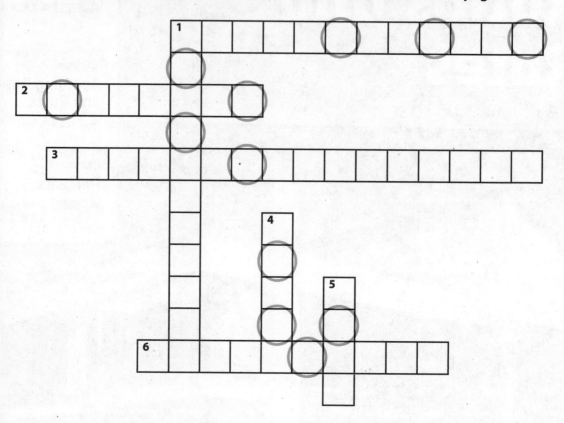

## Down

1. A rate that describes how much smaller or larger the scale drawing is than the real object. (Lesson 8-3)

4. A multiplicative comparison of two quantities expressed with the same units. (Lesson 7-1)

5. A comparison by division of two quantities that have different units. (Lesson 7-2)

## Across

1. Drawing that uses a scale to make an object proportionally smaller or larger than the real object. (Lesson 8-3)

2. A rate in which the second quantity is one unit. (Lesson 7-2)

3. A fraction that compares two equivalent measurements. (Lesson 8-4)

6. An equation that states two ratios are equivalent. (Lesson 8-3)

**Q:** Why was the draftsman excited that the raffle prize was a weighing device?

**A:** It was a ___ ___ ___ ___ ___ – ___ ___ ___ ___ ___ ___ ___!

# Representing Ratios and Rates

### ? ESSENTIAL QUESTION

How can you use ratios and rates to solve real-world problems?

### Real-World Video

Scientists studying sand structures determined that the perfect sand and water mixture is equal to 1 bucket of water for every 100 buckets of sand. This recipe can be written as the ratio $\frac{1}{100}$.

⏻ my.hrw.com

## GO DIGITAL

my.hrw.com

**my.hrw.com**

Go digital with your write-in student edition, accessible on any device.

**Math On the Spot**

Scan with your smart phone to jump directly to the online edition, video tutor, and more.

**Animated Math**

Interactively explore key concepts to see how math works.

**Personal Math Trainer**

Get immediate feedback and help as you work through practice sets.

**177**

# Are YOU Ready?

Complete these exercises to review skills you will need for this chapter.

Personal Math Trainer

Online Assessment and Intervention

my.hrw.com

## Simplify Fractions

**EXAMPLE**  Simplify $\frac{15}{24}$.

15: 1, ③, 5, 15

24: 1, 2, ③, 4, 6, 8, 12, 24

$\frac{15 \div 3}{24 \div 3} = \frac{5}{8}$

List all the factors of the numerator and denominator.

Circle the greatest common factor (GCF).

Divide the numerator and denominator by the GCF.

**Write each fraction in simplest form.**

**1.** $\frac{6}{9}$ _____

**2.** $\frac{4}{10}$ _____

**3.** $\frac{15}{20}$ _____

**4.** $\frac{20}{24}$ _____

**5.** $\frac{16}{56}$ _____

**6.** $\frac{45}{72}$ _____

**7.** $\frac{18}{60}$ _____

**8.** $\frac{32}{72}$ _____

## Write Equivalent Fractions

**EXAMPLE**  $\frac{6}{8} = \frac{6 \times 2}{8 \times 2}$

$= \frac{12}{16}$

$\frac{6}{8} = \frac{6 \div 2}{8 \div 2}$

$= \frac{3}{4}$

Multiply the numerator and denominator by the same number to find an equivalent fraction.

Divide the numerator and denominator by the same number to find an equivalent fraction.

**Write the equivalent fraction.**

**9.** $\frac{12}{15} = \frac{\boxed{\phantom{0}}}{5}$

**10.** $\frac{5}{6} = \frac{\boxed{\phantom{0}}}{30}$

**11.** $\frac{16}{24} = \frac{4}{\boxed{\phantom{0}}}$

**12.** $\frac{3}{9} = \frac{21}{\boxed{\phantom{0}}}$

**13.** $\frac{15}{40} = \frac{\boxed{\phantom{0}}}{8}$

**14.** $\frac{18}{30} = \frac{\boxed{\phantom{0}}}{10}$

**15.** $\frac{48}{64} = \frac{12}{\boxed{\phantom{0}}}$

**16.** $\frac{2}{7} = \frac{18}{\boxed{\phantom{0}}}$

# Reading Start-Up

## Visualize Vocabulary

Use the ✔ words to complete the chart. Choose the review words that describe multiplication and division.

| Understanding Multiplication and Division | | |
|---|---|---|
| **Symbol** | **Operation** | **Term for the answer** |
| × | | |
| ÷ | | |

## Understand Vocabulary

Match the term on the left to the definition on the right.

1. rate

2. ratio

3. unit rate

4. equivalent ratios

**A.** Rate in which the second quantity is one unit.

**B.** Multiplicative comparison of two quantities expressed with the same units.

**C.** Ratios that name the same comparison.

**D.** Comparison by division of two quantities that have different units.

## Active Reading

**Two-Panel Flip Chart** Create a two-panel flip chart, to help you understand the concepts in this module. Label one flap "Ratios" and the other flap "Rates." As you study each lesson, write important ideas under the appropriate flap. Include information about unit rates and any sample equations that will help you remember the concepts when you look back at your notes.

## MODULE 7

# Unpacking the TEKS

Understanding the TEKS and the vocabulary terms in the TEKS will help you know exactly what you are expected to learn in this module.

---

### TEKS 6.4.B

Apply qualitative and quantitative reasoning to solve prediction and comparison of real-world problems involving ratios and rates.

**Key Vocabulary**

**rate** *(tasa)*
A comparison by division of two quantities measured in different units.

### What It Means to You

You will solve real-world problems involving rates.

**UNPACKING EXAMPLE 6.4.B**

A group of 10 friends is in line to see a movie. The table shows how much different groups will pay in all. Predict how much the group of 10 will pay.

| Number in group | 3 | 5 | 6 | 12 |
|---|---|---|---|---|
| Amount paid ($) | 15 | 25 | 30 | 60 |

The rates are all the same.

$$\frac{3}{15} = \frac{1}{5} \qquad \frac{6}{30} = \frac{1}{5} \qquad \frac{5}{25} = \frac{1}{5} \qquad \frac{12}{60} = \frac{1}{5}$$

Find which number in the group is equal to $\frac{1}{5}$.

$$\frac{10}{?} = \frac{1}{5} \quad \rightarrow \quad \frac{10 \div 10}{50 \div 10} = \frac{1}{5} \quad \rightarrow \quad \frac{10}{50} = \frac{1}{5}$$

A group of 10 will pay $50.

---

### TEKS 6.4.D

Give examples of rates as the comparison by division of two quantities having different attributes, including rates as quotients.

**Key Vocabulary**

**unit rate** *(tasa unitaria)*
A rate in which the second quantity in the comparison is one unit.

Visit **my.hrw.com** to see all the **TEKS** unpacked.

my.hrw.com

### What It Means to You

You will solve problems involving unit rates by division.

**UNPACKING EXAMPLE 6.4.D**

A 2-liter bottle of soda costs $2.02. A 3-liter bottle of the same soda costs $2.79. Which is the better deal?

**2-liter bottle**

$$\frac{\$2.02}{2 \text{ liters}}$$

$$\frac{\$2.02 \div 2}{2 \text{ liters} \div 2}$$

$$\frac{\$1.01}{1 \text{ liter}}$$

**3-liter bottle**

$$\frac{\$2.79}{3 \text{ liters}}$$

$$\frac{\$2.79 \div 3}{3 \text{ liters} \div 3}$$

$$\frac{\$0.93}{1 \text{ liter}}$$

The 3-liter bottle is the better deal.

# 7.1 Ratios

TEKS
Proportionality—
6.4.C Give examples
of ratios as multiplicative
comparisons of two quantities
describing the same attribute.
Also 6.4.E

## ESSENTIAL QUESTION

How do you use ratios to compare two quantities?

EXPLORE ACTIVITY · Real World · TEKS 6.4.E

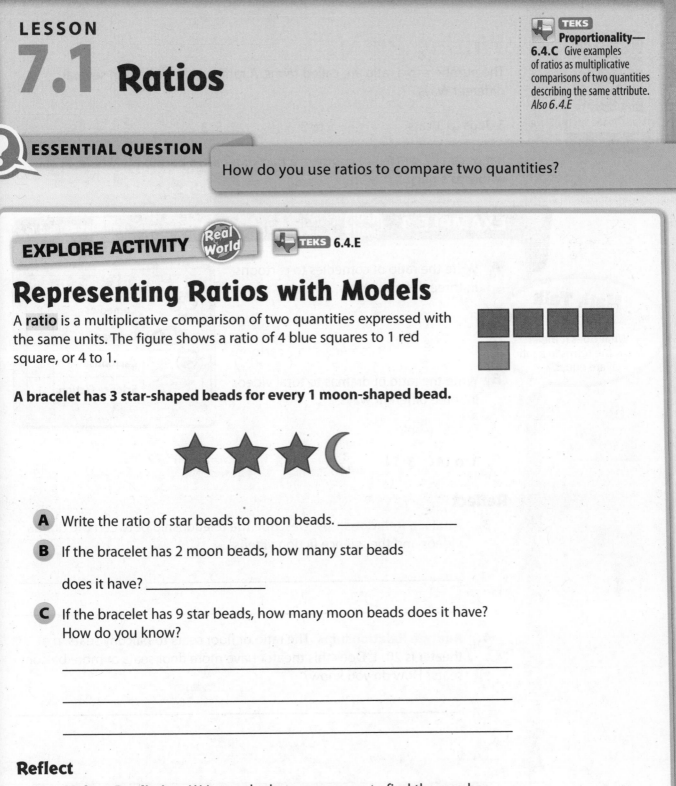

## Representing Ratios with Models

A **ratio** is a multiplicative comparison of two quantities expressed with the same units. The figure shows a ratio of 4 blue squares to 1 red square, or 4 to 1.

**A bracelet has 3 star-shaped beads for every 1 moon-shaped bead.**

**A** Write the ratio of star beads to moon beads. _____

**B** If the bracelet has 2 moon beads, how many star beads

does it have? _____

**C** If the bracelet has 9 star beads, how many moon beads does it have? How do you know?

_____

_____

_____

### Reflect

**1.** **Make a Prediction** Write a rule that you can use to find the number of star beads when you know the number of moon beads.

_____

**2.** **Make a Prediction** Write a rule that you can use to find the number of moon beads when you know the number of star beads.

_____

**Math On the Spot**

⏻ my.hrw.com

# Writing Ratios

The numbers in a ratio are called *terms*. A ratio can be written in several different ways.

5 dogs to 3 cats          5 to 3          5:3          $\frac{5}{3}$

Ratios can be written to compare a part to a part, a part to the whole, or the whole to a part.

## EXAMPLE 1  *Real World*

TEKS 6.4.C

**Math Talk**
Mathematical Processes

What does it mean when the terms in a ratio are equal?

**A** Write the ratio of comedies to cartoons in three different ways.

Part to part

8:2    $\frac{8}{2}$    8 comedies to 2 cartoons

**B** Write the ratio of dramas to total videos in three different ways.

Part to whole

3 to 14    3:14    $\frac{3}{14}$

The total number of videos is $8 + 3 + 2 + 1 = 14$.

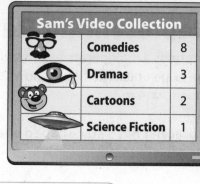

| Sam's Video Collection | |
|---|---|
| Comedies | 8 |
| Dramas | 3 |
| Cartoons | 2 |
| Science Fiction | 1 |

## Reflect

**3. Analyze Relationships** Describe the relationship between the drama videos and the science fiction videos.

_____

_____

**4. Analyze Relationships** The ratio of floor seats to balcony seats in a theater is 20:1. Does this theater have more floor seats or more balcony seats? How do you know?

_____

**Personal Math Trainer**

Online Assessment and Intervention

⏻ my.hrw.com

## YOUR TURN

**Write each ratio in three different ways.**

**5.** bagel chips to peanuts _____

**6.** total party mix to pretzels _____

**7.** cheese crackers to peanuts _____

**Party Mix**
**Makes 8 cups**
4 cups pretzels
2 cups bagel chips
1 cup cheese crackers
1 cup peanuts

# Equivalent Ratios

**Equivalent ratios** are ratios that name the same comparison. You can find equivalent ratios by using a table or by multiplying or dividing both terms of a ratio by the same number.

$$\frac{2}{7} \xrightarrow[\times 2]{\times 2} \frac{4}{14} \qquad \frac{8}{24} \xrightarrow[\div 4]{\div 4} \frac{2}{6}$$

## EXAMPLE 2  Real World

 **TEKS** 6.4.C

A punch recipe makes 5 cups of punch by mixing 3 cups of cranberry juice with 2 cups of apple juice. How much cranberry juice and apple juice do you need to make four times the original recipe?

**Method 1**  Use a table.

**STEP 1**  Make a table comparing the amount of cranberry juice and apple juice needed to make two times, three times, four times, and five times the original recipe.

> Multiply both terms of the original ratio by the same number to find an equivalent ratio.

|  | $2 \times 3$ | $3 \times 3$ | $4 \times 3$ | $5 \times 3$ |
|---|---|---|---|---|
|  | ↓ | ↓ | ↓ | ↓ |
| **Cranberry Juice** | 3 | 6 | 9 | 12 | 15 |
| **Apple Juice** | 2 | 4 | 6 | 8 | 10 |
|  | ↑ | ↑ | ↑ | ↑ |
|  | $2 \times 2$ | $3 \times 2$ | $4 \times 2$ | $5 \times 2$ |

**STEP 2**  Write the original ratio and the ratio that shows the amount of cranberry juice and apple juice needed to make four times the original recipe.

$$\frac{3}{2} = \frac{12}{8}$$

**Method 2**  Multiply both terms of the ratio by the same number.

**STEP 1**  Write the original ratio in fraction form.

$$\frac{3}{2}$$

**STEP 2**  Multiply the numerator and denominator by the same number.

To make four times the original recipe, multiply by 4.

$$\frac{3}{2} \xrightarrow[\times 4]{\times 4} \frac{12}{8}$$

To make four times the original recipe, you will need 12 cups of cranberry juice and 8 cups of apple juice.

My Notes

 **Math Talk**
**Mathematical Processes**

The ratio of apple juice to grape juice in a recipe is 8 cups to 10 cups. How can you find the amount of each juice needed if the recipe is cut in half?

**YOUR TURN**

**Find three ratios equivalent to the given ratio.**

**8.** $\frac{8}{10}$ _____

**9.** $\frac{5}{2}$ _____

# Guided Practice

**The number of dogs compared to the number of cats owned by the residents of an apartment complex is represented by the model shown.**
(Explore Activity)

**1.** Write a ratio that compares the number of dogs to

the number of cats. _____

**2.** If there are 15 cats in the apartment complex, how many dogs are there?

15 ÷ _____ = _____ dogs

**3.** How many cats are there if there are 5 dogs in the apartment complex?

5 × _____ = _____ cats

**The contents of Dana's box of muffins is shown. Write each ratio in three different ways.** (Example 1)

**4.** Banana nut muffins to chocolate chip muffins _____

**5.** Bran muffins to total muffins _____

**Dana's Dozen Muffins**

6 chocolate chip

3 bran

2 banana nut

1 blueberry

**Write three equivalent ratios for the given ratio.** (Example 2)

**6.** $\frac{10}{12}$ _____

**7.** $\frac{14}{2}$ _____

**8.** $\frac{4}{7}$ _____

**? ESSENTIAL QUESTION CHECK-IN**

**9.** Use an example to describe the multiplicative relationship between two equivalent ratios.

_____

_____

# 7.1 Independent Practice

TEKS 6.4.C, 6.4.E

Personal Math Trainer

Online Assessment and Intervention

my.hrw.com

**10.** Draw a model to represent the ratio 1 to 3. Describe how to use the model to find an equivalent ratio.

_____

_____

**11.** The ratio of boys to girls on the bus is $\frac{20}{15}$. Find three ratios equivalent to

the described ratio. _____

**12.** In each bouquet of flowers, there are 4 roses and 6 white carnations. Complete the table to find how many roses and carnations there are in 4 bouquets of flowers. _____

| Roses | 4 | | | | |
|---|---|---|---|---|---|
| Carnations | 6 | | | | |

**13.** Ed is using the recipe shown to make fruit salad. He wants to use 30 diced strawberries in his fruit salad. How many bananas, apples, and pears should Ed use in his fruit salad?

_____

**Fruit Salad Recipe**
4 bananas, diced
3 apples, diced
6 pears, diced
10 strawberries, diced

**14.** A collector has 120 movie posters and 100 band posters. She wants to sell 24 movie posters but still have her poster collection maintain the same ratio of 120 : 100. If she sells 24 movie posters, how many band posters should she sell? Explain.

_____

_____

_____

**15.** Bob needs to mix 2 cups of liquid lemonade concentrate with 3.5 cups of water to make lemonade. Bob has 6 cups of lemonade concentrate. How much lemonade can he make? _____

**16. Multistep** The ratio of North American butterflies to South American butterflies at a butterfly park is 5 : 3. The ratio of South American butterflies to European butterflies is 3 : 2. There are 30 North American butterflies at the butterfly park.

**a.** How many South American butterflies are there? _____

**b.** How many European butterflies are there? _____

**17.** Sinea and Ren are going to the carnival next week. The table shows the amount that each person spent on snacks, games, and souvenirs the last time they went to the carnival.

| | Snacks | Games | Souvenirs |
|---|---|---|---|
| **Sinea** | $5 | $8 | $12 |
| **Ren** | $10 | $8 | $20 |

**a.** Sinea wants to spend money using the same ratios as on her last trip to the carnival. If she spends $26 on games, how much will she spend on souvenirs?

_____

**b.** Ren wants to spend money using the same ratios as on his last trip to the carnival. If he spends $5 on souvenirs, how much will he spend on snacks?

_____

**c.** **What If?** Suppose Sinea and Ren each spend $40 on snacks, and each person spends money using the same ratios as on their last trip. Who spends more on souvenirs? Explain.

_____

_____

_____

 **FOCUS ON HIGHER ORDER THINKING**

Work Area

**18.** **Communicate Mathematical Ideas** Explain why the ratio 2 to 5 is different from the ratio 5 to 2 if both represent the ratio of cats to dogs.

_____

_____

_____

**19.** **Analyze Relationships** How is the process of finding equivalent ratios like the process of finding equivalent fractions?

_____

_____

_____

**20.** **Explain the Error** Tina says that 6:8 is equivalent to 36:64. What did Tina do wrong?

_____

_____

_____

**TEKS**
**Proportionality—**
**6.4.D** Give examples of rates as the comparison by division of two quantities having different attributes, including rates as quotients.

**ESSENTIAL QUESTION**

How do you use rates to compare quantities?

**EXPLORE ACTIVITY** Real World **TEKS** 6.4.D

# Using Rates to Compare Prices

A **rate** is a comparison by division of two quantities that have different units.

Chris drove 107 miles in two hours. You are comparing miles and hours.

The rate is $\frac{107 \text{ miles}}{2 \text{ hours}}$.

**Shana is at the grocery store comparing two brands of juice. Brand A costs $3.84 for a 16-ounce bottle. Brand B costs $4.50 for a 25-ounce bottle.**

To compare the costs, Shana must compare prices for equal amounts of juice. How can she do this?

**Math Talk**
Mathematical Processes

Ryan drove more hours than Chris at the same rate of speed. Who drove the most miles? Explain.

**A** Complete the tables.

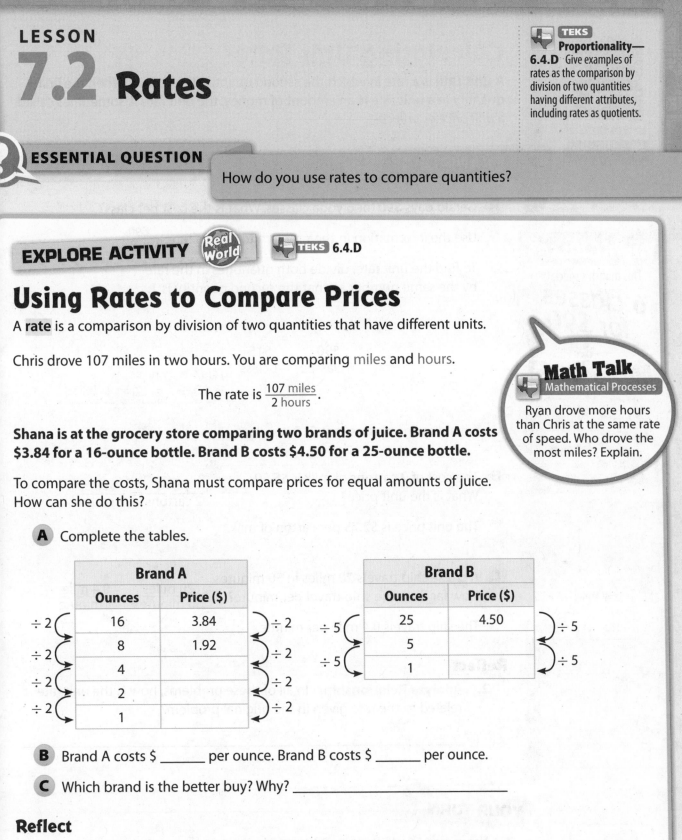

| Brand A | |
|---|---|
| Ounces | Price ($) |
| 16 | 3.84 |
| 8 | 1.92 |
| 4 | |
| 2 | |
| 1 | |

÷ 2, ÷ 2, ÷ 2, ÷ 2

| Brand B | |
|---|---|
| Ounces | Price ($) |
| 25 | 4.50 |
| 5 | |
| 1 | |

÷ 5, ÷ 5

**B** Brand A costs $ _____ per ounce. Brand B costs $ _____ per ounce.

**C** Which brand is the better buy? Why? _____

## Reflect

1. **Analyze Relationships** Describe another method to compare the costs.

_____

_____

# Calculating Unit Rates

A **unit rate** is a rate in which the second quantity is one unit. When the first quantity in a unit rate is an amount of money, the unit rate is sometimes called a *unit price* or *unit cost*.

**EXAMPLE 1** 🌐 Real World                                                    **TEKS** 6.4.D

**A** Gerald pays $90 for 6 yoga classes. What is the cost per class?

Use the information in the problem to write a rate: $\dfrac{\$90}{6 \text{ classes}}$

To find the unit rate, divide both quantities in the rate by the same number so that the second quantity is 1:

*Yoga Classes*

This month's special:

**6 classes for $90**

$$\dfrac{\$90}{6 \text{ classes}} = \dfrac{\$15}{1 \text{ class}}$$

÷6 ... ÷6

The unit rate $\dfrac{\$15}{1 \text{ class}}$ is the same as $15 \div 1 = \$15$ per class.

Gerald's yoga classes cost $15 per class.

**B** The cost of 2 cartons of milk is $5.50. What is the unit price?

$$\dfrac{\$5.50}{2 \text{ cartons}} = \dfrac{\$2.75}{1 \text{ carton}}$$

÷2 ... ÷2

The unit price is $2.75 per carton of milk.

**C** A cruise ship travels 20 miles in 50 minutes. How far does the ship travel per minute?

The first quantity in a unit rate can be less than 1.

$$\dfrac{20 \text{ miles}}{50 \text{ minutes}} = \dfrac{0.4 \text{ mile}}{1 \text{ minute}}$$

÷50 ... ÷50

The ship travels 0.4 mile per minute.

## Reflect

**2. Analyze Relationships** In all of these problems, how is the unit rate related to the rate given in the original problem?

_____

**YOUR TURN**

**3.** There are 156 players on 13 teams. How many players are on each

team? _____ players per team

**4.** A package of 36 photographs costs $18. What is the cost per

photograph? $ _____ per photograph

**Personal Math Trainer**

Online Assessment and Intervention

🔵 my.hrw.com

# Problem Solving with Unit Rates

You can solve rate problems by using a unit rate or by using equivalent rates.

**EXAMPLE 2** 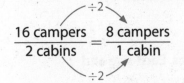       TEKS 6.4.D

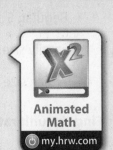

**At a summer camp, the campers are divided into groups. Each group has 16 campers and 2 cabins. How many cabins are needed for 112 campers?**

**Method 1**   Find the unit rate. How many campers per cabin?

$$\frac{16 \text{ campers}}{2 \text{ cabins}} = \frac{8 \text{ campers}}{1 \text{ cabin}}$$
÷2      Divide to find the unit rate.

There are 8 campers per cabin.

$$\frac{112 \text{ campers}}{8 \text{ campers per cabin}} = 14 \text{ cabins}$$
Divide to find the number of cabins.

**Method 2**   Use equivalent rates.

$$\frac{16 \text{ campers}}{2 \text{ cabins}} = \frac{112 \text{ campers}}{14 \text{ cabins}}$$
×7

The camp needs 14 cabins.

## Reflect

5. **What If?** Suppose each group has 12 campers and 3 canoes. Find the unit rate of campers to canoes.

_____

6. Petra jogs 3 miles in 27 minutes. At this rate, how long would it take her to jog 5 miles?

_____

_____

7. When Jerry drives 100 miles on the highway, his car uses 4 gallons of gasoline. How much gasoline would his car use if he drives 275 miles on the highway?

_____

_____

**The sizes and prices of three brands of laundry detergent are shown in the table. Use the table for 1 and 2.** (Explore Activity)

**1.** What is the unit price for each detergent?

Brand A: $ _____ per ounce

Brand B: $ _____ per ounce

Brand C: $ _____ per ounce

| Brand | Size (oz) | Price ($) |
|-------|-----------|-----------|
| A | 32 | 4.80 |
| B | 48 | 5.76 |
| C | 128 | 17.92 |

**2.** Which detergent is the best buy? _____

**Mason's favorite brand of peanut butter is available in two sizes. Each size and its price are shown in the table. Use the table for 3 and 4.** (Explore Activity)

**3.** What is the unit rate for each size of peanut butter?

Regular: $ _____ per ounce

Family size: $ _____ per ounce

| | Size (oz) | Price ($) |
|-------|-----------|-----------|
| Regular | 16 | 3.36 |
| Family Size | 40 | 7.60 |

**4.** Which size is the better buy? _____

**Find the unit rate.** (Example 1)

**5.** Lisa walked 48 blocks in 3 hours.

_____ blocks per hour

**6.** Gordon types 1,800 words in 25 minutes.

_____ words per minute

**Solve.** (Example 2)

**7.** A particular frozen yogurt has 75 calories in 2 ounces. How many calories are in 8 ounces of the yogurt?

_____

**8.** The cost of 10 oranges is $1.00. What is the cost of 5 dozen oranges?

_____

**9.** On Tuesday, Donovan earned $11 for 2 hours of babysitting. On Saturday, he babysat for the same family and earned $38.50. How many hours did he babysit on Saturday?

_____

**? ESSENTIAL QUESTION CHECK-IN**

**10.** How can you use a rate to compare the costs of two boxes of cereal that are different sizes?

_____

_____

## 7.2 Independent Practice

TEKS 6.4.D

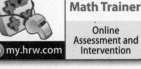

Personal
Math Trainer

Online
Assessment and
Intervention
my.hrw.com

**11.** Abby can buy an 8-pound bag of dog food for $7.40 or a 4-pound bag of the same dog food for $5.38. Which is the better buy?

_____

**12.** A bakery offers a sale price of $3.50 for 4 muffins. What is the price per dozen?

_____

**Taryn and Alastair both mow lawns. Each charges a flat fee to mow a lawn. The table shows the number of lawns mowed in the past week, the time spent mowing lawns, and the money earned.**

|  | Number of Lawns Mowed | Time Spent Mowing Lawns (in hours) | Money Earned |
|---|---|---|---|
| **Taryn** | 9 | 7.5 | $112.50 |
| **Alastair** | 7 | 5 | $122.50 |

**13.** How much does Taryn charge to mow a lawn? _____

**14.** How much does Alastair charge to mow a lawn? _____

**15.** Who earns more per hour, Taryn or Alastair? _____

**16. What If?** If Taryn and Alastair want to earn an additional $735 each, how many additional hours will each spend mowing lawns? Explain.

_____

_____

_____

**17. Multistep** Tomas makes balloon sculptures at a circus. In 180 minutes, he uses 252 balloons to make 36 identical balloon sculptures.

**a.** How many minutes does it take to make 1 balloon sculpture?

_____

**b.** How many balloons are used in one balloon sculpture?

_____

**c.** What is Tomas's unit rate for balloons used per minute?

_____

**18.** Quan and Krystal earned the same number of points playing the same video game. Quan played for 45 minutes and Krystal played for 30 minutes. Whose rate of points earned per minute was higher? Explain.

_____

_____

**Mrs. Jacobsen is a music teacher. She wants to order toy instruments online to give as prizes to her students. The table below shows the prices for various order sizes.**

|  | 25 items | 50 items | 80 items |
|---|---|---|---|
| **Whistles** | $21.25 | $36.00 | $60.00 |
| **Kazoos** | $10.00 | $18.50 | $27.20 |

**19.** What is the highest unit price per kazoo? _____

**20.** **Persevere in Problem Solving** If Mrs. Jacobsen wants to buy the item with the lowest unit price, what item should she order and how many of that item should she order? _____

 **FOCUS ON HIGHER ORDER THINKING**

Work Area

**21.** **Draw Conclusions** There are 2.54 centimeters in 1 inch. How many centimeters are there in 1 foot? in 1 yard? Explain your reasoning.

_____

_____

_____

**22.** **Critique Reasoning** A 2-pound box of spaghetti costs $2.50. Philip says that the unit cost is $\frac{2}{2.50} = \$0.80$ per pound. Explain his error.

_____

_____

_____

**23.** **Look for a Pattern** A grocery store sells three different quantities of sugar. A 1-pound bag costs $1.10, a 2-pound bag costs $1.98, and a 3-pound bag costs $2.85. Describe how the unit cost changes as the quantity of sugar increases.

_____

_____

_____

_____

# LESSON 7.3 Using Ratios and Rates to Solve Problems

**TEKS** Proportionality— 6.4.B Apply qualitative and quantitative reasoning to solve prediction and comparison of real-world problems involving ratios and rates.

## ESSENTIAL QUESTION

How can you use ratios and rates to make comparisons and predictions?

---

**EXPLORE ACTIVITY 1** Real World **TEKS** 6.4.B

# Using Tables to Compare Ratios

Anna's recipe for lemonade calls for 2 cups of lemonade concentrate and 3 cups of water.

**A** In Anna's recipe, the ratio of lemonade concentrate to water is _____.
Use equivalent ratios to complete the table.

> **Math Talk**
> Mathematical Processes
>
> What would happen to the taste of Anna's lemonade if she used more cups of lemonade concentrate to make the same amount of lemonade?

|  | | 2 · 2 | 2 · ☐ | 2 · ☐ |
| --- | --- | --- | --- | --- |
| **Lemonade Concentrate (c)** | 2 | 4 | | |
| **Water (c)** | 3 | | 9 | 15 |
|  | | 3 · 2 | 3 · 3 | 3 · 5 |

Bailey's recipe calls for 3 cups of lemonade concentrate and 5 cups of water.

**B** In Bailey's recipe, the ratio of lemonade concentrate to water is _____.
Use equivalent ratios to complete the table.

|  | | 3 · 3 | 3 · 4 | 3 · ☐ |
| --- | --- | --- | --- | --- |
| **Lemonade Concentrate (c)** | 3 | 9 | 12 | |
| **Water (c)** | 5 | | | 25 |
|  | | 5 · 3 | 5 · ☐ | 5 · ☐ |

**C** Find two columns, one in each table, in which the amount of water is the same. Circle these two columns.

**D** Whose recipe makes stronger lemonade? How do you know?

_____

_____

**E** Compare the ratios: $\frac{10}{15}$ ◯ $\frac{9}{15}$   $\frac{2}{3}$ ◯ $\frac{3}{5}$

## Reflect

**1.** **Explain the Error** Marisol makes the following claim: "Bailey's lemonade is stronger because it has more lemonade concentrate. Bailey's lemonade has 3 cups of lemonade concentrate, and Anna's lemonade has only 2 cups of lemonade concentrate." Explain why Marisol is incorrect.

_____

_____

**Math On the Spot**
my.hrw.com

# Comparing Ratios

You can use equivalent ratios to solve real-world problems.

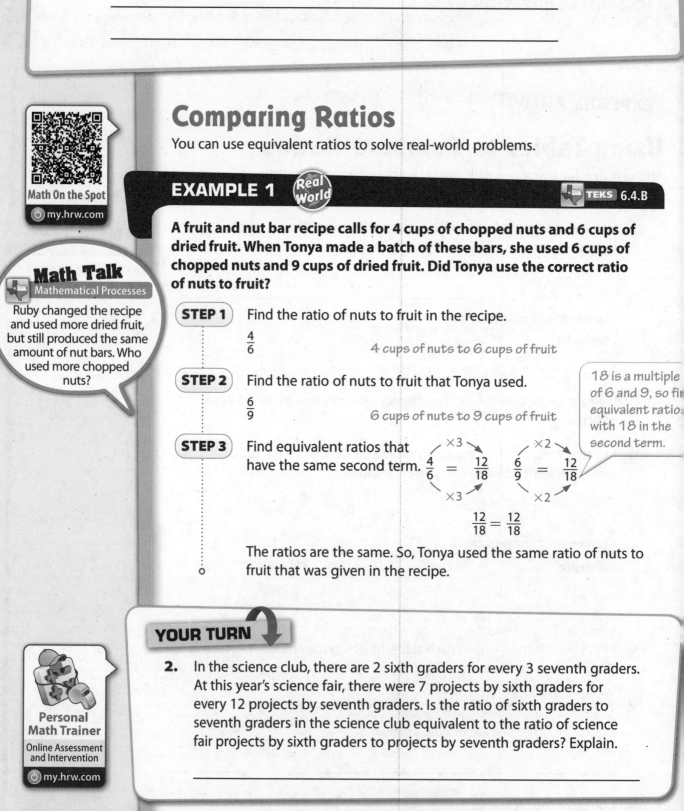

## EXAMPLE 1  *Real World*

TEKS 6.4.B

A fruit and nut bar recipe calls for 4 cups of chopped nuts and 6 cups of dried fruit. When Tonya made a batch of these bars, she used 6 cups of chopped nuts and 9 cups of dried fruit. Did Tonya use the correct ratio of nuts to fruit?

**STEP 1** Find the ratio of nuts to fruit in the recipe.

$\frac{4}{6}$          *4 cups of nuts to 6 cups of fruit*

**STEP 2** Find the ratio of nuts to fruit that Tonya used.

$\frac{6}{9}$          *6 cups of nuts to 9 cups of fruit*

18 is a multiple of 6 and 9, so fi[nd] equivalent ratio[s] with 18 in the second term.

**STEP 3** Find equivalent ratios that have the same second term.

$\frac{4}{6} = \frac{12}{18}$  (×3)     $\frac{6}{9} = \frac{12}{18}$  (×2)

$$\frac{12}{18} = \frac{12}{18}$$

The ratios are the same. So, Tonya used the same ratio of nuts to fruit that was given in the recipe.

**Math Talk**
Mathematical Processes

Ruby changed the recipe and used more dried fruit, but still produced the same amount of nut bars. Who used more chopped nuts?

## YOUR TURN

**2.** In the science club, there are 2 sixth graders for every 3 seventh graders. At this year's science fair, there were 7 projects by sixth graders for every 12 projects by seventh graders. Is the ratio of sixth graders to seventh graders in the science club equivalent to the ratio of science fair projects by sixth graders to projects by seventh graders? Explain.

_____

**Personal Math Trainer**

Online Assessment and Intervention
my.hrw.com

# Using Rates to Make Predictions

You can represent rates on a double number line to make predictions.

**Janet drives from Clarkson to Humbolt in 2 hours. Suppose Janet drives for 10 hours. If she maintains the same driving rate, can she drive more than 600 miles? Justify your answer.**

**Clarkson**  **112 miles**  **Humbolt**

The double number line shows the number of miles Janet drives in various amounts of time.

| Miles | 0 | 112 | 224 | 336 | 448 | ☐ |
|---|---|---|---|---|---|---|
| Hours | 0 | 2 | 4 | 6 | 8 | 10 |

**A** Explain how Janet's rate for two hours is represented on the double number line.

_____

_____

**B** Describe the relationship between Janet's rate for two hours and the other rates shown on the double number line.

_____

_____

**C** Complete the number line.

**D** At this rate, can Janet drive more than 600 miles in 10 hours? Explain.

_____

**E** How would Janet's total distance change if she drove for 10 hours at an increased rate of speed?

_____

## Reflect

**3.** In fifteen minutes, Lena can finish 2 math homework problems. How many math problems can she finish in 75 minutes? Use a double number line to find the answer.

| Minutes | 0 | 15 | ☐ | ☐ | ☐ | ☐ |
|---|---|---|---|---|---|---|
| Problems | 0 | 2 | ☐ | ☐ | ☐ | ☐ |

_____

1. Celeste is making fruit baskets for her service club to take to a local hospital. The directions say to fill the boxes using 5 apples for every 6 oranges. Celeste is filling her baskets with 2 apples for every 3 oranges. (Explore Activity 1)

   **a.** Complete the tables to find equivalent ratios.

   | Apples | 5 | | |
   |---|---|---|---|
   | Oranges | 6 | | |

   | Apples | 2 | | |
   |---|---|---|---|
   | Oranges | 3 | | |

   **b.** Compare the ratios. Is Celeste using the correct ratio of apples to oranges?

   _____

   _____

2. Neha used 4 bananas and 5 oranges in her fruit salad. Daniel used 7 bananas and 9 oranges. Did Neha and Daniel use the same ratio of bananas to oranges? If not, who used the greater ratio of bananas to oranges? (Example 1)

   _____

   _____

3. Tim is a first grader and reads 28 words per minute. Assuming he maintains the same rate, use the double number line to find how many words he can read in 5 minutes. (Explore Activity 2)

   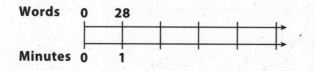

   _____

4. A cafeteria sells 30 drinks every 15 minutes. Predict how many drinks the cafeteria sells every hour. (Explore Activity 2)

   _____

**? ESSENTIAL QUESTION CHECK-IN**

5. Explain how to compare two ratios.

   _____

   _____

   _____

# 7.3 Independent Practice

**Personal Math Trainer**

Online Assessment and Intervention

🏴 **TEKS** 6.4.B

📟 my.hrw.com

**6.** Last week, Gina's art teacher mixed 9 pints of red paint with 6 pints of white paint to make pink. Gina mixed 4 pints of red paint with 3 pints of white paint to make pink.

   **a.** Did Gina use the same ratio of red paint to white paint as her teacher? Explain.

     _____

     _____

   **b.** Yesterday, Gina again mixed red and white paint and made the same amount of paint, but she used one more pint of red paint than she used last week. Predict how the new paint color will compare to the paint she mixed last week.

     _____

**7.** The Suarez family paid $15.75 for 3 movie tickets. How much would they have paid for 12 tickets? _____

**8.** A grocery store sells snacks by weight. A six-ounce bag of mixed nuts costs $3.60. Predict the cost of a two-ounce bag. _____

**9.** The Martin family's truck gets an average of 25 miles per gallon. Predict how many miles they can drive using 7 gallons of gas. _____

**10.** **Multistep** The table shows two cell phone plans that offer free minutes for each given number of paid minutes used. Pablo has Plan A and Sam has Plan B.

   **a.** What is Pablo's ratio of free to paid minutes?

     _____

|  | Cell Phone Plans | |
| --- | --- | --- |
|  | **Plan A** | **Plan B** |
| **Free minutes** | 2 | 8 |
| **Paid minutes** | 10 | 25 |

   **b.** What is Sam's ratio of free to paid minutes? _____

   **c.** Does Pablo's cell phone plan offer the same ratio of free to paid minutes as Sam's? Explain.

     _____

**11.** **Consumer Math** A store has apples on sale for $3.00 for 2 pounds.

   **a.** If an apple is approximately 5 ounces, how many apples can you buy for $9? Explain.

     _____

     _____

   **b.** If Dabney paid less per pound for the same number of apples at a different store, what can you predict about the total cost of the apples?

     _____

**12.** Sophie and Eleanor are making bouquets using daisies and tulips. Each bouquet will have the same total number of flowers. Eleanor uses fewer daisies in her bouquet than Sophie. Whose bouquet will have the greater ratio of daisies to total flowers? Explain.

_____

_____

_____

**13.** A town in east Texas received 10 inches of rain in two weeks. If it kept raining at this rate for a 31-day month, how much rain did the town receive?

_____

_____

**14.** One patterned blue fabric sells for $15.00 every two yards, and another sells for $37.50 every 5 yards. Do these fabrics have the same unit cost? Explain.

_____

**H.O.T.** FOCUS ON HIGHER ORDER THINKING

Work Area

**15. Problem Solving** Complete each ratio table.

| | 12 | 18 | 24 |
|---|---|---|---|
| 4.5 | | | 18 |

| 80.8 | 40.4 | | 10.1 |
|---|---|---|---|
| | 512 | 256 | |

**16. Represent Real-World Problems** Write a real-world problem that compares the ratios 5 to 9 and 12 to 15.

_____

_____

_____

**17. Analyze Relationships** Explain how you can be sure that all the rates you have written on a double number line are correct.

_____

_____

_____

_____

# Ready to Go On?

**Personal Math Trainer**

Online Assessment and Intervention

⏻ my.hrw.com

## 7.1 Ratios

**Use the table to find each ratio.**

**1.** white socks to brown socks _____

**2.** blue socks to nonblue socks _____

**3.** black socks to all of the socks _____

| Color of socks | white | black | blue | brown |
|---|---|---|---|---|
| Number of socks | 8 | 6 | 4 | 5 |

**4.** Find two ratios equivalent to the ratio in Exercise 1.

_____

## 7.2 Rates

**Find each rate.**

**5.** Earl runs 75 meters in 30 seconds. How many meters does Earl run per second? _____

**6.** The cost of 3 scarves is $26.25. What is the unit price? _____

## 7.3 Using Ratios and Rates to Solve Problems

**7.** Danny charges $35 for 3 hours of swimming lessons. Martin charges $24 for 2 hours of swimming lessons. Who offers a better deal? _____

**8.** There are 32 female performers in a dance recital. The ratio of men to women is 3:8. How many men are in the dance recital? _____

**? ESSENTIAL QUESTION**

**9.** How can you use ratios and rates to solve problems?

_____

_____

_____

**MODULE 7 MIXED REVIEW**

# Texas Test Prep

Personal
Math Trainer

Online
Assessment and
Intervention

my.hrw.com

## Selected Response

**1.** Which ratio is **not** equivalent to the other three?

Ⓐ $\frac{2}{3}$    Ⓒ $\frac{12}{15}$

Ⓑ $\frac{6}{9}$    Ⓓ $\frac{18}{27}$

**2.** A lifeguard received 15 hours of first aid training and 10 hours of cardiopulmonary resuscitation (CPR) training. What is the ratio of hours of CPR training to hours of first aid training?

Ⓐ 15:10    Ⓒ 10:15

Ⓑ 15:25    Ⓓ 25:15

**3.** Jerry bought 4 DVDs for $25.20. What was the unit rate?

Ⓐ $3.15    Ⓒ $6.30

Ⓑ $4.20    Ⓓ $8.40

**4.** There are 1,920 fence posts used in a 12-kilometer stretch of fence. How many fence posts are used in 1 kilometer of fence?

Ⓐ 150    Ⓒ 155

Ⓑ 160    Ⓓ 180

**5.** Sheila can ride her bicycle 6,000 meters in 15 minutes. How far can she ride her bicycle in 2 minutes?

Ⓐ 400 meters    Ⓒ 800 meters

Ⓑ 600 meters    Ⓓ 1,000 meters

**6.** Lennon has a checking account. He withdrew $130 from an ATM Tuesday. Wednesday he deposited $240. Friday he wrote a check for $56. What was the total change in Lennon's account?

Ⓐ −$74    Ⓒ $166

Ⓑ $54    Ⓓ $184

**7.** Cheyenne is making a recipe that uses 5 cups of beans and 2 cups of carrots. Which combination below uses the same ratio of beans to carrots?

Ⓐ 10 cups of beans and 3 cups of carrots

Ⓑ 10 cups of beans and 4 cups of carrots

Ⓒ 12 cups of beans and 4 cups of carrots

Ⓓ 12 cups of beans and 5 cups of carrots

**8.** $\frac{5}{8}$ of the 64 musicians in a music contest are guitarists. Some of the guitarists play jazz solos, and the rest play classical solos. The ratio of the number of guitarists playing jazz solos to the total number of guitarists in the contest is 1:4. How many guitarists play classical solos in the contest?

Ⓐ 10    Ⓒ 30

Ⓑ 20    Ⓓ 40

## Gridded Response

**9.** Mikaela is competing in a race in which she both runs and rides a bicycle. She runs 5 kilometers in 0.5 hour and rides her bicycle 20 kilometers in 0.8 hour. At this rate, how many kilometers can Mikaela ride her bicycle in one hour?

| ⊕ | ⓪ | ⓪ | ⓪ | ⓪ | • | ⓪ | ⓪ |
|---|---|---|---|---|---|---|---|
| ⊖ | ① | ① | ① | ① |   | ① | ① |
|   | ② | ② | ② | ② |   | ② | ② |
|   | ③ | ③ | ③ | ③ |   | ③ | ③ |
|   | ④ | ④ | ④ | ④ |   | ④ | ④ |
|   | ⑤ | ⑤ | ⑤ | ⑤ |   | ⑤ | ⑤ |
|   | ⑥ | ⑥ | ⑥ | ⑥ |   | ⑥ | ⑥ |
|   | ⑦ | ⑦ | ⑦ | ⑦ |   | ⑦ | ⑦ |
|   | ⑧ | ⑧ | ⑧ | ⑧ |   | ⑧ | ⑧ |
|   | ⑨ | ⑨ | ⑨ | ⑨ |   | ⑨ | ⑨ |

# Applying Ratios and Rates

**ESSENTIAL QUESTION**

How can you use ratios and rates to solve real-world problems?

**Real-World Video**

Chefs use lots of measurements when preparing meals. If a chef needs more or less of a dish, he can use ratios to scale the recipe up or down. Using proportional reasoning, the chef keeps the ratios of all ingredients constant.

⏻ my.hrw.com

**GO DIGITAL**
my.hrw.com

**my.hrw.com**

Go digital with your write-in student edition, accessible on any device.

**Math On the Spot**

Scan with your smart phone to jump directly to the online edition, video tutor, and more.

**Animated Math**

Interactively explore key concepts to see how math works.

**Personal Math Trainer**

Get immediate feedback and help as you work through practice sets.

**201**

# Are YOU Ready?

Complete these exercises to review skills you will need for this chapter.

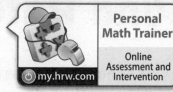

## Graph Ordered Pairs (First Quadrant)

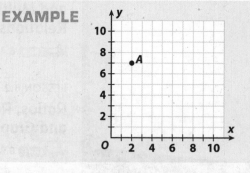

**EXAMPLE**

To graph A(2, 7), start at the origin.
Move 2 units right.
Then move 7 units up.
Graph point A(2, 7).

**Graph each point on the coordinate grid above.**

1. $B(9, 6)$
2. $C(0, 2)$
3. $D(6, 10)$
4. $E(3, 4)$

## Write Equivalent Fractions

**EXAMPLE**   $\frac{14}{21} = \frac{14 \times 2}{21 \times 2} = \frac{28}{42}$   Multiply the numerator and denominator by the same number to find an equivalent fraction.

$\frac{14}{21} = \frac{14 \div 7}{21 \div 7} = \frac{2}{3}$   **Divide** the numerator and denominator by the same number to find an equivalent fraction.

**Write the equivalent fraction.**

5. $\frac{6}{8} = \frac{\boxed{\phantom{0}}}{32}$
6. $\frac{4}{6} = \frac{\boxed{\phantom{0}}}{12}$
7. $\frac{1}{8} = \frac{\boxed{\phantom{0}}}{56}$
8. $\frac{9}{12} = \frac{\boxed{\phantom{0}}}{4}$

9. $\frac{5}{9} = \frac{25}{\boxed{\phantom{0}}}$
10. $\frac{5}{6} = \frac{20}{\boxed{\phantom{0}}}$
11. $\frac{36}{45} = \frac{12}{\boxed{\phantom{0}}}$
12. $\frac{20}{36} = \frac{10}{\boxed{\phantom{0}}}$

## Multiples

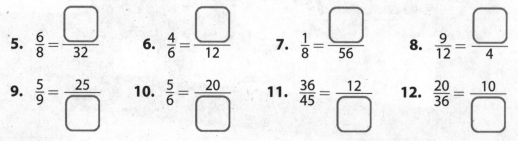

**EXAMPLE**   List the first five multiples of 4.
$4 \times 1 = 4$
$4 \times 2 = 8$
$4 \times 3 = 12$                          Multiply 4 by the numbers 1, 2,
$4 \times 4 = 16$                          3, 4, and 5.
$4 \times 5 = 20$

**List the first five multiples of each number.**

13. 3 _____
14. 7 _____
15. 8 _____

# Reading Start-Up

## Visualize Vocabulary

**Use the ✔ words to complete the graphic.**

**Comparing Unit Rates**

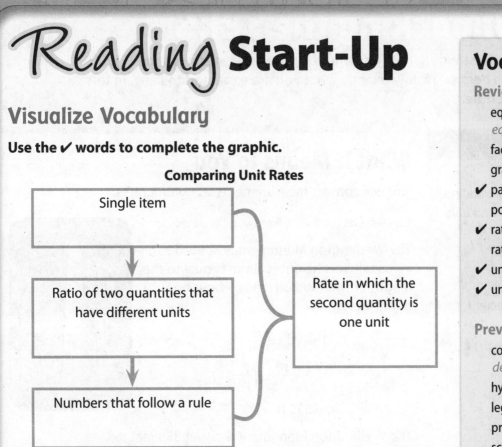

| Single item |
| Ratio of two quantities that have different units |
| Numbers that follow a rule |
| Rate in which the second quantity is one unit |

## Understand Vocabulary

**Complete the sentences using the preview words.**

1. A _____ is a rate that compares two equivalent measurements.

2. The two sides that form the right angle of a right triangle are called _____. The side opposite the right angle in a right triangle is called the _____.

### Vocabulary

**Review Words**

equivalent ratios *(razones equivalentes)*

factor *(factor)*

graph *(gráfica)*

✔ pattern *(patrón)*

point *(punto)*

✔ rate *(tasa)*

ratio *(razón)*

✔ unit *(unidad)*

✔ unit rate *(tasa unitaria)*

**Preview Words**

conversion factor *(factor de conversión)*

hypotenuse *(hipotenusa)*

legs *(catetos)*

proportion *(proporción)*

scale drawing *(dibujo a escala)*

scale factor *(factor de escala)*

## Active Reading

**Tri-Fold** Before beginning the module, create a tri-fold to help you learn the concepts and vocabulary in this module. Fold the paper into three sections. Label one column "Rates and Ratios," the second column "Proportions," and the third column "Converting Measurements." Complete the tri-fold with important vocabulary, examples, and notes as you read the module.

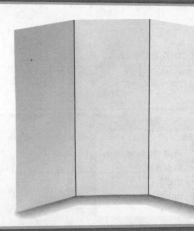

# Unpacking the TEKS

Understanding the TEKS and the vocabulary terms in the TEKS will help you know exactly what you are expected to learn in this module.

---

**TEKS 6.4.H**

Convert units within a measurement system, including the use of proportions and unit rates.

**Key Vocabulary**

**unit rate** (*tasa unitaria*)
A rate in which the second quantity in the comparison is one unit.

## What It Means to You

You will convert measurements using unit rates.

**UNPACKING EXAMPLE 6.4.H**

The Washington Monument is about 185 yards tall. This height is almost equal to the length of two football fields. About how many feet is this?

$$185 \text{ yd} \cdot \frac{3 \text{ ft}}{1 \text{ yd}}$$

$$= \frac{185 \text{ yd}}{1} \cdot \frac{3 \text{ ft}}{1 \text{ yd}}$$

$$= 555 \text{ ft}$$

The Washington Monument is about 555 feet tall.

---

**TEKS 6.5.A**

Represent mathematical and real-world problems involving ratios and rates using scale factors, tables, graphs and proportions.

**Key Vocabulary**

**ratio** (*razón*)
A comparison of two quantities by division.

**rate** (*tasa*)
A ratio that compares two quantities measured in different units.

## What It Means to You

You will use ratios and rates to solve real-world problems such as those involving proportions.

**UNPACKING EXAMPLE 6.5.A**

The distance from Austin to Dallas is about 200 miles. How far apart will these cities appear on a map with the scale of $\frac{1 \text{ in.}}{50 \text{ mi}}$ ?

$$\frac{?}{200} = \frac{1}{50}$$

$$? = 4 \text{ inches}$$

---

Visit **my.hrw.com** to see all the **TEKS** unpacked.

my.hrw.com

# Comparing Additive and Multiplicative Relationships

**TEKS**
Proportionality—
**6.4.A** Compare two rules verbally, numerically, graphically, and symbolically in the form of $y = ax$ or $y = x + a$ in order to differentiate between additive and multiplicative relationships.

## ? ESSENTIAL QUESTION

How do you represent, describe, and compare additive and multiplicative relationships?

---

**EXPLORE ACTIVITY** Real World **TEKS** 6.4.A

## Discovering Additive and Multiplicative Relationships

**A** Every state has two U.S. senators. The number of electoral votes a state has is equal to the total number of U.S. senators and U.S. representatives.

The number of electoral votes is _____ the number of representatives.

Complete the table.

| Representatives | 1 | 2 | 5 | 25 | 41 |
|---|---|---|---|---|---|
| Electoral votes | 3 | 4 | | | |

Describe the rule: The number of electoral votes is equal to

the number of representatives | **plus / times** | _____.

**B** Frannie orders three DVDs per month from her DVD club.

Complete the table.

| Months | 1 | 2 | 4 | 13 | 22 |
|---|---|---|---|---|---|
| DVDs ordered | 3 | 6 | | | |

Describe the rule: The number of DVDs ordered is equal to

the number of months | **plus / times** | _____.

## Reflect

1. **Look for a Pattern** What operation did you use to complete the tables in **A** and **B**?

_____

# Graphing Additive and Multiplicative Relationships

To find the number of electoral votes in part A of the Explore, add 2 to the number of representatives. We call this an *additive relationship*.

To find the number of DVDs Frannie has ordered after a given number of months, multiply the number of months by 3. We call this a *multiplicative relationship*.

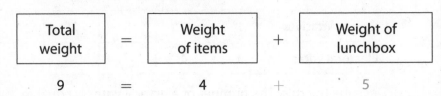

## EXAMPLE 1

TEKS 6.4.A

**A** **Jolene is packing her lunch for school. The empty lunch box weighs five ounces. Graph the relationship between the weight of the items in Jolene's lunch and the total weight of the packed lunchbox.**

**STEP 1** Make a table relating the weight of the items to the total weight.

> The total weight is equal to the weight of the items plus the weight of the lunchbox. The relationship is additive.

| Weight of items (oz) | 1 | 2 | 3 | 4 | 5 |
|---|---|---|---|---|---|
| Total weight (oz) | 6 | 7 | 8 | 9 | 10 |

To find the total weight, add the weight of the items and the weight of the lunchbox.

| Total weight | = | Weight of items | + | Weight of lunchbox |
|---|---|---|---|---|
| 9 | = | 4 | + | 5 |

**STEP 2** List the ordered pairs from the table.

The ordered pairs are (1, 6), (2, 7), (3, 8), (4, 9), and (5, 10).

**STEP 3** Graph the ordered pairs on a coordinate plane.

> To plot (1,6), go right 1 unit from the origin and then up 6 units.

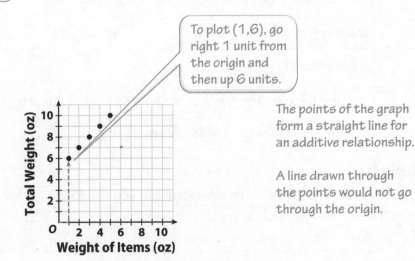

The points of the graph form a straight line for an additive relationship.

A line drawn through the points would not go through the origin.

**B** Oskar sells bracelets for two dollars each and donates the money he collects to a charity. Graph the relationship between the number of bracelets sold and the total donation.

$2.00 Donation

**STEP 1** Complete the table.

| Bracelets sold | 1 | 2 | 3 | 4 | 5 |
|---|---|---|---|---|---|
| Total donation ($) | 2 | 4 | 6 | 8 | 10 |

To find the total donation, multiply the number of bracelets sold by the donation per bracelet.

| Total donation | = | Bracelets sold | × | Donation per bracelet |
|---|---|---|---|---|
| 10 | = | 5 | × | 2 |

> His donation is equal to the number of bracelets sold times the donation for each bracelet. The relationship is multiplicative.

**STEP 2** List the ordered pairs from the table.

The ordered pairs are (1, 2), (2, 4), (3, 6), (4, 8), and (5, 10).

**STEP 3** Graph the ordered pairs on a coordinate plane.

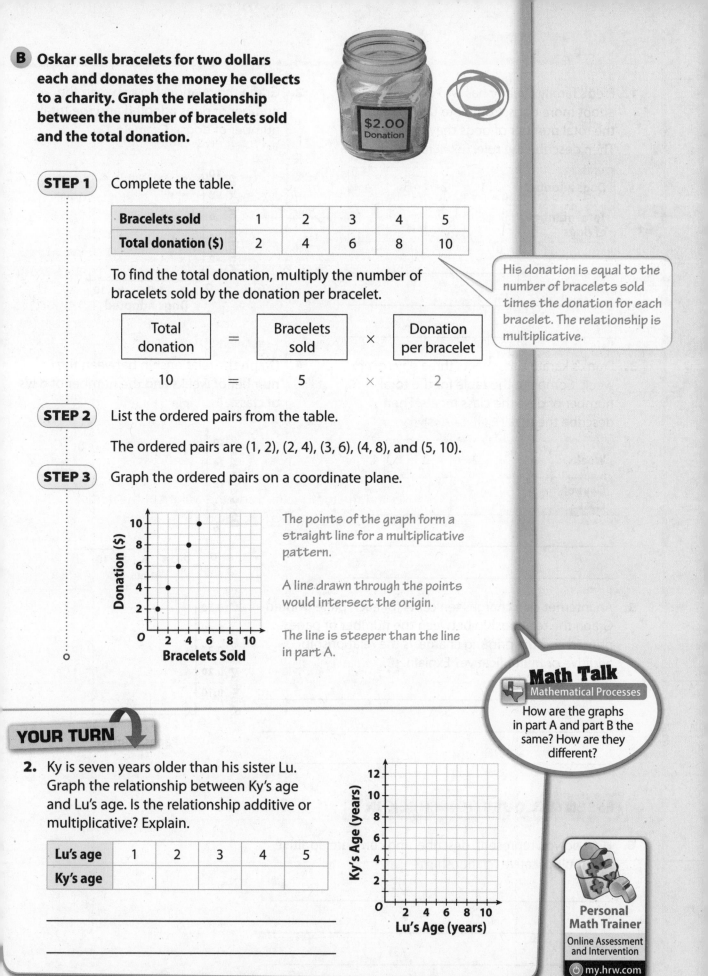

The points of the graph form a straight line for a multiplicative pattern.

A line drawn through the points would intersect the origin.

The line is steeper than the line in part A.

**Math Talk**
Mathematical Processes

How are the graphs in part A and part B the same? How are they different?

**YOUR TURN**

2. Ky is seven years older than his sister Lu. Graph the relationship between Ky's age and Lu's age. Is the relationship additive or multiplicative? Explain.

| Lu's age | 1 | 2 | 3 | 4 | 5 |
|---|---|---|---|---|---|
| Ky's age | | | | | |

_____

_____

**Personal Math Trainer**

Online Assessment and Intervention

⊙ my.hrw.com

**1.** Fred's family already has two dogs. They adopt more dogs. Complete the table for the total number of dogs they will have. Then describe the rule. (Explore Activity)

| Dogs adopted | 1 | 2 | 3 | 4 |
|---|---|---|---|---|
| Total number of dogs | | | | |

_____

_____

_____

**2.** Graph the relationship between the number of dogs adopted and the total number of dogs. (Example 1)

**3.** Frank's karate class meets three days every week. Complete the table for the total number of days the class meets. Then describe the rule. (Explore Activity)

| Weeks | 1 | 2 | 3 | 4 |
|---|---|---|---|---|
| Days of class | | | | |

_____

_____

**4.** Graph the relationship between the number of weeks and the number of days of class. (Example 1)

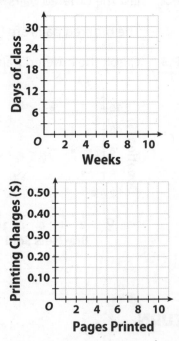

**5.** An internet café charges ten cents for each page printed. Graph the relationship between the number of pages printed and the printing charge. Is the relationship additive or multiplicative? Explain. (Example 1)

_____

_____

_____

## ESSENTIAL QUESTION CHECK-IN

**6.** How do you represent, describe, and compare additive and multiplicative relationships?

_____

_____

_____

Name _____  Class _____  Date _____

# 8.1 Independent Practice

Personal
Math Trainer

Online
Assessment and
Intervention

my.hrw.com

**The tables give the price of a kayak rental from two different companies.**

| Raging River Kayaks | | | | |
|---|---|---|---|---|
| Hours | 1 | 3 | 6 | 8 |
| Cost ($) | 9 | 27 | 54 | 72 |

| Paddlers | | | | |
|---|---|---|---|---|
| Hours | 2 | 4 | 5 | 10 |
| Cost ($) | 42 | 44 | 45 | 50 |

**7.** Is the relationship shown in each table multiplicative or additive? Explain.

_____

_____

_____

_____

**8.** Yvonne wants to rent a kayak for 7 hours. How much would this cost at each company? Which one should she choose?

_____

_____

_____

**9.** After how many hours is the cost for both kayak rental companies the same? Explain how you found your answer.

_____

_____

_____

_____

**The graph represents the distance traveled by a car and the number of hours it takes.**

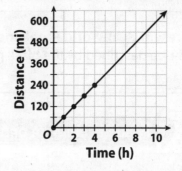

**10. Persevere in Problem Solving** Based on the graph, was the car traveling at a constant speed? At what speed was the car traveling?

_____

_____

**11. Make a Prediction** If the pattern shown in the graph continues, how far will the car have traveled after 6 hours? Explain how you found your answer.

_____

_____

_____

_____

**12. What If?** If the car had been traveling at 40 miles per hour, how would the graph be different?

_____

_____

_____

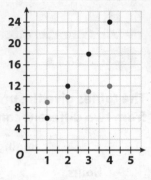

**13.** Which set of points represents an additive relationship? Which set of points represents a multiplicative relationship?

_____

**14.** **Represent Real-World Problems** What is a real-life relationship that might be described by the red points?

_____

**15.** **Represent Real-World Problems** What is a real-life relationship that might be described by the black points?

_____

 **FOCUS ON HIGHER ORDER THINKING**

Work Area

**16.** **Explain the Error** An elevator leaves the ground floor and rises three feet per second. Lili makes the table shown to analyze the relationship. What error did she make?

| Time (s) | 1 | 2 | 3 | 4 |
|---|---|---|---|---|
| Distance (ft) | 4 | 5 | 6 | 7 |

_____

_____

**17.** **Analyze Relationships** Complete each table. Show an additive relationship in the first table and a multiplicative relationship in the second table.

| A | 1 | 2 | 3 |
|---|---|---|---|
| B | | | |

| A | 1 | 2 | 3 |
|---|---|---|---|
| B | 16 | 32 | |

Use two columns of each table. Which table shows equivalent ratios? Name two ratios shown in the table that are equivalent.

_____

**18.** **Represent Real-World Problems** Describe a real-world situation that represents an additive relationship and one that represents a multiplicative relationship.

_____

_____

_____

_____

# LESSON 8.2 Ratios, Rates, Tables, and Graphs

**TEKS** Proportionality—
6.5.A Represent mathematical and real-world problems involving ratios and rates using ... tables, graphs, ...

## ESSENTIAL QUESTION

How can you represent real-world problems involving ratios and rates with tables and graphs?

**EXPLORE ACTIVITY 1** Real World  **TEKS** 6.5.A

# Finding Ratios from Tables

Students in Mr. Webster's science classes are doing an experiment that requires 250 milliliters of distilled water for every 5 milliliters of solvent. The table shows the amount of distilled water needed for various amounts of solvent.

| Solvent (mL) | 2 | 3 | 3.5 | | 5 |
|---|---|---|---|---|---|
| Distilled water (mL) | 100 | | | 200 | 250 |

**A** Use the numbers in the first column of the table to write a ratio of distilled water to solvent. _____

**B** How much distilled water is used for 1 milliliter of solvent? _____

Use your answer to write another ratio of distilled water to solvent.

_____

**C** The ratios in **A** and **B** are **equivalent/not equivalent.**

**D** How can you use your answer to **B** to find the amount of distilled water to add to a given amount of solvent?

_____

_____

**Math Talk**
Mathematical Processes

Is the relationship between the amount of solvent and the amount of distilled water additive or multiplicative? Explain.

**E** Complete the table. What are the equivalent ratios shown in the table?

$$\frac{100}{2} = \frac{\boxed{\phantom{0}}}{3} = \frac{\boxed{\phantom{0}}}{3.5} = \frac{200}{\boxed{\phantom{0}}} = \frac{250}{5}$$

## Reflect

1. **Look for a Pattern** When the amount of solvent increases

   by 1 milliliter, the amount of distilled water increases by _____

   milliliters. So 6 milliliters of solvent requires _____ milliliters of distilled water.

# Graphing with Ratios

**A** Copy the table from Explore Activity 1 that shows the amounts of solvent and distilled water.

| Solvent (mL) | 2 | 3 | 3.5 | | 5 |
|---|---|---|---|---|---|
| Distilled water (mL) | 100 | | | 200 | 250 |

**B** Write the information in the table as ordered pairs. Use the amount of solvent as the *x*-coordinates and the amount of distilled water as the *y*-coordinates.

(2, _____) (3, _____), (3.5, _____), (_____, 200), (5, 250)

Graph the ordered pairs and connect the points.

Describe your graph. _____

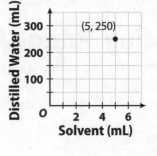

**C** For each ordered pair that you graphed, write the ratio of the *y*-coordinate to the *x*-coordinate. _____

**D** The ratio of distilled water to solvent is $\dfrac{\boxed{\phantom{00}}}{1}$. How are the ratios in **C** related to this ratio? _____

**E** The point (2.5, 125) is on the graph but not in the table. The ratio of the *y*-coordinate to the *x*-coordinate is _____. How is this ratio related to the ratios in **C** and **D**? _____

2.5 milliliters of solvent requires _____ milliliters of distilled water.

**F** **Conjecture** What do you think is true for every point on the graph?

_____

_____

_____

## Reflect

**2.** **Communicate Mathematical Ideas** How can you use the graph to find the amount of distilled water to use for 4.5 milliliters of solvent?

_____

_____

_____

# Representing Rates with Tables and Graphs

You can use tables and graphs to represent real-world problems involving equivalent rates.

## EXAMPLE 1 Real World

TEKS 6.5.A

The Webster family is taking an express train to Washington, D.C. The train travels at a constant speed and makes the trip in 2 hours.

**A** Make a table to show the distance the train travels in various amounts of time.

**STEP 1** Write a ratio of distance to time to find the rate.

$$\frac{distance}{time} = \frac{120 \text{ miles}}{2 \text{ hours}} = \frac{60 \text{ miles}}{1 \text{ hour}} = 60 \text{ miles per hour}$$

**STEP 2** Use the unit rate to make a table.

| Time (h) | 2 | 3 | 3.5 | 4 | 5 |
|---|---|---|---|---|---|
| Distance (mi) | 120 | 180 | 210 | 240 | 300 |

**B** Graph the information from the table.

**STEP 1** Write ordered pairs. Use Time as the x-coordinates and Distance as the y-coordinates.

(2, 120), (3, 180), (3.5, 210), (4, 240), (5, 300)

**STEP 2** Graph the ordered pairs and connect the points.

## YOUR TURN

3. A shower uses 12 gallons of water in 3 minutes. Complete the table and graph.

| Time (min) | 2 | 3 | 3.5 | | 6.5 |
|---|---|---|---|---|---|
| Water used (gal) | | | 20 | | |

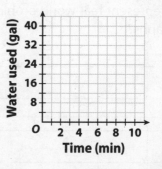

**1.** Sulfur trioxide molecules all have the same ratio of oxygen atoms to sulfur atoms. A number of molecules of sulfur dioxide have 18 oxygen atoms and 6 sulfur atoms. Complete the table. (Explore Activity 1)

| Sulfur atoms | 6 | 9 | 21 | |
|---|---|---|---|---|
| Oxygen atoms | | | | 81 |

What are the equivalent ratios shown in the table?

_____

**2.** Graph the relationship between sulfur atoms and oxygen atoms. (Explore Activity 2)

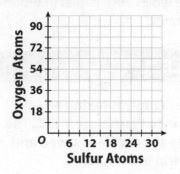

**3.** Stickers are made with the same ratio of width to length. A sticker 2 inches wide has a length of 4 inches. Complete the table. (Explore Activity 1)

| Width (in.) | 2 | 4 | 7 | |
|---|---|---|---|---|
| Length (in.) | | | | 16 |

What are the equivalent ratios shown in the table?

_____

**4.** Graph the relationship between the width and the length of the stickers. (Explore Activity 2)

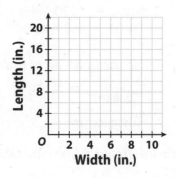

**5.** Five boxes of candles contain a total of 60 candles. Each box holds the same number of candles. Complete the table and graph the relationship. (Example 1)

| Boxes | 5 | 8 | |
|---|---|---|---|
| Candles | | | 120 |

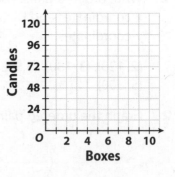

**? ESSENTIAL QUESTION CHECK-IN**

**6.** How do you represent real-world problems involving ratios and rates with tables and graphs?

_____

_____

_____

# 8.2 Independent Practice

TEKS 6.5.A

Personal Math Trainer

Online Assessment and Intervention

my.hrw.com

The table shows information about the number of sweatshirts sold and the money collected at a fundraiser for school athletic programs. For Exercises 7–12, use the table.

| Sweatshirts sold | 3 | 5 | 8 | | 12 |
|---|---|---|---|---|---|
| Money collected ($) | 60 | | | 180 | |

7. Find the rate of money collected per sweatshirt sold. Show your work.

_____

_____

8. Use the unit rate to complete the table.

9. Explain how to graph information from the table.

_____

_____

_____

_____

10. Write the information in the table as ordered pairs. Graph the relationship from the table.

_____

11. **What If?** How much money would be collected if 24 sweatshirts were sold? Show your work.

_____

_____

_____

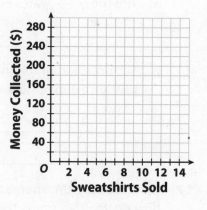

12. **Analyze Relationships** Does the point (5.5, 110) make sense in this context? Explain.

_____

_____

_____

**13. Communicate Mathematical Ideas** The table shows the distance Randy drove on one day of her vacation. Find the distance Randy would have gone if she had driven for one more hour at the same rate. Explain how you solved the problem.

| Time (h) | 1 | 2 | 3 | 4 | 5 |
|---|---|---|---|---|---|
| Distance (mi) | 55 | 110 | 165 | 220 | 275 |

_____

_____

**Use the graph for Exercises 14–15.**

**14. Analyze Relationships** Does the relationship show a ratio or a rate? Explain.

_____

**15. Represent Real-World Problems** What is a real-life relationship that might be described by the graph?

_____

_____

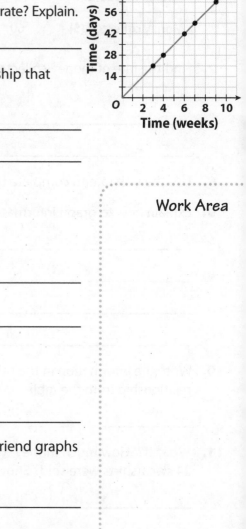

**H.O.T.** FOCUS ON HIGHER ORDER THINKING

Work Area

**16. Make a Conjecture** Complete the table. Then find the rates $\frac{distance}{time}$ and $\frac{time}{distance}$.

| Time (min) | 1 | 2 | 5 | |
|---|---|---|---|---|
| Distance (m) | | | 25 | 100 |

$\frac{distance}{time} =$ _____

$\frac{time}{distance} =$ _____

**a.** Are the $\frac{time}{distance}$ rates equivalent? Explain.

_____

**b.** Suppose you graph the points (time, distance) and your friend graphs (distance, time). How will your graphs be different?

_____

_____

**17. Communicate Mathematical Ideas** To graph a rate or ratio from a table, how do you determine the scales to use on each axis?

_____

_____

_____

_____

# Solving Problems with Proportions

TEKS
**Proportionality—**
**6.5.A** Represent mathematical and real-world problems involving ratios and rates using . . . proportions.

**? ESSENTIAL QUESTION**

How can you solve problems with proportions?

## Using Equivalent Ratios to Solve Proportions

A **proportion** is a statement that two ratios or rates are equivalent.

$\frac{1}{3}$ and $\frac{2}{6}$ are equivalent ratios.     $\frac{1}{3} = \frac{2}{6}$ is a proportion.

Math On the Spot
my.hrw.com

**EXAMPLE 1** Real World                    TEKS 6.5.A

Sheldon and Leonard are partners in a business. Sheldon makes $2 in profits for every $5 that Leonard makes. If Leonard makes $20 profit on the first item they sell, how much profit does Sheldon make?

**STEP 1**   Write a proportion.

Sheldon's profit is unknown.

Sheldon's profit ⟶ $\frac{\$2}{\$5} = \frac{\blacksquare}{\$20}$ ⟵ Sheldon's profit
Leonard's profit ⟶                     ⟵ Leonard's profit

**STEP 2**   Use common denominators to write equivalent ratios.

$\frac{\$2 \times 4}{\$5 \times 4} = \frac{\blacksquare}{\$20}$     *20 is a common denominator.*

$\frac{\$8}{\$20} = \frac{\blacksquare}{\$20}$     *Equivalent ratios with the same denominators have the same numerators.*

$\blacksquare = \$8$

If Leonard makes $20 profit, Sheldon makes $8 profit.

**Math Talk**
Mathematical Processes

How do you know $\frac{8}{20} = \frac{2}{5}$ is a proportion?

**YOUR TURN**

1.  The PTA is ordering pizza for their next meeting. They plan to order 2 cheese pizzas for every 3 pepperoni pizzas they order. How many cheese pizzas will they order if they order 15 pepperoni pizzas?

_____

**Personal Math Trainer**

Online Assessment and Intervention

my.hrw.com

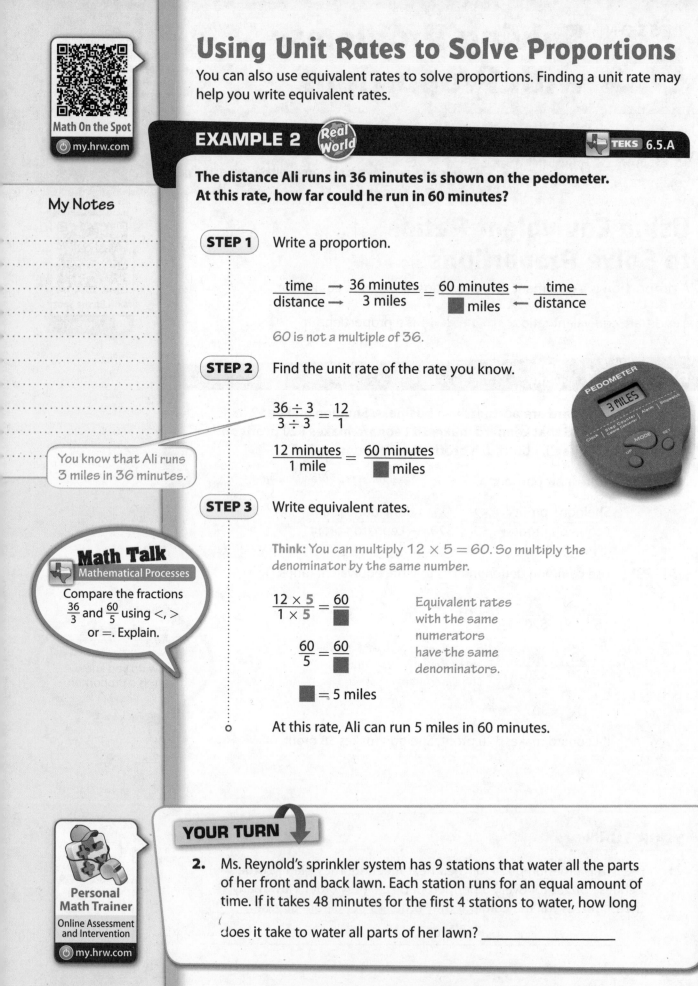
# Using Unit Rates to Solve Proportions

You can also use equivalent rates to solve proportions. Finding a unit rate may help you write equivalent rates.

**My Notes**

**EXAMPLE 2** Real World        🔲 **TEKS** 6.5.A

The distance Ali runs in 36 minutes is shown on the pedometer. At this rate, how far could he run in 60 minutes?

**STEP 1**  Write a proportion.

$$\frac{time \longrightarrow}{distance \longrightarrow} \quad \frac{36\ minutes}{3\ miles} = \frac{60\ minutes}{\blacksquare\ miles} \quad \frac{\longleftarrow time}{\longleftarrow distance}$$

60 is not a multiple of 36.

**STEP 2**  Find the unit rate of the rate you know.

$$\frac{36 \div 3}{3 \div 3} = \frac{12}{1}$$

> You know that Ali runs 3 miles in 36 minutes.

$$\frac{12\ minutes}{1\ mile} = \frac{60\ minutes}{\blacksquare\ miles}$$

PEDOMETER
3 MILES
Clock | Step Counter Calorie Counter | Alarm | Stopwatch
UP   MODE   SET

**STEP 3**  Write equivalent rates.

Think: You can multiply $12 \times 5 = 60$. So multiply the denominator by the same number.

$$\frac{12 \times 5}{1 \times 5} = \frac{60}{\blacksquare}$$    Equivalent rates with the same numerators have the same denominators.

$$\frac{60}{5} = \frac{60}{\blacksquare}$$

$$\blacksquare = 5\ miles$$

At this rate, Ali can run 5 miles in 60 minutes.

**Math Talk**
Mathematical Processes

Compare the fractions $\frac{36}{3}$ and $\frac{60}{5}$ using $<$, $>$ or $=$. Explain.

**YOUR TURN**

**Personal Math Trainer**

Online Assessment and Intervention

⏻ my.hrw.com

2. Ms. Reynold's sprinkler system has 9 stations that water all the parts of her front and back lawn. Each station runs for an equal amount of time. If it takes 48 minutes for the first 4 stations to water, how long does it take to water all parts of her lawn? _____

# Using Proportional Relationships to Find Distance on a Map

A **scale drawing** is a drawing of a real object that is proportionally smaller or larger than the real object. A **scale factor** is a ratio that describes how much smaller or larger the scale drawing is than the real object.

A map is a scale drawing. The measurements on a map are in proportion to the actual distance. If 1 inch on a map equals 2 miles actual distance, the scale factor is $\frac{2 \text{ miles}}{1 \text{ inch}}$.

## EXAMPLE 3 · Real World · TEKS 6.5.A

The distance between two schools on Lehigh Avenue is shown on the map. What is the actual distance between the schools?

**STEP 1** Write a proportion.

$$\frac{2 \text{ miles}}{1 \text{ inch}} = \frac{\blacksquare \text{ miles}}{3 \text{ inches}}$$

The scale factor is a unit rate.

**STEP 2** Use common denominators to write equivalent ratios.

$$\frac{2 \times 3}{1 \times 3} = \frac{\blacksquare}{3}$$

3 is a common denominator.

$$\frac{6 \text{ miles}}{3 \text{ inches}} = \frac{\blacksquare}{3 \text{ inches}}$$

Equivalent ratios with the same denominators have the same numerators.

$$\blacksquare = 6 \text{ miles}$$

The actual distance between the two schools is 6 miles.

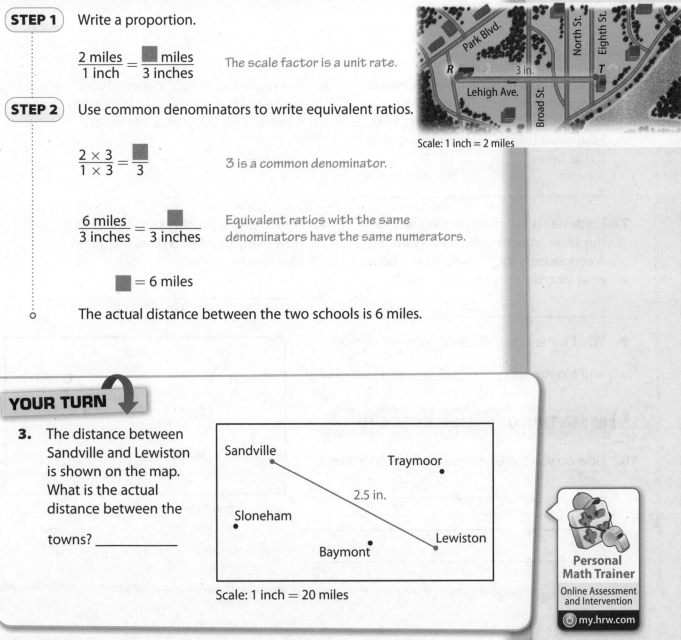

Scale: 1 inch = 2 miles

### YOUR TURN

3. The distance between Sandville and Lewiston is shown on the map. What is the actual distance between the towns? _____

Scale: 1 inch = 20 miles

**Find the unknown value in each proportion.** (Example 1)

1. $\frac{3}{5} = \frac{\blacksquare}{30}$

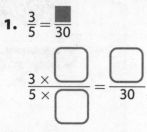

$\frac{3 \times \bigcirc}{5 \times \bigcirc} = \frac{\bigcirc}{30}$

2. $\frac{4}{10} = \frac{\blacksquare}{5}$

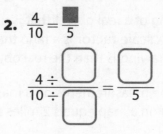

$\frac{4 \div \bigcirc}{10 \div \bigcirc} = \frac{\bigcirc}{5}$

**Solve using equivalent ratios.** (Example 1)

3. Leila and Jo are two of the partners in a business. Leila makes $3 in profits for every $4 that Jo makes. If Jo makes $60 profit on the first item they sell, how much profit does Leila make? _____

4. Hendrick wants to enlarge a photo that is 4 inches wide and 6 inches tall. The enlarged photo keeps the same ratio. How tall is the enlarged photo if it is 12 inches wide? _____

**Solve using unit rates.** (Example 2)

5. A person on a moving sidewalk travels 21 feet in 7 seconds. The moving sidewalk has a length of 180 feet. How long will it take to move from one end to the other?

_____

6. In a repeating musical pattern, there are 56 beats in 7 measures. How many measures are there after 104 beats?

_____

7. Contestants in a dance-a-thon rest for the same amount of time every hour. A couple rests for 25 minutes in 5 hours. How long did they rest in 8 hours?

_____

8. Francis gets 6 paychecks in 12 weeks. How many paychecks does she get in 52 weeks?

_____

9. What is the actual distance between Gendet and Montrose? _____ (Example 3)

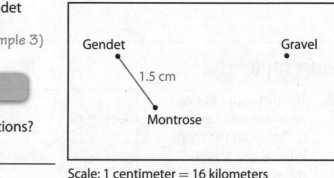

Scale: 1 centimeter = 16 kilometers

**? ESSENTIAL QUESTION CHECK-IN**

10. How do you solve problems with proportions?

_____

_____

_____

# 8.3 Independent Practice

TEKS 6.5.A

Personal
Math Trainer

Online
Assessment and
Intervention

my.hrw.com

11. On an airplane, there are two seats on the left side in each row and three seats on the right side. There are 90 seats on the right side of the plane.

   a. How many seats are on the left side of the plane? _____

   b. How many seats are there altogether? _____

12. The scale of the map is missing. The actual distance from Liberty to West Quall is 72 miles, and it is 6 inches on the map.

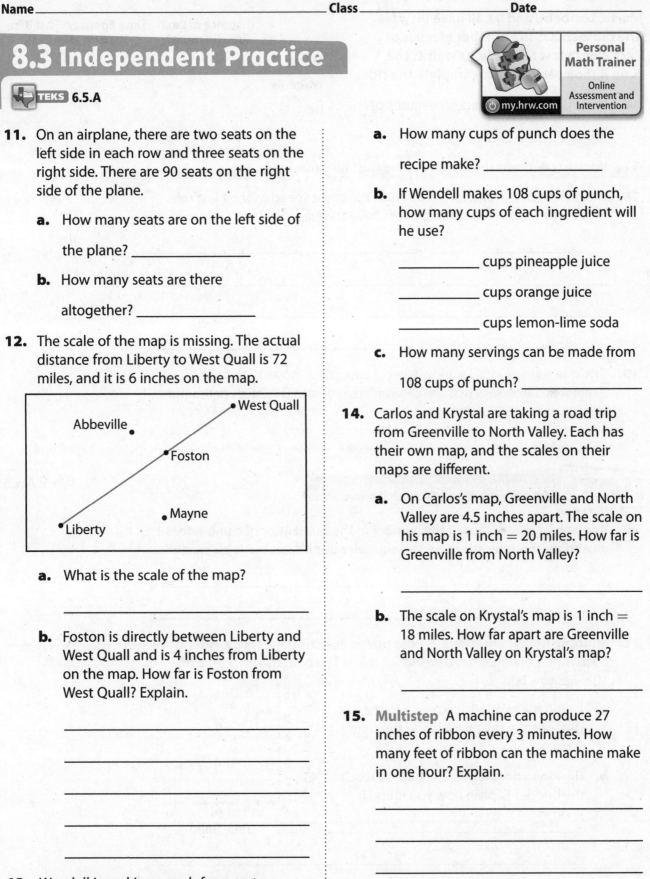

   a. What is the scale of the map?

   _____

   b. Foston is directly between Liberty and West Quall and is 4 inches from Liberty on the map. How far is Foston from West Quall? Explain.

   _____

   _____

   _____

   _____

   _____

13. Wendell is making punch for a party. The recipe he is using says to mix 4 cups pineapple juice, 8 cups orange juice, and 12 cups lemon-lime soda in order to make 18 servings of punch.

   a. How many cups of punch does the recipe make? _____

   b. If Wendell makes 108 cups of punch, how many cups of each ingredient will he use?

   _____ cups pineapple juice

   _____ cups orange juice

   _____ cups lemon-lime soda

   c. How many servings can be made from 108 cups of punch? _____

14. Carlos and Krystal are taking a road trip from Greenville to North Valley. Each has their own map, and the scales on their maps are different.

   a. On Carlos's map, Greenville and North Valley are 4.5 inches apart. The scale on his map is 1 inch = 20 miles. How far is Greenville from North Valley?

   _____

   b. The scale on Krystal's map is 1 inch = 18 miles. How far apart are Greenville and North Valley on Krystal's map?

   _____

15. **Multistep** A machine can produce 27 inches of ribbon every 3 minutes. How many feet of ribbon can the machine make in one hour? Explain.

   _____

   _____

   _____

   _____

**Marta, Loribeth, and Ira all have bicycles. The table shows the number of miles of each rider's last bike ride, as well as the time it took each rider to complete the ride.**

| | Distance of Last Ride (in miles) | Time Spent on Last Bike Ride (in minutes) |
|---|---|---|
| Marta | 8 | 80 |
| Loribeth | 6 | 42 |
| Ira | 15 | 75 |

**16.** What is Marta's unit rate, in minutes per mile? _____

**17.** Whose speed was the fastest on their last bike ride? _____

**18.** If all three riders travel for 3.5 hours at the same speed as their last ride, how many total miles will all 3 riders have traveled? Explain.

_____

_____

_____

_____

**19. Critique Reasoning** Jason watched a caterpillar move 10 feet in 2 minutes. Jason says that the caterpillar's unit rate is 0.2 feet per minute. Is Jason correct? Explain.

_____

_____

 **FOCUS ON HIGHER ORDER THINKING**

**Work Area**

**20. Analyze Relationships** If the number in the numerator of a unit rate is 1, what does this indicate about the equivalent unit rates? Give an example.

_____

_____

**21. Multiple Representations** A boat travels at a constant speed. After 20 minutes, the boat has traveled 2.5 miles. The boat travels a total of 10 miles to a bridge.

**a.** Graph the relationship between the distance the boat travels and the time it takes.

**b.** How long does it take the boat to reach the bridge? Explain how you found it.

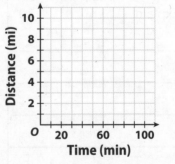

_____

_____

_____

_____

# Converting Measurements

TEKS
**Proportionality—**
**6.4.H** Convert units within a measurement system, including the use of proportions and unit rates.

**?** **ESSENTIAL QUESTION**

How do you convert units within a measurement system?

**EXPLORE ACTIVITY** Real World | TEKS 6.4.H

## Using a Model to Convert Units

The two most common systems of measurement are the customary system and the metric system. You can use a model to convert from one unit to another within the same measurement system.

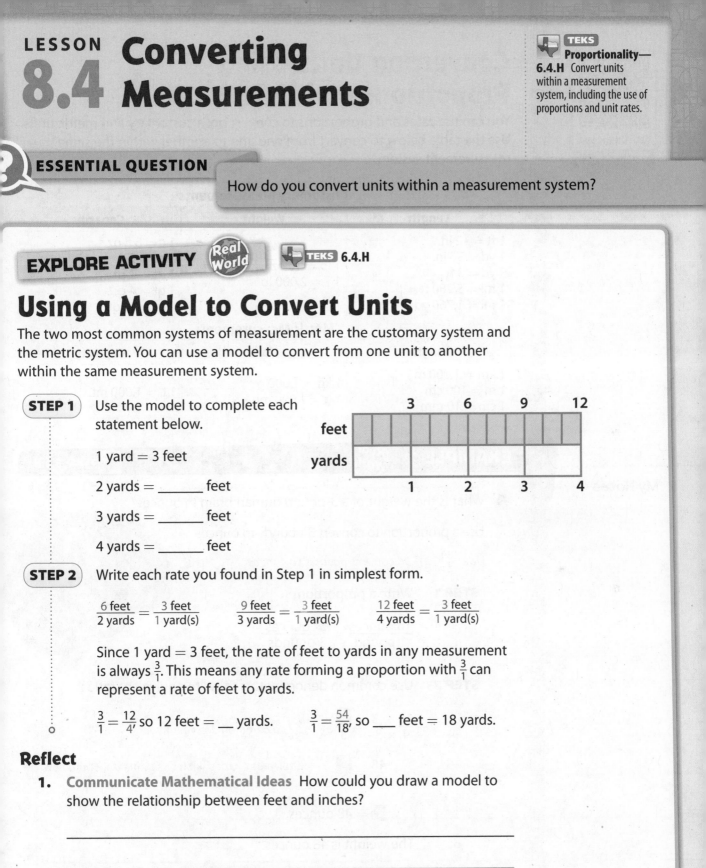

**STEP 1** Use the model to complete each statement below.

1 yard = 3 feet

2 yards = _____ feet

3 yards = _____ feet

4 yards = _____ feet

**STEP 2** Write each rate you found in Step 1 in simplest form.

$\frac{6\ feet}{2\ yards} = \frac{3\ feet}{1\ yard(s)}$     $\frac{9\ feet}{3\ yards} = \frac{3\ feet}{1\ yard(s)}$     $\frac{12\ feet}{4\ yards} = \frac{3\ feet}{1\ yard(s)}$

Since 1 yard = 3 feet, the rate of feet to yards in any measurement is always $\frac{3}{1}$. This means any rate forming a proportion with $\frac{3}{1}$ can represent a rate of feet to yards.

$\frac{3}{1} = \frac{12}{4}$, so 12 feet = __ yards.     $\frac{3}{1} = \frac{54}{18}$, so ___ feet = 18 yards.

### Reflect

1. **Communicate Mathematical Ideas** How could you draw a model to show the relationship between feet and inches?

_____

_____

_____

_____

# Converting Units Using Proportions and Unit Rates

You can use rates and proportions to convert both customary and metric units. Use the table below to convert from one unit to another within the same measurement system.

| Customary Measurements | | |
|---|---|---|
| **Length** | **Weight** | **Capacity** |
| 1 ft = 12 in.<br>1 yd = 36 in.<br>1 yd = 3 ft<br>1 mi = 5,280 ft<br>1 mi = 1,760 yd | 1 lb = 16 oz<br>1 T = 2,000 lb | 1 c = 8 fl oz<br>1 pt = 2 c<br>1 qt = 2 pt<br>1 qt = 4 c<br>1 gal = 4 qt |

| Metric Measurements | | |
|---|---|---|
| **Length** | **Mass** | **Capacity** |
| 1 km = 1,000 m<br>1 m = 100 cm<br>1 cm = 10 mm | 1 kg = 1,000 g<br>1 g = 1,000 mg | 1 L = 1,000 mL |

**EXAMPLE 1** Real World TEKS 6.4.H

**My Notes**

**A** What is the weight of a 3-pound human brain in ounces?

Use a proportion to convert 3 pounds to ounces.

Use $\frac{16\ ounces}{1\ pound}$ to convert pounds to ounces.

**STEP 1** Write a proportion.

$$\frac{16\ ounces}{1\ pound} = \frac{\blacksquare\ ounces}{3\ pounds}$$

**STEP 2** Use common denominators to write equivalent ratios.

$$\frac{16 \times 3}{1 \times 3} = \frac{\blacksquare}{3}$$    3 is a common denominator.

$$\frac{48}{3} = \frac{\blacksquare}{3}$$    Equivalent rates with the same denominators have the same numerators.

$$\blacksquare = 48\ ounces$$

The weight is 48 ounces.

**B** A moderate amount of daily sodium consumption is 2,000 milligrams. What is this mass in grams?

Use a proportion to convert 2,000 milligrams to grams.

Use $\frac{1,000\ mg}{1\ g}$ to convert milligrams to grams.

**STEP 1** Write a proportion.

$$\frac{1{,}000 \text{ mg}}{1 \text{ g}} = \frac{2{,}000 \text{ mg}}{\blacksquare \text{ g}}$$

**STEP 2** Write equivalent rates.

Think: You can multiply $1{,}000 \times 2 = 2{,}000$. So multiply the denominator by the same number.

$$\frac{1{,}000 \times 2}{1 \times 2} = \frac{2{,}000}{\blacksquare}$$

$$\frac{2{,}000}{2} = \frac{2{,}000}{\blacksquare}$$ Equivalent rates with the same numerators have the same denominators.

$$\blacksquare = 2 \text{ grams}$$

The mass is 2 grams.

**Math Talk**
Mathematical Processes
How would you convert 3 liters to milliliters?

**YOUR TURN**

**2.** The height of a doorway is 2 yards. What is the height of the doorway in inches? _____

Personal Math Trainer
Online Assessment and Intervention
my.hrw.com

# Converting Units by Using Conversion Factors

Another way to convert measurements is by using a conversion factor. A **conversion factor** is a rate comparing two equivalent measurements.

Math On the Spot
my.hrw.com

**EXAMPLE 2** Real World                                    TEKS 6.4.H

Elena wants to buy 2 gallons of milk but can only find quart containers for sale. How many quarts does she need?

> You are converting to quarts from gallons.

**STEP 1** Find the conversion factor.

Write 4 quarts = 1 gallon as a rate: $\frac{4 \text{ quarts}}{1 \text{ gallon}}$

**STEP 2** Multiply the given measurement by the conversion factor.

$$2 \text{ gallons} \cdot \frac{4 \text{ quarts}}{1 \text{ gallon}} = \blacksquare \text{ quarts}$$

$$2 \text{ gallons} \cdot \frac{4 \text{ quarts}}{1 \text{ gallon}} = 8 \text{ quarts}$$ Cancel the common unit.

Elena needs 8 quarts of milk.

**Personal Math Trainer**

Online Assessment and Intervention

⏻ my.hrw.com

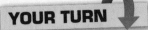

**YOUR TURN**

**3.** An oak tree is planted when it is 250 centimeters tall. What is this height in meters? _____

## Guided Practice

**Use the model below to complete each statement.** (Explore Activity 1)

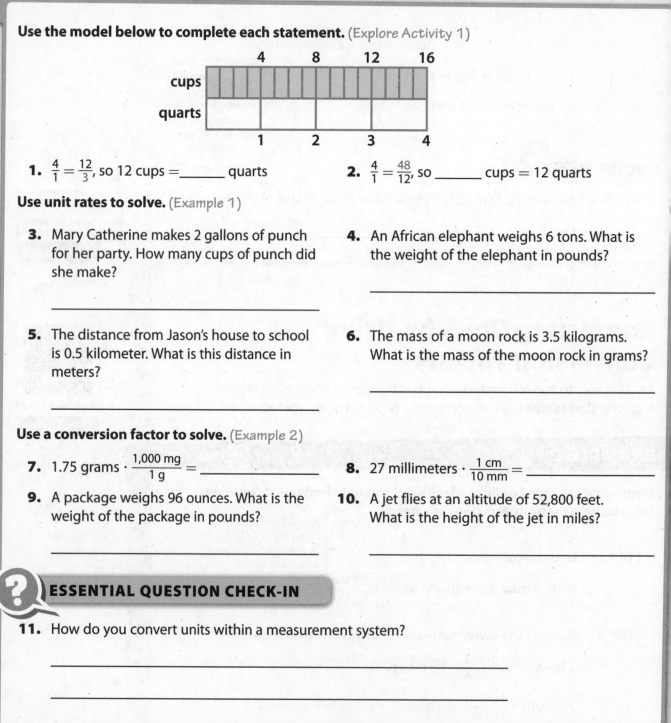

**1.** $\frac{4}{1} = \frac{12}{3}$, so 12 cups = _____ quarts

**2.** $\frac{4}{1} = \frac{48}{12}$, so _____ cups = 12 quarts

**Use unit rates to solve.** (Example 1)

**3.** Mary Catherine makes 2 gallons of punch for her party. How many cups of punch did she make?

_____

**4.** An African elephant weighs 6 tons. What is the weight of the elephant in pounds?

_____

**5.** The distance from Jason's house to school is 0.5 kilometer. What is this distance in meters?

_____

**6.** The mass of a moon rock is 3.5 kilograms. What is the mass of the moon rock in grams?

_____

**Use a conversion factor to solve.** (Example 2)

**7.** 1.75 grams · $\frac{1,000 \text{ mg}}{1 \text{ g}}$ = _____

**8.** 27 millimeters · $\frac{1 \text{ cm}}{10 \text{ mm}}$ = _____

**9.** A package weighs 96 ounces. What is the weight of the package in pounds?

_____

**10.** A jet flies at an altitude of 52,800 feet. What is the height of the jet in miles?

_____

**? ESSENTIAL QUESTION CHECK-IN**

**11.** How do you convert units within a measurement system?

_____

_____

# 8.4 Independent Practice

TEKS 6.4.H

Personal
Math Trainer

my.hrw.com — Online Assessment and Intervention

**12.** What is a conversion factor that you can use to convert gallons to pints? How did you find it?

_____

**13.** Three friends each have some ribbon. Carol has 42 inches of ribbon, Tino has 2.5 feet of ribbon, and Baxter has 1.5 yards of ribbon. Express the total length of ribbon the three friends have in inches, feet and yards.

_____ inches = _____ feet = _____ yards

**14.** Suzanna wants to measure a board, but she doesn't have a ruler to measure with. However, she does have several copies of a book that she knows is 17 centimeters tall.

**a.** Suzanna lays the books end to end and finds that the board is the same length as 21 books. How many centimeters long is the board?

_____

**b.** Suzanna needs a board that is at least 3.5 meters long. Is the board long enough? Explain.

_____

_____

**Sheldon needs to buy 8 gallons of ice cream for a family reunion. The table shows the prices for different sizes of two brands of ice cream.**

|  | Price of small size | Price of large size |
|---|---|---|
| **Cold Farms** | $2.50 for 1 pint | $4.50 for 1 quart |
| **Sweet Dreams** | $4.25 for 1 quart | $9.50 for 1 gallon |

**15.** Which size container of Cold Farm ice cream is the better deal for Sheldon? Explain.

_____

_____

_____

**16.** **Multistep** Which size and brand of ice cream is the best deal?

_____

**17.** In Beijing in 2008, the Women's 3,000 meter Steeplechase became an Olympic event. What is this distance in kilometers? _____

**18.** How would you convert 5 feet 6 inches to inches? _____

_____

  **FOCUS ON HIGHER ORDER THINKING**

**19. Analyze Relationships** A Class 4 truck weighs between 14,000 and 16,000 pounds.

   **a.** What is the weight range in tons? _____

   **b.** If the weight of a Class 4 truck is increased by 2 tons, will it still be classified as a Class 4 truck? Explain.

_____

_____

**Work Area**

**20. Persevere in Problem Solving** A football field is shown at right.

   **a.** What are the dimensions of a football field in feet?

$53\frac{1}{3}$ yd

120 yd

_____

   **b.** A chalk line is placed around the perimeter of the football field. What is the length of this line in feet?

_____

   **c.** About how many laps around the perimeter of the field would equal 1 mile? Explain.

_____

_____

**21. Look for a Pattern** What is the result if you multiply a number of cups by $\frac{8 \text{ ounces}}{1 \text{ cup}}$ and then multiply the result by $\frac{1 \text{ cup}}{8 \text{ ounces}}$? Give an example.

_____

_____

**22. Make a Conjecture** 1 hour = 3,600 seconds and 1 mile = 5,280 feet. Make a conjecture about how you could convert a speed of 15 miles per hour to feet per second. Then convert.

_____

_____

_____

# Ready to Go On?

## 8.1 Comparing Additive and Multiplicative Relationships

**Complete each table and describe the rule for the relationship.**

**1.**

| Meal time | 12:00 | 12:30 | 1:00 | |
|---|---|---|---|---|
| Swim time | 12:45 | | | 2:15 |

_____

**2.**

| Sets of pens | 2 | 3 | 4 | 5 |
|---|---|---|---|---|
| Number of pens | | 9 | | 15 |

_____

## 8.2 Ratios, Rates, Tables, and Graphs

**3.** Charlie runs laps around a track. The table shows how long it takes him to run different numbers of laps. How long would it take Charlie to run 5 laps?

| Number of laps | 2 | 4 | 6 | 8 | 10 |
|---|---|---|---|---|---|
| Time (min) | 10 | 20 | 30 | 40 | 50 |

_____

## 8.3 Solving Problems with Proportions

**4.** Emily is entering a bicycle race for charity. Her mother pledges $0.40 for every 0.25 mile she bikes. If Emily bikes 15 miles, how much will her

mother donate? _____

## 8.4 Converting Measurements

**Convert each measurement.**

**5.** 18 meters = _____ centimeters        **6.** 5 pounds = _____ ounces

**7.** 6 quarts = _____ fluid ounces        **8.** 9 liters = _____ milliliters

### ? ESSENTIAL QUESTION

**9.** Write a real-world problem that could be solved using a proportion.

_____

_____

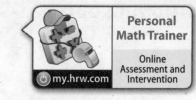
## Selected Response

**1.** The table below shows the number of babies and adults at a nursery.

| Babies | 8 | 12 | 16 | 20 |
|--------|---|----|----|----|
| Adults | 2 | 3  | 4  | 5  |

Which represents the number of babies?

Ⓐ adults × 6

Ⓑ adults × 4

Ⓒ adults + 4

Ⓓ adults + 6

**2.** The graph represents the distance Manuel walks over several hours.

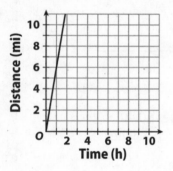

Which is an ordered pair on the line?

Ⓐ (2.5, 14)     Ⓒ (2.25, 12)

Ⓑ (1.25, 5)     Ⓓ (1.5, 9)

**3.** On a map of the city, 1 inch represents 1.5 miles. What distance on the map would represent 12 miles?

Ⓐ 6 inches

Ⓑ 8 inches

Ⓒ 12 inches

Ⓓ 18 inches

**4.** The table below shows the number of petals and leaves for different numbers of flowers.

| Petals | 5 | 10 | 15 | 20 |
|--------|---|----|----|----|
| Leaves | 2 | 4  | 6  | 8  |

How many petals are present when there are 12 leaves?

Ⓐ 25 petals

Ⓑ 30 petals

Ⓒ 35 petals

Ⓓ 36 petals

**5.** A recipe calls for 3 cups of sugar and 9 cups of water. If the recipe is reduced, how many cups of water should be used with 2 cups of sugar?

Ⓐ 3 cups

Ⓑ 4 cups

Ⓒ 6 cups

Ⓓ 8 cups

## Gridded Response

**6.** Janice bought 4 oranges for $3.40. What is the unit price?

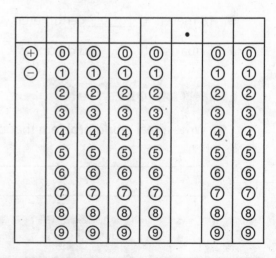

# Percents

## ESSENTIAL QUESTION

How can you use percents to solve real-world problems?

### Real-World Video

When you eat at a restaurant, your bill will include sales tax for most items. It is customary to add a tip for your server in many restaurants. Both taxes and tips are calculated as a percent of the bill.

my.hrw.com

**GO DIGITAL**

my.hrw.com

**my.hrw.com**

Go digital with your write-in student edition, accessible on any device.

**Math On the Spot**

Scan with your smart phone to jump directly to the online edition, video tutor, and more.

**Animated Math**

Interactively explore key concepts to see how math works.

**Personal Math Trainer**

Get immediate feedback and help as you work through practice sets.

Getty Images

# Are YOU Ready?

Complete these exercises to review skills you will need for this chapter.

Personal Math Trainer

Online Assessment and Intervention

my.hrw.com

## Write Equivalent Fractions

**EXAMPLE**   $\dfrac{9}{12} = \dfrac{9 \times 4}{12 \times 4} = \dfrac{36}{48}$   Multiply the numerator and denominator by the same number to find an equivalent fraction.

$\dfrac{9}{12} = \dfrac{9 \div 3}{12 \div 3} = \dfrac{3}{4}$   Divide the numerator and denominator by the same number to find an equivalent fraction.

**Write the equivalent fraction.**

1.  $\dfrac{9}{18} = \dfrac{\boxed{\phantom{0}}}{6}$

2.  $\dfrac{4}{6} = \dfrac{\boxed{\phantom{0}}}{18}$

3.  $\dfrac{25}{30} = \dfrac{5}{\boxed{\phantom{0}}}$

4.  $\dfrac{12}{15} = \dfrac{36}{\boxed{\phantom{0}}}$

5.  $\dfrac{15}{24} = \dfrac{\boxed{\phantom{0}}}{8}$

6.  $\dfrac{24}{32} = \dfrac{\boxed{\phantom{0}}}{8}$

7.  $\dfrac{50}{60} = \dfrac{10}{\boxed{\phantom{0}}}$

8.  $\dfrac{5}{9} = \dfrac{20}{\boxed{\phantom{0}}}$

## Multiply Fractions

**EXAMPLE**   $\dfrac{5}{12} \times \dfrac{3}{10} = \dfrac{\overset{1}{\cancel{5}}}{\cancel{12}_4} \times \dfrac{\overset{1}{\cancel{3}}}{\cancel{10}_2}$   Divide by the common factors.

$= \dfrac{1}{8}$   Simplify.

**Multiply. Write each product in simplest form.**

9.  $\dfrac{3}{8} \times \dfrac{4}{11} = \underline{\hspace{2cm}}$

10.  $\dfrac{8}{15} \times \dfrac{5}{6} = \underline{\hspace{2cm}}$

11.  $\dfrac{7}{12} \times \dfrac{3}{14} = \underline{\hspace{2cm}}$

12.  $\dfrac{9}{20} \times \dfrac{4}{5} = \underline{\hspace{2cm}}$

13.  $\dfrac{7}{10} \times \dfrac{20}{21} = \underline{\hspace{2cm}}$

14.  $\dfrac{8}{18} \times \dfrac{9}{20} = \underline{\hspace{2cm}}$

## Decimal Operations (Multiplication)

**EXAMPLE**   
$\begin{array}{r} 1.6 \\ \times 0.3 \\ \hline 0.48 \end{array}$
   Multiply as you would with whole numbers.
Count the total number of decimal places in the factors.
Place the decimal point that number of places in the product.

**Multiply.**

15. $20 \times 0.25$ _____

16. $0.3 \times 16.99$ _____

17. $0.2 \times 75$ _____

18. $5.5 \times 1.1$ _____

19. $11.99 \times 0.8$ _____

20. $7.25 \times 0.5$ _____

21. $4 \times 0.75$ _____

22. $0.15 \times 12.50$ _____

23. $6.5 \times 0.7$ _____

# Reading Start-Up

## Vocabulary

**Review Words**
✔ decimal (decimal)
✔ equivalent fractions (fracciones equivalentes)
denominator (denominador)
✔ fraction (fracción)
mixed number (número mixto)
numerator (numerador)
✔ ratio (razón)
✔ simplest form (mínima expresión)

**Preview Words**
equivalent decimals (decimales equivalentes)
model (modelo)
percent (porcentaje)
proportional reasoning (razonamiento proporcional)

## Visualize Vocabulary

Use the ✔ words to complete the graphic. You may put more than one word in each box.

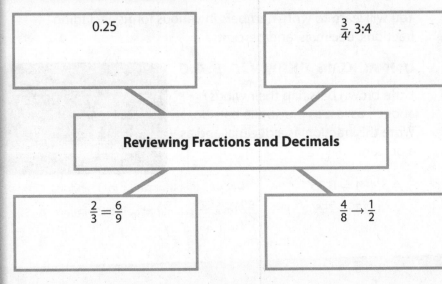

0.25

$\frac{3}{4}$, 3:4

**Reviewing Fractions and Decimals**

$\frac{2}{3} = \frac{6}{9}$

$\frac{4}{8} \rightarrow \frac{1}{2}$

## Understand Vocabulary

Match the term on the left to the correct expression on the right.

**1.** percent

**A.** A ratio that compares a number to 100.

**2.** model

**B.** Decimals that name the same amount.

**3.** equivalent decimals

**C.** Something that represents another thing.

## Active Reading

**Pyramid** Before beginning the module, create a pyramid to help you organize what you learn. Label one side "Decimals," one side "Fractions," and the other side "Percents." As you study the module, write important vocabulary and other notes on the appropriate side.

# Unpacking the TEKS

Understanding the TEKS and the vocabulary terms in the TEKS will help you know exactly what you are expected to learn in this module.

## TEKS 6.4.G

Generate equivalent forms of fractions, decimals, and percents using real-world problems including problems that involve money.

### Key Vocabulary

**equivalent expressions**
*(expresiones equivalentes)*
Expressions that have the same value.

## What It Means to You

You will learn to write numbers in various forms, including fractions, decimals, and percents.

### UNPACKING EXAMPLE 6.4.G

Little brown bats flap their wings about $\frac{3}{4}$ as fast as pipistrelle bats do. Write this fraction as a decimal and as a percent.

$\frac{3}{4} = 3 \div 4 = 0.75$     Divide the numerator by the denominator.

$0.75 = 75\%$     Move the decimal point 2 places to the right.

## TEKS 6.5.B

Solve real-world problems to find the whole given a part and the percent, to find the part given the whole and the percent, and to find the percent given the part and the whole, including the use of concrete and pictorial models.

### Key Vocabulary

**Percent** *(porcentaje)*
A ratio comparing a number to 100.

## What It Means to You

You will solve problems involving percent.

### UNPACKING EXAMPLE 6.5.B

About 67% of a person's total (100%) body weight is water. If Cameron weighs 90 pounds, about how much of his weight is water?

67% of 90

$$\frac{67}{100} \cdot 90$$

$$= \frac{67}{100} \cdot \frac{90}{1}$$

$$= 60.3$$

About 60.3 pounds of Cameron's weight is water.

Visit **my.hrw.com** to see all the **TEKS** unpacked.

my.hrw.com

# LESSON
# 9.1 Understanding Percent

**TEKS**
**Proportionality—**
**6.4.E** Represent percents with concrete models [and] fractions. *Also 6.4.F*

**ESSENTIAL QUESTION**

How can you write a ratio as a percent?

---

**EXPLORE ACTIVITY 1** *Real World* **TEKS** 6.4.E

## Using a Grid to Model Percents

A **percent** is a ratio that compares a number to 100. The symbol % is used to show a percent.

17% is equivalent to

- $\frac{17}{100}$
- 17 to 100
- 17:100

**The free-throw ratios for three basketball players are shown.**

Player 1: $\frac{17}{25}$        Player 2: $\frac{33}{50}$        Player 3: $\frac{15}{20}$

**A** Rewrite each ratio as a number compared to 100. Then shade the grid to represent the free-throw ratio.

Player 1: $\frac{17}{25} = \frac{\boxed{\phantom{00}}}{100}$        Player 2: $\frac{33}{50} = \frac{\boxed{\phantom{00}}}{100}$        Player 3: $\frac{15}{20} = \frac{\boxed{\phantom{00}}}{100}$

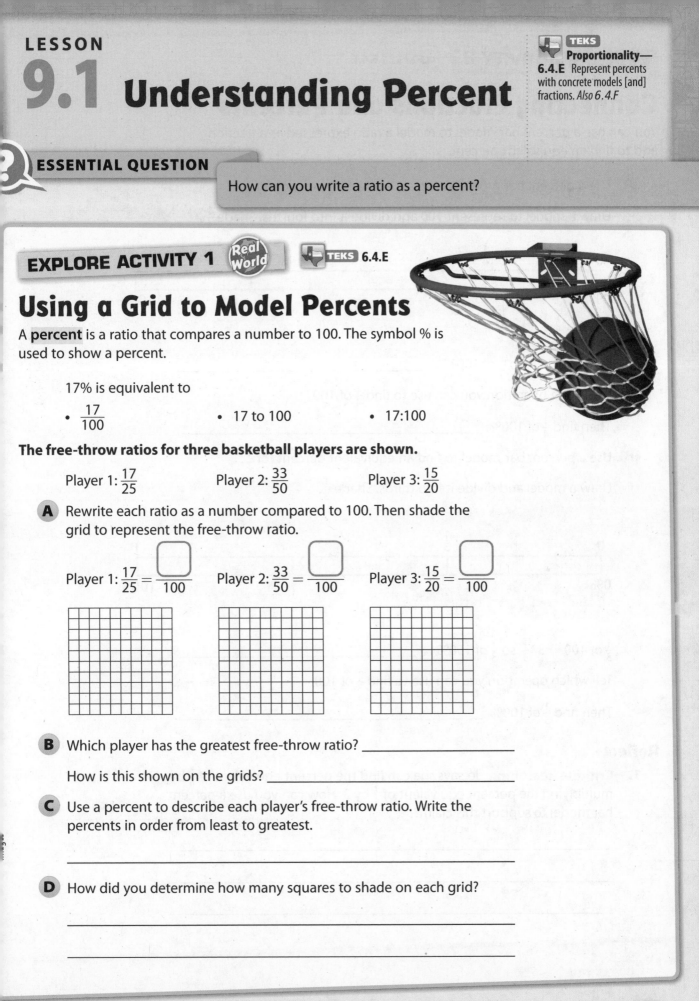

**B** Which player has the greatest free-throw ratio? _____

How is this shown on the grids? _____

**C** Use a percent to describe each player's free-throw ratio. Write the percents in order from least to greatest.

_____

**D** How did you determine how many squares to shade on each grid?

_____

_____

# Connecting Fractions and Percents

You can use a percent bar model to model a ratio expressed as a fraction and to find an equivalent percent.

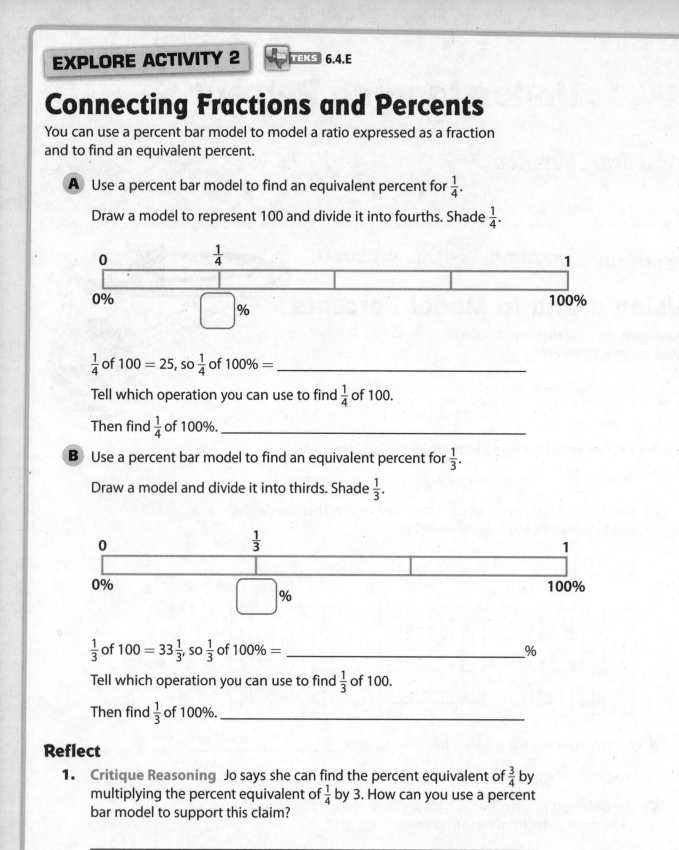

**A** Use a percent bar model to find an equivalent percent for $\frac{1}{4}$.

Draw a model to represent 100 and divide it into fourths. Shade $\frac{1}{4}$.

$\frac{1}{4}$ of 100 = 25, so $\frac{1}{4}$ of 100% = _____

Tell which operation you can use to find $\frac{1}{4}$ of 100.

Then find $\frac{1}{4}$ of 100%. _____

**B** Use a percent bar model to find an equivalent percent for $\frac{1}{3}$.

Draw a model and divide it into thirds. Shade $\frac{1}{3}$.

$\frac{1}{3}$ of 100 = $33\frac{1}{3}$, so $\frac{1}{3}$ of 100% = _____%

Tell which operation you can use to find $\frac{1}{3}$ of 100.

Then find $\frac{1}{3}$ of 100%. _____

## Reflect

1. **Critique Reasoning** Jo says she can find the percent equivalent of $\frac{3}{4}$ by multiplying the percent equivalent of $\frac{1}{4}$ by 3. How can you use a percent bar model to support this claim?

_____

_____

_____

# Using Benchmarks and Proportional Reasoning

You can use certain *benchmark* percents to write other percents and to estimate fractions.

Math On the Spot
my.hrw.com

Number line from 0 to 1 showing benchmark fractions: $\frac{1}{10}$, $\frac{1}{4}$, $\frac{1}{3}$, $\frac{1}{2}$, $\frac{2}{3}$, $\frac{3}{4}$

Number line from 0 to 100 showing benchmark percents: 0, 10%, 25%, 50%, 75%, 100%, with $33\frac{1}{3}\%$ and $66\frac{2}{3}\%$

## EXAMPLE 1 | Real World

TEKS 6.4.F

**A** Find an equivalent percent for $\frac{3}{10}$.

**STEP 1** Write $\frac{3}{10}$ as a multiple of a benchmark fraction.

$$\frac{3}{10} = 3 \cdot \frac{1}{10} \qquad \text{Think: } \frac{3}{10} = \frac{1}{10} + \frac{1}{10} + \frac{1}{10}$$

**STEP 2** Find an equivalent percent for $\frac{1}{10}$.

$$\frac{1}{10} = 10\% \qquad \text{Use the number lines to find the equivalent percent for } \frac{1}{10}.$$

**STEP 3** Multiply.

$$\frac{3}{10} = 3 \cdot \frac{1}{10} = 3 \cdot 10\% = 30\%$$

> **Math Talk**
> Mathematical Processes
>
> Explain how you could use equivalent ratios to write $\frac{3}{10}$ as a percent.

**B** 76% of the students at a middle school bring their own lunch. About what fraction of the students bring their own lunch?

**STEP 1** Note that 76% is close to the benchmark 75%.

**STEP 2** Find a fraction equivalent for 75%:

$$75\% = \frac{3}{4}$$

About $\frac{3}{4}$ of the students bring their own lunch.

## YOUR TURN

**Use a benchmark to find an equivalent percent for each fraction.**

2. $\frac{9}{10}$ _____

3. $\frac{2}{5}$ _____

4. 64% of the animals at an animal shelter are dogs. About what fraction of the animals at the shelter are dogs?

_____

## Guided Practice

1. Shade the grid to represent the ratio $\frac{9}{25}$. Then find a percent equivalent to the given ratio. (Explore Activity 1)

$$\frac{9 \times \boxed{\phantom{0}}}{25 \times \boxed{\phantom{0}}} = \frac{\boxed{\phantom{0}}}{100} = \text{_____}$$

2. Use the percent bar model to find the missing percent. (Explore Activity 2)

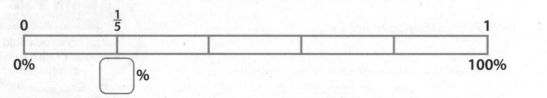

$\boxed{\phantom{0}}$ %

**Identify a benchmark you can use to find an equivalent percent for each ratio. Then find the equivalent percent.** (Example 1)

3. $\frac{6}{10}$ Benchmark: $\dfrac{1}{\boxed{\phantom{0}}}$

4. $\frac{2}{4}$ Benchmark: $\dfrac{\boxed{\phantom{0}}}{4}$

5. $\frac{4}{5}$ Benchmark: $\dfrac{\boxed{\phantom{0}}}{5}$

_____    _____    _____

6. 41% of the students at an art college want to be graphic designers. About what fraction of the students want to be graphic designers? (Example 1)

_____

### ? ESSENTIAL QUESTION CHECK-IN

7. How do you write a ratio as a percent?

_____

_____

## 9.1 Independent Practice

 TEKS 6.4.E, 6.4.F

**Personal Math Trainer**

Online Assessment and Intervention

my.hrw.com

**Shade the grid to represent the ratio. Then find the missing number.**

8. $\frac{23}{50} = \frac{\boxed{\phantom{00}}}{100}$

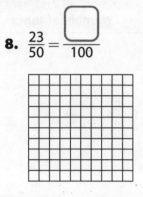

9. $\frac{11}{20} = \frac{\boxed{\phantom{00}}}{100}$

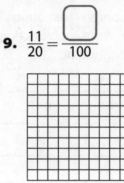

10. Mark wants to use a grid like the ones in Exercises 8 and 9 to model the percent equivalent of the fraction $\frac{2}{3}$. How many grid squares should he shade? What percent would his model show?

_____

11. The ratios of saves to the number of save opportunities are given for three relief pitchers: $\frac{9}{10}, \frac{4}{5}, \frac{17}{20}$. Write each ratio as a percent. Order the percents from least to greatest.

_____

**Circle the greater quantity.**

12. $\frac{1}{3}$ of a box of Corn Krinkles

50% of a box of Corn Krinkles

13. 30% of your minutes are used up

$\frac{1}{4}$ of your minutes are used up

14. **Multiple Representations** Explain how you could write 35% as the sum of two benchmark percents or as a multiple of a percent.

_____

15. Use the percent bar model to find the missing percent.

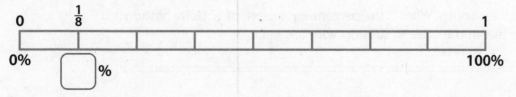

**16. Multistep** Carl buys songs and downloads them to his computer. The bar graph shows the numbers of each type of song he downloaded last year.

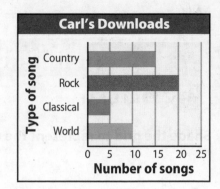

**Carl's Downloads**

a. What is the total number of songs Carl downloaded last year?

_____

b. What fraction of the songs were country? Find the fraction for each type of song. Write each fraction in simplest form and give its percent equivalent.

_____

_____

_____

## H.O.T. FOCUS ON HIGHER ORDER THINKING

**Work Area**

**17. Critique Reasoning** Marcus bought a booklet of tickets to use at the amusement park. He used 50% of the tickets on rides, $\frac{1}{3}$ of the tickets on video games, and the rest of the tickets in the batting cage. Marcus says he used 10% of the tickets in the batting cage. Do you agree? Explain.

_____

_____

_____

_____

**18. Look for a Pattern** Complete the table.

| Fraction | $\frac{1}{5}$ | $\frac{2}{5}$ | $\frac{3}{5}$ | $\frac{4}{5}$ | $\frac{5}{5}$ | $\frac{6}{5}$ |
|----------|------|------|------|------|------|------|
| Percent  | 20%  |      |      |      |      |      |

a. **Analyze Relationships** What is true when the numerator and denominator of the fraction are equal? What is true when the numerator is greater than the denominator?

_____

_____

b. **Justify Reasoning** What is the percent equivalent of $\frac{3}{2}$? Use a pattern like the one in the table to support your answer.

_____

_____

# Percents, Fractions, and Decimals

**TEKS**
**Proportionality—**
**6.4.G** Generate equivalent forms of fractions, decimals, and percents using real-world problems. *Also 6.5.C.*

## ? ESSENTIAL QUESTION

How can you write equivalent percents, fractions, and decimals?

## Writing Percents as Decimals and Fractions

You can write a percent as an equivalent fraction or as an equivalent decimal. Equivalent percents, decimals, and fractions all represent equal parts of the same whole.

**Math On the Spot**
⊙ my.hrw.com

### EXAMPLE 1 Real World

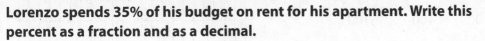
**TEKS** 6.4.G

**Lorenzo spends 35% of his budget on rent for his apartment. Write this percent as a fraction and as a decimal.**

**STEP 1** Write the percent as a fraction.

$$35\% = \frac{35}{100}$$  *Percent means per 100.*

**STEP 2** Write the fraction in simplest form.

$$\frac{35}{100} = \frac{35}{100} = \frac{7}{20}$$  ÷ 5

**STEP 3** Write the percent as a decimal.

$$35\% = \frac{35}{100}$$  *Write the fraction equivalent of 35%.*

$$= 0.35$$  *Write the decimal equivalent of $\frac{35}{100}$.*

So, 35% written as a fraction is $\frac{7}{20}$ and written as a decimal is 0.35.

**Math Talk**
**Mathematical Processes**

Explain why both the numerator and denominator in Step 2 are divided by 5.

### YOUR TURN

**Write each percent as a fraction and as a decimal.**

1. 15% _____

2. 48% _____

3. 80% _____

4. 75% _____

5. 36% _____

6. 40% _____

**Personal Math Trainer**

Online Assessment and Intervention

⊙ my.hrw.com

# Modeling Decimal, Fraction, and Percent Equivalencies

Using models can help you understand how decimals, fractions, and percents are related.

**A** Model 0.78 by shading a 10-by-10 grid.

$$0.78 = \frac{\boxed{\phantom{00}}}{100},$$

_____ out of a hundred, or _____%.

**B** Model 1.42 by shading 10-by-10 grids.

$$1.42 = \frac{\boxed{\phantom{00}}}{100} + \frac{\boxed{\phantom{00}}}{100} = \frac{\boxed{\phantom{00}}}{100} = 1\frac{\boxed{\phantom{00}}}{100}.$$

$$1.42 = 100\% + \text{_____}\% = \text{_____}\%$$

**C** Model 125% by shading 10-by-10 grids.

The model shows 100% + _____% = 125%.

125% = the decimal _____.

$$125\% = \frac{\boxed{\phantom{00}}}{100} + \frac{\boxed{\phantom{00}}}{100} = \frac{\boxed{\phantom{00}}}{100} = 1\frac{\boxed{\phantom{00}}}{100} = 1\frac{\boxed{\phantom{00}}}{\boxed{\phantom{00}}}.$$

## Reflect

7. **Multiple Representations** What decimal, fraction, and percent equivalencies are shown in each model? Explain.

   a. _____

   _____

   _____

   b. _____

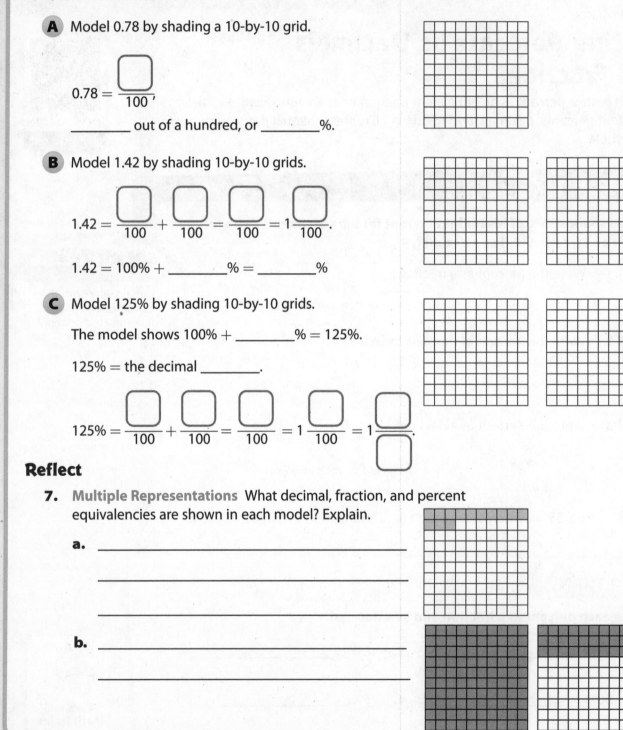

# Writing Fractions as Decimals and Percents

You can write some fractions as percents by writing an equivalent fraction with a denominator of 100. This method is useful when the fraction has a denominator that is a factor or a multiple of 100. If a fraction does not have a denominator that is a factor or multiple of 100, you can use long division.

Math On the Spot
my.hrw.com

**EXAMPLE 2** (Real World)                         TEKS 6.4.G

**A** 96 out of 200 animals treated by a veterinarian are horses. Write $\frac{96}{200}$ as a decimal and as a percent.

> Notice that the denominator is a multiple of 100.

**STEP 1** Write an equivalent fraction with a denominator of 100.

$$\frac{96}{200} = \frac{48}{100}$$   *Divide both the numerator and denominator by 2.*

**STEP 2** Write the decimal equivalent.

$$\frac{48}{100} = 0.48$$

**STEP 3** Write the percent equivalent.

$$\frac{48}{100} = 48\%$$   *Percent means per 100.*

> Notice that the denominator is not a factor or multiple of 100.

**B** $\frac{1}{8}$ of the animals treated by the veterinarian are dogs. Write $\frac{1}{8}$ as a decimal and as a percent.

**STEP 1** Use long division to divide the numerator by the denominator.

$$\frac{1}{8} = 8\overline{)1.000}$$

```
      0.125
  8)1.000
   - 8
     20
   - 16
     40
   - 40
      0
```

*Add a decimal point and zeros to the right of the numerator as needed.*

The decimal equivalent of $\frac{1}{8}$ is 0.125.

**STEP 2** Write the decimal as a percent.

$$0.125 = \frac{125}{1,000}$$   *Write the fraction equivalent of the decimal.*

$$\frac{125}{1,000} = \frac{12.5}{100}$$   *Write an equivalent fraction with a denominator of 100.*
÷ 10

$$\frac{12.5}{100} = 12.5\%$$   *Write as a percent.*

The percent equivalent of $\frac{1}{8}$ is 12.5%.

**YOUR TURN**

**Write each fraction as a decimal and as a percent.**

8. $\frac{9}{25}$ _____

9. $\frac{7}{8}$ _____

## Guided Practice

1. Helene spends 12% of her budget on transportation expenses. Write this percent as a fraction and as a decimal. (Example 1)

_____

**Model the decimal. Then write percent and fraction equivalents.**
(Explore Activity)

2. 0.53

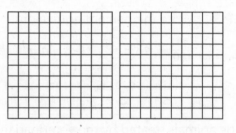

_____

3. 1.07

_____

**Write each fraction as a decimal and as a percent.** (Example 2)

4. $\frac{7}{20}$ of the packages _____

5. $\frac{3}{8}$ of a pie _____

**? ESSENTIAL QUESTION CHECK-IN**

6. How does the definition of *percent* help you write fraction and decimal equivalents?

_____

_____

_____

_____

# 9.2 Independent Practice

TEKS 6.4.G, 6.5.C

**Write each percent as a fraction and as a decimal.**

**7.** 72% full

**8.** 25% successes

**9.** 500% increase

_____

_____

_____

**10.** 5% tax

**11.** 37% profit

**12.** 165% improvement

_____

_____

_____

**Write each fraction as a decimal and as a percent.**

**13.** $\frac{5}{8}$ of an inch

**14.** $\frac{258}{300}$ of the contestants

**15.** $\frac{350}{100}$ of the revenue

_____

_____

_____

**16.** The poster shows how many of its games the football team has won so far. Express this information as a fraction, a percent, and as a decimal.

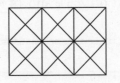

GO TEAM!

12 out of 15 wins!

**17.** Justine answered 68 questions correctly on an 80-question test. Express this amount as a fraction, percent, and decimal.

_____

_____

**Each diagram is made of smaller, identical pieces. Tell how many pieces you would shade to model the given percent.**

**18.** 75% _____

**19.** 25% _____

**20. Multiple Representations** At Brian's Bookstore, 0.3 of the shelves hold mysteries, 25% of the shelves hold travel books, and $\frac{7}{20}$ of the shelves hold children's books. Which type of book covers the most shelf space in the store? Explain how you arrived at your answer.

_____

_____

**H.O.T.** FOCUS ON HIGHER ORDER THINKING

**21. Critical Thinking** A newspaper article reports the results of an election between two candidates. The article says that Smith received 60% of the votes and that Murphy received $\frac{1}{3}$ of the votes. A reader writes in to complain that the article cannot be accurate. What reason might the reader have to say this?

_____

_____

_____

**22. Represent Real-World Problems** Evan budgets $2,000 a month to spend on living expenses for his family. Complete the table to express the portion spent on each cost as a percent, fraction, and decimal.

|          | Food: $500 | Rent: $1,200 | Transportation: $300 |
|----------|------------|--------------|----------------------|
| **Fraction** |        |              |                      |
| **Percent**  |        |              |                      |
| **Decimal**  |        |              |                      |

**23. Communicate Mathematical Ideas** Find the sum of each row in the table. Explain why these sums make sense.

_____

_____

_____

**24. Explain the Error** Your friend says that 14.5% is equivalent to the decimal 14.5. Explain why your friend is incorrect by comparing the fractional equivalents of 14.5% and 14.5.

_____

_____

_____

# Solving Percent Problems

**TEKS**
**Proportionality—**
**6.5.B** Solve real-world problems involving percent.
*Also 6.4.G*

## ESSENTIAL QUESTION

How do you use percents to solve problems?

**EXPLORE ACTIVITY** *Real World*    **TEKS** 6.5.B

# Modeling a Percent Problem

You can use a model to solve a percent problem.

**A sports store received a shipment of 400 baseball gloves. 30% were left-handed. How many left-handed gloves were in the shipment?**

**A** Use the diagram to solve this problem.

30% means 30 out of _____.

There were _____ left-handed gloves for every 100 baseball gloves.

Complete the diagram to model this situation.

**B** Describe how the diagram models the shipment of gloves.

_____

_____

_____

**C** Explain how you can use the diagram to find the total number of left-handed gloves in the shipment.

_____

_____

**D** Use a bar model to solve this problem. The bar represents 100%, or the entire shipment of 400 gloves. The bar is divided into 10 equal parts. Complete the labels along the bottom of the bar.

0%   10%   20%   30%   40%   50%   60%   70%   80%   90%   100%

0    40    80                                              400

**Reflect**

1. **Justify Reasoning** How did you determine the labels along the bottom of the bar model in Step D?

   _____

   _____

2. **Communicate Mathematical Ideas** How can you use the bar model to find the number of left-handed gloves?

   _____

**Math On the Spot**

⏻ my.hrw.com

# Finding a Percent of a Number

A percent is equivalent to the ratio of a part to a whole. To find a percent of a number, you can write a ratio to represent the percent, and find an equivalent ratio that compares the part to the whole.

> The word *of* indicates multiplication.

To find 30% of 400, you can use:

**Proportional Reasoning**

$$\frac{30}{100} = \frac{?}{400} \leftarrow \text{part}$$
$$\phantom{\frac{30}{100}} \leftarrow \text{whole}$$

$$= \frac{120}{400}$$

**Multiplication**

$$30\% \text{ of } 400 = \frac{30}{100} \text{ of } 400$$

$$= \frac{30}{100} \times 400$$

$$= 120$$

---

## EXAMPLE 1

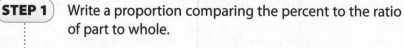

**TEKS** 6.5.B

**A** Use proportional reasoning to find 28% of 25.

**Math Talk**
*Mathematical Processes*

Could you also use the proportion $\frac{28}{100} = \frac{?}{25}$ to find 28% of 25? Explain.

**STEP 1** Write a proportion comparing the percent to the ratio of part to whole.

$$\frac{?}{25} = \frac{28}{100}$$

Notice that 25 is a factor of 100.

**STEP 2** Find the multiplication factor.

$$\begin{array}{l} \text{part} \rightarrow \\ \text{whole} \rightarrow \end{array} \frac{?}{25} = \frac{28}{100}$$

Since $25 \cdot 4 = 100$, find what number times 4 equals 28.

**STEP 3** Find the numerator.

$$\frac{7}{25} = \frac{28}{100}$$

Since $4 \cdot 7 = 28$, 28% of 25 = 7.

28% of 25 is 7.

**B** Multiply by a fraction to find 35% of 60.

**STEP 1** Write the percent as a fraction.

$$35\% \text{ of } 60 = \frac{35}{100} \text{ of } 60$$

**STEP 2** Multiply.

$$\frac{35}{100} \text{ of } 60 = \frac{35}{100} \cdot 60$$

$$= \frac{2{,}100}{100}$$

$$= 21 \quad \text{Simplify.}$$

35% of 60 is 21.

**C** Multiply by a decimal to find 5% of 180.

**STEP 1** Write the percent as a decimal.

$$5\% = \frac{5}{100} = 0.05$$

**STEP 2** Multiply.

$$180 \cdot 0.05 = 9$$

5% of 180 is 9

Animated
Math

my.hrw.com

## Reflect

3. **Analyze Relationships** In B, the percent is 35%. What is the part and what is the whole?

_____

_____

4. **Communicate Mathematical Ideas** Explain how to use proportional reasoning to find 35% of 600.

_____

_____

_____

_____

_____

**YOUR TURN**

Find the percent of each number.

5. 38% of 50 _____    6. 27% of 300 _____    7. 60% of 75 _____

Personal
Math Trainer

Online Assessment
and Intervention

my.hrw.com

# Find a Percent Given a Part and a Whole

You can use proportional reasoning to solve problems in which you need to find a percent.

**EXAMPLE 2** 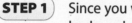 Real World  🗺 **TEKS** 6.5.B

**The school principal spent $2,000 to buy some new computer equipment. Of this money, $120 was used to buy some new keyboards. What percent of the money was spent on keyboards?**

**STEP 1**  Since you want to know the part of the money spent on keyboards, compare the part to the whole.

part → $120
whole → $2,000

**STEP 2**  Write a proportion comparing the percent to the ratio of part to whole.

part → $\frac{?}{100} = \frac{120}{2,000}$ ← part
whole →   ← whole

**STEP 3**  Find the multiplication factor.

$\frac{?}{100} = \frac{120}{2,000}$   Since $100 \cdot 20 = 2,000$, find what number times 20 equals 120.

**STEP 4**  Find the numerator.

$\frac{6}{100} = \frac{120}{2,000}$   Since $20 \cdot 6 = 120$, the percent is 6%.

The principal spent 6% of the money on keyboards.

## Reflect

8.  **Communicate Mathematical Ideas**  Write 57% as a ratio. Which number in the ratio represents the part and which number represents the whole? Explain.

_____

_____

_____

**YOUR TURN**

9.  Out of the 25 students in Mrs. Green's class, 19 have a pet. What percent of the students in Mrs. Green's class have a pet? _____

# Finding a Whole Given a Part and a Percent

You can use proportional reasoning to solve problems in which you know a part and a percent and need to find the whole.

Math On the Spot
my.hrw.com

## EXAMPLE 3 · Real World

**TEKS** 6.5.B

**Twelve of the students in the school choir like to sing solos. These 12 students make up 24% of the choir. How many students are in the choir?**

**Method 1: Use a concrete model.**

24% represents 12 students.

100 squares represent 100%.

24 squares represent 24%.

Since $\frac{12}{24} = \frac{1}{2}$, 1 square represents $\frac{1}{2}$ student.

$100 \cdot \frac{1}{2} = 50$, so 100 squares represent 50 students.

$\frac{1}{2}$ student

24% represents 12 students.

**Method 2: Use a proportion.**

part → $\frac{12}{?} = \frac{24}{100}$ ← part
whole → ← whole

Write a proportion. 12 students represent 24%.

$\frac{12}{?} = \frac{24}{100}$ ×2

Since $12 \cdot 2 = 24$, find what number times $2 = 100$.

$\frac{12}{50} = \frac{24}{100}$

Since $50 \cdot 2 = 100$, the denominator is 50.

There are 50 students in the choir.

**Math Talk**
**Mathematical Processes**

Suppose 10 more students join the choir. None of them are soloists. What percent are soloists now?

## Reflect

**10. Multiple Representations** Sixteen students in the school band play clarinet. Clarinet players make up 20% of the band. Use a bar model to find the number of students in the school band.

| 0% | 10% | 20% | 30% | 40% | 50% | 60% | 70% | 80% | 90% | 100% |
|----|-----|-----|-----|-----|-----|-----|-----|-----|-----|------|

0     16

## YOUR TURN

**11.** 6 is 30% of _____.

**12.** 15% of _____ is 75.

Personal Math Trainer

Online Assessment and Intervention

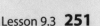

my.hrw.com

**1.** A store has 300 televisions on order, and 80% are high definition. (Explore Activity)

**a.** Use the bar model and complete the bottom of the bar.

| 0% | 10% | 20% | 30% | 40% | 50% | 60% | 70% | 80% | 90% | 100% |
|---|---|---|---|---|---|---|---|---|---|---|

0   30                                                                    300

**b.** Complete the diagram to model this situation.

```
  ┌────────┬──┐
  │   80   │  │
  └────────┴──┘
    100
        ⏟
       300
```

**c.** How many televisions on the order are high definition?

_____

**2.** Use proportional reasoning to find 65% of 200. (Example 1)

part →  $\dfrac{\boxed{\phantom{0}}}{100} = \dfrac{?}{\boxed{\phantom{0}}}$  ← part
whole →                 ← whole

65% of 200 is _____.

**3.** Use multiplication to find 5% of 180. (Example 1)

$\dfrac{5}{100}$ of $180 = \dfrac{5}{100} \boxed{\phantom{0}} 180$

$= \dfrac{\boxed{\phantom{0}}}{100} = \boxed{\phantom{0}}$

5% of 180 is _____.

**4.** Alana spent $21 of her $300 paycheck on a gift. What percent of her paycheck was spent on the gift? (Example 2)

Alana spent _____ of her paycheck on the gift.

**5.** At Pizza Pi, 9% of the pizzas made last week had extra cheese. If 27 pizzas had extra cheese, how many pizzas in all were made last week? (Example 3)

There were _____ pizzas made last week.

**?  ESSENTIAL QUESTION CHECK-IN**

**6.** How can you use proportional reasoning to solve problems involving percent?

_____

_____

_____

# 9.3 Independent Practice

**TEKS** 6.5.B

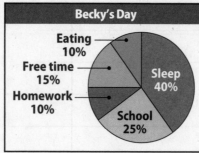

**Personal Math Trainer**

Online Assessment and Intervention

my.hrw.com

## Find the percent of each number.

**7.** 64% of 75 tiles

**8.** 20% of 70 plants

**9.** 32% of 25 pages

_____

_____

_____

**10.** 85% of 40 e-mails

**11.** 72% of 350 friends

**12.** 5% of 220 files

_____

_____

_____

## Complete each sentence.

**13.** 4 students is _____ % of 20 students.

**14.** 2 doctors is _____ % of 25 doctors.

**15.** _____ % of 50 shirts is 35 shirts.

**16.** _____ % of 200 miles is 150 miles.

**17.** 4% of _____ days is 56 days.

**18.** 60 minutes is 20% of _____ minutes.

**19.** 80% of_____ games is 32 games.

**20.** 360 kilometers is 24% of _____ kilometers.

**21.** 75% of _____ peaches is 15 peaches.

**22.** 9 stores is 3% of _____ stores.

**23.** At a shelter, 15% of the dogs are puppies. There are 60 dogs at the shelter.

How many are puppies? _____ puppies

**24.** Carl has 200 songs on his MP3 player. Of these songs, 24 are country songs. What percent of Carl's songs are country songs? _____

**25.** **Consumer Math** The sales tax in the town where Amanda lives is 7%. Amanda paid $35 in sales tax on a new stereo. What was the price of the stereo? _____

**26.** **Financial Literacy** Ashton is saving money to buy a new bike. He needs $120 but has only saved 60% so far. How much more money does Ashton need to buy the scooter? _____

**27.** **Consumer Math** Monica paid sales tax of $1.50 when she bought a new bike helmet. If the sales tax rate was 5%, how much did the store charge for the helmet before tax? _____

**28.** Use the circle graph to determine how many hours per day Becky spends on each activity.

School: _____ hours

Eating: _____ hours

Sleep: _____ hours

Homework: _____ hours

Free time: _____ hours

**Becky's Day**

Eating 10%

Free time 15%

Homework 10%

Sleep 40%

School 25%

**29. Multistep** Marc ordered a rug. He gave a deposit of 30% of the cost and will pay the rest when the rug is delivered. If the deposit was $75, how much more does Marc owe? Explain how you found your answer.

_____

_____

**30. Earth Science** Your weight on different planets is affected by gravity. An object that weighs 150 pounds on Earth weighs only 56.55 pounds on Mars. The same object weighs only 24.9 pounds on the Moon.

**a.** What percent of an object's Earth weight is its weight on Mars and on the Moon?

_____

**b.** Suppose $x$ represents an object's weight on Earth. Write two expressions: one that you can use to find the object's weight on Mars and another that you can use to write the object's weight on the Moon.

_____

**c.** The space suit Neil Armstrong wore when he stepped on the Moon for the first time weighed about 180 pounds on Earth. How much did it weigh on the Moon?

_____

**d. What If?** If you could travel to Jupiter, your weight would be 236.4% of your Earth weight. How much would Neil Armstrong's space suit weigh on Jupiter?

_____

**31. Explain the Error** Fifteen students in the band play clarinet. These 15 students make up 12% of the band. Your friend used the proportion $\frac{12}{100} = \frac{?}{15}$ to find the number of students in the band. Explain why your friend is incorrect and use the grid to find the correct answer.

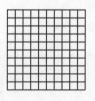

_____

_____

_____

_____

# Ready to Go On?

## 9.1 Understanding Percent

**Shade the grid and write the equivalent percent for each fraction.**

1. $\frac{19}{50}$ _____

2. $\frac{13}{20}$ _____

## 9.2 Percents, Fractions, and Decimals

**Write each number in two equivalent forms.**

3. $\frac{3}{5}$ _____

4. 62.5% _____

5. 0.24 _____

6. $\frac{31}{50}$ _____

7. Selma spent $\frac{7}{10}$ of her allowance on a new backpack. What percent of her allowance did she spend? _____

## 9.3 Solving Percent Problems

**Complete each sentence.**

8. 12 is 30% of _____.

9. 45% of 20 is _____.

10. 18 is _____ % of 30.

11. 56 is 80% of _____.

12. A pack of cinnamon-scented pencils sells for $4.00. What is the sales tax rate if the total cost of the pencils is $4.32? _____

## ? ESSENTIAL QUESTION

13. How can you solve problems involving percents?

_____

_____

_____

_____

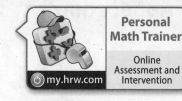
## Selected Response

**1.** What percent does this shaded grid represent?

Ⓐ 42%

Ⓑ 48%

Ⓒ 52%

Ⓓ 58%

**2.** Which expression is **not** equal to one fourth of 52?

Ⓐ 0.25 · 52

Ⓑ 4% of 52

Ⓒ 52 ÷ 4

Ⓓ $\frac{52}{4}$

**3.** Approximately $\frac{4}{5}$ of U.S. homeowners have a cell phone. What percent of homeowners do not have a cell phone?

Ⓐ 20%

Ⓑ 45%

Ⓒ 55%

Ⓓ 80%

**4.** The ratio of rock music to total CDs that Ella owns is $\frac{25}{40}$. Paolo has 50 rock music CDs. The ratio of rock music to total CDs in his collection is equivalent to the ratio of rock music to total CDs in Ella's collection. How many CDs do they own?

Ⓐ 65

Ⓑ 80

Ⓒ 120

Ⓓ 130

**5.** Gabriel saves 40% of his monthly paycheck for college. He earned $270 last month. How much money did Gabriel save for college?

Ⓐ $96

Ⓑ $108

Ⓒ $162

Ⓓ $180

**6.** Forty children from an after-school club went to the matinee. This is 25% of the children in the club. How many children are in the club?

Ⓐ 10

Ⓑ 160

Ⓒ 200

Ⓓ 900

**7.** Dominic answered 43 of the 50 questions on his spelling test correctly. Which decimal represents the fraction of problems he answered incorrectly?

Ⓐ 0.07

Ⓑ 0.14

Ⓒ 0.86

Ⓓ 0.93

## Gridded Response

**8.** Jen bought some bagels. The ratio of the number of sesame bagels to the number of plain bagels that she bought is 1:3. Find the decimal equivalent of the percent of the bagels that are plain.

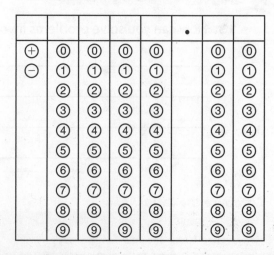

## Representing Ratios and Rates

**Key Vocabulary**
equivalent ratios *(razones equivalentes)*
rate *(tasa)*
ratio *(razón)*
unit rate *(tasa unitaria)*

**? ESSENTIAL QUESTION**

How can you use ratios and rates to solve real-world problems?

### EXAMPLE 1

**Tina pays $45.50 for 13 boxes of wheat crackers. What is the unit price?**

$\dfrac{\$45.50}{13 \text{ boxes}} = \dfrac{\$3.50}{1 \text{ box}}$    The unit price is $3.50 per box of crackers.

### EXAMPLE 2

**A trail mix recipe calls for 3 cups of raisins and 4 cups of peanuts. Mitt made trail mix for a party and used 5 cups of raisins and 6 cups of peanuts. Did Mitt use the correct ratio of raisins to peanuts?**

$\dfrac{3 \text{ cups of raisins}}{4 \text{ cups of peanuts}}$    The ratio of raisins to peanuts in the recipe is $\frac{3}{4}$.

$\dfrac{5 \text{ cups of raisins}}{6 \text{ cups of peanuts}}$    Mitt used a ratio of $\frac{5}{6}$.

$\dfrac{3}{4} \times \dfrac{3}{3} = \dfrac{9}{12}$    $\dfrac{5}{6} \times \dfrac{2}{2} = \dfrac{10}{12}$    $\dfrac{9}{12} < \dfrac{10}{12}$

Mitt used a higher ratio of raisins to peanuts in his trail mix.

### EXERCISES

**Write three equivalent ratios for each ratio.** (Lesson 7.1)

1. $\dfrac{18}{6}$ _____

2. $\dfrac{5}{45}$ _____

3. $\dfrac{3}{5}$ _____

4. To make a dark orange color, Ron mixes 3 ounces of red paint with 2 ounces of yellow paint. Write the ratio of red paint to yellow paint three ways. (Lesson 7.1) _____

5. A box of a dozen fruit tarts costs $15.00. What is the cost of one fruit tart? (Lesson 7.2) _____

**Compare the ratios.** (Lesson 7.3)

6. $\dfrac{2}{5} \bigcirc \dfrac{3}{4}$

7. $\dfrac{9}{2} \bigcirc \dfrac{10}{7}$

8. $\dfrac{2}{11} \bigcirc \dfrac{3}{12}$

9. $\dfrac{6}{7} \bigcirc \dfrac{8}{9}$

# Applying Ratios and Rates

**Key Vocabulary**

conversion factor *(factor de conversión)*

proportion *(proporción)*

scale drawing *(dibujo a escala)*

scale factor *(factor de escala)*

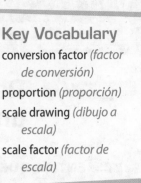

**? ESSENTIAL QUESTION**

How can you use ratios and rates to solve real-world problems?

## EXAMPLE 1

**Jessica earns $5 for each dog she walks. Complete the table, describe the rule, and tell whether the relationship is additive or multiplicative. Then graph the ordered pairs on a coordinate plane.**

| Number of dogs | 1 | 2 | 3 | 4 | 5 |
|---|---|---|---|---|---|
| Profit ($) | 5 | 10 | 15 | 20 | 25 |

Jessica's profit is the number of dogs walked multiplied by $5. The relationship is multiplicative.

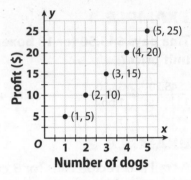

## EXAMPLE 2

**Kim's softball team drank 3 gallons of water during practice. How many cups of water did the team drink?**

$$\frac{16 \text{ cups}}{1 \text{ gallon}} = \frac{? \text{ cups}}{3 \text{ gallons}} \qquad \frac{16 \times 3}{1 \times 3} = \frac{48}{3} \qquad \frac{16 \text{ cups}}{1 \text{ gallon}} = \frac{48 \text{ cups}}{3 \text{ gallons}}$$

The team drank 48 cups of water.

## EXERCISES

**1.** Thaddeus already has $5 saved. He wants to save more to buy a book. Complete the table, and graph the ordered pairs on the coordinate graph. (*Lesson 8.1, 8.2*)

| New savings | 4 | 6 | 8 | 10 |
|---|---|---|---|---|
| Total savings | 9 | | | |

**2.** There are 2 hydrogen atoms and 1 oxygen atom in a water molecule. Complete the table, and list the equivalent ratios shown on the table. (*Lesson 8.1, 8.2*)

| Hydrogen atoms | 8 | | 16 | 20 |
|---|---|---|---|---|
| Oxygen atoms | | 6 | | |

_____

**3.** Sam can solve 30 multiplication problems in 2 minutes. How many can he solve in 20 minutes? (*Lesson 8.3*)

_____

**4.** A male Chihuahua weighs 5 pounds. How many ounces does he weigh? (Lesson 8.4)

_____

# Percents

**? ESSENTIAL QUESTION**

How can you use percents to solve real-world problems?

## EXAMPLE 1

Find an equivalent percent for $\frac{7}{10}$.

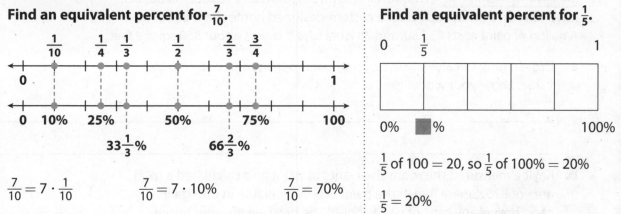

Find an equivalent percent for $\frac{1}{5}$.

$$\frac{7}{10} = 7 \cdot \frac{1}{10} \qquad \frac{7}{10} = 7 \cdot 10\% \qquad \frac{7}{10} = 70\%$$

$\frac{1}{5}$ of $100 = 20$, so $\frac{1}{5}$ of $100\% = 20\%$

$\frac{1}{5} = 20\%$

## EXAMPLE 2

**Thirteen of the 50 states in the United States do not touch the ocean. Write $\frac{13}{50}$ as a decimal and a percent.**

$$\frac{13}{50} = \frac{26}{100} \qquad \frac{26}{100} = 0.26 \qquad 0.26 = 26\% \qquad \frac{13}{50} = 0.26 = 26\%$$

## EXAMPLE 3

**Buckner put $60 of his $400 paycheck into his savings account. Find the percent of his paycheck that Buckner saved.**

$$\frac{60}{400} = \frac{?}{100} \qquad \frac{60 \div 4}{400 \div 4} = \frac{15}{100} \qquad$$ Buckner saved 15% of his paycheck.

## EXERCISES

**Write each fraction as a decimal and a percent.** (Lessons 9.1, 9.2)

**1.** $\frac{3}{4}$ _____  **2.** $\frac{7}{20}$ _____  **3.** $\frac{8}{5}$ _____

**Complete each statement.** (Lessons 9.1, 9.2)

**4.** 25% of 200 is _____.  **5.** 16 is _____ of 20.  **6.** 21 is 70% of _____.

**7.** 42 of the 150 employees at Carlo's Car Repair wear contact lenses. What percent of the employees wear

contact lenses? (Lesson 9.3) _____

**8.** Last week at Best Bargain, 75% of the computers sold were laptops. If 340 computers were sold last week,

how many were laptops? (Lesson 9.3) _____

# Unit 3 Performance Tasks

**1.** **CAREERS IN MATH** Residential Builder Kaylee, a residential builder, is working on a paint budget for a custom-designed home she is building. A gallon of paint costs $38.50, and its label says it covers about 350 square feet.

**a.** Explain how to calculate the cost of paint per square foot. Find this value. Show your work.

_____

_____

**b.** Kaylee measured the room she wants to paint and calculated a total area of 825 square feet. If the paint is only available in one-gallon cans, how many cans of paint should she buy? Justify your answer.

_____

_____

**2.** Davette wants to buy flannel sheets. She reads that a weight of at least 190 grams per square meter is considered high quality.

**a.** Davette finds a sheet that has a weight of 920 grams for 5 square meters. Does this sheet satisfy the requirement for high-quality sheets? If not, what should the weight be for 5 square meters? Explain.

_____

**b.** Davette finds 3 more options for flannel sheets:

Option 1: 1,100 g of flannel in 6 square meters, $45

Option 2: 1,260 g of flannel in 6.6 square meters, $42

Option 3: 1,300 g of flannel in 6.5 square meters, $52

She would like to buy the sheet that meets her requirements for high quality and has the lowest price per square meter. Which option should she buy? Justify your answer.

_____

_____

## Selected Response

**1.** The deepest part of a swimming pool is 12 feet deep. The shallowest part of the pool is 3 feet deep. What is the ratio of the depth of the deepest part of the pool to the depth of the shallowest part of the pool?

Ⓐ 4:1

Ⓑ 12:15

Ⓒ 1:4

Ⓓ 15:12

**2.** How many centimeters are in 15 meters?

Ⓐ 0.15 centimeters

Ⓑ 1.5 centimeters

Ⓒ 150 centimeters

Ⓓ 1,500 centimeters

**3.** Barbara can walk 3,200 meters in 24 minutes. How far can she walk in 3 minutes?

Ⓐ 320 meters

Ⓑ 400 meters

Ⓒ 640 meters

Ⓓ 720 meters

**4.** The table below shows the number of windows and panes of glass in the windows.

| Windows | 2 | 3 | 4 | 5 |
|---|---|---|---|---|
| Panes | 12 | 18 | 24 | 30 |

Which represents the number of panes?

Ⓐ windows × 5

Ⓑ windows × 6

Ⓒ windows + 10

Ⓓ windows + 15

**5.** The graph below represents Donovan's speed while riding his bike.

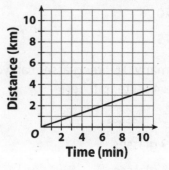

Which would be an ordered pair on the line?

Ⓐ (1, 3)

Ⓑ (2, 2)

Ⓒ (6, 4)

Ⓓ (9, 3)

 **Hot Tip!** Read the graph or diagram as closely as you read the actual test question. These visual aids contain important information.

**6.** Which percent does this shaded grid represent?

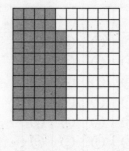

Ⓐ 42%

Ⓑ 48%

Ⓒ 52%

Ⓓ 58%

**7.** Ivan saves 20% of his monthly paycheck for music equipment. He earned $335 last month. How much money did Ivan save for music equipment?

Ⓐ $65

Ⓑ $67

Ⓒ $70

Ⓓ $75

**8.** How many 0.6-liter glasses can you fill up with a 4.5-liter pitcher?

Ⓐ 1.33 glasses

Ⓑ 3.9 glasses

Ⓒ 7.3 glasses

Ⓓ 7.5 glasses

**9.** Which shows the integers in order from greatest to least?

Ⓐ 22, 8, 7, 2, −11

Ⓑ 2, 7, 8, −11, 22

Ⓒ −11, 2, 7, 8, 22

Ⓓ 22, −11, 8, 7, 2

## Gridded Response

**10.** Melinda bought 6 bowls for $13.20. What was the unit rate, in dollars?

**11.** A recipe calls for 6 cups of water and 4 cups of flour. If the recipe is increased, how many cups of water should be used with 6 cups of flour?

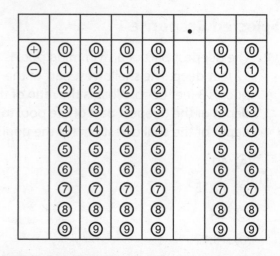

**Hot Tip!** Estimate your answer before solving the question. Use your estimate to check the reasonableness of your answer.

**12.** Broderick answered 21 of the 25 questions on his history test correctly. What decimal represents the fraction of problems he answered incorrectly?

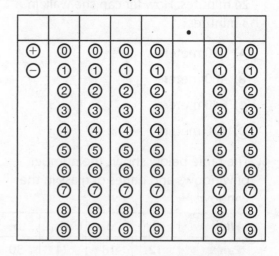

# Expressions, Equations, and Relationships

## CAREERS IN MATH

**Botanist** A botanist is a biologist who studies plants. Botanists use math to analyze data and create models of biological organisms and systems. They use these models to make predictions. They also use statistics to determine correlations. If you are interested in a career in botany, you should study these mathematical subjects:

- Algebra
- Trigonometry
- Probability and Statistics
- Calculus

Research other careers that require the analysis of data and use of mathematical models.

**Unit 4 Performance Task**

At the end of the unit, check out how **botanists** use math.

# UNIT 4
# Vocabulary Preview

Use the puzzle to preview key vocabulary from this unit. Unscramble the circled letters within found words to answer the riddle at the bottom of the page.

```
T O Y H S D F P P O (T) H T J J
(N) E S S V L E B C E R V N N F
E K O P X U C D R A N I U P N
I O F J (S) F P M Y (O) Q H G C I
C F P Z O E E U I N V Z W (I) C
I B N U A M T T Z O Q C C J N
F S O X A F U A D C P Z H L P
F D X V X L D L N V J S A V K
E (E) X P O N E (N) T I O Q (X) W B
O O W S S H Z W T Y D Q E B T
C R U T L O O P R S S R S J A
Z H X R H O P L Y C U X O Q C
U B X F U B Y H J F K P U O E
S B F Q O E K Y K P H C S N C
L F W W Z T V F O P U H U U B
```

- A number that is multiplied by a variable in an algebraic expression. (Lesson 11-1)
- A value of the variable that makes the equation true. (Lesson 12-1)
- The numbers in an ordered pair. (Lesson 14-1)
- The point where the axes intersect to form the coordinate plane. (Lesson 14-1)
- The part of an expression that is added or subtracted. (Lesson 11-1)
- The two number lines that intersect at right angles to form a coordinate plane. (Lesson 14-1)
- Tells how many times the base is used in the product. (Lesson 10-1)

**Q:** Why did the paper rip when the student tried to stretch out the horizontal axis of his graph?

**A:** Too much ___ – ___ ___ ___ ___ ___ ___ ___ !

# Generating Equivalent Numerical Expressions

## ? ESSENTIAL QUESTION

How can you generate equivalent numerical expressions and use them to solve real-world problems?

**Real-World Video**

Assume that you post a video on the internet. Two of your friends view it, then two friends of each of those view it, and so on. The number of views is growing exponentially. Sometimes we say the video went viral.

⏻ my.hrw.com

**GO DIGITAL**
my.hrw.com

**my.hrw.com**

Go digital with your write-in student edition, accessible on any device.

**Math On the Spot**

Scan with your smart phone to jump directly to the online edition, video tutor, and more.

**Animated Math**

Interactively explore key concepts to see how math works.

**Personal Math Trainer**

Get immediate feedback and help as you work through practice sets.

# Are YOU Ready?

Complete these exercises to review skills you will need for this chapter.

Personal Math Trainer

Online Assessment and Intervention

my.hrw.com

## Whole Number Operations

> **EXAMPLE**   $270 \times 83$
>
> $$\begin{array}{r} 270 \\ \times\ 83 \\ \hline 810 \\ +\ 21{,}600 \\ \hline 22{,}410 \end{array}$$
>
> $\leftarrow\ 3 \times 270$
> $\leftarrow\ 80 \times 270$
> $\leftarrow\ (3 \times 270) + (80 \times 270)$

**Find the product.**

**1.** $992 \times 16$ _____

**2.** $578 \times 27$ _____

**3.** $839 \times 65$ _____

**4.** $367 \times 23$ _____

## Use Repeated Multiplication

> **EXAMPLE**   $\underline{5 \times 5} \times 5 \times 5$   Multiply the first two factors.
>
> $\underline{25\ \ \times\ 5}$   Multiply the result by the next factor.
>
> $\underline{125\ \times\ 5}$   Multiply that result by the next factor.
>
> $625$   Continue until there are no more factors to multiply.

**Find the product.**

**5.** $7 \times 7 \times 7$ _____

**6.** $3 \times 3 \times 3 \times 3$ _____

**7.** $6 \times 6 \times 6 \times 6 \times 6$ _____

**8.** $2 \times 2 \times 2 \times 2 \times 2 \times 2$ _____

## Division Facts

> **EXAMPLE**   $54 \div 9 = \blacksquare$   Think:  9 times what number equals 54?
>   $9 \times 6 = 54$
>
> $54 \div 9 = 6$   So, $54 \div 9 = 6$.

**Divide.**

**9.** $20 \div 4$ _____

**10.** $21 \div 7$ _____

**11.** $42 \div 7$ _____

**12.** $56 \div 8$ _____

# Reading Start-Up

## Visualize Vocabulary

Use the ✔ words to complete the graphic. You may put more than one word in each box.

### Reviewing Factorization

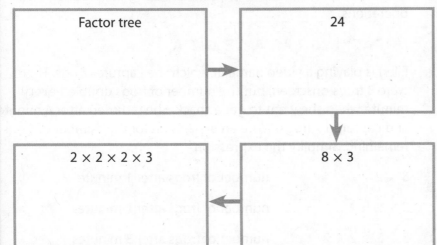

| Factor tree | 24 |
|---|---|

| 2 × 2 × 2 × 3 | 8 × 3 |

### Vocabulary

**Review Words**
✔ factor (*factor*)
  factor tree (*árbol de factores*)
✔ integers (*entero*)
✔ numerical expression (*expresión numérica*)
✔ operations (*operaciones*)
✔ prime factorization (*factorización prima*)
  repeated multiplication (*multiplicación repetida*)
  simplified expression (*expresión simplificada*)

**Preview Words**
  base (*base*)
  exponent (*exponente*)
  order of operations (*orden de las operaciones*)
  power (*potencia*)

## Understand Vocabulary

Complete the sentences using the preview words.

1. A number that is formed by repeated multiplication by the same

   factor is a _____ .

2. A rule for simplifying expressions is _____ .

3. The _____ is a number that is multiplied. The number that

   indicates how many times this number is used as a factor is the _____ .

## Active Reading

**Three-Panel Flip Chart** Before beginning the module, create a three-panel flip chart to help you organize what you learn. Label each flap with one of the lesson titles from this module. As you study each lesson, write important ideas like vocabulary, properties, and formulas under the appropriate flap.

# Unpacking the TEKS

Understanding the TEKS and the vocabulary terms in the TEKS will help you know exactly what you are expected to learn in this module.

---

**TEKS 6.7.A**

Generate equivalent numerical expressions using order of operations, including whole number exponents and prime factorization.

## Key Vocabulary

**exponent** *(exponente)*
The number that indicates how many times the base is used as a factor.

**order of operations** *(orden de las operaciones)* A rule for evaluating expressions: first perform the operations in parentheses, then compute powers and roots, then perform all multiplication and division from left to right, and then perform all addition and subtraction from left to right.

---

# What It Means to You

You will simplify numerical expressions using the order of operations.

## UNPACKING EXAMPLE 6.7.A

Ellen is playing a video game in which she captures frogs. There were 3 frogs onscreen, but the number of frogs doubled every minute when she went to get a snack. She returned after 4 minutes and captured 7 frogs. Write an expression for the number of frogs remaining. Simplify the expression.

| | |
|---|---|
| $3 \times 2$ | number of frogs after 1 minute |
| $3 \times 2 \times 2$ | number of frogs after 2 minutes |
| $3 \times 2 \times 2 \times 2$ | number of frogs after 3 minutes |
| $3 \times 2 \times 2 \times 2 \times 2$ | number of frogs after 4 minutes |

Since 3 and 2 are prime numbers, $3 \times 2 \times 2 \times 2 \times 2$ is the prime factorization of the number of frogs remaining.

$3 \times 2 \times 2 \times 2 \times 2$ can be written with exponents as $3 \times 2^4$.

The expression $3 \times 2^4 - 7$ is the number of frogs remaining after Ellen captured the 7 frogs.

Use the order of operations to simplify $3 \times 2^4 - 7$.

$$3 \times 2^4 - 7 = 3 \times 16 - 7$$
$$= 48 - 7$$
$$= 41$$

41 frogs remain.

---

Visit **my.hrw.com** to see all the **TEKS** unpacked.

⏻ my.hrw.com

# 10.1 Exponents

TEKS
Expressions, equations, and relationships—6.7.A
Generate equivalent numerical expressions using… exponents.

## ESSENTIAL QUESTION

How do you use exponents to represent numbers?

EXPLORE ACTIVITY  Real World  TEKS 6.7.A

# Identifying Repeated Multiplication

A real-world problem may involve repeatedly multiplying a factor by itself.

A scientist observed the hourly growth of bacteria and recorded his observations in a table.

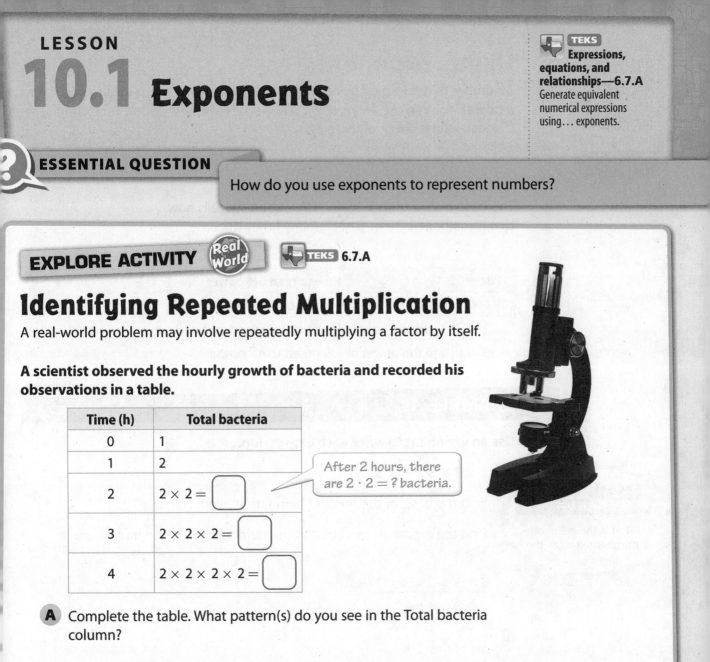

| Time (h) | Total bacteria |
|----------|----------------|
| 0 | 1 |
| 1 | 2 |
| 2 | $2 \times 2 = \boxed{\phantom{0}}$ |
| 3 | $2 \times 2 \times 2 = \boxed{\phantom{0}}$ |
| 4 | $2 \times 2 \times 2 \times 2 = \boxed{\phantom{0}}$ |

After 2 hours, there are $2 \cdot 2 = ?$ bacteria.

**A** Complete the table. What pattern(s) do you see in the Total bacteria column?

_____

_____

**B** Complete each statement.

At 2 hours, the total is equal to the product of two 2s.

At 3 hours, the total is equal to the product of _____ 2s.

At 4 hours, the total is equal to the product of _____ 2s.

## Reflect

1. **Communicate Mathematical Ideas**  How is the time, in hours, related to the number of times 2 is used as a factor?

_____

_____

# Using Exponents

A number that is formed by repeated multiplication by the same factor is called a **power**. You can use an *exponent* and a *base* to write a power. For example, $7^3$ means the product of three 7s:

$$7^3 = 7 \times 7 \times 7$$

The **base** is the number that is multiplied.

The **exponent** tells how many times the base appears in the expression.

| Power | How to read the power |
|-------|----------------------|
| $6^2$ | 6 squared, 6 to the power of 2, 6 raised to the 2nd power |
| $7^3$ | 7 cubed, 7 to the power of 3, 7 raised to the 3rd power |
| $9^4$ | 9 to the power of 4, 9 raised to 4th power |

## EXAMPLE 1

 **TEKS** 6.7.A

**Use an exponent to write each expression.**

**A** $3 \times 3 \times 3 \times 3 \times 3$

Find the base, or the number being multiplied. The base is 3.

Find the exponent by counting the number of 3s being multiplied. The exponent is 5.

$$\underbrace{3 \times 3 \times 3 \times 3 \times 3}_{5 \text{ factors of 3}} = 3^5$$

**B** $\frac{4}{5} \times \frac{4}{5} \times \frac{4}{5} \times \frac{4}{5}$

Find the base, or the number being multiplied. The base is $\frac{4}{5}$.

Find the exponent by counting the number of times $\frac{4}{5}$ appears in the expression. The exponent is 4.

$$\underbrace{\frac{4}{5} \times \frac{4}{5} \times \frac{4}{5} \times \frac{4}{5}}_{4 \text{ factors of } \frac{4}{5}} = \left(\frac{4}{5}\right)^4$$

**Math Talk**

Mathematical Processes

What is the value of a number raised to the power of 1?

## YOUR TURN

**Use exponents to write each expression.**

**2.** $4 \times 4 \times 4$ _____

**3.** $6$ _____

**4.** $\frac{1}{8} \times \frac{1}{8}$ _____

**5.** $5 \times 5 \times 5 \times 5 \times 5 \times 5$ _____

# Finding the Value of a Power

To find the value of a power, remember that the exponent indicates how many times to use the base as a factor.

> ### Property of Zero as an Exponent
>
> The value of any nonzero number raised to the power of 0 is 1.
>
> **Example:** $5^0 = 1$

## EXAMPLE 2      🔲 **TEKS** 6.7.A

**My Notes**

**Find the value of each power.**

**A** $(-10)^4$

Identify the base and the exponent.
The base is $-10$, and the exponent is 4.

Evaluate: $(-10)^4 = -10 \times (-10) \times (-10) \times (-10) = 10,000$

**B** $0.4^3$

Identify the base and the exponent.
The base is 0.4, and the exponent is 3.

Evaluate: $0.4^3 = 0.4 \times 0.4 \times 0.4 = 0.064$

**C** $\left(\dfrac{3}{5}\right)^0$

Identify the base and the exponent.
The base is $\dfrac{3}{5}$, and the exponent is 0.

Evaluate.

$\left(\dfrac{3}{5}\right)^0 = 1$      *Any number raised to the power of 0 is 1.*

> **Math Talk**
> Mathematical Processes
>
> Is the value of $2^3$ the same as the value of $3^2$? Explain.

**D** $-11^2$

Identify the base and the exponent.
The base is 11, and the exponent is 2.

Evaluate.
$-11^2 = -(11 \times 11) = -121$      *The opposite of a positive number squared is a negative number.*

---

### YOUR TURN

**Find the value of each power.**

**6.** $3^4$ _____    **7.** $(-1)^9$ _____    **8.** $\left(\dfrac{2}{5}\right)^3$ _____    **9.** $-12^2$ _____

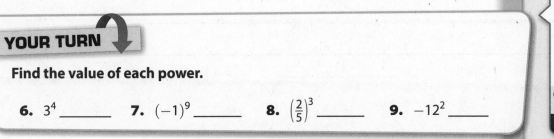

1. Complete the table. (Explore Activity)

| Exponential form | Product | Simplified product |
|---|---|---|
| $5^1$ | 5 | 5 |
| $5^2$ | $5 \times 5$ | |
| $5^3$ | | 125 |
| | $5 \times 5 \times 5 \times 5$ | |
| $5^5$ | | |

Use an exponent to write each expression. (Example 1)

2. $\underline{6 \times 6 \times 6}$ _____

___ factors of 6

3. $10 \times 10 \times 10 \times 10 \times 10 \times 10 \times 10$ _____

4. $\frac{3}{4} \times \frac{3}{4} \times \frac{3}{4} \times \frac{3}{4} \times \frac{3}{4}$ _____

5. $\frac{7}{9} \times \frac{7}{9} \times \frac{7}{9} \times \frac{7}{9} \times \frac{7}{9} \times \frac{7}{9} \times \frac{7}{9} \times \frac{7}{9}$ _____

Find the value of each power. (Example 2)

6. $8^3$ _____

7. $7^4$ _____

8. $10^3$ _____

9. $\left(\frac{1}{4}\right)^2$ _____

10. $\left(\frac{1}{3}\right)^3$ _____

11. $\left(\frac{6}{7}\right)^2$ _____

12. $0.8^2$ _____

13. $0.5^3$ _____

14. $1.1^2$ _____

15. $8^0$ _____

16. $12^1$ _____

17. $\left(\frac{1}{2}\right)^0$ _____

18. $(-2)^3$ _____

19. $\left(-\frac{2}{5}\right)^2$ _____

20. $-9^2$ _____

**? ESSENTIAL QUESTION CHECK-IN**

21. How do you use an exponent to represent a number such as 16?

_____

_____

_____

_____

# 10.1 Independent Practice

 6.7.A

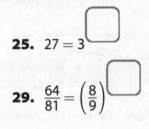
**Write the missing exponent.**

**22.** $100 = 10^{\boxed{\phantom{0}}}$

**23.** $8 = 2^{\boxed{\phantom{0}}}$

**24.** $25 = 5^{\boxed{\phantom{0}}}$

**25.** $27 = 3^{\boxed{\phantom{0}}}$

**26.** $\dfrac{1}{169} = \left(\dfrac{1}{13}\right)^{\boxed{\phantom{0}}}$

**27.** $14 = 14^{\boxed{\phantom{0}}}$

**28.** $32 = 2^{\boxed{\phantom{0}}}$

**29.** $\dfrac{64}{81} = \left(\dfrac{8}{9}\right)^{\boxed{\phantom{0}}}$

**Write the missing base.**

**30.** $1,000 = \boxed{\phantom{0}}^{3}$

**31.** $256 = \boxed{\phantom{0}}^{4}$

**32.** $16 = \boxed{\phantom{0}}^{4}$

**33.** $9 = \boxed{\phantom{0}}^{2}$

**34.** $\dfrac{1}{9} = \left(\boxed{\phantom{0}}\right)^{2}$

**35.** $64 = \boxed{\phantom{0}}^{2}$

**36.** $\dfrac{9}{16} = \left(\boxed{\phantom{0}}\right)^{2}$

**37.** $729 = \boxed{\phantom{0}}^{3}$

**38.** Hadley's softball team has a phone tree in case a game is canceled. The coach calls 3 players. Then each of those players calls 3 players, and so on. How many players will be notified during the third round of calls?

_____

**39.** Tim is reading a book. On Monday he reads 3 pages. On each day after that, he reads triple the number of pages as the previous day. How many pages does he read on Thursday?

_____

**40.** Which power can you write to represent the area of the square shown? Write the power as an expression with a base and an exponent, and then find the area of the square.

8.5 mm

_____

**41.** Antonia is saving for a video game. On the first day, she saves two dollars in her piggy bank. Each day after that, she doubles the number of dollars she saved on the previous day. How many dollars does she save on the sixth day?

_____

**42.** A certain colony of bacteria triples in length every 10 minutes. Its length is now 1 millimeter. How long will it be in 40 minutes?

_____

**43.** Write a power represented with a positive base and a positive exponent whose value is less than the base.

_____

**44.** Which power can you write to represent the volume of the cube shown? Write the power as an expression with a base and an exponent, and then find the volume of the cube.

_____

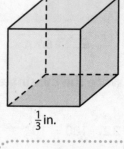

$\frac{1}{3}$ in.

 **FOCUS ON HIGHER ORDER THINKING**

Work Area

**45.** **Communicate Mathematical Ideas** What is the value of 1 raised to the power of any exponent? What is the value of 0 raised to the power of any nonzero exponent? Explain.

_____

_____

_____

_____

**46.** **Look for a Pattern** Find the values of the powers in the following pattern: $10^1$, $10^2$, $10^3$, $10^4$…. Describe the pattern, and use it to evaluate $10^6$ without using multiplication.

_____

_____

_____

_____

**47.** **Critical Thinking** Some numbers can be written as powers of different bases. For example, $81 = 9^2$ and $81 = 3^4$. Write the number 64 using three different bases.

_____

**48.** **Justify Reasoning** Oman said that it is impossible to raise a number to the power of 2 and get a negative value. Do you agree with Oman? Why or why not?

_____

_____

_____

_____

**LESSON**
# 10.2 Prime Factorization

**TEKS**
Expressions, equations, and relationships—
**6.7.A** Generate equivalent numerical expressions using prime factorization.

## ESSENTIAL QUESTION

How do you write the prime factorization of a number?

## Finding Factors of a Number

Whole numbers that are multiplied to find a product are called factors of that product. A number is divisible by its factors. For example, 4 and 2 are factors of 8 because $4 \cdot 2 = 8$, and 8 is divisible by 4 and by 2.

**Math On the Spot**
my.hrw.com

### EXAMPLE 1  Real World    TEKS 6.7.A

**Ana wants to build a rectangular garden with an area of 24 square feet. What are the possible whole number lengths and widths of the garden?**

**STEP 1** Recall that area = length · width. For Ana's garden, $24 \text{ ft}^2 = \text{length} \cdot \text{width}$.

**STEP 2** List the factors of 24 in pairs. List each pair only once.

$24 = 1 \cdot 24$
$24 = 2 \cdot 12$     *$4 \cdot 6 = 6 \cdot 4$, so you only list $4 \cdot 6$.*
$24 = 3 \cdot 8$
$24 = 4 \cdot 6$

You can also use a diagram to show the factor pairs.

**1   2   3   4   6   8   12   24**

The factors of 24 are 1, 2, 3, 4, 6, 8, 12, 24.

**STEP 3** The possible lengths and widths are:

| Length (ft) | 24 | 12 | 8 | 6 |
|---|---|---|---|---|
| Width (ft) | 1 | 2 | 3 | 4 |

**Math Talk**
Mathematical Processes

Give an example of a whole number that has exactly two factors? What type of number has exactly two factors?

### YOUR TURN

List all the factors of each number.

1. 21 _____

2. 37 _____

3. 42 _____

4. 30 _____

**Personal Math Trainer**

Online Assessment and Intervention

my.hrw.com

# Finding the Prime Factorization of a Number

The prime factorization of a number is the number written as the product of its prime factors. For example, the prime factors of 12 are 3, 2, and 2.

The prime factorization of 12 is $2 \cdot 3 \cdot 2$ or $2^2 \cdot 3$.

> Use exponents to show repeated factors.

Animated Math

my.hrw.com

**Use a factor tree to find the prime factorization of 240.**

**A** List the factor pairs of 240.

_____

_____

**B** Choose any factor pair to begin the tree. If a number in this pair is prime, circle it. If a number in the pair can be written as a product of two factors, draw additional branches and write the factors.

**C** Continue adding branches until the factors at the ends of the branches are prime numbers.

**D** Write the prime factorization of 240.

_____

Then write the prime factorization using exponents.

_____

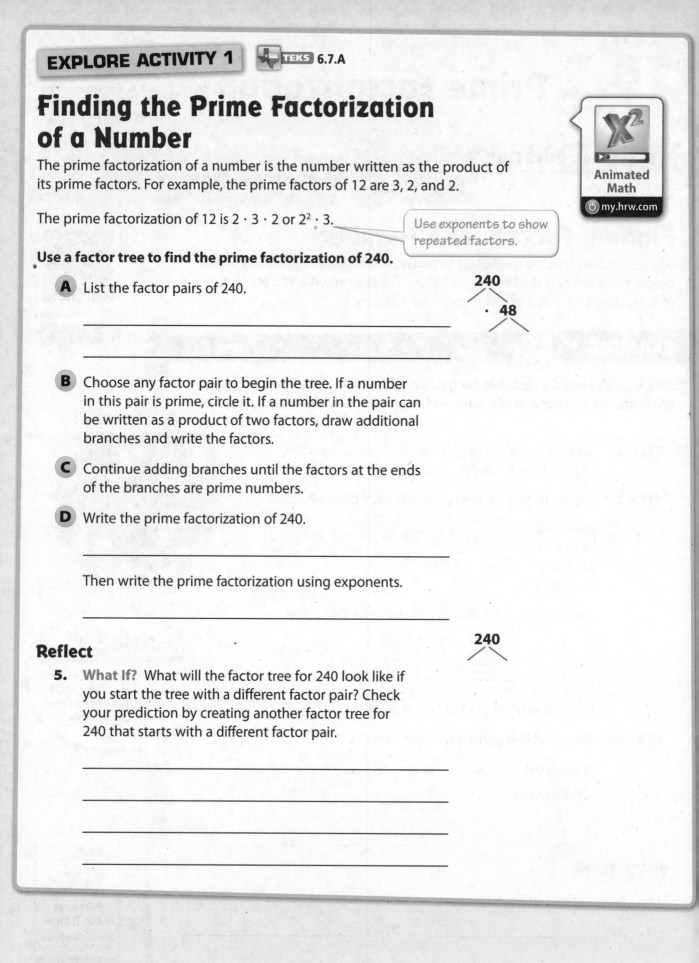

240

48

240

## Reflect

**5.** **What If?** What will the factor tree for 240 look like if you start the tree with a different factor pair? Check your prediction by creating another factor tree for 240 that starts with a different factor pair.

_____

_____

_____

_____

# Using a Ladder Diagram

A ladder diagram is another way to find the prime factorization of a number.

**Use a ladder diagram to find the prime factorization of 132.**

**A** Write 132 in the top "step" of the ladder. Choose a prime factor of 132 to write next to the step with 132. Choose 2. Divide 132 by 2 and write the quotient 66 in the next step of the ladder.

$$
\begin{array}{r|r}
2 & 132 \\
\hline
\square & 66 \\
\end{array}
$$

**B** Now choose a prime factor of 66. Write the prime factor next to the step with 66. Divide 66 by that prime factor and write the quotient in the next step of the ladder.

**C** Keep choosing prime factors, dividing, and adding to the ladder until you get a quotient of 1.

**D** What are the prime factors of 132? How can you tell from the ladder diagram?

_____

_____

**E** Write the prime factorization of 132 using exponents.

_____

## Reflect

**6.** Complete a factor tree and a ladder diagram to find the prime factorization of 54.

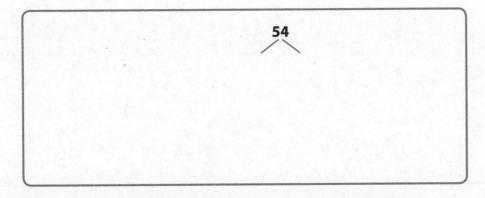

**7.** **Communicate Mathematical Ideas** If one person uses a ladder diagram and another uses a factor tree to write a prime factorization, will they get the same result? Explain.

_____

_____

## Guided Practice

**Use a diagram to list the factor pairs of each number.** (Example 1)

**1.** 18

**2.** 52

_____

_____

**3.** Karl needs to build a stage that has an area of 72 square feet. The length of the stage should be longer than the width. What are the possible whole number measurements for the length and width of the stage? (Example 1)

Complete the table with possible measurements of the stage.

| Length (ft) | 72 | | | | |
|---|---|---|---|---|---|
| Width (ft) | | 2 | | | |

**Use a factor tree to find the prime factorization of each number.**
(Explore Activity 1)

**4.** 402

**402**
  /\
**201** ·

**5.** 36

_____

_____

**Use a ladder diagram to find the prime factorization of each number.**
(Explore Activity 2)

**6.** 32

**7.** 27

_____

_____

? **ESSENTIAL QUESTION CHECK-IN**

**8.** Tell how you know when you have found the prime factorization of a number.

_____

_____

## 10.2 Independent Practice

TEKS 6.7.A

Personal Math Trainer

my.hrw.com

Online Assessment and Intervention

9. **Multiple Representations** Use the grid to draw three different rectangles so that each has an area of 12 square units and they all have different widths. What are the dimensions of the rectangles?

_____

_____

10. Brandon has 32 stamps. He wants to display the stamps in rows, with the same number of stamps in each row. How many different ways can he display the stamps? Explain.

_____

_____

_____

11. **Communicate Mathematical Ideas** How is finding the factors of a number different from finding the prime factorization of a number?

_____

_____

_____

_____

**Find the prime factorization of each number.**

12. 891 _____    13. 504 _____

14. 23 _____    15. 230 _____

16. The number 2 is chosen to begin a ladder diagram to find the prime factorization of 66. What other numbers could have been used to start the ladder diagram for 66? How does starting with a different number change the diagram?

_____

_____

_____

17. **Critical Thinking** List five numbers that have 3, 5, and 7 as prime factors.

_____

**18.** In a game, you draw a card with three consecutive numbers on it. You can choose one of the numbers and find the sum of its prime factors. Then you can move that many spaces. You draw a card with the numbers 25, 26, 27. Which number should you choose if you want to move as many spaces as possible? Explain.

_____

_____

_____

_____

**19. Explain the Error** When asked to write the prime factorization of the number 27, a student wrote $9 \cdot 3$. Explain the error and write the correct answer.

_____

_____

**H.O.T.** FOCUS ON HIGHER ORDER THINKING

**20. Communicate Mathematical Ideas** Explain why it is possible to draw more than two different rectangles with an area of 36 square units, but it is not possible to draw more than two different rectangles with an area of 15 square units. The sides of the rectangles are whole numbers.

_____

_____

_____

**21. Critique Reasoning** Alice wants to find all the prime factors of the number you get when you multiply $17 \cdot 11 \cdot 13 \cdot 7$. She thinks she has to use a calculator to perform all the multiplications and then find the prime factorization of the resulting number. Do you agree? Why or why not?

_____

_____

_____

**22. Look for a Pattern** Ryan wrote the prime factorizations shown below. If he continues this pattern, what prime factorization will he show for the number one million? What prime factorization will he show for one billion?

$10 = 5 \cdot 2$

$100 = 5^2 \cdot 2^2$

$1,000 = 5^3 \cdot 2^3$

_____

LESSON
# 10.3 Order of Operations

TEKS
Expressions,
equations, and
relationships— 6.7.A
Generate equivalent
numerical expressions using
order of operations ...

## ESSENTIAL QUESTION

How do you use the order of operations to simplify expressions with exponents?

**EXPLORE ACTIVITY** Real World — TEKS 6.7.A

# Exploring the Order of Operations

> **Order of Operations**
>
> 1. Perform operations in parentheses.
> 2. Find the value of numbers with exponents.
> 3. Multiply or divide from left to right.
> 4. Add or subtract from left to right.

Amy and three friends launch a new website. Each friend emails the web address to three new friends. These new friends forward the web address to three more friends. If no one receives the e-mail more than once, how many people will receive the web address in the second wave of e-mails?

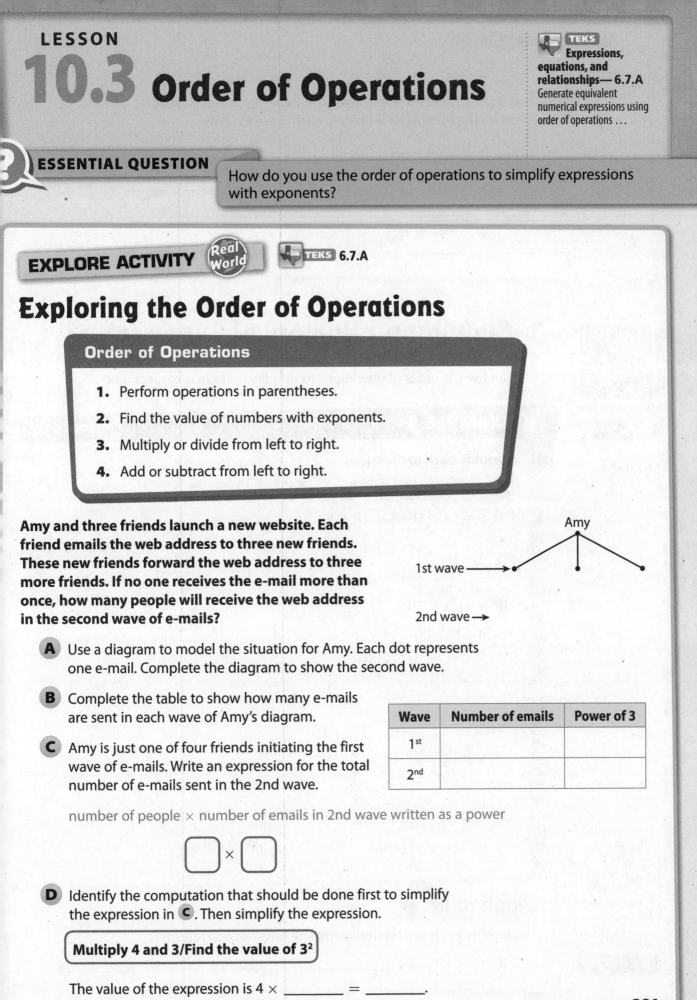

Amy

1st wave ⟶

2nd wave ⟶

**A** Use a diagram to model the situation for Amy. Each dot represents one e-mail. Complete the diagram to show the second wave.

**B** Complete the table to show how many e-mails are sent in each wave of Amy's diagram.

**C** Amy is just one of four friends initiating the first wave of e-mails. Write an expression for the total number of e-mails sent in the 2nd wave.

| Wave | Number of emails | Power of 3 |
|------|------------------|-----------|
| 1st  |                  |           |
| 2nd  |                  |           |

number of people × number of emails in 2nd wave written as a power

☐ × ☐

**D** Identify the computation that should be done first to simplify the expression in **C**. Then simplify the expression.

> **Multiply 4 and 3/Find the value of $3^2$**

The value of the expression is $4 \times$ _____ = _____ .

**Reflect**

1. In ⓒ, why does it makes sense to write the values as powers? What is the pattern for the number of e-mails in each wave for Amy?

_____

_____

_____

_____

**Math On the Spot**

⏻ my.hrw.com

**My Notes**

# Simplifying Numerical Expressions

A numerical expression is an expression involving numbers and operations. You can use the order of operations to simplify numerical expressions.

## EXAMPLE 1

**TEKS** 6.7.A

**Simplify each expression.**

**A** $5 + 18 \div 3^2$

$$5 + 18 \div 3^2 = 5 + 18 \div 9 \qquad \text{Evaluate } 3^2.$$
$$= 5 + 2 \qquad \text{Divide.}$$
$$= 7 \qquad \text{Add.}$$

**B** $4 \times (9 \div 3)^2$

$$4 \times (9 \div 3)^2 = 4 \times 3^2 \qquad \text{Perform operations inside parentheses.}$$
$$= 4 \times 9 \qquad \text{Evaluate } 3^2.$$
$$= 36 \qquad \text{Multiply.}$$

**C** $8 + \dfrac{(12 - 8)^2}{2}$

$$8 + \dfrac{(12 - 8)^2}{2} = 8 + \dfrac{4^2}{2} \qquad \text{Perform operations inside parentheses.}$$
$$= 8 + \dfrac{16}{2} \qquad \text{Evaluate } 4^2.$$
$$= 8 + 8 \qquad \text{Divide.}$$
$$= 16 \qquad \text{Add.}$$

**Personal Math Trainer**

Online Assessment and Intervention

⏻ my.hrw.com

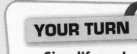

**YOUR TURN**

**Simplify each expression using the order of operations.**

2. $(3 - 1)^4 + 3$ _____

3. $24 \div (3 \times 2^2)$ _____

# Using the Order of Operations with Integers

You can use the order of operations to simplify expressions involving integers.

Math On the Spot

my.hrw.com

## EXAMPLE 2

TEKS 6.7.A

**Simplify each expression using the order of operations.**

**A**  $-4(3 - 9) + (-2)^2$

$$-4(3 - 9) + (-2)^2 = -4(-6) + (-2)^2 \qquad \text{Perform operations inside parentheses.}$$

$$= -4(-6) + 4 \qquad \text{Evaluate } (-2)^2.$$

$$= 24 + 4 \qquad \text{Multiply.}$$

$$= 28 \qquad \text{Add.}$$

**B**  $-21 + \dfrac{(-3)^2}{3}$

$$-21 + \frac{(-3)^2}{3} = -21 + \frac{9}{3} \qquad \text{Evaluate } (-3)^2.$$

$$= -21 + 3 \qquad \text{Divide.}$$

$$= -18 \qquad \text{Add.}$$

**C**  $6 \times (-2)^3 \div 3 + 1$

$$6 \times (-2)^3 \div 3 + 1 = 6 \times (-8) \div 3 + 1 \qquad \text{Evaluate } (-2)^3.$$

$$= -48 \div 3 + 1 \qquad \text{Multiply.}$$

$$= -16 + 1 \qquad \text{Divide.}$$

$$= -15 \qquad \text{Add.}$$

## YOUR TURN

**Simplify each expression using the order of operations.**

**4.**  $-7 \times (-4) \div 14 - 2^2$

**5.**  $-5 (-3 + 1)^3 - 3$

**Personal Math Trainer**

Online Assessment and Intervention

my.hrw.com

1. In a video game, a guppy that escapes a net turns into three goldfish. Each goldfish can turn into two betta fish. Each betta fish can turn into two angelfish. Complete the diagram and write the number of fish at each stage. Write and evaluate an expression for the number of angelfish that can be formed from one guppy. (Explore Activity)

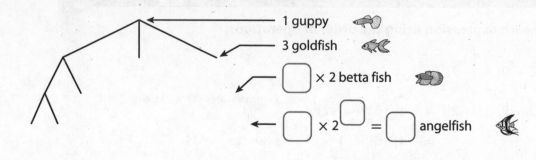

1 guppy

3 goldfish

☐ × 2 betta fish

☐ × 2$^{☐}$ = ☐ angelfish

_____

**Complete to simplify each expression.** (Examples 1 and 2)

2. $4 + (10 - 7)^2 \div 3 = 4 + (\underline{\hspace{0.6cm}})^2 \div 3$

$= 4 + \underline{\hspace{0.6cm}} \div 3$

$= 4 + \underline{\hspace{0.6cm}}$

$= \underline{\hspace{0.6cm}}$

3. $36 \div 2^2 - 4 \times 2 = 36 \div \underline{\hspace{0.8cm}} - 4 \times 2$

$= \underline{\hspace{0.8cm}} - 4 \times 2$

$= \underline{\hspace{0.8cm}} - 8$

$= \underline{\hspace{0.6cm}}$

4. $2 + (-24 \div 2^3) - 9 = 2 + (-24 \div \underline{\hspace{0.6cm}}) - 9$

$= 2 + \underline{\hspace{0.8cm}} - 9$

$= \underline{\hspace{0.6cm}} - 9$

$= \underline{\hspace{0.6cm}}$

5. $-4^2 \times (-3 \times 2 + 8) = -4^2 \times (\underline{\hspace{0.5cm}} + 8)$

$= -4^2 \times \underline{\hspace{0.8cm}}$

$= \underline{\hspace{0.8cm}} \times \underline{\hspace{0.8cm}}$

$= \underline{\hspace{0.6cm}}$

**? ESSENTIAL QUESTION CHECK-IN**

6. How do you use the order of operations to simplify expressions with exponents?

_____

_____

_____

_____

# 10.3 Independent Practice

TEKS 6.7.A

**Simplify each expression using the order of operations.**

**7.** $5 \times 2 + 3^2$ _____

**8.** $15 - 7 \times 2 + 2^3$ _____

**9.** $(11 - 8)^2 - 2 \times 6$ _____

**10.** $6 + 3(13 - 2) - 5^2$ _____

**11.** $12 + \dfrac{9^2}{3}$ _____

**12.** $\dfrac{8 + 6^2}{11} + 7 \times 2$ _____

**13. Explain the Error** Jay simplified the expression $-3 \times (3 + 12 \div 3) - 4$. For his first step, he added $3 + 12$ to get 15. What was Jay's error? Find the correct answer.

_____

_____

**14. Multistep** A clothing store has the sign shown in the shop window. Pani sees the sign and wants to buy 3 shirts and 2 pairs of jeans. The cost of each shirt before the discount is $12, and the cost of each pair of jeans is $19 before the discount.

**a.** Write and simplify an expression to find the amount Pani pays if a $3 discount is applied to her total.

_____

**b.** Pani says she should get a $3 discount on the price of each shirt and a $3 discount on the price of each pair of jeans. Write and simplify an expression to find the amount she would pay if this is true.

_____

**c. Analyze Relationships** Why are the amounts Pani pays in **a** and **b** different?

_____

_____

**d.** If you were the shop owner, how would you change the sign? Explain.

_____

_____

_____

_____

**15.** Ellen is playing a video game in which she captures butterflies. There are 3 butterflies onscreen, but the number of butterflies doubles every minute. After 4 minutes, she was able to capture 7 of the butterflies.

**a.** **Look for a Pattern** Write an expression for the number of butterflies after 4 minutes. Use a power of 2 in your answer.

_____

**b.** Write an expression for the number of butterflies remaining after Ellen captured the 7 butterflies. Simplify the expression.

_____

_____

**16.** Show how to write, evaluate and simplify an expression to represent and solve this problem: Jeff and his friend each text four classmates about a concert. Each classmate then texts four students from another school about the concert. If no one receives the message more than once, how many students from the other school receive a text about the concert?

_____

Work Area

**17.** **Geometry** The figure shown is a rectangle. The green shape in the figure is a square. The blue and white shapes are rectangles, and the area of the blue rectangle is 24 square inches.

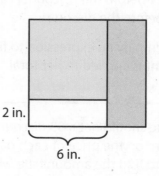

2 in.

6 in.

**a.** Write an expression for the area of the entire figure that includes an exponent. Then find the area.

_____

**b.** Find the dimensions of the entire figure.

_____

**18.** **Analyze Relationships** Roberto's teacher writes the following statement on the board: The cube of a number plus one more than the square of the number is equal to the opposite of the number. Show that the number is $-1$.

_____

_____

**19.** **Persevere in Problem Solving** Use parentheses to make this statement true: $8 \times 4 - 2 \times 3 + 8 \div 2 = 25$

_____

# Ready to Go On?

Personal Math Trainer

Online Assessment and Intervention

⏻ my.hrw.com

## 10.1 Exponents

**Find the value of each power.**

**1.** $7^3$ _____   **2.** $9^2$ _____   **3.** $\left(\frac{7}{9}\right)^2$ _____   **4.** $\left(\frac{1}{2}\right)^6$ _____

**5.** $\left(\frac{2}{3}\right)^3$ _____   **6.** $(-3)^5$ _____   **7.** $(-2)^4$ _____   **8.** $1.4^2$ _____

## 10.2 Prime Factorization

**Find the factors of each number.**

**9.** 96 _____

**10.** 120 _____

**Find the prime factorization of each number.**

**11.** 58 _____   **12.** 212 _____

**13.** 2,800 _____   **14.** 900 _____

## 10.3 Order of Operations

**Simplify each expression using the order of operations.**

**15.** $(21 - 3) \div 3^2$ _____   **16.** $7^2 \times (6 \div 3)$ _____

**17.** $17 + 15 \div 3 - 2^4$ _____   **18.** $(8 + 56) \div 4 - 3^2$ _____

**19.** The nature park has a pride of 7 adult lions and 4 cubs. The adults eat 6 pounds of meat each day and the cubs eat 3 pounds. Simplify $7 \times 6 + 4 \times 3$ to find the amount of meat consumed each day by the lions. _____

**?** **ESSENTIAL QUESTION**

**20.** How do you use numerical expressions to solve real-world problems?

_____

_____

_____

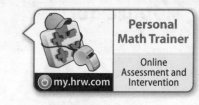

## Selected Response

**1.** Which expression has a value that is less than the base of that expression?

Ⓐ $2^3$

Ⓑ $\left(\frac{5}{6}\right)^2$

Ⓒ $3^2$

Ⓓ $4^4$

**2.** After the game the coach bought 9 chicken meals for $5 each and 15 burger meals for $6 each. What percent of the total amount the coach spent was used for the chicken meals?

Ⓐ $33\frac{1}{3}\%$

Ⓑ 45%

Ⓒ $66\frac{2}{3}\%$

Ⓓ 90%

**3.** Which operation should you perform first when you simplify $75 - (8 + 45 \div 3) \times 7$?

Ⓐ addition

Ⓑ division

Ⓒ multiplication

Ⓓ subtraction

**4.** At Tanika's school, three people are chosen in the first round. Each of those people chooses 3 people in the second round, and so on. How many people are chosen in the sixth round?

Ⓐ 18

Ⓑ 216

Ⓒ 243

Ⓓ 729

**5.** Which expression shows the prime factorization of 100?

Ⓐ $2^2 \times 5^2$     Ⓒ $10^{10}$

Ⓑ $10 \times 10$     Ⓓ $2 \times 5 \times 10$

**6.** Which number has only two factors?

Ⓐ 21     Ⓒ 25

Ⓑ 23     Ⓓ 27

**7.** Which expression is equivalent to $3.6 \times 3.6 \times 3.6 \times 3.6$?

Ⓐ $3.6 \times 4$     Ⓒ $3^4 \times 6^4$

Ⓑ $36^3$     Ⓓ $3.6^4$

**8.** Which expression gives the prime factorization of 80?

Ⓐ $2^4 \times 10$     Ⓒ $2^3 \times 5$

Ⓑ $2 \times 5 \times 8$     Ⓓ $2^4 \times 5$

## Gridded Response

**9.** Alison raised 10 to the 5th power. Then she divided this value by 100. What was the quotient?

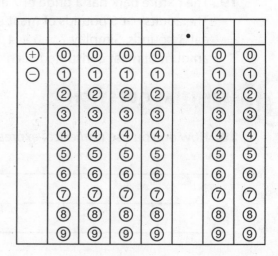

# Generating Equivalent Algebraic Expressions

**?** **ESSENTIAL QUESTION**

How can you generate equivalent algebraic expressions and use them to solve real-world problems?

⊙ my.hrw.com

**Real-World Video**

Carpenters use formulas to calculate a project's materials supply. Sometimes formulas can be written in different forms. The perimeter of a rectangle can be written as $P = 2(l + w)$ or $P = 2l + 2w$.

## GO DIGITAL
my.hrw.com

**my.hrw.com**

Go digital with your write-in student edition, accessible on any device.

**Math On the Spot**

Scan with your smart phone to jump directly to the online edition, video tutor, and more.

**Animated Math**

Interactively explore key concepts to see how math works.

**Personal Math Trainer**

Get immediate feedback and help as you work through practice sets.

**289**

# Are YOU Ready?

Complete these exercises to review skills you will need for this chapter.

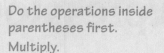
## Use of Parentheses

**EXAMPLE**     $(6 + 4) \times (3 + 8 + 1) = 10 \times 12$     Do the operations inside parentheses first.

                                        $= 120$     Multiply.

**Evaluate.**

**1.** $11 + (20 - 13)$

_____

**2.** $(10 - 7) - (14 - 12)$

_____

**3.** $(4 + 17) - (16 - 9)$

_____

**4.** $(23 - 15) - (18 - 13)$

_____

**5.** $8 \times (4 + 5 + 7)$

_____

**6.** $(2 + 3) \times (11 - 5)$

_____

## Words for Operations

**EXAMPLE**     Write a numerical expression for the quotient of 20 and 5.     Think: *Quotient* means to divide.

            $20 \div 5$     Write 20 divided by 5.

**Write a numerical expression for the word expression.**

**7.** the difference between 42 and 19 _____

**8.** the product of 7 and 12 _____

**9.** 30 more than 20 _____

**10.** 100 decreased by 77 _____

## Evaluate Expressions

**EXAMPLE**     Evaluate $2(5) - 3^2$.

            $2(5) - 3^2 = 2(5) - 9$     Evaluate exponents.
                      $= 10 - 9$     Multiply.
                      $= 1$     Subtract.

**Evaluate the expression.**

**11.** $3(8) - 15$ _____

**12.** $4(12) + 11$ _____

**13.** $3(7) - 4(2)$ _____

**14.** $4(2 + 3) - 12$ _____

**15.** $9(14 - 5) - 42$ _____

**16.** $7(8) - 5(8)$ _____

# Reading Start-Up

## Visualize Vocabulary

Use the review words to complete the graphic. You may put more than one word in each oval.

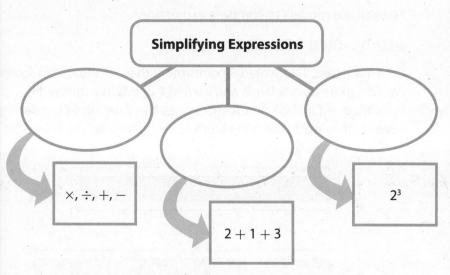

Simplifying Expressions

$\times, \div, +, -$

$2 + 1 + 3$

$2^3$

**Vocabulary**

**Review Words**
   base *(base)*
   exponent *(exponente)*
   numerical expression
   *(expresión numérica)*
   operations *(operaciones)*
   order of operations *(orden de las operaciones)*

**Preview Words**
   algebraic expression
   *(expresión algebraica)*
   coefficient *(coeficiente)*
   constant *(constante)*
   equivalent expression
   *(expresión equivalente)*
   evaluating *(evaluar)*
   like terms *(términos semejantes)*
   term *(término, en una expresión)*
   variable *(variable)*

## Understand Vocabulary

Complete the sentences using the preview words.

1. An expression that contains at least one variable is an

   _____ .

2. A part of an expression that is added or subtracted is a _____ .

3. A _____ is a specific number whose value does not change.

## Active Reading

**Key-Term Fold** Before beginning the module, create a key-term fold to help you learn the vocabulary in this module. Write the highlighted vocabulary words on one side of the flap. Write the definition for each word on the other side of the flap. Use the key-term fold to quiz yourself on the definitions used in this module.

## MODULE 11

# Unpacking the TEKS

Understanding the TEKS and the vocabulary terms in the TEKS will help you know exactly what you are expected to learn in this module.

---

TEKS **6.7.C**

Determine if two expressions are equivalent using concrete models, pictorial models, and algebraic representations.

### Key Vocabulary

**equivalent expressions**
*(expresión equivalente)*
Expressions that have the same value for all values of the variables.

## What It Means to You

You will use models to compare expressions.

### UNPACKING EXAMPLE 6.7.C

On a math quiz, Tina scored 3 points more than Yolanda. Juan scored 2 points more than Yolanda and earned 2 points as extra credit. Draw models for Tina's and Juan's scores. Use your models to decide whether they made the same score.

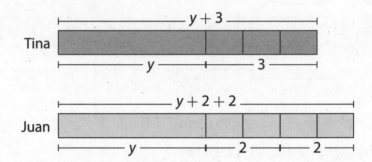

Tina and Juan did not make the same score because the models do not show equivalent expressions.

---

TEKS **6.7.D**

Generate equivalent expressions using the properties of operations: inverse, identity, commutative, associative, and distributive properties.

## What It Means to You

You will use the properties of operations to find an equivalent expression.

### UNPACKING EXAMPLE 6.7.D

William earns \$13 an hour working at a movie theater. He worked $h$ hours in concessions and three times as many hours at the ticket counter. Write and simplify an expression for the amount of money William earned.

\$13 · hours at concessions + \$13 · hours at ticket counter

$13h + 13(3h)$

$13h + 39h$      Multiply $13 \cdot 3h$.

$h(13 + 39)$     Distributive Property

# Modeling Equivalent Expressions

TEKS
Expressions, equations, and relationships—
6.7.C Determine if two expressions are equivalent using concrete models, pictorial models, and algebraic representations.

**? ESSENTIAL QUESTION**

How can you write algebraic expressions and use models to decide if expressions are equivalent?

---

**EXPLORE ACTIVITY**  TEKS 6.7.C

## Modeling Equivalent Expressions

**Equivalent expressions** are expressions that have the same value.

**The scale shown to the right is balanced.**

**A** Write an expression to represent the circles on the left side of the balance. _____

**B** The value of the expression on the left side is _____.

**C** Write an expression to represent the circles on the right side of the balance. _____

**D** The value of the expression on the right side is _____.

**E** Since the expressions have the same value, the expressions are _____.

**F** What will happen if you remove a circle from the right side of the balance?

_____

**G** If you add a circle to the left side of the balance, what can you do to the right side to keep the scale in balance?

_____

## Reflect

1. **What If?** Suppose there were 2 + 5 circles on the right side of the balance and 3 on the left side of the balance. What can you do to balance the scale? Explain how the scale models equivalent expressions.

_____

_____

Math On the Spot
my.hrw.com

# Writing Algebraic Expressions

An **algebraic expression** is an expression that contains one or more variables and may also contain operation symbols, such as + or −.

A **variable** is a letter or symbol used to represent an unknown or unspecified number. The value of a variable may change.

A **constant** is a specific number whose value does not change.

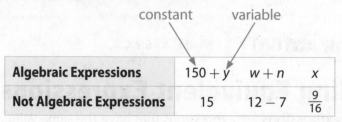

constant      variable

| Algebraic Expressions | $150 + y$ | $w + n$ | $x$ |
|---|---|---|---|
| **Not Algebraic Expressions** | 15 | $12 - 7$ | $\frac{9}{16}$ |

In algebraic expressions, multiplication and division are usually written without the symbols × and ÷.

- Write $3 \times n$ as $3n$, $3 \cdot n$, or $n \cdot 3$.
- Write $3 \div n$ as $\frac{3}{n}$.

There are several different ways to describe expressions with words.

| Operation | Addition | Subtraction | Multiplication | Division |
|---|---|---|---|---|
| **Words** | • added to<br>• plus<br>• sum<br>• more than | • subtracted from<br>• minus<br>• difference<br>• less than<br>• take away<br>• taken from | • times<br>• multiplied by<br>• product<br>• groups of | • divided by<br>• divided into<br>• quotient |

## EXAMPLE 1

TEKS 6.7.C

**A** **Write each phrase as an algebraic expression.**

The sum of 7 and x          *The operation is addition.*

The algebraic expression is $7 + x$.

The quotient of z and 3          *The operation is division.*

The algebraic expression is $\frac{z}{3}$.

**B** **Write a phrase for each expression.**

$11x$          *The operation is multiplication.*

The product of 11 and x

$8 - y$          *The operation is subtraction.*

y less than 8

## YOUR TURN

**Write each phrase as an algebraic expression.**

**2.** *n* times 7 _____     **3.** 4 minus *y* _____     **4.** 13 added to *x* _____

**Write a phrase for each expression.**

**5.** $\frac{x}{12}$ _____     **6.** 10*y* _____

# Modeling Algebraic Expressions

Algebraic expressions can also be represented with models.

## EXAMPLE 2

TEKS 6.7.C

**Use a bar model to represent each expression.**

**A** $7 + x$     *Combine 7 and x.*

**B** $\frac{z}{3}$     *Divide z into 3 equal parts.*

## YOUR TURN

**Draw a bar model to represent each expression.**

**7.** $t - 2$     **8.** $4y$

# Comparing Expressions Using Models

Algebraic expressions are *equivalent* if they are equal for all values of the variable. For example, $x + 2$ and $x + 1 + 1$ are equivalent.

## EXAMPLE 3  *Real World*                            TEKS 6.7.C

**Katriana and Andrew started the day with the same amount of money. Katriana spent 5 dollars on lunch. Andrew spent 3 dollars on lunch and 2 dollars on an afterschool snack.**

Do Katriana and Andrew have the same amount of money left?

**STEP 1**  Write an algebraic expression to represent the money Katriana has left. Represent the expression with a model.

> The variable represents the amount of money both Katriana and Andrew have at the beginning of the day.

$x - 5$

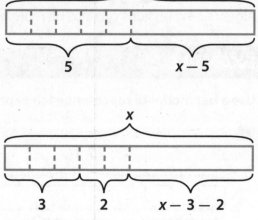

**STEP 2**  Write an algebraic expression to represent the money Andrew has left. Represent the expression with a model.

$x - 3 - 2$

**STEP 3**  Compare the models.

The models are equivalent, so the expressions are equivalent.

Andrew and Katriana have the same amount of money left.

## YOUR TURN

9.  On a math quiz, Tina scored 3 points more than Julia. Juan scored 2 points more than Julia and earned 2 points in extra credit. Write an expression and draw a bar model to represent Tina's score and Juan's score. Did Tina and Juan make the same grade on the quiz? Explain.

## Guided Practice

**1.** Write an expression in the right side of the scale that will keep the scale balanced. (Explore Activity)

**Write each phrase as an algebraic expression.** (Example 1)

**2.** 3 less than $y$ _____

**3.** The product of 2 and $p$ _____

**Write a phrase for each algebraic expression.** (Example 1)

**4.** $y + 12$ _____

**5.** $\dfrac{p}{10}$ _____

**6.** Draw a bar model to represent the expression $m \div 4$. (Example 2)

**At 6 p.m., the temperature in Phoenix, AZ, $t$, is the same as the temperature in Tucson, AZ. By 9 p.m., the temperature in Phoenix has dropped 2 degrees and in Tucson it has dropped 4 degrees. By 11 p.m., the temperature in Phoenix has dropped another 3 degrees.** (Example 3)

**7.** Represent the temperature in each city with an algebraic expression and a bar model.

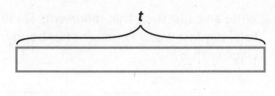

_____          _____

**8.** Are the expressions that represent the temperatures in the two cities equivalent? Justify your answer.

_____

_____

### ? ESSENTIAL QUESTION CHECK-IN

**9.** How can you use expressions and models to determine if expressions are equivalent?

_____

_____

# 11.1 Independent Practice

**TEKS** 6.7.C

**10.** Write an algebraic expression with the constant 7 and the variable $y$.

_____

**11.** Write an algebraic expression with two variables and one constant.

_____

**12.** What are the variables in the expression $x + 8 - y$?

_____

**13.** Identify the parts of the algebraic expression $x + 15$.

Constant(s) _____

Variable(s) _____

**Write each phrase as an algebraic expression.**

**14.** $n$ divided by 8 _____

**15.** $p$ multiplied by 4 _____

**16.** $b$ plus 14 _____

**17.** 90 times $x$ _____

**18.** $a$ take away 16 _____

**19.** $k$ less than 24 _____

**20.** 3 groups of $w$ _____

**21.** the sum of 1 and $q$ _____

**22.** the quotient of 13 and $z$ _____

**23.** $c$ added to 45 _____

**Write a phrase in words for each algebraic expression.**

**24.** $m + 83$ _____

**25.** $42s$ _____

**26.** $\frac{9}{d}$ _____

**27.** $t - 29$ _____

**28.** $2 + g$ _____

**29.** $11x$ _____

**30.** $\frac{h}{12}$ _____

**31.** $5 - k$ _____

**Sarah and Noah work at Read On Bookstore and get paid the same hourly wage. The table shows their work schedule for last week.**

| Read On Bookstore Work Schedule (hours) | | | |
|---|---|---|---|
| | **Monday** | **Tuesday** | **Wednesday** |
| **Sarah** | 5 | 3 | |
| **Noah** | | | 8 |

**32.** Write an expression that represents Sarah's total pay last week. Represent her hourly wage with $w$.

_____

**33.** Write an expression that represents Noah's total pay last week. Represent his hourly wage with $w$.

_____

**34.** Are the expressions equivalent? Did Sarah and Noah earn the same amount last week? Use models to justify your answer.

_____

_____

_____

_____

_____

**35. Critique Reasoning** Lisa concluded that $3 \cdot 2$ and $3^2$ are equivalent expressions. Is Lisa correct? Explain.

_____

_____

**36. Multiple Representations** How could you represent the expressions $x - 5$ and $x - 3 - 3$ on a scale like the one you used in the Explore Activity? Would the scale balance?

_____

_____

_____

**37. Multistep** Will, Hector, and Lydia volunteered at the animal shelter in March and April. The table shows the number of hours Will and Hector volunteered in March. Let $x$ represent the number of hours Lydia volunteered in March.

| March Volunteering | |
|---|---|
| Will | 3 hours |
| Hector | 5 hours |

a. Will's volunteer hours in April were equal to his March volunteer hours plus Lydia's March volunteer hours. Write an expression to represent Will's volunteer hours in April.

_____

b. Hector's volunteer hours in April were equal to 2 hours less than his March volunteer hours plus Lydia's March volunteer hours. Write an expression to represent Hector's volunteer hours in April.

_____

c. Did Will and Hector volunteer the same number of hours in April? Explain.

_____

**38.** The town of Rayburn received 6 more inches of snow than the town of Greenville. Let $g$ represent the amount of snow in Greenville. Write an algebraic expression to represent the amount of snow in Rayburn.

_____

**39.** Abby baked 48 cookies and divided them evenly into bags. Let $b$ represent the number of bags. Write an algebraic expression to represent the number of cookies in each bag.

_____

**40.** Eli is driving at a speed of 55 miles per hour. Let $h$ represent the number of hours that Eli drives at this speed. Write an algebraic expression to represent the number of miles that Eli travels during this time.

_____

 **FOCUS ON HIGHER ORDER THINKING**

Work Area

**41. Represent Real-World Problems** If the number of shoes in a closet is $s$, then how many pairs of shoes are in the closet? Explain.

_____

_____

**42. Communicate Mathematical Ideas** Is $12x$ an algebraic expression? Explain why or why not.

_____

_____

**43. Problem Solving** Write an expression that has three terms, two different variables, and one constant.

_____

**44. Represent Real-World Problems** Describe a situation that can be modeled by the expression $x - 8$.

_____

_____

_____

**45. Critique Reasoning** Ricardo says that the expression $y + 4$ is equivalent to the expression $1y + 4$. Is he correct? Explain.

_____

_____

_____

_____

# Evaluating Expressions

**TEKS**
Expressions, equations, and relationships—6.7.A
Generate equivalent numerical expressions using order of operations, including whole number exponents and prime factorization.

## ESSENTIAL QUESTION

How can you use the order of operations to evaluate algebraic expressions?

# Evaluating Expressions

Recall that an algebraic expression contains one or more variables. You can substitute a number for that variable and then find the value of the expression. This is called **evaluating** the expression.

Math On the Spot

my.hrw.com

### EXAMPLE 1                                    **TEKS** 6.7.A

**Evaluate each expression for the given value of the variable.**

**A** $x - 9$; $x = 15$

$15 - 9$       Substitute 15 for x.

$6$            Subtract.

When $x = 15$, $x - 9 = 6$.

**B** $\frac{16}{n}$; $n = 8$

$\frac{16}{8}$       Substitute 8 for n.

$2$            Divide.

When $n = 8$, $\frac{16}{n} = 2$.

**C** $0.5y$; $y = 1.4$

$0.5(1.4)$     Substitute 1.4 for y.

$0.7$          Multiply.

When $y = 1.4$, $0.5y = 0.7$.

**D** $6k$; $k = \frac{1}{3}$

HINT: Think of 6 as $\frac{6}{1}$.

$6\left(\frac{1}{3}\right)$       Substitute $\frac{1}{3}$ for k.

$2$            Multiply.

When $k = \frac{1}{3}$, $6k = 2$.

**Personal Math Trainer**

Online Assessment and Intervention

⏻ my.hrw.com

**Math On the Spot**

⏻ my.hrw.com

**YOUR TURN**

Evaluate each expression for the given value of the variable.

**1.** $4x$; $x = 8$ _____ **2.** $6.5 - n$; $n = 1.8$ _____ **3.** $\frac{m}{6}$; $m = 18$ _____

# Using the Order of Operations

Expressions may have more than one operation or more than one variable. To evaluate these expressions, substitute the given value for each variable and then use the order of operations.

**EXAMPLE 2**  TEKS 6.7.A

Evaluate each expression for the given value of the variable.

**A** $4(x - 4)$; $x = 7$

$4(7 - 4)$ — Substitute 7 for x.

$4(3)$ — Subtract inside the parentheses.

$12$ — Multiply.

When $x = 7$, $4(x - 4) = 12$.

**B** $4x - 4$; $x = 7$

$4(7) - 4$ — Substitute 7 for x.

$28 - 4$ — Multiply.

$24$ — Subtract.

When $x = 7$, $4x - 4 = 24$.

**C** $w - x + y$; $w = 6$, $x = 5$, $y = 3$

$(6) - (5) + (3)$ — Substitute 6 for w, 5 for x, and 3 for y.

$1 + 3$ — Subtract.

$4$ — Add.

When $w = 6$, $x = 5$, $y = 3$, $w - x + y = 4$.

**Math Talk**

Mathematical Processes

Is $w - x + y$ equivalent to $w - y + x$? Explain any difference in the order the math operations are performed.

**D** $x^2 - x$; $x = 9$

$(9)^2 - (9)$ — Substitute 9 for each x.

$81 - 9$ — Evaluate exponents.

$72$ — Subtract.

When $x = 9$, $x^2 - x = 72$.

Evaluate each expression for $n = 5$.

**4.** $3(n + 1)$ _____ **5.** $4(n - 4) + 14$ _____ **6.** $6n + n^2$ _____

Evaluate each expression for $a = 3$, $b = 4$, and $c = -6$.

**7.** $ab - c$ _____ **8.** $bc + 5a$ _____ **9.** $a^2 - (b + c)$ _____

**Personal Math Trainer**

Online Assessment and Intervention

⏻ my.hrw.com

# Evaluating Real-World Expressions

You can evaluate expressions to solve real-world problems.

**Math On the Spot**

⏻ my.hrw.com

## EXAMPLE 3  Real World

TEKS 6.7.A

**The expression $1.8c + 32$ gives the temperature in degrees Fahrenheit for a given temperature in degrees Celsius $c$. Find the temperature in degrees Fahrenheit that is equivalent to $30\,°C$.**

**STEP 1**  Find the value of $c$.

$c = 30\,°C$

**STEP 2**  Substitute the value into the expression.

$1.8c + 32$

$1.8(30) + 32$   Substitute 30 for $c$.

$54 + 32$   Multiply.

$86$   Add.

$86\,°F$ is equivalent to $30\,°C$.

**10.** The expression $6x^2$ gives the surface area of a cube, and the expression $x^3$ gives the volume of a cube, where $x$ is the length of one side of the cube. Find the surface area and the volume of a cube with a side length of 2 m.

$S =$ _____ $m^2$ ; $V =$ _____ $m^3$

**11.** The expression $60m$ gives the number of seconds in $m$ minutes. How many seconds are there in 7 minutes?

_____ seconds

**Personal Math Trainer**

Online Assessment and Intervention

⏻ my.hrw.com

## Guided Practice

**Evaluate each expression for the given value(s) of the variable(s).**
(Examples 1 and 2)

**1.** $x - 7; x = 23$ _____

**2.** $3a - b; a = 4, b = 6$ _____

**3.** $\frac{8}{t}; t = 4$ _____

**4.** $9 + m; m = 1.5$ _____

**5.** $\frac{1}{2}w + 2; w = \frac{1}{9}$ _____

**6.** $5(6.2 + z); z = 3.8$ _____

**7.** The table shows the prices for games in Bella's soccer league. Her parents and grandmother attended a soccer game. How much did they spend if they all went together in one car? (Example 3)

| Women's Soccer Game Prices | |
|---|---|
| Student tickets | $6 |
| Nonstudent tickets | $12 |
| Parking | $5 |

    **a.** Write an expression that represents the cost of one carful of nonstudent soccer fans. Use $x$ as the number of people who rode in the car and attended the game.

    _____ is an expression that represents the cost of one carful of nonstudent soccer fans.

    **b.** Since there are three attendees, evaluate the expression $12x + 5$ for $x = 3$.

    $12(\underline{\quad}) + 5 = \underline{\quad\quad} + 5 = \underline{\quad\quad}$

    The family spent _____ to attend the game.

**8.** Stan wants to add trim all around the edge of a rectangular tablecloth that measures 5 feet long by 7 feet wide. The perimeter of the rectangular tablecloth is twice the length added to twice the width. How much trim does Stan need to buy? (Example 3)

    **a.** Write an expression that represents the perimeter of the rectangular tablecloth. Let $l$ represent the length of the tablecloth and $w$ represent its width. The expression would be _____.

    **b.** Evaluate the expression $P = 2w + 2l$ for $l = 5$ and $w = 7$.

    $2(\underline{\quad\quad}) + 2(\underline{\quad\quad}) = 14 + \underline{\quad\quad} = \underline{\quad\quad}$

    Stan bought _____ of trim to sew onto the tablecloth.

**9.** **Essential Question Follow Up** How do you know the correct order in which to evaluate algebraic expressions?

_____

_____

_____

## 11.2 Independent Practice

**TEKS** 6.7.A

**10.** The table shows ticket prices at the Movie 16 theater. Let $a$ represent the number of adult tickets, $c$ the number of children's tickets, and $s$ the number of senior citizen tickets.

| Movie 16 Ticket Prices | |
|---|---|
| Adults | $8.75 |
| Children | $6.50 |
| Seniors | $6.50 |

**a.** Write an expression for the total cost of tickets.

_____

_____

**b.** The Andrews family bought 2 adult tickets, 3 children's tickets, and 1 senior ticket. Evaluate your expression in part a to find the total cost of the tickets.

_____

_____

**c.** The Spencer family bought 4 adult tickets and 2 children's tickets. Did they spend the same as the Andrews family? Explain.

_____

**11.** The area of a triangular sail is given by the expression $\frac{1}{2}bh$, where $b$ is the length of the base and $h$ is the height. What is the area of a triangular sail in a model sailboat when $b = 12$ inches and $h = 7$ inches?

$A =$ _____ in.$^2$

**12.** Ramon wants to balance his checking account. He has $2,340 in the account. He writes a check for $140. He deposits a check for $268. How much does Ramon have left

in his checking account? _____

**13.** **Look for a Pattern** Evaluate the expression $6x - x^2$ for $x = 0, 1, 2, 3, 4, 5,$ and 6. Use your results to fill in the table and describe any pattern that you see.

| $x$ | 0 | 1 | 2 | 3 | 4 | 5 | 6 |
|---|---|---|---|---|---|---|---|
| $6x - x^2$ | | | | | | | |

_____

_____

_____

_____

_____

_____

_____

**14.** The kinetic energy (in joules) of a moving object can be calculated from the expression $\frac{1}{2}mv^2$, where $m$ is the mass of the object in kilograms and $v$ is its speed in meters per second. Find the kinetic energy of a 0.145-kg baseball that is thrown at a speed of 40 meters per second.

$E =$ _____ joules

**15.** The area of a square is given by $x^2$, where $x$ is the length of one side. Mary's original garden was in the shape of a square. She has decided to double the area of her garden. Write an expression that represents the area of Mary's new garden. Evaluate the expression if the side length of Mary's original garden was 8 feet.

_____

**16.** The volume of a pyramid with a square base is given by the expression $\frac{1}{3}s^2h$, where $s$ is the length of a side of the base and $h$ is the height. Find the volume of a pyramid with a square base of side length 24 feet and a height of 30 feet.

_____

Work Area

**17. Draw Conclusions** Consider the expressions $3x(x - 2) + 2$ and $2x^2 + 3x - 12$.

**a.** Evaluate each expression for $x = 2$ and for $x = 7$. Based on your results, do you know whether the two expressions are equivalent? Explain.

_____

_____

_____

_____

_____

**b.** Evaluate each expression for $x = 1$. Based on your results, do you know whether the two expressions are equivalent? Explain.

_____

_____

_____

_____

_____

**18. Critique Reasoning** Marjorie evaluated the expression $3x + 2$ for $x = 5$ as shown:

$$3x + 2 = 35 + 2 = 37$$

What was Marjorie's mistake? What is the correct value of $3x + 2$ for $x = 5$?

_____

_____

_____

# LESSON 11.3 Generating Equivalent Expressions

**TEKS**
Expressions, equations, and relationships—
**6.7.D** Generate equivalent expressions using the properties of operations: inverse, identity, commutative, associative, and distributive properties.
*Also 6.7.C*

**? ESSENTIAL QUESTION**

How can you identify and write equivalent expressions?

---

**EXPLORE ACTIVITY 1** | **TEKS** 6.7.C

## Identifying Equivalent Expressions

One way to test whether two expressions might be equivalent is to evaluate them for the same value of the variable.

**Match the expressions in List A with their equivalent expressions in List B.**

| List A | List B |
|--------|--------|
| $5x + 65$ | $5x + 1$ |
| $5(x + 1)$ | $5x + 5$ |
| $1 + 5x$ | $5(13 + x)$ |

**A** Evaluate each of the expressions in the lists for $x = 3$.

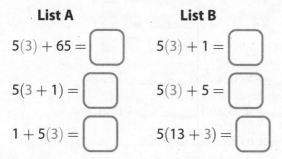

**List A**

$5(3) + 65 = \boxed{\phantom{00}}$

$5(3 + 1) = \boxed{\phantom{00}}$

$1 + 5(3) = \boxed{\phantom{00}}$

**List B**

$5(3) + 1 = \boxed{\phantom{00}}$

$5(3) + 5 = \boxed{\phantom{00}}$

$5(13 + 3) = \boxed{\phantom{00}}$

**B** Which pair(s) of expressions have the same value for $x = 3$?

_____

_____

**C** How could you further test whether the expressions in each pair are equivalent?

_____

**D** Do you think the expressions in each pair are equivalent? Why or why not?

_____

_____

**Reflect**

1. **Error Analysis** Lisa evaluated the expressions $2x$ and $x^2$ for $x = 2$ and found that both expressions were equal to 4. Lisa concluded that $2x$ and $x^2$ are equivalent expressions. How could you show Lisa that she is incorrect?

_____

_____

**EXPLORE ACTIVITY 2**  TEKS 6.7.C

# Modeling Equivalent Expressions

You can also use models to determine if two expressions are equivalent. *Algebra tiles* are one way to model expressions.

**Algebra Tiles**

$\boxed{+} = 1$

$\boxed{-} = -1$

$\boxed{\ +\ } = x$

**Determine if the expression $3(x + 2)$ is equivalent to $3x + 6$.**

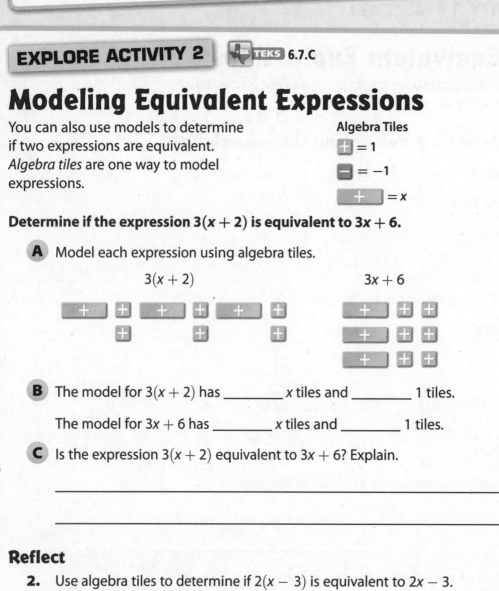

**A** Model each expression using algebra tiles.

$3(x + 2)$ 　　　　　　　　　 $3x + 6$

**B** The model for $3(x + 2)$ has _____ x tiles and _____ 1 tiles.

The model for $3x + 6$ has _____ x tiles and _____ 1 tiles.

**C** Is the expression $3(x + 2)$ equivalent to $3x + 6$? Explain.

_____

_____

**Reflect**

2. Use algebra tiles to determine if $2(x - 3)$ is equivalent to $2x - 3$. Explain your answer.

_____

_____

# Writing Equivalent Expressions Using Properties

Math On the Spot
my.hrw.com

**Properties of operations can be used to identify equivalent expressions.**

| Properties of Operations | Examples |
|---|---|
| **Commutative Property of Addition:** When adding, changing the order of the numbers does not change the sum. | $3 + 4 = 4 + 3$ |
| **Commutative Property of Multiplication:** When multiplying, changing the order of the numbers does not change the product. | $2 \times 4 = 4 \times 2$ |
| **Associative Property of Addition:** When adding more than two numbers, the grouping of the numbers does not change the sum. | $(3 + 4) + 5 = 3 + (4 + 5)$ |
| **Associative Property of Multiplication:** When multiplying more than two numbers, the grouping of the numbers does not change the product. | $(2 \times 4) \times 3 = 2 \times (4 \times 3)$ |
| **Distributive Property:** Multiplying a number by a sum or difference is the same as multiplying by each number in the sum or difference and then adding or subtracting. | $6(2 + 4) = 6(2) + 6(4)$ $8(5 - 3) = 8(5) - 8(3)$ |
| **Identity Property of Addition:** Adding zero to a number does not change its value. | $9 + 0 = 9$ |
| **Identity Property of Multiplication:** Multiplying a number by one does not change its value. | $1 \times 7 = 7$ |
| **Inverse Property of Addition:** The sum of a number and its opposite, or additive inverse, is zero. | $-3 + 3 = 0$ |

**Math Talk**
Mathematical Processes

What property can you use to write an expression that is equivalent to $0 + c$? What is the equivalent expression?

## EXAMPLE 1

TEKS 6.7.D

**Use a property to write an expression that is equivalent to $x + 3$.**

The operation in the expression is addition.

You can use the Commutative Property of Addition to write an equivalent expression: $x + 3 = 3 + x$

### YOUR TURN

**For each expression, use a property to write an equivalent expression. Tell which property you used.**

3. $(ab)c = $ _____

4. $3y + 4y = $ _____

Personal Math Trainer

Online Assessment and Intervention

my.hrw.com

# Identifying Equivalent Expressions Using Properties

## EXAMPLE 2

Use the properties of operations to determine if the expressions are equivalent.

**A** $3(x - 2)$; $3x - 6$

$3(x - 2) = 3x - 6$                    Distributive Property

$3(x - 2)$ and $3x - 6$ are equivalent expressions.

**B** $2 + x$; $\frac{1}{2}(4 + x)$

$\frac{1}{2}(x + 4) = \frac{1}{2}x + 2$              Distributive Property

$= 2 + \frac{1}{2}x$                   Commutative Property

$2 + x$ does not equal $2 + \frac{1}{2}x$.

They are not equivalent expressions.

**Math Talk**

**Mathematical Processes**

Explain how you could use algebra tiles to represent the Distributive Property in A.

### YOUR TURN

Use the properties of operations to determine if the expressions are equivalent.

**5.** $6x - 8$; $2(3x - 5)$

**6.** $2 - 2 + 5x$; $5x$

_____        _____

_____        _____

**7.** Jamal bought 2 packs of stickers and 8 individual stickers. Use $x$ to represent the number of stickers in a pack of stickers and write an expression to represent the number of stickers Jamal bought. Is the expression equivalent to $2(4 + x)$? Check your answer with algebra tile models.

_____

_____

_____

# Generating Equivalent Expressions

| Parts of an algebraic expression | | |
|---|---|---|
| terms | The parts of the expression that are separated by $+$ or $-$ signs | $12 + 3y^2 + 4x + 2y^2 + 4$ |
| coefficients | Numbers that are multiplied by at least one variable | $12 + 3y^2 + 4x + 2y^2 + 4$ |
| like terms | Terms with the same variable(s) raised to the same power(s) | $12 + 3y^2 + 4x + 2y^2 + 4$ |

Math On the Spot

my.hrw.com

When an expression contains like terms, you can use properties to combine the like terms into a single term. This results in an expression that is equivalent to the original expression.

## EXAMPLE 3

TEKS 6.7.D

**Combine like terms.**

**A** $6x^2 - 4x^2$

$6x^2$ and $4x^2$ are like terms.

| | |
|---|---|
| $6x^2 - 4x^2 = x^2(6 - 4)$ | Distributive Property |
| $= x^2(2)$ | Subtract inside the parentheses. |
| $= 2x^2$ | Commutative Property of Multiplication |
| $6x^2 - 4x^2 = 2x^2$ | |

> **Math Talk**
> Mathematical Processes
> Write 2 terms that can be combined with $7y^4$.

**B** $3a + 2(b + 5a)$

| | |
|---|---|
| $3a + 2(b + 5a) = 3a + 2b + 2(5a)$ | Distributive Property |
| $= 3a + 2b + (2 \cdot 5)a$ | Associative Property of Multiplication |
| $= 3a + 2b + 10a$ | Multiply 2 and 5. |
| $= 3a + 10a + 2b$ | Commutative Property of Addition |
| $= (3 + 10)a + 2b$ | Distributive Property |
| $= 13a + 2b$ | Add inside the parentheses. |
| $3a + 2(b + 5a) = 13a + 2b$ | |

**C** $y + 11x - 7x + 7y$

| | |
|---|---|
| | $y$ and $7y$ are like terms; $11x$ and $7x$ are like terms. |
| $y + 11x - 7x + 7y = y + 7y + 11x - 7x$ | Commutative Property |
| $= y(1 + 7) + x(11 - 7)$ | Distributive Property |
| $= 8y + 4x$ | Commutative Property |
| $y + 11x - 7x + 7y = 8y + 4x$ | |

**YOUR TURN**

**Combine like terms.**

**8.** $8y - 3y = $ _____

**9.** $6x^2 + 4(x^2 - 1) = $ _____

**10.** $4a^5 - 2a^5 + 4b + b = $

_____

**11.** $8m + 14 - 12 + 4n = $

_____

# Guided Practice

**1.** Evaluate each of the expressions in the list for $y = 5$. Then, draw lines to match the expressions in List A with their equivalent expressions in List B.
(Explore Activity 1)

**List A**

$4 + 4y = $ _____

$4(y - 1) = $ _____

$4y + 1 = $ _____

**List B**

$4y - 4 = $ _____

$4(y + 1) = $ _____

$1 + 4y = $ _____

**2.** Determine if the expressions are equivalent by comparing the models. (Explore Activity 2) _____

$$x - 4 \qquad\qquad 2(x - 2)$$

**For each expression, use a property to write an equivalent expression. Tell which property you used.** (Example 1)

**3.** $ab = $ _____

_____

**4.** $5(3x - 2) = $ _____

_____

**Use the properties of operations to determine if each pair of expressions is equivalent.** (Example 2)

**5.** $\frac{1}{2}(4 - 2x); 2 - 2x$ _____

**6.** $\frac{1}{2}(6x - 2); 3 - x$ _____

**Combine like terms.** (Example 3)

**7.** $32y + 12y = $ _____

**8.** $12 + 3x - x - 12 = $ _____

**? ESSENTIAL QUESTION CHECK-IN**

**9.** Describe two ways to write equivalent algebraic expressions.

_____

_____

## 11.3 Independent Practice

TEKS 6.7.D, 6.7.C

Personal Math Trainer

Online Assessment and Intervention

my.hrw.com

**For each expression, use a property to write an equivalent expression. Tell which property you used.**

10. $cd =$ _____

_____

11. $x + 13 =$ _____

_____

12. $4(2x - 3) =$ _____

_____

13. $2 + (a + b) =$ _____

_____

14. Draw algebra tile models to prove that $4 + 8x$ and $4(2x + 1)$ are equivalent.

_____ _____

**Combine like terms.**

15. $7x^4 - 5x^4 =$ _____

16. $32y + 5y =$ _____

17. $6b + 7b - 10 =$ _____

18. $2x + 3x + 4 =$ _____

19. $y + 4 + 3(y + 2) =$ _____

20. $7a^2 - a^2 + 16 =$ _____

21. $3y^2 + 3(4y^2 - 2) =$ _____

22. $z^2 + z + 4z^3 + 4z^2 =$ _____

23. $0.5(x^4 - 3) + 12 =$ _____

24. $\frac{1}{4}(16 + 4p) =$ _____

25. **Justify Reasoning** Is $3x + 12 - 2x$ equivalent to $x + 12$? Use two properties of operations to justify your answer.

_____

_____

_____

26. William earns $13 an hour working at a movie theater. Last week he worked $h$ hours at the concession stand and three times as many hours at the ticket counter. Write and simplify an expression for the amount of money William earned last week.

_____

**27. Multiple Representations** Use the information in the table to write and simplify an expression to find the total weight of the medals won by the top medal-winning nations in the 2012 London Olympic Games. The three types of medals have different weights.

| 2012 Summer Olympics | | | |
|---|---|---|---|
| | Gold | Silver | Bronze |
| United States | 46 | 29 | 29 |
| China | 38 | 27 | 23 |
| Great Britain | 29 | 17 | 19 |

_____

_____

**Write an expression for the perimeters of each given figure. Simplify the expressions.**

28. _____     29. _____

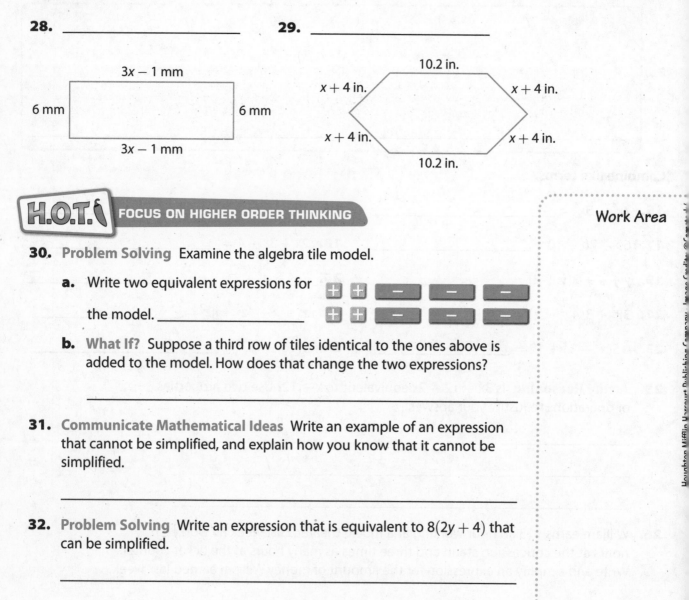

**30. Problem Solving** Examine the algebra tile model.

**a.** Write two equivalent expressions for the model. _____

**b. What If?** Suppose a third row of tiles identical to the ones above is added to the model. How does that change the two expressions?

_____

**31. Communicate Mathematical Ideas** Write an example of an expression that cannot be simplified, and explain how you know that it cannot be simplified.

_____

**32. Problem Solving** Write an expression that is equivalent to $8(2y + 4)$ that can be simplified.

_____

**Work Area**

Houghton Mifflin Harcourt Publishing Company • Image Credits: ©Getty

# Ready to Go On?

## 11.1 Modeling Equivalent Expressions

**Write each phrase as an algebraic expression.**

**1.** $p$ divided by 6 _____

**2.** 65 less than $j$ _____

**3.** the sum of 185 and $h$ _____

**4.** the product of 16 and $g$ _____

**5.** Let $x$ represent the number of television show episodes that are taped in a season. Write an expression for the number of episodes taped in

4 seasons. _____

## 11.2 Evaluating Expressions

**Evaluate each expression for the given value of the variable.**

**6.** $8p; p = 9$ _____

**7.** $11 + r; r = 7$ _____

**8.** $4(d + 7); d = -2$ _____

**9.** $\frac{-60}{m}; m = 5$ _____

**10.** To find the area of a triangle, you can use the expression $b \times h \div 2$, where $b$ is the base of the triangle and $h$ is its height. What is the area

of a triangle with a base of 6 and a height of 8? _____

## 11.3 Generating Equivalent Expressions

**11.** Draw lines to match the expressions in List A with their equivalent expressions in List B.

| List A | List B |
|--------|--------|
| $7x + 14$ | $7(1 + x)$ |
| $7 + 7x$ | $7x - 7$ |
| $7(x - 1)$ | $7(x + 2)$ |

**? ESSENTIAL QUESTION**

**12.** How can you determine if two algebraic expressions are equivalent?

_____

_____

_____

_____

## Selected Response

**1.** Which expression represents the product of 83 and $x$?

Ⓐ $83 + x$

Ⓑ $83 \div x$

Ⓒ $83x$

Ⓓ $83 - x$

**2.** Which phrase describes the algebraic expression $\frac{r}{9}$?

Ⓐ the product of $r$ and 9

Ⓑ the quotient of $r$ and 9

Ⓒ 9 less than $r$

Ⓓ $r$ more than 9

**3.** Rhonda was organizing photos in a photo album. She took 60 photos and divided them evenly among $p$ pages. Which algebraic expression represents the number of photos on each page?

Ⓐ $p - 60$     Ⓒ $\frac{p}{60}$

Ⓑ $60 - p$     Ⓓ $\frac{60}{p}$

**4.** Using the algebraic expression $4n + 6$, what is the greatest whole-number value of $n$ that will give you a result less than 100?

Ⓐ 22     Ⓒ 24

Ⓑ 23     Ⓓ 25

**5.** Evaluate $7w - 14$ for $w = 9$.

Ⓐ 2

Ⓑ 18

Ⓒ 49

Ⓓ 77

**6.** Katie has read 32% of a book. If she has read 80 pages, how many more pages does Katie have left to read?

Ⓐ 40

Ⓑ 170

Ⓒ 200

Ⓓ 250

**7.** The expression $12(x + 4)$ represents the total cost of CDs Mei bought in April and May at $12 each. Which property is applied to write the equivalent expression $12x + 48$?

Ⓐ Associative Property of Addition

Ⓑ Associative Property of Multiplication

Ⓒ Commutative Property of Multiplication

Ⓓ Distributive Property

## Gridded Response

**8.** When traveling in Europe, Bailey converts the temperature given in degrees Celsius to a Fahrenheit temperature by using the expression $9x \div 5 + 32$, where $x$ is the Celsius temperature. Find the temperature in degrees Fahrenheit when it is $15\,°C$.

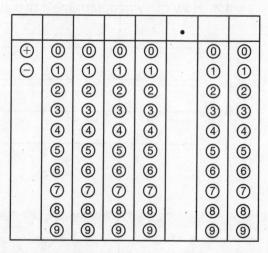

# Equations and Relationships

## ESSENTIAL QUESTION

How can you use equations and relationships to solve real-world problems?

**Real-World Video**

People often attempt to break World Records. To model how many seconds faster $f$ an athlete's time $a$ seconds must be to match a record time $r$ seconds, write the equation $f = a - r$.

my.hrw.com

# GO DIGITAL
my.hrw.com

**my.hrw.com**

Go digital with your write-in student edition, accessible on any device.

**Math On the Spot**

Scan with your smart phone to jump directly to the online edition, video tutor, and more.

**Animated Math**

Interactively explore key concepts to see how math works.

**Personal Math Trainer**

Get immediate feedback and help as you work through practice sets.

# Are YOU Ready?

Complete these exercises to review skills you will need for this chapter.

**Personal Math Trainer**

Online Assessment and Intervention

my.hrw.com

## Evaluate Expressions

| EXAMPLE | Evaluate $8(3+2) - 5^2$ | |
|---|---|---|
| | $8(3+2) - 5^2 = 8(5) - 5^2$ | Perform operations inside parentheses first. |
| | $= 8(5) - 25$ | Evaluate exponents. |
| | $= 40 - 25$ | Multiply. |
| | $= 15$ | Subtract. |

**Evaluate the expression.**

**1.** $4(5 + 6) - 15$ _____

**2.** $8(2 + 4) + 16$ _____

**3.** $3(14 - 7) - 16$ _____

**4.** $6(8 - 3) + 3(7 - 4)$ _____

**5.** $10(6 - 5) - 3(9 - 6)$ _____

**6.** $7(4 + 5 + 2) - 6(3 + 5)$ _____

**7.** $2(8 + 3) + 4^2$ _____

**8.** $7(14 - 8) - 6^2$ _____

**9.** $8(2 + 1)^2 - 4^2$ _____

## Connect Words and Equations

| EXAMPLE | The product of a number and 4 is 32. | |
|---|---|---|
| | The product of $x$ and 4 is 32. | Represent the unknown with a variable. |
| | $4 \times x$ is 32. | Determine the operation. |
| | $4 \times x = 32$. | Determine the placement of the equal sign. |

**Write an algebraic equation for the word sentence.**

**10.** A number increased by 7.9 is 8.3. _____

**11.** 17 is the sum of a number and 6. _____

**12.** The quotient of a number and 8 is 4. _____

**13.** 81 is three times a number. _____

**14.** The difference between 31 and a number is 7. _____

**15.** Eight less than a number is 19. _____

# Reading Start-Up

## Visualize Vocabulary

**Use the ✔ words to complete the graphic.**

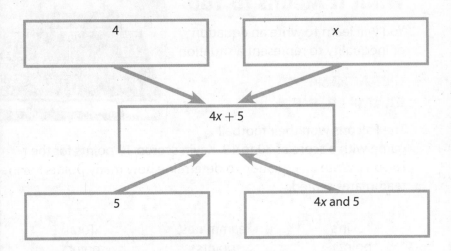

| 4 | | x |
|---|---|---|

$4x + 5$

| 5 | | 4x and 5 |
|---|---|---|

## Vocabulary

**Review Words**

✔ algebraic expression (expresión algebraica)

✔ coefficient (coeficiente)

✔ constant (constante)

evaluating (evaluar)

like terms (términos semejantes)

✔ term (término, en una expresión)

✔ variable (variable)

**Preview Words**

equation (ecuación)

equivalent expression (expresión equivalente)

properties of operations (propiedades de las operaciones)

solution (solución)

## Understand Vocabulary

**Match the term on the left to the correct expression on the right.**

**1.** algebraic expression

**A.** A mathematical statement that two expressions are equal.

**2.** equation

**B.** A value of the variable that makes the statement true.

**3.** solution

**C.** A mathematical statement that includes one or more variables.

## Active Reading

**Booklet** Before beginning the module, create a booklet to help you learn the concepts in this module. Write the main idea of each lesson on each page of the booklet. As you study each lesson, write important details that support the main idea, such as vocabulary and formulas. Refer to your finished booklet as you work on assignments and study for tests.

# Unpacking the TEKS

Understanding the TEKS and the vocabulary terms in the TEKS will help you know exactly what you are expected to learn in this module.

---

### TEKS 6.9.A

Write one-variable, one-step equations and inequalities to represent constraints or conditions within problems.

#### Key Vocabulary

**equation** *(ecuación)*
A mathematical sentence that shows that two expressions are equivalent.

**inequality** *(desigualdad)*
A mathematical sentence that shows the relationship between quantities that are not equal.

## What It Means to You

You will learn to write an equation or inequality to represent a situation.

### UNPACKING EXAMPLE 6.9.A

The Falcons won their football game with a score of 30 to 19. Kevin scored 12 points for the Falcons. Write an equation to determine how many points Kevin's teammates scored.

| Kevin's points | + | Teammates' points | = | Total points |
|:---:|:---:|:---:|:---:|:---:|
| 12 | + | $t$ | = | 30 |

---

### TEKS 6.10.B

Determine if the given value(s) make(s) one-variable, one-step equations or inequalities true.

## What It Means to You

You can substitute a given value for the variable in an equation or inequality to check if that value makes the equation or inequality true.

### UNPACKING EXAMPLE 6.10.B

Melanie bought 6 tickets to a play. She paid a total of $156. Write an equation to determine whether each ticket cost $26 or $28.

| Number of tickets bought | · | Price per ticket | = | Total cost |
|:---:|:---:|:---:|:---:|:---:|
| 6 | · | $p$ | = | 156 |

Substitute 26 and 28 for $p$ to see which equation is true.

$6p = 156$                     $6p = 156$

$6 \cdot 26 \overset{?}{=} 156$          $6 \cdot 28 \overset{?}{=} 156$

$156 \overset{?}{=} 156$ ✓          $168 \overset{?}{=} 156$ ✗

The cost of a ticket to the play was $26.

# Writing Equations to Represent Situations

**TEKS**
Expressions, equations, and relationships—6.9.A
Write one-variable, one-step equations ... to represent constraints or conditions within problems. *Also 6.7.B, 6.10.B*

**? ESSENTIAL QUESTION**

How do you write equations and determine whether a number is a solution of an equation?

## Determining Whether Values Are Solutions

An **equation** is a mathematical statement that two *expressions* are equal. An equation may or may not contain variables. For an equation that has a variable, a **solution** of the equation is a value of the variable that makes the equation true.

Math On the Spot
my.hrw.com

An expression represents a single value.

An equation represents a relationship between two values.

|  | Expression | Equation |
|---|---|---|
| **Numerical** | $5 + 4$ | $5 + 4 = 9$ |
| **Words** | a number *plus* 4 | a number *plus* 4 *is* 9. |
| **Algebraic** | $n + 4$ | $n + 4 = 9$ |

An equation relates two expressions using symbols for *is* or *equals*.

---

## EXAMPLE 1

**TEKS** 6.10.B

**Determine whether the given value is a solution of the equation.**

**A** $x + 9 = 15; x = 6$

$6 + 9 \overset{?}{=} 15$ ⠀⠀ Substitute 6 for x.

$15 \overset{?}{=} 15$ ⠀⠀ Add.

6 is a solution of $x + 9 = 15$.

**B** $\dfrac{y}{4} = -32; y = -8$

$\dfrac{-8}{4} \overset{?}{=} -32$ ⠀⠀ Substitute −8 for y.

$-2 \overset{?}{=} -32$ ⠀⠀ Divide.

−8 is not a solution of the equation $\dfrac{y}{4} = -32$.

**C** $8x = 72; x = 9$

$8(9) \overset{?}{=} 72$ ⠀⠀ Substitute 9 for x.

$72 \overset{?}{=} 72$ ⠀⠀ Multiply.

9 is a solution of $8x = 72$.

**YOUR TURN**

Determine whether the given value is a solution of the equation.

**1.** $11 = n + 6; n = 5$     **2.** $y - 6 = 24; y = 18$     **3.** $\frac{36}{x} = 9; x = 4$

_____     _____     _____

**Math On the Spot**

⏻ my.hrw.com

# Writing Equations to Represent Situations

You can represent some real-world situations with an equation. Making a model first can help you organize the information.

**EXAMPLE 2** Real World        ⬛ TEKS 6.9.A

Mark scored 17 points for the home team in a basketball game. His teammates as a group scored $p$ points. Write an equation to represent this situation.

| Mark's points | + | Teammates' points | = | Total points |
|:---:|:---:|:---:|:---:|:---:|
| ↓ | | ↓ | | ↓ |
| 17 | + | $p$ | = | 46 |

HOME **46**   PERIOD **4**   GUEST **42**

0:00

**Math Talk**

Mathematical Processes

Use words to describe two expressions that represent the total points scored. What does the equation say about the expressions you wrote?

**YOUR TURN**

Write an equation to represent each situation.

**4.** Marilyn has a fish tank that contains 38 fish. There are 9 goldfish and $f$ other fish.

_____

**5.** Juanita has 102 beads to make $n$ necklaces. Each necklace will have 17 beads.

_____

**6.** Craig is $c$ years old. His 12-year-old sister Becky is 3 years younger than Craig.

_____

**7.** Sonia rented ice skates for $h$ hours. The rental fee was $2 per hour and she paid a total of $8.

_____

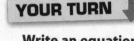

# Writing an Equation and Checking Solutions

You can substitute a given value for the variable in an equation to check if that value makes the equation true.

Math On the Spot
my.hrw.com

## EXAMPLE 3

**TEKS** 6.10.B

Sarah used a gift card to buy $47 worth of groceries. Now she has $18 left on her gift card. Write an equation to determine whether Sarah had $65 or $59 on the gift card before buying groceries.

**STEP 1** Identify the three quantities given in the problem.

$$\boxed{\text{Amount on card}} - \boxed{\text{Amount spent}} = \boxed{\text{Amount left on card}}$$

**STEP 2** Rewrite the equation using a variable for the unknown quantity and the given values for the known quantities.

Let $x$ be the amount on the card.

$$\boxed{\text{Amount on card}} - \boxed{\text{Amount spent}} = \boxed{\text{Amount left on card}}$$
$$x \quad - \quad 47 \quad = \quad 18$$

> The amount spent and the amount left on the card are the known quantities. Substitute those values in the equation.

**STEP 3** Substitute 65 and 59 for $x$ to see which equation is true.

$$x - 47 = 18 \qquad\qquad x - 47 = 18$$
$$65 - 47 \overset{?}{=} 18 \qquad 59 - 47 \overset{?}{=} 18$$
$$18 \overset{?}{=} 18 \qquad\qquad 12 \overset{?}{=} 18$$

The amount on Sarah's gift card before she bought groceries was $65.

## Reflect

8. What expressions are represented in the equation $x - 47 = 18$? How does the relationship represented in the equation help you determine if the equation is true?

_____

_____

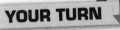 **YOUR TURN**

9. On Saturday morning, Owen earned $24 raking leaves. By the end of the afternoon he had earned a total of $62. Write an equation to determine whether Owen earned $38 or $31 on Saturday afternoon.

_____

Personal Math Trainer
Online Assessment and Intervention
my.hrw.com

**Determine whether the given value is a solution of the equation.** (Example 1)

**1.** $23 = x - 9$; $x = 14$ _____

$23 \stackrel{?}{=} \boxed{\phantom{0}} - 9$

$23 \stackrel{?}{=} \boxed{\phantom{0}}$

**2.** $\frac{n}{13} = 4$; $n = 52$ _____

$\dfrac{\boxed{\phantom{0}}}{13} \stackrel{?}{=} 4$

$\boxed{\phantom{0}} \stackrel{?}{=} 4$

**3.** $14 + x = 46$; $x = 32$ _____

**4.** $17y = 85$; $y = 5$ _____

**5.** $25 = \frac{k}{5}$; $k = 5$ _____

**6.** $2.5n = 45$; $n = 18$ _____

**7.** $21 = m + 9$; $m = 11$ _____

**8.** $21 - h = 15$; $h = 6$ _____

**9.** $d - 4 = 19$; $d = 15$ _____

**10.** $5 + x = 47$; $x = 52$ _____

**11.** $w - 9 = 0$; $w = 9$ _____

**12.** $5q = 31$; $q = 13$ _____

**13.** Each floor of a hotel has $r$ rooms. On 8 floors, there are a total of 256 rooms. Write an equation to represent this situation. (Example 2)

| Number | | Number of rooms | | | |
|---|---|---|---|---|---|
| _____ | × | _____ | = | _____ | _____ |

**14.** In the school band, there are 5 trumpet players and $f$ flute players. There are twice as many flute players as there are trumpet players. Write an equation to represent this situation. (Example 3)

_____

**15.** Pedro bought 8 tickets to a basketball game. He paid a total of $208. Write an equation to determine whether each ticket cost $26 or $28. (Example 3)

_____

**16.** The high temperature was 92°F. This was 24°F higher than the overnight low temperature. Write an equation to determine whether the low temperature was 62°F or 68°F. (Example 3)

_____

## ? ESSENTIAL QUESTION CHECK-IN

**17.** Tell how you can determine whether a number is a solution of an equation.

_____

_____

# 12.1 Independent Practice

TEKS 6.7.B, 6.9.A, 6.10.B

**Personal Math Trainer**

Online Assessment and Intervention

my.hrw.com

**18.** Andy is one-fourth as old as his grandfather, who is 76 years old. Write an equation to determine whether Andy is 19 or 22 years old.

_____

**19.** A sleeping bag weighs 8 pounds. Your backpack and sleeping bag together weigh 31 pounds. Write an equation to determine whether the backpack without the sleeping bag weighs 25 or 23 pounds.

_____

**20.** Halfway through a bus route, 23 students have been dropped off and 48 students remain on the bus. Write an equation to determine whether there are 61 or 71 students on the bus at the beginning of the route.

_____

**21.** The table shows the distance between Greenville and nearby towns. The distance between Artaville and Greenville is 13 miles less than the distance between Greenville and Jonesborough.

| Distance between Greenville and Nearby Towns (miles) | |
|---|---|
| Jonesborough | 29 |
| Maybern | 32 |

**a.** Write two equations that state the relationship of the distances between Greenville, Artaville, and Jonesborough.

_____

**b.** Describe what your variable represents.

_____

**22.** Write an equation that involves multiplication, contains a variable, and has a solution of 5. Can you write another equation that has the same solution and includes the same variable and numbers but uses division? If not, explain. If possible, write the equation.

_____

_____

**23.** How are expressions and equations different? Explain using a numerical example.

_____

_____

_____

_____

_____

_____

_____

_____

_____

**24.** **Explain the Error** The problem states that Ursula earns $9 per hour. To write an expression that tells how much money Ursula earns for $h$ hours, Joshua wrote $\frac{9}{h}$. Sarah wrote $9h$. Whose expression is correct and why?

_____

_____

_____

_____

**25. Communicate Mathematical Ideas**  A dog weighs 44 pounds and the veterinarian thinks it needs to lose 7 pounds. Mikala wrote the equation $x + 7 = 44$ to represent the situation. Kirk wrote the equation $44 - x = 7$. Which equation is correct? Can you write another equation that represents the situation?

_____

_____

**26. Multiple Representations**  The table shows ages of Cindy and her dad.

| Dad's Age | Cindy's Age |
|---|---|
| 28 years old | 2 years old |
| 36 years old | 10 years old |
| ? | 18 years old |

**a.** Write an equation that relates Cindy's age to her dad's age when Cindy is 18.

_____

**b.** Determine if 42 is a solution to the equation. Show your work.

_____

**c.** Explain the meaning of your answer in part b.

_____

 **FOCUS ON HIGHER ORDER THINKING**

**Work Area**

**27. Critical Thinking**  In the school band, there are 4 trumpet players and *f* flute players. The total number of trumpet and flute players is 12. Are there twice as many flute players as trumpet players? Explain.

_____

_____

**28. Problem Solving**  Ronald paid $162 for 6 tickets to a basketball game. During the game he noticed that his friend paid $130 for 5 tickets. The price of each ticket was $26. Was Ronald overcharged? Justify your answer.

_____

_____

**29. Communicate Mathematical Ideas**  Tariq said you can write an equation by setting an expression equal to itself. Would an equation like this be true? Explain.

_____

_____

_____

# Addition and Subtraction Equations

**TEKS**
Expressions, equations, and relationships—6.10.A
Model and solve one-variable, one-step equations ... that represent problems, including geometric concepts.
*Also 6.9.B, 6.9.C*

**? ESSENTIAL QUESTION**

How do you solve equations that contain addition or subtraction?

---

**EXPLORE ACTIVITY** (Real World)     **TEKS** 6.10.A

## Modeling Equations

A puppy weighed 6 ounces at birth. After two weeks, the puppy weighed 14 ounces. How much weight did the puppy gain?

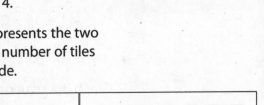

Let $x$ represent the number of ounces gained.

| Weight at birth | + | Weight gained | = | Weight after 2 weeks |
|:---:|:---:|:---:|:---:|:---:|
| ↓ | | ↓ | | ↓ |
| 6 | + | $x$ | = | 14 |

To answer this question, you can solve the equation $6 + x = 14$.

Algebra tiles can model some equations. An equation mat represents the two sides of an equation. To solve the equation, remove the same number of tiles from both sides of the mat until the $x$ tile is by itself on one side.

**A** Model $6 + x = 14$.

**B** How many 1 tiles must you remove on the left side so that the $x$ tile is by itself? _____ Cross out these tiles on the equation mat.

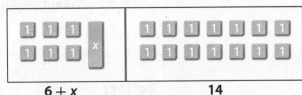

$6 + x$          $14$

**C** Whenever you remove tiles from one side of the mat, you must remove the same number of tiles from the other side of the mat. Cross out the tiles that should be removed on the right side of the mat.

**D** How many tiles remain on the right side of the mat? _____ This is the solution of the equation.

The puppy gained _____ ounces.

> **Math Talk**
> Mathematical Processes
>
> Why did you remove tiles from each side of your model?

### Reflect

1. **Communicate Mathematical Ideas** How do you know when the model shows the final solution? How do you read the solution?

_____

_____

# Using Subtraction to Solve Equations

Removing the same number of tiles from each side of an equation mat models subtracting the same number from both sides of an equation.

## Subtraction Property of Equality

You can subtract the same number from both sides of an equation, and the two sides will remain equal.

When an equation contains addition, solve by subtracting the same number from both sides.

## EXAMPLE 1

TEKS 6.10.A, 6.9.B

**Solve the equation $a + 15 = 26$. Graph the solution on a number line.**

$a + 15 = 26$     Notice that the number 15 is added to a.

$$
\begin{array}{r}
a + 15 = 26 \\
-15 \quad -15 \\
\hline
a \quad = 11
\end{array}
$$

Subtract 15 from both sides of the equation.

Check: $a + 15 = 26$

$11 + 15 \overset{?}{=} 26$     Substitute 11 for a.

$26 = 26$     Add on the left side.

Graph the solution on a number line.

5  6  7  8  9  10  11  12  13  14  15

### Reflect

2. **Communicate Mathematical Ideas** How do you decide which number to subtract from both sides?

_____

_____

### YOUR TURN

3. Solve the equation $5 = w + 1.5$.

Graph the solution on a number line.

−5 −4 −3 −2 −1  0  1  2  3  4  5

$w =$ _____

# Using Addition to Solve Equations

When an equation contains subtraction, solve by adding the same number to both sides.

**Math On the Spot**
⏻ my.hrw.com

> ### Addition Property of Equality
>
> You can add the same number to both sides of an equation, and the two sides will remain equal.

## EXAMPLE 2
**TEKS** 6.10.A, 6.9.B

**Solve the equation $y - 21 = 18$. Graph the solution on a number line.**

$y - 21 = 18$     *Notice that the number 21 is subtracted from y.*

$$\begin{array}{r} y - 21 = 18 \\ +21 \quad +21 \\ \hline y \quad = 39 \end{array}$$     *Add 21 to both sides of the equation.*

Check: $y - 21 = 18$

$39 - 21 \overset{?}{=} 18$     *Substitute 39 for y.*

$18 = 18$     *Subtract.*

Graph the solution on a number line.

```
35 36 37 38 39 40 41 42 43 44 45
```

## Reflect

4. **Communicate Mathematical Ideas** How do you know whether to add on both sides or subtract on both sides when solving an equation?

_____

_____

_____

### YOUR TURN

5. Solve the equation $h - \frac{1}{2} = \frac{3}{4}$.

```
-2   -1   0   1   2
```

Graph the solution on a number line.

$h = $ _____

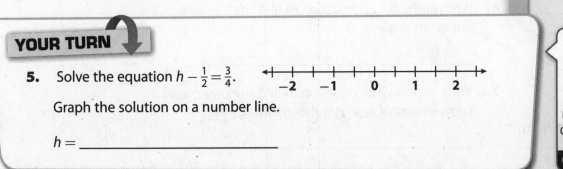
**Personal Math Trainer**

Online Assessment and Intervention

⏻ my.hrw.com

# Solving Equations that Represent Geometric Concepts

You can write equations to represent geometric relationships.

Recall that a straight line has an angle measure of 180°. Two angles whose measures have a sum of 180° are called supplementary angles. Two angles whose measures have a sum of 90° are called complementary angles.

## EXAMPLE 3

**TEKS** 6.10.A

**Find the measure of the unknown angle.**

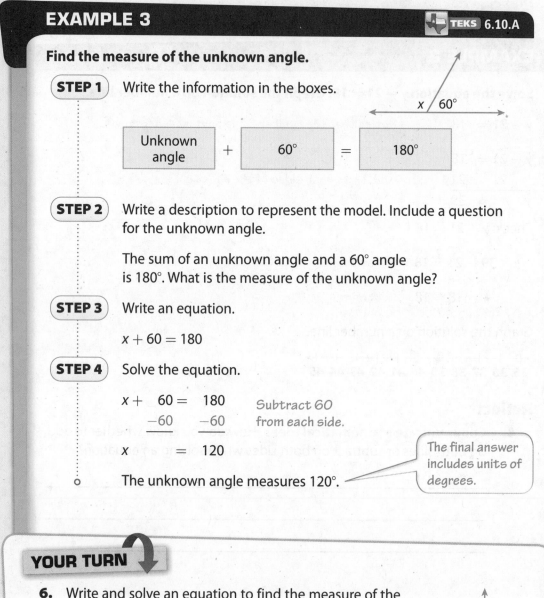

**STEP 1** Write the information in the boxes.

| Unknown angle | + | 60° | = | 180° |

**STEP 2** Write a description to represent the model. Include a question for the unknown angle.

The sum of an unknown angle and a 60° angle is 180°. What is the measure of the unknown angle?

**STEP 3** Write an equation.

$x + 60 = 180$

**STEP 4** Solve the equation.

$$x + 60 = 180$$
$$\phantom{x +} -60 \quad -60$$
$$x \phantom{+ 60} = 120$$

*Subtract 60 from each side.*

The unknown angle measures 120°.

*The final answer includes units of degrees.*

## YOUR TURN

6. Write and solve an equation to find the measure of the unknown angle.

_____

7. Write and solve an equation to find the measure of a complement of an angle that measures 42°.

_____

# Writing Real-World Problems for a Given Equation

You can write a real-world problem for a given equation. Examine each number and mathematical operation in the equation.

**EXAMPLE 4** (Real World)      **TEKS** 6.9.C

**Write a real-world problem for the equation $21.79 + x = 25$. Then solve the equation.**

$$21.79 + x = 25$$

**STEP 1**   Examine each part of the equation.

     $x$ is the unknown or quantity we are looking for.

     $21.79$ is added to $x$.

     $= 25$ means that after adding $21.79$ and $x$, the result is $25$.

**STEP 2**   Write a real-world situation that involves *adding* two quantities.

     Joshua wants to buy his mother flowers and a card for Mother's Day. Joshua has $25 to spend and selects roses for $21.79. How much can he spend on a card?

**STEP 3**   Solve the equation.

$$21.79 + x = 25$$
$$\underline{-21.79 \qquad -21.79}$$
$$x = 3.21$$

> The final answer includes units of money in dollars.

     Joshua can spend $3.21 on a Mother's Day card.

> **Math Talk**
> Mathematical Processes
>
> How is the question in a real-world problem related to its equation?

## Reflect

8. **What If?** How might the real-world problem change if the equation were $x - 21.79 = 25$ and Joshua still spent $21.79 on roses?

_____

_____

_____

**YOUR TURN**

9. Write a real-world problem for the equation $x - 100 = 40$. Then solve the equation.

_____

**Personal Math Trainer**

Online Assessment and Intervention

my.hrw.com

**1.** A total of 14 guests attended a birthday party. Three guests stayed after the party to help clean up. How many guests left when the party ended? (Explore Activity)

**a.** Let $x$ represent the _____

**b.**
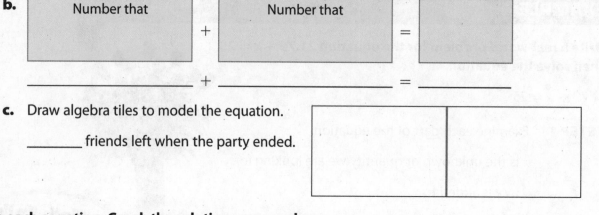

**c.** Draw algebra tiles to model the equation.

_____ friends left when the party ended.

**Solve each equation. Graph the solution on a number line.** (Examples 1 and 2)

**2.** $2 = x - 3$        $x =$ _____

$$\xleftarrow{\;\;\;\;} \underset{-5\;-4\;-3\;-2\;-1\;\;\;0\;\;\;1\;\;\;2\;\;\;3\;\;\;4\;\;\;5}{+\!+\!+\!+\!+\!+\!+\!+\!+\!+\!+} \xrightarrow{\;\;\;\;}$$

**3.** $s + 12.5 = 14$        $s =$ _____

$$\xleftarrow{\;\;\;\;} \underset{-5\;-4\;-3\;-2\;-1\;\;\;0\;\;\;1\;\;\;2\;\;\;3\;\;\;4\;\;\;5}{+\!+\!+\!+\!+\!+\!+\!+\!+\!+\!+} \xrightarrow{\;\;\;\;}$$

**Solve each equation.** (Examples 1 and 2)

**4.** $h + 6.9 = 11.4$

$h =$ _____

**5.** $82 + p = 122$

$p =$ _____

**6.** $n + \frac{1}{2} = \frac{7}{4}$

$n =$ _____

**7.** Write and solve an equation to find the measure of the unknown angle. (Example 3)

_____

$45°$  $x$

**8.** Write a real-world problem for the equation $x - 75 = 200$. Then solve the equation. (Example 4)

_____

**? ESSENTIAL QUESTION CHECK-IN**

**9.** How do you solve equations that contain addition or subtraction?

_____

_____

_____

# 12.2 Independent Practice

**TEKS** 6.9.B, 6.9.C, 6.10.A

Personal Math Trainer

Online Assessment and Intervention

my.hrw.com

**Write and solve an equation to answer each question.**

**10.** A wildlife reserve had 8 elephant calves born during the summer and now has 31 total elephants. How many elephants were in the reserve before summer began?

_____

_____

**11.** My sister is 14 years old. My brother says that his age minus twelve is equal to my sister's age. How old is my brother?

_____

**12.** Kim bought a poster that cost $8.95 and some colored pencils. The total cost was $21.35. How much did the colored pencils cost?

_____

_____

**13.** The Acme Car Company sold 37 vehicles in June. How many compact cars were sold in June?

| Acme Car Company — June Sales | |
|---|---|
| **Type of car** | **Number sold** |
| SUV | 8 |
| Compact | ? |

_____

_____

**14.** Sandra wants to buy a new MP3 player that is on sale for $95. She has saved $73. How much more money does she need?

_____

_____

**15.** Ronald spent $123.45 on school clothes. He counted his money and discovered that he had $36.55 left. How much money did he originally have?

_____

_____

**16.** Brita withdrew $225 from her bank account. After her withdrawal, there was $548 left in Brita's account. How much money did Brita have in her account before the withdrawal?

_____

_____

**17. Represent Real-World Problems** Write a real-world situation that can be represented by $15 + c = 17.50$. Then solve the equation and describe what your answer represents for the problem situation.

_____

_____

_____

**18. Critique Reasoning** Paula solved the equation $7 + x = 10$ and got 17, but she is not certain if she got the correct answer. How could you explain Paula's mistake to her?

_____

_____

_____

_____

**Work Area**

**19. Multistep** Handy Dandy Grocery is having a sale this week. If you buy a 5-pound bag of apples for the regular price, you can get another bag for $1.49. If you buy a 5-pound bag of oranges at the regular price, you can get another bag for $2.49.

| Handy Dandy Grocery | |
|---|---|
| | **Regular price** |
| 5-pound bag of apples | $2.99 |
| 5-pound bag of oranges | $3.99 |

**a.** Write an equation to find the discount for each situation using *a* for apples and *r* for oranges.

_____

**b.** Which fruit has a greater discount? Explain.

_____

_____

**20. Critical Thinking** An orchestra has twice as many woodwind instruments as brass instruments. There are a total of 150 brass and woodwind instruments.

**a.** Write two different addition equations that describe this situation. Use *w* for woodwinds and *b* for brass.

_____

**b.** How many woodwinds and how many brass instruments satisfy the given information?

_____

**21. Look for a Pattern** Assume the following: $a + 1 = 2$, $b + 10 = 20$, $c + 100 = 200$, $d + 1{,}000 = 2{,}000$, ...

**a.** Solve each equation for each variable.

_____

**b.** What pattern do you notice between the variables?

_____

**c.** What would be the value of *g* if the pattern continues?

_____

# Multiplication and Division Equations

**TEKS**
Expressions, equations, and relationships—6.10.A
Model and solve one-variable, one-step equations . . . that represent problems, including geometric concepts. *Also* 6.9.B, 6.9.C

## ESSENTIAL QUESTION

How do you solve equations that contain multiplication or division?

**EXPLORE ACTIVITY** *Real World*    **TEKS** 6.9.B, 6.9.C, 6.10.A

## Modeling Equations

**Deanna has a cookie recipe that requires 12 eggs to make 3 batches of cookies. How many eggs are needed per batch of cookies?**

Let *x* represent the number of eggs needed per batch.

| Number of batches | · | Number of eggs per batch | = | Total eggs |
|---|---|---|---|---|

$$3 \quad \cdot \quad x \quad = \quad 12$$

To answer this question, you can use algebra tiles to solve $3x = 12$.

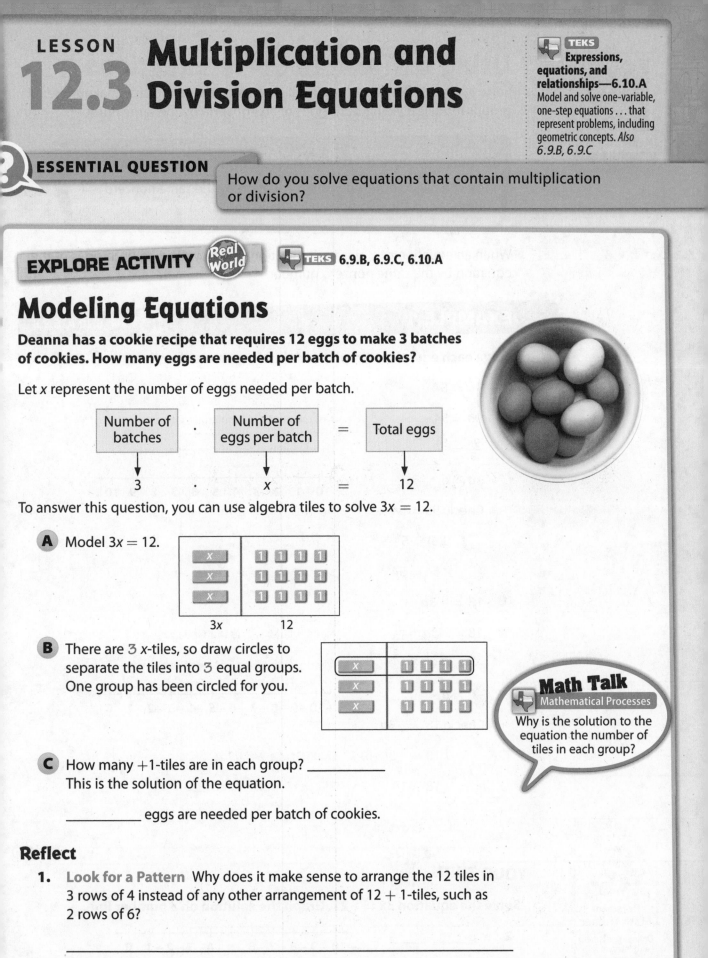

**A** Model $3x = 12$.

| | |
|---|---|
| x | 1 1 1 1 |
| x | 1 1 1 1 |
| x | 1 1 1 1 |

$3x$      $12$

**B** There are 3 *x*-tiles, so draw circles to separate the tiles into 3 equal groups. One group has been circled for you.

| | |
|---|---|
| x | 1 1 1 1 |
| x | 1 1 1 1 |
| x | 1 1 1 1 |

**Math Talk**
Mathematical Processes

Why is the solution to the equation the number of tiles in each group?

**C** How many +1-tiles are in each group? _____ This is the solution of the equation.

_____ eggs are needed per batch of cookies.

## Reflect

**1.** **Look for a Pattern** Why does it make sense to arrange the 12 tiles in 3 rows of 4 instead of any other arrangement of 12 + 1-tiles, such as 2 rows of 6?

_____

# Using Division to Solve Equations

Separating the tiles on both sides of an equation mat into an equal number of groups models dividing both sides of an equation by the same number.

### Division Property of Equality

You can divide both sides of an equation by the same nonzero number, and the two sides will remain equal.

When an equation contains multiplication, solve by dividing both sides of the equation by the same nonzero number.

## EXAMPLE 1

**TEKS** 6.10.A, 6.9.B

**Solve each equation. Graph the solution on a number line.**

**A** $9a = 54$

| | |
|---|---|
| $9a = 54$ | Notice that 9 is multiplied by $a$. |
| $\dfrac{9a}{9} = \dfrac{54}{9}$ | Divide both sides of the equation by 9. |
| $a = 6$ | |

Check: $9a = 54$

$9(6) \stackrel{?}{=} 54$     Substitute 6 for $a$.

$54 = 54$     Multiply on the left side.

**B** $18 = -3d$

| | |
|---|---|
| $18 = -3d$ | Notice that $-3$ is multiplied by $d$. |
| $\dfrac{18}{-3} = \dfrac{-3d}{-3}$ | Divide both sides of the equation by $-3$. |
| $-6 = d$ | |

Check: $18 = -3d$

$18 \stackrel{?}{=} -3(-6)$     Substitute $-6$ for $d$.

$18 = 18$     Multiply on the right side.

## YOUR TURN

**Solve the equation $3x = -21$. Graph the solution on a number line.**

**2.** $x =$ _____

# Using Multiplication to Solve Equations

When an equation contains division, solve by multiplying both sides of the equation by the same number.

Math On the Spot
my.hrw.com

### Multiplication Property of Equality

You can multiply both sides of an equation by the same number, and the two sides will remain equal.

## EXAMPLE 2

**TEKS** 6.10.A, 6.9.B

Solve each equation. Graph the solution on a number line.

**A** $\frac{x}{5} = 10$

$\frac{x}{5} = 10$      Notice that $x$ is divided by the number 5.

$5 \cdot \frac{x}{5} = 5 \cdot 10$      Multiply both sides of the equation by 5.

$x = 50$

(number line from −20 to 50, point at 50)
−20 −10  0  10  20  30  40  50

Check: $\frac{x}{5} = 10$

$\frac{50}{5} \stackrel{?}{=} 10$      Substitute 50 for $x$.

$10 = 10$      Divide on the left side.

**B** $15 = \frac{r}{2}$

$15 = \frac{r}{2}$      Notice that $r$ is divided by the number 2.

$2 \cdot 15 = 2 \cdot \frac{r}{2}$      Multiply both sides of the equation by 2.

$30 = r$

(number line, point at 30)
0  5  10  15  20  25  30  35  40  45  50

Check: $15 = \frac{r}{2}$

$15 \stackrel{?}{=} \frac{30}{2}$      Substitute 30 for $r$.

$15 = 15$      Divide on the right side.

> **Math Talk**
> Mathematical Processes
>
> How is solving a multiplication equation similar to solving a division equation? How are they different?

## YOUR TURN

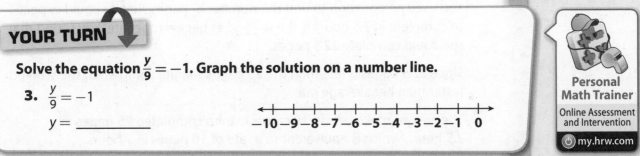

Solve the equation $\frac{y}{9} = -1$. Graph the solution on a number line.

**3.** $\frac{y}{9} = -1$

$y =$ _____

(number line from −10 to 0)
−10 −9 −8 −7 −6 −5 −4 −3 −2 −1  0

Personal Math Trainer
Online Assessment and Intervention
my.hrw.com

My Notes

# Using Equations to Solve Problems

You can use equations to solve real-world problems.

**EXAMPLE 3**  Problem Solving

TEKS 6.9.C

Juanita is scrapbooking. She usually completes about 9 pages per hour. One night last week she completed pages 23 through 47 in 2.5 hours. Did she work at her average rate?

### Analyze Information

Identify the important information.

- Worked for 2.5 hours
- Starting page: 23        Ending page: 47
- Scrapbooking rate: 9 pages per hour

### Formulate a Plan

- Solve an equation to find the number of pages Juanita can expect to complete.

- Compare the number of pages Juanita can expect to complete with the number of pages she actually completed.

### Solve

Let $n$ represent the number of pages Juanita can expect to complete in 2.5 hours if she works at her average rate of 9 pages per hour.

Write an equation.

$$\frac{n}{2.5} = 9 \qquad \text{Write the equation.}$$

$$2.5 \cdot \frac{n}{2.5} = 2.5 \cdot 9 \qquad \text{Multiply both sides by 2.5.}$$

$$n = 22.5$$

Juanita can expect to complete 22.5 pages in 2.5 hours.

Juanita completed pages 23 through 47, a total of 25 pages. Because 25 > 22.5, she worked faster than her expected rate.

### Justify and Evaluate

You used an equation to find the number of pages Juanita could expect to complete in 2.5 hours if she worked at her average rate. You found that she could complete 22.5 pages.

Since 22.5 pages is less than the 25 pages Juanita completed, she worked faster than her average rate.

The answer makes sense, because Juanita completed 25 pages in 2.5 hours, which is equivalent to a rate of 10 pages in 1 hour. Since 10 > 9, you know that she worked faster than her average rate.

## YOUR TURN

**4.** Roberto is dividing his baseball cards equally among himself, his brother, and his 3 friends. Roberto was left with 9 cards. How many cards did Roberto give away? Write and solve an equation to solve the problem.

_____

_____

# Writing Real-World Problems

You can write a real-world problem for a given equation.

**Math On the Spot**

⏻ my.hrw.com

**EXAMPLE 4** (Real World)　　　　　　　🔲 TEKS 6.9.C

Write a real-world problem for the equation $8x = 72$. Then solve the equation.

$$8x = 72$$

**STEP 1** Examine each part of the equation.

$x$ is the unknown or quantity we are looking for.

8 is multiplied by $x$.

$= 72$ means that after multiplying 8 and $x$, the result is 72.

**STEP 2** Write a real-world situation that involves multiplying two quantities.

A hot air balloon flew at 8 miles per hour. How many hours did it take this balloon to travel 72 miles?

**STEP 3** Solve the equation.

$$8x = 72$$

$$\frac{8x}{8} = \frac{72}{8} \qquad \textit{Divide both sides by 8.}$$

$$x = 9$$

The balloon traveled for 9 hours.

## YOUR TURN

**5.** Write a real-world problem for the equation $11x = 385$. Then solve the equation.

_____

_____

**Personal Math Trainer**

Online Assessment and Intervention

⏻ my.hrw.com

1. Caroline ran 15 miles in 5 days. She ran the same distance each day. Write and solve an equation to determine the number of miles she ran each day. (Explore Activity)

   a. Let $x$ represent the _____.

   b.
   | Number of | . | Number of | = | |
   |---|---|---|---|---|

   _____ . _____ = _____

   c. Draw algebra tiles to model the equation.

   Caroline ran _____ miles each day.

**Solve each equation. Graph the solution on a number line.**
(Examples 1 and 2)

2. $x \div 3 = 3$

   $x =$ _____

   <---+---+---+---+---+---+---+---+---+---+--->
     0   1   2   3   4   5   6   7   8   9  10

3. $4x = -32$

   $x =$ _____

   <---+---+---+---+---+---+---+---+---+---+--->
   −10 −9 −8 −7 −6 −5 −4 −3 −2 −1  0

4. The area of the rectangle shown is 24 square inches. How much longer is its length than its width? (Example 3)

   _____

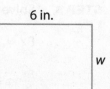

6 in.

$w$

5. How do you solve equations that contain multiplication or division?

   _____

   _____

   _____

## 12.3 Independent Practice

TEKS 6.9.B, 6.9.C, 6.10.A

**Write and solve an equation to answer each question.**

**6.** Jorge baked cookies for his math class's end-of-year party. There are 28 people in Jorge's math class including Jorge and his teacher. Jorge baked enough cookies for everyone to get 3 cookies each. How many cookies did Jorge bake?

_____

**7.** Sam divided a rectangle into 8 congruent rectangles that each have the area shown. What is the area of the rectangle before Sam divided it?

| Area = 5 cm² | | |
|---|---|---|
| | | |

_____

**8.** Carmen participated in a read-a-thon. Mr. Cole pledged $4.00 per book and gave Carmen $44. How many books did Carmen read?

_____

**9.** Lee drove 420 miles and used 15 gallons of gasoline. How many miles did Lee's car travel per gallon of gasoline?

_____

**10.** On some days, Melvin commutes 3.5 hours per day to the city for business meetings. Last week he commuted for a total of 14 hours. How many days did he commute to the city?

_____

**11.** Dharmesh has a square garden with a perimeter of 132 feet. Is the area of the garden greater than 1,000 square feet?

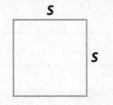

_____
_____
_____
_____
_____

**12.** Ingrid walked her dog and washed her car. The time she spent walking her dog was one-fourth the time it took her to wash her car. It took Ingrid 14 minutes to walk the dog. How long did it take Ingrid to wash her car?

_____

**13.** **Representing Real-World Problems** Write and solve a problem involving money that can be solved with a multiplication equation.

_____
_____
_____
_____
_____
_____
_____

14. **Representing Real-World Problems** Write and solve a problem involving money that can be solved with a division equation and has a solution of 1,350.

## H.O.T. FOCUS ON HIGHER ORDER THINKING

Work Area

15. **Communicate Mathematical Ideas** Explain why $7 \cdot \frac{x}{7} = x$. How does this relate to solving division equations?

16. **Critical Thinking** A number tripled and tripled again is 729. What is the number?

17. **Multistep** Andre has 4 times as many model cars as Peter, and Peter has one-third as many model cars as Jade. Andre has 36 model cars.

   **a.** Write and solve an equation to find how many model cars Peter has.

   **b.** Using your answer from part a, write and solve an equation to find how many model cars Jade has.

# Ready to Go On?

**Personal Math Trainer**

Online Assessment and Intervention

⏻ my.hrw.com

## 12.1 Writing Equations to Represent Situations

**Determine whether the given value is a solution of the equation.**

**1.** $p - 6 = 19; p = 13$ _____

**2.** $62 + j = 74; j = 12$ _____

**3.** $\frac{b}{12} = 5; b = 60$ _____

**4.** $7w = 87; w = 12$ _____

**5.** $18 - h = 13; h = -5$ _____

**6.** $6g = -86; g = -16$ _____

**Write an equation to represent the situation.**

**7.** The number of eggs in the refrigerator $e$ decreased by 5 equals 18.

_____

**8.** The number of new photos $p$ added to the 17 old photos equals 29.

_____

## 12.2 Addition and Subtraction Equations

**Solve each equation.**

**9.** $r - 38 = 9$ _____

**10.** $h + 17 = 40$ _____

**11.** $n + 75 = 155$ _____

**12.** $q - 17 = 18$ _____

## 12.3 Multiplication and Division Equations

**Solve each equation.**

**13.** $8z = 112$ _____

**14.** $\frac{d}{14} = 7$ _____

**15.** $\frac{f}{28} = 24$ _____

**16.** $3a = 57$ _____

**?** **ESSENTIAL QUESTION**

**17.** How can you solve problems involving equations that contain addition, subtraction, multiplication, or division?

_____

_____

## Selected Response

**1.** Kate has gone up to the chalkboard to do math problems 5 more times than Andre. Kate has gone up 11 times. Which equation represents this situation?

Ⓐ $a - 11 = 5$

Ⓑ $5a = 11$

Ⓒ $a - 5 = 11$

Ⓓ $a + 5 = 11$

**2.** For which equation is $y = 7$ a solution?

Ⓐ $7y = 1$

Ⓑ $y - 26 = -19$

Ⓒ $y + 7 = 0$

Ⓓ $\frac{y}{2} = 14$

**3.** Which is an equation?

Ⓐ $17 + x$

Ⓒ $20x = 200$

Ⓑ $45 \div x$

Ⓓ $90 - x$

**4.** The number line below represents which equation?

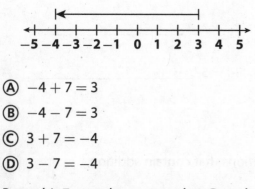

Ⓐ $-4 + 7 = 3$

Ⓑ $-4 - 7 = 3$

Ⓒ $3 + 7 = -4$

Ⓓ $3 - 7 = -4$

**5.** Becca hit 7 more home runs than Beverly. Becca hit 21 home runs. How many home runs did Beverly hit?

Ⓐ 3

Ⓒ 21

Ⓑ 14

Ⓓ 28

**6.** Jeordie spreads out a rectangular picnic blanket with an area of 42 square feet. Its width is 6 feet. Which equation could you use to find its length?

Ⓐ $6x = 42$

Ⓒ $\frac{6}{x} = 42$

Ⓑ $42 - x = 6$

Ⓓ $6 + x = 42$

**7.** What is a solution to the equation $6t = 114$?

Ⓐ $t = 19$

Ⓒ $t = 120$

Ⓑ $t = 108$

Ⓓ $t = 684$

**8.** The area of a rectangular deck is 680 square feet. The deck's width is 17 feet. What is its length?

Ⓐ 17 feet

Ⓒ 40 feet

Ⓑ 20 feet

Ⓓ 51 feet

## Gridded Response

**9.** Sylvia earns $7 per hour at her afterschool job. One week she worked several hours and received a paycheck for $91. Write and solve an equation to find the number of hours in which Sylvia would earn $91.

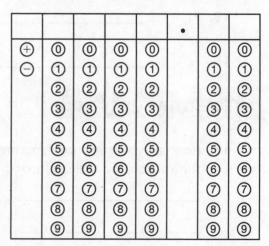

# Inequalities and Relationships

## ESSENTIAL QUESTION

How can you use inequalities and relationships to solve real-world problems?

**Real-World Video**

Some rides at amusement parks indicate a minimum height required for riders. You can model all the heights that are allowed to get on the ride with an inequality.

my.hrw.com

**GO DIGITAL**

my.hrw.com

**my.hrw.com**

Go digital with your write-in student edition, accessible on any device.

**Math On the Spot**

Scan with your smart phone to jump directly to the online edition, video tutor, and more.

**Animated Math**

Interactively explore key concepts to see how math works.

**Personal Math Trainer**

Get immediate feedback and help as you work through practice sets.

# Are YOU Ready?

Complete these exercises to review skills you will need for this chapter.

## Understand Integers

**EXAMPLE** A water well was drilled 735 feet into the ground.

$-735$

Decide whether the integer is positive or negative:
*into the ground → negative*

*Write the integer.*

**Write an integer to represent each situation.**

1. a loss of $75 _____

2. a football player's gain of 9 yards _____

3. spending $1,200 on a flat screen TV _____

4. a climb of 2,400 feet _____

## Integer Operations

**EXAMPLE**
$3 \times 8 = 24$
$-30 \div (-5) = 6$

*The product or quotient of two integers is positive if the signs of the integers are the same.*

$7 \times (-4) = -28$
$-72 \div 9 = -8$

*The product or quotient of two integers is negative if the signs of the integers are different.*

**Find the product or quotient.**

5. $6 \times 9$ _____

6. $15 \div (-5)$ \_\_\_\_

7. $-8 \times 6$ _____

8. $-100 \div (10)$ \_\_\_\_

9. $3 \times (-7)$ \_\_\_\_

10. $-64 \div 8$ \_\_\_\_\_

11. $-8 \times (-2)$ \_\_\_

12. $32 \div 2$ _____

## Solve Multiplication Equations

**EXAMPLE**
$\frac{3}{4}h = 15$

*Write the equation.*

$\frac{4}{3} \cdot \frac{3}{4}h = 15 \cdot \frac{4}{3}$

*$h$ is multiplied by $\frac{3}{4}$. Multiply both sides by the reciprocal, $\frac{4}{3}$, to isolate the variable.*

$h = \frac{15 \cdot 4}{3}$

$h = 20$

*Simplify.*

**Solve.**

13. $9p = 108$ \_\_\_\_

14. $\frac{3}{5}n = 21$ \_\_\_\_

15. $\frac{4}{7}k = 84$ \_\_\_\_

16. $\frac{3}{20}e = 24$ \_\_\_\_

# Reading Start-Up

## Visualize Vocabulary

Use the ✔ words to complete the graphic.

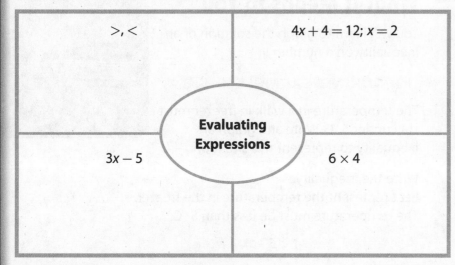

| | |
|---|---|
| $>, <$ | $4x + 4 = 12; x = 2$ |
| $3x - 5$ | $6 \times 4$ |

Center: **Evaluating Expressions**

## Understand Vocabulary

**Match the term on the left to the correct expression on the right.**

1. solution of an inequality
2. coefficient
3. constant

**A.** A value or values that make the inequality true.

**B.** A specific number whose value does not change.

**C.** The number that is multiplied by the variable in an algebraic expression.

## Active Reading

**Two-Panel Flip Chart** Create a two-panel flip chart to help you understand the concepts in this module. Label one flap "Adding and Subtracting Inequalities." Label the other flap "Multiplying and Dividing Inequalities." As you study each lesson, write important ideas under the appropriate flap.

# Unpacking the TEKS

Understanding the TEKS and the vocabulary terms in the TEKS will help you know exactly what you are expected to learn in this module.

---

**TEKS 6.9.B**

Represent solutions for one-variable, one-step equations and inequalities on number lines.

### Key Vocabulary

**equation** (*ecuación*)
A mathematical sentence that shows that two expressions are equivalent.

**inequality** (*desigualdad*)
A mathematical sentence that shows the relationship between quantities that are not equal.

**solution of an inequality** (*solución de una desigualdad*)
A value or values that make the inequality true.

## What It Means to You

You will learn to graph the solution of an inequality on a number line.

**UNPACKING EXAMPLE 6.9.B**

The temperature in a walk-in freezer must stay under 5 °C. Write and graph an inequality to represent this situation.

Write the inequality.
Let *t* represent the temperature in the freezer.
The temperature must be less than 5 °C.

$$t < 5$$

Graph the inequality.

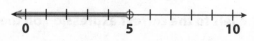

---

**TEKS 6.10.A**

Model and solve one-variable, one-step equations and inequalities that represent problems, including geometric concepts.

## What It Means to You

You can model and solve a one-variable, one-step inequality.

**UNPACKING EXAMPLE 6.10.A**

Donny buys 3 binders and spends more than $9. How much did he spend on each binder?

Let *x* represent the cost of one binder.

| Number of binders | · | Cost of a binder | > | Total cost of binders |
|---|---|---|---|---|
| ↓ | | ↓ | | ↓ |
| 3 | · | *x* | > | 9 |

Use algebra tiles to model $3x > 9$ and solve the inequality.

$$x > 3$$

Donny spent more than $3 on each binder.

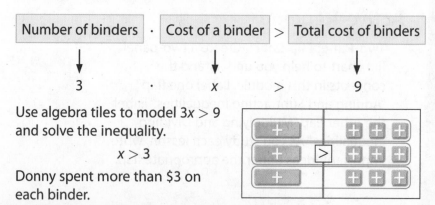

Visit **my.hrw.com** to see all the **TEKS** unpacked.

my.hrw.com

TEKS
Expressions, equations, and relationships—
**6.9.A** Write ... inequalities to represent constraints or conditions within problems.
*Also 6.9.B, 6.10.B.*

## ESSENTIAL QUESTION

How can you use inequalities to represent real-world constraints or conditions?

**EXPLORE ACTIVITY** Real World  TEKS 6.9.A

# Using Inequalities to Describe Quantities

You can use inequality symbols with variables to describe quantities that can have many values.

| Symbol | Meaning | Word Phrases |
|--------|---------|--------------|
| $<$ | Is less than | Fewer than, below |
| $>$ | Is greater than | More than, above |
| $\leq$ | Is less than or equal to | At most, no more than |
| $\geq$ | Is greater than or equal to | At least, no less than |

**A** The lowest temperature ever recorded in Florida was −2 °F. Graph this temperature on the number line.

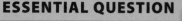

-8 -7 -6 -5 -4 -3 -2 -1  0  1  2  3  4  5  6  7  8

**B** The temperatures 0 °F, 3 °F, 6 °F, 5 °F, and −1 °F have also been recorded in Florida. Graph these temperatures on the number line.

**C** How do the temperatures in **B** compare to −2? How can you see this relationship on the number line?

_____

_____

**D** How many other numbers have the same relationship to −2 as the temperatures in **B** ? Give some examples.

_____

**E** Suppose you could graph all of the possible answers to **D** on a number line. What would the graph look like?

_____

**F** Let *x* represent all the possible answers to **D** .

Complete this inequality: *x* ☐ −2

# Graphing the Solutions of an Inequality

A **solution of an inequality** that contains a variable is any value of the variable that makes the inequality true. For example, 7 is a solution of $x > -2$, since $7 > -2$ is a true statement.

## EXAMPLE 1

**TEKS** 6.9.B

**Graph the solutions of each inequality. Check the solutions.**

**A** $y \leq -3$

**STEP 1** Draw a solid circle at $-3$ to show that $-3$ is a solution.

**STEP 2** Shade the number line to the left of $-3$ to show that numbers less than $-3$ are solutions.

> Use a solid circle for an inequality that uses $\geq$ or $\leq$.

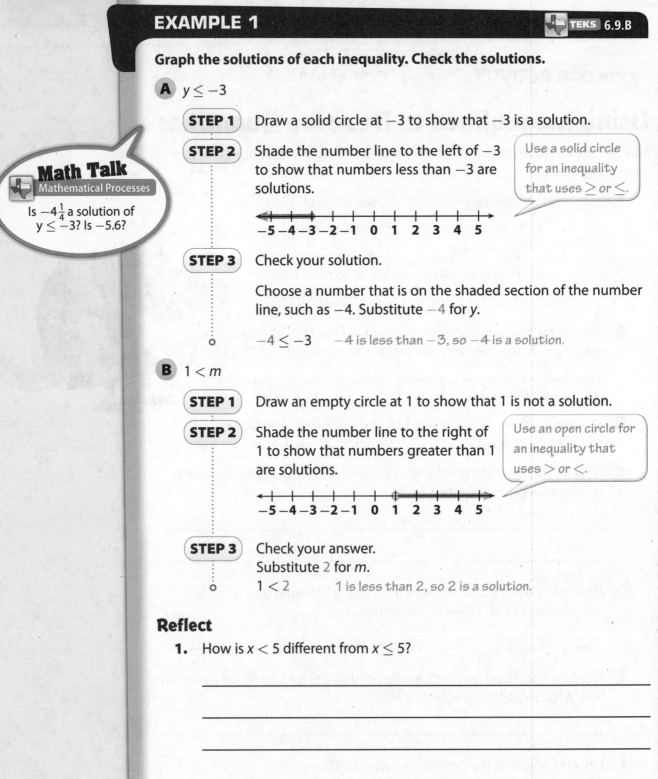

**STEP 3** Check your solution.

Choose a number that is on the shaded section of the number line, such as $-4$. Substitute $-4$ for $y$.

$-4 \leq -3$     $-4$ is less than $-3$, so $-4$ is a solution.

**B** $1 < m$

**STEP 1** Draw an empty circle at 1 to show that 1 is not a solution.

**STEP 2** Shade the number line to the right of 1 to show that numbers greater than 1 are solutions.

> Use an open circle for an inequality that uses $>$ or $<$.

**STEP 3** Check your answer.
Substitute 2 for $m$.

$1 < 2$     1 is less than 2, so 2 is a solution.

**Math Talk**
Mathematical Processes

Is $-4\frac{1}{4}$ a solution of $y \leq -3$? Is $-5.6$?

## Reflect

**1.** How is $x < 5$ different from $x \leq 5$?

_____

_____

_____

_____

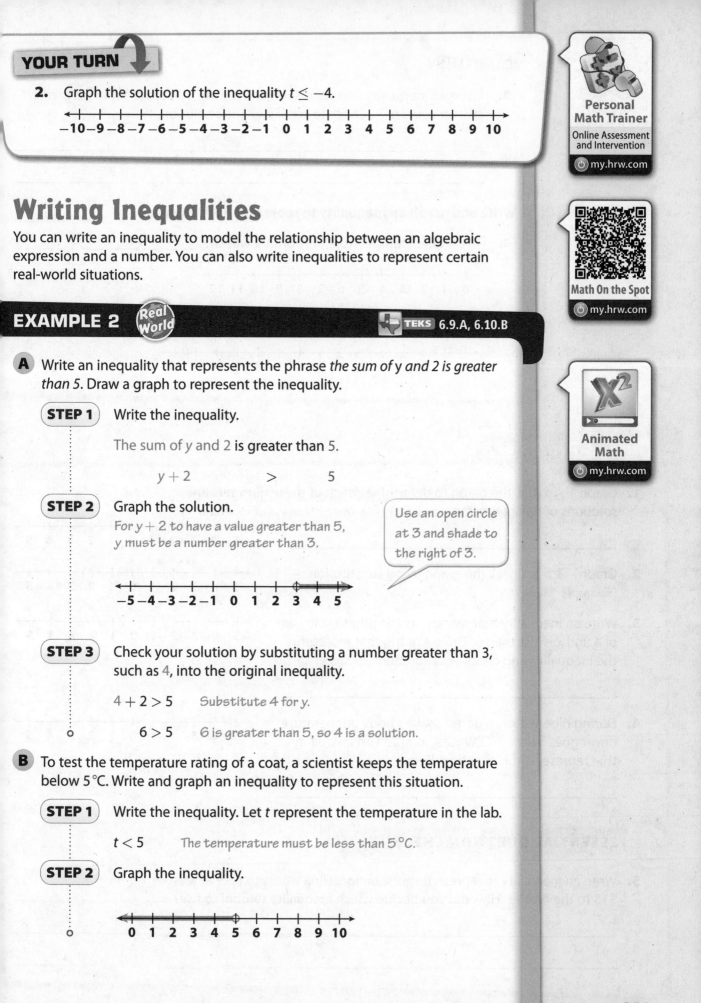

**2.** Graph the solution of the inequality $t \leq -4$.

$$-10\ -9\ -8\ -7\ -6\ -5\ -4\ -3\ -2\ -1\ \ 0\ \ 1\ \ 2\ \ 3\ \ 4\ \ 5\ \ 6\ \ 7\ \ 8\ \ 9\ \ 10$$

**Personal Math Trainer**

Online Assessment and Intervention

⏻ my.hrw.com

# Writing Inequalities

You can write an inequality to model the relationship between an algebraic expression and a number. You can also write inequalities to represent certain real-world situations.

**Math On the Spot**

⏻ my.hrw.com

## EXAMPLE 2 · Real World

**TEKS** 6.9.A, 6.10.B

**A** Write an inequality that represents the phrase *the sum of y and 2 is greater than 5*. Draw a graph to represent the inequality.

**STEP 1** Write the inequality.

The sum of *y* and 2 **is greater than** 5.

$$y + 2 \qquad > \qquad 5$$

**STEP 2** Graph the solution.

For $y + 2$ to have a value greater than 5, $y$ must be a number greater than 3.

> Use an open circle at 3 and shade to the right of 3.

$$-5\ -4\ -3\ -2\ -1\ \ 0\ \ 1\ \ 2\ \ 3\ \ 4\ \ 5$$

**STEP 3** Check your solution by substituting a number greater than 3, such as 4, into the original inequality.

$4 + 2 > 5$    Substitute 4 for *y*.

$6 > 5$    6 is greater than 5, so 4 is a solution.

**Animated Math**

⏻ my.hrw.com

**B** To test the temperature rating of a coat, a scientist keeps the temperature below 5 °C. Write and graph an inequality to represent this situation.

**STEP 1** Write the inequality. Let *t* represent the temperature in the lab.

$t < 5$    The temperature must be less than 5 °C.

**STEP 2** Graph the inequality.

$$0\ \ 1\ \ 2\ \ 3\ \ 4\ \ 5\ \ 6\ \ 7\ \ 8\ \ 9\ \ 10$$

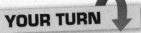

**YOUR TURN**

3. Write an inequality that represents the phrase *the sum of 1 and* y *is greater than or equal to 3* . Check to see if $y = 1$ is a solution.

_____

_____

**Write and graph an inequality to represent each situation.**

4. The highest temperature in February was 6°F. _____

```
<-+--+--+--+--+--+--+--+--+--+--+--+--+->
  0  1  2  3  4  5  6  7  8  9  10 11 12
```

5. Each package must weigh more than 2 ounces. _____

```
<-+--+--+--+--+--+--+--+--+--+--+--+--+--+->
 -2 -1  0  1  2  3  4  5  6  7  8  9  10 11 12
```

## Guided Practice

1. Graph $1 \leq x$. Use the graph to determine which of these numbers are solutions of the inequality: −1, 3, 0, 1 (Explore Activity and Example 1)

   _____

   ```
   <-+--+--+--+--+--+--+--+--+--+--+->
    -5 -4 -3 -2 -1  0  1  2  3  4  5
   ```

2. Graph $-3 > z$. Check the graph using substitution. (Example 1)

   ```
   <-+--+--+--+--+--+--+--+--+--+--+->
    -5 -4 -3 -2 -1  0  1  2  3  4  5
   ```

3. Write an inequality that represents the phrase "the sum of 4 and *x* is less than 6." Draw a graph that represents the inequality, and check your solution. (Example 2)

   ```
   <-+--+--+--+--+--+--+--+--+--+--+->
    -5 -4 -3 -2 -1  0  1  2  3  4  5
   ```

   _____

4. During hibernation, a garter snake's body temperature never goes below 3 °C. Write and graph an inequality that represents this situation. (Example 2)

   ```
   <-+--+--+--+--+--+--+--+--+--+--+->
    -5 -4 -3 -2 -1  0  1  2  3  4  5
   ```

   _____

**? ESSENTIAL QUESTION CHECK-IN**

5. Write an inequality to represent this situation: Nina wants to take at least $15 to the movies. How did you decide which inequality symbol to use?

   _____

   _____

# 13.1 Independent Practice

TEKS 6.9.A, 6.9.B, 6.10.B

**Personal Math Trainer**

Online Assessment and Intervention

my.hrw.com

**6.** Which of the following numbers are solutions to $x \geq 0$?

$-5, 0.03, -1, 0, 1.5, -6, \frac{1}{2}$ _____

Graph each inequality.

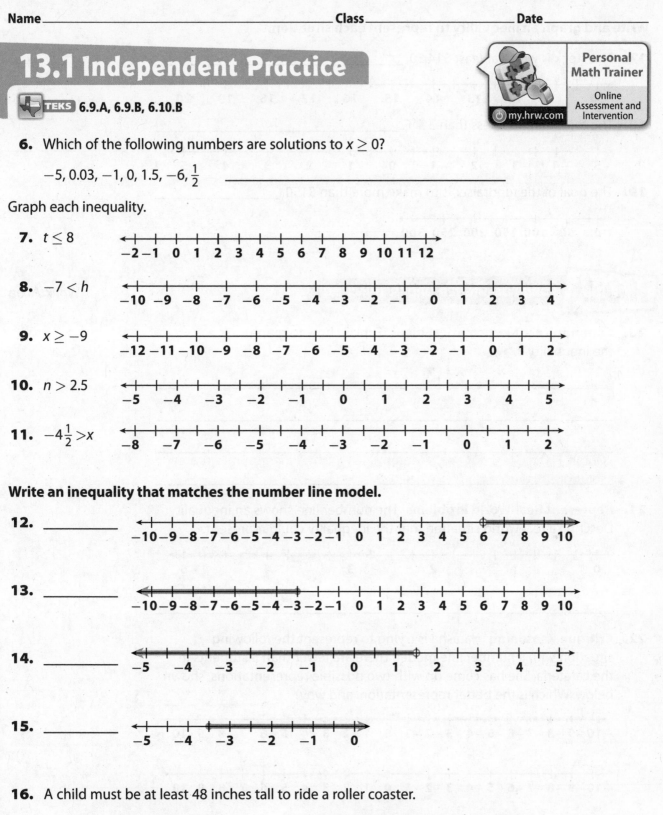

**7.** $t \leq 8$

**8.** $-7 < h$

**9.** $x \geq -9$

**10.** $n > 2.5$

**11.** $-4\frac{1}{2} > x$

**Write an inequality that matches the number line model.**

**12.** _____

**13.** _____

**14.** _____

**15.** _____

**16.** A child must be at least 48 inches tall to ride a roller coaster.

**a.** Write and graph an inequality to represent this situation.

38 40 42 44 46 48 50 52 54 56 58

_____

**b.** Can a child who is 46 inches tall ride the roller coaster? Explain.

_____

**Write and graph an inequality to represent each situation.**

**17.** The stock is worth at least $14.50. _____

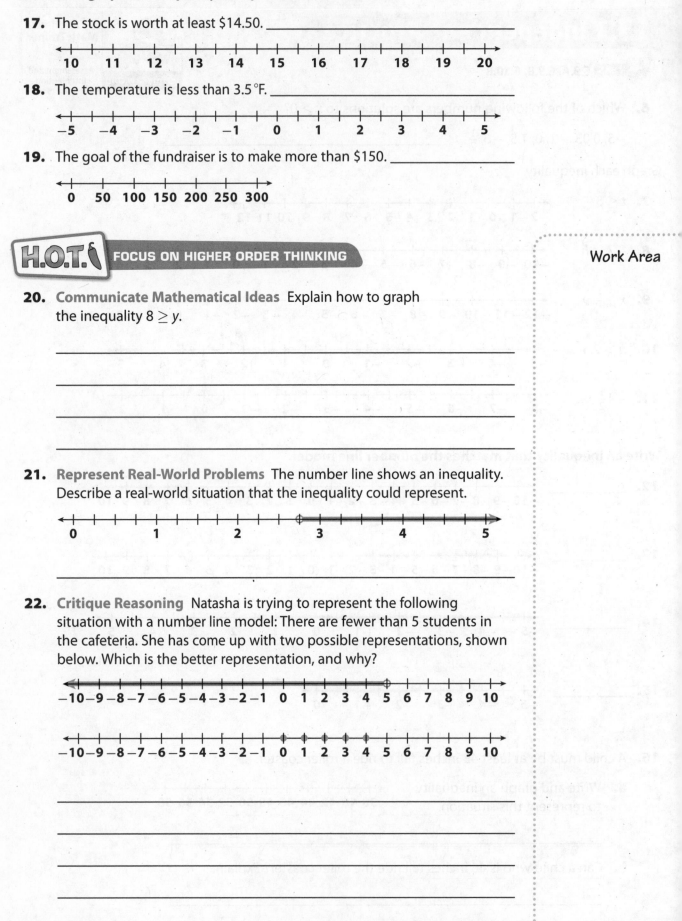

**18.** The temperature is less than 3.5 °F. _____

**19.** The goal of the fundraiser is to make more than $150. _____

## H.O.T. FOCUS ON HIGHER ORDER THINKING

Work Area

**20. Communicate Mathematical Ideas** Explain how to graph the inequality $8 \geq y$.

_____

_____

_____

_____

**21. Represent Real-World Problems** The number line shows an inequality. Describe a real-world situation that the inequality could represent.

_____

**22. Critique Reasoning** Natasha is trying to represent the following situation with a number line model: There are fewer than 5 students in the cafeteria. She has come up with two possible representations, shown below. Which is the better representation, and why?

_____

_____

_____

_____

# Addition and Subtraction Inequalities

TEKS
Expressions, equations, and relationships—6.10.A
Model and solve one-variable, one-step... inequalities that represent problems. *Also* 6.9.B, 6.9.C, 6.10.B.

**ESSENTIAL QUESTION**

How can you solve an inequality involving addition or subtraction?

**EXPLORE ACTIVITY** Real World  TEKS 6.10.A

## Modeling One-Step Inequalities

You can use algebra tiles to model an inequality involving addition.

**On a day in January in Watertown, NY, the temperature was 5 °F at dawn. By noon it was at least 8 °F. By how many degrees did the temperature increase?**

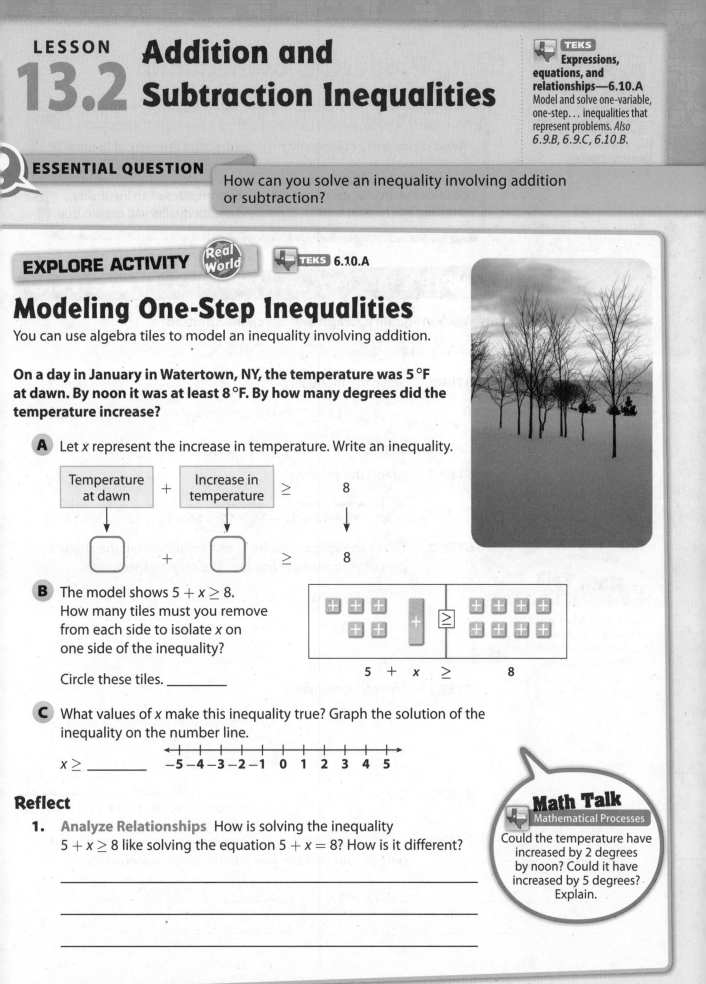

**A** Let *x* represent the increase in temperature. Write an inequality.

| Temperature at dawn | + | Increase in temperature | $\geq$ | 8 |

$\boxed{\phantom{xx}}$ + $\boxed{\phantom{xx}}$ $\geq$ 8

**B** The model shows $5 + x \geq 8$. How many tiles must you remove from each side to isolate *x* on one side of the inequality?

Circle these tiles. _____

$5 + x \geq 8$

**C** What values of *x* make this inequality true? Graph the solution of the inequality on the number line.

$x \geq$ _____   −5 −4 −3 −2 −1  0  1  2  3  4  5

## Reflect

**1. Analyze Relationships** How is solving the inequality $5 + x \geq 8$ like solving the equation $5 + x = 8$? How is it different?

_____

_____

_____

**Math Talk**
Mathematical Processes

Could the temperature have increased by 2 degrees by noon? Could it have increased by 5 degrees? Explain.

**Math On the Spot**

⏻ my.hrw.com

# Using Properties of Inequalities

| Addition and Subtraction Properties of Inequality | |
| --- | --- |
| **Addition Property of Inequality** | **Subtraction Property of Inequality** |
| You can add the same number to both sides of an inequality and the inequality will remain true. | You can subtract the same number from both sides of an inequality and the inequality will remain true. |

## EXAMPLE 1

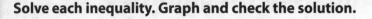 **TEKS** 6.9.B, 6.10.B

**Solve each inequality. Graph and check the solution.**

**A** $x + 5 < -12$

**STEP 1** Solve the inequality.

$$x + 5 < -12 \qquad \text{Use the Subtraction Property of Inequality.}$$

$$\frac{-5 \qquad -5}{x \qquad < -17} \qquad \text{Subtract 5 from both sides.}$$

**STEP 2** Graph the solution.

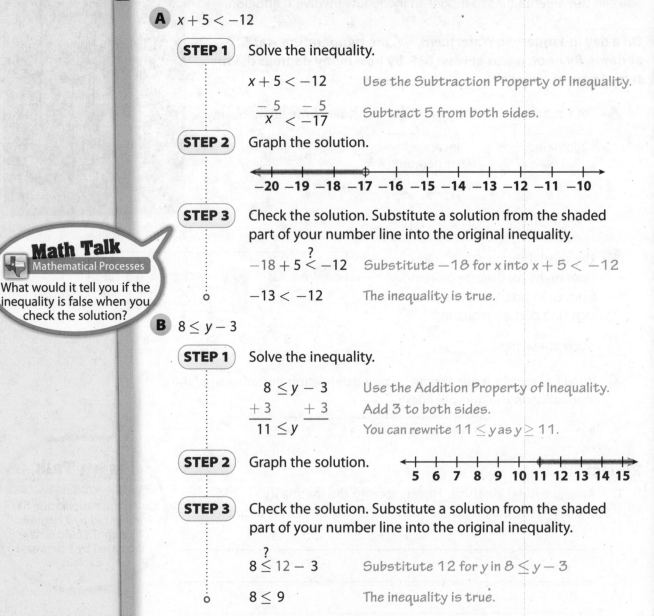

**STEP 3** Check the solution. Substitute a solution from the shaded part of your number line into the original inequality.

$$-18 + 5 \overset{?}{<} -12 \qquad \text{Substitute } -18 \text{ for } x \text{ into } x + 5 < -12$$

$$-13 < -12 \qquad \text{The inequality is true.}$$

**Math Talk**

**Mathematical Processes**

What would it tell you if the inequality is false when you check the solution?

**B** $8 \leq y - 3$

**STEP 1** Solve the inequality.

$$8 \leq y - 3 \qquad \text{Use the Addition Property of Inequality.}$$

$$\frac{+3 \qquad +3}{11 \leq y} \qquad \text{Add 3 to both sides.}$$

You can rewrite $11 \leq y$ as $y \geq 11$.

**STEP 2** Graph the solution.

**STEP 3** Check the solution. Substitute a solution from the shaded part of your number line into the original inequality.

$$8 \overset{?}{\leq} 12 - 3 \qquad \text{Substitute 12 for } y \text{ in } 8 \leq y - 3$$

$$8 \leq 9 \qquad \text{The inequality is true.}$$

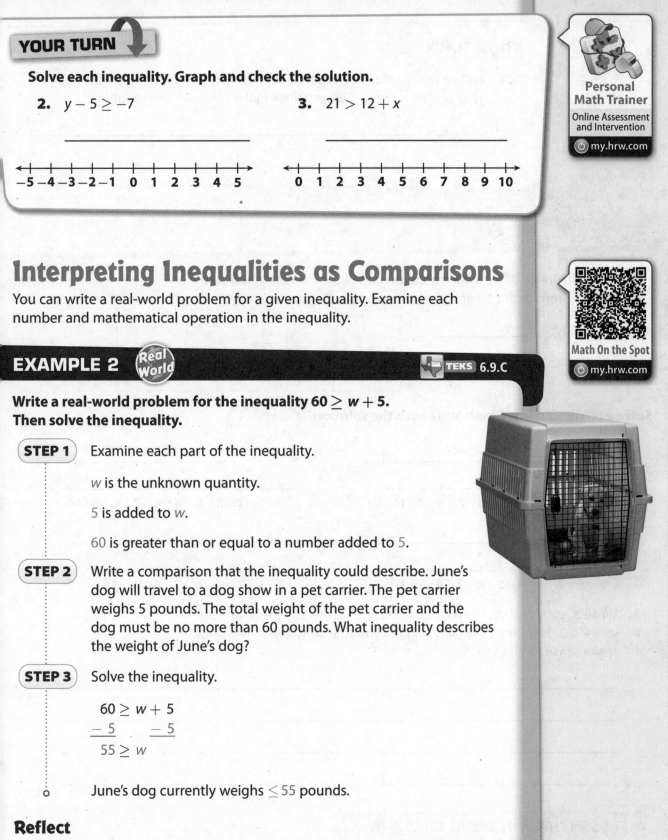

Solve each inequality. Graph and check the solution.

**2.** $y - 5 \geq -7$

**3.** $21 > 12 + x$

_____

_____

Personal
Math Trainer
Online Assessment
and Intervention
ⓞ my.hrw.com

# Interpreting Inequalities as Comparisons

You can write a real-world problem for a given inequality. Examine each number and mathematical operation in the inequality.

Math On the Spot
ⓞ my.hrw.com

## EXAMPLE 2  Real World

TEKS 6.9.C

Write a real-world problem for the inequality $60 \geq w + 5$.
Then solve the inequality.

**STEP 1**  Examine each part of the inequality.

$w$ is the unknown quantity.

5 is added to $w$.

60 is greater than or equal to a number added to 5.

**STEP 2**  Write a comparison that the inequality could describe. June's dog will travel to a dog show in a pet carrier. The pet carrier weighs 5 pounds. The total weight of the pet carrier and the dog must be no more than 60 pounds. What inequality describes the weight of June's dog?

**STEP 3**  Solve the inequality.

$$60 \geq w + 5$$
$$\underline{-5} \quad \underline{-5}$$
$$55 \geq w$$

June's dog currently weighs $\leq 55$ pounds.

## Reflect

**4.** If you were to graph the solution, would all points on the graph make sense for the situation?

_____

_____

**YOUR TURN**

5. Write a real-world problem that can be modeled by $x - 13 > 20$. Solve your problem and tell what values make sense for the situation.

_____

_____

## Guided Practice

1. Write the inequality shown on the model. Circle the tiles you would remove from each side and give the solution. (Explore Activity)

   Inequality: _____

   Solution: _____

**Solve each inequality. Graph and check the solution.** (Example 1)

2. $x + 4 \geq 9$ _____

   ⟵+—+—+—+—+—+—+—+—+—+—+⟶
   0  1  2  3  4  5  6  7  8  9  10

3. $5 > z - 3$ _____

   ⟵+—+—+—+—+—+—+—+—+—+—+⟶
   0  1  2  3  4  5  6  7  8  9  10

4. $t + 5 > 12$ _____

   ⟵+—+—+—+—+—+—+—+—+—+—+⟶
   0  1  2  3  4  5  6  7  8  9  10

5. $y - 4 < 2$ _____

   ⟵+—+—+—+—+—+—+—+—+—+—+⟶
   0  1  2  3  4  5  6  7  8  9  10

6. Write a real-world problem that can be represented by the inequality $y - 4 < 2$. Solve the inequality and tell whether all values in the solution make sense for the situation. (Example 2)

_____

_____

_____

_____

**? ESSENTIAL QUESTION CHECK-IN**

7. Explain how to solve $7 + x \geq 12$. Tell what property of inequality you would use.

_____

_____

# 13.2 Independent Practice

TEKS 6.9.B, 6.9.C, 6.10.A, 6.10.B

Personal Math Trainer

Online Assessment and Intervention

my.hrw.com

**Solve each inequality. Graph and check the solution.**

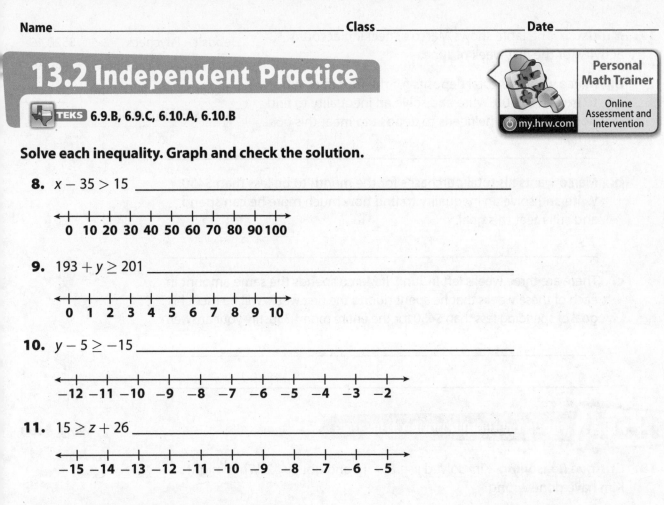

**8.** $x - 35 > 15$ _____

**9.** $193 + y \geq 201$ _____

**10.** $y - 5 \geq -15$ _____

**11.** $15 \geq z + 26$ _____

**Write an inequality to solve each problem.**

**12.** The water level in the aquarium's shark tank is always greater than 25 feet. If the water level decreased by 6 feet during cleaning, what was the water level before the cleaners took out any water?

_____

**13.** Danny has at least $15 more than his big brother. Danny's big brother has $72. How much money does Danny have?

_____

**14.** The vet says that Ray's puppy will grow to be at most 28 inches tall. Ray's puppy is currently 1 foot tall. How much more will the puppy grow?

_____

**15.** Pierre's parents ordered some pizzas for a party. 4.5 pizzas were eaten at the party. There were at least $5\frac{1}{2}$ whole pizzas left over. How many pizzas did Pierre's parents order?

_____

**16.** To get a free meal at his favorite restaurant, Tom needs to spend $50 or more at the restaurant. He has already spent $30.25. How much more does Tom need to spent to get his free meal?

_____

**17. Multistep** The table shows Marco's checking account activity for the first week of June.

| | |
|---|---|
| Deposit – Paycheck | $520.45 |
| Purchase – Grocery Store | $46.50 |
| Purchase – Movie Theatre | $24.00 |
| Purchase – Water bill | $22.82 |

**a.** Marco wants his total deposits for the month of June to exceed $1,500. Write and solve an inequality to find how much more he needs to deposit to meet this goal.

_____

**b.** Marco wants his total purchases for the month to be less than $450. Write and solve an inequality to find how much more he can spend and still meet this goal.

_____

**c.** There are three weeks left in June. If Marco spends the same amount in each of these weeks that he spent during the first week, will he meet his goal of spending less than $450 for the entire month? Justify your answer.

_____

_____

**H.O.T.** FOCUS ON HIGHER ORDER THINKING

Work Area

**18. Critique Reasoning** Kim solved $y - 8 \leq 10$ and got $y \leq 2$. What might Kim have done wrong?

_____

_____

_____

**19. Critical Thinking** José solved the inequality $3 > x + 4$ and got $x < 1$. Then, to check his solution, he substituted $-2$ into the original inequality to check his solution. Since his check worked, he believes that his answer is correct. Describe another check José could perform that will show his solution is not correct. Then explain how to solve the inequality.

_____

_____

_____

**20. Look for a Pattern** Solve $x + 1 > 10$, $x + 11 > 20$, and $x + 21 > 30$. Describe a pattern. Then use the pattern to predict the solution of $x + 9,991 > 10,000$.

_____

_____

_____

LESSON
**13.3**

TEKS
Expressions,
equations, and
relationships—6.10.A
Model and solve one-variable,
one-step inequalities that
represent problems. *Also*
*6.9.B, 6.9.C, 6.10.B.*

# Multiplication and Division Inequalities with Positive Numbers

**?** **ESSENTIAL QUESTION**

How can you solve an inequality involving multiplication or division with positive numbers?

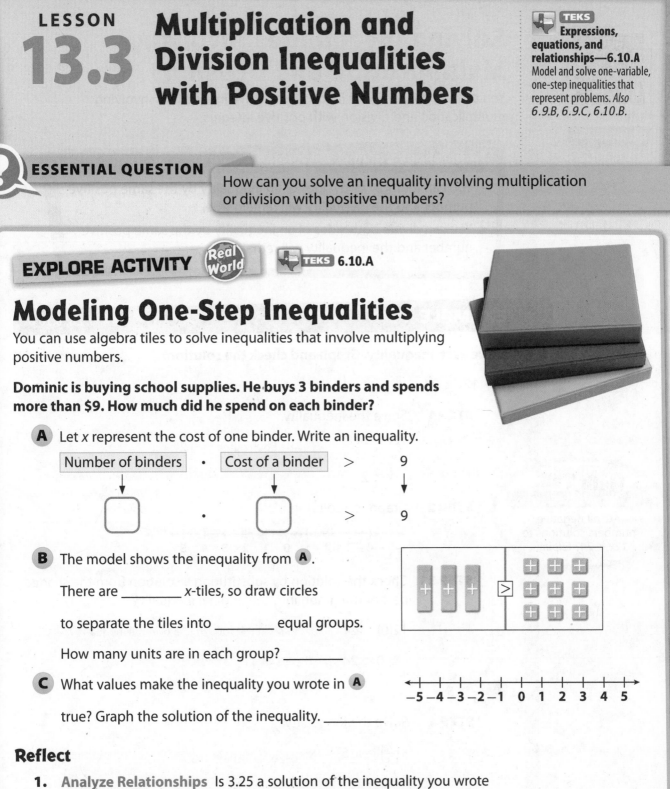

**EXPLORE ACTIVITY** Real World  TEKS 6.10.A

## Modeling One-Step Inequalities

You can use algebra tiles to solve inequalities that involve multiplying positive numbers.

**Dominic is buying school supplies. He buys 3 binders and spends more than $9. How much did he spend on each binder?**

**A** Let $x$ represent the cost of one binder. Write an inequality.

| Number of binders | · | Cost of a binder | > | 9 |

☐ · ☐ > 9

**B** The model shows the inequality from **A**.

There are _____ $x$-tiles, so draw circles

to separate the tiles into _____ equal groups.

How many units are in each group? _____

**C** What values make the inequality you wrote in **A**

true? Graph the solution of the inequality. _____

### Reflect

**1.** **Analyze Relationships** Is 3.25 a solution of the inequality you wrote in **A**? If so, does that solution make sense for the situation?

_____

**2.** **Represent Real-World Problems** Rewrite the situation in **A** to represent the inequality $3x < 9$.

_____

_____

# Solving Inequalities Involving Multiplication and Division

You can use properties of inequality to solve inequalities involving multiplication and division with positive integers.

> ## Multiplication and Division Properties of Inequality
>
> - You can multiply both sides of an inequality by the same positive number and the inequality will remain true.
> - You can divide both sides of an inequality by the same positive number and the inequality will remain true.

## EXAMPLE 1
 **TEKS** 6.9.B, 6.10.B

Solve each inequality. Graph and check the solution.

**A** $12x < 24$

> **STEP 1** Solve the inequality.
>
> $$\frac{12x}{12} < \frac{24}{12} \qquad \text{Divide both sides by 12.}$$
>
> $$x < 2$$

> **STEP 2** Graph the solution.
>
> Use an open circle to show that 2 is not a solution.
>
> ```
> ←——+——+——+——+——+——+——○——+——+——+——→
>   -5  -4  -3  -2  -1   0   1   2   3   4   5
> ```

> **STEP 3** Check the solution by substituting a solution from the shaded part of the graph into the original inequality.
>
> $$12(0) \overset{?}{<} 24 \qquad \text{Substitute 0 for } x \text{ in the original inequality.}$$
>
> $$0 < 24 \qquad \text{The inequality is true.}$$

**B** $\frac{y}{3} \geq 5$

> **STEP 1** Solve the inequality.
>
> $$3\left(\frac{y}{3}\right) \geq 3(5) \qquad \text{Multiply both sides by 3.}$$
>
> $$y \geq 15$$
>
> Use a closed circle to show that 15 is a solution.

> **STEP 2** Graph the solution.
>
> ```
> ←——+——+——+——+——+——+——+——+——+——+——●——+——+——+——+——+——→
>    5   6   7   8   9  10  11  12  13  14  15  16  17  18  19  20
> ```

> **STEP 3** Check the solution by substituting a solution from the shaded part of the graph into the original inequality.
>
> $$\frac{18}{3} \overset{?}{\geq} 5 \qquad \text{Substitute 18 for } x \text{ in the original inequality.}$$
>
> $$6 \geq 5 \qquad \text{The inequality is true.}$$

Solve each inequality. Graph and check the solution.

**3.** $5x \geq 100$

<----+----+----+----+----+----+----+----+----+----+---->
15  16  17  18  19  20  21  22  23  24  25

_____

**4.** $\frac{z}{4} < 11$

<----+----+----+----+----+----+----+----+----+----+---->
40  41  42  43  44  45  46  47  48  49  50

_____

# Solving Real-World Problems

You can use multiplication and division inequalities to model and solve real-world problems.

**EXAMPLE 2**   *Problem Solving*     🏴 **TEKS** 6.10.A

**Cy is making a square flag. He wants the perimeter to be at least 22 inches. Write and solve an inequality to find the possible side lengths.**

🧩 **Analyze Information**

Find the possible lengths of 1 side of a square that has a perimeter of at least 22 inches.

🧩 **Formulate a Plan**

Write and solve a multiplication inequality. Use the fact that the perimeter of a square is 4 times its side length.

🧩 **Solve**

$4x \geq 22$     Let $x$ represent a side length.

$\frac{4x}{4} \geq \frac{22}{4}$     Divide both sides by 4.

$x \geq 5.5$     The side lengths must be greater than or equal to 5.5 in.

Cy's flag should have a side length of 5.5 inches or more.

🧩 **Justify and Evaluate**

Check the solution by substituting a value in the solution set in the original inequality. Try $x = 6$.

$4(6) \overset{?}{\geq} 22$     Substitute 6 for $x$.

$24 \geq 22$     The statement is true.

Cy's flag could have a side length of 6 inches.

## Reflect

**5. Represent Real-World Problems** Write and solve a real-world problem for the inequality $4x \leq 60$.

_____

_____

_____

**YOUR TURN**

6. A paperweight must weigh less than 4 ounces. Brittany wants to make 6 paperweights using sand. Write and solve an inequality to find the possible weight of the sand she needs.

_____

# Guided Practice

1. Write the inequality shown on the model. Circle groups of tiles to show the solution. Then write the solution. (Explore Activity)

   Inequality: _____

   Solution: _____

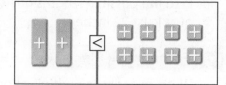

**Solve each inequality. Graph and check the solution.** (Example 1)

2. $8y < 320$ _____

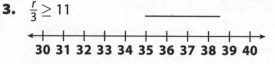
35 36 37 38 39 40 41 42 43 44 45

3. $\frac{r}{3} \geq 11$ _____

30 31 32 33 34 35 36 37 38 39 40

4. Karen divided her books and put them on 6 shelves. There were at least 14 books on each shelf. How many books did she have? Write and solve an inequality to represent this situation. (Example 2)

_____

**? ESSENTIAL QUESTION CHECK-IN**

5. Explain how to solve and check the solution to $5x < 40$ using properties of inequalities.

_____

_____

# 13.3 Independent Practice

**TEKS** 6.9.B, 6.9.C, 6.10.A, 6.10.B

Personal Math Trainer

Online Assessment and Intervention

my.hrw.com

**Write and solve an inequality for each problem.**

**6. Geometry** The perimeter of a regular hexagon is at most 42 inches. Find the possible side lengths of the hexagon.

_____

_____

**7.** Tamar needs to make at least $84 at work on Tuesday to afford dinner and a movie on Wednesday night. She makes $14 an hour at her job. How many hours does she need to work on Tuesday?

_____

**8.** In a litter of 7 kittens, each kitten weighs more than 3.5 ounces. Find the possible total weight of the litter.

_____

_____

**9.** To cover his rectangular backyard, Will needs at least 170.5 square feet of sod. The length of Will's yard is 15.5 feet. What are the possible widths of Will's yard?

_____

_____

**Solve each inequality. Graph and check the solution.**

**10.** $10x \leq 60$ _____

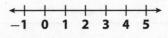

**11.** $\frac{t}{2} > 0$ _____

-5 -4 -3 -2 -1 0 1 2 3 4 5

**12.** Steve pays less than $32 per day to rent his apartment. August has 31 days. What are the possible amounts Steve could pay for rent in August?

_____

**13.** If you were to graph the solution for exercise 12, would all points on the graph make sense for the situation? Explain.

_____

_____

_____

**14. Multistep** Lina bought 4 smoothies at a health food store. The bill was less than $16.

**a.** Write and solve an inequality to represent the cost of each smoothie.

_____

_____

**b.** What values make sense for this situation? Explain.

_____

_____

_____

**c.** Graph the values that make sense for this situation on the number line.

-1 0 1 2 3 4 5

**Solve each inequality.**

**15.** $\frac{p}{13} \leq 30$ _____

**16.** $2t > 324$ _____

**17.** $12y \geq 1$ _____

**18.** $\frac{x}{9.5} < 11$ _____

**The sign shows some prices at a produce stand.**

| Produce | Price per Pound |
|---|---|
| Onions | $1.25 |
| Yellow Squash | $0.99 |
| Spinach | $3.00 |
| Potatoes | $0.50 |

**19.** Tom has $10. What is the greatest amount of spinach he can buy?

_____

**20.** Gary has enough money to buy at most 5.5 pounds of potatoes. How much money does Gary have?

_____

**21.** Florence wants to spend no more than $3 on onions. Will she be able to buy 2.5 pounds of onions? Explain.

_____

_____

**22.** The produce buyer for a local restaurant wants to buy more than 30 lb of onions. The produce buyer at a local hotel buys exactly 12 pounds of spinach. Who spends more at the produce stand? Explain.

_____

_____

 **FOCUS ON HIGHER ORDER THINKING**

**Work Area**

**23. Critique Reasoning** A student solves $\frac{r}{5} \leq \frac{2}{5}$ and gets $r \leq \frac{2}{25}$. What is the correct solution? What mistake might the student have made?

_____

_____

**24. Represent Real-World Problems** Write and solve a word problem that can be represented with $240 \leq 2x$.

_____

_____

_____

**25. Persevere in Problem Solving** A rectangular prism has a length of 13 inches and a width of $\frac{1}{2}$ inch. The volume of the prism is at most 65 cubic inches. Find all possible heights of the prism. Show your work.

_____

_____

# Multiplication and Division Inequalities with Rational Numbers

**TEKS**
Expressions, equations, and relationships—6.9.B Represent solutions for one-step inequalities on number lines. *Also 6.10.A, 6.10.B*

**ESSENTIAL QUESTION**

How do you solve inequalities that involve multiplication and division of integers?

---

**EXPLORE ACTIVITY** **TEKS** 6.10.A

# Investigating Inequality Symbols

You have seen that multiplying or dividing both sides of an inequality by the same *positive* number results in an equivalent inequality. How does multiplying or dividing both sides by the same *negative* number affect an inequality?

**A** Complete the tables.

| Inequality | Multiply each side by: | New inequality | New inequality is true or false? |
|---|---|---|---|
| 3 < 4 | 2 | | |
| 2 ≥ −3 | 3 | | |
| 5 > 2 | −1 | | |
| −8 > −10 | −8 | | |

| Inequality | Divide each side by: | New inequality | New inequality is true or false? |
|---|---|---|---|
| 4 < 8 | 4 | | |
| 12 ≥ −15 | 3 | | |
| −16 ≤ 12 | −4 | | |
| 15 > 5 | −5 | | |

**B** What do you notice when you multiply or divide both sides of an inequality by the same negative number?

_____

**C** How could you make each of the multiplication and division inequalities that were not true into true statements?

_____

# Multiplication and Division Properties of Inequality

Recall that you can multiply or divide both sides of an inequality by the same positive number, and the statement will still be true.

> ### Multiplication and Division Properties of Inequality
>
> - If you multiply or divide both sides of an inequality by the same negative number, you must reverse the inequality symbol for the statement to still be true.

## EXAMPLE 1    📋 TEKS  6.9.B, 6.10.B

**Solve each inequality. Graph and check the solution.**

**A** $-4x > 52$

**STEP 1**  Solve the inequality.

$$-4x > 52$$

$$\frac{-4x}{-4} < \frac{52}{-4}$$    Divide both sides by $-4$.
Reverse the inequality symbol.

$$x < -13$$

**STEP 2**  Graph the solution.

-15 -14 -13 -12 -11 -10 -9 -8

**STEP 3**  Check your answer using substitution.

$$-4(-15) \overset{?}{>} 52$$    Substitute $-15$ for $x$ in $-4x > 52$.

$$60 > 52$$    The statement is true.

**B** $-\frac{y}{3} < -5$

**STEP 1**  Solve the inequality.

$$-\frac{y}{3} < -5$$

$$-3\left(-\frac{y}{3}\right) > -3(-5)$$    Multiply both sides by $-3$.
Reverse the inequality symbol.

$$y > 15$$

**STEP 2**  Graph the solution.

10 11 12 13 14 15 16 17 18 19 20

**STEP 3**  Check your answer using substitution.

$$-\frac{18}{3} \overset{?}{<} -5$$    Substitute 18 for $y$ in $-\frac{y}{3} < -5$.

$$-6 < -5$$    The inequality is true.

### My Notes

## YOUR TURN

Solve each inequality. Graph and check the solution.

**1.** $-10y < 60$ _____

$$\overset{\longleftrightarrow}{{\underset{-10\,-9\,-8\,-7\,-6\,-5\,-4\,-3\,-2\,-1\ \ \ 0\ \ \ 1}{\mid\mid\mid\mid\mid\mid\mid\mid\mid\mid\mid\mid}}}$$

**2.** $7 \geq -\dfrac{t}{6}$ _____

$$\overset{\longleftrightarrow}{{\underset{-47\ -46\ -45\ -44\ -43\ -42\ -41\ -40}{\mid\ \ \mid\ \ \mid\ \ \mid\ \ \mid\ \ \mid\ \ \mid\ \ \mid}}}$$

# Solving a Real-World Problem

Although elevations below sea level are represented by negative numbers, we often use absolute value to describe these elevations. For example, −50 feet relative to sea level might be described as 50 feet below sea level.

### EXAMPLE 2   Problem Solving

**TEKS** 6.10.A

A marine submersible descends more than 40 feet below sea level. As it descends from sea level, the change in elevation is −5 feet per second. For how many seconds does it descend?

#### Analyze Information

Rewrite the question as a statement.

- Find the number of seconds that the submersible decends below sea level.

**List the important information:**

- The final elevation is greater than 40 feet below sea level or $< -40$ feet.
- The rate of descent is −5 feet per second.

#### Formulate a Plan

Write and solve an inequality. Use this fact:

Rate of change in elevation × Time in seconds = Total change in elevation

#### Solve

$$-5t < -40 \qquad \textit{Rate of change} \times \textit{Time} < \textit{Maximum elevation}$$

$$\frac{-5t}{-5} > \frac{-40}{-5} \qquad \textit{Divide both sides by −5. Reverse the inequality symbol.}$$

$$t > 8$$

The submersible descends for more than 8 seconds.

#### Justify and Evaluate

Check your answer by substituting a value greater than 8 seconds in the original inequality.

$$-5(9) \overset{?}{<} -40 \qquad \textit{Substitute 9 for t in the inequality } -5t < -40.$$

$$-45 < -40 \qquad \textit{The statement is true.}$$

**YOUR TURN**

3. Every month, $35 is withdrawn from Tom's savings account to pay for his gym membership. He has enough savings to withdraw no more than $315. For how many months can Tony pay for his gym membership?

_____

_____

## Guided Practice

**Solve each inequality. Graph and check the solution.**
(Explore Activity and Example 1)

1. $-7z \geq 21$ _____

$$\overset{\longleftrightarrow}{\underset{-10\ -9\ -8\ -7\ -6\ -5\ -4\ -3\ -2\ -1\ \ \ 0}{|\ |\ |\ |\ |\ |\ |\ |\ |\ |\ |}}$$

2. $-\dfrac{t}{4} > 5$ _____

$$\overset{\longleftrightarrow}{\underset{-50\ -40\ -30\ -20\ -10\ \ \ 0\ \ \ 10\ \ \ 20\ \ \ 30\ \ \ 40\ \ \ 50}{|\ |\ |\ |\ |\ |\ |\ |\ |\ |\ |}}$$

3. $11x < -66$ _____

$$\overset{\longleftrightarrow}{\underset{-8\ -7\ -6\ -5\ -4\ -3\ -2\ -1\ \ \ 0\ \ \ 1\ \ \ 2}{|\ |\ |\ |\ |\ |\ |\ |\ |\ |\ |}}$$

4. $-\dfrac{t}{10} > 5$ _____

$$\overset{\longleftrightarrow}{\underset{-100\ -90\ -80\ -70\ -60\ -50\ -40\ -30\ -20\ -10\ \ \ 0}{|\ |\ |\ |\ |\ |\ |\ |\ |\ |\ |}}$$

5. For a scientific experiment, a physicist must make sure that the temperature of a metal does not get colder than −80 °C. The metal begins the experiment at 0 °C and is cooled at a steady rate of −4 °C per hour. How long can the experiment run? (Example 2)

a. Let $t$ represent time in hours. Write an inequality. Use the fact that the rate of change in temperature times the number of seconds equals the final temperature.

_____

b. Solve the inequality in part **a**. How long will it take the physicist to change the temperature of the metal?

_____

c. The physicist has to repeat the experiment if the metal gets cooler than −80 °C. How many hours would the physicist have to cool the metal for this to happen?

_____

**?** **ESSENTIAL QUESTION CHECK-IN**

6. Suppose you are solving an inequality. Under what circumstances do you reverse the inequality symbol?

_____

# 13.4 Independent Practice

**Personal Math Trainer**

Online Assessment and Intervention

my.hrw.com

**TEKS** 6.9.B, 6.10.A, 6.10.B

**Solve each inequality. Graph and check your solution.**

**7.** $-\frac{q}{7} \geq -1$ _____

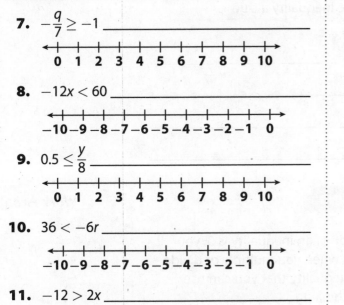

**8.** $-12x < 60$ _____

**9.** $0.5 \leq \frac{y}{8}$ _____

**10.** $36 < -6r$ _____

**11.** $-12 > 2x$ _____

**12.** $-\frac{x}{6} \leq -0.5$ _____

**13. Multistep** Parav is playing a game in which he flips a counter that can land on either a −6 or a 6. He adds the point values of all the flips to find his total score. To win, he needs to get a score less than −48.

**a.** Assuming Parav only gets −6s when he flips the counter, how many times does he have to flip the counter?

_____

**b.** Suppose Parav flips the counter and gets five 6s and twelve −6s when he plays the game. Does he win? Explain.

_____

_____

**14.** A veterinarian tells Max that his cat should lose no more than 30 ounces. The veterinarian suggests that the cat should lose 7 ounces or less per week. What is the shortest time in weeks and days it would take Max's cat to lose the 30 ounces?

_____

_____

**15.** The elevation of an underwater cave is −120 feet relative to sea level. A submarine descends to the cave. The submarine's rate of change in elevation is no greater than −12 feet per second. How long will it take to reach the cave?

_____

_____

**16.** The temperature of a freezer is never greater than −2 °C. Yesterday the temperature was −10 °C, but it increased at a steady rate of 1.5 °C per hour. How long in hours and minutes did the temperature increase inside the freezer?

_____

_____

**17. Explain the Error** A student's solution to the inequality $-6x > 42$ was $x > -7$. What error did the student make in the solution? What is the correct answer?

_____

_____

_____

_____

_____

**Solve each inequality.**

**18.** $18 \leq -2x$ _____

**19.** $-\frac{x}{7} \leq -23$ _____

**20.** $-\frac{x}{8} < -\frac{1}{2}$ _____

**21.** $0.4 < -x$ _____

**22.** $4x < \frac{1}{5}$ _____

**23.** $-\frac{x}{0.8} \leq -30$ _____

**24.** Use the order of operations to simplify the left side of the inequality below. What values of $x$ make the inequality a true statement? $-\frac{1}{2}(3^2 + 7)x > 32$

_____

_____

_____

_____

**H.O.T.**   **FOCUS ON HIGHER ORDER THINKING**

Work Area

**25. Counterexamples**  John says that if one side of an inequality is 0, you don't have to reverse the inequality symbol when you multiply or divide both sides by a negative number. Find an inequality that you can use to disprove John's statement. Explain your thinking.

_____

_____

_____

_____

_____

**26. Communicate Mathematical Thinking**  Van thinks that the answer to $-3x < 12$ is $x < -4$. How would you convince him that his answer is incorrect?

_____

_____

_____

_____

_____

_____

# Ready to Go On?

**Personal Math Trainer**

Online Assessment and Intervention

⏻ my.hrw.com

## 13.1 Writing Inequalities

**Write an inequality to represent each situation, then graph the solutions.**

1. There are fewer than 8 gallons of gas in the tank. _____

   ↤┼─┼─┼─┼─┼─┼─┼─┼─┼─┼─↦
   　0　1　2　3　4　5　6　7　8　9　10

2. There are at least 3 pieces of gum left in the pack. _____

   ↤┼─┼─┼─┼─┼─┼─┼─┼─┼─┼─↦
   　0　1　2　3　4　5　6　7　8　9　10

3. The valley was at least 4 feet below sea level. _____

   ↤┼─┼─┼─┼─┼─┼─┼─┼─┼─┼─┼─┼─┼─┼─┼─┼─┼─┼─┼─┼─↦
   −10−9−8−7−6−5−4−3−2−1　0　1　2　3　4　5　6　7　8　9　10

## 13.2 Addition and Subtraction Inequalities

**Solve each inequality. Graph the solution.**

4. $c - 28 > -32$ _____

   ↤┼─┼─┼─┼─┼─┼─┼─┼─┼─┼─↦
   −10−9−8−7−6−5−4−3−2−1　0

5. $v + 17 \leq 20$ _____

   ↤┼─┼─┼─┼─┼─┼─┼─┼─┼─┼─↦
   　0　1　2　3　4　5　6　7　8　9　10

6. Today's high temperature of 80 °F is at least 16° warmer than yesterday's high

   temperature. What was yesterday's high temperature? _____

## 13.3, 13.4 Multiplication and Division Inequalities

**Solve each inequality. Graph the solution.**

7. $7f \leq 35$ _____

   ↤┼─┼─┼─┼─┼─┼─┼─┼─┼─┼─↦
   　0　1　2　3　4　5　6　7　8　9　10

8. $\frac{a}{2} < 4$ _____

   ↤┼─┼─┼─┼─┼─┼─┼─┼─┼─┼─↦
   　0　1　2　3　4　5　6　7　8　9　10

9. $-25g \geq 150$ _____

   ↤┼─┼─┼─┼─┼─┼─┼─┼─┼─┼─↦
   −10−9−8−7−6−5−4−3−2−1　0

10. $\frac{k}{-3} < 3$ _____

   ↤┼─┼─┼─┼─┼─┼─┼─┼─┼─┼─↦
   −10−9−8−7−6−5−4−3−2−1　0

**MODULE 13 MIXED REVIEW**

# Texas Test Prep

Personal
Math Trainer

Online
Assessment and
Intervention

my.hrw.com

## Selected Response

1. Em saves at least 20% of what she earns each week. If she earns $140 each week for 4 weeks, which inequality describes the total amount she saves?

   Ⓐ $t > 112$

   Ⓑ $t \geq 112$

   Ⓒ $t < 28$

   Ⓓ $t \leq 28$

2. Which number line represents the inequality $r > 6$?

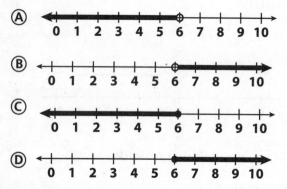

3. For which inequality below is $z = 3$ a solution?

   Ⓐ $z + 5 \geq 9$

   Ⓑ $z + 5 > 9$

   Ⓒ $z + 5 \leq 8$

   Ⓓ $z + 5 < 8$

4. What is the solution to the inequality $-6x < -18$?

   Ⓐ $x > 3$

   Ⓑ $x < 3$

   Ⓒ $x \geq 3$

   Ⓓ $x \leq 3$

5. The number line below represents the solution to which inequality?

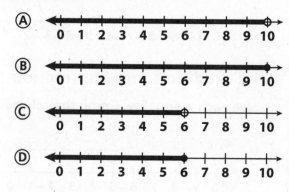

   Ⓐ $\frac{m}{4} > 2.2$       Ⓒ $\frac{m}{3} > 2.5$

   Ⓑ $2m < 17.6$       Ⓓ $5m > 40$

6. Which number line shows the solution to $w - 2 \leq 8$?

   Ⓐ

   Ⓑ

   Ⓒ

   Ⓓ

## Gridded Response

7. Hank needs to save at least $150 to ride the bus to his grandparent's home. If he saves $12 a week, what is the least number of weeks he needs to save?

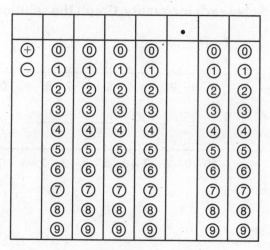

# Relationships in Two Variables

**? ESSENTIAL QUESTION**

How can you use relationships in two variables to solve real-world problems?

**Real-World Video**

A two-variable equation can represent an animal's distance over time. A graph can display the relationship between the variables. You can graph two or more animals' data to visually compare them.

my.hrw.com

**DIGITAL**
my.hrw.com

**my.hrw.com**

Go digital with your write-in student edition, accessible on any device.

**Math On the Spot**

Scan with your smart phone to jump directly to the online edition, video tutor, and more.

**Animated Math**

Interactively explore key concepts to see how math works.

**Personal Math Trainer**

Get immediate feedback and help as you work through practice sets.

# Are YOU Ready?

Complete these exercises to review skills you will need for this chapter.

**Personal Math Trainer**

Online Assessment and Intervention

my.hrw.com

## Multiplication Facts

**EXAMPLE**   $8 \times 7 = \boxed{\phantom{00}}$

Use a related fact you know.
$7 \times 7 = 49$
Think: $8 \times 7 = (7 \times 7) + 7$
$= 49 + 7$
$= 56$

**Multiply.**

**1.** $7 \times 6$ _____

**2.** $10 \times 9$ _____

**3.** $13 \times 12$ _____

**4.** $8 \times 9$ _____

**Write the rule for each table.**

**5.**

| $x$ | 1 | 2 | 3 | 4 |
|---|---|---|---|---|
| $y$ | 7 | 14 | 21 | 28 |

_____

**6.**

| $x$ | 1 | 2 | 3 | 4 |
|---|---|---|---|---|
| $y$ | 7 | 8 | 9 | 10 |

_____

**7.**

| $x$ | 1 | 2 | 3 | 4 |
|---|---|---|---|---|
| $y$ | −5 | −10 | −15 | −20 |

_____

**8.**

| $x$ | 0 | 4 | 8 | 12 |
|---|---|---|---|---|
| $y$ | 0 | 2 | 4 | 6 |

_____

## Graph Ordered Pairs (First Quadrant)

**EXAMPLE**

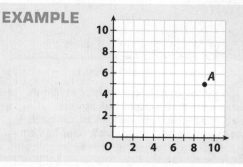

Start at the origin.
Move 9 units right.
Then move 5 units up.
Graph point A(9, 5).

**Graph each point on the coordinate grid above.**

**9.**  $B\,(0, 8)$

**10.**  $C\,(2, 3)$

**11.**  $D\,(6, 7)$

**12.**  $E\,(5, 0)$

# Reading Start-Up

## Visualize Vocabulary

**Use the ✔ words to complete the chart.**

| Parts of the Algebraic Expression $14 + 3x$ | | |
|---|---|---|
| **Definition** | **Mathematical Representation** | **Review Word** |
| A specific number whose value does not change | 14 | |
| A number that is multiplied by a variable in an algebraic expression | 3 | |
| A letter or symbol used to represent an unknown | $x$ | |

## Understand Vocabulary

**Complete the sentences using the preview words.**

1. The numbers in an ordered pair are _____.

2. A _____ is formed by two number lines that intersect at right angles.

## Vocabulary

**Review Words**
✔ coefficient *(coeficiente)*
✔ constant *(constante)*
  equation *(ecuación)*
  negative number *(número negativo)*
  positive number *(número positivo)*
  scale *(escala)*
✔ variable *(variable)*

**Preview Words**
  axes *(ejes)*
  coordinate plane *(plano cartesiano)*
  coordinates *(coordenadas)*
  dependent variable *(variable dependiente)*
  independent variable *(variable independiente)*
  ordered pair *(par ordenado)*
  origin *(origen)*
  quadrants *(cuadrantes)*
  *x*-axis *(eje x)*
  *x*-coordinate *(coordenada x)*
  *y*-axis *(eje y)*
  *y*-coordinate *(coordenada y)*

## Active Reading

**Layered Book** Before beginning the module, create a layered book to help you learn the concepts in this module. Label each flap with lesson titles from this module. As you study each lesson, write important ideas such as vocabulary and formulas under the appropriate flap. Refer to your finished layered book as you work on exercises from this module.

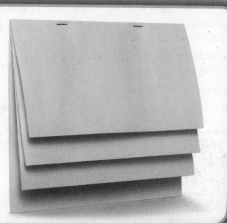

# Unpacking the TEKS

Understanding the TEKS and the vocabulary terms in the TEKS will help you know exactly what you are expected to learn in this module.

---

**TEKS 6.6.B**

Write an equation that represents the relationship between independent and dependent quantities from a table.

**Key Vocabulary**

**equation** *(ecuación)*
A mathematical sentence that shows that two expressions are equivalent.

## What It Means to You

You will learn to write an equation that represents the relationship in a table.

**UNPACKING EXAMPLE 6.6.B**

Emily has a dog-walking service. She charges a daily fee of $7 to walk a dog twice a day. Create a table that shows how much Emily earns for walking 1, 6, 10, and 15 dogs. Write an equation that represents the situation.

| Dogs walked | 1 | 6 | 10 | 15 |
|---|---|---|---|---|
| Earnings ($) | 7 | 42 | 70 | 105 |

Earnings is 7 times the number of dogs walked. Let the variable $e$ represent earnings and the variable $d$ represent the number of dogs walked.

$$e = 7 \times d$$

---

**TEKS 6.6.C**

Represent a given situation using verbal descriptions, tables, graphs, and equations in the form $y = kx$ or $y = x + b$.

**Key Vocabulary**

**coordinate plane**
*(plano cartesiano)*
A plane formed by the intersection of a horizontal number line called the $x$-axis and a vertical number line called the $y$-axis.

## What It Means to You

You can use words, a table, a graph, or an equation to model the same mathematical relationship.

**UNPACKING EXAMPLE 6.6.C**

The equation $y = 4x$ represents the total cost $y$ for $x$ games of miniature golf. Make a table of values and a graph for this situation.

| Number of games, $x$ | 1 | 2 | 3 | 4 |
|---|---|---|---|---|
| Total cost ($), $y$ | 4 | 8 | 12 | 16 |

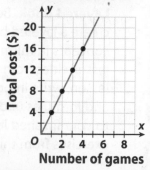

# Graphing on the Coordinate Plane

**TEKS**
**Measurement and data—6.11** Graph points in all four quadrants using ordered pairs of rational numbers.

Math On the Spot
my.hrw.com

**?** **ESSENTIAL QUESTION**

How do you locate and name points in the coordinate plane?

## Naming Points in the Coordinate Plane

A **coordinate plane** is formed by two number lines that intersect at right angles. The point of intersection is 0 on each number line.

- The two number lines are called the **axes**.

- The horizontal axis is called the **x-axis**.

- The vertical axis is called the **y-axis**.

- The point where the axes intersect is called the **origin**.

- The two axes divide the coordinate plane into four **quadrants**.

An **ordered pair** is a pair of numbers that gives the location of a point on a coordinate plane. The first number tells how far to the right (positive) or left (negative) the point is located from the origin. The second number tells how far up (positive) or down (negative) the point is located from the origin.

The numbers in an ordered pair are called **coordinates**. The first number is the **x-coordinate** and the second number is the **y-coordinate**.

## EXAMPLE 1

**TEKS** 6.11

**Identify the coordinates of each point. Name the quadrant where each point is located.**

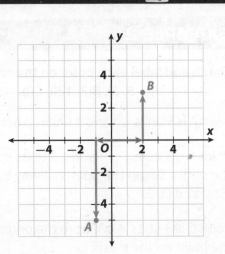

Point *A* is 1 unit *left* of the origin, and 5 units *down*. It has *x*-coordinate $-1$ and *y*-coordinate $-5$, written $(-1, -5)$. It is located in Quadrant III.

Point *B* is 2 units *right* of the origin, and 3 units *up*. It has *x*-coordinate 2 and *y*-coordinate 3, written $(2, 3)$. It is located in Quadrant I.

## Reflect

1. If both coordinates of a point are negative, in which quadrant is the point located? _____

2. Describe the coordinates of all points in Quadrant I.

   _____

3. **Communicate Mathematical Ideas** Explain why $(-3, 5)$ represents a different location than $(3, 5)$.

   _____

   _____

   _____

### YOUR TURN

**Identify the coordinates of each point. Name the quadrant where each point is located.**

4. G _____

   E _____

5. F _____

   H _____

# Graphing Points in the Coordinate Plane

Points that are located on the axes are not located in any quadrant. Points on the x-axis have a y-coordinate of 0, and points on the y-axis have an x-coordinate of 0.

### EXAMPLE 2

TEKS 6.11

**Graph and label each point on the coordinate plane.**
   $A(-5, 2), B(3, 1.5), C(0, -3)$

Point A is 5 units *left* and 2 units *up* from the origin.

Point B is 3 units *right* and 1.5 units *up* from the origin. Graph the point halfway between $(3, 1)$ and $(3, 2)$.

Point C is 3 units *down* from the origin. Graph the point on the y-axis.

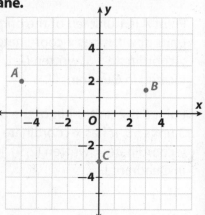

## YOUR TURN

**Graph and label each point on the coordinate plane.**

6.  $P(-4, 2)$

7.  $Q(3, 2.5)$

8.  $R(-4.5, -5)$

9.  $S(4, -5)$

10.  $T(-2.5, 0)$

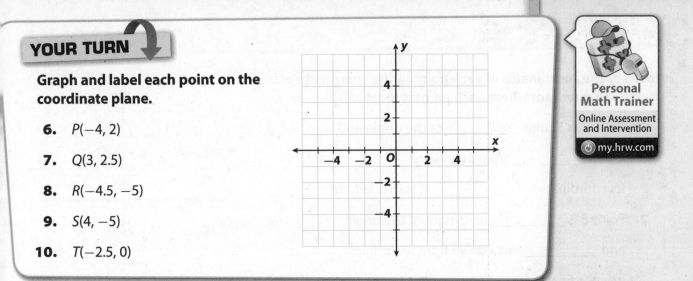

# Reading Scales on Axes

The *scale* of an axis is the number of units that each grid line represents.
So far, the graphs in this lesson have a scale of 1 unit, but graphs frequently
use other units.

**Math On the Spot**
my.hrw.com

## EXAMPLE 3 Real World

TEKS 6.11

**The graph shows the location of a city.
It also shows the location of Gary's and
Jen's houses. The scale on each axis
represents miles.**

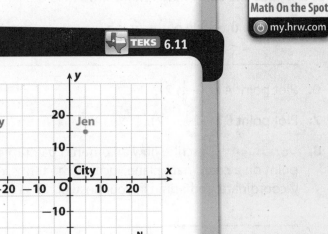

**A** Use the scale to describe Gary's
location relative to the city.

Each grid square is 5 miles on a side.

Gary's house is at $(-25, 15)$, which
is 25 miles west and 15 miles north
of the city.

**B** Describe the location of Jen's house relative to Gary's house.

Jen's house is located 6 grid squares to the right of Gary's house.
Since each grid square is 5 miles on a side, her house is
$6 \cdot 5 = 30$ miles east of Gary's.

**Math Talk**
Mathematical Processes

How are north, south,
east, and west represented
on the graph in
Example 3?

## YOUR TURN

**Use the graph in the Example.**

11.  Ted lives 20 miles south and 20 miles west of the city represented on
the graph in Example 3. His brother Ned lives 50 miles north of Ted's
house. Give the coordinates of each brother's house.

_____

Personal
Math Trainer

Online Assessment
and Intervention

my.hrw.com

**Identify the coordinates of each point in the coordinate plane. Name the quadrant where each point is located.** (Example 1)

**1.** Point *A* is 5 units _____ of the origin and

1 unit _____ from the origin.

Its coordinates are _____. It is in quadrant _____.

**2.** Point *B* is _____ units right of the origin

and _____ units down from the origin.

Its coordinates are _____. It is in quadrant _____.

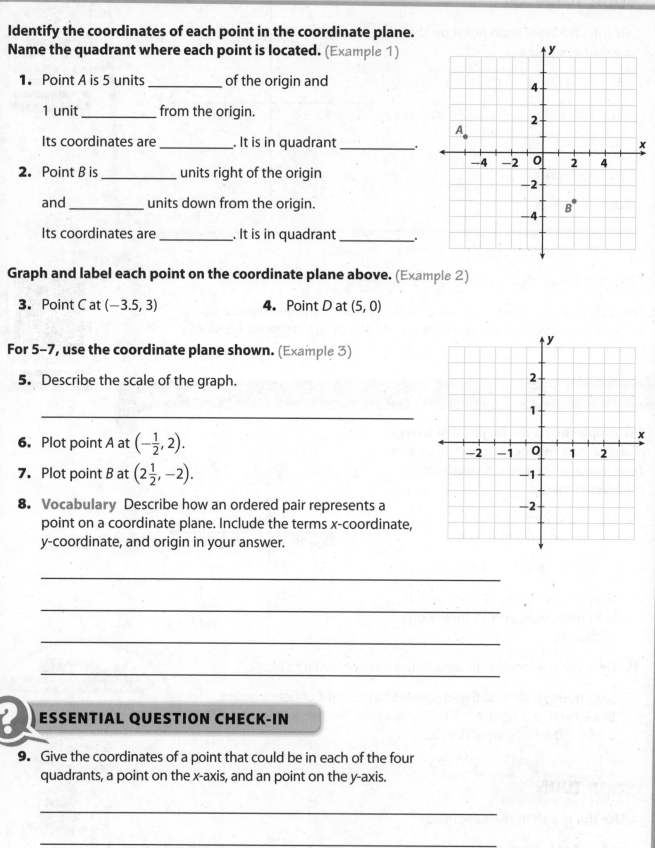

**Graph and label each point on the coordinate plane above.** (Example 2)

**3.** Point *C* at (−3.5, 3)

**4.** Point *D* at (5, 0)

**For 5–7, use the coordinate plane shown.** (Example 3)

**5.** Describe the scale of the graph.

_____

**6.** Plot point *A* at $\left(-\frac{1}{2}, 2\right)$.

**7.** Plot point *B* at $\left(2\frac{1}{2}, -2\right)$.

**8.** **Vocabulary** Describe how an ordered pair represents a point on a coordinate plane. Include the terms *x*-coordinate, *y*-coordinate, and origin in your answer.

_____

_____

_____

_____

**?** **ESSENTIAL QUESTION CHECK-IN**

**9.** Give the coordinates of a point that could be in each of the four quadrants, a point on the *x*-axis, and an point on the *y*-axis.

_____

_____

_____

# 14.1 Independent Practice

TEKS 6.11

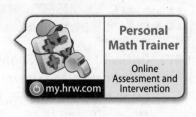
**For 10–13, use the coordinate plane shown. Each unit represents 1 kilometer.**

**10.** Write the ordered pairs that represent the location of Sam and the theater.

_____

**11.** Describe Sam's location relative to the theater.

_____

_____

**12.** Sam wants to meet his friend Beth at a restaurant before they go to the theater. The restaurant is 9 km south of the theater. Plot and label a point representing the restaurant. What are the coordinates of the point?

_____

**13.** Beth describes her current location: "I'm directly south of the theater, halfway to the restaurant." Plot and label a point representing Beth's location. What are the coordinates of the point?

_____

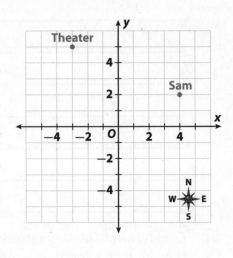

**For 14–15, use the coordinate plane shown.**

**14.** Find the coordinates of points *T*, *U*, and *V*.

_____

**15.** Points *T*, *U*, and *V* are the vertices of a rectangle. Point *W* is the fourth vertex. Plot point *W* and give its coordinates.

_____

**16.** **Explain the Error** Janine tells her friend that ordered pairs that have an *x*-coordinate of 0 lie on the *x*-axis. She uses the origin as an example. Describe Janine's error. Use a counterexample to explain why Janine's statement is false.

_____

_____

_____

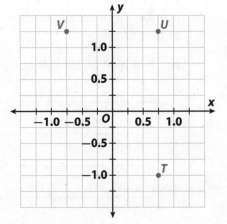

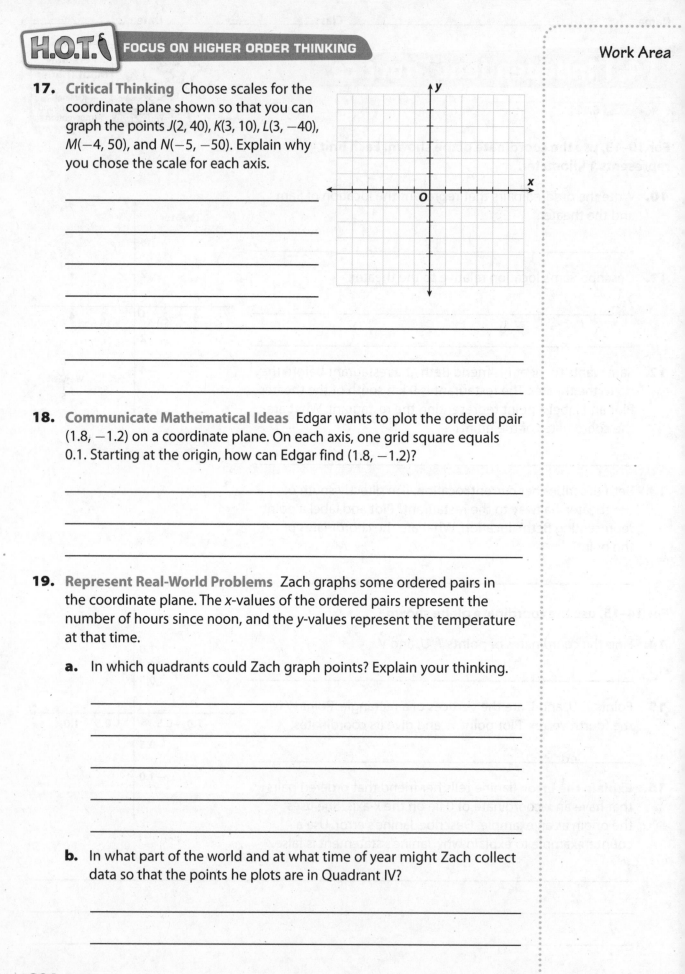

**17. Critical Thinking** Choose scales for the coordinate plane shown so that you can graph the points $J(2, 40)$, $K(3, 10)$, $L(3, -40)$, $M(-4, 50)$, and $N(-5, -50)$. Explain why you chose the scale for each axis.

_____

_____

_____

_____

_____

_____

**18. Communicate Mathematical Ideas** Edgar wants to plot the ordered pair $(1.8, -1.2)$ on a coordinate plane. On each axis, one grid square equals 0.1. Starting at the origin, how can Edgar find $(1.8, -1.2)$?

_____

_____

_____

**19. Represent Real-World Problems** Zach graphs some ordered pairs in the coordinate plane. The $x$-values of the ordered pairs represent the number of hours since noon, and the $y$-values represent the temperature at that time.

**a.** In which quadrants could Zach graph points? Explain your thinking.

_____

_____

_____

_____

**b.** In what part of the world and at what time of year might Zach collect data so that the points he plots are in Quadrant IV?

_____

_____

# LESSON
# 14.2

**TEKS**
Expressions, equations, and relationships—6.6.A Identify independent and dependent quantities from tables and graphs. *Also 6.6.C.*

# Independent and Dependent Variables in Tables and Graphs

**ESSENTIAL QUESTION**

How can you identify independent and dependent quantities from tables and graphs?

---

**EXPLORE ACTIVITY 1**  **TEKS** 6.6.A

# Identifying Independent and Dependent Quantities from a Table

Many real-world situations involve two variable quantities in which one quantity depends on the other. The quantity that depends on the other quantity is called the **dependent variable**, and the quantity it depends on is called the **independent variable**.

**A freight train moves at a constant speed. The distance $y$ in miles that the train has traveled after $x$ hours is shown in the table.**

| Time $x$ (h) | 0 | 1 | 2 | 3 |
|---|---|---|---|---|
| Distance $y$ (mi) | 0 | 50 | 100 | 150 |

**A** What are the two quantities in this situation?

_____

Which of these quantities depends on the other?

_____

What is the independent variable? _____

What is the dependent variable? _____

**B** How far does the train travel each hour? _____

The relationship between the distance traveled by the train and the time in hours can be represented by an equation in two variables.

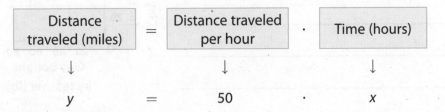

| Distance traveled (miles) | = | Distance traveled per hour | · | Time (hours) |
|---|---|---|---|---|
| ↓ | | ↓ | | ↓ |
| $y$ | = | 50 | · | $x$ |

### Reflect

1. **Analyze Relationships** Describe how the value of the independent variable is related to the value of the dependent variable. Is the relationship additive or multiplicative?

   _____

2. What are the units of the independent variable and of the dependent variable?

   _____

   _____

3. A rate is used in the equation. What is the rate?

   _____

---

### EXPLORE ACTIVITY 2 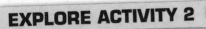 TEKS 6.6.A

# Identifying Independent and Dependent Variables from a Graph

In Explore Activity 1, you used a table to represent a relationship between an independent variable (time) and a dependent variable (distance). You can also use a graph to show a relationship of this sort.

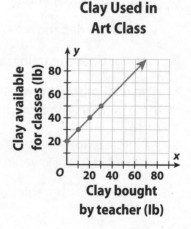

**An art teacher has 20 pounds of clay but wants to buy more clay for her class. The amount of clay x purchased by the teacher and the amount of clay y available for the class are shown on the graph.**

**A** If the teacher buys 10 more pounds of clay, how many

pounds will be available for the art class? _____ lb

If the art class has a total of 50 pounds of clay available, how many pounds of clay did the teacher buy?

How can you use the graph to find this information?

_____

_____

_____

**Clay Used in Art Class**

*y-axis:* Clay available for classes (lb) — 20, 40, 60, 80

*x-axis:* Clay bought by teacher (lb) — 20, 40, 60, 80

**B** What are the two quantities in this situation?

_____

_____

Which of these quantities depends on the other?

_____

_____

What is the independent variable? _____

What is the dependent variable? _____

**C** The relationship between the amount of clay purchased by the teacher and the amount of clay available to the class can be represented by an equation in two variables.

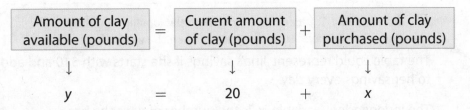

| Amount of clay available (pounds) | = | Current amount of clay (pounds) | + | Amount of clay purchased (pounds) |
| :---: | :---: | :---: | :---: | :---: |
| ↓ | | ↓ | | ↓ |
| $y$ | = | 20 | + | $x$ |

**D** Describe in words how the value of the independent variable is related to the value of the dependent variable.

_____

_____

## Reflect

**4.** In this situation, the same units are used for the independent and dependent variables. How is this different from the situation involving the train in the first Explore?

_____

_____

**5.** **Analyze Relationships** Tell whether the relationship between the independent variable and the dependent variable is a multiplicative or an additive relationship.

_____

**6.** What are the units of the independent variable, and what are the units of the dependent variable?

independent variable: _____; dependent variable: _____

# Describing Relationships Between Independent and Dependent Variables

Thinking about how one quantity depends on another helps you identify which quantity is the independent variable and which quantity is the dependent variable. In a graph, the independent variable is usually shown on the horizontal axis and the dependent variable on the vertical axis.

**EXAMPLE 1** Real World

TEKS 6.6.A

**A** The table shows a relationship between two variables, $x$ and $y$. Describe a possible situation the table could represent. Describe the independent and dependent variables in the situation.

| Independent variable, $x$ | 0 | 1 | 2 | 3 |
|---|---|---|---|---|
| Dependent variable, $y$ | 10 | 11 | 12 | 13 |

As $x$ increases by 1, $y$ increases by 1. The relationship is additive. The value of $y$ is always 10 units greater than the value of $x$.

The table could represent Jina's savings if she starts with $10 and adds $1 to her savings every day.

The independent variable, $x$, is the number of days she has been adding money to her savings.
The dependent variable, $y$, is her savings after $x$ days.

**B** The graph shows a relationship between two variables. Describe a possible situation that the graph could represent. Describe the independent and dependent variables.

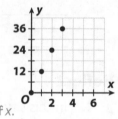

As $x$ increases by 1, $y$ increases by 12. The relationship is multiplicative. The value of $y$ is always 12 times the value of $x$.

The graph could represent the number of eggs in cartons that each hold 12 eggs.

The independent variable, $x$, is the number of cartons.
The dependent variable, $y$, is the total number of eggs.

## Reflect

**7.** What are other possible situations that the table and graph in Example 1 could represent?

_____

_____

_____

_____

_____

## YOUR TURN

Describe a real-world situation that the variables could represent. Describe the relationship between the independent and dependent variables.

8.

| x | 0 | 1 | 2 | 3 |
|---|---|---|---|---|
| y | 15 | 16 | 17 | 18 |

_____

_____

_____

_____

_____

9.

| x | 0 | 1 | 2 | 3 | 4 |
|---|---|---|---|---|---|
| y | 0 | 16 | 32 | 48 | 64 |

_____

_____

_____

_____

_____

10.

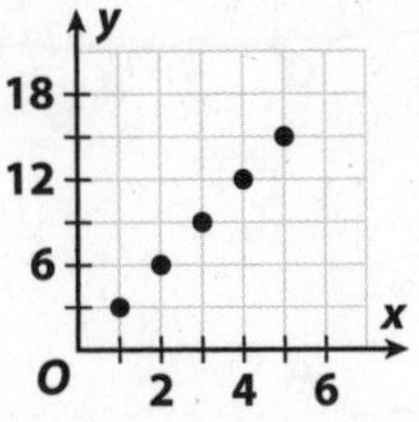

_____

_____

_____

_____

_____

**1.** A boat rental shop rents paddleboats for a fee plus an additional cost per hour. The cost of renting for different numbers of hours is shown in the table.

| Time (hours) | 0 | 1 | 2 | 3 |
|---|---|---|---|---|
| Cost ($) | 10 | 11 | 12 | 13 |

What is the independent variable, and what is the dependent variable? How do you know? (Explore Activity 1)

_____

_____

_____

**2.** A car travels at a constant rate of 60 miles per hour. (Explore Activity 1)

| Time x (h) | 0 | 1 | 2 | 3 |
|---|---|---|---|---|
| Distance y (mi) | | | | |

**a.** Complete the table.

**b.** What is the independent variable, and what is the dependent variable?

_____

_____

**c.** Describe how the value of the dependent variable is related to the value of the independent variable.

_____

**Use the graph to answer the questions.**

**3.** Describe in words how the value of the dependent variable is related to the value of the independent variable. (Explore Activity 2)

_____

_____

**4.** Describe a real-world situation that the graph could represent. (Example 1)

_____

_____

**ESSENTIAL QUESTION CHECK-IN**

**5.** How can you identify the dependent and independent variables in a real-world situation modeled by a graph?

_____

_____

_____

# 14.2 Independent Practice

TEKS 6.6.A, 6.6.C

Personal
Math Trainer

Online
Assessment and
Intervention

my.hrw.com

6. The graph shows the relationship between the hours a soccer team
practiced after the season started and their total practice time for the year.

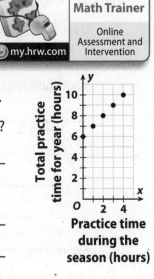

a. How many hours did the soccer team practice before the season began?

_____

b. What are the two quantities in this situation?

_____

_____

c. What are the dependent and independent variables?

_____

_____

d. **Analyze Relationships** Describe the relationship between the
quantities in words.

_____

_____

e. Is the relationship between the variables additive or multiplicative?
Explain.

_____

_____

7. **Multistep** Teresa is buying glitter markers
to put in gift bags. The table shows the
relationship between the number of gift
bags and the number of glitter markers
she needs to buy.

| Number of gift bags, x | 0 | 1 | 2 | 3 |
|---|---|---|---|---|
| Number of markers, y | 0 | 5 | 10 | 15 |

a. What is the dependent variable? _____

b. What is the independent variable? _____

c. Describe the relationship between the quantities in words.

_____

d. Is the relationship additive or multiplicative? Explain.

_____

_____

**8.** Ty borrowed $500 from his parents. The graph shows how much he owes them each month if he pays back a certain amount each month.

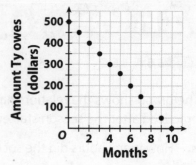

**a.** Describe the relationship between the number of months and the amount Ty owes. Identify an independent and dependent variable and explain your thinking.

_____

_____

_____

_____

**b.** How long will it take Ty to pay back his parents?

_____

**H.O.T.** FOCUS ON HIGHER ORDER THINKING

Work Area

**9. Error Analysis** A discount store has a special: 8 cans of juice for a dollar. A shopper decides that since the number of cans purchased is 8 times the number of dollars spent, the cost is the independent variable and the number of cans is the dependent variable. Do you agree? Explain.

_____

_____

_____

_____

_____

**10. Analyze Relationships** Provide an example of a real-world relationship where there is no clear independent or dependent variable. Explain.

_____

_____

_____

_____

_____

_____

# Writing Equations from Tables

**TEKS**
Expressions, equations, and relationships—6.6.B
Write an equation that represents the relationship between independent and dependent quantities from a table. *Also 6.6.C.*

? **ESSENTIAL QUESTION**

How can you use an equation to show a relationship between two variables?

**EXPLORE ACTIVITY**   **TEKS** 6.6.B, 6.6.C

## Writing an Equation to Represent a Real-World Relationship

Many real-world situations involve two variable quantities in which one quantity depends on the other. This type of relationship can be represented by a table. You can also use an equation to model the relationship.

**The table shows how much Amanda earns for walking 1, 2, or 3 dogs. Use the table to determine how much Amanda earns per dog. Then write an equation that models the relationship between number of dogs walked and earnings. Use your equation to complete the table.**

| Dogs walked | 1 | 2 | 3 | 5 | 10 | 20 |
|---|---|---|---|---|---|---|
| Earnings | $8 | $16 | $24 | | | |

> For 1 dog, Amanda earns $1 \cdot 8 = \$8$. For 2 dogs, she earns $2 \cdot 8 = \$16$.

**A** For each column, compare the number of dogs walked and earnings. What is the pattern?

_____

_____

**B** Based on the pattern, Amanda earns $ _____ for each dog she walks.

**C** Write an equation that relates the number of dogs Amanda walks to the amount she earns. Let *e* represent earnings and *d* represent dogs.

_____

**D** Use your equation to complete the table for 5, 10, and 20 walked dogs.

**E** Amanda's earnings depend on _____.

## Reflect

1. **What If?** If Amanda changed the amount earned per dog to $11, what equation could you write to model the relationship between number of dogs walked and earnings? _____

# Writing an Equation Based on a Table

The relationship between two variables where one variable depends on the other can be represented in a table or by an equation. An equation expresses the dependent variable in terms of the independent variable.

When there is no real-world situation to consider, we usually say $x$ is the independent variable and $y$ is the dependent variable. The value of $y$ depends on the value of $x$.

## EXAMPLE 1

TEKS 6.6.B, 6.6.C

**Write an equation that expresses $y$ in terms of $x$.**

**A**

| x | 1 | 2 | 3 | 4 | 5 |
|---|---|---|---|---|---|
| y | 0.5 | 1 | 1.5 | 2 | 2.5 |

**STEP 1** Compare the $x$- and $y$-values to find a pattern.

Each $y$-value is $\frac{1}{2}$, or 0.5 times, the corresponding $x$-value.

**STEP 2** Use the pattern to write an equation expressing $y$ in terms of $x$.

$y = 0.5x$

**B**

| x | 2 | 4 | 6 | 8 | 10 |
|---|---|---|---|---|----|
| y | 5 | 7 | 9 | 11 | 13 |

**STEP 1** Compare the $x$- and $y$-values to find a pattern.

Each $y$-value is 3 more than the corresponding $x$-value.

**STEP 2** Use the pattern to write an equation expressing $y$ in terms of $x$.

$y = x + 3$

**Math Talk**
**Mathematical Processes**

How can you check that your equations are correct?

### YOUR TURN

**For each table, write an equation that expresses $y$ in terms of $x$.**

**2.**

| x | 12 | 11 | 10 |
|---|----|----|----|
| y | 10 | 9 | 8 |

_____

**3.**

| x | 10 | 12 | 14 |
|---|----|----|----|
| y | 25 | 30 | 35 |

_____

**4.**

| x | 5 | 4 | 3 |
|---|---|---|---|
| y | 10 | 9 | 8 |

_____

**5.**

| x | 0 | 1 | 2 |
|---|---|---|---|
| y | 0 | 2 | 4 |

_____

# Using Tables and Equations to Solve Problems

You can use tables and equations to solve real-world problems.

**EXAMPLE 2** *Problem Solving*

 TEKS 6.6.B, 6.6.C

A certain percent of the sale price of paintings at a gallery will be donated to charity. The donation will be $50 if a painting sells for $200. The donation will be $75 if a painting sells for $300. Find the amount of the donation if a painting sells for $1,200.

### Analyze Information

You know the donation amount when the sale price of a painting is $200 and $300. You need to find the donation amount if a painting sells for $1,200.

### Formulate a Plan

You can make a table to help you determine the relationship between sale price and donation amount. Then you can write an equation that models the relationship. Use the equation to find the unknown donation amount.

### Solve

Make a table.

| Sale price ($) | 200 | 300 |
|---|---|---|
| Donation amount ($) | 50 | 75 |

> One way to determine the relationship between sale price and donation amount is to find the percent.

$$\frac{50}{200} = \frac{50 \div 2}{200 \div 2} = \frac{25}{100} = 25\% \qquad \frac{75}{300} = \frac{75 \div 3}{300 \div 3} = \frac{25}{100} = 25\%$$

Write an equation. Let $p$ represent the sale price of the painting. Let $d$ represent the donation amount to charity.

The donation amount is equal to 25% of the sale price.

$d = 0.25 \cdot p$

> $p$ is the independent variable; its value does not depend on any other value. $d$ is the dependent variable; its value depends on the price of the painting.

Find the donation amount when the sale price is $1,200.

$d = 0.25 \cdot p$

$d = 0.25 \cdot 1,200$     *Substitute $1,200 for the sale price of the painting.*

$d = 300$     *Simplify to find the donation amount.*

When the sale price is $1,200, the donation to charity is $300.

### Justify and Evaluate

Substitute values from the table for $p$ and $d$ to check that they are solutions of the equation $d = 0.25 \cdot p$. Then check your answer of $300 by substituting for $d$ and solving for $p$.

| | | |
|---|---|---|
| $d = 0.25 \cdot p$ | $d = 0.25 \cdot p$ | $d = 0.25 \cdot p$ |
| $d = 0.25 \cdot 200$ | $d = 0.25 \cdot 300$ | $300 = 0.25 \cdot p$ |
| $d = 50$   ✓ | $d = 75$   ✓ | $p = 1,200$   ✓ |

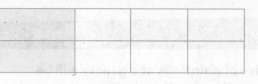

**YOUR TURN**

6. When Ryan is 10, his brother Kyle is 15. When Ryan is 16, Kyle will be 21. When Ryan is 21, Kyle will be 26. Complete the table for Ryan and Kyle. Write and solve an equation to find Kyle's age when Ryan is 52.

|  |  |  |  |
|--|--|--|--|
|  |  |  |  |

_____

## Guided Practice

**Write an equation to express y in terms of x.** (Explore Activity, Example 1)

1.

| x | 10 | 20 | 30 | 40 |
|---|----|----|----|----|
| y | 6 | 16 | 26 | 36 |

_____

2.

| x | 0 | 1 | 2 | 3 |
|---|---|---|---|---|
| y | 0 | 4 | 8 | 12 |

_____

3.

| x | 4 | 6 | 8 | 10 |
|---|---|---|---|----|
| y | 7 | 9 | 11 | 13 |

_____

4.

| x | 12 | 24 | 36 | 48 |
|---|----|----|----|----|
| y | 2 | 4 | 6 | 8 |

_____

5. Jameson downloaded one digital song for $1.35, two digital songs for $2.70, and 5 digital songs for $6.75. Complete the table. Write and solve an equation to find the cost to download 25 digital songs. (Example 2)

| Songs downloaded | 1 | 2 | 5 |
|------------------|---|---|---|
| Total cost ($) | 1.35 |  |  |

Number of songs = $n$; Cost = _____

The total cost of 25 songs is _____.

**? ESSENTIAL QUESTION CHECK-IN**

6. Explain how to use a table to write an equation that represents the relationship in the table.

_____

_____

# 14.3 Independent Practice

**TEKS** 6.6.B, 6.6.C

Personal Math Trainer

my.hrw.com — Online Assessment and Intervention

**7. Vocabulary** What does it mean for an equation to express $y$ in terms of $x$?

_____

_____

_____

**8.** The length of a rectangle is 2 inches more than twice its width.

Write an equation relating the length $l$ of the rectangle to its width $w$.

_____

**9. Look for a Pattern** Compare the $y$-values in the table to the corresponding $x$-values. What pattern do you see? How is this pattern used to write an equation that represents the relationship between the $x$- and $y$-values?

| x | 20 | 24 | 28 | 32 |
|---|----|----|----|----|
| y | 5 | 6 | 7 | 8 |

_____

_____

**10. Explain the Error** A student modeled the relationship in the table with the equation $x = 4y$. Explain the student's error. Write an equation that correctly models the relationship.

| x | 2 | 4 | 6 | 8 |
|---|---|---|---|---|
| y | 8 | 16 | 24 | 32 |

_____

_____

**11. Multistep** Marvin earns $8.25 per hour at his summer job. He wants to buy a video game system that costs $206.25.

**a.** Write an equation to model the relationship between number of hours worked $h$ and amount earned $e$.

_____

**b.** Solve your equation to find the number of hours Marvin needs to work in order to afford the video game system.

_____

**12. Communicate Mathematical Ideas** For every hour that Noah studies, his test score goes up 3 points. Explain which is the independent variable and which is the dependent variable. Write an equation modeling the relationship between hours studied *h* and the increase in Noah's test score *s*.

_____

_____

_____

 **FOCUS ON HIGHER ORDER THINKING**

**13. Make a Conjecture** Compare the *y*-values in the table to the corresponding *x*-values. Determine whether there is an additive relationship or a multiplicative relationship between *x* and *y*. If possible, write an equation modeling the relationship. If not, explain why.

| x | 1 | 3 | 5 | 7 |
|---|---|---|---|---|
| y | 3 | 6 | 8 | 21 |

_____

_____

**14. Represent Real-World Problems** Describe a real-world situation in which there is an additive or multiplicative relationship between two quantities. Make a table that includes at least three pairs of values. Then write an equation that models the relationship between the quantities.

_____

_____

_____

| | | | | |
|---|---|---|---|---|
| | | | | |

**15. Critical Thinking** Georgia knows that there is either an additive or multiplicative relationship between *x* and *y*. She only knows a single pair of data values. Explain whether Georgia has enough information to write an equation that models the relationship between *x* and *y*.

_____

_____

_____

# Representing Algebraic Relationships in Tables and Graphs

TEKS
Expressions, equations, and relationships—6.6.C
Represent a given situation using tables, graphs, and equations.... *Also 6.6.A, 6.6.B*

**ESSENTIAL QUESTION**

How can you use verbal descriptions, tables, and graphs to represent algebraic relationships?

**EXPLORE ACTIVITY 1** *Real World*  TEKS 6.6.C

## Representing Algebraic Relationships

Angie's walking speed is 5 kilometers per hour, and May's is 4 kilometers per hour. Use tables and graphs to show how the distance each girl walks is related to time.

**A** For each girl, make a table comparing time and distance.

| Time (h) | 0 | 1 | 2 | 3 | 4 |
|---|---|---|---|---|---|
| Angie's distance (km) | 0 | 5 | 10 | | |

*For every hour Angie walks, she travels 5 km.*

| Time (h) | 0 | 1 | 2 | 3 | 4 |
|---|---|---|---|---|---|
| May's distance (km) | 0 | 4 | 8 | | |

*For every hour May walks, she travels 4 km.*

**B** For each girl, make a graph showing her distance *y* as it depends on time *x*. Plot points from the table and connect them with a line.

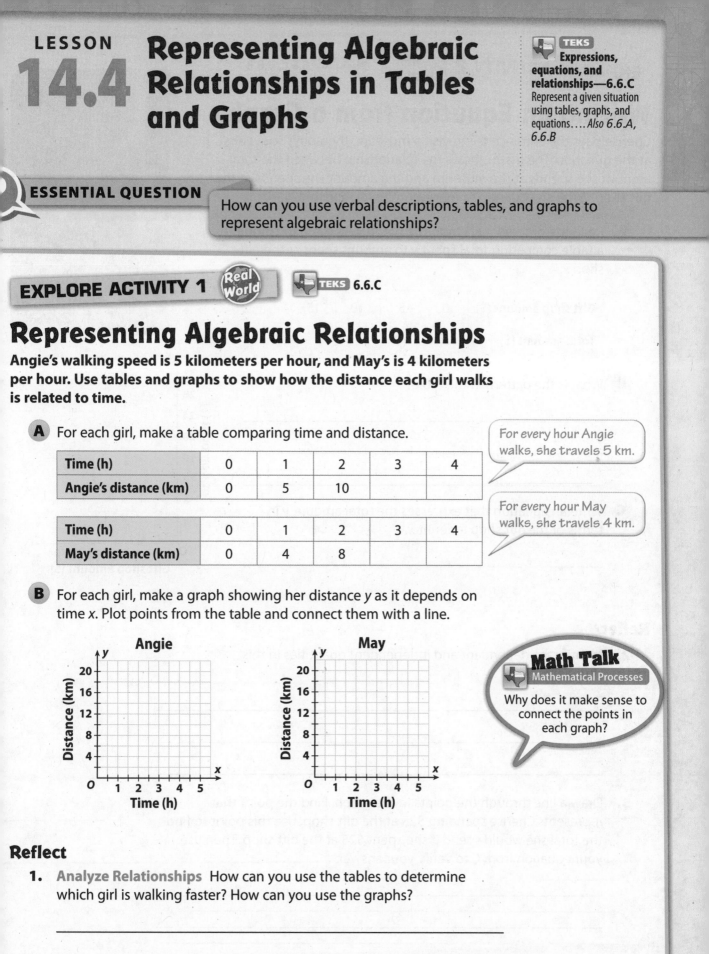

**Math Talk**
Mathematical Processes

Why does it make sense to connect the points in each graph?

## Reflect

1. **Analyze Relationships** How can you use the tables to determine which girl is walking faster? How can you use the graphs?

_____

_____

**EXPLORE ACTIVITY 2** Real World    TEKS 6.6.C, 6.6.B

# Writing an Equation from a Graph

Cherise pays the entrance fee to visit a museum, then buys souvenirs at the gift shop. The graph shows the relationship between the total amount she spends at the museum and the amount she spends at the gift shop. Write an equation to represent the relationship.

**A**  Read the ordered pairs from the graph. Use them to complete a table comparing total spent *y* to amount spent at the gift shop *x*.

| Gift shop amount ($) | 0 | 5 | 10 | 15 | |
|---|---|---|---|---|---|
| Total amount ($) | 5 | 10 | | | |

**B**  What is the pattern in the table?

_____

_____

_____

**C**  Write an equation that expresses the total amount *y* in terms of the gift shop amount *x*.

_____

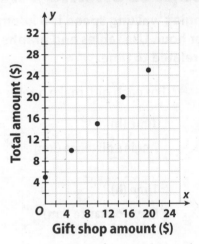

## Reflect

**2.**  Identify the dependent and independent quantities in this situation.

_____

_____

**3.**  Draw a line through the points in the graph. Find the point that represents Cherise spending $25 at the gift shop. Use this point to find the total she would spend if she spent $25 at the gift shop. Then use your equation from C to verify your answer.

_____

_____

# Graphing an Equation

An ordered pair $(x, y)$ that makes an equation like $y = x + 1$ true is called a **solution** of the equation. The graph of an equation represents all the ordered pairs that are solutions.

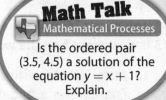

**Math On the Spot**

⏻ my.hrw.com

## EXAMPLE 1

**TEKS** 6.6.C

**Graph each equation.**

**A** $y = x + 1$

> **STEP 1** Make a table of values. Choose some values for $x$ and use the equation to find the corresponding values for $y$.
>
> **STEP 2** Plot the ordered pairs from the table.
>
> **STEP 3** Draw a line through the plotted points to represent all of the ordered pair solutions of the equation.

**Math Talk**

Mathematical Processes

Is the ordered pair (3.5, 4.5) a solution of the equation $y = x + 1$? Explain.

| x | x + 1 = y | (x, y) |
|---|-----------|--------|
| 1 | 1 + 1 = 2 | (1, 2) |
| 2 | 2 + 1 = 3 | (2, 3) |
| 3 | 3 + 1 = 4 | (3, 4) |
| 4 | 4 + 1 = 5 | (4, 5) |
| 5 | 5 + 1 = 6 | (5, 6) |

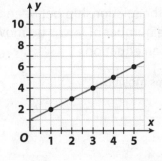

**B** $y = 2x$

> **STEP 1** Make a table of values. Choose some values for $x$ and use the equation to find the corresponding values for $y$.
>
> **STEP 2** Plot the ordered pairs from the table.
>
> **STEP 3** Draw a line through the plotted points to represent all of the ordered pair solutions of the equation.

| x | 2x = y | (x, y) |
|---|--------|--------|
| 1 | 2 × 1 = 2 | (1, 2) |
| 2 | 2 × 2 = 4 | (2, 4) |
| 3 | 2 × 3 = 6 | (3, 6) |
| 4 | 2 × 4 = 8 | (4, 8) |
| 5 | 2 × 5 = 10 | (5, 10) |

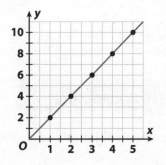

**YOUR TURN**

4. **Graph** $y = x + 2.5$.

| x | x + 2.5 = y | (x, y) |
|---|---|---|
|   |   |   |
|   |   |   |
|   |   |   |
|   |   |   |

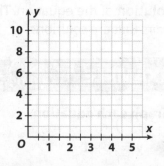

## Guided Practice

**Frank mows lawns in the summer to earn extra money. He can mow 3 lawns every hour he works.** (Explore Activity 1 and Explore Activity 2)

1. Make a table to show the relationship between the number of hours Frank works, x, and the number of lawns he mows, y. Graph the relationship and write an equation.

| Hours worked | Lawns mowed |
|---|---|
| 0 |   |
| 1 |   |
|   |   |
|   |   |

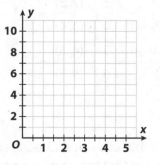

_____

**Graph** $y = 1.5x$. (Example 1)

2. Make a table to show the relationship.

| x |   |   |   |   |
|---|---|---|---|---|
| y |   |   |   |   |

3. Plot the points and draw a line through them.

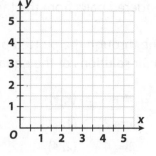

**? ESSENTIAL QUESTION CHECK-IN**

4. How can a table represent an algebraic relationship between two variables?

_____

_____

# 14.4 Independent Practice

TEKS 6.6.A, 6.6.B, 6.6.C

**Students at Mills Middle School are required to work a certain number of community service hours. Students may work additional hours beyond the requirement.**

**5.** Read the ordered pairs from the graph to make a table.

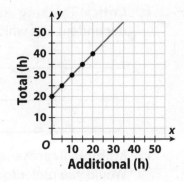

| Additional hours | | | | | |
|---|---|---|---|---|---|
| Total hours | | | | | |

**6.** Write an equation that expresses the total hours in terms of the additional hours.

_____

**7. Analyze Relationships** How many community service hours are students required to work? Explain.

_____

_____

_____

**Beth is using a map. Let $x$ represent a distance in centimeters on the map. To find an actual distance $y$ in kilometers, Beth uses the equation $y = 8x$.**

**8.** Make a table comparing a distance on the map to the actual distance.

| Map distance (cm) | | | | | |
|---|---|---|---|---|---|
| Actual distance (km) | | | | | |

**9.** Make a graph that compares the map distance to the actual distance.

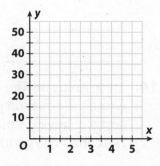

**10. Critical Thinking** The actual distance between Town A and Town B is 64 kilometers. What is the distance on Beth's map? Did you use the graph or the equation to find the answer? Why?

_____

_____

_____

**11. Multistep** The equation $y = 9x$ represents the total cost $y$ for $x$ movie tickets.

**a.** Make a table and a graph to represent the relationship between $x$ and $y$.

| Number of tickets, $x$ | | | | | |
|---|---|---|---|---|---|
| Total cost ($), $y$ | | | | | |

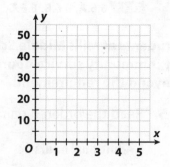

**b. Critical Thinking** In this situation, which quantity is dependent and which is independent? Justify your answer.

_____

_____

_____

**c. Multiple Representations** Eight friends want to go see a movie. Would you prefer to use an equation, a table, or a graph to find the cost of 8 movie tickets? Explain how you would use your chosen method to find the cost.

_____

_____

 **FOCUS ON HIGHER ORDER THINKING**

Work Area

**12. Critical Thinking** Think about graphing the equations $y = 5x$ and $y = x + 500$. Which line would be steeper? Why?

_____

_____

**13. Persevere in Problem Solving** Marcus plotted the points (0, 0), (6, 2), (18, 6), and (21, 7) on a graph. He wrote an equation for the relationship. Find another ordered pair that could be a solution of Marcus's equation. Justify your answer.

_____

_____

**14. Error Analysis** The cost of a personal pizza is $4. A drink costs $1. Anna wrote the equation $y = 4x + 1$ to represent the relationship between total cost $y$ of buying $x$ meals that include one personal pizza and one drink. Describe Anna's error and write the correct equation.

_____

_____

# Ready to Go On?

## 14.1 Graphing on the Coordinate Plane

**Graph each point on the coordinate plane.**

**1.** $A(-2, 4)$

**2.** $B(3, 5)$

**3.** $C(6, -4)$

**4.** $D(-3, -5)$

**5.** $E(7, 2)$

**6.** $F(-4, 6)$

## 14.2 Independent and Dependent Variables in Tables and Graphs

**7.** Jon buys packages of pens for $5 each. Identify the independent and dependent variables in the situation.

_____

## 14.3 Writing Equations from Tables

**Write an equation that represents the data in the table.**

**8.**

| x | 3 | 5 | 8 | 10 |
|---|---|---|---|----|
| y | 21 | 35 | 56 | 70 |

**9.**

| x | 5 | 10 | 15 | 20 |
|---|---|----|----|----|
| y | 17 | 22 | 27 | 32 |

_____        _____

## 14.4 Representing Algebraic Relationships in Tables and Graphs

**Graph each equation.**

**10.** $y = x + 3$

**11.** $y = 5x$

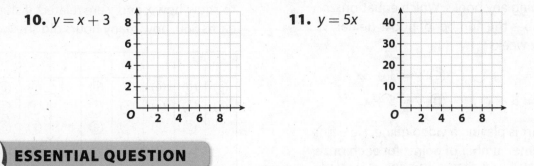

## ? ESSENTIAL QUESTION

**12.** How can you write an equation in two variables to solve a problem?

_____

_____

## Selected Response

**1.** What are the coordinates of point *G* on the coordinate grid below?

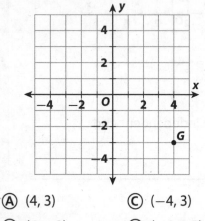

Ⓐ (4, 3)          Ⓒ (−4, 3)

Ⓑ (4, −3)         Ⓓ (−4, −3)

**2.** A point is located in quadrant II of a coordinate plane. Which of the following could be the coordinates of that point?

Ⓐ (−5, −7)        Ⓒ (−5, 7)

Ⓑ (5, 7)          Ⓓ (5, −7)

**3.** Matt had 5 library books. He checked 1 additional book out every week without returning any books. Which equation describes the number of books he has, *y*, after *x* weeks?

Ⓐ $y = 5x$         Ⓒ $y = 1 + 5x$

Ⓑ $y = 5 - x$      Ⓓ $y = 5 + x$

**4.** Stewart is playing a video game. He earns the same number of points for each prize he captures. He earned 1,200 points for 6 prizes, 2,000 points for 10 prizes, and 2,600 points for 13 prizes. Which is the dependent variable in the situation?

Ⓐ the number of prizes captured

Ⓑ the number of points earned

Ⓒ the number of hours

Ⓓ the number of prizes available

**5.** Dwayne graphed the equation $y = 10 + x$. Which point does the graph *not* pass through?

Ⓐ (0, 10)         Ⓒ (8, 2)

Ⓑ (3, 13)         Ⓓ (5, 15)

**6.** Amy gets paid by the hour. Her little sister helps. As shown below, Amy gives her sister part of her earnings. Which equation represents Amy's pay when her sister's pay is $13?

| Amy's pay in dollars | 10 | 20 | 30 | 40 |
|---|---|---|---|---|
| Sister's pay in dollars | 2 | 4 | 6 | 8 |

Ⓐ $y = \frac{13}{5}$      Ⓒ $5y = 13$

Ⓑ $13 = \frac{x}{5}$      Ⓓ $13 = 5x$

## Gridded Response

**7.** Betty earns $7.50 per hour at a part-time job. Let *x* be the number of hours and *y* be the amount she earns. Betty makes a graph to show how *x* and *y* are related. If she earns $60, how many hours did she work?

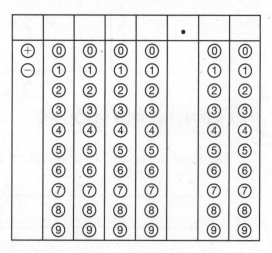

# Study Guide Review

## MODULE 10 Generating Equivalent Numerical Expressions

### ? ESSENTIAL QUESTION

How can you generate equivalent numerical expressions and use them to solve real-world problems?

### EXAMPLE 1

**Find the value of each power.**

**A.** $0.9^2$

$0.9^2 = 0.9 \times 0.9 = 0.81$

**B.** $18^0$

Any number raised to the power of 0 is 1.

$18^0 = 1$

**C.** $\left(\frac{1}{4}\right)^4$

$\left(\frac{1}{4}\right)^4 = \left(\frac{1}{4}\right)\left(\frac{1}{4}\right)\left(\frac{1}{4}\right)\left(\frac{1}{4}\right) = \frac{1}{256}$

### EXAMPLE 2

**Find the prime factorization of 60.**

$$\begin{array}{r|r} 2 & 60 \\ 2 & 30 \\ 3 & 15 \\ 5 & 5 \\ & 1 \end{array}$$

$60 = 2 \times 2 \times 3 \times 5$

$60 = 2^2 \times 3 \times 5$

The prime factorization of 60 is $2^2 \times 3 \times 5$.

### EXAMPLE 3

**Simplify each expression.**

**A.** $4 \times (2^3 + 5)$

| | |
|---|---|
| $= 4 \times (8 + 5)$ | $2^3 = 8$ |
| $= 4 \times 13$ | Add. |
| $= 52$ | Multiply. |

**B.** $27 \div 3^2 \times 6$

| | |
|---|---|
| $= 27 \div 9 \times 6$ | $3^2 = 9$ |
| $= 3 \times 6$ | Divide. |
| $= 18$ | Multiply. |

### EXERCISES

**Use exponents to write each expression.** (Lesson 10.1)

**1.** $3.6 \times 3.6$ _____

**2.** $9 \times 9 \times 9 \times 9$ _____

**3.** $\frac{4}{5} \times \frac{4}{5} \times \frac{4}{5}$ _____

**Find the value of each power.** (Lesson 10.1)

**4.** $12^0$ _____  **5.** $13^2$ _____  **6.** $\left(\frac{2}{7}\right)^3$ _____

**Write the prime factorization of each number.** (Lesson 10.2)

**7.** 75 _____  **8.** 29 _____  **9.** 168 _____

**10.** Eduardo is building a sandbox that has an area of 84 square feet. What are the possible whole number measurements for the length and width of the sandbox? (Lesson 10.2)

**11.** $2 \times 5^2 - (4 + 1)$ _____  **12.** $\dfrac{22 - (3^2 + 4)}{12 \div 4}$ _____

---

MODULE **11** # Generating Equivalent Algebraic Expressions

**Key Vocabulary**
algebraic expression
   (*expresión algebraica*)
coefficients (*coeficiente*)
constant (*constante*)
equivalent expressions
   (*expresiónes equivalente*)
evaluating (*evaluar*)
term (*término (en una expresión)*)

**? ESSENTIAL QUESTION**

How can you generate equivalent algebraic expressions and use them to solve real-world problems?

## EXAMPLE 1

**Evaluate each expression for the given value of the variable.**

**A.** $2(x^2 - 9)$; $x = 5$

$2(5^2 - 9)$          $5^2 = 25$

$= 2(16)$          Subtract.

$= 32$          Multiply.

When $x = 5$, $2(x^2 - 9) = 32$.

**B.** $w - y^2 + 3w$; $w = 2$, $y = 6$

$2 - 6^2 + 3(2)$          $6^2 = 36$

$= 2 - 36 + 6$          Multiply.

$= -28$          Add and subtract
                  from left to right.

When $w = 2$ and $y = 6$, $w - y^2 + 3w = -28$.

## EXAMPLE 2

**Determine whether the algebraic expressions are equivalent:**
$5(x + 2)$ **and** $10 + 5x$.

$5(x + 2) = 5x + 10$          Distributive Property

$\quad\quad\quad = 10 + 5x$          Commutative Property

$5(x + 2)$ is equal to $10 + 5x$. They are equivalent expressions.

## EXERCISES

**Write each phrase as an algebraic expression.** (Lesson 11.1)

**1.** $x$ subtracted from 15 _____  **2.** 12 divided by $t$ _____

**Write a phrase for each algebraic expression.** (Lesson 11.1)

**3.** $8p$ _____.

**4.** $s + 7$ _____

**Evaluate each expression for the given value of the variable.**
(Lesson 11.2)

**5.** $8z + 3; z = 8$ _____

**6.** $3(7 + x^2); x = 2$ _____

**7.** $s - 5t + s^2; s = 4, t = -1$ _____

**8.** $x - y^3; x = -7, y = 3$ _____

**9.** The expression $\frac{1}{2}(h)(b_1 + b_2)$ gives the area of a trapezoid, with $b_1$ and $b_2$ representing the two base lengths of a trapezoid and $h$ representing the height. Find the area of a trapezoid with base lengths 4 in. and 6 in. and a height of 8 in. (Lesson 11.2)

_____

**Determine if the expressions are equivalent.** (Lesson 11.3)

**10.** $7 + 7x; 7\left(x + \frac{1}{7}\right)$ _____

**11.** $2.5(3 + x); 2.5x + 7.5$ _____

**Combine like terms.** (Lesson 11.3)

**12.** $3m - 6 + m^2 - 5m + 1$ _____

**13.** $7x + 4(2x - 6)$ _____

**MODULE 12** **Equations and Relationships**

**Key Vocabulary**

equation *(ecuación)*

solution *(solución)*

**? ESSENTIAL QUESTION**

How can you use equations and relationships to solve real-world problems?

**EXAMPLE 1**

**Determine if the given value is a solution of the equation.**

**A.** $r - 5 = 17; r = 12$

$12 - 5 \overset{?}{=} 17$     Substitute.

$7 \neq 17$

12 is not a solution of $r - 5 = 17$.

**B.** $\frac{x}{6} = -7; x = -42$

$\frac{-42}{6} \overset{?}{=} -7$     Substitute.

$-7 = -7$

$-42$ is a solution of $\frac{x}{6} = -7$.

## EXAMPLE 2

**Solve each equation. Check your answer.**

**A.** $y - 12 = 10$

$\underline{+12 = +12}$

$y = 22$    *Add 12 to both sides.*

Check: $22 - 12 \overset{?}{=} 10$ *Substitute.*

$10 = 10$

**B.** $5p = -30$

$\dfrac{5p}{5} = \dfrac{-30}{5}$

$p = -6$    *Divide both sides by 5.*

Check: $5(-6) \overset{?}{=} -30$ *Substitute.*

$-30 = -30$

## EXERCISES

**Determine whether the given value is a solution of the equation.**
(Lesson 12.1)

**1.** $7x = 14; x = 3$ _____

**2.** $y + 13 = -4; y = -17$ _____

**Write an equation to represent the situation.** (Lesson 12.1)

**3.** Don has three times as much money as his brother,

who has $25. _____

**4.** There are $s$ students enrolled in Mr. Rodriguez's class.
There are 6 students absent and 18 students present

today. _____

**Solve each equation. Check your answer.** (Lessons 12.2, 12.3)

**5.** $p - 5 = 18$ _____

**6.** $\dfrac{t}{4} = -12$ _____

**7.** $9q = 18.9$ _____

**8.** $3.5 + x = 7$ _____

**9.** $18 = x - 31$ _____

**10.** $\dfrac{2}{7} = 2x$ _____

**11.** Sonia used $12.50 to buy a new journal. She has $34.25 left in her savings account. How much money did Sonia have before she bought the journal? Write and solve an equation to solve

the problem. (Lesson 12.2) _____

**12.** Tom read 132 pages in 4 days. He read the same number of pages each day. How many pages did he read each day? Write and solve an

equation to solve the problem. (Lesson 12.3) _____

# Inequalities and Relationships

**Key Vocabulary**
solution of an inequality
*(solución de una desigualdad)*

**?** **ESSENTIAL QUESTION**

How can you use inequalities and relationships to solve real-world problems?

## EXAMPLE 1

**Write and graph an inequality to represent each situation.**

**A.** There are at least 5 gallons of water in an aquarium.

$g \geq 5$

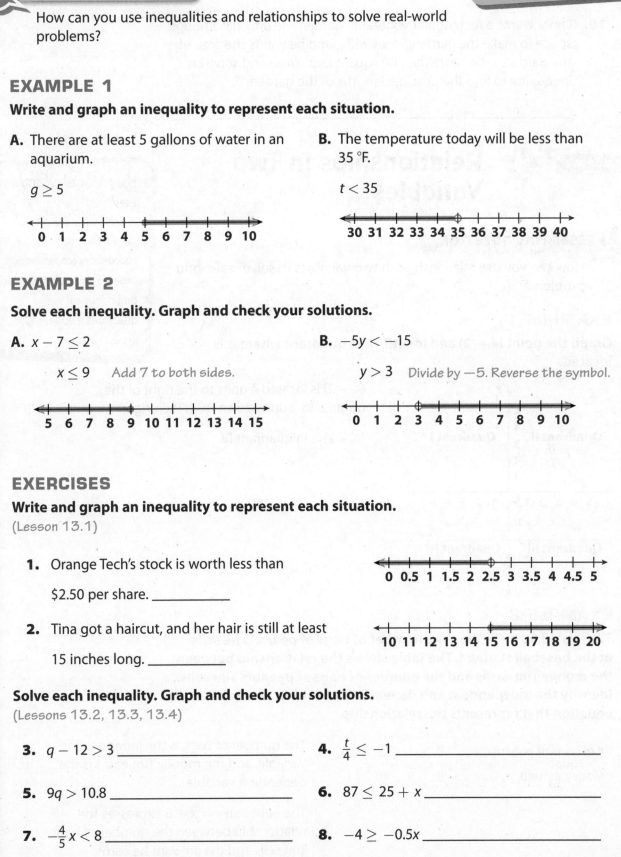

**B.** The temperature today will be less than 35 °F.

$t < 35$

## EXAMPLE 2

**Solve each inequality. Graph and check your solutions.**

**A.** $x - 7 \leq 2$

$x \leq 9$    Add 7 to both sides.

**B.** $-5y < -15$

$y > 3$    Divide by $-5$. Reverse the symbol.

## EXERCISES

**Write and graph an inequality to represent each situation.**

(Lesson 13.1)

**1.** Orange Tech's stock is worth less than $2.50 per share. _____

**2.** Tina got a haircut, and her hair is still at least 15 inches long. _____

**Solve each inequality. Graph and check your solutions.**

(Lessons 13.2, 13.3, 13.4)

**3.** $q - 12 > 3$ _____

**4.** $\frac{t}{4} \leq -1$ _____

**5.** $9q > 10.8$ _____

**6.** $87 \leq 25 + x$ _____

**7.** $-\frac{4}{5}x < 8$ _____

**8.** $-4 \geq -0.5x$ _____

**9.** Write a real-world comparison that can be described by $x - 3 \geq 11$.
(Lesson 13.2)

_____

_____

**10.** Omar wants a rectangular vegetable garden. He only has enough space to make the garden 5 feet wide, and he wants the area of the garden to be more than 80 square feet. Write and solve an inequality to find the possible lengths of the garden. (Lesson 13.3)

_____

# Relationships in Two Variables

**?** **ESSENTIAL QUESTION**

How can you use relationships in two variables to solve real-world problems?

## EXAMPLE 1

**Graph the point (4, −2) and identify the quadrant where it is located.**

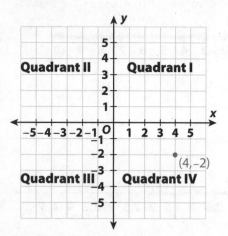

(4, −2) is located 4 units to the right of the origin and 2 units down from the origin.

(4, −2) is in quadrant IV.

## EXAMPLE 2

**Tim is paid $8 more than the number of bags of peanuts he sells at the baseball stadium. The table shows the relationship between the money Tim earns and the number of bags of peanuts Tim sells. Identify the independent and dependent variables, and write an equation that represents the relationship.**

| # of bags of peanuts, x | 0 | 1 | 2 | 3 |
|---|---|---|---|---|
| Money earned, y | 8 | 9 | 10 | 11 |

The number of bags is the independent variable, and the money Tim earns is the dependent variable.

The equation $y = x + 8$ expresses the relationship between the number of bags Tim sells and the amount he earns.

## EXERCISES

**Graph and label each point on the coordinate plane.** (Lesson 14.1)

1. (4, 4)

2. (−3, −1)

3. (−1, 4)

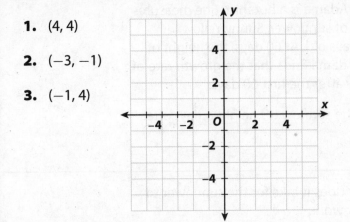

**Use the graph to answer the questions.** (Lesson 14.2)

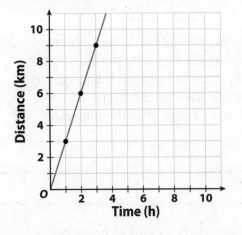

4. What is the independent variable? _____

5. What is the dependent variable? _____

6. Describe the relationship between the independent variable and the dependent variable.

   _____

7. Use the data on the table to write an equation to express $y$ in terms of $x$. Then graph the equation. (Lessons 14.3, 14.4)

| x | 0 | 1 | 2 | 3 |
|---|---|---|---|---|
| y | −2 | −1 | 0 | 1 |

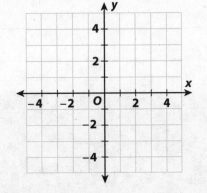

_____

# Unit 4 Performance Tasks

1. **CAREERS IN MATH** | Botanist Dr. Adama is a botanist. She measures the daily height of a particular variety of sunflower, Sunny Yellow, beginning when the sunflower is 60 days old. At 60 days, the height of the sunflower is 205 centimeters. Dr. Adama finds that the growth rate of this sunflower is 2 centimeters per day after the first 60 days.

   **a.** Write an expression to represent the sunflower's height $d$ days after the 60th day.

   _____

   **b.** How many days after the 60th day does it take for the sunflower to reach 235 centimeters? Show your work.

   _____

   _____

   **c.** Dr. Adama is studying a different variety of sunflower, Suntracker, which grows at a rate of 2.5 centimeters per day after the first 60 days. If this sunflower is 195 centimeters tall when it is 60 days old, write an expression to represent Suntracker's height $d$ days after the 60th day. Which sunflower will be taller 22 days after the 60th day? Explain how you found your answer.

   _____

   _____

2. Vernon practiced soccer $5\frac{3}{4}$ hours this week. He practiced $4\frac{1}{3}$ hours on weekdays and the rest over the weekend.

   **a.** Write an equation that represents the situation. Define your variable.

   _____

   _____

   **b.** What is the least common multiple of the denominators of $5\frac{3}{4}$ and $4\frac{1}{3}$? Show your work.

   _____

   **c.** Solve the equation and interpret the solution. Show your work.

   _____

   _____

## Selected Response

**1.** Which expression is equivalent to $2.3 \times 2.3 \times 2.3 \times 2.3 \times 2.3$?

Ⓐ $2.3 \times 5$

Ⓑ $23^5$

Ⓒ $2^5 \times 3^5$

Ⓓ $2.3^5$

**2.** Which operation should you perform first when you simplify $63 - (2 + 54 \times 6) \div 5$?

Ⓐ addition

Ⓑ division

Ⓒ multiplication

Ⓓ subtraction

**3.** Sheena was organizing items in a scrapbook. She took 25 photos and divided them evenly among $p$ pages. Which algebraic expression represents the number of photos on each page?

Ⓐ $p - 25$

Ⓑ $25 - p$

Ⓒ $\frac{p}{25}$

Ⓓ $\frac{25}{p}$

**4.** The number line below represents which equation?

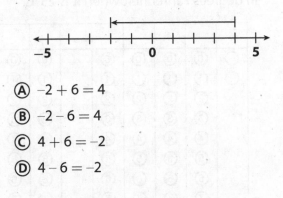

Ⓐ $-2 + 6 = 4$

Ⓑ $-2 - 6 = 4$

Ⓒ $4 + 6 = -2$

Ⓓ $4 - 6 = -2$

**5.** No more than 7 copies of a newspaper are left in the newspaper rack. Which inequality represents this situation?

Ⓐ $n < 7$

Ⓑ $n \leq 7$

Ⓒ $n > 7$

Ⓓ $n \geq 7$

**6.** For which of the inequalities below is $v = 4$ a solution?

Ⓐ $v + 5 \geq 9$

Ⓑ $v + 5 > 9$

Ⓒ $v + 5 \leq 8$

Ⓓ $v + 5 < 8$

**7.** Sarah has read aloud in class 3 more times than Joel. Sarah has read 9 times. Which equation represents this situation?

Ⓐ $j - 9 = 3$

Ⓑ $3j = 9$

Ⓒ $j - 3 = 9$

Ⓓ $j + 3 = 9$

**8.** The number line below represents the solution to which inequality?

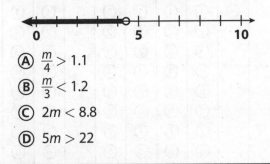

Ⓐ $\frac{m}{4} > 1.1$

Ⓑ $\frac{m}{3} < 1.2$

Ⓒ $2m < 8.8$

Ⓓ $5m > 22$

**Hot Tip!** When possible, use logic to eliminate at least two answer choices.

**9.** Brian is playing a video game. He earns the same number of points for each star he picks up. He earned 2,400 points for 6 stars, 4,000 points for 10 stars, and 5,200 points for 13 stars. Which is the independent variable in the situation?

Ⓐ the number of stars picked up

Ⓑ the number of points earned

Ⓒ the number of hours played

Ⓓ the number of stars available

**10.** Which ratio is **not** equivalent to the other three?

Ⓐ $\frac{2}{5}$  Ⓒ $\frac{6}{15}$

Ⓑ $\frac{12}{25}$  Ⓓ $\frac{18}{45}$

**11.** One inch is 2.54 centimeters. About how many centimeters is 4.5 inches?

Ⓐ 1.8 centimeters

Ⓑ 11.4 centimeters

Ⓒ 13.7 centimeters

Ⓓ 114 centimeters

## Gridded Response

**12.** The area of a rectangular mural is 84 square feet. The mural's width is 7 feet. What is its length in feet?

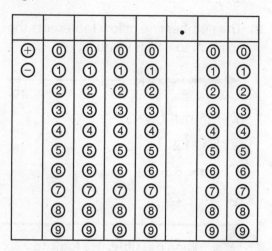

**13.** What is the *y*-coordinate of point *G* on the coordinate grid below?

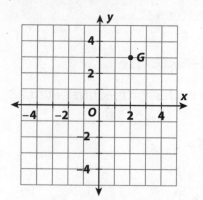

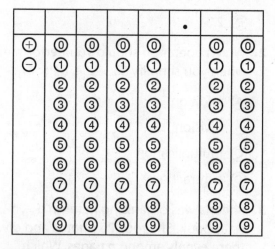

 **Gridded responses can be positive or negative numbers. Enter any negative signs in the first column. Check your work!**

**14.** When traveling in Canada, Patricia converts the temperature given in degrees Celsius to a Fahrenheit temperature by using the expression $9x \div 5 + 32$, where *x* is the Celsius temperature. Find the temperature in degrees Fahrenheit when it is 25 °C.

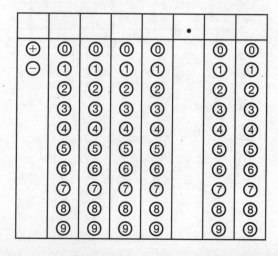

# Relationships in Geometry

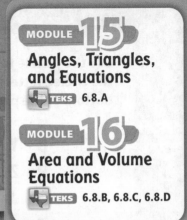

**MODULE 15**

**Angles, Triangles, and Equations**

TEKS 6.8.A

**MODULE 16**

**Area and Volume Equations**

TEKS 6.8.B, 6.8.C, 6.8.D

## AREERS IN MATH

**Theater Set Construction** A person who works in theater set construction works with the set designer to create scenery and needs technical precision when scaling and building sets based on the dimensions of the models.

If you are interested in a career in theater set construction, you should study these mathematical subjects:

- Geometry
- Algebra
- Trigonometry

Research other careers that require technical precision in scaling and building models.

**Unit 5 Performance Task**

At the end of the unit, check out how **theater set construction** workers use math.

# Vocabulary Preview

Use the puzzle to preview key vocabulary from this unit. Unscramble the circled letters within found words to answer the riddle at the bottom of the page.

```
B Y W (P) R E V L P G E J Z V S
P Z O A V P N K L T B L F C U
D J M R Q W O E H Z B F Z O B
Z J W A B N B G L W W M C E M
K P O L G Z I E G A G B Q S O
M H D L L R Y J V V C U J G H
Q F H E Q L I T G S (I) S G Q (R)
Q T W L Y V D Y K L P M C N Q
O S O O E K B Z A U B U D P B
Q B L G S K U T N E D L G C N
F H F R T S E L E C (S) O S I A
W Q F A T R L V A P M H E T M
H L G (M) A I X G D Z F W W D W
X Y K L V A U P L V V J P C A
Z J H L K Q C A P I Q A D J L
```

- A triangle that has three congruent sides and three congruent angles. (Lesson 15-2)
- A triangle that has two congruent sides. (Lesson 15-3)
- A triangle that contains a right angle. (Lesson 15-2)
- A triangle that has no congruent sides. (Lesson 15-3)
- A quadrilateral where opposite sides are congruent and parallel. (Lesson 16-1)
- A quadrilateral in which all sides are congruent and opposite sides are parallel. (Lesson 16-1)

**Q:** Where does a mathematician go when she commits a crime?

**A:** __ __ __ __ __!

# Angles, Triangles, and Equations

## ESSENTIAL QUESTION

How can you use angles, triangles, and equations to solve real-world problems?

**Real-World Video**

You can find examples of triangles all around you. Some buildings, such as the Transamerica Tower, have triangular faces.

⏻ my.hrw.com

**GO DIGITAL**

my.hrw.com

**my.hrw.com**

Go digital with your write-in student edition, accessible on any device.

**Math On the Spot**

Scan with your smart phone to jump directly to the online edition, video tutor, and more.

**Animated Math**

Interactively explore key concepts to see how math works.

**Personal Math Trainer**

Get immediate feedback and help as you work through practice sets.

Photodisc/Getty Images

# Are YOU Ready?

Complete these exercises to review skills you will need for this chapter.

**Personal Math Trainer**

Online Assessment and Intervention

my.hrw.com

## Inverse Operations

**EXAMPLE**

$7k = 35$    $k$ is multiplied by 7.

$\frac{7k}{7} = \frac{35}{7}$    To solve the equation, use the inverse operation, division.

$k = 5$

$k + 7 = 9$    7 is added to $k$.

$k + 7 - 7 = 9 - 7$    To solve the equation, use the inverse operation, subtraction.

$k = 2$

**Solve each equation using the inverse operation.**

**1.** $9p = 54$ _____

**2.** $m - 15 = 9$ _____

**3.** $\frac{b}{8} = 4$ _____

**4.** $z + 17 = 23$ _____

## Name Angles

**EXAMPLE**

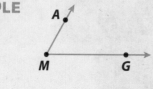

Use three points of an angle, including the vertex, to name the angle. If there is only one angle at the vertex, you can name the angle by the vertex. Write the vertex between the other two points. $\angle AMG$, $\angle GMA$, or $\angle M$.

**Give two names for the angle formed by the dashed rays.**

**5.** _____    **6.** _____    **7.** _____

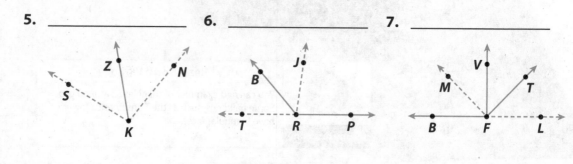

# Reading Start-Up

## Visualize Vocabulary

Use the ✔ words to complete the graphic. You will put one word in each oval.

| Types of Angles | |
| --- | --- |
| **Description** | **Angle** |
| angle measure > 0° and < 90° | |
| angle measure > 90° and < 180° | |
| angle measure = 90° | |

## Understand Vocabulary

**Complete the sentences using the review words.**

1. A triangle that contains a right angle is a _____.

2. An _____ has three congruent sides and three congruent angles.

3. The sides of triangles are _____. Where two lines

   meet to form an angle of a triangle is called a _____.

### Vocabulary

**Review Words**

✔ acute angle (*ángulo agudo*)
angle (*ángulo*)
equilateral triangle (*triángulo equilátero*)
inequalities (*desigualdad*)
line segments (*segmentos de línea*)
✔ obtuse angle (*ángulo obtuso*)
✔ right angle (*ángulo recto*)
right triangle (*triángulo rectángulo*)
vertex (*vértice*)

## Active Reading

**Pyramid** Before beginning the module, create a pyramid to help you organize what you learn. Label each side with one of the lesson titles from this module. As you study each lesson, write important ideas like vocabulary, properties, and formulas on the appropriate side.

# Unpacking the TEKS

Understanding the TEKS and the vocabulary terms in the TEKS will help you know exactly what you are expected to learn in this module.

---

**TEKS 6.8.A**

Extend previous knowledge of triangles and their properties to include the sum of angles of a triangle, the relationship between the lengths of sides and measures of angles in a triangle, and **determining when three lengths form a triangle**.

## What It Means to You

You will learn to determine if three lengths can form a triangle.

**UNPACKING EXAMPLE 6.8.A**

A map of a new dog park shows that it is triangular and that the sides measure 18 yd, 37 yd, and 17 yd. Are the dimensions possible? Explain your reasoning.

Find the sum of the lengths of each pair of sides. Compare the sum to the third side.

$$18 + 37 \overset{?}{>} 17 \qquad 18 + 17 \overset{?}{>} 37 \qquad 37 + 17 \overset{?}{>} 18$$

$$55 > 17 \ ✔ \qquad 35 \not> 34 \ ✗ \qquad 54 > 18 \ ✔$$

The sum of two of the given lengths is not greater than the third length. So, the dog park cannot have these side lengths.

---

**TEKS 6.8.A**

Extend previous knowledge of triangles and their properties to include **the sum of angles of a triangle**, the relationship between the lengths of sides and measures of angles in a triangle, and determining when three lengths form a triangle.

## What It Means to You

You will learn how to find the measure of an angle of a triangle if you know the measures of the other two angles.

The measures of two of the angles of a triangle are 47° and 81°. What is the measure of the third angle of the triangle?

$$m\angle A + m\angle B + m\angle C = 180°$$

$$47° + 81° + x = 180°$$

$$128° + x = 180°$$

$$x = 52°$$

The third angle of the triangle measures 52°.

# Determining When Three Lengths Form a Triangle

**TEKS**
Expressions, equations, and relationships—
**6.8.A** Extend previous knowledge of triangles and their properties to include ... determining when three lengths form a triangle.

**? ESSENTIAL QUESTION**

How can you use the relationship between side lengths to determine when three lengths form a triangle?

---

**EXPLORE ACTIVITY** **TEKS** 6.8.A

## Drawing Three Sides

Use geometry software to draw a triangle whose sides have the following lengths: 2 units, 3 units, and 4 units.

**A** Draw three line segments of 2, 3, and 4 units of length.

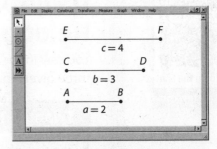

**B** Let $\overline{AB}$ be the base of the triangle. Place endpoint C on top of endpoint B and endpoint E on top of endpoint A. These will become two of the vertices of the triangle.

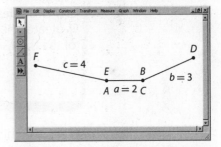

**C** Using the endpoints C and E as fixed vertices, rotate endpoints F and D to see if they will meet in a single point.

The line segments of 2, 3, and 4 units **do / do not** form a triangle.

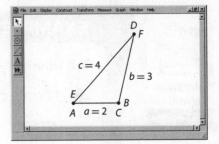

**D** Repeat Steps 2 and 3, but start with a different base length. Do the line segments make the exact same triangle as the original?

The line segments **do / do not** make the same triangle as the original.

**E** Draw three line segments of 2, 3, and 6 units. Can you form a triangle with the given segments?

The line segments of 2, 3, and 6 units **do / do not** form a triangle.

## Reflect

1. **Conjecture** Try to make triangles using real world objects such as three straws of different lengths. Find three side lengths that form a triangle and three side lengths that do not form a triangle. What do you notice about the lengths that do not form a triangle?

_____

_____

_____

**Math On the Spot**

my.hrw.com

# Using Triangle Side Length Relationships

You saw in the Explore Activity that you cannot always form a triangle from three given line segments.

### Triangle Inequality

The sum of the lengths of any two sides of a triangle is greater than the length of the third side.

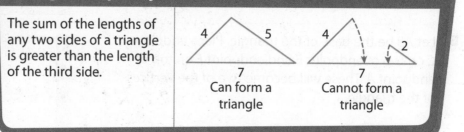

Can form a triangle

Cannot form a triangle

You can use this relationship to determine if given side lengths can form a triangle.

**Animated Math**

my.hrw.com

## EXAMPLE 1

**TEKS** 6.8.A

**Tell whether a triangle can have sides with the given lengths.**

**A** 11 cm, 6 cm, 13 cm

**STEP 1** Find the sum of the lengths of each pair of sides.

$$11 + 6 \overset{?}{>} 13 \quad 6 + 13 \overset{?}{>} 11 \quad 11 + 13 \overset{?}{>} 6$$

**STEP 2** Compare the sum to the third side.

$$17 > 13 \checkmark \quad 19 > 11 \checkmark \quad 24 > 6 \checkmark$$

The sum of any two of the given lengths is greater than the third length.

So, a triangle **can** have these side lengths.

**B** 5 ft, 15 ft, 9 ft

**STEP 1** Find the sum of the lengths of each pair of sides.

$5 + 15 \overset{?}{>} 9$    $15 + 9 \overset{?}{>} 5$    $5 + 9 \overset{?}{>} 15$

**STEP 2** Compare the sum to the third side.

$20 > 9$ ✓    $24 > 5$ ✓    $14 \not> 15$

The sum of any two of the given lengths is **not** greater than the third length.

So, a triangle **cannot** have these side lengths.

**Math Talk**
Mathematical Processes

Explain why a triangle with sides measuring 5 in., 5 in., and 1 foot cannot be constructed.

**YOUR TURN**

Tell whether a triangle can have sides with the given lengths. Explain.

**2.** 3 cm, 6 cm, 9 cm

**3.** 4 m, 5 m, 8 m

_____    _____

_____    _____

_____    _____

**Personal Math Trainer**

Online Assessment and Intervention

⊕ my.hrw.com

# Using Inequalities to Represent the Relationship Between Triangle Side Lengths

You can use what you know about the relationship among the lengths of the sides of a triangle to write an inequality. Then you can use the inequality to determine if a given value can be the length of an unknown side.

**Math On the Spot**

⊕ my.hrw.com

**EXAMPLE 2**    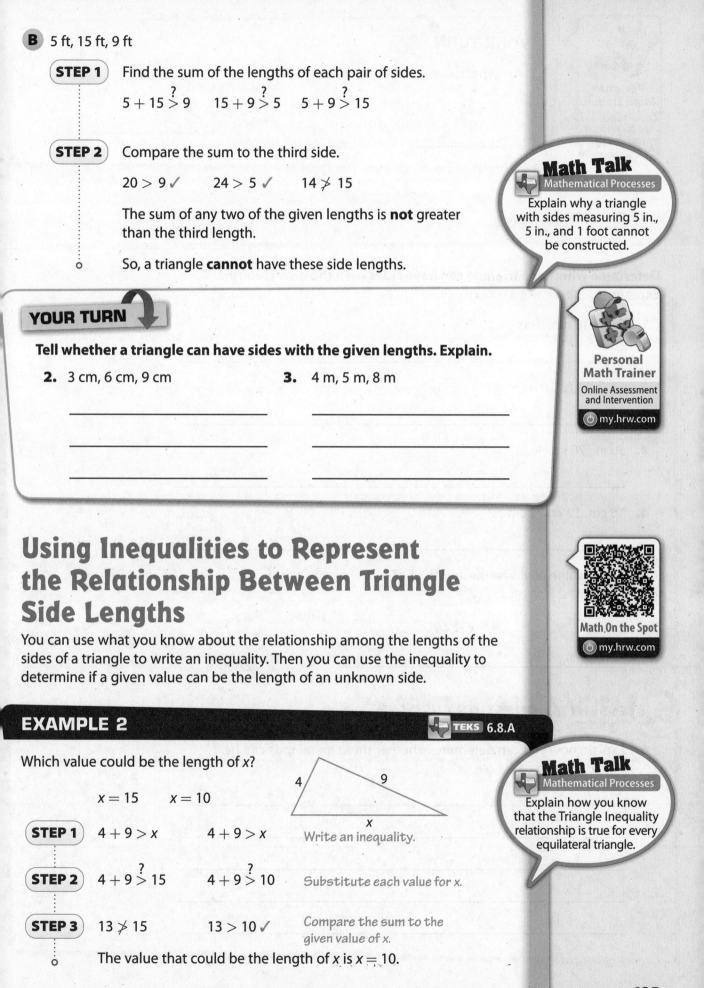TEKS 6.8.A

Which value could be the length of $x$?

$x = 15$    $x = 10$

**STEP 1** $4 + 9 > x$    $4 + 9 > x$    Write an inequality.

**STEP 2** $4 + 9 \overset{?}{>} 15$    $4 + 9 \overset{?}{>} 10$    Substitute each value for x.

**STEP 3** $13 \not> 15$    $13 > 10$ ✓    Compare the sum to the given value of x.

The value that could be the length of $x$ is $x = 10$.

**Math Talk**
Mathematical Processes

Explain how you know that the Triangle Inequality relationship is true for every equilateral triangle.

4. Which value could be the length of x?

   x = 35               x = 13

   _____

20    13

x

## Guided Practice

**Determine whether a triangle can have sides with the given lengths. Explain.** (Explore Activity and Example 1)

1. 3 cm, 10 cm, 8 cm

   _____

2. 10 ft, 10 ft, 18 ft

   _____

3. 30 in., 20 in., 40 in.

   _____

4. 16 cm, 12 cm, 3 cm

   _____

5. Which value could be the length of x?
   (Example 2)

   x = 29               x = 45

   _____

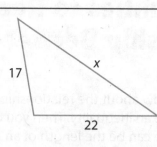

17    x

22

### ? ESSENTIAL QUESTION CHECK-IN

6. Explain how you can determine whether three metal rods can be joined to form a triangle.

   _____

   _____

   _____

   _____

# 15.1 Independent Practice

**TEKS** 6.8.A

Personal
Math Trainer

Online
Assessment and
Intervention

my.hrw.com

**7.** A map of a new dog park shows that it is triangular and that the sides measure 18.5 m, 36.9 m, and 16.9 m. Are the dimensions correct? Explain your reasoning.

_____

_____

_____

_____

_____

**8.** Choose a real world object that you can cut into three different lengths to form a triangle. Find three side lengths that form a triangle and three lengths that do not form a triangle. For each triangle, give the side lengths and explain why those lengths do or do not form a triangle.

Triangle 1: _____

_____

_____

_____

Triangle 2: _____

_____

_____

_____

**9.** Could the three sides of a triangular shopping mall measure $\frac{1}{2}$ mi, $\frac{1}{3}$ mi, and $\frac{1}{4}$ mi? Show how you found your answer.

_____

_____

_____

_____

**10. Geography** The map shows the distance in air miles from Houston to both Austin and San Antonio.

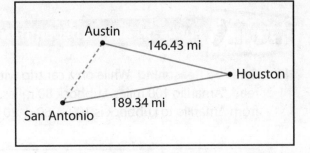

**a.** What is the greatest possible distance from Austin to San Antonio?

_____

**b.** How did you find the answer?

_____

_____

_____

_____

**c.** What is the least possible distance from Austin to San Antonio?

_____

**d.** How did you find the answer?

_____

_____

_____

_____

_____

_____

_____

_____

_____

**11. Critical Thinking** Two sides of an isosceles triangle measure 3 inches and 13 inches respectively. Find the length of the third side. Explain your reasoning.

_____

_____

_____

_____

**H.O.T.** FOCUS ON HIGHER ORDER THINKING

Work Area

**12. Critique Reasoning** While on a car trip with her family, Erin saw a sign that read, "Amarillo 100 miles, Lubbock 80 miles." She concluded that the distance from Amarillo to Lubbock is $100 - 80 = 20$ miles. Was she right? Explain.

_____

_____

_____

_____

_____

**13. Make a Conjecture** Is there a value of $n$ for which there could be a triangle with sides of length $n$, $2n$, and $3n$? Explain.

_____

_____

_____

**14. Persevere in Problem Solving** A metalworker cut an 8-foot length of pipe into three pieces and welded them to form a triangle. Each of the 3 sections measured a whole number of feet in length. How long was each section? Explain your reasoning.

_____

_____

_____

_____

_____

# LESSON
# 15.2

# Sum of Angle Measures in a Triangle

**TEKS**
Expressions, equations, and relationships—6.8.A
Extend previous knowledge of triangles and their properties to include the sum of angles in a triangle . . .

**? ESSENTIAL QUESTION**

How do you use the sum of angles in a triangle to find an unknown angle measure?

---

**EXPLORE ACTIVITY** **TEKS** 6.8.A

## Exploring Angles in a Triangle

Recall that a triangle is a closed figure with three line segments and three angles. The measures of the angles of a triangle have a special relationship with one another.

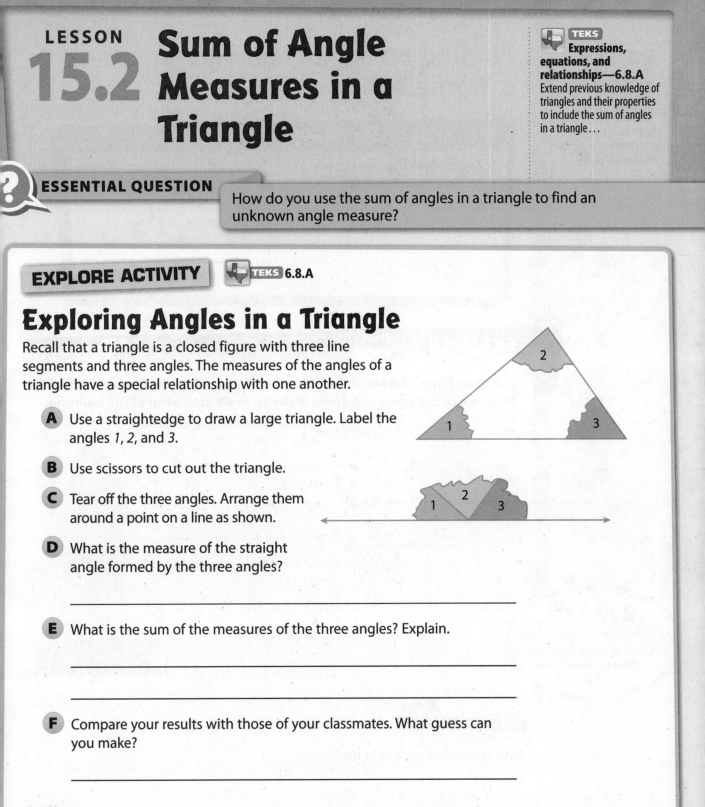

**A** Use a straightedge to draw a large triangle. Label the angles *1*, *2*, and *3*.

**B** Use scissors to cut out the triangle.

**C** Tear off the three angles. Arrange them around a point on a line as shown.

**D** What is the measure of the straight angle formed by the three angles?

_____

**E** What is the sum of the measures of the three angles? Explain.

_____

_____

**F** Compare your results with those of your classmates. What guess can you make?

_____

### Reflect

**1. Justify Reasoning** How can you show that your guess is correct?

_____

_____

_____

# Finding an Angle Measure in a Triangle

## Sum of Angle Measures of a Triangle

The sum of the measures of the angles in a triangle is 180°.

$m\angle 1 + m\angle 2 + m\angle 3 = 180°$

## EXAMPLE 1 · Real World

TEKS 6.8.A

Fountain Place, shown to the right, is a 720-foot Dallas skyscraper. Find the measure of the unknown angle in the triangle at the top of the building.

$m\angle 1 + m\angle 2 + m\angle 3 = 180°$    The sum of the angle measures in a triangle is 180°.

$65° + 65° + x = 180°$    Write an equation.

$130° + x = 180°$    Add.

$\underline{-130° \qquad -130°}$    Subtract 130° from both sides.

$x = 50°$

The angle at the top of the triangle measures 50°.

### Math Talk
**Mathematical Processes**

Can a triangle have two obtuse angles? Why or why not?

## YOUR TURN

Find the unknown angle measures.

2.

$D$   100°   $x$   $E$

55°

$F$

$x =$ _____

3.

$K$

$x$

71°     56°

$J$         $L$

$x =$ _____

**Personal Math Trainer**

Online Assessment and Intervention

⏼ my.hrw.com

# Finding Angles in an Equilateral Triangle

Recall that an *equilateral* triangle has three congruent sides and three congruent angles.

## EXAMPLE 2

TEKS 6.8.A

**Find the angle measures in the equilateral triangle.**

$3x = 180°$      *Write an equation.*

$\dfrac{3x}{3} = \dfrac{180°}{3}$      *Divide both sides by 3.*

$x = 60°$

Each angle in an equilateral triangle measures 60°.

## Reflect

4. **Multiple Representations** Write a different equation to find the angle measures in Example 2. Will the answer be the same? Explain.

_____

_____

5. **Draw Conclusions** Triangle *ABC* is a right triangle. What conclusions can you draw about the measures of the angles of the triangle?

_____

_____

_____

### YOUR TURN

**Write an equation to find the unknown angle measure in each triangle.**

6. The measures of two of the angles are 25° and 65°.

_____

7. The measures of two of the angles are 60°.

_____

8. The measures of two of the angles are 35°.

_____

**Personal Math Trainer**

Online Assessment and Intervention

my.hrw.com

1. The sum of the angle measures in a triangle is _____.
   (Explore Activity)

**Find the unknown angle measure in each triangle.** (Examples 1 and 2)

2. $m\angle R + m\angle S + m\angle T =$ _____

   _____ + _____ + x = _____

   _____ + x = _____

   – _____    – _____

   x = _____

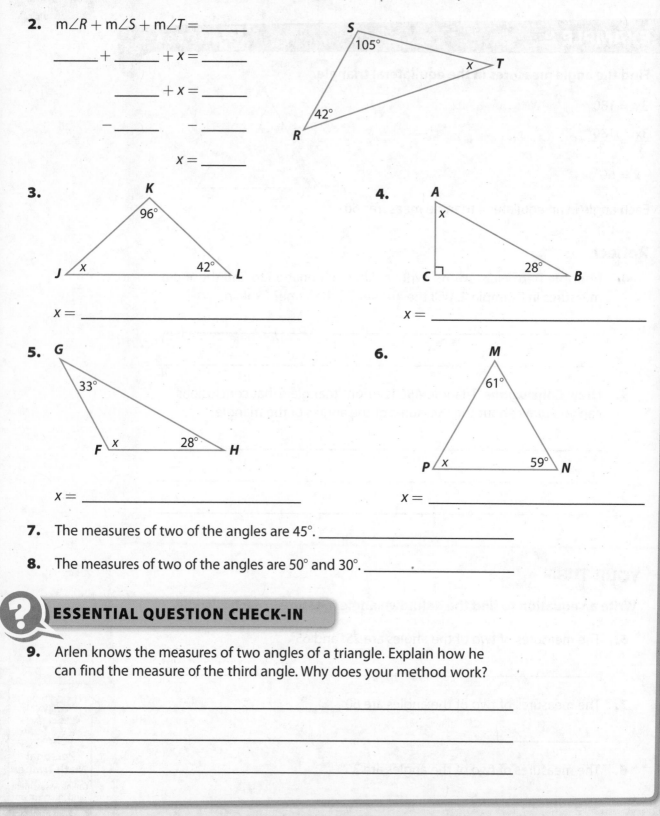

3. x = _____

4. x = _____

5. x = _____

6. x = _____

7. The measures of two of the angles are 45°. _____

8. The measures of two of the angles are 50° and 30°. _____

9. Arlen knows the measures of two angles of a triangle. Explain how he
   can find the measure of the third angle. Why does your method work?

   _____

   _____

   _____

# 15.2 Independent Practice

**Personal Math Trainer**

Online Assessment and Intervention

my.hrw.com

**Figure *ABCD* represents a garden crossed by straight walkway $\overline{AC}$. Use the figure for 10–15.**

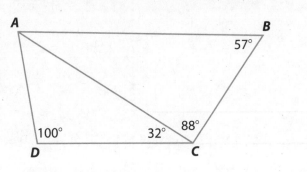

**10.** Find m∠*DAC*.

_____

**11.** Explain how you found m∠*DAC*.

_____

_____

_____

**12.** Find m∠*BAC*.

_____

**13.** Explain how you found m∠*BAC*.

_____

_____

_____

**14.** Find m∠*DAB*.

_____

**15.** Explain how you found m∠*DAB*.

_____

_____

_____

_____

**16.** An observer at point *O* sees airplane *P* directly over airport *A*. The observer measures the angle of the plane at 40.5°.

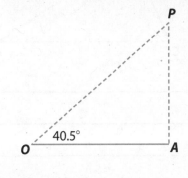

Find m∠*P*. _____

**The map shows the intersection of three streets in San Antonio's River Walk district. Use the map for 17–18.**

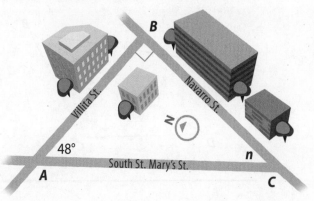

**17.** Find the measures of the three angles of the triangle.

_____

_____

**18.** Explain how you found the angle measures.

_____

_____

_____

**19. Persevere in Problem Solving** Find the measure of ∠ACB. Explain how you found your answer.

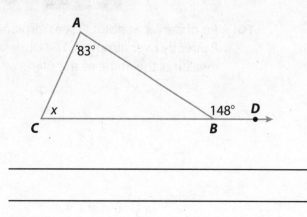

_____

_____

_____

_____

**20. Communicate Mathematical Ideas** Explain how you can use the figure to find the sum of the measures of the angles of quadrilateral *ABCD*. What is the sum?

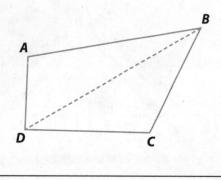

_____

_____

_____

_____

**21. Draw Conclusions** Recall that a right triangle is a triangle with one right angle. One angle of a triangle measures 89.99 degrees. Can the triangle be a right triangle? Explain your reasoning.

_____

_____

_____

_____

# Relationships Between Sides and Angles in a Triangle

**TEKS**
Expressions, equations, and relationships—6.8.A
Extend previous knowledge of triangles and their properties to include...the relationship between the lengths of sides and measures of angles in a triangle...

## ESSENTIAL QUESTION

How can you use the relationships between side lengths and angle measures in a triangle to solve problems?

**EXPLORE ACTIVITY**  **TEKS** 6.8.A

## Exploring the Relationship Between Sides and Angles in a Triangle

There is a special relationship between the lengths of sides and the measures of angles in a triangle.

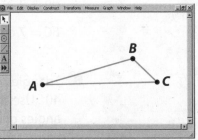

**A** Use geometry software to make triangle *ABC*. Make ∠*A* the smallest angle.

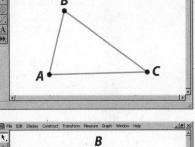

**B** Choose one vertex and drag it so that you lengthen the side of the triangle opposite angle *A*. Describe what happens to ∠*A*.

_____

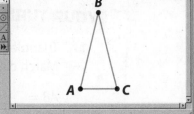

**C** Drag the vertex to shorten the side opposite ∠*B*. What happens to ∠*B*?

_____

**D** Make several new triangles. In each case, note the locations of the longest and shortest sides in relation to the largest and smallest angles. Describe your results.

_____

_____

_____

**My Notes**

# Using the Relationship Between Sides and Angles in a Triangle

You have seen that in a triangle the largest angle is opposite the longest side and the smallest angle is opposite the shortest side. It follows that the midsize angle is opposite the midsize side.

## EXAMPLE 1

TEKS 6.8.A

**A** Triangle *ABC* has side lengths of 7 cm, 9 cm, and 4.5 cm. Use the relationship between the sides and angles of a triangle to match each side with its correct length.

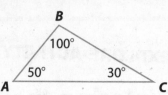

$AC = 9$ cm    The longest side is opposite the largest angle.

$AB = 4.5$ cm    The shortest side is opposite the smallest angle.

$BC = 7$ cm    The midsize side is opposite the midsize angle.

**B** Triangle *ABC* has angles measuring 60°, 80°, and 40°. Use the relationship between the sides and angles of a triangle to match each angle with its correct measure.

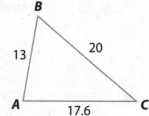

$m\angle A = 80°$    The largest angle is opposite the longest side.

$m\angle C = 40°$    The smallest angle is opposite the shortest side.

$m\angle B = 60°$    The midsize angle is opposite the midsize side.

### YOUR TURN

**1.** Triangle *ABC* has side lengths of 11, 16, and 19. Match each side with its correct length.

$AB = $ _____ $AC = $ _____ $BC = $ _____

**2.** Triangle *ABC* has angle measures of 45°, 58°, and 77°. Match each angle with its correct measure.

$m\angle A = $ _____ $m\angle B = $ _____ $m\angle C = $ _____

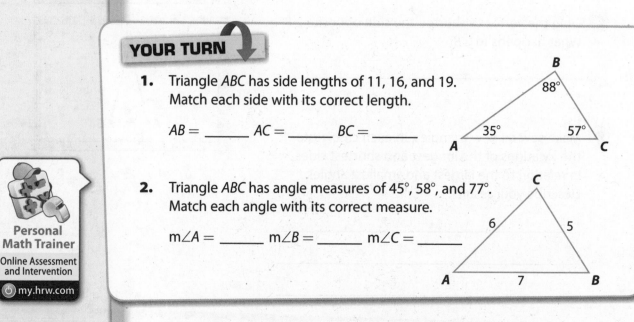

# Solving Problems Using Triangle Relationships

Math On the Spot
my.hrw.com

Recall that triangles can be classified by the lengths of their sides. A *scalene* triangle has no congruent sides. An *isosceles* triangle has two congruent sides. An *equilateral* triangle has three congruent sides.

**EXAMPLE 2** Problem Solving                                    TEKS 6.8.A

Brandy is making a quilt. Each block of the quilt is made up of four triangles. Each triangle is in the shape of a right isosceles triangle. Two of the side measures of one triangle are 6.4 inches and 9 inches. Brandy wants to add a ribbon border around one of the triangles. How much ribbon will she need?

### Analyze Information

Rewrite the question as a statement.

- Find the amount of ribbon Brandy will need for a border around one triangle.

**Identify the important information.**

- Each quilt piece has the shape of a right isosceles triangle.
- Two sides of the triangle measure 6.4 inches and 9 inches.

### Formulate a Plan

You can draw a model and label it with the important information to find the total length of ribbon that Brandy needs for one triangle.

### Solve

*Think:* A right triangle will have one 90° angle. Since the sum of the angles is 180°, the other two angles will be congruent and will have a combined measure of 90°.

$90° \div 2 = 45°$

Label the new information on the model.

90° is the greatest angle measure, so the side opposite the 90° angle will be the longest side. The other two angles are congruent, so the sides opposite those angles are congruent.

The shortest side lengths are 6.4 inches and 6.4 inches. So, Brandy will need $6.4 + 6.4 + 9 = 21.8$ inches of ribbon.

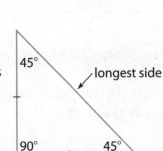

### Justify and Evaluate

The solution is reasonable because the quilt piece is in the shape of an isosceles right triangle and it has two sides measuring 6.4 inches and 9 inches.

**YOUR TURN**

3. A fence around a rock garden is in the shape of a right triangle. Two angles measure 30° and 60°. Two sides measure 10 feet and 17.3 feet. The total length of the fence is 47.3 feet. How long is the side opposite

the right angle? _____

## Guided Practice

1. Triangle ABC has side lengths of 17, 13, and 24. Match each side with its correct length. (Example 1)

   _____ = 24        _____ = 13        _____ = 17

2. The figure represents a traffic island that has angles measuring 60°, 20°, and 100°. Match each angle with its correct measure. (Example 1)

   m∠_____ = 100°   m∠_____ = 20°   m∠_____ = 60°

3. **Vocabulary** Explain how the relationship between the sides and angles of a triangle applies to equilateral triangles. (Example 2)

   _____

4. Ramone is building a fence around a vegetable garden in his backyard. The fence will be in the shape of a right isosceles triangle. Two of the side measures are 12 feet and 16 feet. Use a problem solving model to find the total length of fencing he needs. Explain. (Example 2)

   _____

   _____

   _____

   _____

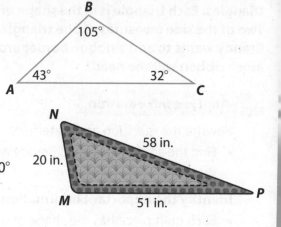

**? ESSENTIAL QUESTION CHECK-IN**

5. Describe the relationship between the lengths of the sides and the measures of the angles in a triangle.

   _____

   _____

   _____

# 15.3 Independent Practice

TEKS 6.8.A

**Use the figure for 6–8.**

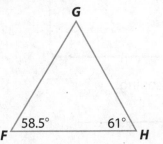

6. **Critique Reasoning** Dustin says that △FGH is an equilateral triangle because the sides appear to be the same length. Is his reasoning valid? Explain.

_____

_____

_____

_____

_____

7. What additional information do you need to know before you can determine which side of the triangle is the longest? How can you find it?

_____

_____

_____

_____

8. Which side of the triangle is the longest? Explain how you found the answer.

_____

_____

_____

_____

_____

_____

**The figure shows the angle measurements formed by two fenced-in animal pens that share a side. Use the figure for 9–10.**

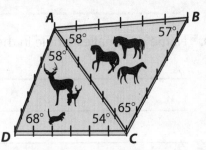

9. Caitlin says that $\overline{AC}$ is the longest segment of fencing because it is opposite 68°, the largest angle measure in the figure. Is her reasoning valid? Explain.

_____

_____

_____

_____

_____

_____

_____

_____

10. What is the longest segment of fencing in △ABC? Explain your reasoning.

_____

_____

11. Find the longest segment of fencing in the figure. Explain your reasoning.

_____

_____

_____

_____

**12.** In triangle $ABC$, $\overline{AB}$ is longer than $\overline{BC}$ and $\overline{BC}$ is longer than $\overline{AC}$.

   **a.** Draw a sketch of triangle $ABC$.

   **b.** Name the smallest angle in the triangle. Explain your reasoning.

_____

_____

_____

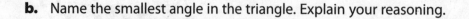

**H.O.T.**    **FOCUS ON HIGHER ORDER THINKING**

                                                              **Work Area**

**13.** **Persevere in Problem Solving**
Determine the shortest line segment in the
figure. Explain how you found the answer.

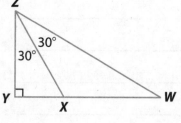

_____

_____

_____

_____

_____

_____

**14.** **Communicate Mathematical Ideas** Explain how the relationship
between the sides and angles of a triangle applies to isosceles triangles.

_____

_____

_____

**15.** **Critical Thinking** Can a scalene triangle contain a pair of congruent
angles? Explain.

_____

_____

_____

# Ready to Go On?

## 15.1 Determining When Three Lengths Form a Triangle

**Determine whether the three side lengths form a triangle.**

**1.** 3, 5, 7 _____

**2.** 9, 15, 4 _____

**3.** 17, 5, 23 _____

**4.** 28, 16, 38 _____

## 15.2 Sum of Angle Measures in a Triangle

**Find the unknown angle measures.**

**5.** _____

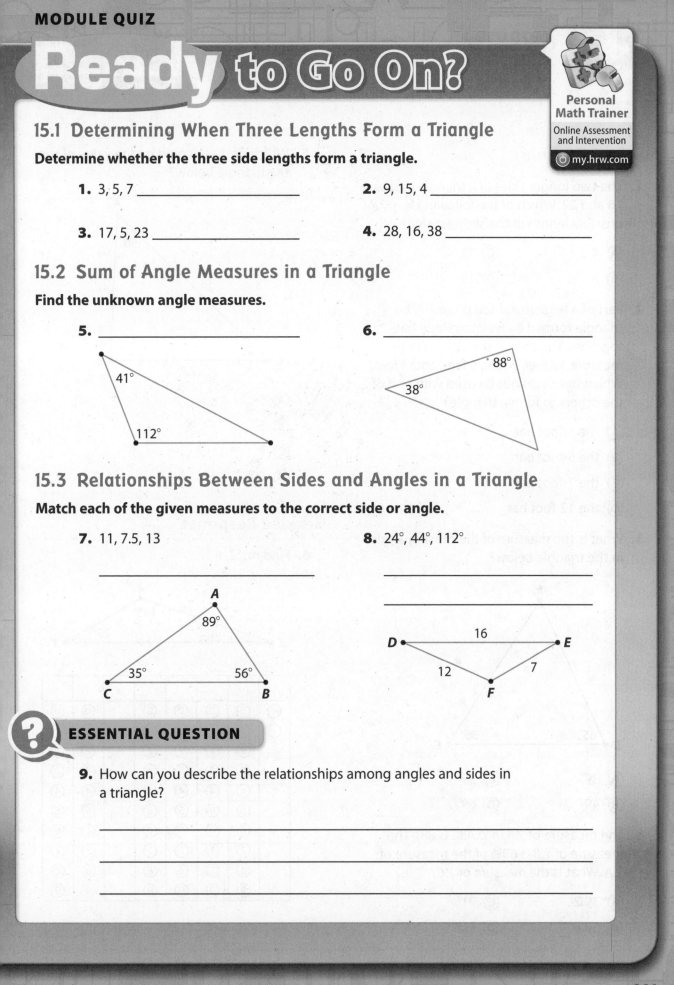

**6.** _____

## 15.3 Relationships Between Sides and Angles in a Triangle

**Match each of the given measures to the correct side or angle.**

**7.** 11, 7.5, 13

_____

**8.** 24°, 44°, 112°

_____

_____

**ESSENTIAL QUESTION**

**9.** How can you describe the relationships among angles and sides in a triangle?

_____

_____

_____

## Selected Response

**1.** The two longer sides of a triangle measure 16 and 22. Which of the following is a possible length of the shortest side?

Ⓐ 4          Ⓒ 11

Ⓑ 6          Ⓓ 19

**2.** Part of a large metal sculpture will be a triangle formed by welding three bars together. The artist has four bars that measure 12 feet, 7 feet, 5 feet, and 3 feet. Which bar could not be used with two of the others to form a triangle?

Ⓐ the 3-foot bar

Ⓑ the 5-foot bar

Ⓒ the 7-foot bar

Ⓓ the 12-foot bar

**3.** What is the measure of the missing angle in the triangle below?

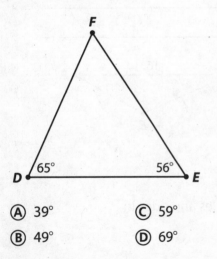

Ⓐ 39°          Ⓒ 59°

Ⓑ 49°          Ⓓ 69°

**4.** The measure of ∠A in △ABC is 88°. The measure of ∠B is 60% of the measure of ∠A. What is the measure of ∠C?

Ⓐ 39.2°          Ⓒ 91°

Ⓑ 52.8°          Ⓓ 127.2°

**5.** Which of these could be the value of x in the triangle below?

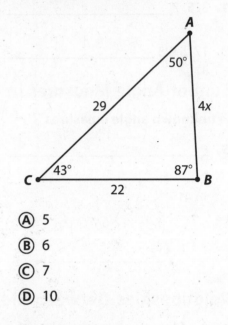

Ⓐ 5

Ⓑ 6

Ⓒ 7

Ⓓ 10

## Gridded Response

**6.** Find m∠Z.

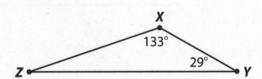

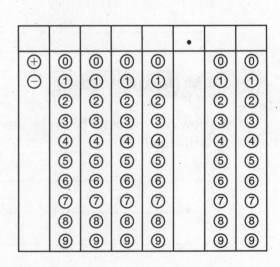

# Area and Volume Equations

**? ESSENTIAL QUESTION**

How can you use area and volume equations to solve real-world problems?

**Real-World Video**

Quilting, painting, and other art forms use familiar geometric shapes, such as triangles and rectangles. To buy enough supplies for a project, you need to find or estimate the areas of each shape in the project.

⏻ my.hrw.com

**GO DIGITAL**
my.hrw.com

**my.hrw.com**
Go digital with your write-in student edition, accessible on any device.

**Math On the Spot**
Scan with your smart phone to jump directly to the online edition, video tutor, and more.

**Animated Math**
Interactively explore key concepts to see how math works.

**Personal Math Trainer**
Get immediate feedback and help as you work through practice sets.

# Are YOU Ready?

Complete these exercises to review skills you will need for this chapter.

## Use of Parentheses

**EXAMPLE** $\frac{1}{2}(14)(12 + 18) = \frac{1}{2}(14)(30)$  Perform operations inside parentheses first.

$= 7(30)$  Multiply left to right.

$= 210$  Multiply again.

**Evaluate.**

1. $\frac{1}{2}(3)(5 + 7)$  **2.** $\frac{1}{2}(15)(13 + 17)$  **3.** $\frac{1}{2}(10)(9.4 + 3.6)$  **4.** $\frac{1}{2}(2.1)(3.5 + 5.7)$

_____    _____    _____    _____

## Area of Square, Rectangles, Triangle

**EXAMPLE** Find the area of the rectangle.

8 ft

3 ft

$A = bh$  Use the formula for area of a rectangle.

$= 8 \cdot 3$  Substitute for base and height.

$= 24$  Multiply.

Area equals 24 square feet.

**Find the area of each figure.**

5. a triangle with base 6 in. and height 3 in. _____

6. a square with sides of 7.6 m _____

7. a rectangle with length $3\frac{1}{4}$ ft and width $2\frac{1}{2}$ ft _____

8. a triangle with base 8.2 cm and height 5.1 cm _____

# Reading Start-Up

## Visualize Vocabulary

Use the ✔ words to complete the graphic. You will put one word in each oval.

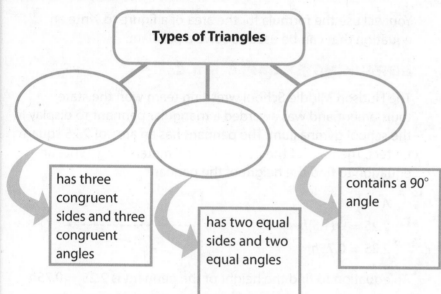

**Types of Triangles**

has three congruent sides and three congruent angles

has two equal sides and two equal angles

contains a 90° angle

## Understand Vocabulary

Match the term on the left to the correct expression on the right.

**1.** parallelogram

    **A.** A quadrilateral in which all sides are congruent and opposite sides are parallel.

**2.** trapezoid

    **B.** A quadrilateral in which opposite sides are parallel and congruent.

**3.** rhombus

    **C.** A quadrilateral in which two sides are parallel.

## Active Reading

**Booklet** Before beginning the module, create a booklet to help you learn the concepts in this module. Write the main idea of each lesson on each page of the booklet. As you study each lesson, write important details that support the main idea, such as vocabulary and formulas. Refer to your finished booklet as you work on assignments and study for tests.

# Unpacking the TEKS

Understanding the TEKS and the vocabulary terms in the TEKS will help you know exactly what you are expected to learn in this module.

---

**TEKS 6.8.C**

Write equations that represent problems related to the area of rectangles, parallelograms, trapezoids, and triangles and volume of right rectangular prisms where dimensions are positive rational numbers.

## What It Means to You

You will use the formula for the area of a figure to write an equation that can be used to solve a problem.

**UNPACKING EXAMPLE 6.8.C**

The Hudson Middle School wrestling team won the state tournament and was awarded a triangular pennant to display in the school gymnasium. The pennant has an area of 2.25 square meters. The base of the pennant is 1.5 meters long. Write an equation to find the height of the pennant.

$$A = \frac{1}{2}bh$$
$$2.25 = \frac{1}{2}(1.5)h$$
$$2.25 = 0.75h$$

1.5 m

An equation to find the height of the pennant is $2.25 = 0.75h$.

---

**TEKS 6.8.D**

Determine solutions for problems involving the area of rectangles, parallelograms, trapezoids, and triangles and volume of right rectangular prisms where dimensions are positive rational numbers.

## What It Means to You

You will use the formula for the volume of a rectangular prism.

**UNPACKING EXAMPLE 6.8.D**

Jala has an aquarium in the shape of a rectangular prism with a volume of 2,160 cubic inches. The length is 15 inches and the width is 12 inches. Find the height of the aquarium.

$$v = l \cdot w \cdot h$$
$$2,160 = 15 \cdot 12 \cdot h$$
$$2,160 = 180 \cdot h$$
$$\frac{2,160}{180} = h$$
$$12 = h$$

The height of the aquarium is 12 inches.

Visit **my.hrw.com** to see all the **TEKS** unpacked.

my.hrw.com

# Area of Quadrilaterals

TEKS
Expressions, equations, and relationships—
6.8.B Model area formulas for parallelograms, trapezoids ... by decomposing and rearranging parts of these shapes. Also 6.8.D

**ESSENTIAL QUESTION**

How can you find the areas of parallelograms, rhombuses, and trapezoids?

**EXPLORE ACTIVITY** TEKS 6.8.B

## Area of a Parallelogram

Recall that a rectangle is a special type of parallelogram.

**A** Draw a large parallelogram on grid paper. Cut out your parallelogram.

**B** Cut your parallelogram on the dashed line as shown. Then move the triangular piece to the other side of the parallelogram.

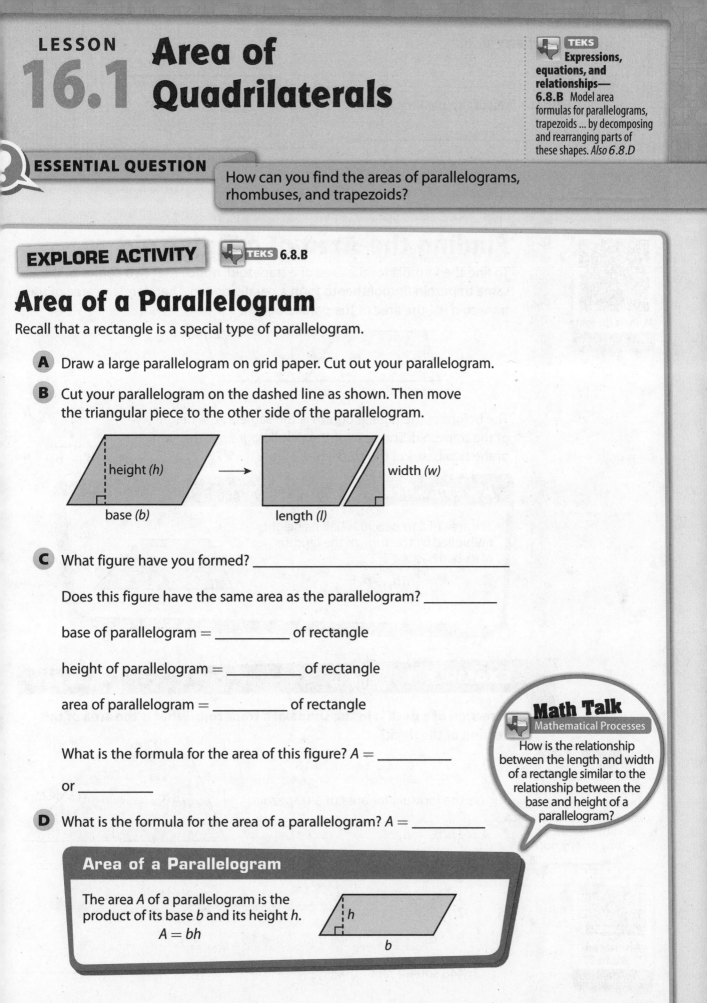

height (h)

base (b)

width (w)

length (l)

**C** What figure have you formed? _____

Does this figure have the same area as the parallelogram? _____

base of parallelogram = _____ of rectangle

height of parallelogram = _____ of rectangle

area of parallelogram = _____ of rectangle

What is the formula for the area of this figure? $A =$ _____

or _____

**D** What is the formula for the area of a parallelogram? $A =$ _____

**Math Talk**
Mathematical Processes

How is the relationship between the length and width of a rectangle similar to the relationship between the base and height of a parallelogram?

### Area of a Parallelogram

The area $A$ of a parallelogram is the product of its base $b$ and its height $h$.

$$A = bh$$

h

b

## Reflect

**1.** Find the area of the parallelogram.

$A = $ _____

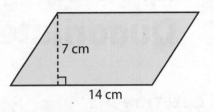

7 cm

14 cm

# Finding the Area of a Trapezoid

To find the formula for the area of a trapezoid, notice that two copies of the same trapezoid fit together to form a parallelogram. Therefore, the area of the trapezoid is $\frac{1}{2}$ the area of the parallelogram.

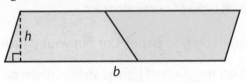

$h$

$b$

The height of the parallelogram is the same as the height of the trapezoid. The base of the parallelogram is the sum of the two bases of the trapezoid.

$A = b \cdot h$

$A = (b_1 + b_2) \cdot h$

## Area of a Trapezoid

The area of a trapezoid is half its height multiplied by the sum of the lengths of its two bases.

$$A = \frac{1}{2}h(b_1 + b_2)$$

$b_1$

$h$

$b_2$

## EXAMPLE 1

Real World

TEKS 6.8.D

**A section of a deck is in the shape of a trapezoid. What is the area of this section of the deck?**

$b_1 = 17 \qquad b_2 = 39 \qquad h = 16$

Use the formula for area of a trapezoid.

$A = \frac{1}{2}h(b_1 + b_2)$

$= \frac{1}{2} \cdot 16(17 + 39)$    Substitute.

$= \frac{1}{2} \cdot 16(56)$    Add inside the parentheses.

$= 8 \cdot 56$    Multiply $\frac{1}{2}$ and 16.

$= 448$ square feet    Multiply.

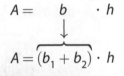

17 ft

16 ft

39 ft

**YOUR TURN**

**2.** Another section of the deck is also shaped like a trapezoid. For this section, the length of one base is 27 feet, and the length of the other base is 34 feet. The height is 12 feet. What is the area of this section of the deck? $A =$ _____ $\text{ft}^2$

# Finding the Area of a Rhombus

A **rhombus** is a quadrilateral in which all sides are congruent and opposite sides are parallel. A rhombus can be divided into four triangles that can then be rearranged into a rectangle.

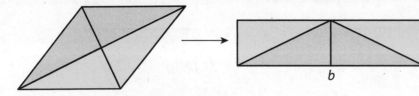

The base of the rectangle is the same length as one of the diagonals of the rhombus. The height of the rectangle is $\frac{1}{2}$ the length of the other diagonal.

$$A = b \cdot h$$
$$\downarrow \qquad \downarrow$$
$$A = d_1 \cdot \tfrac{1}{2}d_2$$

## Area of a Rhombus

The area of a rhombus is half of the product of its two diagonals.

$$A = \tfrac{1}{2}d_1 d_2$$

$d_2$ $\qquad$ $d_1$

**EXAMPLE 2** *Real World*

**TEKS** 6.8.B

Cedric is constructing a kite in the shape of a rhombus. The spars of the kite measure 15 inches and 24 inches. How much fabric will Cedric need for the kite?

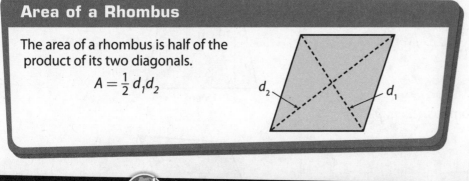

To determine the amount of fabric needed, find the area of the kite.

$d_1 = 15 \qquad\qquad d_2 = 24$

Use the formula for area of a rhombus.

$$A = \tfrac{1}{2}d_1 d_2$$

$$= \tfrac{1}{2}(15)(24) \qquad\qquad \text{Substitute.}$$

$$= 180 \text{ square inches} \qquad \text{Multiply.}$$

—15 in.

24 in.

## YOUR TURN

**Find the area of each rhombus.**

**3.** $d_1 = 35$ m; $d_2 = 12$ m

$A =$ _____ m²

**4.** $d_1 = 9.5$ in.; $d_2 = 14$ in.

$A =$ _____ in²

**5.** $d_1 = 10$ m; $d_2 = 18$ m

$A =$ _____ m²

**6.** $d_1 = 8\frac{1}{4}$ ft; $d_2 = 40$ ft

$A =$ _____ ft²

## Guided Practice

**1.** Find the area of the parallelogram. (Explore Activity)

$A = bh$

$= ($ _____ $)($ _____ $)$

$=$ _____ in.²

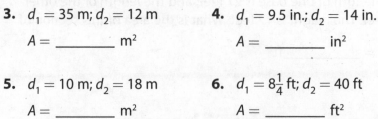

9 in.

13 in.

**2.** Find the area of the trapezoid. (Example 1)

$A = \frac{1}{2}h(b_1 + b_2)$

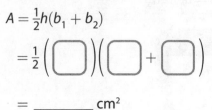

$=$ _____ cm²

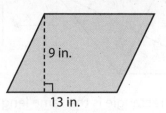

9 cm

14 cm

15 cm

**3.** Find the area of the rhombus. (Example 2)

$A = \frac{1}{2}d_1d_2$

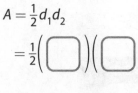

$=$ _____ in.²

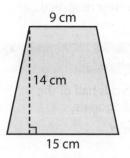

18 in.

11 in.

## ? ESSENTIAL QUESTION CHECK-IN

**4.** How can you find the areas of parallelograms, rhombuses, and trapezoids?

_____

_____

_____

_____

# 16.1 Independent Practice

**TEKS** 6.8.B, 6.8.D

**5.** Rearrange the parts of the parallelogram to form a rectangle. Find the area of the parallelogram and the area of the rectangle. What is the relationship between the areas?

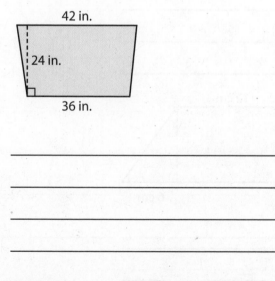

6 cm

14 cm

_____

_____

_____

**6.** What is the area of a parallelogram that has a base of $12\frac{3}{4}$ in. and a height of $2\frac{1}{2}$ in.?

_____

**7.** Draw a copy of the trapezoid to form a parallelogram. Find the area of the trapezoid and the area of the parallelogram. What is the relationship between the areas?

42 in.

24 in.

36 in.

_____

_____

_____

_____

**8.** The bases of a trapezoid are 11 meters and 14 meters. Its height is 10 meters. What is the area of the trapezoid?

_____

**9.** The seat of a bench is in the shape of a trapezoid with bases of 6 feet and 5 feet and a height of 1.5 feet. What is the area of the seat?

_____

**10.** A kite in the shape of a rhombus has diagonals that are 25 inches long and 15 inches long. What is the area of the kite?

_____

**11.** A window in the shape of a parallelogram has a base of 36 inches and a height of 45 inches. What is the area of the window?

_____

**12.** **Communicate Mathematical Ideas** Find the area of the figure. Explain how you found your answer.

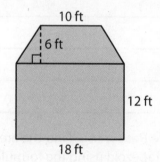

10 ft

6 ft

12 ft

18 ft

_____

_____

_____

_____

_____

_____

**13. Multistep** A parking space shaped like a parallelogram has a base of 17 feet and a height is 9 feet. A car parked in the space is 16 feet long and 6 feet wide. How much of the parking space is not covered by the car?

_____

Work Area

**14. Critique Reasoning** Simon says that to find the area of a trapezoid, you can multiply the height by the top base and the height by the bottom base. Then add the two products together and divide the sum by 2. Is Simon correct? Explain your answer.

_____

_____

_____

_____

**15. Multistep** The height of a trapezoid is 8 in. and its area is 96 in². One base of the trapezoid is 6 inches longer than the other base. What are the lengths of the bases? Explain how you found your answer.

_____

_____

_____

_____

_____

_____

**16. Critique Reasoning** Find the area of the trapezoid using the formula $A = \frac{1}{2}h(b_1 + b_2)$. Decompose the trapezoid into a rectangle and a triangle and find the area of each. Then find the sum of the two areas. Compare this sum with the area of the trapezoid.

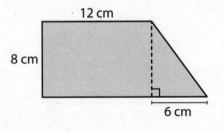

12 cm

8 cm

6 cm

_____

_____

_____

_____

# 16.2 Area of Triangles

**TEKS** Expressions, equations, and relationships— **6.8.B** Model area formulas for ... triangles by decomposing and rearranging parts of these shapes. *Also* 6.8.D

**? ESSENTIAL QUESTION**

How do you find the area of a triangle?

---

**EXPLORE ACTIVITY 1**   **TEKS** 6.8.B

## Area of a Right Triangle

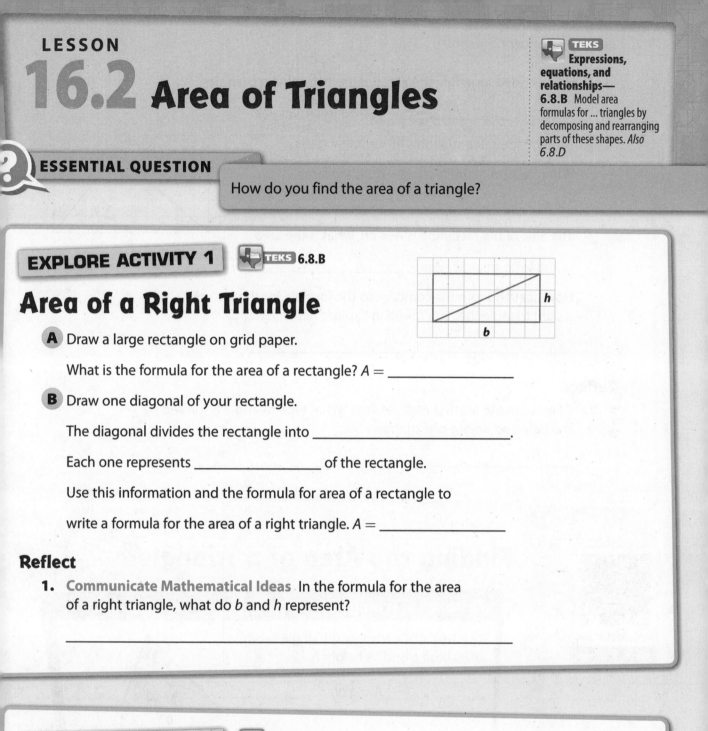

**A** Draw a large rectangle on grid paper.

What is the formula for the area of a rectangle? $A = $ _____

**B** Draw one diagonal of your rectangle.

The diagonal divides the rectangle into _____.

Each one represents _____ of the rectangle.

Use this information and the formula for area of a rectangle to

write a formula for the area of a right triangle. $A = $ _____

### Reflect

1. **Communicate Mathematical Ideas** In the formula for the area of a right triangle, what do $b$ and $h$ represent?

_____

---

**EXPLORE ACTIVITY 2**   **TEKS** 6.8.B

## Area of a Triangle

**A** Draw a large triangle on grid paper. Do not draw a right triangle.

**B** Cut out your triangle. Then trace around it to make a copy of your triangle. Cut out the copy.

**C** Cut one of your triangles into two pieces by cutting through one angle directly across to the opposite side. Now you have three triangles — one large triangle and two smaller triangles.

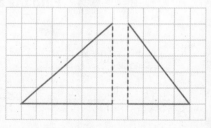

When added together, the areas of the two smaller triangles

equal the _____ of the large triangle.

**D** Arrange the three triangles into a rectangle.

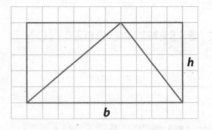

What fraction of the rectangle does the large

triangle represent? _____

The area of the rectangle is $A = bh$. What is the area

of the large triangle? $A =$ _____

How does this formula compare to the formula for the area of
a right triangle that you found in Explore Activity 1?

_____

### Reflect

2. **Communicate Mathematical Ideas** What type of angle is formed by
   the base and height of a triangle?

   _____

Math On the Spot

my.hrw.com

# Finding the Area of a Triangle

### Area of a Triangle

The area $A$ of a triangle is half the product
of its base $b$ and its height $h$.

$$A = \frac{1}{2}bh$$

## EXAMPLE 1

TEKS 6.8.D

**Find the area of each triangle.**

**A**

8 m

20 m

$b = 20$ meters    $h = 8$ meters

$A = \frac{1}{2}bh$

$= \frac{1}{2}(20 \text{ meters})(8 \text{ meters})$    Substitute.

$= 80$ square meters    Multiply.

**Find the area of each triangle.**

**B**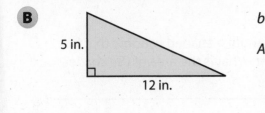

$b = 12$ inches   $h = 5$ inches

$A = \frac{1}{2}bh$

$\quad = \frac{1}{2}(12 \text{ inches})(5 \text{ inches})$   Substitute.

$\quad = 30$ square inches   Multiply.

---

**YOUR TURN**

**Find the area of the triangle.**

**3.**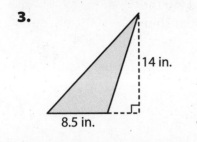

14 in.

8.5 in.   $A = \underline{\hspace{3cm}}$

**Personal Math Trainer**

Online Assessment and Intervention

my.hrw.com

**Math Talk**
Mathematical Processes

Why can you also write the formula for the area of a triangle as $A = \frac{bh}{2}$?

# Problem Solving Using Area of Triangles

You can use the formula for the area of a triangle to solve real-world problems.

**Math On the Spot**

my.hrw.com

**EXAMPLE 2** Real World

TEKS 6.8.D

Each triangular face of the Pyramid of Peace in Kazakhstan is made up of 25 smaller equilateral triangles. These triangles have measurements as shown in the diagram. What is the area of one of the smaller equilateral triangles?

10.4 m

12 m

**STEP 1** Identify the length of the base and the height of the triangle.

$b = 12$ m and $h = 10.4$ m

**STEP 2** Use the formula to find the area of the triangle.

$A = \frac{1}{2}bh$   Substitute.

$\quad = \frac{1}{2}(12)(10.4)$   Multiply.

$\quad = 62.4$

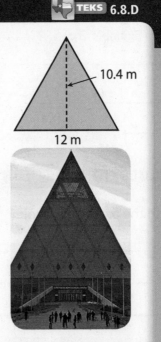

The area of one small equilateral triangle is 62.4 m².

**YOUR TURN**

4. Amy needs to order a shade for a triangular-shaped window that has a base of 6 feet and a height of 4 feet. What is the area of the shade?

_____

## Guided Practice

1. Show how you can use a copy of the triangle to form a rectangle. Find the area of the triangle and the area of the rectangle. What is the relationship between the areas? (Explore Activities 1 and 2, Example 1)

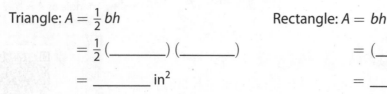

8 in.

14 in.

Triangle: $A = \frac{1}{2} bh$          Rectangle: $A = bh$

$= \frac{1}{2}$ (_____) (_____)          $=$ (_____) (_____)

$=$ _____ in²          $=$ _____ in²

_____

2. A pennant in the shape of a triangle has a base of 12 inches and a height of 30 inches. What is the area of the pennant? (Example 2)

$A = \frac{1}{2} bh$

$= \frac{1}{2}$ (_____) (_____)

$=$ _____ in²

**GO COYOTES!**

**? ESSENTIAL QUESTION CHECK-IN**

3. How do you find the area of a triangle?

_____

_____

_____

# 16.2 Independent Practice

TEKS 6.8.B, 6.8.D

**Find the area of each triangle.**

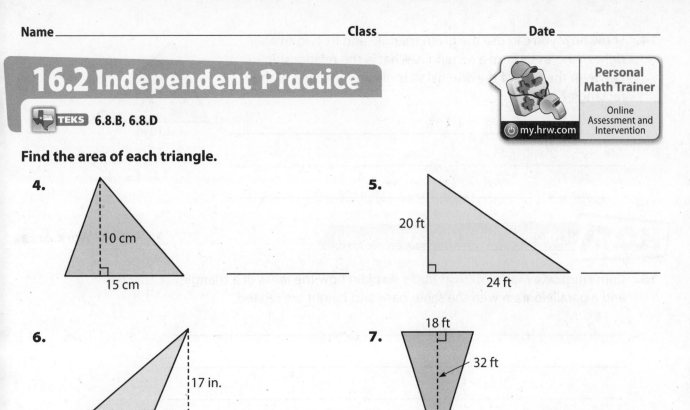

**4.**

10 cm

15 cm

_____

**5.**

20 ft

24 ft

_____

**6.**

17 in.

12 in.

_____

**7.**

18 ft

32 ft

_____

**8.** What is the area of a triangle that has a base of $15\frac{1}{4}$ in. and a height of 18 in.?

_____

**9.** A right triangle has legs that are 11 in. and 13 in. long. What is the area of the triangle?

_____

**10.** A triangular plot of land has the dimensions shown in the diagram. What is the area of the land?

_____

20 km

30 km

**11.** The front part of a tent has the dimensions shown in the diagram. What is the area of this part of the tent?

_____

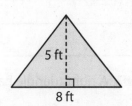

5 ft

8 ft

**12.** **Multistep** The sixth-grade art students are making a mosaic using tiles in the shape of right triangles. Each tile has leg measures of 3 centimeters and 5 centimeters. If there are 200 tiles in the mosaic, what is the area of the mosaic?

_____

**13.** **Critique Reasoning** Monica has a triangular piece of fabric. The height of the triangle is 15 inches and the triangle's base is 6 inches. Monica says that the area of the fabric is 90 in.² What error did Monica make? Explain your answer.

_____

_____

**14.** Show how you can use the given triangle and its two smaller right triangles to form a rectangle. What is the relationship between the area of the original triangle and the area of the rectangle?

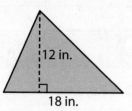
12 in.
18 in.

_____

_____

_____

 **FOCUS ON HIGHER ORDER THINKING**

**15. Communicate Mathematical Ideas** Explain how the areas of a triangle and a parallelogram with the same base and height are related.

_____

_____

_____

_____

_____

**16. Analyze Relationships** A rectangle and a triangle have the same area. If their bases are the same lengths, how do their heights compare? Justify your answer.

_____

_____

_____

_____

_____

_____

**17. What If?** A right triangle has an area of 18 square inches.

**a.** If the triangle is an isosceles triangle, what are the lengths of the legs of the triangle?

_____

**b.** If the triangle is not an isosceles triangle, what are all the possible lengths of the legs, if the lengths are whole numbers?

_____

_____

# Solving Area Equations

**TEKS**
Expressions, equations, and relationships—6.8.C
Write equations that represent problems related to the area of rectangles, parallelograms, trapezoids, and triangles ... where dimensions are positive rational numbers. *Also 6.8.D*

## ESSENTIAL QUESTION

How do you use equations to solve problems about area of rectangles, parallelograms, trapezoids, and triangles?

# Problem Solving Using the Area of a Triangle

Recall that the formula for the area of a triangle is $A = \frac{1}{2}bh$. You can also use the formula to find missing dimensions if you know the area and one dimension.

**Math On the Spot**
my.hrw.com

## EXAMPLE 1 Real World

**TEKS** 6.8.D

The Hudson High School wrestling team just won the state tournament and has been awarded a triangular pennant to hang on the wall in the school gymnasium. The base of the pennant is 1.5 feet long. It has an area of 2.25 square feet. What is the height of the pennant?

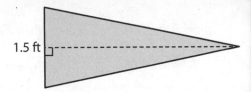

1.5 ft

| | |
|---|---|
| $A = \frac{1}{2}bh$ | Write the formula. |
| $2.25 = \frac{1}{2}(1.5)h$ | Use the formula to write an equation. |
| $2.25 = 0.75h$ | Multiply $\frac{1}{2}$ and 1.5. |
| $\dfrac{2.25}{0.75} = \dfrac{0.75}{0.75}h$ | Divide both sides of the equation by 0.75. |
| $3 = h$ | |

The height of the pennant is 3 feet.

**Math Talk**
Mathematical Processes

How can you use units in the formula to confirm that the units for the height are in feet?

## YOUR TURN

1. Renee is sewing a quilt whose pattern contains right triangles. Each quilt piece has a height of 6 in. and an area of 24 in².

   How long is the base of each quilt piece? _____

**Personal Math Trainer**

Online Assessment and Intervention

my.hrw.com

# Writing Equations Using the Area of a Trapezoid

You can use the formula for area of a trapezoid to write an equation to solve a problem.

## EXAMPLE 2  Real World

TEKS 6.8.C

A garden in the shape of a trapezoid has an area of 44.4 square meters. One base is 4.3 meters and the other base is 10.5 meters long. The height of the trapezoid is the width of the garden. How wide is the garden?

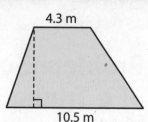

4.3 m

10.5 m

| | |
|---|---|
| $A = \frac{1}{2}h(b_1 + b_2)$ | Write the formula. |
| $44.4 = \frac{1}{2}h(4.3 + 10.5)$ | Use the formula to write an equation. |
| $44.4 = \frac{1}{2}h(14.8)$ | Add inside parentheses. |
| $44.4 = 7.4h$ | Multiply $\frac{1}{2}$ and 14.8. |
| $\frac{44.4}{7.4} = \frac{7.4}{7.4}h$ | Divide both sides of the equation by 7.4. |
| $6 = h$ | |

The garden is 6 meters wide.

**Math Talk**
Mathematical Processes

How can you check that the answer is reasonable?

### Reflect

2. **Communicate Mathematical Ideas** Explain why the first step after substituting is addition.

_____

_____

_____

## YOUR TURN

3. The cross section of a water bin is shaped like a trapezoid. The bases of the trapezoid are 18 feet and 8 feet long. It has an area of 52 square feet. What is the height of the cross section?

_____

# Solving Multistep Problems

You can write equations to solve real-world problems using relationships in geometry.

Math On the Spot

my.hrw.com

**EXAMPLE 3** Problem Solving      TEKS 6.8.D

John and Mary are using rolls of fabric to make a rectangular stage curtain for their class play. The rectangular piece of fabric on each roll measures 2.5 feet by 15 feet. If the area of the curtain is 200 square feet, what is the least number of rolls they need?

### Analyze Information

Rewrite the question as a statement.

- Find the least number of rolls of fabric needed to cover an area of 200 ft$^2$.

**List the important information.**

- Each roll of fabric is a 2.5 foot by 15 foot rectangle.
- The area of the curtain is 200 square feet.

### Formulate a Plan

Write an equation to find the area of each roll of fabric.

Use the area of the curtain and the area of each roll to write an equation to find the least number of rolls.

### Solve

**STEP 1**    Write an equation to find the area of each roll of fabric.

$$A = lw$$
$$A = 15 \cdot 2.5$$
$$A = 37.5 \text{ ft}^2$$

**STEP 2**    Write an equation to find the least number of rolls.

$$n = 200 \div 37.5$$
$$n = 5\frac{1}{3}$$

**STEP 3**    The problem asks for the least number of rolls needed. Since 5 rolls will not be enough, they will need 6 rolls to make the curtain.

John and Mary will need 6 rolls of fabric to make the curtain.

### Justify and Evaluate

The area of each roll is about 38 ft$^2$. Since 38 ft$^2$ · 6 = 228 ft$^2$, the answer is reasonable.

**Personal Math Trainer**

Online Assessment and Intervention

⏻ my.hrw.com

**YOUR TURN**

**4.** A parallelogram-shaped field in a park needs sod. The parallelogram has a base of 21.5 meters and a height of 18 meters. The sod is sold in pallets of 50 square meters. How many pallets of sod are needed to fill the field?

_____

# Guided Practice

**1.** A triangular bandana has an area of 70 square inches. The height of the triangle is $8\frac{3}{4}$ inches. Write and solve an equation to find the length of the base of the triangle. (Example 1)

_____

**2.** The top of a desk is shaped like a trapezoid. The bases of the trapezoid are 26.5 and 30 centimeters long. The area of the desk is 791 square centimeters. The height of the trapezoid is the width of the desk. Write and solve an equation to find the width of the desk. (Example 2)

_____

**3.** Taylor wants to paint his rectangular deck that is 42 feet long and 28 feet wide. A gallon of paint covers about 350 square feet. How many gallons of paint will Taylor need to cover the entire deck? (Example 3)

Write an equation to find the _____ of the deck.

Write and solve the equation.

Write an equation to find the _____.

Write and solve the equation.

Taylor will need _____ gallons of paint.

**?** **ESSENTIAL QUESTION CHECK-IN**

**4.** How do you use equations to solve problems about area of rectangles, parallelograms, trapezoids, and triangles?

_____

# 16.3 Independent Practice

TEKS 6.8.C, 6.8.D

**Personal Math Trainer**

Online Assessment and Intervention

my.hrw.com

**5.** A window shaped like a parallelogram has an area of $18\frac{1}{3}$ square feet. The height of the window is $3\frac{1}{3}$ feet. How long is the base of the window?

_____

**6.** A triangular sail has a base length of 2.5 meters. The area of the sail is 3.75 square meters. How tall is the sail?

_____

**7.** A section in a stained glass window is shaped like a trapezoid. The top base is 4 centimeters and the bottom base is 2.5 centimeters long. If the area of the section of glass is 3.9 square centimeters, how tall is the section?

_____

**8. Multistep** Amelia wants to paint three walls in her family room. Two walls are 26 feet long by 9 feet wide. The other wall is 18 feet long by 9 feet wide.

**a.** What is the total area of the walls that Amelia wants to paint?

_____

**b.** Each gallon of paint covers about 250 square feet. How many gallons of paint should Amelia buy to paint the walls?

_____

**9. Critical Thinking** The area of a triangular block is 64 square inches. If the base of the triangle is twice the height, how long are the base and the height of the triangle?

_____

**10. Multistep** Alex needs to varnish the top and the bottom of a dozen rectangular wooden planks. The planks are 8 feet long and 3 feet wide. Each pint of varnish covers about 125 square feet and costs $3.50.

**a.** What is the total area that Alex needs to varnish?

_____

**b.** How much will it cost Alex to varnish all the wooden planks?

_____

**11. Multistep** Leia cuts congruent triangular patches with an area of 45 square centimeters from a rectangular piece of fabric that is 18 centimeters long and 10 centimeters wide. How many of the patches can Leia cut from 32 pieces of the fabric?

_____

**12. Multistep** A farmer needs to buy fertilizer for two fields. One field is shaped like a trapezoid, and the other is shaped like a triangle. The trapezoidal field has bases that are 35 and 48 yards and a height of 26 yards. The triangular field has the same height and a base of 39 yards. Each bag of fertilizer covers 150 square yards. Use a problem solving model to find how many bags of fertilizer the farmer needs to buy.

_____

**13.** A tennis court for singles play is 78 feet long and 27 feet wide.

**a.** The court for doubles play has the same length but is 9 feet wider than the court for singles play. How much more area is covered by the tennis court used for doubles play? _____

**b.** The junior court for players 8 and under is 36 feet long and 18 feet wide. How much more area is covered by the tennis court used for singles play than by the junior court? _____

**c.** The court for players 10 and under has the same width but is 18 feet shorter than the court for singles play. How much more area is covered by the tennis court used for singles play? _____

**14. Draw Conclusions** The cross section of a metal ingot is a trapezoid. The cross section has an area of 39 square centimeters. The top base of the cross section is 12 centimeters. The length of the bottom base is 2 centimeters greater than the top base. How tall is the metal ingot? Explain.

_____

_____

_____

**H.O.T.**   **FOCUS ON HIGHER ORDER THINKING**

Work Area

**15. Analyze Relationships** A mirror is made of two congruent parallelograms as shown in the diagram. The parallelograms have a combined area of $9\frac{1}{3}$ square yards. The height of each parallelogram is $1\frac{1}{3}$ yards.

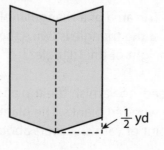
$\frac{1}{2}$ yd

**a.** How long is the base of each parallelogram?

_____

**b.** What is the area of the smallest *rectangle* of wall that the mirror could fit on?

_____

**16. Persevere in Problem Solving** A watercolor painting is 20 inches long by 9 inches wide. Ramon makes a mat that adds a 1-inch-wide border around the painting. What is the area of the mat?

1 in.

20 in.

9 in.

_____

LESSON
16.4

TEKS
Equations,
expressions, and
relationships—
6.8.C Write equations
that represent problems
related to . . . volume of right
rectangular prisms where
dimensions are positive
rational numbers. *Also 6.8.D*

# Solving Volume Equations

How do you write equations to solve problems involving volume of right rectangular prisms?

## Problem Solving by Finding Volume

To find the volume of a box, which is in the shape of a rectangular prism, you can multiply the length, the width, and the height. The volume of a three-dimensional shape is always in cubic units, such as cubic meters or cubic inches.

**Math On the Spot**
my.hrw.com

### Volume of a Rectangular Prism

The volume $V$ of a rectangular prism is the product of its length $\ell$, its width $w$, and its height $h$.

$$V = \ell wh$$

**Math Talk**
Mathematical Processes

Why are $V = \ell wh$ and $V = Bh$ both formulas for the volume of a rectangular prism?

### EXAMPLE 1 Real World

TEKS 6.8.D

A rectangular swimming pool is 25 meters long and $17\frac{1}{2}$ meters wide. It has an average depth of $1\frac{1}{2}$ meters. What is the volume of the pool?

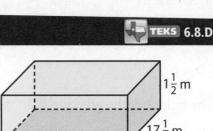
$1\frac{1}{2}$ m
$17\frac{1}{2}$ m
25 m

Label the rectangular prism to represent the pool.

$\ell = 25$ meters      $w = 17\frac{1}{2}$ meters      $h = 1\frac{1}{2}$ meters

Use the formula to write an equation.

$V = \ell wh$

$V = 25 \cdot 17\frac{1}{2} \cdot 1\frac{1}{2}$

$\quad = 25 \cdot \frac{35}{2} \cdot \frac{3}{2}$          Write mixed numbers as fractions greater than 1.

$\quad = \frac{2{,}625}{4}$              Multiply.

$\quad = 656\frac{1}{4}$ cubic meters      Write as a mixed number in simplest form.

**YOUR TURN**

1. Miguel has a toolbox that measures $18\frac{1}{2}$ inches by $12\frac{1}{2}$ inches by 4 inches. What is the volume of the toolbox?

$V =$ _____ cubic inches

# Writing Equations Using the Volume of a Rectangular Prism

You can use the formula for the volume of a rectangular prism to write an equation. Then solve the equation to find missing measurements for a prism.

**EXAMPLE 2** *Real World*

TEKS 6.8.C

Samuel has an ant farm with a volume of 375 cubic inches. The width of the ant farm is 2.5 inches and the length is 15 inches. What is the height of Samuel's ant farm?

| | |
|---|---|
| $V = \ell wh$ | Write the formula. |
| $375 = 15 \cdot 2.5 \cdot h$ | Use the formula to write an equation. |
| $375 = 37.5h$ | Multiply. |
| $\dfrac{375}{37.5} = \dfrac{37.5h}{37.5}$ | Divide both sides of the equation by 37.5. |
| $10 = h$ | |

The height of the ant farm is 10 inches.

## Reflect

2. **Communicate Mathematical Ideas** Explain how you would find the solution to Example 2 using the formula $V = Bh$.

_____

_____

**Personal Math Trainer**

Online Assessment and Intervention

⏻ my.hrw.com

**YOUR TURN**

3. Find the height of this shape, which has a volume of $\frac{15}{16}$ cubic feet.

_____

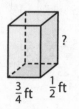

$\frac{3}{4}$ ft   $\frac{1}{2}$ ft

# Solving Multistep Problems

One cubic foot of water equals approximately 7.5 gallons and weighs approximately 62.43 pounds.

## EXAMPLE 3 · Real World

TEKS 6.8.D

**The classroom aquarium holds 30 gallons of water. It is 0.8 feet wide and has a height of 2 feet. Find the length of the aquarium.**

**STEP 1** Find the volume of the classroom aquarium in cubic feet.

> Divide the total number of gallons by the unit rate to find the number of cubic feet.

$$\frac{30 \text{ gallons}}{7.5 \text{ gallons per cubic foot}} = 4 \text{ cubic feet}$$

The volume of the classroom aquarium is 4 cubic feet.

**STEP 2** Find the length of the aquarium.

| | |
|---|---|
| $V = \ell wh$ | Write the formula for volume. |
| $4 = \ell \cdot 0.8 \cdot 2$ | Use the formula to write an equation. |
| $4 = \ell(1.6)$ | Multiply. |
| $\dfrac{4}{1.6} = \dfrac{\ell(1.6)}{1.6}$ | Divide both sides of the equation by 1.6. |
| $2.5 = \ell$ | |

The length of the classroom aquarium is 2.5 feet.

## Reflect

4. **Persevere in Problem Solving** How much does the water in the classroom aquarium weigh? Explain.

_____

_____

_____

## YOUR TURN

5. An aquarium holds 33.75 gallons of water. It has a length of 2 feet and a height of 1.5 feet. What is the volume of the aquarium? What is the width of the aquarium? Explain.

_____

_____

**Personal Math Trainer**

Online Assessment and Intervention

my.hrw.com

1. Find the volume of this rectangular prism. (Example 1)

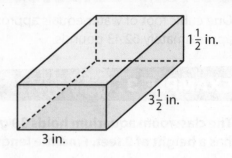

$V = \ell w h$

$V = 3\frac{1}{2} \cdot \boxed{\phantom{0}} \cdot \boxed{\phantom{0}}$

$V = \dfrac{\boxed{\phantom{0}}}{2} \cdot \dfrac{\boxed{\phantom{0}}}{1} \cdot \dfrac{\boxed{\phantom{0}}}{2} \cdot \dfrac{\boxed{\phantom{0}}}{4}$

$V = \boxed{\phantom{0}}$

The volume of the rectangular prism is _____ cubic inches.

2. Write an equation to find the width of the rectangular prism. Show your work. (Example 2)

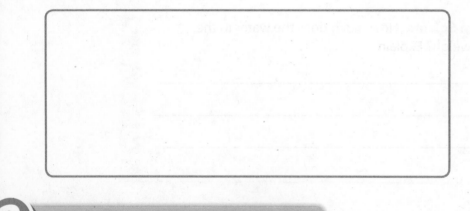

3. One red clay brick weighs 5.76 pounds. The brick is 8 inches long and $2\frac{1}{4}$ inches wide. If the clay weighs 0.08 pounds per cubic inch, what is the volume of the brick? Write an equation to find the height of the brick. Show your work. (Example 3)

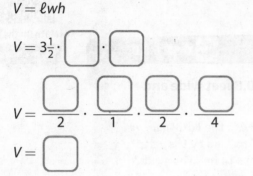

**? ESSENTIAL QUESTION CHECK-IN**

4. How do you solve problems about volume of right rectangular prisms?

_____

_____

# 16.4 Independent Practice

TEKS 6.8.C, 6.8.D

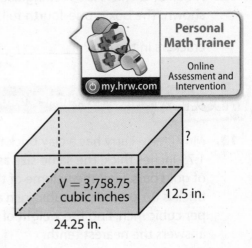

Personal Math Trainer

Online Assessment and Intervention

my.hrw.com

**5.** Jala has an aquarium in the shape of a rectangular prism with the dimensions shown. What is the height of the aquarium?

$V = 3,758.75$ cubic inches
12.5 in.
24.25 in.

Height = _____

**6.** Find the volume of a juice box that is 3 in. by $1\frac{1}{2}$ in. by 4 in.

Volume = _____

**7.** Find the width of a cereal box that has a volume of 3,600 cm³ and is 20 cm long and 30 cm high.

Width = _____

**8.** Bill has a box of markers that has a base of 8 cm by 20 cm and a height of 6 cm. Martin's pencil box has a height of 4 cm and a base that is 15 cm by 16 cm. Bill says his marker box has the same volume as Martin's pencil box. Is Bill right? Explain.

_____

_____

**9.** **Physical Science** A small bar of gold measures 40 mm by 25 mm by 2 mm. One cubic millimeter of gold weighs about 0.0005 ounces. Find the volume in cubic millimeters and the weight in ounces of this small bar of gold.

_____

_____

**10.** **History** The average stone on the lowest level of the Great Pyramid in Egypt was a rectangular prism 5 feet long by 5 feet high by 6 feet deep and weighed 15 tons. What was the volume of the average stone? How much did one cubic foot of this stone weigh?

_____

**11.** A freshwater fish is healthiest when there is at least one gallon of water for every inch of its body length. Roshel wants to put a goldfish that is about $2\frac{1}{2}$ inches long in her tank. Roshel's tank is 7 inches long, 5 inches wide, and 7 inches high. The volume of 1 gallon of water is about 231 cubic inches.

**a.** How many gallons of water would Roshel need for the fish? _____

**b.** What is the volume of Roshel's tank? _____

**c.** Is her fish tank large enough for the fish? Explain. _____

_____

**12.** A box of crackers is a rectangular box with the dimensions shown. The box is one-fourth full. What is the volume of

crackers in the box? _____

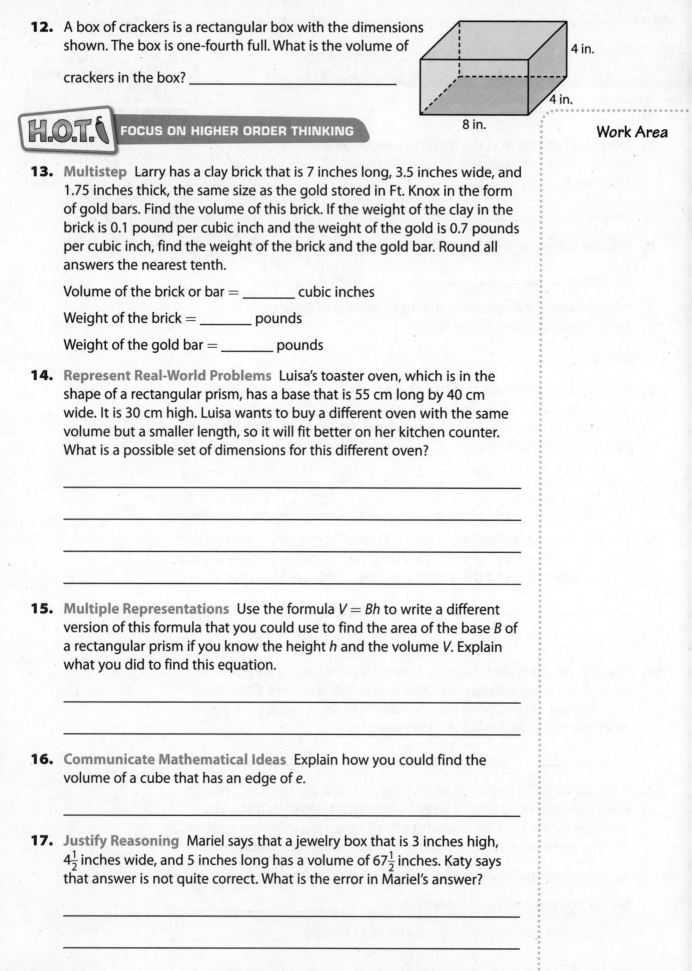

4 in.

4 in.

8 in.

## H.O.T. FOCUS ON HIGHER ORDER THINKING

**13. Multistep** Larry has a clay brick that is 7 inches long, 3.5 inches wide, and 1.75 inches thick, the same size as the gold stored in Ft. Knox in the form of gold bars. Find the volume of this brick. If the weight of the clay in the brick is 0.1 pound per cubic inch and the weight of the gold is 0.7 pounds per cubic inch, find the weight of the brick and the gold bar. Round all answers the nearest tenth.

Volume of the brick or bar = _____ cubic inches

Weight of the brick = _____ pounds

Weight of the gold bar = _____ pounds

**14. Represent Real-World Problems** Luisa's toaster oven, which is in the shape of a rectangular prism, has a base that is 55 cm long by 40 cm wide. It is 30 cm high. Luisa wants to buy a different oven with the same volume but a smaller length, so it will fit better on her kitchen counter. What is a possible set of dimensions for this different oven?

_____

_____

_____

_____

**15. Multiple Representations** Use the formula $V = Bh$ to write a different version of this formula that you could use to find the area of the base $B$ of a rectangular prism if you know the height $h$ and the volume $V$. Explain what you did to find this equation.

_____

_____

**16. Communicate Mathematical Ideas** Explain how you could find the volume of a cube that has an edge of $e$.

_____

**17. Justify Reasoning** Mariel says that a jewelry box that is 3 inches high, $4\frac{1}{2}$ inches wide, and 5 inches long has a volume of $67\frac{1}{2}$ inches. Katy says that answer is not quite correct. What is the error in Mariel's answer?

_____

_____

# Ready to Go On?

**Personal Math Trainer**

Online Assessment and Intervention

my.hrw.com

## 16.1 Area of Quadrilaterals

**1.** Find the area of the figure.

_____

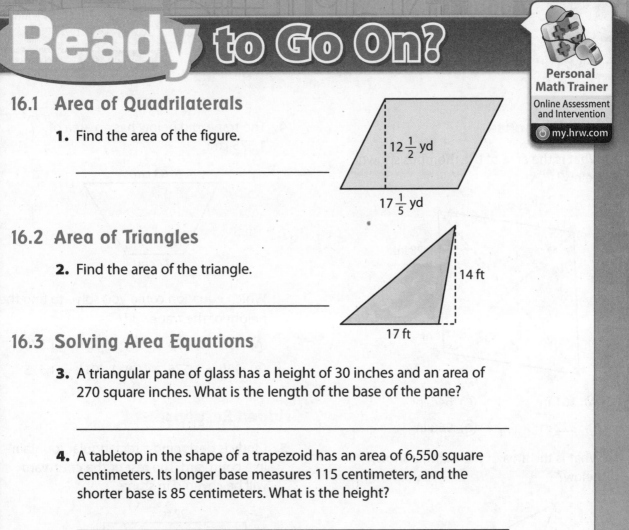

$12\frac{1}{2}$ yd

$17\frac{1}{5}$ yd

## 16.2 Area of Triangles

**2.** Find the area of the triangle.

_____

14 ft

17 ft

## 16.3 Solving Area Equations

**3.** A triangular pane of glass has a height of 30 inches and an area of 270 square inches. What is the length of the base of the pane?

_____

**4.** A tabletop in the shape of a trapezoid has an area of 6,550 square centimeters. Its longer base measures 115 centimeters, and the shorter base is 85 centimeters. What is the height?

_____

## 16.4 Solving Volume Equations

**5.** A rectangular shoebox has a volume of 728 cubic inches. The base of the shoebox measures 8 inches by 6.5 inches. How long is the shoebox?

_____

## ? ESSENTIAL QUESTION

**6.** How can you use equations to solve problems involving area and volume?

_____

_____

_____

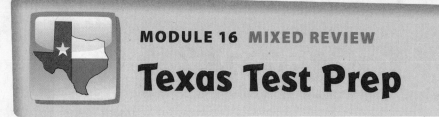

## Selected Response

**1.** What is the area of the rhombus shown below?

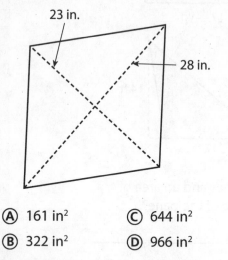

23 in.

28 in.

Ⓐ 161 in²     Ⓒ 644 in²

Ⓑ 322 in²     Ⓓ 966 in²

**2.** What is the area of the triangle shown below?

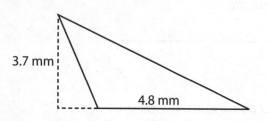

3.7 mm

4.8 mm

Ⓐ 4.44 mm²

Ⓑ 5.92 mm²

Ⓒ 8.88 mm²

Ⓓ 17.76 mm²

**3.** A rectangular prism has a volume of 912 cubic meters. It has a length of 19 meters and a width of 12 meters. Which equation could be solved to find the height of the rectangular prism?

Ⓐ $114h = 912$

Ⓑ $228h = 912$

Ⓒ $15.5h = 912$

Ⓓ $31h = 912$

**4.** The trapezoid below has an area of 1,575 cm².

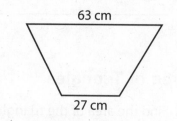

63 cm

27 cm

Which equation could you solve to find the height of the trapezoid?

Ⓐ $45h = 1{,}575$     Ⓒ $850.5h = 1{,}575$

Ⓑ $90h = 1{,}575$     Ⓓ $1{,}701h = 1{,}575$

## Gridded Response

**5.** Cindy is designing a rectangular fountain in a courtyard. The rest of the courtyard will be covered in stone.

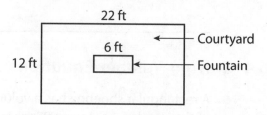

22 ft

6 ft — Courtyard

12 ft — Fountain

The part of the courtyard that will be covered in stone has an area of 246 ft². What is the width of the fountain in feet?

| ⊕ | ⓪ | ⓪ | ⓪ | ⓪ | • | ⓪ | ⓪ |
|---|---|---|---|---|---|---|---|
| ⊖ | ① | ① | ① | ① | | ① | ① |
| | ② | ② | ② | ② | | ② | ② |
| | ③ | ③ | ③ | ③ | | ③ | ③ |
| | ④ | ④ | ④ | ④ | | ④ | ④ |
| | ⑤ | ⑤ | ⑤ | ⑤ | | ⑤ | ⑤ |
| | ⑥ | ⑥ | ⑥ | ⑥ | | ⑥ | ⑥ |
| | ⑦ | ⑦ | ⑦ | ⑦ | | ⑦ | ⑦ |
| | ⑧ | ⑧ | ⑧ | ⑧ | | ⑧ | ⑧ |
| | ⑨ | ⑨ | ⑨ | ⑨ | | ⑨ | ⑨ |

## MODULE 15 · Angles, Triangles, and Equations

**Key Vocabulary**
parallelogram
(paralelogramo)
rhombus (rombo)
trapezoid (trapecio)

### ? ESSENTIAL QUESTION

How can you use angles, triangles, and equations to solve real-world problems?

## EXAMPLE 1

**Find the missing angle measure in each triangle.**

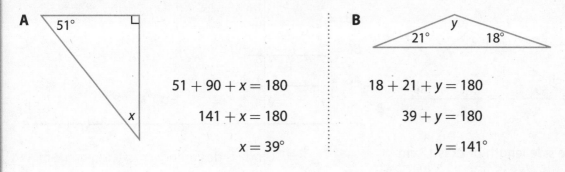

**A**

51°

$x$

$$51 + 90 + x = 180$$
$$141 + x = 180$$
$$x = 39°$$

**B**

$y$

21°      18°

$$18 + 21 + y = 180$$
$$39 + y = 180$$
$$y = 141°$$

## EXAMPLE 2

**The triangle shown has approximate side lengths of 5 cm, 5.8 cm, and 3 cm. Match each side with its correct length.**

*A*

31°

59°

*C*      *B*

$AB = 5$ cm

$BC = 3$ cm     The shortest side is opposite the smallest angle.

$AC = 5.8$ cm    The longest side is opposite the largest angle.

## EXERCISES

**Tell whether a triangle can have sides with the given lengths. If it cannot, give an inequality that shows why not.** (Lesson 15.1)

**1.** 5 in., 12 in., 13 in. _____

**2.** 4.5 ft, 5.5 ft, 11 ft _____

**Find each missing angle measure. Classify each triangle as acute, obtuse, or right.** (Lesson 15.2)

**3.**

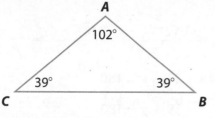

**4.**

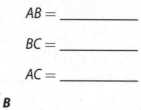

_____  _____

**Match each side length with its correct measure. Classify each triangle as scalene, isosceles, or equilateral.** (Lesson 15.3)

**5.** The side lengths of triangle *ABC* are 6.4 ft, 10 ft, and 6.4 ft.

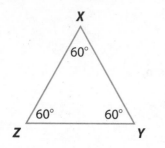

$AB =$ _____

$BC =$ _____

$AC =$ _____

_____

**6.** The side length of *ZX* is 17 cm.

$XY =$ _____

$YZ =$ _____

_____

**Area and Volume Equations**

**Key Vocabulary**
parallelogram
  *(paralelogramo)*
rhombus *(rombo)*
trapezoid *(trapecio)*

**? ESSENTIAL QUESTION**

How can you use area and volume equations to solve real-world problems?

**EXAMPLE 1**

**Find the area of the trapezoid.**

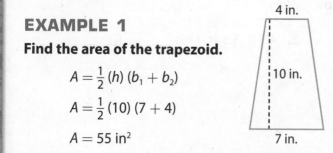

$A = \frac{1}{2}(h)(b_1 + b_2)$

$A = \frac{1}{2}(10)(7 + 4)$

$A = 55 \text{ in}^2$

## EXAMPLE 2

A triangular sail for a sailboat has a height of 30 feet and an area of 330 square feet. Find the base length of the sail.

$$A = \frac{1}{2}bh$$

$$330 = \left(\frac{1}{2}\right)30b$$

$$b = 22 \text{ ft}$$

## EXAMPLE 3

A cubic centimeter of gold weighs approximately 19.32 grams. Find the weight of a brick of gold that has a height of 6 centimeters, width of 3 centimeters, and length of 8 centimeters.

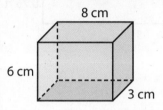

$$V = lwh$$

$$V = 8\,(3)\,(6)$$

$$V = 144 \text{ cm}^3$$

The weight of the gold is $144 \times 19.32$ grams, which is 2,782.08 grams.

## EXERCISES

**Find the area of each figure.** (Lessons 16.1, 16.2)

**1.**

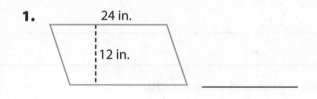

24 in.

12 in.

_____

**2.**

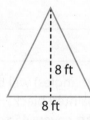

8 ft

8 ft

_____

**Find the missing measurement.** (Lesson 16.3)

**3.**

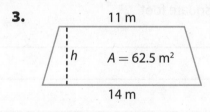

11 m

$h$   $A = 62.5 \text{ m}^2$

14 m

_____

**4.**

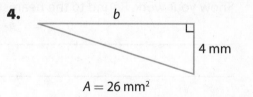

$b$

4 mm

$A = 26 \text{ mm}^2$

_____

**Find the volume of each rectangular prism.** (Lesson 16.4)

**5.**

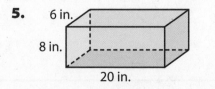

6 in.

8 in.

20 in.

_____

**6.** A rectangular prism with a width of 7 units, a length of 8 units, and a height of 2 units _____

**7.** Jelani is ordering a piece of glass in the shape of a trapezoid to create a patio table top. Each square foot of glass costs $25. The trapezoid has base lengths of 5 feet and 3 feet and a height of 4 feet. Find the cost of the glass. (Lesson 16.1) _____

# Unit 5 Performance Tasks

**1.** | **CAREERS IN MATH** | Theater Set Construction  Ahmed and Karina are building scenery of the Egyptian pyramids out of plywood for a community play. The pyramids are represented by triangles on a rectangular base. The diagram shows the measurements of the piece of scenery.

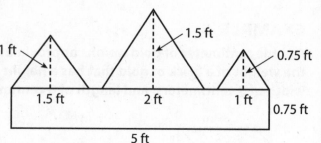

**a.** They have one sheet of plywood, 3 ft by 6 ft. Will they be able to make the piece using this one sheet? Explain.

_____

_____

_____

**b.** How many square feet of plywood is in the completed piece? Show your work.

_____

_____

**c.** The pyramids (the triangles) will be painted gray, and the base (the rectangle) will be painted black. How much of each paint color will they use, if one quart covers 45 square feet? Only one side of the model needs to be painted, but two coats of paint will be needed. Show your work. Round to the nearest hundredth of a square foot.

_____

_____

_____

**2.** Cassandra is making a design for a logo. One part of the design is a triangle with two congruent sides. She must draw the triangle with at least one side with length 6 centimeters, and at least one side with length 4 centimeters. Sketch two possible figures that Cassandra could use. Label the side lengths in both figures.

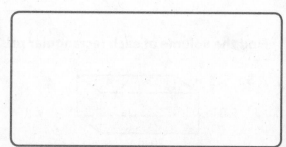

**Personal Math Trainer**

Online Assessment and Intervention

my.hrw.com

## Selected Response

**1.** Part of a large wooden art project will be a triangle formed by joining three boards together. The artist has four boards that measure 16 feet, 11 feet, 7 feet, and 3 feet. Which board could not be used with two of the others to form a triangle?

- Ⓐ the 3-foot board
- Ⓑ the 7-foot board
- Ⓒ the 11-foot board
- Ⓓ the 16-foot board

**2.** Which of these could be the value of *x* in the triangle below?

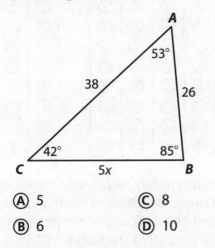

- Ⓐ 5
- Ⓒ 8
- Ⓑ 6
- Ⓓ 10

**3.** What is the area of a trapezoid that has bases measuring 19 centimeters and 23 centimeters, and a height of 14 centimeters?

- Ⓐ 105 square centimeters
- Ⓑ 266 square centimeters
- Ⓒ 294 square centimeters
- Ⓓ 322 square centimeters

**4.** What is the area of the triangle shown below?

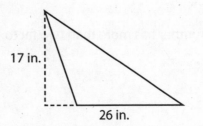

- Ⓐ 110.5 square inches
- Ⓑ 221 square inches
- Ⓒ 442 square inches
- Ⓓ 884 square inches

**5.** The trapezoid below has an area of 475 square meters.

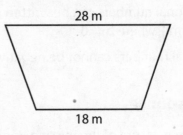

Which equation could you solve to find the height of the trapezoid?

- Ⓐ $23h = 475$
- Ⓑ $252h = 475$
- Ⓒ $46h = 475$
- Ⓓ $504h = 475$

**6.** A rectangular prism has a volume of 1,500 cubic centimeters. It has a length of 34 centimeters and a width of 22 centimeters. Which equation could be solved to find the height of the rectangular prism?

- Ⓐ $374h = 1,500$
- Ⓑ $28h = 1,500$
- Ⓒ $748h = 1,500$
- Ⓓ $56h = 1,500$

**7.** Which expression represents the sum of 59 and *x*?

Ⓐ $59 + x$

Ⓑ $59 \div x$

Ⓒ $59x$

Ⓓ $59 - x$

**8.** Which number has more than two factors?

Ⓐ 19

Ⓑ 23

Ⓒ 25

Ⓓ 29

**9.** Which of the following statements about rational numbers is **not** correct?

Ⓐ All whole numbers are also rational numbers.

Ⓑ All integers are also rational numbers.

Ⓒ All rational numbers can be written in the form $\frac{a}{b}$ where b ≠ 0.

Ⓓ Rational numbers cannot be negative.

## Gridded Response

**10.** What is the measure of the missing angle in a triangle that contains angle measures of 37° and 59°?

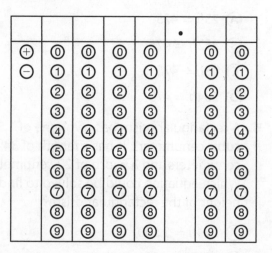

**Hot Tip!** It is helpful to draw or redraw a figure. Answers to geometry problems may become clearer as you redraw the figure.

**11.** What is the measure, in degrees, of the missing angle in the triangle below?

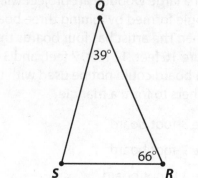

**12.** Janice wants to buy carpet for a trapezoid-shaped room. The bases of the trapezoid are 12 feet and 14 feet, and the height is 15 feet. If the carpet she likes is $5.50 per square foot, how much will new carpet for the room cost in dollars?

# Measurement and Data

## CAREERS IN MATH

**Geneticist** A geneticist is a scientist who studies and applies genetics, a branch of biology that focuses on heredity and variation in organisms. Geneticists analyze how different traits are passed from parents to offspring.

If you are interested in a career as a geneticist, you should study these mathematical subjects:
- Algebra
- Trigonometry
- Probability and Statistics
- Calculus

Research other careers that require the analysis of data.

### Unit 6 Performance Task

At the end of the unit, check out how **geneticists** use math.

Use the puzzle to preview key vocabulary from this unit. Unscramble the circled letters to answer the riddle at the bottom of the page.

1. **OBX LOTP**

2. **TOD TOLP**

3. **HOSTIARMG**

4. **NIADEM**

5. **PEPRU LAETURQI**

6. **LETVIEAR QUYFENREC**

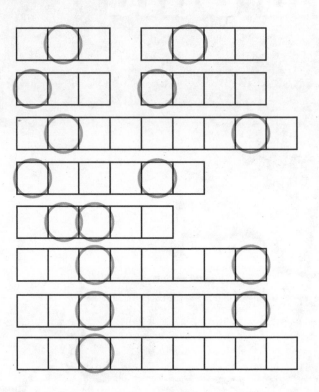

1. A display that shows how the values in a data set are distributed. (Lesson 17-2)

2. A display in which each piece of data is represented by a dot above the number line. (Lesson 17-3)

3. A type of bar graph whose bars represent frequencies of numerical data within intervals. (Lesson 17-4)

4. The middle value of an ordered data set. (Lesson 17-1)

5. The median of the upper half of the data in a box plot. (Lesson 17-2)

6. The ratio of the frequency and the total amount of data. (Lesson 17-5)

**Q:** What is a math teacher's favorite dessert?

**A:** __ __ __ __ __ __ __ __ __ __

__ __ __ __ __ __ __ __!

# Displaying, Analyzing, and Summarizing Data

 **ESSENTIAL QUESTION**

How can you use solve real-world problems by displaying, analyzing, and summarizing data?

**Real-World Video**

Biologists collect data on different animals. They can describe the data using measures of center or spread, and by displaying the data in plots or graphs, they may see trends related to the animal population.

my.hrw.com

 **GO DIGITAL**
my.hrw.com

 **my.hrw.com**
Go digital with your write-in student edition, accessible on any device.

 **Math On the Spot**
Scan with your smart phone to jump directly to the online edition, video tutor, and more.

 **Animated Math**
Interactively explore key concepts to see how math works.

 **Personal Math Trainer**
Get immediate feedback and help as you work through practice sets.

# Are YOU Ready?

Complete these exercises to review skills you will need for this chapter.

## Remainders

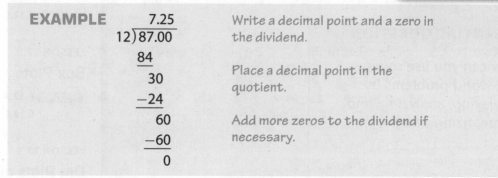

**EXAMPLE**

$$\begin{array}{r} 7.25 \\ 12\overline{)87.00} \\ \underline{84} \\ 30 \\ \underline{-24} \\ 60 \\ \underline{-60} \\ 0 \end{array}$$

Write a decimal point and a zero in the dividend.

Place a decimal point in the quotient.

Add more zeros to the dividend if necessary.

**Find the quotient.**

1. $15\overline{)42}$ _____
2. $75\overline{)93}$ _____
3. $52\overline{)91}$ _____
4. $24\overline{)57}$ _____

## Read Bar Graphs

**EXAMPLE**   How many goals did Alec score?

The first bar shows how many goals Alec scored.

The bar extends to a height of 5.

Alec scored 5 goals.

5. How many goals did Dion score? _____

6. Which two players together scored the same number of goals

   as Jeff? _____

7. How many fewer goals than Cesar did Alec score? _____

# Reading Start-Up

## Visualize Vocabulary

**Use the review words to complete the chart.**

| Introduction to Statistics | | |
|---|---|---|
| **Definition** | **Example** | **Review word** |
| A group of facts | The grades of all of the students in a school | |
| A tool used to gather information from individuals | A questionnaire given to all students to find the number of hours each student spends studying in 1 week | |
| A value that summarizes a set of unequal values, found by addition and division | Results of the survey show that students typically spend 5 hours a week studying | |

## Understand Vocabulary

**Complete the sentences using the preview words.**

1. The average of a data set is the _____.

2. The _____ is the middle value of a data set.

3. The number or category that occurs most frequently in a data set is

   the _____.

## Vocabulary

**Review Words**
  average *(promedio)*
  data *(datos)*
  survey *(encuesta)*

**Preview Words**
  box plot *(diagrama de caja)*
  categorical data *(datos categóricos)*
  dot plot *(diagrama de puntos)*
  histogram *(histograma)*
  interquartile range *(rango entre cuartiles)*
  lower quartile *(cuartil inferior)*
  ✔ mean *(media)*
  ✔ median *(mediana)*
  measure of center *(medida central)*
  measure of spread *(medida de dispersión)*
  ✔ mode *(moda)*
  range *(rango)*
  relative frequency *(frecuencia relativa)*
  statistical question *(pregunta estadística)*
  upper quartile *(cuartil superior)*

## Active Reading

**Layered Book**  Before beginning the module, create a layered book to help you learn the concepts in this module. Label each flap with lesson titles from this module. As you study each lesson, write important ideas, such as vocabulary and formulas under the appropriate flap. Refer to your finished layered book as you work on exercises from this module.

# Unpacking the TEKS

Understanding the TEKS and the vocabulary terms in the TEKS will help you know exactly what you are expected to learn in this module.

---

## TEKS 6.12.C

Summarize numeric data with numerical summaries, including the mean and median (measures of center) and the range and interquartile range (IQR) (measures of spread), and use these summaries to describe the center, spread, and shape of the data distribution.

## What It Means to You

You will use measures of center to describe a data set.

### UNPACKING EXAMPLE 6.12.C

Several students' scores on a history test are shown. Find the mean score and the median score. Which measure better describes the typical score for these students? Explain.

| History Test Scores |
|---|
| 73  48  88  90  90  81  83 |

Mean: $\frac{73 + 48 + 88 + 90 + 90 + 81 + 83}{7} = \frac{553}{7} = 79$

To find the median, write the data values in order from least to greatest and find the middle value.

Median: 48  73  81  83  88  90  90

The median better describes the typical score. The mean is affected by the low score of 48.

---

## TEKS 6.13.A

Interpret numeric data summarized in dot plots, stem-and-leaf plots, histograms, and box plots.

## What It Means to You

You will interpret the data from a dot plot, stem-and-leaf plot, histogram, or box plot.

### UNPACKING EXAMPLE 6.13.A

Kim has started rating each movie she sees using a scale of 1 to10 on an online site. She made a histogram that shows how she rated the movies. What does the shape of the distribution tell you about the movies Kim has rated?

Of the 15 movies that Kim rated, she rated almost half a 7 or an 8 and did not generally give extreme ratings.

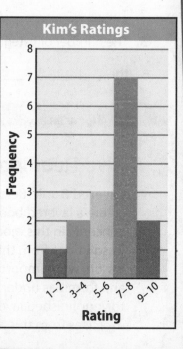

Kim's Ratings

---

Visit **my.hrw.com** to see all the **TEKS** unpacked.

my.hrw.com

LESSON
# 17.1 Measures of Center

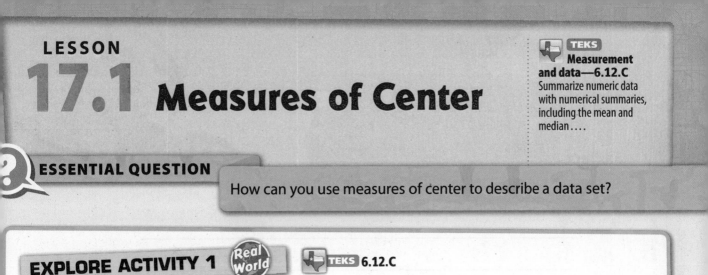

TEKS
**Measurement
and data—6.12.C**
Summarize numeric data
with numerical summaries,
including the mean and
median....

**?** **ESSENTIAL QUESTION**

How can you use measures of center to describe a data set?

---

**EXPLORE ACTIVITY 1** (Real World)  TEKS 6.12.C

## Finding the Mean

A **measure of center** is a single number used to describe a set of numeric data.
A measure of center describes a typical value from the data set.

One measure of center is the *mean*. The **mean**, or average, of a data set is the
sum of the data values divided by the number of data values in the set.

Tami surveyed five of her friends to find out how many
brothers and sisters they have. Her results are shown in
the table.

| Number of Siblings | | | | |
|---|---|---|---|---|
| Amy | Ben | Cal | Don | Eva |
| 2 | 3 | 1 | 1 | 3 |

**A** Model each person's response as a group of counters.

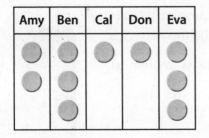

**B** Now rearrange the counters so that each group has the same number
of counters.

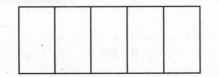

Each group now has _____ counter(s). This value is the mean. This
model demonstrates how the mean "evens out" the data values.

**C** Use numbers to calculate the mean.

The sum of the data values is $2 + 3 + \boxed{\phantom{0}} + \boxed{\phantom{0}} + \boxed{\phantom{0}} = \boxed{\phantom{0}}$.

How many data values are in the set? _____

**Math Talk**
Mathematical Processes

Suppose you have a data set in which all of the values are 2. What is the mean?

Mean = $\dfrac{\text{sum of data values}}{\text{number of data values}}$ = $\dfrac{\boxed{\phantom{0}}}{\boxed{\phantom{0}}}$ = $\boxed{\phantom{0}}$

### Reflect

1. Can the mean be greater than the greatest value in a data set? Why or why not?

_____

_____

_____

_____

**Math On the Spot**
my.hrw.com

# Finding the Median

Another measure of center is the *median*. The **median** represents the middle value of an ordered data set.

## EXAMPLE 1  Real World

TEKS 6.12.C

**A** A coach records the distances that some cross-country team members ran last week. Find the median.

Write the data values in order from least to greatest.

3  4  5  5  6  7  7  8  10  10  10

This value is the median.

Equal number of values on either side of the median

| Distances Run | |
|---|---|
| Cara | 3 mi |
| Rob | 5 mi |
| Maria | 7 mi |
| Olivia | 10 mi |
| Paul | 10 mi |
| Chris | 4 mi |
| Amir | 7 mi |
| Iris | 5 mi |
| Alex | 8 mi |
| Tara | 10 mi |
| Ned | 6 mi |

The median is 7.

**Math Talk**
Mathematical Processes

Why does the data set in **A** have one middle value while the data set in **B** has two middle values?

**B** Find the median of these test scores: 87, 90, 77, 83, 99, 94, 93, 90, 85, 83.

Write the data values in order from least to greatest.

77  83  83  85  87  90  90  93  94  99

This data set has two middle values: 87 and 90.

The median is the average of these two values:

Median = $\dfrac{87 + 90}{2}$ = 88.5

The median is 88.5.

## Reflect

2. **What If?** Which units are used for the data in **A**? If the coach had recorded some distances in kilometers and some in miles, can you still find the median of the data? Explain.

_____

_____

3. Charlotte recorded the number of minutes she spent exercising in the past ten days: 12, 4, 5, 6, 8, 7, 9, 8, 2, 1. Find the median of the data.

_____

**Personal Math Trainer**

Online Assessment and Intervention

⏻ my.hrw.com

---

**EXPLORE ACTIVITY 2** Real World    TEKS 6.12.C

# Comparing the Mean and the Median

The mean and median of a data set may be equal, very close to each other, or very different from each other. For data sets where the mean and median differ greatly, one likely describes the data set better than the other.

**The monthly earnings of several teenagers are $200, $320, $275, $250, $750, $350, and $310.**

A   Find the mean.

$$\frac{\bigcirc + \bigcirc + \bigcirc + \bigcirc + \bigcirc + \bigcirc + \bigcirc}{\bigcirc} = \frac{\bigcirc}{\bigcirc} \approx \bigcirc$$

B   Write the data values in order from least to greatest and find the median.

_____

C   The mean and the median differ by about $_____. Why?

_____

_____

D   Which measure of center better describes the typical monthly earnings for this group of teenagers—the mean or the median? Explain.

_____

_____

Lesson 17.1 **487**

**EXPLORE ACTIVITY 2** *(cont'd)*

## Reflect

4. **Communicate Mathematical Ideas** Luka's final exam scores for this semester are 70, 72, 99, 72, and 69. Find the mean and median. Which is a better description of Luka's typical exam score? Explain your thinking.

_____

_____

# Guided Practice

1. Spencer surveyed five of his friends to find out how many pets they have. His results are shown in the table. What is the mean number of pets? (Explore Activity 1)

| Number of Pets | | | | |
|------|------|-----|------|-------|
| Lara | Cody | Sam | Ella | Maria |
| 3 | 5 | 2 | 4 | 1 |

$$\text{Mean} = \frac{\text{sum of data values}}{\text{number of data values}} = \frac{\boxed{\phantom{00}}}{\boxed{\phantom{00}}} = \boxed{\phantom{00}}$$

The mean number of pets is _____

2. The following are the weights, in pounds, of some dogs at a kennel: 36, 45, 29, 39, 51, 49. (Example 1)

   a. Find the median. _____

   b. Suppose one of the weights were given in kilograms. Can you still find the median? Explain.

   _____

3. a. Find the mean and the median of this data set: 9, 6, 5, 3, 28, 6, 4, 7. (Explore Activity 2)

   _____

   b. Which better describes the data set, the mean or the median? Explain.

   _____

   _____

## ? ESSENTIAL QUESTION CHECK-IN

4. How can you use measures of center to describe a data set?

   _____

   _____

# 17.1 Independent Practice

**TEKS** 6.12.C

Several students in Ashton's class were randomly selected and asked how many text messages they sent yesterday. Their answers were 1, 0, 10, 7, 13, 2, 9, 15, 0, 3.

**5.** How many students were asked? How do you know?

_____

_____

_____

**6.** Find the mean and the median for these data.

Mean = _____     Median = _____

The points scored by a basketball team in its last 6 games are shown. Use these data for 7 and 8.

| Points Scored | | | | | |
|---|---|---|---|---|---|
| 73 | 77 | 85 | 84 | 37 | 115 |

**7.** Find the mean score and the median score.

Mean = _____     Median = _____

**8.** Which measure better describes the typical number of points scored? Explain.

_____

_____

_____

Some people were asked how long it takes them to commute to work. Use the data for 9–11.

**9.** What units are used for the data? What should you do before finding the mean and median number of minutes?

_____

| 16 min | 5 min |
|---|---|
| 7 min | 8 min |
| 14 min | 12 min |
| 0.5 hr | 1 hr |

**10.** Find the mean and median number of minutes.

Mean = _____     Median = _____

**11.** Which measure do you think is more typical of the data?

_____

_____

_____

**12. Critique Reasoning** For two weeks, the school librarian recorded the number of library books returned each morning. The data are shown in the dot plot. The librarian found the mean number of books returned each morning.

**Books Returned**

**Books**

$$\frac{8+6+10+5+9+8+3+6}{8} = \frac{55}{8} = 6.9$$

Is this the correct mean of this data set? If not, explain and correct the answer.

_____

_____

**13. Critical Thinking** Lauren's scores on her math tests are 93, 91, 98, 100, 95, 92, and 96. What score could Lauren get on her next math test so that the mean and median remain the same? Explain your answer.

_____

_____

_____

**14. Persevere in Problem Solving** Yuko wants to take a job selling cars. Since she will get a commission for every car she sells, she finds out the sale price of the last four cars sold at each company.

Company A: $16,000; $20,000; $25,000; $35,000;

Company B: $21,000, $23,000, $36,000, $48,000

**a.** Find the mean selling price at each company.

_____

**b.** Find the median selling price at each company.

_____

**c. Communicate Mathematical Ideas** At either company, Yuko will get paid a commission of 20% of the sale price of each car she sells. Based on the data, where do you recommend she take a job? Why?

_____

_____

_____

# 17.2 Box Plots

**TEKS**
**Measurement and data—6.12.A** Represent numeric data graphically, including box plots. *Also* *6.12.B, 6.12.C, 6.13.A*

**? ESSENTIAL QUESTION**

How can you use a box plot and measures of spread to describe a data set?

## Using a Box Plot

A **box plot** is a display that shows how the values in a data set are distributed, or spread out.

To make a box plot, first find five values for the data set:

- the least value
- the **lower quartile** — the median of the lower half of the data
- the median
- the **upper quartile** — the median of the upper half of the data
- the greatest value

**Math On the Spot**
⏻ my.hrw.com

---

### EXAMPLE 1 Real World

**TEKS** 6.12.A, 6.12.C

The heights of several students are shown. Make a box plot for the data.

| Students' Heights (in.) | | | | | |
|---|---|---|---|---|---|
| 60 | 58 | 54 | 56 | 63 | 61 |
| 65 | 61 | 62 | 59 | 56 | 58 |

**STEP 1** Order the data and find the needed values.

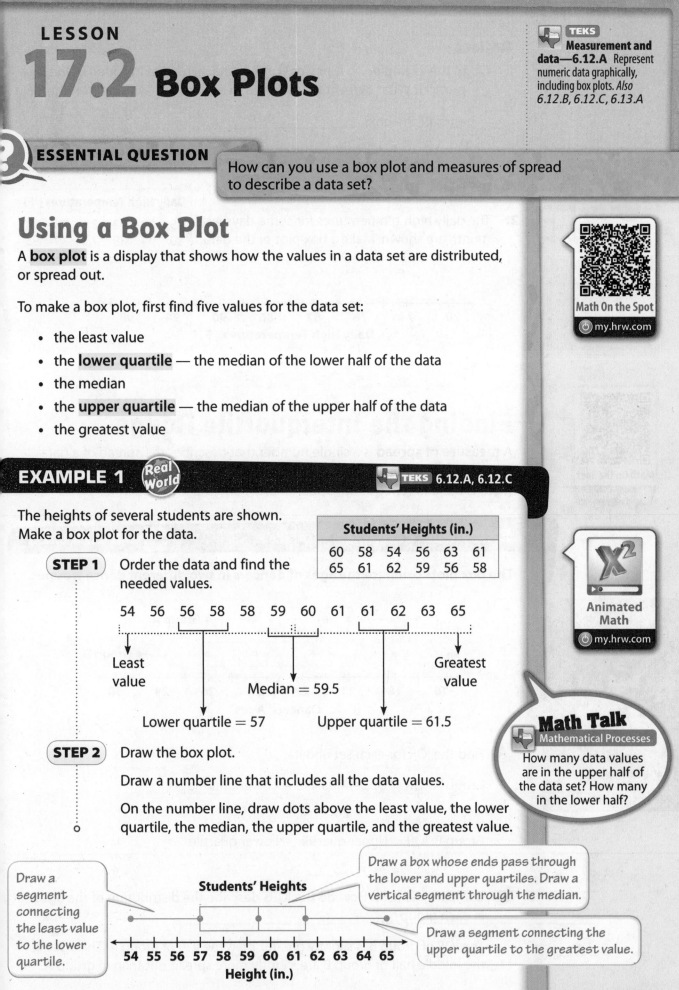

54  56  56  58  58  59  60  61  61  62  63  65

Least value

Greatest value

Median = 59.5

Lower quartile = 57

Upper quartile = 61.5

**STEP 2** Draw the box plot.

Draw a number line that includes all the data values.

On the number line, draw dots above the least value, the lower quartile, the median, the upper quartile, and the greatest value.

**X²**
**Animated Math**
⏻ my.hrw.com

**Math Talk**
**Mathematical Processes**
How many data values are in the upper half of the data set? How many in the lower half?

Draw a segment connecting the least value to the lower quartile.

**Students' Heights**

Draw a box whose ends pass through the lower and upper quartiles. Draw a vertical segment through the median.

Draw a segment connecting the upper quartile to the greatest value.

54  55  56  57  58  59  60  61  62  63  64  65
**Height (in.)**

## Reflect

1. In the example, what percent of the data values are included in the box portion? What percent are included in each of the "whiskers" on the ends of the box? _____

**YOUR TURN**

2. The daily high temperatures for some days last month are shown. Make a box plot of the data.

| Daily High Temperatures (°F) | | | | | |
|---|---|---|---|---|---|
| 85 | 78 | 92 | 88 | 78 | 84 |
| 80 | 94 | 89 | 75 | 79 | 83 |

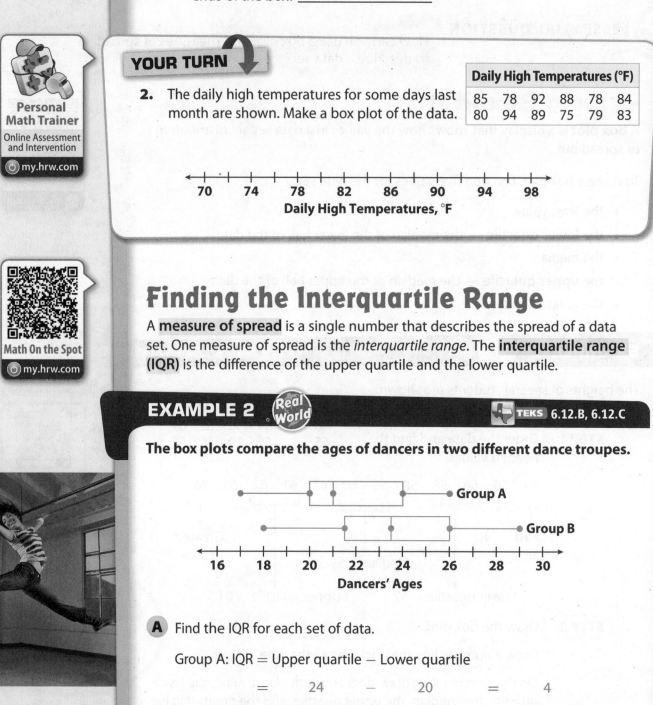

70  74  78  82  86  90  94  98

**Daily High Temperatures, °F**

# Finding the Interquartile Range

A **measure of spread** is a single number that describes the spread of a data set. One measure of spread is the *interquartile range*. The **interquartile range (IQR)** is the difference of the upper quartile and the lower quartile.

**EXAMPLE 2**  Real World          TEKS 6.12.B, 6.12.C

The box plots compare the ages of dancers in two different dance troupes.

16  18  20  22  24  26  28  30

**Dancers' Ages**

Ⓐ Find the IQR for each set of data.

Group A: IQR = Upper quartile − Lower quartile

       =       24      −      20      =      4

Group B: IQR = Upper quartile − Lower quartile

       =       26      −      21.5      =      4.5

Ⓑ Compare the IQRs. How do the IQRs describe the distribution of the ages in each group?

The IQR of group B is slightly greater than the IQR of group A. The ages in the middle half of group B are slightly more spread out than in group A.

**492** Unit 6

3. The box plots compare the weekly earnings of two groups of salespeople from different clothing stores. Find and compare the IQRs of the box plots.

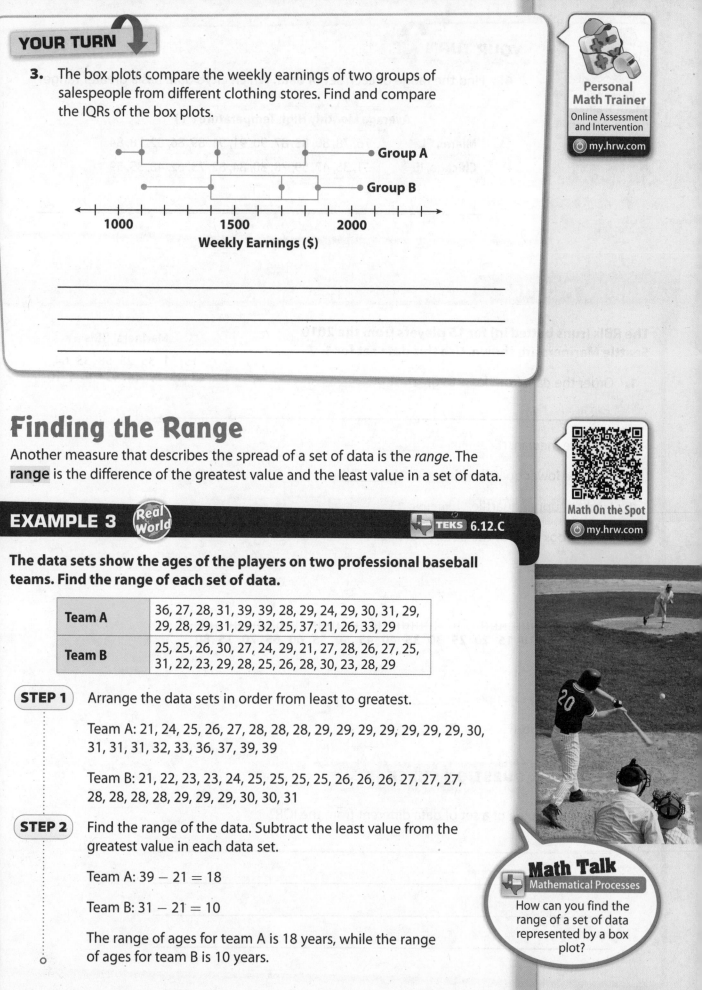

Weekly Earnings ($)

# Finding the Range

Another measure that describes the spread of a set of data is the *range*. The **range** is the difference of the greatest value and the least value in a set of data.

Math On the Spot

my.hrw.com

## EXAMPLE 3 Real World

TEKS 6.12.C

The data sets show the ages of the players on two professional baseball teams. Find the range of each set of data.

| Team A | 36, 27, 28, 31, 39, 39, 28, 29, 24, 29, 30, 31, 29, 29, 28, 29, 31, 29, 32, 25, 37, 21, 26, 33, 29 |
|--------|--------|
| Team B | 25, 25, 26, 30, 27, 24, 29, 21, 27, 28, 26, 27, 25, 31, 22, 23, 29, 28, 25, 26, 28, 30, 23, 28, 29 |

**STEP 1** Arrange the data sets in order from least to greatest.

Team A: 21, 24, 25, 26, 27, 28, 28, 28, 29, 29, 29, 29, 29, 29, 29, 30, 31, 31, 31, 32, 33, 36, 37, 39, 39

Team B: 21, 22, 23, 23, 24, 25, 25, 25, 25, 26, 26, 26, 27, 27, 27, 28, 28, 28, 28, 29, 29, 29, 30, 30, 31

**STEP 2** Find the range of the data. Subtract the least value from the greatest value in each data set.

Team A: $39 - 21 = 18$

Team B: $31 - 21 = 10$

The range of ages for team A is 18 years, while the range of ages for team B is 10 years.

**Math Talk**
Mathematical Processes

How can you find the range of a set of data represented by a box plot?

**Personal Math Trainer**

Online Assessment and Intervention

my.hrw.com

**4.** Find the range of each set of data. Which city's data has a greater range?

| Average Monthly High Temperature (°F) | |
|---|---|
| **Miami, FL** | 76, 78, 80, 83, 87, 90, 91, 91, 89, 86, 82, 78, 84 |
| **Chicago, IL** | 31, 35, 47, 59, 70, 80, 84, 82, 75, 62, 48, 35, 59 |

_____

## Guided Practice

The RBIs (runs batted in) for 15 players from the 2010 Seattle Mariners are shown. Use this data set for 1–7.

| Mariners' RBIs |
|---|
| 15  51  35  25  58  33  64 |
| 43  33  29  14  13  11  4  10 |

**1.** Order the data from least to greatest. (Example 1)

_____

**2.** Find the median. (Example 1) _____

**3.** Find the lower quartile. (Example 1) _____

**4.** Find the upper quartile. (Example 1) _____

**5.** Make a box plot for the data. (Example 1)

0  5  10  15  20  25  30  35  40  45  50  55  60  65  70  75  80

**6.** Find the IQR. (Example 2) _____

**7.** Find the range. (Example 3) _____

### ? ESSENTIAL QUESTION CHECK-IN

**8.** How is the range of a set of data different from the IQR?

_____

_____

_____

_____

# 17.2 Independent Practice

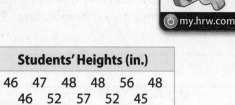

Personal Math Trainer

Online Assessment and Intervention

my.hrw.com

**TEKS** 6.12.A, 6.12.B, 6.12.C, 6.13.A

**For 9–12, use the data set of the heights of several different students.**

| Students' Heights (in.) |
|---|
| 46  47  48  48  56  48 |
| 46  52  57  52  45 |

**9.** Draw a box plot of the data.

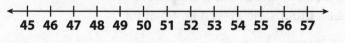

```
45 46 47 48 49 50 51 52 53 54 55 56 57
```

**10.** How many students are included in the data set? _____

**11.** What method could have been used to collect the data?

_____

**12.** **Represent Real-World Problems** What other data could you collect from the students to create a box plot? Provide several examples with units of measurement, if applicable.

_____

**For 13–15, use the box plots of the total precipitation for the same group of cities for the months of January and June.**

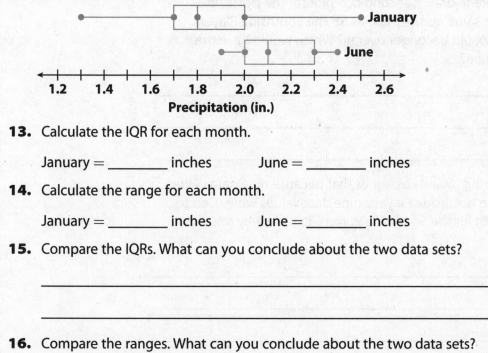

**13.** Calculate the IQR for each month.

January = _____ inches        June = _____ inches

**14.** Calculate the range for each month.

January = _____ inches        June = _____ inches

**15.** Compare the IQRs. What can you conclude about the two data sets?

_____

_____

**16.** Compare the ranges. What can you conclude about the two data sets?

_____

**17. Analyze Relationships** Can two box plots have the same range and IQR and yet represent completely different data? Explain.

_____

_____

_____

_____

**18. Multiple Representations** Matthew collected data about the ages of the actors in two different community theater groups. He drew a box plot for one of the sets of data.

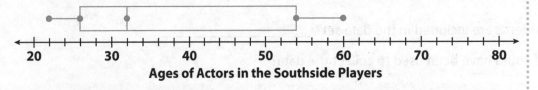

**Ages of Actors in the Southside Players**

| Ages of Actors in the Northside Players | 71, 62, 63, 21, 63, 39, 25, 26, 30 |
|---|---|

**a.** Find the median, range, and IQR for each set of data.

| Theater Group | Median | Range | IQR |
|---|---|---|---|
| Northside Players | | | |
| Southside Players | | | |

**b.** Suppose you were to draw a second box plot for the Northside Players using the same number line as for the Southside Players. Which box plot would be longer overall? Which would have the longest box portion?

_____

_____

_____

**c. Critique Reasoning** Mandy assumes that because nine data values are shown for the Northside Players, nine data values were used to make the box plot for the Southside Players. Explain why this is not necessarily true.

_____

_____

_____

_____

# LESSON
# 17.3  Dot Plots and Data Distribution

**TEKS** **Measurement and data—6.13.A** Interpret numeric data summarized in dot plots. *Also 6.12.A, 6.12B, 6.13.B*

**? ESSENTIAL QUESTION**

How can you summarize and display numeric data?

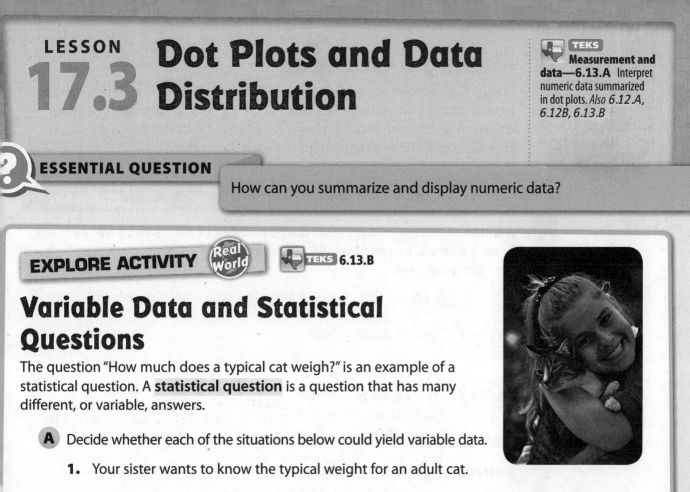

**EXPLORE ACTIVITY** *Real World*    **TEKS** 6.13.B

## Variable Data and Statistical Questions

The question "How much does a typical cat weigh?" is an example of a statistical question. A **statistical question** is a question that has many different, or variable, answers.

**A** Decide whether each of the situations below could yield variable data.

**1.** Your sister wants to know the typical weight for an adult cat.

_____

**2.** You want to know how tall your friend is. _____

**3.** You want to know how far your house is from school. _____

**4.** A car owner wants to know how much money people usually pay

for a new tire. _____

**5.** How many students were in line for lunch at the cafeteria today

at 12:30? _____

**B** For which of the situations in part **A** can you write a statistical question? Write questions for these situations.

_____

_____

## Reflect

**1.** Choose one of the questions you wrote in part **B**. How might you find answers to this question? What units would you use for the answers?

_____

_____

_____

Lesson 17.3    **497**

# Making a Dot Plot

Statistical questions are answered by collecting and analyzing data. One way to understand a set of data is to make a visual display. A **dot plot** is a visual display in which each piece of data is represented by a dot above a number line. A dot plot shows the frequency of each data value.

## EXAMPLE 1 · Real World

TEKS 6.12.A

**A baseball team manager records the number of runs scored by the team in each game for several weeks. Use the data to make a dot plot.**

1, 3, 1, 7, 2, 0, 11, 2, 2, 3, 1, 3, 4, 2, 2, 4, 5, 2, 6

> The team usually scores between 0 and 7 runs in a game, but in one game they scored 11 runs.

**STEP 1** Make a number line.

Data values range from 0 to 11, so use a scale from 0 to 11.

**STEP 2** Draw a dot above the number line for each data value.

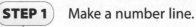

**Runs Scored**

## Reflect

2. How many games did the team play during the season? How can you tell from looking at the dot plot?

_____

_____

3. At how many games did the team score 2 runs or fewer? How do you know?

_____

_____

## YOUR TURN

4. A different baseball team scores the following numbers of runs in its games for several weeks:
4, 4, 6, 1, 2, 4, 1, 2, 5, 3, 3, 5, 4, 2

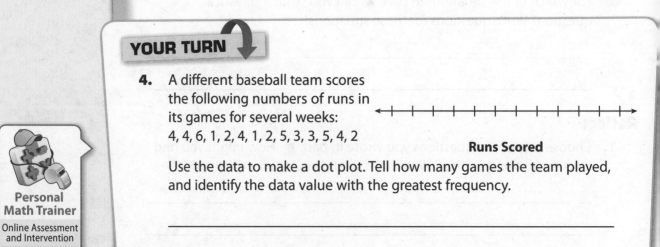

**Runs Scored**

Use the data to make a dot plot. Tell how many games the team played, and identify the data value with the greatest frequency.

_____

_____

# Interpreting a Dot Plot

A dot plot can give you a visual picture of the spread, center, and shape of a data distribution.

You can describe the spread of a data set by identifying the least and greatest values. You can also look for **outliers** which are data values that are either much greater or much less than the other data values.

You can describe the center and shape of a data set in terms of *peaks, clusters,* or *symmetry*. A symmetric distribution has approximately the same number of data values on either side of the center.

## EXAMPLE 2

TEKS 6.12.B

**Describe the spread, center, and shape of each data distribution.**

**A** The data values are spread out from 3 to 7 with no outliers.

The data has a cluster from 3 to 7 with one peak at 5, which is the center of the distribution.

The distribution is symmetric. The data values are clustered around the center of the distribution.

**B** The data values are spread out from 1 to 9. The data value 1 appears to be an outlier.

The data has a cluster from 6 to 9 with one peak at 9, which is the greatest value in the data set.

The distribution is not symmetric. The data values are clustered at one end of the distribution.

**My Notes**

### YOUR TURN

**5.** Describe the spread, center, and shape of the data distribution from Example 1.

_____

_____

_____

_____

# Finding Measures from a Dot Plot

You can also find and calculate measures of center and spread from a dot plot.

**EXAMPLE 3** *Real World*                                    **TEKS** 6.12.B

**The dot plot shows the number of runs scored by a baseball team in each game for several weeks from Example 1.**

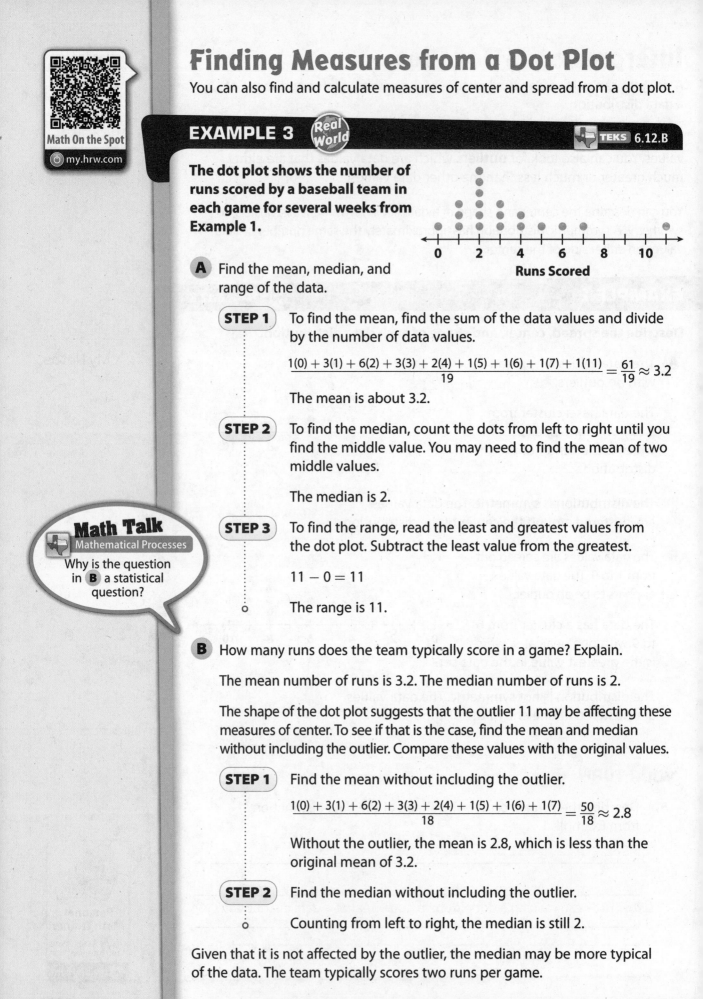

**Runs Scored**

**A** Find the mean, median, and range of the data.

**STEP 1** To find the mean, find the sum of the data values and divide by the number of data values.

$$\frac{1(0) + 3(1) + 6(2) + 3(3) + 2(4) + 1(5) + 1(6) + 1(7) + 1(11)}{19} = \frac{61}{19} \approx 3.2$$

The mean is about 3.2.

**STEP 2** To find the median, count the dots from left to right until you find the middle value. You may need to find the mean of two middle values.

The median is 2.

**STEP 3** To find the range, read the least and greatest values from the dot plot. Subtract the least value from the greatest.

$$11 - 0 = 11$$

The range is 11.

**B** How many runs does the team typically score in a game? Explain.

The mean number of runs is 3.2. The median number of runs is 2.

The shape of the dot plot suggests that the outlier 11 may be affecting these measures of center. To see if that is the case, find the mean and median without including the outlier. Compare these values with the original values.

**STEP 1** Find the mean without including the outlier.

$$\frac{1(0) + 3(1) + 6(2) + 3(3) + 2(4) + 1(5) + 1(6) + 1(7)}{18} = \frac{50}{18} \approx 2.8$$

Without the outlier, the mean is 2.8, which is less than the original mean of 3.2.

**STEP 2** Find the median without including the outlier.

Counting from left to right, the median is still 2.

Given that it is not affected by the outlier, the median may be more typical of the data. The team typically scores two runs per game.

6. Find the mean, median, and range of the data from Your Turn question 4. What is the typical number of runs the team scores in a game? Justify your answer.

_____

_____

_____

# Guided Practice

**Tell whether the situation could yield variable data. If possible, write a statistical question.** (Explore Activity)

1. The town council members want to know how much recyclable trash a typical household in town generates each week.

_____

_____

**Kate asked some friends how many movies they saw last winter. Use her data for 2 and 3.**

| Movies Seen Last Winter |
|---|
| 0, 1, 1, 2, 2, 3, 3, 3, 4, 4, 4, 4, 5, 5, 5, 5, 6, 6, 7, 7, 7, 8, 8, 9, 9, 17 |

2. Make a dot plot of the data. (Example 1)

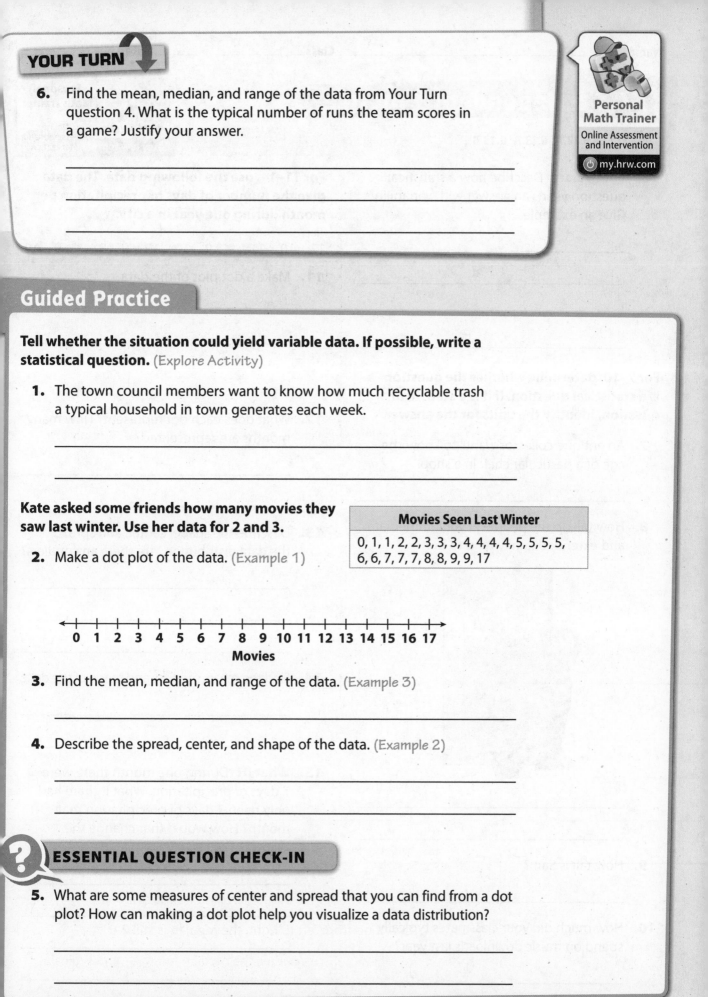

```
<---+--+--+--+--+--+--+--+--+--+--+--+--+--+--+--+--+--+--->
    0  1  2  3  4  5  6  7  8  9 10 11 12 13 14 15 16 17
                          Movies
```

3. Find the mean, median, and range of the data. (Example 3)

_____

4. Describe the spread, center, and shape of the data. (Example 2)

_____

_____

**? ESSENTIAL QUESTION CHECK-IN**

5. What are some measures of center and spread that you can find from a dot plot? How can making a dot plot help you visualize a data distribution?

_____

_____

# 17.3 Independent Practice

**TEKS** 6.12.A, 6.13.A, 6.13.B

Personal
Math Trainer

Online
Assessment and
Intervention

my.hrw.com

**6.** **Vocabulary** Describe how a statistical question yields an answer with variability. Give an example.

_____

_____

_____

_____

**For 7–10, determine whether the question is a statistical question. If it is a statistical question, identify the units for the answer.**

**7.** An antique collector wants to know the age of a particular chair in a shop.

_____

**8.** How tall do the people in your immediate and extended family tend to be?

_____

_____

**9.** How tall is Sam?

_____

**10.** How much did your classmates typically spend on music downloads last year?

_____

**For 11–14, use the following data. The data give the number of days of precipitation per month during one year in a city.**

12  10  11  9  9  10  12  9  8  7  9  10

**11.** Make a dot plot of the data.

←——+——+——+——+——+——+——+——+——+——+——+——+——→

**12.** What does each dot represent? How many months are represented?

_____

_____

**13.** Describe the shape, center, and spread of the data distribution. Are there any outliers?

_____

_____

_____

**14.** Find the mean, median, and range of the data.

_____

_____

**15.** **What If?** During one month there were 7 days of precipitation. What if there had only been 3 days of precipitation that month? How would that change the measures of center?

_____

_____

_____

_____

**For 16 and 17, use the dot plot of the number of cars sold at a car dealership per week during the first half of the year.**

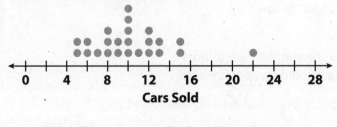

Cars Sold

**16.** Find the mean, median, and range.

Mean = _____    Median = _____

Range = _____

**17.** The owner of the car dealership decides to treat the value 22 as an outlier. Which measure of center or spread is affected the most if the owner removes this outlier? Explain.

_____

_____

_____

**18.** How many cars are sold in a typical week at the dealership? Explain.

_____

_____

**19.** Write an expression that represents the total number of cars sold during the first half of the year.

_____

_____

**20.** Describe the spread, center, and shape of the data distribution.

_____

_____

_____

_____

**21.** Vocabulary Explain how you can tell the frequency of a data value by looking at a dot plot.

_____

_____

**For 22–26 use the following data. The data give the number of runs scored by opponents of the Boston Red Sox in June 2010.**

4, 4, 9, 0, 2, 4, 1, 2, 11, 8, 2, 2, 5, 3, 2, 5, 6, 4, 0

**22.** Make a dot plot for the data.

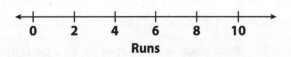

Runs

**23.** How many games did the Boston Red Sox play in June 2010? Explain.

_____

_____

**24.** Which data value in your dot plot has the greatest frequency? Explain what that frequency means for this data.

_____

_____

_____

**25.** Find the mean, median, and range of the data.

_____

_____

**26.** What is a statistical question that you could answer using the dot plot? Answer your question and justify your response.

_____

_____

_____

_____

**27.** A pediatrician records the ages of the patients seen in one day:
1, 2, 5, 7, 9, 17, 13, 16, 18, 12, 3, 5, 1.

**a. Explain the Error** Assuming that some of the patients are infants who are less than 1 year old, what information did the pediatrician forget to write down?

_____

**b. Critical Thinking** Can you make a dot plot of the pediatrician's data? Can you find the mean, median, and range? Why or why not?

_____

_____

_____

**28. Multistep** A nurse measured a patient's heart rate at different times over several days.

| Heart Rate (beats per minute) |
|---|
| 86, 87, 89, 87, 86, 88, 90, |
| 85, 82, 86, 83, 85, 84, 86 |

**a.** Make a dot plot.

**b.** Describe the shape, center, and spread of the data. Then find the mean, median, range, and IQR for the data.

_____

_____

_____

_____

**c. What If?** The nurse collected the data when the patient was resting. How might the dot plot and the measures change if the nurse collects the data when the patient is exercising?

_____

_____

**TEKS**
**Measurement and data— 6.12.A** Represent numeric data graphically, including . . . stem-and-leaf plots [and] histograms. . . . *Also 6.12.B, 6.13.A*

**?** **ESSENTIAL QUESTION**

How can you display data in a stem-and-leaf plot and in a histogram?

---

**EXPLORE ACTIVITY**  **TEKS 6.12.A**

## Making a Stem-and-Leaf Plot

You can use a **stem-and-leaf plot** to display numeric data. Each data value consists of a stem and a leaf.

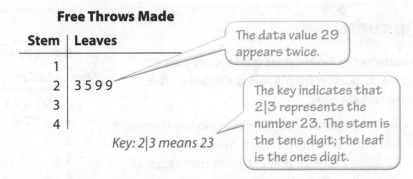

The 12 members of the high-school basketball team have a free-throw drill. Each player attempts 50 free throws. The number of free throws made by each player is given.

44, 35, 29, 25, 33, 36, 35, 23, 30, 29, 19, 32

**A** Group the data by tens digits. Then order the data from least to greatest.

19 23 25 29 29 30 32 ____ ____ ____ ____ ____

**B** Organize the data in a stem-and-leaf plot.

Use the tens digits as stems. Use the ones digits as leaves. Write the leaves in increasing order.

**Free Throws Made**

| Stem | Leaves |
|------|--------|
| 1 | |
| 2 | 3 5 9 9 |
| 3 | |
| 4 | |

*Key: 2|3 means 23*

> The data value 29 appears twice.

> The key indicates that 2|3 represents the number 23. The stem is the tens digit; the leaf is the ones digit.

## Reflect

**1.** Where are most of the data values? How can you tell from looking at the stem-and-leaf plot?

_____

_____

# Analyzing a Stem-and-Leaf Plot

A stem-and-leaf plot gives a picture of the distribution of a set of data. You can find measures of center and spread from a stem-and-leaf plot.

## EXAMPLE 1 ⓡ Real World

**TEKS** 6.12.A, 6.12.B

**Val's quiz scores are shown in the stem-and-leaf plot.**

**Ⓐ** Find the median and the mean.

**Median:** There are 15 quiz scores. The median is the eighth value.

Count the leaves from the top until you reach the 8th leaf.

The median is 87 because the 8th value has a stem of 8 and a leaf of 7.

**Mean:** Find the sum of the data values and divide by 15.

**Val's Quiz Scores**

| Stem | Leaves |
|------|--------|
| 3 | 2 |
| 4 | |
| 5 | |
| 6 | |
| 7 | 0 5 5 |
| 8 | 2 4 4 7 7 7 |
| 9 | 0 0 3 5 9 |

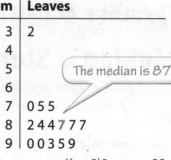

The median is 87.

*Key: 3|2 means 32*

$$\frac{32 + 70 + 75 + 75 + 82 + 84 + 84 + 87 + 87 + 87 + 90 + 90 + 93 + 95 + 99}{15} = \frac{1{,}230}{15} = 82$$

The mean is 82.

**Ⓑ** Which measure of center better represents the data? Justify your answer.

Look at the shape of the distribution. The quiz score of 32 is much lower than the other scores, so it is an outlier.

If the outlier were not included, the mean score would be higher. The median, 87, better represents the data.

### Math Talk
**Mathematical Processes**

A stem-and-leaf plot shows rows for all intervals, even ones without leaves. How does this help you see the shape of the data distribution?

## YOUR TURN

**The number of home runs a baseball player hit in each season he played is shown in the stem-and-leaf plot.**

2. How many seasons are included in the stem-and-leaf plot? What is the least number of home runs the baseball player had in one season?

_____

3. Find the median and the mean. Which measure of center better represents the data? Justify your answer.

_____

_____

**Home Runs**

| Stem | Leaves |
|------|--------|
| 0 | 0 5 5 7 7 8 9 |
| 1 | 0 0 7 9 |
| 2 | |
| 3 | |
| 4 | 4 |

*Key: 1|7 means 17*

# Using a Histogram

A **histogram** is a type of bar graph whose bars represent the frequencies of numeric data within intervals.

Math On the Spot
⏱ my.hrw.com

## EXAMPLE 2 · Real World

TEKS 6.12.A, 6.13.A

A birdwatcher counts and records the number of birds at a birdfeeder every morning at 9:00 for several days.

12, 3, 8, 1, 1, 6, 10, 14, 3, 6, 2, 1, 3, 2, 7

**A** Make a histogram of the data.

  **STEP 1**  Make a frequency table.

Divide the data into equal-sized intervals of 4. Make a frequency table.

| Interval | Frequency |
|----------|-----------|
| 1–4 | 8 |
| 5–8 | 4 |
| 9–12 | 2 |
| 13–16 | 1 |

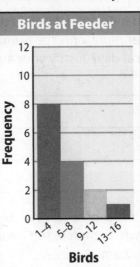

**STEP 2**  Make a histogram.

The intervals are listed along the horizontal axis. The vertical axis shows the frequencies. For each interval, draw a bar to show the number of days in that interval. The bars should have equal widths. They should touch but not overlap.

**B** What does the shape of the distribution tell you about the situation?

The highest bar is for the interval 1–4, which means that on more than half the days (8 out of 15), the birdwatcher saw only 1–4 birds at the feeder. The bars decrease in height, so it was more likely for the birdwatcher to see fewer birds.

### Math Talk
**Mathematical Processes**

How does the histogram show the number of days the birdwatcher counted birds at the feeder?

## YOUR TURN

**4.** Kim has started rating each movie she sees using a scale of 1 to 10 on an online site. Here are her ratings so far:

6, 9, 8, 5, 7, 4, 8, 8, 3, 7, 8, 7, 5, 1, 10

Make a histogram of the data. What does the shape of the distribution tell you about Kim's rating?

_____

_____

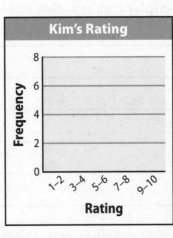

**Personal Math Trainer**

Online Assessment and Intervention

⏱ my.hrw.com

Wendy kept track of the number of text messages she sent each day for two weeks. Use her data for 1 and 2.

**Wendy's Text Messages**
**35, 20, 46, 29, 27, 33, 15, 52, 27, 30, 35, 24, 34, 42.**

1. Complete the stem-and-leaf plot. (Explore Activity)

2. Find the mean and median of Wendy's data. Which measure of center, if any, better represents the number of text messages she sent on a typical day? Justify your answer. (Example 1)

_____

_____

_____

_____

**Wendy's Text Messages**

| Stem | Leaves |
|------|--------|
|      |        |

*Key:*

3. Ed counted the number of seats available in each café in his town. Complete the frequency table and the histogram. (Example 2)

18, 20, 22, 26, 10, 12, 16, 18, 7, 8

| Interval | Frequency |
|----------|-----------|
| 1–7      |           |
| 8–14     |           |
| 15–21    |           |
| 22–28    |           |

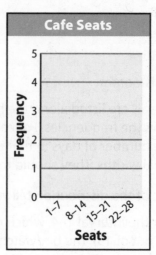

**Cafe Seats**

?  **ESSENTIAL QUESTION CHECK-IN**

4. How can you display data in a stem-and-leaf plot and in a histogram?

_____

_____

_____

_____

_____

# 17.4 Independent Practice

TEKS 6.12.A, 6.12.B, 6.13.A

Personal Math Trainer

Online Assessment and Intervention

my.hrw.com

**An amusement park employee records the ages of the people who ride the new roller coaster during a fifteen–minute period.**

**Ages of riders: 47, 16, 16, 35, 45, 43, 11, 29, 31, 50, 23, 18, 18, 20, 29, 17, 18, 48, 56, 24, 18, 21, 38, 12, 23.**

**5.** Complete the frequency table. Then make a histogram of the data.

| Interval | Frequency |
|----------|-----------|
| 10–19    |           |
|          |           |
|          |           |
|          |           |
|          |           |

**Roller Coaster Riders**

**6.** Describe two things you know about the riders who are represented by the data.

_____

_____

_____

_____

**7.** Use the same data to make a stem-and-leaf plot.

**8.** Find the mean, median, and range of the data.

_____

**9.** How are the two displays similar? How are they different?

_____

_____

_____

_____

**Roller Coaster Rider Ages**

| Stem | Leaves |
|------|--------|
|      |        |

*Key:*

**10.** West Middle School has classes of many different sizes during first period. The number of students in each class is shown.

9, 23, 18, 14, 20, 26, 14, 18, 18, 12, 8, 13, 21, 22, 28, 10, 7, 19, 24, 20

**a.** Complete each frequency table.

| Interval | Frequency |
|----------|-----------|
| 1–5      |           |
|          |           |
|          |           |
|          |           |
|          |           |
|          |           |

| Interval | Frequency |
|----------|-----------|
| 0–9      |           |
|          |           |
|          |           |

**b.** Suppose you were to make a stem-and-leaf plot and a histogram of the data. Which frequency table would you use if you wanted the two displays to use the same intervals?

_____

_____

**11.** **Critical Thinking** The bars on a histogram all have the same height. What is true about the frequencies for the intervals? Give an example of a set of data that could be represented by such a histogram.

_____

_____

_____

**12.** **Multiple Representations** Suppose someone shows you a stem-and-leaf plot with data values ranging from 0 to 100.

**a.** What other types of displays that you learned about in this module could you use to show the data?

_____

**b.** What measures of center and spread could you find from the stem-and-leaf plot?

_____

TEKS
Measurement and data—6.12.D Summarize categorical data with numerical and graphical summaries, including the mode, ... relative frequency table, and the percent bar graph, and use these ... to describe the data distribution.

**?** **ESSENTIAL QUESTION**

How can you summarize and describe categorical data?

**EXPLORE ACTIVITY** Real World TEKS 6.12.D

# Describing Categorical Data

Some data are quantitative, such as height or number of siblings of all students in a class. Other data are qualitative, such as eye color or favorite type of music. **Categorical data** are data that are sorted into categories on the basis of qualitative characteristics.

You can use the *mode* to summarize or describe categorical data. The **mode** of a categorical data set is the category that occurs most often. If all categories have the same frequency, there is no mode.

**Karl sells red, blue, black, white, and green shirts online. One day Karl received orders for 4 red, 5 blue, 6 black, 6 white, and 3 green shirts.**

**A** Complete the dot plot of Karl's shirt orders for the day.

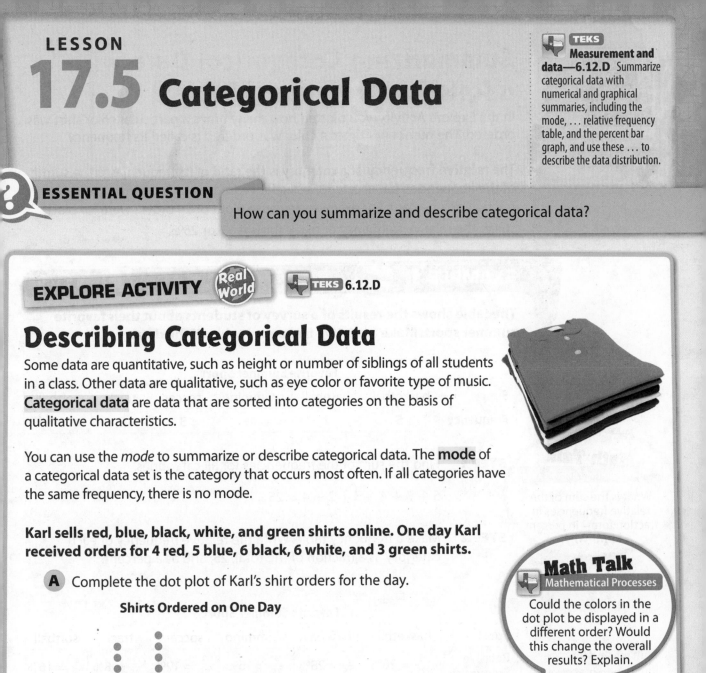

Shirts Ordered on One Day

Red   Blue   Black   White   Green

> **Math Talk**
> Mathematical Processes
>
> Could the colors in the dot plot be displayed in a different order? Would this change the overall results? Explain.

**B** Which shirt color or colors were the most and least popular that day?

_____

**C** Identify the mode(s) of the data. _____

## Reflect

**1. Justify Reasoning** Is it possible to find the mean or median of Karl's data set? Explain.

_____

_____

**Math On the Spot**

my.hrw.com

# Summarizing Categorical Data with a Relative Frequency Table

In the Explore Activity, you plotted how many times a particular color shirt was ordered. The number of times a color was ordered is called its frequency.

The **relative frequency** of a category is the ratio of its frequency to the sum of the frequencies for all categories. Relative frequency is often written as a fraction or a percent. For example, because 6 out of 24 orders were for black shirts, the relative frequency of black shirts is $\frac{6}{24}$ or 25%.

## EXAMPLE 1    Real World

TEKS 6.12.D

The table shows the results of a survey of students about their favorite summer sport. Make a relative frequency table of the data.

| Favorite Summer Sport | | | | | | |
|---|---|---|---|---|---|---|
| **Sport** | basketball | baseball | swimming | soccer | track | softball |
| **Frequency** | 5 | 7 | 4 | 3 | 2 | 4 |

**Math Talk**
Mathematical Processes

What is the sum of the relative frequencies in fraction form? in percent form? Why?

**STEP 1**   Find the sum of the frequencies for all categories.

$$5 + 7 + 4 + 3 + 2 + 4 = 25$$

**STEP 2**   Make a frequency table. Write the relative frequency of each category as a fraction of the total, 25, and as a percent.

Multiply numerator and denominator by 4:
$\frac{5 \times 4}{25 \times 4} = \frac{20}{100} = 20\%.$

| Favorite Summer Sport | | | | | | |
|---|---|---|---|---|---|---|
| **Sport** | basketball | baseball | swimming | soccer | track | softball |
| **Relative Frequency** | $\frac{5}{25} = 20\%$ | $\frac{7}{25} = 28\%$ | $\frac{4}{25} = 16\%$ | $\frac{3}{25} = 12\%$ | $\frac{2}{25} = 8\%$ | $\frac{4}{25} = 16\%$ |

## YOUR TURN

2. Chuy has 40 dimes, 20 pennies, 10 nickels, and 10 quarters in his coin jar. Make a relative frequency table of the coins in the jar.

| Coins in a Jar | | | | |
|---|---|---|---|---|
| **Type of coin** | | | | |
| **Relative frequency** | | | | |

**Personal Math Trainer**

Online Assessment and Intervention

my.hrw.com

# Using a Percent Bar Graph to Describe a Data Distribution

You can graph relative frequencies in a percent bar graph to help you visualize how the data are distributed.

Math On the Spot
my.hrw.com

## EXAMPLE 2  Real World

TEKS 6.12.D

The table shows the results of a survey taken in Mr. Jenk's music class about the students' favorite musical instruments. Make a percent bar graph. Then find the mode and describe how the data are distributed.

| Favorite Musical Instrument | | | | | | |
|---|---|---|---|---|---|---|
| Instrument | drums | guitar | bass | saxophone | trumpet | clarinet |
| Frequency | 6 | 5 | 3 | 3 | 2 | 1 |
| Relative frequency | $\frac{6}{20} = 30\%$ | $\frac{5}{20} = 25\%$ | $\frac{3}{20} = 15\%$ | $\frac{3}{20} = 15\%$ | $\frac{2}{20} = 10\%$ | $\frac{1}{20} = 5\%$ |

**STEP 1** Make a percent bar graph of the relative frequencies. The height of each bar shows the percent of students surveyed who favor that instrument.

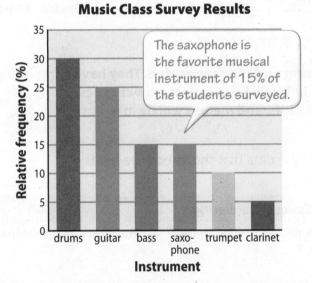

**Music Class Survey Results**

The saxophone is the favorite musical instrument of 15% of the students surveyed.

**STEP 2** The instrument mentioned most often is drums, so the mode is drums, although the guitar is nearly as popular. More than half the students (55%) favor drums or the guitar. About a third of students (30%) favor the bass or saxophone. All other students (15%) favor the trumpet or clarinet.

## Reflect

3. **Analyze Relationships** Why is it helpful to arrange the categories in the order of their relative frequencies?

_____

_____

_____

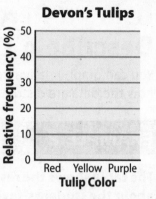

## YOUR TURN

**4.** Devon is growing tulips in his garden. He has 24 red tulips, 11 yellow tulips, and 15 purple tulips. Make a percent bar graph and describe the distribution.

_____

_____

_____

**Devon's Tulips**

| | |
|---|---|
| Relative frequency (%) | Red  Yellow  Purple |

**Tulip Color**

**Personal Math Trainer**
Online Assessment and Intervention
my.hrw.com

# Guided Practice

**Mrs. Valentine surveyed her class about their favorite summer activity. Four students chose reading, 7 chose movies, 7 chose sports, and 5 chose travel.** (Explore Activity)

**1.** Make a dot plot of the data.

**2.** Identify the mode(s) of the data set.

_____

**Favorite Summer Activities**

_____

Reading  Movies  Sports  Travel

**The garden club is planning their spring and summer garden. They have 20 plots. Tomatoes will be in 3 plots, kale will be in 5 plots, strawberries will be in 6 plots, zucchini will be in 2 plots, and melons will be in 4 plots.** (Examples 1 and 2)

**3.** Make a relative frequency table of the data that shows both fractions and percents.

| Summer Garden Plots | | | | | |
|---|---|---|---|---|---|
| **Plant** | tomatoes | kale | strawberries | zucchini | melons |
| **Relative frequency** | | | | | |

**4.** Make a percent bar graph of the relative frequencies of the garden plots.

**Summer Garden Plots**

| | |
|---|---|
| Relative frequency (%) | Tomatoes  Kale  Strawberries  Zucchini  Melons |

**Plant**

## ? ESSENTIAL QUESTION CHECK-IN

**5.** How can you calculate relative frequencies as percents?

_____

_____

_____

# 17.5 Independent Practice

**Mr. Anderson's fifth grade class is getting a class pet. Seven students vote to get a gerbil, 3 vote for a fish, 6 vote for a mouse, and 4 vote for a lizard.**

**6.** What is the mode of the data set? What does it mean for this situation?

_____

**7.** If each pet had received 9 votes, what would the mode have been?

_____

**8.** **Analyze Relationships** Make a dot plot of the data. Use the dot plot to describe the data.

_____

_____

_____   Gerbil   Fish   Mouse  Lizard

**9.** The service club sells snacks at school basketball games. In the first quarter they sell 6 servings of nachos, 4 bags of popcorn, 7 pieces of fruit, and 3 bags of nuts.

**a.** Make a relative frequency table. Include both fractions and percents.

| Snacks Sold in the First Quarter | | | |
|---|---|---|---|
| Snack | nachos | popcorn | fruit | nuts |
| Relative frequency | | | | |

**b.** **Analyze Relationships** Deloria says she can find the relative frequency of nuts based on another relative frequency. What might she be doing?

_____

_____

_____

**c.** **Draw Conclusions** If 9 bags of popcorn were sold rather than 4, which relative frequencies would be affected? Explain.

_____

_____

_____

**The percent bar graph shows the relative frequencies that resulted from of a survey about eye color.**

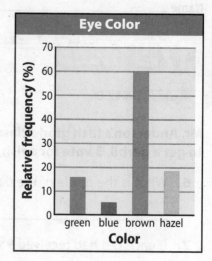

**10. Draw Conclusions** Can you tell from the bar graph how many people were surveyed? Why or why not?

_____

_____

_____

**11. Communicate Mathematical Ideas** Describe how the data are distributed.

_____

_____

_____

_____

**H.O.T.** FOCUS ON HIGHER ORDER THINKING

**12. What If?** Suppose 250 people were surveyed to create the eye color data shown in the graph for Exercises 10 and 11. How many people would have brown eyes? Justify your answer.

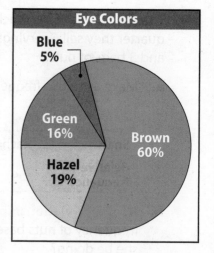

_____

**13. Multiple Representations** Describe how this circle graph is similar to and different from the percent bar graph shown for Exercises 10–11.

_____

_____

_____

_____

Work Area

**14. Justify Reasoning** Jayshree says the number of dots in a dot plot for Exercise 8 shows that the data is numeric and not categorical. Is she right? Explain. If not, what is her mistake?

_____

_____

_____

_____

# Ready to Go On?

## 17.1 Measures of Center

**1.** Find the mean and median of the data set. _____

| 2   5   9   11   17   19 |

## 17.2 Box Plots

**2.** Make a box plot for the data set.

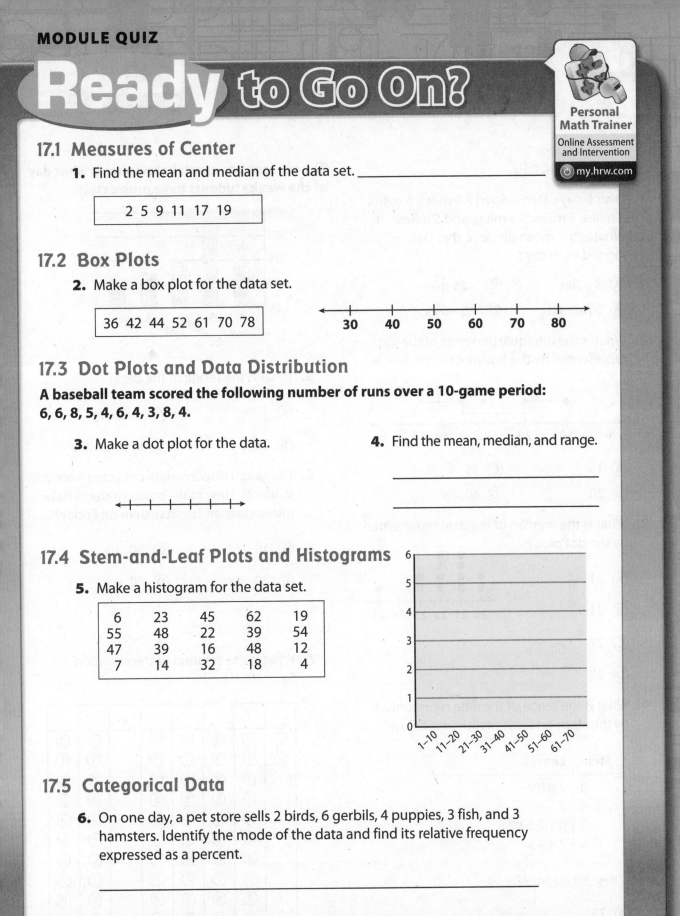

| 36   42   44   52   61   70   78 |

## 17.3 Dot Plots and Data Distribution

**A baseball team scored the following number of runs over a 10-game period:
6, 6, 8, 5, 4, 6, 4, 3, 8, 4.**

**3.** Make a dot plot for the data.

**4.** Find the mean, median, and range.

_____

_____

## 17.4 Stem-and-Leaf Plots and Histograms

**5.** Make a histogram for the data set.

| 6  | 23 | 45 | 62 | 19 |
| 55 | 48 | 22 | 39 | 54 |
| 47 | 39 | 16 | 48 | 12 |
| 7  | 14 | 32 | 18 | 4  |

## 17.5 Categorical Data

**6.** On one day, a pet store sells 2 birds, 6 gerbils, 4 puppies, 3 fish, and 3 hamsters. Identify the mode of the data and find its relative frequency expressed as a percent.

_____

**MODULE 17 MIXED REVIEW**

# Texas Test Prep

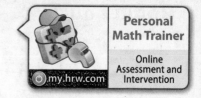

Personal
Math Trainer

Online
Assessment and
Intervention

my.hrw.com

## Selected Response

**1.** Over 6 days, Dan jogged 7.5 miles, 6 miles, 3 miles, 3 miles, 5.5 miles, and 5 miles. What is the mean distance that Dan jogged each day?

Ⓐ 3 miles     Ⓒ 5.25 miles

Ⓑ 5 miles     Ⓓ 7.5 miles

**2.** What is the interquartile range of the data represented by the box plot shown below?

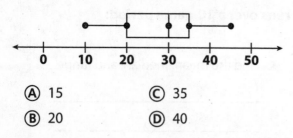

Ⓐ 15     Ⓒ 35

Ⓑ 20     Ⓓ 40

**3.** What is the median of the data represented by the dot plot?

Ⓐ 21

Ⓑ 21.5

Ⓒ 22

Ⓓ 25

20 21 22 23 24 25

**4.** What is the range of the data represented by the stem-and-leaf plot shown below?

| Stem | Leaves |
|------|--------|
| 3 | 7 8 8 9 |
| 4 | 3 |
| 5 | 0 1 2 2 3 7 8 |
| 6 | 2 4 4 5 |

Key: 3|7 means 37

Ⓐ 25     Ⓒ 28

Ⓑ 26     Ⓓ 65

**The percent bar graph below shows what day of the week students have music class.**

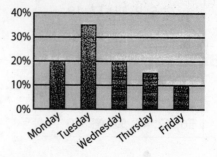

**5.** What is the mode of the data?

Ⓐ 20%     Ⓒ Tuesday

Ⓑ 35%     Ⓓ Wednesday

**6.** The graph displays data collected from 200 students. How many more students have music class on Tuesday than on Friday?

Ⓐ 10     Ⓒ 50

Ⓑ 20     Ⓓ 70

## Gridded Response

**7.** What is the solution of the equation $5x = 195.5$?

| ⊕ | ⓪ | ⓪ | ⓪ | ⓪ | • | ⓪ | ⓪ |
|---|---|---|---|---|---|---|---|
| ⊖ | ① | ① | ① | ① | | ① | ① |
| | ② | ② | ② | ② | | ② | ② |
| | ③ | ③ | ③ | ③ | | ③ | ③ |
| | ④ | ④ | ④ | ④ | | ④ | ④ |
| | ⑤ | ⑤ | ⑤ | ⑤ | | ⑤ | ⑤ |
| | ⑥ | ⑥ | ⑥ | ⑥ | | ⑥ | ⑥ |
| | ⑦ | ⑦ | ⑦ | ⑦ | | ⑦ | ⑦ |
| | ⑧ | ⑧ | ⑧ | ⑧ | | ⑧ | ⑧ |
| | ⑨ | ⑨ | ⑨ | ⑨ | | ⑨ | ⑨ |

# Study Guide Review

## MODULE 17 Displaying, Analyzing, and Summarizing Data

### Key Vocabulary
*box plot* (diagrama de caja)
*categorical data* (datos categóricos)
*dot plot* (diagrama de puntos)
*histogram* (histograma)
*interquartile range* (rango entre cuartiles)
*lower quartile* (cuartil inferior)
*mean* (media)
*median* (mediana)
*measure of center* (medida central)
*measure of spread* (medida de dispersión)
*mode* (moda)
*range* (rango)
*relative frequency* (frecuencia relativa)
*statistical question* (pregunta estadística)
*upper quartile* (cuartil superior)

**? ESSENTIAL QUESTION**

How can you solve real-world problems by displaying, analyzing, and summarizing data?

### EXAMPLE 1

**The ages of Thomas's neighbors are shown.**

| Ages of Thomas's Neighbors |
|---|
| 30, 48, 31, 45, 42, 32, 32, 38, 34, 50, 49, 48 |

**Make a box plot of the data.**

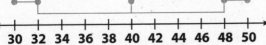

30  31  **32  32**  34  **38  42**  45  **48  48**  49  50

Lower quartile = 32    Median = 40    Upper quartile = 48

30 32 34 36 38 40 42 44 46 48 50

### EXAMPLE 2

**Find the mean, median, and range of the data shown on the dot plot.**

9 10 11 12 13 14 15 16 17

The mean is 13.    $\dfrac{2(9) + 4(13) + 5(14) + 16}{12} = 13$

The median is 13.5.    9, 9, 13, 13, 13, <u>13, 14</u>, 14, 14, 14, 14, 16

The range is 7.    $16 - 9 = 7$

### EXERCISES

1. Find the mean and median of the data set: 4, 6, 2, 8, 14, 2. _____

2. The number of goals for the 13 players on a soccer team are 4, 9, 0, 1, 1, 2, 0, 0, 2, 8, 8, 3, 1. Find the median, lower quartile, and upper quartile. Then make a box plot for the data. (Lesson 17.2) _____

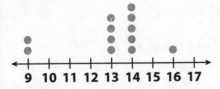

0 1 2 3 4 5 6 7 8 9 10

**3.** Use the dot plot to find the mean, median, and range of the data. (Lesson 17.3)

mean _____ median _____ range _____

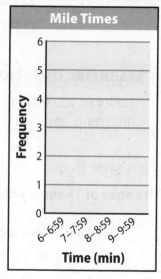

17 18 19 20 21 22 23

**4.** The coach recorded the time it took 14 students to run a mile. The times are as follows: 9:23, 8:15, 9:23, 9:01, 6:45, 6:55, 7:20, 9:14, 6:21, 7:12, 7:34, 6:10, 9:15, 9:18. (Lesson 17.4)

Use the data to complete the frequency table. Then use the table to make a histogram.

| Interval | Frequency |
|----------|-----------|
| 6–6:59 | |
| | |
| | |
| | |

**Mile Times**

Frequency (0–6) vs Time (min): 6–6:59, 7–7:59, 8–8:59, 9–9:59

**5.** The 16 students in Mr. Wu's algebra class took a survey on their favorite color. The results are shown in the frequency table. (Lesson 17.5)

| Favorite Color | | | | |
|----------|------|-------|--------|-----|
| Color | blue | green | yellow | red |
| Frequency | 5 | 4 | 3 | 4 |

Make a relative frequency table of the data that shows each data item as a fraction of the total and as a percent.

| Blue | Green | Yellow | Red |
|------|-------|--------|-----|
| | | | |

# Unit 6 Performance Tasks

**1.** **CAREERS IN MATH** **Geneticist** Kinesha collects data about the eye colors of the students in her science class.

**a.** Which measure or measures of center are appropriate for this data? Explain your answer.

_____

_____

**b.** Which measure or measures of variation are appropriate for this data? Explain your answer.

_____

_____

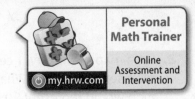
## Selected Response

**1.** Over 6 days, Jim jogged 6.5 miles, 5 miles, 3 miles, 2 miles, 3.5 miles, and 4 miles. What is the mean distance that Jim jogged each day?

Ⓐ 3.75 miles     Ⓒ 4.5 miles

Ⓑ 4 miles     Ⓓ 6.5 miles

**2.** What is the range of the data represented by the stem-and-leaf plot shown below?

| Stem | Leaf |
|------|------|
| 3 | 3 5 7 9 |
| 4 | 8 9 |
| 5 | 1 1 2 3 3 5 6 |
| 6 | 0 3 7 9 |

Key: $\frac{3}{5}$ means 35

Ⓐ 27

Ⓑ 30

Ⓒ 33

Ⓓ 36

**3.** The percent bar graph below shows the day of the week on which students have their weekly spelling quiz. On which day do most students have their weekly spelling quiz?

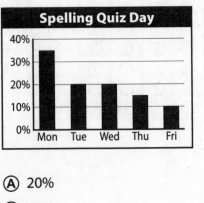

**Spelling Quiz Day**

Ⓐ 20%

Ⓑ 35%

Ⓒ Tuesday

Ⓓ Monday

**4.** The ages of the volunteers at a local food bank are shown below.

34, 25, 24, 50, 18, 46, 43, 36, 32

What is the median of this set of data?

Ⓐ 32     Ⓒ 34

Ⓑ 33.1     Ⓓ 50

**5.** The dot plot shows the number of participants in each age group in a science fair.

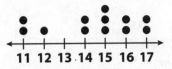

11 12 13 14 15 16 17

Which of the following is **not** supported by the dot plot?

Ⓐ The range is 6.

Ⓑ The mean of the ages is about 14.4.

Ⓒ The mode of the ages is 13.

Ⓓ The median of the ages is 15.

**6.** Which expression shows the prime factorization of 120?

Ⓐ $2^3 \times 3 \times 5$

Ⓑ $2 \times 3 \times 5$

Ⓒ $10^{12}$

Ⓓ $2 \times 5 \times 12$

**7.** The two longer sides of a triangle measure 22 units and 29 units. Which of the following is a possible length of the shortest side?

Ⓐ 4     Ⓒ 24

Ⓑ 14     Ⓓ 34

**8.** On a map of the city, 1 centimeter represents 2.5 miles. What distance on the map would represent 20 miles?

   Ⓐ 6 centimeters

   Ⓑ 8 centimeters

   Ⓒ 12 centimeters

   Ⓓ 18 centimeters

**9.** Which expression is equal to 0?

   Ⓐ $\dfrac{-56}{7} - 8$

   Ⓑ $\dfrac{-56}{-7} + 8$

   Ⓒ $\dfrac{56}{7} + 8$

   Ⓓ $\dfrac{-56}{-7} - 8$

## Gridded Response

**10.** What is the median of the data represented by the dot plot?

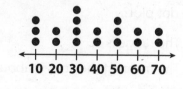

**11.** The heights (in inches) of 8 students are 50, 53, 52, 68, 54, 49, 55, and 51. What is the mean height if the outlier is removed from the data?

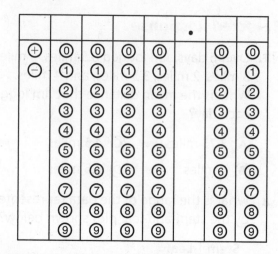

> **Hot Tip!** Read a graph or diagram as closely as you read the actual test question. These visual aids contain important information.

**12.** What is the interquartile range of the data represented by the box plot shown below?

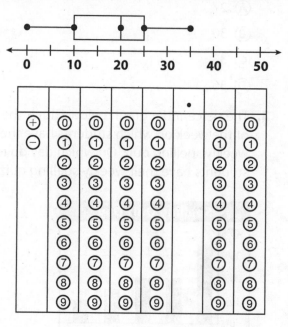

# Personal Financial Literacy

## CAREERS IN MATH

**Bicycle Tour Operator** A bike tour operator organizes cycling trips for tourists all over the world. Bike tour operators use math to calculate expenses, determine rates, and compute payroll information for their employees. If tours include travel in another country, operators must understand how to calculate currency exchange rates.

If you are interested in a career as a bicycle tour operator, you should study these mathematical subjects:
- Basic Math
- Business Math

Research other careers that require the understanding of business mathematics.

**Unit 7 Performance Task**

At the end of the unit, check out how **bicycle tour operators** use math.

# Vocabulary Preview

**Use the puzzle to preview key vocabulary from this unit. Unscramble the circled letters to answer the riddle at the bottom of the page.**

Plastic payment card you can use to purchase goods or services; the money is deducted immediately from your bank account. (Lesson 18-1)

__ __ __ (__) __     __ __ __ __ __

The summary of information about how well you manage your money and pay your bills. (Lesson 18-2)

__ __ (__) __ __     __ __ __ __ (__) __

Plastic payment card you can use to make purchases and pay for them later in a bill at the end of the month. (Lesson 18-1)

__ (__) __ (__) __ __     __ __ __ __

A number calculated by information in credit reports and credit history to determine the quality of your credit. (Lesson 18-2)

(__) __ __ __ __ __     __ (__) __ __ __ __

College funding awarded to students based on achievement. (Lesson 18-3)

__ __ __ __ (__) __ __ (__) __ __ __

College funding from the government or other organizations, usually for students who need money the most. (Lesson 18-3)

__ __ (__) __ __ __ __

**Q:** Where can you always find money?

**A:** in the __ __ __ __ __ __ __ __ __ __

# Becoming a Knowledgeable Consumer and Investor

**? ESSENTIAL QUESTION**

How can you become a knowledgeable consumer and investor?

**Real-World Video**

Your spending and saving habits can help you save for expenses such as college tuition. Debit cards, credit cards, and ATMs make it easy to buy things, but responsible spending can protect your future.

my.hrw.com

**GO DIGITAL**
my.hrw.com

**my.hrw.com**
Go digital with your write-in student edition, accessible on any device.

**Math On the Spot**
Scan with your smart phone to jump directly to the online edition, video tutor, and more.

**Animated Math**
Interactively explore key concepts to see how math works.

**Personal Math Trainer**
Get immediate feedback and help as you work through practice sets.

# Are YOU Ready?

Complete these exercises to review skills you will need for this chapter.

## Fractions, Decimals, Percents

**EXAMPLE**   Write $\frac{3}{4}$ as a decimal and a percent.

$$4)\overline{3.00}$$
$$\begin{array}{r} 0.75 \\ \underline{-28} \\ 20 \\ \underline{-20} \\ 0 \end{array}$$

Write the fraction as a division problem.

Write a decimal point and zeros in the dividend.

Place a decimal point in the quotient.

$0.75 = 75\%$   Write the decimal as a percent.

**Write the fraction as a decimal and a percent.**

1. $\frac{1}{4}$ _____

2. $\frac{4}{5}$ _____

3. $\frac{1}{10}$ _____

4. $\frac{5}{8}$ _____

## Decimal Operations

**EXAMPLE**   $6.3 + 14.67 \rightarrow$
$$\begin{array}{r} 6.30 \\ +14.67 \\ \hline 20.97 \end{array}$$

To add decimals, align the decimal points.

Add zeros if necessary.

**Find the sum.**

5. $4.9 + 26.78$

6. $3 + 13.792$

7. $65.8 + 88.39$

8. $2.789 + 58.3$

_____   _____   _____   _____

## Find the Percent of a Number

**EXAMPLE**   $40\%$ of $66 = ?$

$40\% = 0.40$   Write the percent as a decimal.

$$\begin{array}{r} 66 \\ \times 0.4 \\ \hline 26.4 \end{array}$$   Multiply.

**Find the percent.**

9. $20\%$ of $50$ _____

10. $8\%$ of $72$ _____

11. $35\%$ of $240$ _____

12. $14\%$ of $18$ _____

13. $145\%$ of $80$ _____

14. $4.3\%$ of $700$ _____

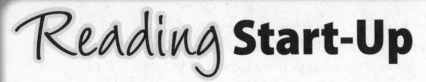

# Reading Start-Up

## Visualize Vocabulary

**Use the ✔ words to complete the graphic.**

**You and Your Bank**

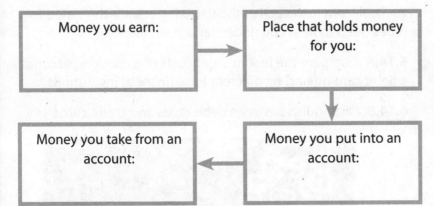

| Money you earn: | → | Place that holds money for you: |
| Money you take from an account: | ← | Money you put into an account: |

## Understand Vocabulary

**Complete the sentences using the preview words.**

1. When you use a _____, the money you spend is deducted immediately from your checking or savings account.

   When you use a _____, you pay for your purchases later.

2. A _____ includes information about how well you manage money.

3. Banks use your _____ to decide whether to give you a loan or credit card.

## Vocabulary

### Review Words
✔ bank *(banco)*
career *(carrera)*
✔ deposit *(depósito)*
✔ income *(ingreso)*
✔ salary *(salario)*
✔ withdrawal *(retirada)*

### Preview Words
checking account *(cuenta corriente)*
credit card *(tarjeta de crédito)*
credit history *(historia crediticia)*
credit report *(crediticio informe)*
credit score *(calificación crediticia)*
debit card *(tarjeta de débito)*
grant *(beca)*
scholarships *(becas)*
work-study programs *(programas de trabajo y estudio)*

## Active Reading

**Tri-Fold** Before beginning the module, create a tri-fold to help you learn the concepts and vocabulary in this module. Fold the paper into three sections. Label the columns "What I Know," "What I Need to Know," and "What I Learned." Complete the first two columns before you read. After studying the chapter, complete the third column.

# Unpacking the TEKS

Understanding the TEKS and the vocabulary terms in the TEKS will help you know exactly what you are expected to learn in this module.

## TEKS 6.14

Develop an economic way of thinking and problem solving useful in one's life as a knowledgeable consumer and investor.

### Key Vocabulary

**debit card** *(tarjeta de débito)*
A plastic card used to purchase goods or services. The money is deducted immediately from your account.

**credit card** *(tarjeta de crédito)*
A plastic card used to purchase goods or services. You receive a monthly bill, and you will pay interest on any balance you carry.

**grant** *(beca)*
Money awarded to students that does not need to be repaid.

**work-study program** *(programas de trabajo y estudio)*
Job on campus or at local organizations that pay toward tuition.

**scholarship** *(becas)*
Money awarded to students based on achievement.

## What It Means to You

You will learn how each of the following standards related to 6.14 is designed to help you understand your finances.

**6.14.A** Compare the features and costs of a checking account and a debit card offered by different local financial institutions.

**6.14.B** Distinguish between debit cards and credit cards.

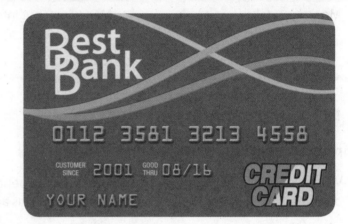

**6.14.C** Balance a check register that includes deposits, withdrawals, and transfers.

**6.14.G** Explain various methods to pay for college, including through savings, grants, scholarships, student loans, and work-study.

**6.14.H** Compare the annual salary of several occupations requiring various levels of post-secondary education or vocational training and calculate the effects of the different annual salaries on lifetime income.

Visit **my.hrw.com** to see all the **TEKS** unpacked.

my.hrw.com

# LESSON
# 18.1 Choosing a Bank

**TEKS**
**Personal financial literacy—**
**6.14.A** Compare the features and costs of a checking account and a debit card offered by different local financial institutions. *Also 6.14.B, 6.14.C*

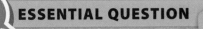

**? ESSENTIAL QUESTION**

How do you compare services offered by different banks?

**EXPLORE ACTIVITY 1**  **TEKS** 6.14.A

## Comparing the Costs of Checking Accounts and Debit Cards

You can withdraw money from your bank account in several ways. With a **checking account**, you write checks or use a debit card to withdraw money. A **debit card** is a plastic card you can use to purchase goods or services. When you use a debit card, the money you spend is deducted immediately from your checking or savings account.

> **Math Talk**
> Mathematical Processes
>
> Margaret wants to open a new checking account. What are some things she should consider when choosing a bank?

**A** The table shows the fees for certain features at two banks. Complete the table to show which bank has the better deal for each feature.

|  | Township Bank fees | Peachtree Bank fees | Better deal |
|---|---|---|---|
| **Checks** | $0.50 per check | free |  |
| **ATM transactions (nonbank ATM)** | $1 per withdrawal | $2 per withdrawal |  |
| **ATM transactions (bank ATM)** | free | free |  |
| **Debit cards** | $2.50 per month | $0.50 per withdrawal |  |

**B** During one month, Carmen wrote 4 checks and used her debit card for two nonbank ATM transactions. Which bank is better for her? Explain.

_____

_____

_____

_____

# Debit Cards or Credit Cards?

A **credit card** is a plastic payment card you can use to purchase goods or services. Using a credit card is like getting a loan. You pay for your purchases later when you receive a monthly bill. You also pay interest on the balance.

**Sam and Kong bought identical guitars that cost $600. Sam paid for his guitar with his debit card so $600 was deducted from his checking account on the day of the purchase. Kong charged his guitar on his credit card. He made payments each month until the guitar was paid off. Over time, he paid the credit card company $600 plus an additional $32 in interest.**

**A** Describe how the payment methods used by Sam and Kong to pay for their guitars affected the amount of money they had in the bank.

_____

_____

_____

_____

**B** The table shows some features of debit cards and credit cards. Write A next to the features you think are advantages. Write D next to the features you think are disadvantages.

| Debit Cards | | Credit Cards | |
|---|---|---|---|
| Do not have to carry cash or a checkbook | _____ | Balances can quickly increase and be difficult to pay off each month. | _____ |
| May include a fee for each purchase | _____ | May include a yearly fee | _____ |
| Need a PIN to access the account | _____ | Statements provide a record of expenses. | _____ |
| Need enough money in account to cover the cost of purchases | _____ | Can make purchases without having money to cover the full price | _____ |
| Easy access to cash at ATM machines | _____ | Must pay interest on any unpaid monthly balance | _____ |

**C** Jolene bought a new helmet from the bike shop. She recorded her purchase in her check register. Which type of card did she use? Explain.

_____

_____

_____

## Reflect

1. **Analyze Relationships** Terrance has $54.29 in his checking account. He needs to purchase a football uniform for $56.50. Should Terrance use his debit card or his credit card? Explain your reasoning.

_____

_____

---

**EXPLORE ACTIVITY 3**  Real World    TEKS 6.14.C

# Balancing a Check Register

Your checkbook includes a check register to help you keep track of deposits, withdrawals, and transfers. Your balance tells you how much money is actually in your account. To balance the check register, add deposits to the balance and subtract withdrawals and transfers from the balance.

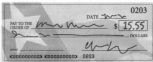

**The check register shows Annie's checking account transactions.**

| Check # | Date | Transaction | Deposit | | Withdrawal | | Balance | |
|---------|------|-------------|---------|---|------------|---|---------|---|
| | | beginning balance | | | | | $236 | 75 |
| | 2/1 | deposit (lawn mowing money) | $25 | 00 | | | $261 | 75 |
| 202 | 2/9 | beauty salon | | | $28 | 29 | $233 | 46 |
| | 2/12 | transfer to savings account | | | $20 | 00 | | |
| | 2/20 | ATM withdrawal | | | $40 | 00 | | |
| | 2/20 | ATM fee | | | $1 | 00 | | |
| | | | | | | | | |
| | | | | | | | | |

> Add the deposit to the beginning balance.

> Subtract the withdrawal from the previous balance.

**A** Complete the check register to show Annie's balance after the transfer and the ATM withdrawal.

**B** Add these transactions to Annie's check register.

- deposited $25.00 dog walking money on 2/24

- wrote a check to The Sport Resort for $15.55 on 2/28

**Animated Math**

my.hrw.com

**Use the table for Exercise 1.** (Explore Activity 1)

1. Graciella is shopping for a bank. She does not write checks or use the ATM. She pays for lunch with her debit card 20 times each month.

   **a.** What services does Graciella use?

   _____

   **b.** Calculate her monthly costs.

   _____

   **c.** Which bank is a better deal for her? Explain.

   _____

   _____

|  | A+ Bank | NextGen Bank |
|---|---|---|
| Checks | $0.25 each | free |
| Monthly checking fee | $1 | none |
| ATM fee | free | $1.50 |
| Debit card fee | $2.50 per month | $0.50 per withdrawal |

**Which type of card was used, debit or credit? Explain.** (Explore Activity 2)

2. Carol bought art supplies at the craft store. She paid for the supplies at the end of the month.

   _____

3. Stephen wanted a mouth guard for football that costs $23. He bought a less expensive guard so he would not overdraw his account.

   _____

4. Fill in the missing items in the check register. (Explore Activity 3)

| Check # | Date | Transaction | Deposit | | Withdrawal | | Balance | |
|---|---|---|---|---|---|---|---|---|
| | | beginning balance | | | | | $311 | 25 |
| | 12/1 | deposit (allowance) | $25 | 00 | | | $336 | 25 |
| 180 | 12/2 | Rick's Barber shop | | | $15 | 00 | | |
| | 12/6 | transfer to savings account | | | $40 | 00 | | |
| | 12/12 | ATM withdrawal | | | $20 | 00 | | |
| | 12/15 | deposit (allowance) | $25 | 00 | | | | |

**?** **ESSENTIAL QUESTION CHECK-IN**

5. What information do you need to compare the services of different banks?

   _____

   _____

# 18.1 Independent Practice

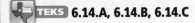

TEKS 6.14.A, 6.14.B, 6.14.C

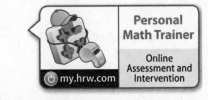

**Personal Math Trainer**

Online Assessment and Intervention

my.hrw.com

**Use the table for Exercises 6–10.**

|  | First City Bank | Transnational Bank | Hometown Bank |
|---|---|---|---|
| **Checks** | free checks | $5 per month checking fee | $0.50 per check |
| **ATM transactions** | $1 per transaction | no ATM fees | bank ATM: free nonbank ATM: $2 per transaction |
| **Debit cards** | $0.25 per debit card transaction | $0.25 per debit card transaction | no debit card fees |

6. **Draw Conclusions** Compare the check and debit card fees at Hometown Bank. When would it be cheaper to use checks and not a debit card?

_____

_____

7. **Multistep** Charlie has a checking account at Transnational Bank. In December he wrote 4 checks and made 3 debit card transactions. Would Charlie's monthly fee be cheaper if his account were at First City Bank? Explain.

_____

_____

8. **Multiple Representations** Kim has an account at Hometown Bank. In March, she paid $16 in ATM fees. Write an equation showing the number of times she used a nonbank ATM.

_____

9. **What If?** The balance in Jake's checking account is $45.55. What would happen if he wrote 3 checks for $20 each? Show your work.

_____

_____

10. **Critique Reasoning** First City Bank's TV commercial states they offer the best deal because they do not charge for checks. Do you agree? Explain.

_____

_____

**11.** Enter the following information into the check register. Balance the check register.

- deposit of $150.00 on 4/1

- check 34 to Harv's Games for $65.98 on 4/3

- ATM withdrawal of $60 on 4/5

- ATM fee of $1.00 on 4/5

- transfer to savings account of $20 on 4/7

| Check # | Date | Transaction | Deposit | | Withdrawal | | Balance | |
|---------|------|-------------|---------|---|------------|---|---------|----|
| | | beginning balance | | | | | $300 | 00 |
| | | | | | | | | |
| | | | | | | | | |
| | | | | | | | | |
| | | | | | | | | |
| | | | | | | | | |

**FOCUS ON HIGHER ORDER THINKING**

Work Area

**12. What If?** Suppose you are offered a credit card that has 0% interest for 6 months and 25.9% interest after the introductory period. Why might you choose a credit card with 14.9% interest instead?

_____

_____

_____

**13. Critique Reasoning** Consider the following statement: "People who use credit cards always end up owing more money than they have. No one should use a credit card." Do you agree with this opinion? Explain your answer.

_____

_____

_____

_____

**14. Communicate Mathematical Ideas** Kate has a balance of $1,080 on her credit card. If she makes no purchases and pays $90 each month, will her credit card balance be paid off in a year? Explain.

_____

_____

**TEKS**
**Personal financial literacy—**
**6.14.D** Explain why it is important to establish a positive credit history.
*Also 6.14.E, 6.14.F*

## ESSENTIAL QUESTION

How do you establish a positive credit history?

**EXPLORE ACTIVITY 1** Real World  **TEKS** 6.14.D

# Establishing Credit History

Your **credit history** includes information about how well you manage your money and pay your bills. To build a positive credit history, you must first obtain a small loan or begin buying on credit. Then you must make regular payments to repay your debt.

Banks and other lenders use this information to decide whether they should loan you money for large purchases. Landlords use your credit history to decide whether or not to rent an apartment or house to you.

**Raphael's older brother has applied for a bank loan to buy a jet ski. Each statement below tells something about the brother's credit history. Decide whether the bank would regard each statement as a positive or negative factor in deciding whether to approve the loan application.**

**A** Pays credit card balance monthly and on time

_____

_____

**B** Recently lost his job and is looking for work

_____

_____

**C** Is currently repaying student loans and a loan to start a business

_____

_____

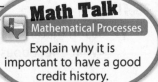
**Math Talk**
Mathematical Processes

Explain why it is important to have a good credit history.

**D** Answered all questions on the application honestly, even those that reflected poorly on his past credit history

_____

_____

# Credit Reports

**Credit reports** are compiled by agencies to help lenders decide whether or not to loan money to consumers. A credit report includes a person's credit history as well as personal information, employment background, and income.

**Sort the following information about Christina into the table.**

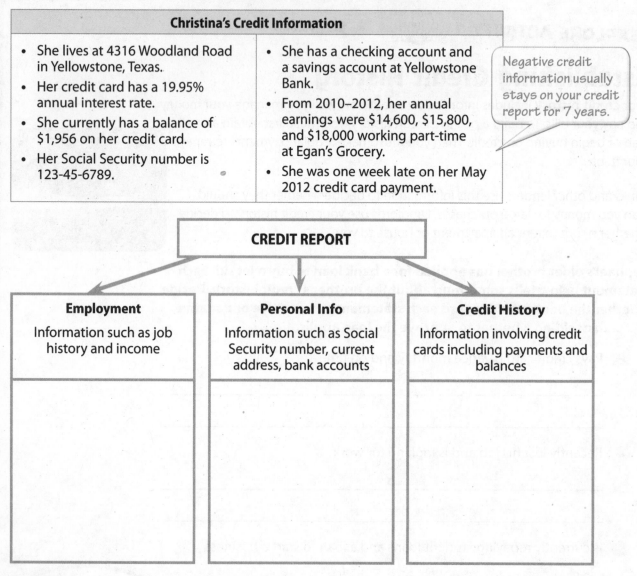

| Christina's Credit Information |
|---|

- She lives at 4316 Woodland Road in Yellowstone, Texas.
- Her credit card has a 19.95% annual interest rate.
- She currently has a balance of $1,956 on her credit card.
- Her Social Security number is 123-45-6789.

- She has a checking account and a savings account at Yellowstone Bank.
- From 2010–2012, her annual earnings were $14,600, $15,800, and $18,000 working part-time at Egan's Grocery.
- She was one week late on her May 2012 credit card payment.

*Negative credit information usually stays on your credit report for 7 years.*

**CREDIT REPORT**

| **Employment** | **Personal Info** | **Credit History** |
|---|---|---|
| Information such as job history and income | Information such as Social Security number, current address, bank accounts | Information involving credit cards including payments and balances |

## Reflect

1. Jason made several late payments on his credit card four years ago. What effect does that have on his credit report now? Explain.

_____

_____

_____

# How Credit Reports Are Used

The information in your credit report is used to calculate a **credit score**. A good credit history will give you a high credit score. Late payments, high credit card balances or owing a lot of money are likely to result in a low credit score. Lenders use credit scores to decide whether to give you a loan or a credit card. Your credit score can also affect the interest rate you have to pay for a loan or a credit card.

**Math On the Spot**
my.hrw.com

## EXAMPLE 1 · Real World

TEKS 6.14.F

Credit histories for Deena and Ariel are given below. One received a credit score of 760, which is considered an excellent credit score by most lenders. The other received a credit score of 590, which is considered a poor credit score by many lenders. Match the person with the score.

| Deena | Ariel |
|---|---|
| • Monthly income: $3,200 <br> • Time at present job: 8 months <br> • Monthly debt payments: $350 on car loan, $180 on credit card, $300 on student loan <br> • Late payments: 3 times on credit card | • Monthly income: $2,250 <br> • Time at present job: 4 years <br> • Monthly debt payments: $45 on credit card <br> • Late payments: 0 times |

**STEP 1** Compare monthly debt with monthly income.

Deena: $\frac{350 + 180 + 300}{3,200} = \frac{830}{3,200} \approx 25.9\%$     Ariel: $\frac{45}{2,250} = 2\%$

Ariel has the lower monthly income of the two. But she spends only 2% of her income on debt repayment. Deena spends more than one-quarter of her income on debt repayment.

**STEP 2** Compare other factors.

Deena has been at her job for less than a year. That and her 3 late payments will lower her score even more. Ariel has held her job for 4 years and has never missed a credit card payment.

**STEP 3** Match the score with the person.

Ariel: 760     Low debt-to-income ratio, excellent job and credit history

Deena: 590     High debt-to-income ratio, good job history, poor credit history

**Math Talk**
Mathematical Processes

How might Deena's credit score affect her search for a new job?

## Reflect

**2.** Which of the two women would be more likely to get a car loan? Explain.

_____

_____

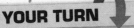

**YOUR TURN**

Match the credit score with the credit history. Credit scores: 760, 600

**3.** Monthly income: $1,900
Credit card payment: $48
Credit card balance: 3,857
Car loan payment: $218
Two late car loan payments

_____

**4.** Monthly income: $3,300
Credit card balance:
pays full balance
Monthly student loan
payment: $100

_____

## Guided Practice

**1.** Explain why it is important to have a good credit history. (Explore Activity 1)

_____

_____

**2.** List two items that could appear on a person's credit report that might hinder the person in his or her effort to get a loan to buy a boat.
(Explore Activity 2)

_____

**Match the credit score with the credit history. Credit scores: 700, 620**
(Example 1)

**3.** Monthly income: $3,200. Credit card
1 payment: $151. Credit card 2 payment:
$61. Car loan payment: $365. Three late
credit card payments

_____

**4.** Monthly income: $2,800. Student loan
payment: $140. Car loan payment: $276.
Credit card balance: pays full balance
monthly; no late payments

_____

**? ESSENTIAL QUESTION CHECK-IN**

**5.** Angela has a credit score of 800. Describe reasons why her score might
be so high.

_____

_____

_____

_____

# 18.2 Independent Practice

TEKS 6.14.D, 6.14.E, 6.14.F

Personal
Math Trainer

my.hrw.com

Online
Assessment and
Intervention

Five factors are used to calculate your credit score. The circle graph shows the relative importance of each factor. The two factors represented by 10% on the graph are (1) new credit and (2) the types of credit you use.

The other factors represented on the graph are (3) length of time you have been borrowing on credit, (4) your record of paying on time, and (5) the total amount you owe.

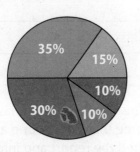

**6.** Which factor do you think is represented by the 35% sector of the graph? Explain your reasoning.

_____
_____
_____
_____
_____
_____

**7.** Which factor do you think is represented by the 30% sector of the graph? Explain your reasoning.

_____
_____
_____
_____
_____
_____
_____

**8.** Describe possible consequences of each of the following.

**a.** failing to pay your cell phone bill

_____
_____
_____
_____

**b.** failing to pay your credit card bill on time

_____
_____
_____
_____

**9.** Whitney and Jonathan each take out a $15,000 loan for a new car. Each has to repay the loan in 4 years. Whitney will pay an interest rate of 3% per year. Her monthly payments will be $332.01. Because Jonathan has a lower credit score, he will have to pay an interest rate of 3.5% per year. His monthly payments will be $335.34.

**a.** How much will Whitney repay the lender in 4 years?

_____

**b.** How much will Jonathan repay the lender in 4 years?

_____

**c.** How much more will a $15,000 loan cost Jonathan than it will cost Whitney?

_____

**H.O.T.** FOCUS ON HIGHER ORDER THINKING

Work Area

**10. Critical Thinking** You have just obtained a copy of your credit report and are disappointed with your score. Describe steps you could take to raise the score.

**11. Critical Thinking** Tom Smith obtains a copy of his credit report and is certain that it contains errors. Should he (a) assume that he is wrong and do nothing, or (b) contact the company that issued the report and inform them of the errors? Explain.

**12. Critical Thinking** You are a bank loan officer. Elena comes to you seeking a loan. She tells you that she has a sure-fire idea for a business that simply cannot fail. She states further that the bank will not be risking a penny by granting her the loan. Do Elena's claims encourage you or discourage you from approving the loan?

# 18.3 Paying for College

TEKS
**Personal financial literacy—6.14.G** Explain various methods to pay for college including through savings, grants, scholarships, student loans, and work-study.

**ESSENTIAL QUESTION**

How can you pay for college?

---

EXPLORE ACTIVITY 1 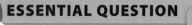 Real World    TEKS 6.14.G

## Exploring Methods to Pay for College

What you do in middle school affects your future so learning about ways to pay for college now is a good idea. The government and other organizations offer help. There are **grants**, usually for students who need money the most; **work-study programs** which allow students to earn money; and **scholarships**, awarded to students based on achievement.

**Work with a partner to research online and complete the following table.**

| How to Pay for College | | |
|---|---|---|
| | **What is it?** | **How can I qualify?** |
| **Grants** | | |
| **Savings** | | |
| **Scholarship** | | |
| **Loans** | | |
| **Work-study** | | |

## Reflect

1. **Communicate Mathematical Ideas** Which methods would you choose to pay for college? Explain why you would choose those methods.

_____

_____

_____

# Explaining Different Methods to Pay for College

Websites are a common tool for sharing information. Website designers sometimes create a storyboard to plan and organize the information they want to include in the website.

**Complete the storyboard for a website to help others learn about different ways to pay for college. Include a brief description and a benefit for each method listed on the storyboard.**

| Paying for College Website storyboard | |
|---|---|
| Grants | |
| Students with the most need for financial assistance may qualify for grants such as the Federal Pell Grant or the Federal Supplemental Education Opportunity Grant. Students do not have to repay grants. | |
| Savings | |
| | |
| Scholarships | |
| | |
| Loans | |
| | |

## Reflect

2. **Critical Thinking** Explain how you chose what information to include about each method of paying for college.

_____

_____

# Solving Problems About Paying for College

Many students use a combination of methods to pay for college.

Math On the Spot

my.hrw.com

## EXAMPLE 1 Problem Solving

TEKS 6.14.G

One year of classes at the University of North Texas costs $10,000. Mariano has received a grant that will pay $500 and a scholarship for $4,500. He wants to get a job to pay 25% of the remainder of the costs and hopes to get a loan to cover the rest of the costs for one year. How much does he need to earn on his job, and how much will he need to borrow?

### Analyze Information

Rewrite the question as a statement.

- Find the amount Mariano will need to make to earn 25% of the costs of one year of classes after deducting the grant and scholarship.
- Find the amount he will need to borrow to cover the remainder.

**List the important information:**

- One year of classes costs $10,000.
- Mariano has a grant for $500 and a scholarship for $4,500.

### Formulate a Plan

Add his grant and scholarship and subtract this from his expenses to find the amount he needs. Then find 25% of that amount. This is what Mariano plans to earn. The remaining amount he plans to borrow.

### Solve

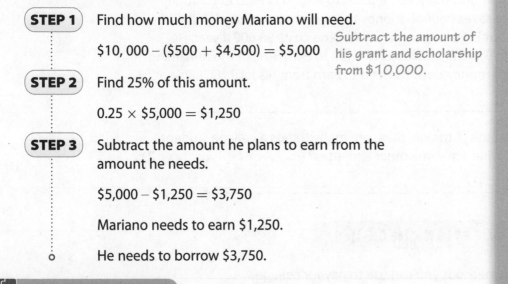

**STEP 1** Find how much money Mariano will need.

$10,000 - (\$500 + \$4,500) = \$5,000$     Subtract the amount of his grant and scholarship from $10,000.

**STEP 2** Find 25% of this amount.

$0.25 \times \$5,000 = \$1,250$

**STEP 3** Subtract the amount he plans to earn from the amount he needs.

$\$5,000 - \$1,250 = \$3,750$

Mariano needs to earn $1,250.

He needs to borrow $3,750.

### Justify and Evaluate

The sum of Mariano's grant, scholarship, job earnings, and amount borrowed is equal to $10,000. The answer is reasonable.

**Personal Math Trainer**

Online Assessment and Intervention

⏻ my.hrw.com

**3.** Angela is attending the University of Texas, where the tuition is $12,000 a year. She has a scholarship that pays $6,000 and a grant for $1,000. She also has a job at the campus bookstore. If her job pays her $50 every day that she works, how many days would she need to work to pay for 50% of the

remaining amount? _____

## Guided Practice

**1.** Michael is graduating from high school soon and wants to attend college. He did not earn any scholarships or save any money to help pay for college. What are some methods you would suggest for Michael to use to pay for college? Why? (Explore Activities 1 and 2)

_____

_____

**2.** Kiera is in her last year of college at the University of Houston. She has a scholarship that pays 75% of her costs. Her classes cost $14,000 for the year. How much money does she still need to pay the costs not paid by her scholarship? What are some methods she can use to pay them? (Explore Activities 1 and 2, Example 1)

_____

_____

**3.** Jim wants to go to college. He does not have enough money to attend a four-year university, so he plans to attend El Paso Community College until he saves enough money to transfer to a university. Jim has $2,300 saved, but El Paso Community College costs $8,000 a year. He received a $1,000 grant and wants to work to earn 50% of the remaining cost. How much money does he need to earn from his job? (Example 1)

_____

**4.** Other than the cost of tuition, there are many things a college student has to pay for. What are some other expenses? (Explore Activities 1 and 2)

_____

## ? ESSENTIAL QUESTION CHECK-IN

**5.** What are some methods you can use to pay for college?

_____

# 18.3 Independent Practice

Personal
Math Trainer

Online
Assessment and
Intervention

my.hrw.com

**6.** College tuition usually increases over time. You are interested in two colleges, A and B. College A plans to increase tuition by $500 per year for the next 6 years. College B plans to increase tuition by $850 for each of the next 6 years.

|  | College A | College B |
|---|---|---|
| 2012 | $12,000 | $10,000 |
| 2013 | | |
| 2014 | | |
| 2015 | | |
| 2016 | | |
| 2017 | | |
| 2018 | | |

**a.** Complete the table to determine which college will cost more in 6 years.

_____

**b.** Suppose you attend College A or College B in 2018. College A offers a grant that will pay $5,000 and a scholarship that pays 25% of your tuition, while College B only offers a scholarship that covers 60% of your tuition. How much do you still need to pay for each college? Show your work.

_____

_____

_____

_____

**c.** Suppose that College B reduces its scholarship to 50% of your tuition but adds a grant worth $2,000. Which college costs more in 2018? Explain.

**7. Make a Prediction** Suppose your parents started saving for your college education when you were 5 years old. Assume they saved $300 the first year, $325 the second year, $350 the third year, and so on, increasing each year's contribution by $25. If you are 17 in the last year of contributions, how much will have been saved in all?

_____

**8. Communicate Mathematical Ideas** Explain the difference between a scholarship and a loan.

_____

_____

_____

**9.** Lisa has a scholarship that pays for 75% of her tuition for all four years she attends college. What is the total amount the scholarship is worth if Lisa's classes cost

$12,000 per year? _____

**10.** Darren wants to attend a college that costs $15,000 per year. His parents have enough money saved to pay for 45% of his costs for two years. How much money have Darren's parents saved for his college costs? Explain your answer.

_____

_____

**11. Multistep** Susan is trying to decide whether to attend Texas A&M University or Midland College. She made a table to compare the costs of the two colleges, including tuition and fees. She also considered financial aid offers by each college.

|  | Scholarships | Grants | Total cost per year |
|---|---|---|---|
| **Texas A&M** | 30% of tuition | $2,000 | twice the cost of Midland College |
| **Midland College** | 0 | 0 | $4,500 |

**a.** What is the total cost per year for Texas A&M? _____

**b.** How much would Susan have to pay to go to Texas A&M? _____

Work Area

FOCUS ON HIGHER ORDER THINKING

**12. Critique Reasoning** William will be attending college next year. He thinks that even though the tuition is higher at College A it will cost less overall because it is in-state and College B is not. Do you agree with William? Explain.

_____

_____

_____

**13. Multistep** There are 4 years left until Desmond attends college. He wants to go full time for 4 years to a college that costs $25,000 a year. His parents' goal is to save enough to pay 75% of the cost. There is currently $60,000 in an account they set up. Assume that college costs do not increase each year.

**a.** How much will Desmond's college of choice cost for 4 years?

_____

**b.** About how much more money do Desmond's parents need to save to meet their goal?

_____

**c.** How many months are left for them to save money in his college savings account?

_____

**d.** How much money do Desmond's parents need to save each month to meet their goal?

_____

**e.** How much money will Desmond still need for college tuition?

_____

# Wages, Salaries, and Careers

🖱 TEKS
**Personal financial literacy—**
**6.14.H** Compare the annual salary of several occupations requiring various levels of post-secondary education or vocational training and calculate the effects of the different annual salaries on lifetime income.

**?** **ESSENTIAL QUESTION**

How can you compare the salaries of different occupations?

**EXPLORE ACTIVITY 1** *Real World* 🖱 TEKS 6.14.H

## Exploring Salaries and Careers

The U.S. Bureau of Labor Statistics website can help you research the salary and educational requirements for a variety of occupations. Look up each of these occupations and complete the table.

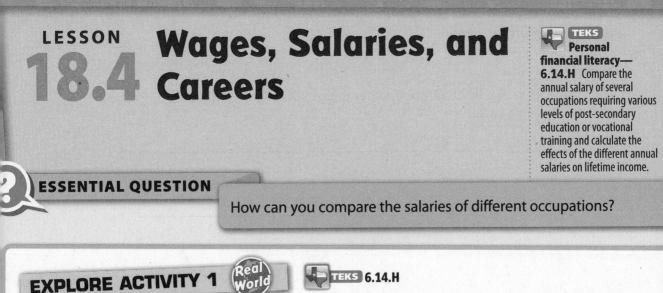

| | Environmental Engineers | Fitness Trainers | Veterinarians |
|---|---|---|---|
| **Description of the occupation** | | | |
| **Training and/or education needed** | | | |
| **Median income** | | | |
| **Other important factors** | | | |

> Median income represents the middle value of a range of incomes.

### Reflect

**1.** Besides salary, what are some other things you might consider in choosing a career?

_____

_____

_____

**EXPLORE ACTIVITY 2** Real World     TEKS 6.14.H

# Choosing a Career

Use the Bureau of Labor Statistics website to research the career you are considering. Read about its median income, educational requirements, and job outlook. Then complete the bubble map.

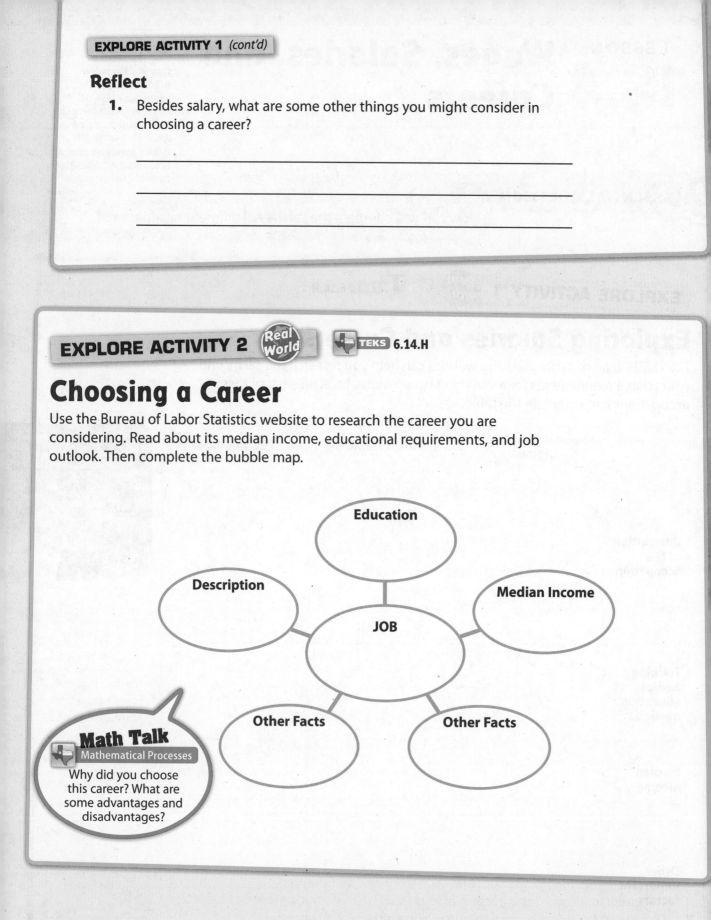

Education

Description

Median Income

JOB

Other Facts

Other Facts

**Math Talk**
Mathematical Processes

Why did you choose this career? What are some advantages and disadvantages?

# Calculating the Effects on Lifetime Income

Many people stay in a career for most of their lives. One way to compare careers is to consider the total income over many years.

**EXAMPLE 1** Real World     TEKS 6.14.H

The annual median income for an economist is **$89,450**. The annual median income for a software developer is **$90,530**. Compare the salaries of these careers over 30 years. How much more can a software developer expect to earn over that time?

**STEP 1**   Estimate the total income of an economist over 30 years.

$89,450 × 30 = $2,683,500    *Multiply the annual income by 30.*

**STEP 2**   Estimate the total income of a software developer over 30 years.

$90,530 × 30 = $2,715,900    *Multiply the annual income by 30.*

**STEP 3**   Find the difference between these total incomes.

$2,715,900 − $2,683,500 = $32,400

A software developer can expect to earn about $32,400 more than an economist over 30 years.

## Reflect

2. **Communicate Mathematical Ideas** What is another way to find how much more the software developer can earn over 30 years?

_____

_____

3. **Select Tools** What are two tools you could use to find the total income over 30 years?

_____

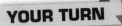

4. The annual median income for a dental assistant is $33,470. The annual median income for a nursing aide is $25,010. How much more can a dental assistant expect to earn than a nursing aide over 30 years?

_____

**Personal Math Trainer**
Online Assessment and Intervention

⊙ my.hrw.com

The table shows information about two occupations.

| | Construction managers | Microbiologists |
|---|---|---|
| Description | Supervise construction projects, including planning, managing employees and sticking to a budget | Study microorganisms, such as bacteria, fungi, and algae |
| Educational requirements | Associate's degree | Bachelor's degree |
| Median income | $83,860 per year $40.32 per hour | $65,920 per year $31.69 per hour |
| Other facts | Many are self-employed. Most work from a field office on the construction site, but they may have another office where they manage finances and do paperwork. | Microbiologists might work in the lab of a research facility at a university, hospital, or government agency. |

1. Compare and contrast these two occupations based on the information in the table. (Explore Activities 1 and 2)

   _____

   _____

   _____

   _____

   _____

2. Using the information from the table, determine how much less a microbiologist would earn over 30 years than a construction manager. (Example 1)

   _____

   _____

   _____

**? ESSENTIAL QUESTION CHECK-IN**

3. How can you compare salaries of different occupations?

   _____

   _____

   _____

# 18.4 Independent Practice

TEKS 6.14.H

Personal Math Trainer

Online Assessment and Intervention

my.hrw.com

**4.** Simon earns $2,470 per month and Amaress earns $2,340 per month. Amaress also gets a yearly bonus in the amount of $750.

   **a.** How much does Simon earn per year? _____

   **b.** How much does Amaress earn per year? _____

   **c.** What is the difference between the amount that Simon could earn in 30 years and the amount that Amaress could earn in 30 years?

   _____

**For 5–7, use the table of median yearly income for various kinds of drivers in three states that Timothy is interested in moving to.**

|  | City bus driver | Truck driver | Delivery driver | Taxi driver |
|---|---|---|---|---|
| **California** | $40,790 | $41,990 | $34,810 | $24,690 |
| **Florida** | $31,650 | $36,360 | $31,670 | $22,410 |
| **North Carolina** | $30,670 | $37,970 | $31,420 | $21,740 |

**5.** How much can Timothy earn in 30 years as a delivery driver in

   California? _____

**6.** Compare the salaries of a Florida truck driver and a North Carolina city bus driver. How much more money can Timothy earn as a Florida truck

   driver in 30 years? _____

**7.** What is the difference between the income earned over 30 years at the highest paying job and the income earned over 30 years at the lowest

   paying job? _____

**8.** Harris and Georgina both work in a clothing store. Harris earns $2,360 per month and Georgina earns $2,120 per month. Every month, the employee with the highest sales gets a $250 bonus. In the past year, Georgina got the monthly bonus 7 times, and Harris got the monthly bonus 1 time.

   **a.** How much did Harris earn in the past year? Explain. _____

   _____

   **b.** How much did Georgina earn in the past year? Explain. _____

   _____

   _____

**9.** Janelle earns $950 a week. Carter earns $50,320 a year. Each works 52 weeks a year. What is the difference between the amounts Janelle and Carter earn in 30 years? Explain.

_____

_____

_____

**Rayshawn is trying to decide between three job offers. Each job offer is 40 hours a week and 52 weeks a year. The table shows the wage for each of Rayshawn's three job offers.**

|  | Hourly wage | Weekly wage | Yearly wage |
|---|---|---|---|
| **Air conditioning repair** | $20.15 |  |  |
| **Internet service repair** |  | $1,042 |  |
| **Automotive glass repair** |  |  | $32,256 |

**10.** Calculate the hourly, weekly, and yearly wages to complete the table.

**11.** What is the difference between the yearly wage of the internet service repair offer and the yearly wage of the air conditioning repair

offer? _____

 **FOCUS ON HIGHER ORDER THINKING**

Work Area

**12. Critique Reasoning** Carlotta earns $2,400 a month. She thinks she will earn $720,000 in 30 years. Is Carlotta correct? Explain.

_____

_____

**13. Communicate Mathematical Ideas** If you know a job pays *k* dollars per hour, how can you use unit rates to find the job's yearly salary? Explain.

_____

_____

_____

**14. Critical Thinking** Tara earns more per hour than Ed, but Ed earns more money per year than Tara. What might make Ed's yearly salary higher than Tara's?

_____

_____

# Ready to Go On?

**Personal
Math Trainer**

Online Assessment
and Intervention

⏻ my.hrw.com

## 18.1 Choosing a Bank

**1.** Ruby is trying to choose a bank. She does not write checks. She makes a withdrawal from the ATM once a week and buys coffee with her debit card 5 times a week.

What is Ruby's monthly cost for each bank?

|  | FN Bank | Community Bank |
|---|---|---|
| Checks | free | $0.25 each |
| Monthly checking fee | none | $2 |
| ATM fee | $2 per withdrawal | Free |
| Debit card fee | $1.50 per month | $0.50 per use |

_____

## 18.2 Protecting Your Credit

**2.** Would one late credit card payment 2 years ago make you more likely

or less likely to get a car loan? _____

## 18.3 Paying for College

**3.** The cost for Roberta's college next year is $11,000. She has a grant for $1,500 and a scholarship of $5,000. She plans to earn 40% of the

remaining amount. How much will still be left to pay? _____

## 18.4 Wages, Salaries, and Careers

**4.** The annual median income for an entry-level auto mechanic is $33,934. The annual median income for a senior auto mechanic is $50,856. How much more can a senior auto mechanic earn than an

entry-level auto mechanic over 10 years? _____

**? ESSENTIAL QUESTION**

**5.** What are some things you can do to be a knowledgeable consumer?

_____

_____

_____

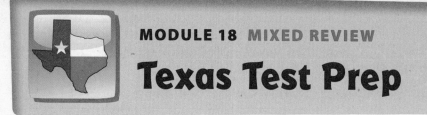

## Selected Response

**1.** Which situation describes the use of a credit card?

Ⓐ Ryan entered his PIN to complete a transaction.

Ⓑ Ryan overdrew his checking account.

Ⓒ Ryan bought groceries and paid for them at the end of the month.

Ⓓ After making a purchase, Ryan recorded the information in his check register.

**2.** Which of these can have a positive effect on your credit score?

Ⓐ paying credit card balance monthly

Ⓑ late payments

Ⓒ a new job

Ⓓ high monthly debt repayment

**3.** Joel has an annual salary of $34,840. He works 40 hours a week, 52 weeks a year. How much does Joel earn per hour?

Ⓐ $13　　　Ⓒ $16.75

Ⓑ $15　　　Ⓓ $18

**4.** Traci's bank charges $2 for withdrawals at nonbank ATMs and a fee of $2.50 per month for a debit card. Last month she paid $10.50 in ATM and debit card fees. How many nonbank ATM withdrawals did she make?

Ⓐ 2

Ⓑ 4

Ⓒ 5

Ⓓ 8

**5.** Lacey is attending a university where the cost for one year is $10,500. She has a scholarship worth $6,000 and a grant worth $900. She earns $45 a day at her job. How many days does she need to work to pay for 50% of the remaining amount?

Ⓐ 40　　　Ⓒ 60

Ⓑ 50　　　Ⓓ 80

**6.** The annual median income for a senior accounting clerk is $42,294. The annual median income for a senior accountant is $64,473. How much more can a senior accountant earn than a senior accounting clerk over 30 years?

Ⓐ $22,179　　　Ⓒ $221,790

Ⓑ $66,537　　　Ⓓ $665,370

## Gridded Response

**7.** Sally recorded the distances she ran for 5 days: 5 miles, 3.5 miles, 6 miles, 4.5 miles, and 5.5 miles. What is the mean number of miles Sally ran per day?

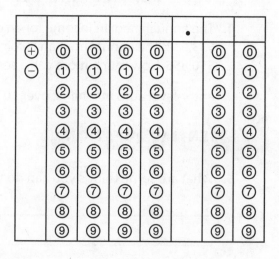

## MODULE 18 Becoming a Knowledgeable Consumer and Investor

### Key Vocabulary
checking account (cuenta corriente)

credit card (tarjeta de crédito)

credit history (historia crediticia)

credit report (informe crediticio)

credit score (calificación crediticia)

debit card (tarjeta de débito)

grant (beca)

scholarships (becas)

work-study programs (programas de trabajo y estudio)

### ? ESSENTIAL QUESTION

How can you become a knowledgeable consumer and investor?

### EXAMPLE 1

The table shows fees charged by Jeremy's bank. He uses his checking account to pay for his 10 monthly bills, and he uses his debit card to pay for lunch about 20 times each month. Calculate his monthly bank fees.

| Item | Jeremy's bank fees |
|------|--------------------|
| checks | $0.15 each |
| monthly checking fee | $10 |
| ATM fee | free |
| debit card fee | $2.50 per month |

Write 10 checks: $10 \times \$0.15 = \$1.50$

Monthly checking fee:        $10.00

Debit card fee:              $2.50

Total:                       $14.00

Jeremy's monthly bank fees are $14.00.

### EXAMPLE 2

Calculate the debt-to-income ratio for Alicia. Her monthly income is $1,400, and she has a monthly payment of $120 for her car and $75 for her credit card.

Compare her monthly debt with her monthly income.

Debt-to-income ratio is $\frac{120 + 75}{1,400} \approx 0.139 \approx 14\%$

### EXAMPLE 3

The average median income for a cashier is $24,000. The average median income for a programmer is $78,000.

   **a.** What is the total income of a cashier over 20 years?
     $20 \times \$24,000 = \$480,000$

   **b.** What is the total income of a programmer over 20 years?
     $20 \times \$78,000 = \$1,560,000$

   **c.** How much more will the programmer make than the cashier over the 20 years?
     $\$1,560,000 - \$480,000 = \$1,080,000$

## EXERCISES

1. Emily is looking for a bank. Compare the two banks in the table. Emily has an average balance of $500, writes 15 checks per month, and uses her debit card at an ATM 17 times per month. (Lesson 18.1)

| Item | Uptown Bank | First Bank |
|---|---|---|
| checks | $0.20 each | $2 for less than 20<br>$4 for more than 20 |
| monthly checking fee | $5 | $10 |
| monthly ATM fee | free | $.05 per use |
| debit card fee | $3.50 per month | $2.50 per month |

a. Calculate her total monthly fee for each bank.

_____

b. Which is the best choice for her? Explain.

_____

_____

## Calculate the debt-to-income ratio for the following. (Lesson 18.2)

2. Damien has a monthly income of $2,500, a car payment of $400, and credit card payments of $100. _____

3. Mara has a monthly income of $1,000, a credit card payment of $50, and a student loan payment of $75. _____

4. Alicia has a monthly income of $4,000 and a student loan payment of $300. _____

5. Steven has a monthly income of $500 and a credit card payment of $25. _____

6. Median income is $35,000 per year for a truck driver, $3,400 per month for a middle school teacher, and $450 per week for a bank teller. (Lesson 18.4)

a. Which profession makes the most per year?

_____

b. Compare the incomes of a truck driver and a bank teller over 20 years. Show your work.

_____

_____

_____

c. Compare the income of a truck driver to a middle school teacher over 20 years. Show your work.

_____

_____

_____

1. **CAREERS IN MATH** | Bicycle Tour Operator  Viktor is a bike tour operator and needs to replace two of his touring bikes. He orders two bikes from the sporting goods store for a total of $2,000 and pays using his credit card. When the bill arrives, he reads the following information:

> **Balance:** $2,000
> **Annual interest rate:** 14.9%
> **Minimum payment due:** $40
> **Late fee:** $10 if payment not received by 3/1/2013

a. To keep his good credit, Viktor promptly sends in a minimum payment of $40. When the next bill arrives, it looks a lot like the previous bill.

> Balance: $1,984.34
> Annual interest rate: 14.9%
> Minimum payment due: $40
> Late fee: $10 if payment not received by 4/1/2013

Explain how the credit card company calculated the new balance. Notice that the given interest rate is annual, but the payment is monthly.

_____

_____

_____

b. Viktor was upset about the new bill, so he decided to send in $150 for his April payment. The minimum payment on his bill is calculated as 2% of the balance (rounded to the nearest dollar) or $20, whichever is greater. Fill out the details for Viktor's new bill.

> **Balance:**
> **Annual interest rate:**
> **Minimum payment due:**
> **Late fee: $10 if payment not received by**

c. Viktor's bank offers a credit card with an introductory annual interest rate of 9.9%. He can transfer his current balance for a fee of $40. After one year, the rate will return to the bank's normal rate, which is 13.9%. The bank charges a late fee of $15. Give two reasons why Viktor should transfer the balance, and two reasons why he should not.

_____

_____

_____

_____

**2.** Manuel has a monthly income of $440. Currently, his only monthly payment is his portion of the rent, which is $110. However, he is considering buying a used car.

   **a.** Calculate Manuel's current debt-to-income ratio.

_____

   **b.** If Manuel would like to maintain a debt-to-income ratio that is less than 60%, can he afford a monthly car payment of $175? Show your work.

_____

   **c.** Manuel thinks he can maintain a debt-to-income ratio that is less than 60% if his car payment is less than $154. Is he correct? Explain.

_____

_____

_____

**3.** Lillian is a high school science teacher. She makes $50,230 per year and plans to teach for another 16 years. Lillian's family is moving, so she will need to find a new school at which to teach. Lillian's real estate agent said, "In the city you are moving to, salaries for teaching high school are 12% higher than the national average for a high school teacher."

   **a.** Lillian currently makes $3,000 less than the national average for a high school teacher. How much could she make in the city she moves to, based on the real estate agent's comment? Round your answer to the nearest dollar.

_____

   **b.** Compare the total incomes for her current job and potential new job, for the remainder of time that Lillian plans to teach. Assume that Lillian's yearly income remains constant in both locations.

_____

_____

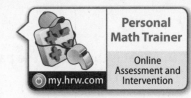
## Selected Response

1. Which situation describes the use of a debit card?

   Ⓐ Phillip bought groceries and paid for them at the end of the month.

   Ⓑ Phillip received change from the cashier after making a purchase.

   Ⓒ Phillip entered his PIN at an ATM to complete a transaction.

   Ⓓ Phillip missed a monthly payment and was charged a late fee.

2. Which number line models the expression $-1 + 4$?

   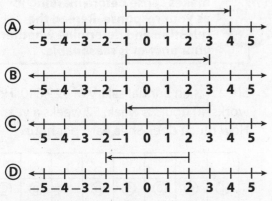

3. Which of these can have a positive effect on your credit score?

   Ⓐ high debt-to-income ratio

   Ⓑ making payments on time

   Ⓒ losing your job

   Ⓓ high credit card balance

4. Armando saves 30% of his monthly paycheck for college. He earned $450 last month. How much money did Armando save for college?

   Ⓐ $135        Ⓒ $300

   Ⓑ $150        Ⓓ $315

5. What is the debt-to-income ratio for the data below?

   Monthly income: $1,500
   Credit card payment: $55
   Student loan payment: $125

   Ⓐ 3.67%

   Ⓑ 8.33%

   Ⓒ 12%

   Ⓓ 18%

6. For which equation is $y = 9$ a solution?

   Ⓐ $9y = 9$

   Ⓑ $y - 17 = -8$

   Ⓒ $y + 9 = 0$

   Ⓓ $\frac{y}{2} = 18$

7. The median annual income for an aerospace engineer is $62,640. The median annual income for an aircraft electrician is $43,235. How much more can an aerospace engineer earn than an aircraft electrician over 20 years?

   Ⓐ $19,405

   Ⓑ $38,810

   Ⓒ $194,050

   Ⓓ $388,100

Hot Tip!

Underline key words given in the test question so you know for certain what the question is asking.

**8.** What is the area of the parallelogram shown below?

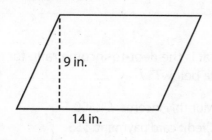

9 in.

14 in.

Ⓐ 42 square inches

Ⓑ 63 square inches

Ⓒ 126 square inches

Ⓓ 252 square inches

**9.** Which shows the integers in order from least to greatest?

Ⓐ 17, 3, 2, −5, −16

Ⓑ −5, 2, 3, −16, 17

Ⓒ −16, −5, 2, 3, 17

Ⓓ 17, −16, 3, 2, −5

## Gridded Response

**10.** What is the debt-to-income ratio for the data below written as a percent?

Monthly income: $2,750
Car loan payment: $375
Credit card payment: $120

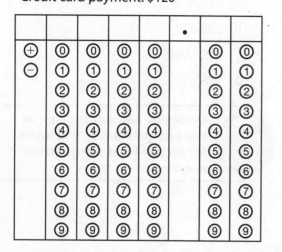

**11.** Andrea is attending a university where the cost for one year is $13,500. She has a scholarship worth $5,000 and a grant worth $1,700. She earns $40 a day at her job. How many days does she need to work to pay for 30% of the remaining amount?

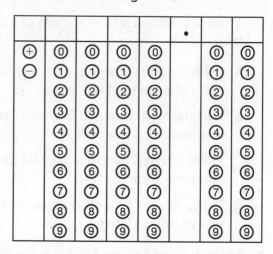

**Make sure that your answer makes sense before marking it as your response. Reread the question and determine whether your answer is reasonable.**

Hot Tip!

**12.** Shea has an annual salary of $29,640. He works 40 hours a week, 52 weeks a year. How much does Shea earn per hour?

# UNIT 1 Selected Answers

## MODULE 1

### LESSON 1.1

**Your Turn**

**6.**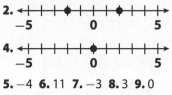
**8.** −10 **9.** 5 **10.** 0 **11.** 6

**Guided Practice**

**2.** 
   −5   0   5
**4.** 
   −5   0   5
**5.** −4 **6.** 11 **7.** −3 **8.** 3 **9.** 0
**10.** −22

**Independent Practice**

**13.** 17 **15.** 2 **17.** 12 **19a.** gain
**b.** Tino **c.** Tino and Luis **d.** −6
**e.** No; −6 pound change means
Frankie lost 6 pounds. **21.** 4 units
**23.** 14 units **25.** −9; it is 9 units
away from 0 on a number line, and
6 is only 6 units away from 0.

### LESSON 1.2

**Your Turn**

**2.** 4, 2, 0, −3, −5, −6

   −6   0   4

**3.** 9, 8, 5, 2, 0, −1, −6, −10

   −10  −6  −2   2   6   10

**4.** < **5.** < **6.** >
**7.** −2 > −18; −18 < −2
**8.** −39 < 39; 39 > −39

**Guided Practice**

**1b.** A **c.** B **2.** −9, −6, −3, 0, 1, 4, 8
**3.** −65, −13, −7, 7, 34, 55, 62
**4.** −17 > −22; −22 < −17 **5.** <
**6.** < **7.** > **8.** > **9.** > **10.** < **11.** <
**12.** > **13a.** −3 < 2 **b.** 0 > −4

**Independent Practice**

**15b.** E. Simpson **17.** 167 > −65
**19b.** −5, −2, 2, 4, 7 **21.** 377 > 249
**23.** Argentina **25.** No; −12 °F <
−3 °F, so it was getting colder
outside. **27.** −10, −3, 5, 16 and
−3, 5, −10, 16

### LESSON 1.3

**Your Turn**

**4.** The temperature at night
reached 13 °F below zero.
**5.** 12 **6.** 91 **7.** 55 **8.** 0 **9.** 88 **10.** 1

**Guided Practice**

**1.** negative **2a.** late fee of $10; it
is a fee, so it represents a change
of −$10 in the amount of money
Ryan has.
**b.** |−10| = 10

   −10              0

**3a.** more than 100 **b.** less than
Leo **c.** more than 50

**Independent Practice**

**5.** The first week his balance
changed by +$80. The second
week his balance changed by
−$85. **7b.** April **9a.** −5, 4, −1, 3, −2
**b.** The spinner landing on red
results in a change of −$5 to Lisa's
amount of money. **13.** No;
−|−4| = −4; |−(−4)| = |4| = 4.

## MODULE 2

### LESSON 2.1

**Your Turn**

**3.** $\frac{-15}{1}$ **4.** $\frac{31}{100}$ **5.** $\frac{41}{9}$ **6.** $\frac{62}{1}$
**9.** rational numbers **10.** rational
numbers **11.** integers and rational
numbers **12.** whole numbers,
integers, and rational numbers

**Guided Practice**

**1a.** 4 rolls of ribbon divided evenly
among the 5 friends. 4 ÷ 5.
**b.** $\frac{4}{5}$ roll **2.** $\frac{7}{10}$ **3.** $\frac{-29}{1}$ **4.** $\frac{25}{3}$
**5.** integers, rational numbers
**6.** rational numbers

**Independent Practice**

**11.** $\frac{22}{5}$, or $4.40 **13.** Venn **15.** $\frac{35}{2}$,
rational numbers **17.** $\frac{8}{15}$ cup

### LESSON 2.2

**Your Turn**

**2.** −7, 3.5, −2.25, and $9\frac{1}{3}$. **4.** 4.5
**5.** $1\frac{1}{2}$ **6.** 4 **7.** $3\frac{1}{4}$

**Guided Practice**

**1.** 
   −5   0   5
**2.** 
   −5   0   5
**3.** 
   −5   0   5
**4.** 
   −5   0   5
**5.** −3.78 **6.** $7\frac{5}{12}$ **7.** 0 **8.** −4.2
**9.** −12.1 **10.** −2.6 **11.** They are
the same distance from 0 on the
number line. **12.** 5.23 **13.** $4\frac{2}{11}$
**14.** 0 **15.** $6\frac{3}{5}$ **16.** 2.12 **17.** 8.2

**Independent Practice**

**19a.** Girardi $85.23, Lewis
−$20.44, Stein $116.33, Yuan
−$13.50, Wenner $9.85
**b.** Wenner **c.** Stein **23.** to the left
**25a.** −25,344 ft **b.** −5 and −4
**c.** 
   −5   0   5

### LESSON 2.3

**Your Turn**

**3.** 0.15, $\frac{3}{5}$, $\frac{7}{10}$, 0.85 **5.** −1.8, −1.25,
1, $1\frac{2}{5}$, $1\frac{9}{10}$

**Guided Practice**

**1.** $\frac{3}{5}$ **2.** 0.25 **3.** $\frac{9}{10}$ **4.** $\frac{1}{10}$ **5.** 0.3
**6.** $1\frac{2}{5}$ **7.** 0.8 **8.** $\frac{2}{5}$ **9.** 0.75
**10.** $\frac{1}{5}$, 0.4, $\frac{1}{2}$, 0.75 **11.** $12\frac{3}{4}$, 12.7, $12\frac{3}{5}$
**12.** 2.3, 2.6, $2\frac{4}{5}$ **13.** $\frac{5}{48}$, $\frac{3}{16}$, 0.5, 0.75
**14.** $\frac{1}{5}$, 0.35, $\frac{12}{25}$, 0.5, $\frac{4}{5}$ **15.** $-\frac{3}{4}$, $-\frac{7}{10}$,
$\frac{3}{4}$, $\frac{8}{10}$ **16.** −0.65, $-\frac{3}{8}$, $\frac{5}{16}$, $\frac{2}{4}$ **17.** $-2\frac{4}{5}$,
−2.6, −2.3 **18.** −0.72, $-\frac{5}{8}$, −0.6, $-\frac{7}{12}$
**19.** 1.2, $1\frac{1}{3}$, 1.45, $1\frac{1}{2}$ **20.** −0.35, −0.3,
0.5, 0.55

**Independent Practice**

**23a.** $6\frac{1}{6}$, 5.5, $4\frac{3}{8}$, 4.3, $\frac{15}{4}$ **b.** Claire,
Peter, Brenda, and Jim; Micah
**c.** Yes; the smallest donation is
$\frac{15}{4}$ pounds. $\frac{1}{2}$ pound is equal to $\frac{2}{4}$
pound. $\frac{15}{4} + \frac{2}{4} = \frac{17}{4} = 4\frac{1}{4} = 4.25$ lb,
which is just enough to win a free
movie coupon.

# UNIT 2 Selected Answers

## LESSON 3.1

**Your Turn**

**9.** 15 **10.** 12 **11.** $\frac{8}{3}$ **12.** $\frac{7}{2}$ **13.** $\frac{49}{10}$
**14.** 7

**Guided Practice**

**1a.**

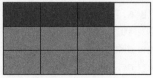

**b.** $\frac{1}{4}$ **c.** $\frac{1}{3} \times \frac{3}{4} = \frac{1}{4}$ **d.** Decrease
**2.** $\frac{5}{16}$ **3.** $\frac{1}{3}$ **4.** $\frac{3}{20}$ **5.** 3 **6.** 16 **7.** 24
**8.** 15

**Independent Practice**

**11a.** $\frac{5}{8} \times 16 = 10$, so she buys
10 pounds. **b.** No, she will need to
buy five more bags. **13a.** Oranges
$= 1\frac{1}{2}$, apples $= 1\frac{4}{5}$, blueberries $= \frac{3}{4}$
cup, peaches $= 2$ **17.** $300.00
**19.** The answer is not affected
because dividing by 1 does not
change the number.

## LESSON 3.2

**Your Turn**

**2.** $\frac{5}{2}$, or $2\frac{1}{2}$ **3.** $\frac{9}{10}$ **4.** $\frac{55}{24}$, or $2\frac{7}{24}$
**5.** $\frac{33}{25}$, or $1\frac{8}{25}$ **6.** $\frac{39}{10}$, or $3\frac{9}{10}$ **7.** $\frac{31}{48}$ **9.** $\frac{64}{21}$,
or $3\frac{1}{21}$ **10.** $\frac{19}{5}$, or $3\frac{4}{5}$ **11.** $\frac{108}{7}$, or $15\frac{3}{7}$
**12.** $\frac{49}{2}$, or $24\frac{1}{2}$

**Guided Practice**

**1a.**

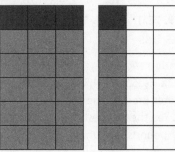

**b.** $\frac{2}{9}$ acre **c.** $\frac{1}{6} \times 1\frac{1}{3} = \frac{2}{9}$ **d.** Decrease
**2.** $\frac{18}{25}$ **3.** 1 **4.** $\frac{11}{15}$ **5.** $\frac{34}{25}$, or $1\frac{9}{25}$ **6.** $\frac{13}{6}$,
or $2\frac{1}{6}$ **7.** $\frac{35}{12}$, or $2\frac{11}{12}$ **8.** $\frac{143}{25}$, or $5\frac{18}{25}$
**9.** $\frac{361}{20}$, or $18\frac{1}{20}$

**Independent Practice**

**11.** Estimate: $4 \times 2 = 8$; Actual: $8\frac{1}{6}$
cups **13.** Estimate: $1 \times \frac{1}{5} = \frac{1}{5}$,
total $= \frac{1}{5} + 1\frac{2}{5} = 1\frac{3}{5}$; Actual: $1\frac{17}{25}$
bags **15.** 20, $112\frac{1}{2}$ meters **17a.** $22\frac{1}{2}$
minutes **b.** Yes **c.** There are $7\frac{1}{2}$
minutes left. **21.** It is not possible.

## LESSON 3.3

**Your Turn**

**5.** $\frac{8}{7}$ **6.** $\frac{1}{9}$ **7.** 11 **10.** $2\frac{1}{4}$ **11.** $1\frac{1}{2}$

**Guided Practice**

**1.** $\frac{5}{2}$ **2.** 9 **3.** $\frac{3}{10}$ **4.** $\frac{4}{5}$ **5.** $\frac{3}{8}$ **6.** $1\frac{1}{4}$

**Independent Practice**

**9.** 4 runners will be needed. **11.** $\frac{1}{10}$
pound **13.** 9 bags **15.** 8 **17.** 2
**19.** Greater than $\frac{1}{2}$ **21.** Robyn

## LESSON 3.4

**Your Turn**

**6.** 9; $10\frac{1}{2} \div 1\frac{1}{4} = 8\frac{2}{5}$; she will need
9 containers. **8.** $4\frac{1}{2}$ meters **9.** $3\frac{1}{4}$
yards

**Guided Practice**

**1.** 17; 17; 4; 3; $5\frac{2}{3}$ **2.** 3; 9; 3; 4; 9; $\frac{2}{3}$
**3.** $3\frac{5}{9}$ **4.** $2\frac{4}{5}$ **5.** $3\frac{1}{3}$ **6.** 4 **7.** $26 \div 5\frac{1}{2}$;
The width is $4\frac{8}{11}$ feet. **8.** $230 \div 12\frac{1}{2}$;
$18\frac{2}{5}$ feet

**Independent Practice**

**11.** $5\frac{1}{2}$ pieces **13a.** No, it only
makes $7\frac{1}{3}$ servings. **b.** $\frac{11}{20}$ of a cup;
$5\frac{1}{2}$ cups $\div$ 10 people $= \frac{11}{2} \times \frac{1}{10} = \frac{11}{20}$
**c.** She would need $7\frac{1}{2}$ cups total,
so she would need 2 more cups
of trail mix. **15.** yes because the
height is $4\frac{1}{4}$ feet **17.** $5\frac{1}{4}$ feet
**19.** He used the reciprocal of $\frac{3}{4}$
instead of the reciprocal of $2\frac{3}{4}$.

## LESSON 4.1

**Your Turn**

**3.** 1; 1; 6,300; 12,600; 192.78; 2
**4.** 2; 2; 5,856; 39,040; 4.4896; 4
**5.** 49,980; 428,400; 48.4092
**6.** 8,043; 22,980; 919,200; 95.0223
**7.** 38.75

**Guided Practice**

**1.** 0.28

**2.** 2.64

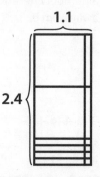

**3.** 0.0108 **4.** 130.055 **5.** 0.1152
**6.** 2,021.175 **7.** 14.858 **8.** 2.48292
**9.** 23.63 **10.** 173.90 **11.** 29.21
**12.** 1.06

**Independent Practice**

**15.** 14 inches **17.** $342 **19.** $15.50
**21.** $23.58 **23.** 20.425 miles
**25.** 14.425 miles **27.** 3.48 is
closer to 3 and 7.33 is closer to 7;
$7 \times 3 = 21$. **29.** The 22-karat gold
object; 24.3285 ounces

## LESSON 4.2

**Your Turn**
**3.** 1.95 **4.** 0.92 **5.** 8.5 **6.** 18

**Guided Practice**
**1.** 7.375 **2.** 3.31 **3.** 7 **4.** 0.15
**5.** 77 **6.** 2.65 **7.** 33.16 **8.** 1.95
**9.** 19 **10.** 0.3 **11.** 6.2 **12.** 405
**13.** 250 **14.** 11.8 **15.** 0.8 pound
**16.** 3.5 pounds **17.** 18.1 seconds
**18.** 18 **19.** $2.73 per gallon
**20.** 20 inches

**Independent Practice**
**23.** $8.50 **25a.** 10 movies
**27.** beef **29a.** 0.42 **b.** 0.25
**c.** 0.15 **31.** 42 **33.** 20 weeks

## LESSON 4.3

**Your Turn**
**1.** He paid $\frac{29}{2} \times \frac{3}{5} = 8\frac{7}{10}$ dollars
or $14.5 \times 0.6 = $8.70. **2.** $49.20

**Guided Practice**
**1.** $3\frac{1}{2}$ gallons; $8\frac{3}{4} \times \frac{2}{5} = 3\frac{1}{2}$
**2.** $134\frac{1}{2}$ miles; $188\frac{3}{10} \times \frac{5}{7} = 134\frac{1}{2}$
**3.** $397.80; $0.75 \times 530.40 = 397.8$
**4.** 14.525; $17.5 \times 0.17 = 2.975$ lb;
$17.5 - 2.975 = 14.525$
**5.** $8 per hour; $54 \div (2.5 + 4.25) = 8$
**6.** $12.60; $(3 + 4.2) \times 1.75 = 12.6$

**Independent Practice**
**9.** $(11.5 + 10.7) \times 0.40 = 8.88$;
$8.88 \div 2.96 = 3$ movies **11.** $1\frac{5}{8}$ bags;
$1\frac{1}{10}$ pounds left over **13.** 3 games
**17.** 35

MODULE 5

## LESSON 5.1

**Your Turn**
**7.** −9 **8.** −10 **9.** −60 **10.** −70
**11.** 300 **12.** −145 **13.** −1,650
**14.** −1,000

**Guided Practice**
**1a.** 6 **b.** negative **c.** −6 **2a.** 9
**b.** negative **c.** −9 **3.** −7

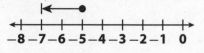

**4.** −4

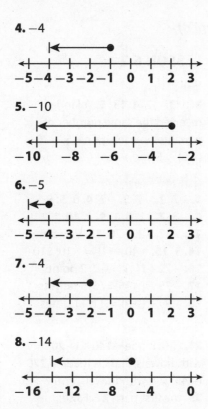

**5.** −10

**6.** −5

**7.** −4

**8.** −14

**9.** −9 **10.** −11 **11.** −10 **12.** −110
**13.** −100 **14.** 203 **15.** −15
**16.** −570

**Independent Practice**
**19.** −11 **21.** −54 **23.** −100 +
(−75) + (−85) = −260

## LESSON 5.2

**Your Turn**
**3.** 4 **4.** −2 **5.** −6 **6.** −1 **7.** −28
**8.** −8 **9.** 0 **10.** −1

**Guided Practice**
**1.** 6

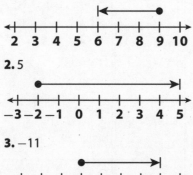

**2.** 5

**3.** −11

**4.** −3

**5.** 1 **6.** 0 **7.** −3 **8.** 4 **9.** 6 **10.** 2
**11.** −16 **12.** 0 **13.** −5 **14.** 24

**Independent Practice**
**17.** −8 **19.** 25 **21.** −95 **23.** −7
**25.** 100 **27.** −55 + 275 = 220. The
team's profit was $220.

## LESSON 5.3

**Your Turn**
**4.** −9 **5.** 2 **6.** −2 **7.** −4

**Guided Practice**
**1.** −3 **2.** −2 **3.** (−5); −9 **4.** −4; −3
**5.** −3 **6.** 2 **7.** −6 **8.** −18 **9.** 5
**10.** 19 **11.** 14 **12.** 42 **13.** 38 **14.** 0

**Independent Practice**
**17.** −127 − (−225) = 98 feet
**19.** −150 points **21.** Diet Chow
**25.** −16, −21, −26

## LESSON 5.4

**Your Turn**
**1.** −40 − 13 + 18; −35; 35 feet
below the cave entrance
**3.** −35 + (−45) + 180 = 100;
$100 increase **4.** Jim

**Guided Practice**
**1.** −15 + 9 − 12 = −18; 18 feet
below sea level **2.** −23 + 5 − 7 =
−25; −25 °F **3.** 50 − 40 + 87 − 30
= 67 **4.** 24 **5.** −12 **6.** 18 **7.** 21
**8.** 97 **9.** 27 **10.** (−12 + 6 − 4) <
(−34 − 3 + 39) **11.** (21 − 3 + 8)
> (−14 + 31 − 6)

**Independent Practice**
**13a.** 5 − 1 + 6 − 1 = 9 **b.** over par
**c.** yes **15.** The Commutative
Property does not apply to
subtraction. 3 − 6 + 5 = 2 and
3 − 5 + 6 = 4 **17a.** 3:00 to 4:00
**b.** 87 **19.** $24 **23.** The sum of
the other two numbers must be
greater than the value of the first
number.

MODULE **6**

## LESSON 6.1

**Your Turn**

**4.** $-15$ **5.** $20$ **6.** $-42$ **7.** $0$
**8.** $45$ **9.** $32$

**Guided Practice**

**1.** $-9$ **2.** $-28$ **3.** $54$ **4.** $-100$
**5.** $-60$ **6.** $0$ **7.** $49$ **8.** $-135$
**9.** $-96$ **10.** $300$ **11.** $0$ **12.** $-192$
**13.** $7(-75) = -525$; $-\$525$
**14.** Start at zero and move 5 units
to the left 3 times. $3(-5) = -15$;
$-15$ yards **15.** $6(-2) = -12$;
$-12\,°F$ **16.** $4(-5) = -20$; $-\$20$
**17.** $5(-50) = -250$; $-250$ feet

**Independent Practice**

**19.** No **21.** $5(-4) = -20$; $\$20$
decrease **23.** $7(-6) = -42$; the
cost of the jeans decreased by $42
over the 7 weeks. **25.** $7(-8) =$
$-56$; $7(-5) = -35$; $-56 + (-35)$
$= -91$. The savings decreased by
$91. **27a.** $-27$ **b.** $27$ **c.** $-27$
**d.** $-81$ **e.** $81$ **f.** $-81$ **g.** negative;
positive

## LESSON 6.2

**Your Turn**

**2.** $0$ **3.** $-2$ **4.** $13$ **5.** Yolanda
received the same number of
penalties in each game; 5. $-25 \div$
$(-5) = 5$ and $-35 \div (-7) = 5$.

**Guided Practice**

**1.** $-7$ **2.** $-7$ **3.** $-2$ **4.** $0$ **5.** $9$
**6.** $-3$ **7.** $11$ **8.** $1$ **9.** $0$ **10.** $11$
**11.** $-12$ **12.** $-20$ **13.** undefined
**14.** $3$ **15.** $-40 \div (4) = -10$; $\$10$
**16.** $-22 \div (11) = -2$; 2 points
**17.** $-75 \div (-15) = 5$; 5 targets
**18.** $-99 \div (-9) = 11$; 11 times

**Independent Practice**

**21.** Elisa made $-140 \div (-20) = 7$
withdrawals; Francis made $-270 \div$
$(-45) = 6$ withdrawals, and $7 > 6$.
**23.** the first part **27.** False;
division by 0 is undefined for any
dividend. **29.** $12$

## LESSON 6.3

**Your Turn**

**1.** Reggie earned 110 points;
$3(-30) + 200 = -90 + 200 = 110$.
**2.** $-78 - 21 = -99$ **4.** $0$ **5.** $20$
**6.** $22$ **7.** $-28$ **8.** Will **9.** $-7$; $-6$;
$(-28) \div 4 + 1$ **10.** $-5$; $-6$; $42 \div$
$(-3) + 9$

**Guided Practice**

**1.** $42$ **2.** $-21$ **3.** $-9$ **4.** $-32$
**5.** $-4$ **6.** $-1$ **7.** $7(-5) + 20 =$
$-15$; 15 dollars less **8.** $7(-10) +$
$(-100) = -170$; 170 fewer points
**9.** $6(-4) + 10 = -14$; lost 14
points **10.** $4(-12) + 10 = -38$;
$38 less **11.** $>$ **12.** $=$ **13.** $>$
**14.** $<$

**Independent Practice**

**17.** $4$ **19.** $0$ **21.** $2$ **23.** $5(-4) - 8$
$= -28$ **25a.** $4(-35) - 9 = -149$;
$149 less **b.** Yes **29.** $80$ inches

 **Selected Answers**

# UNIT 3 Selected Answers

MODULE 7

## LESSON 7.1

**Your Turn**

**5.** 2 : 1; 2 to 1; $\frac{2}{1}$  **6.** 8 : 4; 8 to 4; $\frac{8}{4}$
**7.** 1 : 1; 1 to 1; $\frac{1}{1}$

**Guided Practice**

**1.** 1 dog to 5 cats  **2.** 5; 3  **3.** 5; 25
**4.** Sample answer: 2 to 6; 2 : 6; $\frac{2}{6}$
**5.** Sample answer: 3 to 12; 3 : 12; $\frac{3}{12}$
**6.** Sample answer: $\frac{5}{6}, \frac{20}{24}, \frac{25}{30}$
**7.** Sample answer: $\frac{7}{1}, \frac{21}{3}, \frac{28}{4}$
**8.** Sample answer: $\frac{8}{14}, \frac{12}{21}, \frac{16}{28}$

**Independent Practice**

**11.** $\frac{4}{3}, \frac{40}{30}, \frac{100}{75}$
**13.** 12 bananas, 9 apples, and
18 pears  **15.** 16.5 cups  **17a.** $39
**b.** $2.50

## LESSON 7.2

**Your Turn**

**3.** 12  **4.** 0.50

**6.** $\frac{27 \text{ minutes}}{3 \text{ miles}} \div \frac{3}{3} = \frac{9 \text{ minutes}}{1 \text{ miles}}$
$\frac{9 \text{ minutes}}{1 \text{ mile}} \times \frac{5}{5} = \frac{45 \text{ minutes}}{5 \text{ miles}}$
**7.** $\frac{100 \text{ miles}}{4 \text{ gallons}} \div \frac{4}{4} = \frac{25 \text{ miles}}{1 \text{ gallon}}$
$\frac{275 \text{ miles}}{25 \text{ miles per gallon}} = 11 \text{ gallons}$

**Guided Practice**

**1.** 0.15; 0.12; 0.14  **2.** B  **3.** 0.21; 0.19
**4.** family size  **5.** 16  **6.** 72  **7.** 300
calories  **8.** $6.00  **9.** 7 hours

**Independent Practice**

**11.** 8-pound bag  **13.** $12.50
per lawn  **15.** Alastair  **17a.** 5
minutes  **b.** 7 balloons  **c.** 1.4
balloons per minute  **19.** $0.40
per kazoo  **21.** 2.54 × 12 = 30.48
centimeters per foot; 30.48 cm × 3
= 91.44 centimeters per yard.
**23.** The unit cost decreases as the
quantity of sugar increases.

## LESSON 7.3

**Your Turn**

**2.** No, the ratios are not
equivalent. $\frac{2 \times 4}{3 \times 4} = \frac{8}{12}; \frac{8}{12} > \frac{7}{12}$

**Guided Practice**

**1b.** No, Celeste is not using
the correct ratio of apples to
oranges; $\frac{10}{12} > \frac{8}{12}$  **2.** No; Neha used
the greater ratio of bananas to
oranges in her fruit salad.  **3.** Tim
can read 140 words in 5 minutes.
**4.** On average, the cafeteria sells
120 drinks per hour.

**Independent Practice**

**7.** $63  **9.** 175 miles
**11.** approximately 18 apples
**13.** approximately 22 inches
**17.** All of the rates should be
equivalent to each other.

MODULE 8

## LESSON 8.1

**Your Turn**

**2.** Additive; Sample answer: Ky's
age is equal to Lu's age plus 7.

| Lu's age | 1 | 2 | 3 | 4 | 5 |
|---|---|---|---|---|---|
| Ky's age | 8 | 9 | 10 | 11 | 12 |

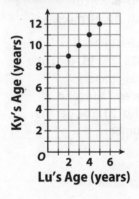

**Guided Practice**

**1.** The total number of dogs is
equal to the number of dogs
adopted plus 2.

**2.**

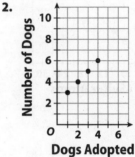

**3.** The number of days of class is 3
times the number of weeks.

**4.**

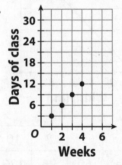

**5.** Multiplicative

**Independent Practice**

**7.** Raging River: multiplicative;
Paddlers: additive  **9.** 5 hours
**11.** 360 miles  **13.** red points:
additive; black points: multiplicative

## LESSON 8.2

**Your Turn**

**3.**

| Time (min) | 2 | 3 | 3.5 | 5 | 6.5 |
|---|---|---|---|---|---|
| Water used (gal) | 8 | 12 | 14 | 20 | 26 |

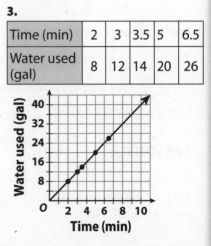

**Guided Practice**

**1.** $\frac{18}{6} = \frac{27}{9} = \frac{63}{21} = \frac{81}{27}$

**2.**

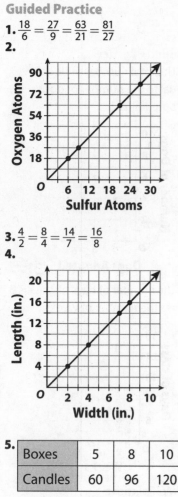

**3.** $\frac{4}{2} = \frac{8}{4} = \frac{14}{7} = \frac{16}{8}$

**4.**

**5.**

| Boxes | 5 | 8 | 10 |
|---|---|---|---|
| Candles | 60 | 96 | 120 |

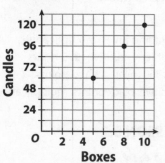

**Independent Practice**

**7.** $\frac{\text{money collected}}{\text{sweatshirts sold}} = \frac{\$60}{3 \text{ sweatshirts}}$
$= \frac{\$20}{1 \text{ sweatshirt}} = \$20$ per sweatshirt
sold  **11.** $480  **13.** 330 mi

## LESSON 8.3

**Your Turn**

**1.** 10 cheese pizzas  **2.** 108 minutes  **3.** 50 miles

**Guided Practice**

**1.** 6; 6; 18  **2.** 2; 2; 2  **3.** $45
**4.** 18 inches tall  **5.** 60 seconds
**6.** 13 measures  **7.** 40 minutes
**8.** 26 paychecks  **9.** 24 kilometers

**Independent Practice**

**11a.** 60 seats  **b.** 150 seats
**13a.** 24 cups  **b.** 18; 36; 54
**c.** 81 servings  **15.** 45 ft
**17.** Ira  **19.** No, the caterpillar's unit rate should be 5 feet per minute.
**21a.**

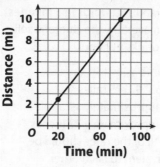

**b.** 80 minutes

## LESSON 8.4

**Your Turn**

**2.** 72 inches  **3.** 2.5 meters

**Guided Practice**

**1.** 3  **2.** 48  **3.** 32 cups
**4.** 12,000 pounds
**5.** 500 meters  **6.** 3,500 grams
**7.** 1,750 mg  **8.** 2.7 cm
**9.** 6 pounds  **10.** 10 miles

**Independent Practice**

**13.** 126; 10.5; 3.5  **15.** the large size  **17.** 3 kilometers
**19a.** between 7 tons and 8 tons  **b.** No  **21.** You get the original number.

## LESSON 9.1

**Your Turn**

**2.** 90%  **3.** 40%  **4.** about $\frac{2}{3}$

**Guided Practice**

**1.** 4; 4; 36; 36%

**2.**

**3.** 10; 60%  **4.** 1; 50%  **5.** 1; 80%
**6.** about $\frac{2}{5}$

**Independent Practice**

**9.** 55  **11.** $\frac{9}{10} = 90\%$, $\frac{4}{5} = 80\%$, $\frac{17}{20} = 85\%$, 80%, 85%, 90%
**13.** 30% of your minutes are used up.  **17.** No

## LESSON 9.2

**Your Turn**

**1.** $\frac{3}{20}$, 0.15  **2.** $\frac{12}{25}$, 0.48  **3.** $\frac{4}{5}$, 0.8
**4.** $\frac{3}{4}$, 0.75  **5.** $\frac{9}{25}$, 0.36  **6.** $\frac{2}{5}$, 0.4
**8.** 0.36, 36%  **9.** 0.875, 87.5%

**Guided Practice**

**1.** $\frac{3}{25}$; 0.12  **2.** 53%, $\frac{53}{100}$  **3.** 107%;
$\frac{107}{100} = 1\frac{7}{100}$  **4.** 0.35; 35%  **5.** 0.375; 37.5%

**Independent Practice**

**7.** $\frac{18}{25}$; 0.72  **9.** $\frac{500}{100}$, $\frac{5}{1}$, 5  **11.** $\frac{37}{100}$; 0.37  **13.** 0.625, 62.5%  **15.** 3.5, 350%  **17.** $\frac{68}{80} = \frac{17}{20}$; 85%; 0.85
**19.** 6  **23.** 1, 100%, 1

## LESSON 9.3

**Your Turn**

**5.** 19  **6.** 81  **7.** 45  **9.** 76%
**11.** 20  **12.** 500

**Guided Practice**

**1.** 240 televisions are high definition.  **2.** 65; 200; 130
**3.** $\times$; 900; 9; 9  **4.** 21; 100; 300; 7%
**5.** 9; 300

**Independent Practice**

**7.** 48 tiles  **9.** 8 pages  **11.** 252 friends  **13.** 20  **15.** 70  **17.** 1,400
**19.** 40  **21.** 20  **23.** 9  **25.** $500
**27.** $30  **29.** $175  **31.** $\frac{25}{100} = \frac{?}{50}$; 25% of 50 is 12.5.

# UNIT 4 Selected Answers

 **MODULE 10**

## LESSON 10.1

**Your Turn**

**2.** $4^3$ **3.** $6^1$ **4.** $\left(\frac{1}{8}\right)^2$ **5.** $5^6$ **6.** 81
**7.** $-1$ **8.** $\frac{8}{125}$ **9.** $-144$

**Guided Practice**

**2.** $6^3$ **3.** $10^7$ **4.** $\left(\frac{3}{4}\right)^5$ **5.** $\left(\frac{7}{9}\right)^8$ **6.** 512
**7.** 2,401 **8.** 1,000 **9.** $\frac{1}{16}$ **10.** $\frac{1}{27}$
**11.** $\frac{36}{49}$ **12.** 0.64 **13.** 0.125
**14.** 1.21 **15.** 1 **16.** 12 **17.** 1
**18.** $-8$ **19.** $\frac{4}{25}$ **20.** $-81$

**Independent Practice**

**23.** 3 **25.** 3 **27.** 1 **29.** 2 **31.** 4
**33.** 3 **35.** 8 **37.** 9 **39.** $3^4$ pages, or
81 pages **41.** $2^6$ dollars, or $64
**47.** $2^6$, $4^3$, and $8^2$

## LESSON 10.2

**Your Turn**

**1.** 1, 3, 7, 21 **2.** 1, 37 **3.** 1, 2, 3, 6, 7,
14, 21, 42 **4.** 1, 2, 3, 5, 6, 10, 15, 30

**Guided Practice**

**1.** 1, 2, 3, 6, 9, 18 **2.** 1, 2, 4, 13, 26,
52 **4.** $2 \cdot 3 \cdot 67$ **5.** $2^2 \cdot 3^2$ **6.** $2^5$
**7.** $3 \cdot 3 \cdot 3$ or $3^3$

**Independent Practice**

**9.** $1 \times 12$; $2 \times 6$; $3 \times 4$
**13.** $2^3 \cdot 3^2 \cdot 7$ **15.** $2 \cdot 5 \cdot 23$
**19.** prime factorization of $27 = 3^3$

## LESSON 10.3

**Your Turn**

**2.** 19 **3.** 2 **4.** $-2$ **5.** 37

**Guided Practice**

**1.** $3 \times 2^2 = 12$ angelfish **2.** 3; 9; 3;
7 **3.** 4; 9; 9; 1 **4.** 8; $-3$; $-6$; $-15$
**5.** $-6$; 2; $-16$; 2; $-32$

**Independent Practice**

**7.** 19 **9.** $-3$ **11.** 39 **13.** $-25$.
**15a.** $3 \times 2 \times 2 \times 2 \times 2 = 3 \times 2^4$
**b.** $3 \times 2^4 - 7 = 3 \times 16 \times - 7$
$= 48 - 7 = 41$ butterflies
**17a.** $6^2 + 2 \times 6 + 24 = 72$ square
inches
**b.** 8 in. by 9 in.
**19.** $8 \times 4 - (2 \times 3 + 8) \div 2$

## LESSON 11.1

**Your Turn**

**2.** $7n$ **3.** $4 - y$ **4.** $x + 13$
**5.** Sample answer: the quotient of $x$ and 12 **6.** Sample answers 10 multiplied by $y$
**7.**

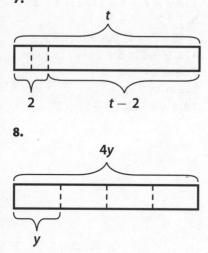

**8.**

**9.** No; the expressions are not equivalent.

**Guided Practice**

**1.** Sample answer given. 5; 5
**2.** $y - 3$ **3.** $2p$ **4.** Sample answers are given. 12 added to $y$
**5.** Sample answers are given. 10 divided into $p$
**6.**

$m$

$\frac{m}{4}$

**7.**

Phoenix $t$

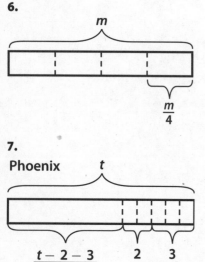

$t - 2 - 3$ $2$ $3$

Tucson $t$

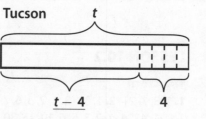

$t - 4$ $4$

**8.** No

**Independent Practice**

**13.** $15; x$ **15.** $4p$ **17.** $90x$
**19.** $24 - k$ **21.** $1 + q$ **23.** $45 + c$
**25.** Sample answer: 42 times $s$
**27.** Sample answer: $t$ minus 29
**29.** Sample answer: the product of 11 and $x$ **31.** Sample answer: $k$ less than 5 **33.** $8w$ **35.** No
**37a.** $3 + x$ **b.** $5 - 2 + x$
**c.** Yes **39.** $\frac{48}{b}$ **41.** $\frac{s}{2}$ **43.** Sample answer: $2x - 8y + 7$.

## LESSON 11.2

**Your Turn**

**1.** 32 **2.** 4.7 **3.** 3 **4.** 18 **5.** 18
**6.** 55 **7.** 18 **8.** $-9$ **9.** 11
**10.** 24; 8 **11.** 420

**Guided Practice**

**1.** 16 **2.** 6 **3.** 2 **4.** 10.5 **5.** $2\frac{1}{18}$
**6.** 50 **7a.** $12x + 5$ **b.** 3; 36; 41; $41 **8a.** $2w + 2l$ **b.** 7; 5; 10; 24; 24 feet

**Independent Practice**

**11.** 42 **15.** $2(x^2)$; $2(64) = 128$ square feet

## LESSON 11.3

**Your Turn**

**3.** Sample answer: $a(bc)$; Associative Property of Multiplication **4.** Sample answer: $(3 + 4)y$; Distributive Property **5.** $2(3x - 5) = 6x - 10$; not equivalent **6.** $2 - 2 + 5x = 5x$; equivalent **7.** Jamal bought $2x + 8$ stickers. $2(4 + x) = 8 + 2x = 2x + 8$; yes **8.** $5y$ **9.** $10x^2 - 4$

**10.** $2a^5 + 5b$ **11.** $8m + 2 + 4n$

**Guided Practice**

**2.** not equivalent **3.** Sample answer: $ba$; Commutative Prop. of Mult. **4.** Sample answer: $5(3x) - 5(2)$; Distributive Prop. **5.** not equivalent **6.** not equivalent
**7.** $44y$ **8.** $2x$

**Independent Practice**

**11.** Sample answer: $13 + x$; Commutative Prop. of Addition
**13.** Sample answer: $(2 + a) + b$; Associative Prop. of Addition
**15.** $2x^4$ **17.** $13b - 10$ **19.** $4y + 10$
**21.** $15y^2 - 6$ **23.** $0.5x^4 + 10.5$
**25.** $3x + 12 + x$ is equivalent to $4(3 + x)$. **27.** $(46 + 38 + 29)g + (29 + 27 + 17)s + (29 + 23 + 19)b$; $113g + 73s + 71b$ **29.** $36.4 + 4x$ in. **31.** $3x^2 - 4x + 7$; it does not have any like terms.

## LESSON 12.1

**Your Turn**

**1.** yes **2.** no **3.** yes **4.** $f + 9 = 38$
**5.** $17n = 102$ **6.** $c - 3 = 12$
**7.** $2h = 8$

**Guided Practice**

**1.** no; 14; 5 **2.** yes; 52; 4 **3.** yes
**4.** yes **5.** no **6.** yes **7.** no
**8.** yes **9.** no **10.** no **11.** yes
**12.** no **13.** $8r = 256$ **14.** Sample answer: $\frac{f}{2} = 5$ **15.** Sample equation: $8x = 208$; $26
**16.** Sample equation: $x + 24 = 92$; 68 °F

**Independent Practice**

**19.** $x + 8 = 31$; 23 pounds
**21a.** $29 - 13 = x$; $13 + x = 29$
**b.** $x$ is the distance between Artavelle and Greenville. **25.** Both equations are correct. Another correct equation is $44 - 7 = x$.

**27.** Yes, because $4 + f = 12$ means there are 8 flute players, and 8 is twice 4. **29.** Yes

## LESSON 12.2

**Your Turn**

**4.** 3.5

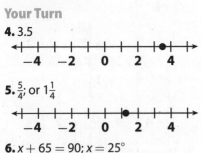

**5.** $\frac{5}{4}$, or $1\frac{1}{4}$

**6.** $x + 65 = 90$; $x = 25°$
**7.** $x + 42 = 90$; $x = 48°$

**Guided Practice**

**1a.** number of guests who left when the party ended. **c.** 11 **2.** 5

**3.** 1.5

**4.** 4.5 **5.** 40 **6.** $\frac{5}{4}$ **7.** $x + 45 = 180$; $x = 135°$ **8.** $x = 275$

**Independent Practice**

**11.** Sample answer: $14 = b - 12$; $b = 26$ **13.** Sample answer: $x + 8 = 37$; 29 compact cars **15.** Sample answer: $m - 123.45 = 36.55$; $160 **17.** $c = 2.50$ **19a.** $1.49 + a = 2.99$; $2.49 + r = 3.99$ **b.** Both $a$ and $r$ are equal to $1.50, so the discount is the same. **21a.** $a = 1$; $b = 10$, $c = 100$, $d = 1,000$ **b.** Every variable is ten times the one before it. **c.** $g = 1,000,000$

## LESSON 12.3

**Your Turn**

**2.** −7

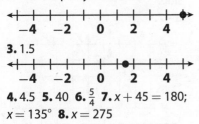

**3.** −9

**5.** $x = 35$

**Guided Practice**

**1a.** number of miles run each day **c.** 3 **2.** 9

**3.** −8

**Independent Practice**

**7.** $\frac{a}{8} = 5$; 40 square centimeters
**9.** $15m = 420$; 28 mi/gal
**11.** $4s = 132$; $s = 33$ ft; $33 \times 33 = 1,089$ square feet
**15.** $7 \cdot \frac{x}{7} = \frac{7x}{7} = 1x = x$; 7 divided by 7 is 1. $1x$ is the same as $x$.
**17a.** $4p = 36$; $p = 9$; Peter has 9 model cars.
**b.** $\frac{1}{3}j = 9$; $j = 27$; Jade has 27 model cars.

## MODULE 13

## LESSON 13.1

**Your Turn**

**2.**

**3.** $1 + y \geq 3$; $y = 1$ is not a solution because $1 + 1$ is not greater than or equal to 3. **4.** $t \leq 6$

**5.** $w \not> 2$

**Guided Practice**

**1.** 3, 1

**2.**

**3.** $4 + x < 6$

**4.** Let $t$ be temperature in °C; $t \geq 3$

**Independent Practice**

**7.**

**11.**

**13.** $x \leq -3$ **15.** $x \geq -3.5$
**19.** $g > 150$

## LESSON 13.2

**Your Turn**

**2.** $y \geq -2$

**3.** $x < 9$

**5.** Check students' problems.

**Guided Practice**

**1.** $3 + x \leq 5$; $x \leq 2$
**2.** $x \geq 5$

**3.** $z < 8$

**4.** $t > 7$

**5.** $y < 6$

**Independent Practice**

**9.** $y \geq 8$

**11.** $z \leq -11$

**13.** $72 \leq d - 15$; $d \geq 87$ dollars
**15.** $p - 4.5 \geq 5.5$; $p \geq 10$ pizzas
**17a.** $x + 520.45 > 1,500$; $x > 979.55$ **b.** $x + 93.32 < 450$; $x < 356.68$ **c.** Yes

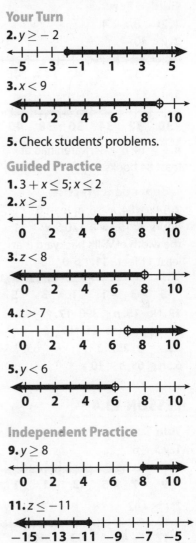

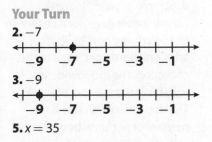

## LESSON 13.3

**Your Turn**

**3.** $x \geq 20$

15 17 19 21 23 25

**4.** $z < 44$

40 42 44 46 48 50

**6.** $\frac{w}{6} < 4$; $w < 24$; Brittany must use less than 24 oz of sand.

**Guided Practice**

**1.** $2x < 8$; $x < 4$

**2.** $y < 40$

35 37 39 41 43 45

**3.** $r \geq 33$

30 32 34 36 38 40

**4.** $\frac{b}{6} \geq 14$; $b \geq 84$; Karen had at least 84 books.

**Independent Practice**

**7.** $14x \geq 84$; $x \geq 6$; at least 6 hours **9.** $15.5w \geq 170.5$; $w \geq 11$; the width of Will's backyard is at least 11 feet. **11.** $t > 0$

−5 −3 −1 1 3 5

**13.** No **15.** $p \leq 390$ **17.** $y \geq \frac{1}{12}$
**19.** $3\frac{1}{3}$ pounds **21.** No
**23.** $r \leq 2$ **25.** $13 \cdot \left(\frac{1}{2}\right) \cdot h \leq 65$;
$6.5h \leq 65$; $h < 10$

## LESSON 13.4

**Your Turn**

**1.** $y > -6$

−9 −7 −5 −3 −1 1

**2.** $t \geq -42$

−47 −45 −43 −41

**4.** $m \leq 9$

**Guided Practice**

**3.** $z \leq -3$

−10 −8 −6 −4 −2 0

**2.** $t < -20$

−40 −20 0 20

**3.** $x < -6$

−8 −6 −4 −2 0 2

**4.** $t < -50$

−100 −80 −60 −40

**5a.** $-4 \cdot t \geq -80$ **b.** 20 or fewer hours **c.** more than 20 hours

**Independent Practice**

**7.** $q \leq 7$

0 2 4 6 8 10

**9.** $y \geq 4$

0 2 4 6 8 10

**11.** $x < -6$

−8 −6 −4 −2 0 2

**13a.** $-6x < -48$; $x > 8$; 9 times
**b.** No **15.** no less than 10 seconds
**17.** The student did not reverse the inequality sign. The answer should be $x < -7$. **19.** $x \geq 161$
**21.** $x < -0.4$ **23.** $x \geq 24$

MODULE **14**

## LESSON 14.1

**Your Turn**

**4.** $G(4, -4)$; IV; $E(-2, 4)$; II
**5.** $F(3, 2)$; I; $H(-1, -3)$; III
**6–10.**

**11.** Ted $(-20, -20)$, Ned $(-20, 30)$

**Guided Practice**

**1.** left; up; $(-5, 1)$; II **2.** 2; 3;
$(2, -3)$; IV
**3–4.**

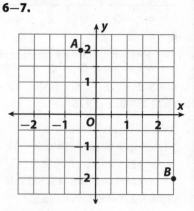

**5.** Each grid square is $\frac{1}{2}$ unit on a side.
**6–7.**

**Independent Practice**
**11.** Sam is 3 km south and 7 km east of the theater.
**13.** $(-3, 0.5)$
**15.** $W(-0.75, -1.0)$

## LESSON 14.2

**Your Turn**

**8.** Sample answer: Bridget's grandmother gave her a collection of 15 perfume bottles. Bridget adds one bottle per week to the collection. The independent variable is the number of weeks. The dependent variable is the number of perfume bottles in her collection. The value of $y$ is always 15 units greater than the value of $x$.

## Guided Practice

**1.** Time is the independent variable and cost is the dependent variable.

**2a.**

| Time $x$ (h) | 0 | 1 | 2 | 3 |
|---|---|---|---|---|
| Distance $y$ (mi) | 0 | 60 | 120 | 180 |

**b.** Time is the independent variable and distance is the dependent variable. **c.** The value of $y$ is always 60 times the value of $x$. **3.** The dependent variable is 5 times the value of the independent variable.

### Independent Practice

**7a.** number of markers **b.** number of gift bags **c.** The relationship is multiplicative because $y$ increases by a factor of 5 as $x$ increases by 1. **d.** The number of glitter markers is 5 times the number of gift bags.

## LESSON 14.3

### Your Turn

**2.** $y = x - 2$ **3.** $y = 2.5x$ **4.** $y = x + 5$
**5.** $y = 2x$ **6.** $k = r + 5$; 57 years old

### Guided Practice

**1.** $y = x - 4$ **2.** $y = 4x$ **3.** $y = x + 3$
**4.** $y = \frac{x}{6}$
**5.** $1.35n$; $33.75

### Independent Practice

**9.** The $y$-value is $\frac{1}{4}$ of the $x$-value.
**11a.** $e = 8.25h$ **b.** $206.25 =$ $8.25h$; $25 = h$; 25 hours **13.** Not possible; there is no consistent pattern between the $y$-values and corresponding $x$-values. **15.** No

## LESSON 14.4

### Your Turn

**4.**

| $x$ | $x + 2.5 = y$ | $(x, y)$ |
|---|---|---|
| 0 | $0 + 2.5 = 2.5$ | $(0, 2.5)$ |
| 1 | $1 + 2.5 = 3.5$ | $(1, 3.5)$ |
| 2 | $2 + 2.5 = 4.5$ | $(2, 4.5)$ |
| 3 | $3 + 2.5 = 5.5$ | $(3, 5.5)$ |

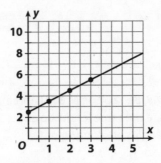

### Guided Practice

**1.** $y = 3x$

| Hours worked | Lawns mowed |
|---|---|
| 0 | 0 |
| 1 | 3 |
| 2 | 6 |
| 3 | 9 |

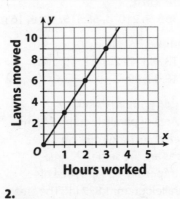

**2.**

| $x$ | 0 | 1 | 2 | 3 |
|---|---|---|---|---|
| $y$ | 0 | 1.5 | 3 | 4.5 |

**3.**

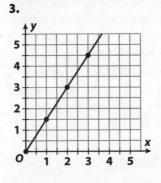

### Independent Practice

**5.**

| Additional hours | 0 | 5 | 10 | 15 | 20 |
|---|---|---|---|---|---|
| Total hours | 20 | 25 | 30 | 35 | 40 |

**7.** 20 hours; when 0 additional hours are worked, the total is 20 hours.

**9.**

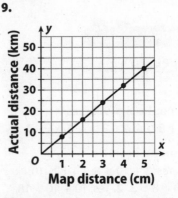

**Map distance (cm)**

**11a.**

| Number of tickets, $x$ | 1 | 2 | 3 | 4 | 5 |
|---|---|---|---|---|---|
| Total cost ($), $y$ | 9 | 18 | 27 | 36 | 45 |

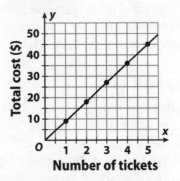

**Number of tickets**

**b.** Dependent: total cost; independent: number of tickets

## UNIT 5 Selected Answers

### LESSON 15.1

**Your Turn**
**2.** no; $3 + 6 \not> 9$ **3.** yes; $4 + 5 > 8$; $5 + 8 > 4$; $4 + 8 > 5$ **4.** $x = 13$

**Guided Practice**
**1.** Yes; $3 + 10 > 8$; $3 + 8 > 10$; $10 + 8 > 3$ **2.** Yes; $10 + 10 > 18$; $10 + 18 > 10$ **3.** Yes; $30 + 20 > 40$; $30 + 40 > 20$; $20 + 40 > 30$
**4.** No; $3 + 12 \not> 16$ **5.** $x = 29$

**Independent Practice**
**7.** No; the combined lengths of the two shortest sides is less than the length of the longest side. So the three lengths cannot form a triangle. **9.** Yes **11.** 13 in. **13.** No

### LESSON 15.2

**Your Turn**
**2.** $25°$ **3.** $53°$ **6.** $25° + 65° + x = 180$; $x = 90°$ **7.** $60° + 60° + x = 180$; $x = 60°$ **8.** $35° + 35° + x = 180$; $x = 110°$

**Guided Practice**
**1.** $180°$ **2.** $33°$ **3.** $42°$ **4.** $62°$
**5.** $119°$ **6.** $60°$ **7.** $90°$ **8.** $100°$

**Independent Practice**
**11.** $m\angle DAC = 48°$.
**13.** $m\angle BAC = 35°$. **15.** $\angle DAB$ is formed by $\angle DAC$ and $\angle BAC$; $48° + 35° = 83°$. **17.** $m\angle A = 48°$; $m\angle B = 90°$; $m\angle C = 42°$ **19.** $65°$ **21.** Yes

### LESSON 15.3

**Your Turn**
**1.** 16; 19; 11 **2.** $45°$; $58°$; $77°$
**3.** 20 feet

**Guided Practice**
**1.** $AC$, $AB$, $BC$ **2.** $M$; $P$; $N$ **3.** All three sides are the same length so all three angles are congruent.
**4.** 40 feet

**Independent Practice**
**7.** Find $m\angle G$ by subtracting the sum of the measures of the other two angles from $180°$. **9.** No
**11.** $\overline{AB}$ **13.** $\overline{YX}$ **15.** No

### LESSON 16.1

**Your Turn**
**2.** 366 **3.** 210 **4.** 66.5 **5.** 90 **6.** 165

**Guided Practice**
**1.** 13; 9; 117 **2.** 14; 9; 15; 168
**3.** 18; 11; 99

**Independent Practice**
**5.** Area of parallelogram: 84 cm²; Area of rectangle: 84 cm²; The areas are the same. **7.** Area of trapezoid: 936 in²; Area of parallelogram: 1,872 in²; The area of the trapezoid is $\frac{1}{2}$ the area of the parallelogram. **9.** 8.25 ft²
**11.** 1,620 in² **13.** 57 ft² **15.** 9 in. and 15 in.; use the formula for the area of a trapezoid. Substitute 96 for $A$ and 8 for $h$ and simplify the equation to find $24 = (b_1 + b_2)$. Use guess and check to find two numbers that add to 24 with one number 6 more than the other and get 9 and 15.

### LESSON 16.2

**Your Turn**
**3.** 59.5 in² **5.** 12 ft²

**Guided Practice**
**1.** 14; 8; 56 **2.** 12; 30; 180

**Independent Practice**
**5.** 240 ft² **7.** 288 ft² **9.** 71.5 in²
**11.** 20 ft² **13.** Monica forgot to multiply by $\frac{1}{2}$. The area of the fabric is 45 in². **17a.** 6 in. **b.** 1 in. and 36 in., 2 in. and 18 in., 3 in. and 12 in., 4 in. and 9 in.

### LESSON 16.3

**Your Turn**
**1.** 8 in. **3.** 4 ft **4.** 8 pallets

**Guided Practice**
**1.** $70 = \frac{1}{2}\left(8\frac{3}{4}\right) b$; 16 inches **2.** $791 = \frac{1}{2}h(26.5 + 30)$; 28 centimeters
**3.** area; $A = 42(28) = 1{,}176$ ft²; number of gallons of paint; $n = 1{,}176 \div 350 = 3.36$; 4

**Independent Practice**
**5.** $5\frac{1}{2}$ ft **7.** 1.2 cm **9.** 16 in. and 8 in. **11.** 128 patches **13a.** 702 ft²
**b.** 1,458 ft² **c.** 486 ft² **15a.** $3\frac{1}{2}$ yd
**b.** $10\frac{2}{3}$ yd²

### LESSON 16.4

**Your Turn**
**1.** 925 **3.** The height is $\frac{5}{2}$ ft or $2\frac{1}{2}$ ft.
**5.** $33.75 \div 7.5 = 4.5$ so $V = 4.5$ cubic feet; $4.5 = 2(w)(1.5)$; $w = 1.5$ feet

**Guided Practice**
**1.** $15\frac{3}{4}$ **2.** 22 cm $= w$ **3.** 4 inches $= h$

**Independent Practice**
**5.** 12.4 in. **7.** 6 cm **9.** The volume is 2,000 cubic millimeters and the weight is 1 ounce.
**11a.** 2.5 gallons **b.** 245 cubic inches **c.** No, the fish would need 577.5 cubic inches of water.
**13.** 42.9; 4.3; 30.0 **15.** Begin with $V = Bh$ and divide both sides of the equation by $h$ to get $B = \frac{V}{h}$.
**17.** The volume is correct but the units should be cubic inches, not inches.

## MODULE 17

### LESSON 17.1

**Your Turn**

**3.** median = 6.5 minutes

**Guided Practice**

**1.** 15; 5; 3; 3  **2a.** 42  **b.** No
**3a.** mean: 8.5; median: 6  **b.** The median; sample answer: the median is closer to most of the data values than the mean is.

**Independent Practice**

**5.** Ten students were asked, because there are 10 data values in the list.  **7.** 78.5; 80.5  **9.** Minutes and hours; convert all times to minutes.  **11.** Median; it is closer to most of the data values; the data values of 0.5 hr and 1 hr raise the mean a great deal.  **13.** 95

### LESSON 17.2

**Your Turn**

**3.** Group A IQR = $700. Group B IQR = $450. Group A's IQR is greater, so the salaries in the middle 50% for group A are more spread out than those for group B.
**4.** Miami = 15, Chicago = 53; Chicago

**Guided Practice**

**1.** 4; 10; 11; 13; 14; 15; 25; 29; 33; 33; 35; 43; 51; 58; 64  **2.** 29  **3.** 13  **4.** 43  **6.** 30  **7.** 60

**Independent Practice**

**11.** Sample answer: Students could have measured each others' heights.  **13.** 0.3; 0.3  **15.** The IQRs are the same. The spreads of the middle 50% of the data values are the same for the two data sets.  **17.** Yes

### LESSON 17.3

**Your Turn**

**4.** 14 games; the value with the greatest frequency is 4; there were 4 games in which the team scored 4 runs.  **6.** Mean: about 3.3, median: 3.5, range: 5; sample answer: between 3 and 4 runs. The mean and median are close in value, and there are no outliers.

**Guided Practice**

**1.** Variable data  **3.** Mean: about 5.2; median = 5; range = 17.
**4.** spread: 0 to 17. 17 appears to be an outlier. The distribution is not symmetric.

**Independent Practice**

**7.** not statistical  **9.** not statistical
**11.**

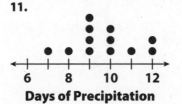

**Days of Precipitation**

**15.** The mean would change to about 9.3; the median would stay at 9.5; the range would change to 9 days.  **19.** 5(2) + 6(2) + 7 + 8(3) + 9(2) + 10(5) + 11 + 12(3) + 13(2) + 15(2) + 22  **21.** Count the number of dots above that data value.  **23.** 19; Each dot represents one game.  **25.** Mean: about 3.9 runs; median: 4 runs; range: 11 runs  **27a.** the units for the ages (years, months, weeks)  **b.** No

### LESSON 17.4

**Your Turn**

**2.** 12 seasons; 0 home runs
**3.** Median: 8.5, mean: 11.75; the median; 44 appears to be an outlier that raises the value of the mean.

**Guided Practice**

**1.**

**Wendy's Text Messages**

| Stem | Leaves |
|------|--------|
| 1 | 5 |
| 2 | 0 4 7 7 9 |
| 3 | 0 3 4 5 5 |
| 4 | 2 6 |
| 5 | 2 |

*Key: 1|5 means 15*

**2.** Mean: about 32.1, median: 31.5; either measure of center could be used because there are no outliers and the measures are close in value.
**3.**

| Interval | Frequency |
|----------|-----------|
| 1–7 | 1 |
| 8–14 | 3 |
| 15–21 | 4 |
| 22–28 | 2 |

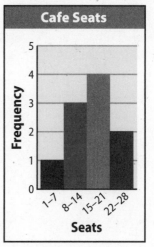

Cafe Seats

**Independent Practice**

**5.**

| Interval | Frequency |
|----------|-----------|
| 10–19 | 9 |
| 20–29 | 7 |
| 30–39 | 3 |
| 40–49 | 4 |
| 50–59 | 2 |

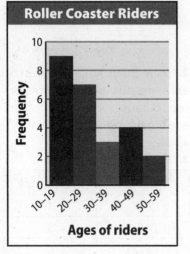

**Roller Coaster Riders**

Ages of riders

**7.**

**Roller Coaster Rider Ages**

| Stem | Leaves |
|------|--------|
| 1 | 1 2 6 6 7 8 8 8 8 |
| 2 | 0 1 3 3 4 9 9 |
| 3 | 1 5 8 |
| 4 | 3 5 7 8 |
| 5 | 0 6 |

*Key: 1|1 means 11*

**11.** The intervals all have the same frequency.

# LESSON 17.5

**Your Turn**

**4.** About half of the tulips (48%) are red. The other half is split between yellow (22%) and purple (30%) tulips.

**Guided Practice**

**2.** movies and sports

**Independent Practice**

**7.** If no pet had more votes than any other, there would be no mode.  **13.** Both graphs show the percent for each eye color and a visual comparison of their relative sizes. The circle graph also shows the relative frequencies as parts of a whole (adding together to make 100% and a full circle).

## LESSON 18.1

**Guided Practice**

**1a.** debit card **b.** A+ bank: $2.50; NextGen Bank: $10 **c.** A+ bank; the fees for using a debit card are less. **2.** Credit card; she paid when she received her credit card bill. **3.** Debit card; the cost was deducted from his account at the time of purchase.

**Independent Practice**

**7.** Yes **9.** His account would have a negative balance.

## LESSON 18.2

**Your Turn**

**3.** 600 **4.** 760

**Guided Practice**

**1.** no late payments, low debt-to-income ratio **2.** late payments, high balance on a credit card **3.** 620 **4.** 700

**Independent Practice**

**9a.** $15,936.48 **b.** $16,096.32 **c.** $159.84

## LESSON 18.3

**Your Turn**

**3.** 50 days

**Guided Practice**

**1.** He could look for grants. He could also take out loans or apply for the work-study program at the college he attends. **2.** She still needs $3,500. She could take out a loan, apply for a grant, or apply for a work-study program. **3.** $2,350

**Independent Practice**

**7.** $5,850 **9.** $36,000
**11a.** $9,000 **b.** $4,300
**13a.** $100,000 **b.** $15,000
**c.** 48 months **d.** $312.50 a month
**e.** $25,000

## LESSON 18.4

**Your Turn**

**4.** $253,800

**Guided Practice**

**2.** Sample answer: ($83,860 · 30) − ($65,920 · 30 ) = $2,515,800 − $1,977,600 = $538,200

**Independent Practice**

**5.** $1,044,300 **7.** $607,500
**9.** $27,600 **11.** $12,272
**13.** Multiply $k$ dollars per hour by the unit rate $\frac{40 \text{ hours}}{1 \text{ work week}}$ to find the job's weekly wage, and then multiply the answer by $\frac{52 \text{ work weeks}}{1 \text{ year}}$ to find the job's yearly salary.

# Glossary/Glosario

## A

| ENGLISH | SPANISH | EXAMPLES |
|---|---|---|
| **absolute value** The distance of a number from zero on a number line; shown by \| \|. | **valor absoluto** Distancia a la que está un número de 0 en una recta numérica. El símbolo del valor absoluto es \| \|. | $\|-5\| = 5$ |
| **acute angle** An angle that measures greater than 0° and less than 90°. | **ángulo agudo** Ángulo que mide más de 0° y menos de 90°. | |
| **acute triangle** A triangle with all angles measuring less than 90°. | **triángulo acutángulo** Triángulo en el que todos los ángulos miden menos de 90°. | |
| **addend** A number added to one or more other numbers to form a sum. | **sumando** Número que se suma a uno o más números para formar una suma. | In the expression $4 + 6 + 7$, the numbers 4, 6, and 7 are addends. |
| **Addition Property of Opposites** The property that states that the sum of a number and its opposite equals zero. | **Propiedad de la suma de los opuestos** Propiedad que establece que la suma de un número y su opuesto es cero. | $12 + (-12) = 0$ |
| **additive inverse** The opposite of a number. | **inverso aditivo** El opuesto de un número | $-4$ is the additive inverse of 4 |
| **adjacent angles** Angles in the same plane that have a common vertex and a common side. | **ángulos adyacentes** Ángulos en el mismo plano que comparten un vértice y un lado. | $\angle 1$ and $\angle 2$ are adjacent angles. |
| **algebraic expression** An expression that contains at least one variable. | **expresión algebraica** Expresión que contiene al menos una variable. | $x + 8$<br>$4(m - b)$ |
| **algebraic inequality** An inequality that contains at least one variable. | **desigualdad algebraica** Desigualdad que contiene al menos una variable. | $x + 3 > 10$<br>$5a > b + 3$ |
| **alternate exterior angles** For two lines intersected by a transversal, a pair of angles that lie on opposite sides of the transversal and outside the other two lines. | **ángulos alternos externos** Dadas dos rectas cortadas por una transversal, par de ángulos no adyacentes ubicados en los lados opuestos de la transversal y fuera de las otras dos rectas. | $\angle 4$ and $\angle 5$ are alternate exterior angles. |

| ENGLISH | SPANISH | EXAMPLES |
|---|---|---|
| **alternate interior angles** For two lines intersected by a transversal, a pair of nonadjacent angles that lie on opposite sides of the transversal and between the other two lines. | **ángulos alternos internos** Dadas dos rectas cortadas por una transversal, par de ángulos no adyacentes ubicados en los lados opuestos de la transversal y entre las otras dos rectas. | <br>∠3 and ∠6 are alternate interior angles. |
| **angle** A figure formed by two rays with a common endpoint called the vertex. | **ángulo** Figura formada por dos rayos con un extremo común llamado vértice. | |
| **area** The number of square units needed to cover a given surface. | **área** El número de unidades cuadradas que se necesitan para cubrir una superficie dada. | <br>The area is 10 square units. |
| **arithmetic sequence** A sequence in which the terms change by the same amount each time. | **secuencia aritmética** Una sucesión en la que los términos cambian la misma cantidad cada vez. | The sequence 2, 5, 8, 11, 14 . . . is an arthmetic sequence. |
| **Associative Property of Addition** The property that states that for three or more numbers, their sum is always the same, regardless of their grouping. | **Propiedad asociativa de la suma** Propiedad que establece que agrupar tres o más números en cualquier orden siempre da como resultado la misma suma. | $2 + 3 + 8 = (2 + 3) + 8 = 2 + (3 + 8)$ |
| **Associative Property of Multiplication** The property that states that for three or more numbers, their product is always the same, regardless of their grouping. | **Propiedad asociativa de la multiplicación** Propiedad que establece que agrupar tres o más números en cualquier orden siempre da como resultado el mismo producto. | $2 \cdot 3 \cdot 8 = (2 \cdot 3) \cdot 8 = 2 \cdot (3 \cdot 8)$ |
| **asymmetrical** Not identical on either side of a central line; not symmetrical. | **asimétrico** Que no es idéntico a ambos lados de una línea central; no simétrico. | |
| **average** The sum of the items in a set of data divided by the number of items in the set; also called *mean*. | **promedio** La suma de los elementos de un conjunto de datos dividida entre el número de elementos del conjunto. También se le llama *media*. | Data set: 4, 6, 7, 8, 10<br>Average: $\frac{4 + 6 + 7 + 8 + 10}{5} =$ $\frac{35}{5} = 7$ |
| **axes** The two perpendicular lines of a coordinate plane that intersect at the origin. singular: axis | **ejes** Las dos rectas numéricas perpendiculares del plano cartesiano que se intersecan en el origen. | |

## B

**bar graph** A graph that uses vertical or horizontal bars to display data.

**gráfica de barras** Gráfica en la que se usan barras verticales u horizontales para presentar datos.

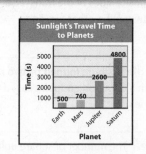

**base (in numeration)** When a number is raised to a power, the number that is used as a factor is the base.

**base (en numeración)** Cuando un número es elevado a una potencia, el número que se usa como factor es la base.

$3^5 = 3 \cdot 3 \cdot 3 \cdot 3 \cdot 3$; 3 is the base.

**base (of a polygon or three-dimensional figure)** A side of a polygon; a face of a three-dimensional figure by which the figure is measured or classified.

**base (de un polígono o figura tridimensional)** Lado de un polígono; la cara de una figura tridimensional, a partir de la cual se mide o se clasifica la figura.

bases of    bases of
a cylinder    a prism

base of    base of
a cone    a pyramid

**bisect** To divide into two congruent parts.

**trazar una bisectriz** Dividir en dos partes congruentes.

**box plot** A graph that shows how data are distributed by using the median, quartiles, least value, and greatest value; also called a box-and-whisker plot.

**gráfica de caja** Gráfica para demostrar la distribución de datos utilizando la mediana, los cuartiles y los valores menos y más grande; también llamado gráfica de mediana y rango.

First quartile   Third quartile
Minimum   Median   Maximum

2   4   6   8   10   12   14

**break (graph)** A zigzag on a horizontal or vertical scale of a graph that indicates that some of the numbers on the scale have been omitted.

**discontinuidad (gráfica)** Zig-zag en la escala horizontal o vertical de una gráfica que indica la omisión de algunos de los números de la escala.

65

60

55

0

## C

**capacity** The amount a container can hold when filled.

**capacidad** Cantidad que cabe en un recipiente cuando se llena.

**categorical data** Data that consists of non numeric information.

**datos categóricos** Datos que constan de información no numérica.

**Celsius** A metric scale for measuring temperature in which 0°C is the freezing point of water and 100°C is the boiling point of water; also called *centigrade*.

**Celsius** Escala métrica para medir la temperatura, en la que 0° C es el punto de congelación del agua y 100° C es el punto de ebullición. También se llama *centígrado*.

---

**center (of a circle)** The point inside a circle that is the same distance from all the points on the circle.

**centro (de un círculo)** Punto interior de un círculo que se encuentra a la misma distancia de todos los puntos de la circunferencia.

---

**center (of rotation)** The point about which a figure is rotated.

**centro (de una rotación)** Punto alrededor del cual se hace girar una figura.

---

**checking account** An account at a financial institution that allows for withdrawals and deposits.

**cuenta corriente** Cuenta bancaria de la cual puedes retirar dinero mediante el uso de un cheque o una tarjeta de débito.

---

**chord** A line segment whose endpoints lie on a circle.

**cuerda** Segmento cuyos extremos se encuentran en un círculo.

---

**circle** The set of all points in a plane that are the same distance from a given point called the center.

**círculo** Conjunto de todos los puntos en un plano que se encuentran a la misma distancia de un punto dado llamado centro.

---

**circle graph** A graph that uses sections of a circle to compare parts to the whole and parts to other parts.

**gráfica circular** Gráfica que usa secciones de un círculo para comparar partes con el todo y con otras partes.

---

**circumference** The distance around a circle.

**circunferencia** Distancia alrededor de un círculo.

---

**clockwise** A circular movement in the direction shown.

**en el sentido de las manecillas del reloj** Movimiento circular en la dirección que se indica.

Glossary/Glosario

| ENGLISH | SPANISH | EXAMPLES |
|---|---|---|
| **clustering** A method used to estimate a sum when all addends are close to the same value. | **agrupación** Método que se usa para estimar una suma cuando todos los sumandos se aproximan al mismo valor. | 27, 29, 24, and 23 all cluster around 25. |
| **coefficient** The number that is multiplied by the variable in an algebraic expression. | **coeficiente** Número que se multiplica por la variable en una expresión algebraica. | 5 is the coefficient in $5b$. |
| **combination** An arrangement of items or events in which order does not matter. | **combinación** Agrupación de objetos o sucesos en la cual el orden no es importante. | For objects $A$, $B$, $C$, and $D$, there are 6 different combinations of 2 objects: $AB$, $AC$, $AD$, $BC$, $BD$, $CD$. |
| **common denominator** A denominator that is the same in two or more fractions. | **denominador común** Denominador que es común a doso más fracciones. | The common denominator of $\frac{5}{8}$ and $\frac{2}{8}$ is 8. |
| **common factor** A number that is a factor of two or more numbers. | **factor común** Número que es factor de dos o más números. | 8 is a common factor of 16 and 40. |
| **common multiple** A number that is a multiple of each of two or more numbers. | **múltiplo común** Un número que es múltiplo de dos o más números. | 15 is a common multiple of 3 and 5. |
| **Commutative Property of Addition** The property that states that two or more numbers can be added in any order without changing the sum. | **Propiedad conmutativa de la suma** Propiedad que establece que sumar dos o más números en cualquier orden no altera la suma. | $8 + 20 = 20 + 8$ |
| **Commutative Property of Multiplication** The property that states that two or more numbers can be multiplied in any order without changing the product. | **Propiedad conmutativa de la multiplicación** Propiedad que establece que multiplicar dos o más números en cualquier orden no altera el producto. | $6 \cdot 12 = 12 \cdot 6$ |
| **compatible numbers** Numbers that are close to the given numbers that make estimation or mental calculation easier. | **números compatibles** Números que están cerca de los números dados y hacen más fácil la estimación o el cálculo mental. | To estimate $7,957 + 5,009$, use the compatible numbers 8,000 and 5,000: $8,000 + 5,000 = 13,000$ |
| **compensation** When a number in a problem is close to another number that is easier to calculate with, the easier number is used to find the answer. Then the answer is adjusted by adding to it or subtracting from it. | **compensación** Cuando un número de un problema está cerca de otro con el que es más fácil hacer cálculos, se usa el número más fácil para hallar la respuesta. Luego, se ajusta la respuesta sumando o restando. | |
| **complement** The set of all outcomes that are not the event. | **complemento** La serie de resultados que no están en el suceso. | When rolling a number cube, the complement of rolling a 3 is rolling a 1, 2, 4, 5, or 6. |

Glossary/Glosario

| ENGLISH | SPANISH | EXAMPLES |
|---|---|---|
| **complementary angles** Two angles whose measures add to 90°. | **ángulos complementarios** Dos ángulos cuyas medidas suman 90°. |  The complement of a 53° angle is a 37° angle. |
| **composite number** A number greater than 1 that has more than two whole-number factors. | **número compuesto** Número mayor que 1 que tiene más de dos factores que son números cabales. | 4, 6, 8, and 9 are composite numbers. |
| **compound inequality** A combination of more than one inequality. | **desigualdad compuesta** Combinación de dos o más desigualdades. | $-2 \leq x < 10$ |
| **cone** A three-dimensional figure with one vertex and one circular base. | **cono** Figura tridimensional con un vértice y una base circular. | |
| **congruent** Having the same size and shape. | **congruentes** Que tienen la misma forma y el mismo tamaño. | |
| **congruent angles** Angles that have the same measure. | **ángulos congruentes** Ángulos que tienen la misma medida. |  m $\angle ABC$ = m $\angle DEF$ |
| **congruent figures** Two figures whose corresponding sides and angles are congruent. | **figuras congruentes** Figuras que tienen el mismo tamaño y forma. | |
| **congruent line segments** Two line segments that have the same length. | **segmentos congruentes** Dos segmentos que tienen la misma longitud. | |
| **conjecture** A statement that is believed to be true. | **conjetura** Enunciado que se supone verdadero. | |
| **constant** A value that does not change. | **constante** Valor que no cambia. | $3, 0, \pi$ |
| **coordinates** The numbers of an ordered pair that locate a point on a coordinate graph. | **coordenadas** Los números de un par ordenado que ubican un punto en una gráfica de coordenadas. |  The coordinates of B are (−2, 3) |

| ENGLISH | SPANISH | EXAMPLES |
| --- | --- | --- |

**coordinate grid**  A grid formed by the intersection of horizontal and vertical lines that is used to locate points.

**cuadrícula de coordenadas**  Cuadricula formado por la intersección de líneas horizontales y líneas verticales que se usando por localizar puntos.

---

**coordinate plane**  A plane formed by the intersection of a horizontal number line called the *x*-axis and a vertical number line called the *y*-axis.

**plano cartesiano**  Plano formado por la intersección de una recta numérica horizontal llamada eje *x* y otra vertical llamada eje *y*.

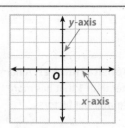

---

**correspondence**  The relationship between two or more objects that are matched.

**correspondencia**  La relación entre dos o más objetos que coinciden.

---

**corresponding angles (for lines)**  Angles in the same position formed when a third line intersects two lines.

**ángulos correspondientes (en líneas)**  Ángulos en la misma posición formaron cuando una tercera linea interseca dos lineas.

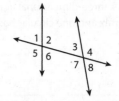

$\angle 1$ and $\angle 3$ are corresponding angles.

---

**corresponding angles (in polygons)**  Angles in the same relative position in polygons with an equal number of sides.

**ángulos correspondientes (en polígonos)**  Ángulos que se ubican en la misma posición relativa en polígonos que tienen el mismo número de lados.

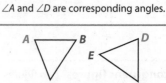

$\angle A$ and $\angle D$ are corresponding angles.

---

**corresponding sides**  Sides in the same relative position in polygons with an equal number of sides.

**lados correspondientes**  Lados que se ubican en la misma posición relativa en polígonos que tienen el mismo número de lados.

$\overline{AB}$ and $\overline{DE}$ are corresponding sides.

---

**counterclockwise**  A circular movement in the direction shown.

**en sentido contrario a las manecillas del reloj**  Movimiento circular en la dirección que se indica.

---

**credit card**  A plastic card issued by a financial company allowing a customer to buy goods or services on credit.

**tarjeta de crédito**  Tarjeta de pago plástica que un cliente puede utilizar para comprar bienes o servicios. El cliente puede pagar por las compras a plazos, pero pagará intereses en el saldo restante.

---

**credit history**  Information about how a consumer has borrowed and repaid debt.

**historia crediticia**  Información del buen manejo de dinero y pago de cuentas por parte de un cliente.

Glossary/Glosario

**credit report** A report containing detailed information on a person's credit history.

**informe crediticio** Informe que recopilan las agencias acerca de la historia crediticia de un cliente y que ayuda a los prestamistas a decidir si dan dinero a crédito a los clientes.

---

**credit score** A number based on information in a consumer's credit report that measures an individual's creditworthiness.

**calificación crediticia** Número basado en información de un informe crediticio de un cliente. Se usa para predecir la posibilidad de que una persona se retrase en hacer pagos o que no pague una deuda.

---

**cross product** The product of numbers on the diagonal when comparing two ratios.

**producto cruzado** El producto de los números multiplicados en diagonal cuando se comparan dos razones.

For the proportion $\frac{2}{3} = \frac{4}{6}$, the cross products are $2 \cdot 6 = 12$ and $3 \cdot 4 = 12$.

---

**cube (geometric figure)** A rectangular prism with six congruent square faces.

**cubo (figura geométrica)** Prisma rectangular con seis caras cuadradas congruentes.

---

**cube (in numeration)** A number raised to the third power.

**cubo (en numeración)** Número elevado a la tercera potencia.

$5^3 = 5 \cdot 5 \cdot 5 = 125$

---

**cumulative frequency** The frequency of all data values that are less than or equal to a given value.

**frecuencia acumulativa** Muestra el total acumulado de las frecuencias.

---

**customary system** The measurement system often used in the United States.

**sistema usual de medidas** El sistema de medidas que se usa comúnmente en Estados Unidos.

inches, feet, miles, ounces, pounds, tons, cups, quarts, gallons

---

**cylinder** A three-dimensional figure with two parallel, congruent circular bases connected by a curved lateral surface.

**cilindro** Figura tridimensional con dos bases circulares paralelas y congruentes, unidas por una superficie lateral curva.

## D

**debit card** An electronic card issued by a financial institution that allows a customer to access their account to withdraw cash or pay for goods and services

**tarjeta de débito** Tarjeta de pago plástica que un cliente puede usar para pagar por bienes o servicios. El dinero se retira inmediatamente de la cuenta corriente o de ahorros del cliente.

---

**degree** The unit of measure for angles or temperature.

**grado** Unidad de medida para ángulos y temperaturas.

**Glossary/Glosario**

**denominator** The bottom number of a fraction that tells how many equal parts are in the whole.

**denominador** Número de abajo en una fracción que indica en cuántas partes iguales se divide el entero.

$\frac{3}{4}$ ◀── denominator

---

**dependent events** Events for which the outcome of one event affects the probability of the other.

**sucesos dependientes** Dos sucesos son dependientes si el resultado de uno afecta la probabilidad del otro.

A bag contains 3 red marbles and 2 blue marbles. Drawing a red marble and then drawing a blue marble without replacing the first marble is an example of dependent events.

---

**dependent variable** The output of a function; a variable whose value depends on the value of the input, or independent variable.

**variable dependiente** Salida de una función; variable cuyo valor depende del valor de la entrada, o variable independiente.

For $y = 2x + 1$, $y$ is the dependent variable. input: $x$ output: $y$

---

**diagonal** A line segment that connects two non-adjacent vertices of a polygon.

**diagonal** Segmento de recta que une dos vértices no adyacentes de un polígono.

---

**diameter** A line segment that passes through the center of a circle and has endpoints on the circle, or the length of that segment.

**diámetro** Segmento de recta que pasa por el centro de un círculo y tiene sus extremos en la circunferencia, o bien la longitud de ese segmento.

---

**difference** The result when one number is subtracted from another.

**diferencia** El resultado de restar un número de otro.

---

**dimension** The length, width, or height of a figure.

**dimensión** Longitud, ancho o altura de una figura.

---

**discount** The amount by which the original price is reduced.

**descuento** Cantidad que se resta del precio original de un artículo.

---

**Distributive Property** The property that states if you multiply a sum by a number, you will get the same result if you multiply each addend by that number and then add the products.

**Propiedad distributiva** Propiedad que establece que, si multiplicas una suma por un número, obtendrás el mismo resultado que si multiplicas cada sumando por ese número y luego sumas los productos.

$5(20 + 1) = 5 \cdot 20 + 5 \cdot 1$

---

**dividend** The number to be divided in a division problem.

**dividendo** Número que se divide en un problema de división.

In $8 \div 4 = 2$, 8 is the dividend.

---

**divisible** Can be divided by a number without leaving a remainder.

**divisible** Que se puede dividir entre un número sin dejar residuo.

18 is divisible by 3.

---

**divisor** The number you are dividing by in a division problem.

**divisor** El número entre el que se divide en un problema de división.

In $8 \div 4 = 2$, 4 is the divisor.

---

**dot plot** A visual display in which each piece of data is represented by a dot above a number line.

**diagrama de puntos** Despliegue visual en que cada dato se representa con un punto sobre una recta numérica.

**double-bar graph** A bar graph that compares two related sets of data.

**gráfica de doble barra** Gráfica de barras que compara dos conjuntos de datos relacionados.

Students at Hill Middle School

**double-line graph** A graph that shows how two related sets of data change over time.

**gráfica de doble línea** Gráfica lineal que muestra cómo cambian con el tiempo dos conjuntos de datos relacionados.

Population Growth

## E

**edge** The line segment along which two faces of a polyhedron intersect.

**arista** Segmento de recta donde se intersecan dos caras de un poliedro.

Edge

**elements** The words, numbers, or objects in a set.

**elementos** Palabras, números u objetos que forman un conjunto.

Elements of A: 1, 2, 3, 4

**empty set** A set that has no elements.

**conjunto vacío** Un conjunto que no tiene elementos.

**endpoint** A point at the end of a line segment or ray.

**extremo** Un punto ubicado al final de un segmento de recta o rayo.

$A$        $B$

$D$

**equally likely** Outcomes that have the same probability.

**igualmente probables** Resultados que tienen la misma probabilidad de ocurrir.

When you toss a coin, the outcomes "heads" and "tails" are equally likely.

**equation** A mathematical sentence that shows that two expressions are equivalent.

**ecuación** Enunciado matemático que indica que dos expresiones son equivalentes.

$x + 4 = 7$
$6 + 1 = 10 - 3$

**equilateral triangle** A triangle with three congruent sides.

**triángulo equilátero** Triángulo con tres lados congruentes.

**equivalent** Having the same value.

**equivalentes** Que tienen el mismo valor.

**equivalent expression** Equivalent expressions have the same value for all values of the variables.

**expresión equivalente** Las expresiones equivalentes tienen el mismo valor para todos los valores de las variables.

$4x + 5x$ and $9x$ are equivalent expressions.

| ENGLISH | SPANISH | EXAMPLES |
|---|---|---|
| **equivalent fractions** Fractions that name the same amount or part. | **fracciones equivalentes** Fracciones que representan la misma cantidad o parte. | $\frac{1}{2}$ and $\frac{2}{4}$ are equivalent fractions. |
| **equivalent ratios** Ratios that name the same comparison. | **razones equivalentes** Razones que representan la misma comparación. | $\frac{1}{2}$ and $\frac{2}{4}$ are equivalent ratios. |
| **estimate (n)** An answer that is close to the exact answer and is found by rounding or other methods. | **estimación (s)** Una solución aproximada a la respuesta exacta que se halla mediante el redondeo u otros métodos. | |
| **estimate (v)** To find an answer close to the exact answer by rounding or other methods. | **estimar (v)** Hallar una solución aproximada a la respuesta exacta mediante el redondeo u otros métodos. | |
| **evaluate** To find the value of a numerical or algebraic expression. | **evaluar** Hallar el valor de una expresión numérica o algebraica. | Evaluate $2x + 7$ for $x = 3$. $2x + 7$ $2(3) + 7$ $6 + 7$ $13$ |
| **even number** A whole number that is divisible by two. | **número par** Un número cabal que es divisible entre dos. | |
| **event** An outcome or set of outcomes of an experiment or situation. | **suceso** Un resultado o una serie de resultados de un experimento o una situación. | |
| **expanded form** A number written as the sum of the values of its digits. | **forma desarrollada** Número escrito como suma de los valores de sus dígitos. | 236,536 written in expanded form is $200,000 + 30,000 + 6,000 + 500 + 30 + 6$. |
| **experiment** In probability, any activity based on chance. | **experimento** En probabilidad, cualquier actividad basada en la posibilidad. | Tossing a coin 10 times and noting the number of "heads." |
| **experimental probability** The ratio of the number of times an event occurs to the total number of trials, or times that the activity is performed. | **probabilidad experimental** Razón del número de veces que ocurre un suceso al número total de pruebas o al número de veces que se realiza el experimento. | Kendra attempted 27 free throws and made 16 of them. Her experimental probability of making a free throw is $\frac{\text{number made}}{\text{number attempted}} = \frac{16}{27} \approx 0.59$. |
| **exponent** The number that indicates how many times the base is used as a factor. | **exponente** Número que indica cuántas veces se usa la base como factor. | $2^3 = 2 \cdot 2 \cdot 2 = 8$; 3 is the exponent. |
| **exponential form** A number is in exponential form when it is written with a base and an exponent. | **forma exponencial** Cuando se escribe un número con una base y un exponente, está en forma exponencial. | $4^2$ is the exponential form for $4 \cdot 4$. |
| **expression** A mathematical phrase that contains operations, numbers, and/or variables. | **expresión** Enunciado matemático que contiene operaciones, números y/o variables. | $6x + 1$ |

**F**

| | | |
|---|---|---|
| **face** A flat surface of a polyhedron. | **cara** Lado plano de un poliedro. | Face |
| **factor** A number that is multiplied by another number to get a product. | **factor** Número que se multiplica por otro para hallar un producto. | 7 is a factor of 21 since $7 \cdot 3 = 21$. |
| **factor tree** A diagram showing how a whole number breaks down into its prime factors. | **árbol de factores** Diagrama que muestra cómo se descompone un número cabal en sus factores primos. | 12<br>3 · 4<br>2 · 2<br>$12 = 3 \cdot 2 \cdot 2$ |
| **Fahrenheit** A temperature scale in which 32 °F is the freezing point of water and 212 °F is the boiling point of water. | **Fahrenheit** Escala de temperatura en la que 32 °F es el punto de congelación del agua y 212 °F es el punto de ebullición. | |
| **fair** When all outcomes of an experiment are equally likely, the experiment is said to be fair. | **justo** Se dice de un experimento donde todos los resultados posibles son igualmente probables. | When tossing a fair coin, heads and tails are equally likely. Each has a probability of $\frac{1}{2}$. |
| **formula** A rule showing relationships among quantities. | **fórmula** Regla que muestra relaciones entre cantidades. | $A = \ell w$ is the formula for the area of a rectangle. |
| **fraction** A number in the form $\frac{a}{b}$, where $b \neq 0$. | **fracción** Número escrito en la forma $\frac{a}{b}$, donde $b \neq 0$. | |
| **frequency** The number of times a data value occurs. | **frecuencia** Cantidad de veces que aparece el valor en un conjunto de datos. | In the data set 5, 6, 7, 8, 6, the data value 6 has a frequency of 2. |
| **frequency table** A table that lists items together according to the number of times, or frequency, that the items occur. | **tabla de frecuencia** Una tabla en la que se organizan los datos de acuerdo con el número de veces que aparece cada valor (o la frecuencia). | Data set: 1, 1, 2, 2, 3, 4, 5, 5, 5, 6, 6<br>Frequency table: |
| **front-end estimation** An estimating technique in which the front digits of the addends are added. | **estimación por partes** Técnica en la que se suman sólo los números enteros de los sumandos. y luego se ajusta la suma para tener una estimacion mas exacta. | Estimate 25.05 + 14.671 with the sum 25 + 14 = 39. The actual value is 39 or greater. |
| **function** An input-output relationship that has exactly one output for each input. | **función** Relación de entrada-salida en la que a cada valor de entrada corresponde un valor de salida. | 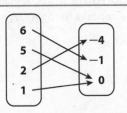 |

Frequency table:

| Date | Frequency |
|---|---|
| 1 | 2 |
| 2 | 2 |
| 3 | 1 |
| 4 | 1 |
| 5 | 3 |
| 6 | 2 |

| | ENGLISH | SPANISH | EXAMPLES |
|---|---|---|---|

**function table** A table of ordered pairs that represent solutions of a function.

**tabla de funciónes** Tabla de pares ordenados que representan soluciones de una función.

| x | 3 | 4 | 5 | 6 |
|---|---|---|---|---|
| y | 7 | 9 | 11 | 13 |

## G

**grants** Money awarded to students that does not need to be repaid.

**beca** Dinero que se otorga a estudiantes y el cual no se necesita devolver.

**graph of an equation** A graph of the set of ordered pairs that are solutions of the equation.

**gráfica de una ecuación** Gráfica del conjunto de pares ordenados que son soluciones de la ecuación.

**greatest common factor (GCF)** The largest common factor of two or more given numbers.

**máximo común divisor (MCD)** El mayor de los factores comunes compartidos por dos o más números dados.

The GCF of 27 and 45 is 9.

## H

**height** In a triangle or quadrilateral, the perpendicular distance from the base to the opposite vertex or side. In a prism or cylinder, the perpendicular distance between the bases.

**altura** En un triángulo o cuadrilátero, la distancia perpendicular desde la base de la figura al vértice o lado opuesto. En un prisma o cilindro, la distancia perpendicular entre las bases.

**heptagon** A seven-sided polygon.

**heptágono** Polígono de siete lados.

**hexagon** A six-sided polygon.

**hexágono** Polígono de seis lados.

**histogram** A bar graph that shows the frequency of data within equal intervals.

**histograma** Gráfica de barras que muestra la frecuencia de los datos en intervalos iguales.

**Starting Salaries**

Frequency: 40, 30, 20, 10, 0
Salary range (thousand $): 20–29, 30–39, 40–49, 50–59

**hypotenuse** In a right triangle, the side opposite the right angle.

**hipotenusa** En un triángulo rectángulo, el lado opuesto al ángulo recto.

hypotenuse

Glossary/Glosario

**I**

| ENGLISH | SPANISH | EXAMPLES |
|---|---|---|
| **Identity Property (for Multiplication)** The property that states that the product of 1 and any number is that number. | **Propiedad de identidad (de la multiplicación)** Propiedad que establece que el producto de 1 y cualquier número es ese número. | $5 \times 1 = 5$<br>$-8 \times 1 = -8$ |
| **Identity Property (for Addition)** The property that states the sum of zero and any number is that number. | **Propiedad de identidad (de la suma)** Propiedad que establece que la suma de cero y cualquier número es ese número. | $7 + 0 = 7$<br>$-9 + 0 = -9$ |
| **improper fraction** A fraction in which the numerator is greater than or equal to the denominator. | **fracción impropia** Fracción cuyo numerador es mayor que o igual al denominador. | $\frac{5}{5}$<br><br>$\frac{7}{3}$ |
| **independent variable** The input of a function; a variable whose value determines the value of the output, or dependent variable. | **variable independiente** Entrada de una función; variable cuyo valor determina el valor de la salida, o variable dependiente. | For $y = 2x + 1$, $x$ is the dependent variable. Input: $x$ output: $y$ |
| **indirect measurement** The technique of using similar figures and proportions to find a measure. | **medición indirecta** La técnica de usar figuras semejantes y proporciones para hallar una medida. | |
| **inequality** A mathematical sentence that shows the relationship between quantities that are not equal. | **desigualdad** Enunciado matemático que muestra una relación entre cantidades que no son iguales. | $5 < 8$<br>$5x + 2 \geq 12$ |
| **input** The value substituted into an expression or function. | **valor de entrada** Valor que se usa para sustituir una variable en una expresión o función. | For the rule $y = 6x$, the input 4 produces an output of 24. |
| **integer** A member of the set of whole numbers and their opposites. | **entero** Un miembro del conjunto de los números cabales y sus opuestos. | $\ldots -3, -2, -1, 0, 1, 2, 3, \ldots$ |
| **interest** The amount of money charged for borrowing or using money, or the amount of money earned by saving money. | **interés** Cantidad de dinero que se cobra por el préstamo o uso del dinero, o la cantidad que se gana al ahorrar dinero. | |
| **interquartile range (IQR)** The difference of the third (upper) and first (lower) quartiles in a data set, representing the middle half of the data. | **rango intercuartil (RIC)** Diferencia entre el tercer cuartil (superior) y el primer cuartil (inferior) de un conjunto de datos, que representa la mitad central de los datos. | Lower half    Upper half<br>18, (23), 28,    29, (36), 42<br>First quartile    Third quartile<br>Interquartile range:<br>$36 - 23 = 13$ |
| **intersecting lines** Lines that cross at exactly one point. | **rectas secantes** Líneas que se cruzan en un solo punto. | |

**Glossary/Glosario**

**intersection (sets)** The set of elements common to two or more sets.

**intersección (de conjuntos)** Conjunto de elementos comunes a dos o más conjuntos.

**interval** The space between marked values on a number line or the scale of a graph.

**intervalo** El espacio entre los valores marcados en una recta numérica o en la escala de una gráfica.

**inverse operations** Operations that undo each other: addition and subtraction, or multiplication and division.

**operaciones inversas** Operaciones que se cancelan mutuamente: suma y resta, o multiplicación y división.

**isosceles triangle** A triangle with at least two congruent sides.

**triángulo isósceles** Triángulo que tiene al menos dos lados congruentes.

**L**

**lateral surface** In a cylinder, the curved surface connecting the circular bases; in a cone, the curved surface that is not a base.

**superficie lateral** En un cilindro, superficie curva que une las bases circulares; en un cono, la superficie curva que no es la base.

Lateral surface

**least common denominator (LCD)** The least common multiple of two or more denominators.

**mínimo común denominador (m.c.d.)** El mínimo común múltiplo de dos o más denominadores.

The LCD of $\frac{3}{4}$ and $\frac{5}{6}$ is 12.

**least common multiple (LCM)** The smallest number, other than zero, that is a multiple of two or more given numbers.

**mínimo común múltiplo (m.c.m.)** El menor de los múltiplos (distinto de cero) de dos o más números.

The LCM of 10 and 18 is 90.

**like fractions** Fractions that have the same denominator.

**fracciones semejantes** Fracciones que tienen el mismo denominador.

$\frac{5}{12}$ and $\frac{3}{12}$ are like fractions.

**like terms** Terms with the same variables raised to the same exponents.

**términos semejantes** Términos con las mismas variables elevadas a los mismos exponentes.

$3a^2b^2$ and $7a^2b^2$

**line** A straight path that has no thickness and extends forever.

**recta** Trayectoria recta que no tiene ningún grueso y que se extiende por siempre.

$\ell$

**line graph** A graph that uses line segments to show how data changes.

**gráfica lineal** Gráfica que muestra cómo cambian los datos mediante segmentos de recta.

**Marlon's Video Game Scores**

Score — 1200, 800, 400

Game number — 1 2 3 4 5 6

| ENGLISH | SPANISH | EXAMPLES |
|---------|---------|----------|
| **line plot** A number line with marks or dots that show frequency. | **diagrama de puntos** Recta numérica con marcas o puntos que indican la frecuencia. | **Number of Pets** |
| **line of reflection** A line that a figure is flipped across to create a mirror image of the original figure. | **línea de reflexión** Línea sobre la cual se invierte una figura para crear una imagen reflejada de la figura original. | **Line of reflection** |
| **line of symmetry** The imaginary "mirror" in line symmetry. | **eje de simetría** El <<espejo>> imaginario en la simetría axial. | |
| **line segment** A part of a line between two endpoints. | **segmento de recta** Parte de una línea con dos extremos. | $\overset{\bullet}{A} \overset{\bullet}{B}$ |
| **line symmetry** A figure has line symmetry if one half is a mirror image of the other half. | **simetría axial** Una figura tiene simetría axial si una de sus mitades es la imagen reflejada de la otra. | |
| **linear equation** An equation whose solutions form a straight line on a coordinate plane. | **ecuación lineal** Ecuación en la que las soluciones forman una línea recta en un plano cartesiano. | $y = 2x + 1$ |

## M

| | | |
|---------|---------|----------|
| **mean** The sum of the items in a set of data divided by the number of items in the set; also called *average*. | **media** La suma de todos los elementos de un conjunto de datos dividida entre el número de elementos del conjunto. | Data set: 4, 6, 7, 8, 10 <br> Mean: $\frac{4+6+7+8+10}{5} = \frac{35}{5} = 7$ |
| **median** The middle number or the mean (average) of the two middle numbers in an ordered set of data. | **mediana** El número intermedio o la media (el promedio) de los dos números intermedios en un conjunto ordenado de datos. | Data set: 4, 6, 7, 8, 10 <br> Median: 7 |
| **measure of center** A measure used to describe the middle of a data set. Also called measure of central tendency. | **medida central** Medida que se usa para describir el centro de un conjunto de datos; la media, la mediana y la moda son medidas centrales. También se conocen como medidas de tendencia central. | |

**Glossary/Glosario**

**measure of spread** A measure that describes how far apart the data are distributed.

**medida de dispersión** Medida que describe la separación en una distribución de datos.

---

**metric system** A decimal system of weights and measures that is used universally in science and commonly throughout the world.

**sistema métrico** Sistema decimal de pesos y medidas empleado universalmente en las ciencias y por lo general en todo el mundo.

centimeters, meters, kilometers, grams, kilograms, milliliters, liters

---

**midpoint** The point that divides a line segment into two congruent line segments.

**punto medio** El punto que divide un segmento de recta en dos segmentos de recta congruentes.

$A$    $B$    $C$

$B$ is the midpoint of $\overline{AC}$.

---

**mixed number** A number made up of a whole number that is not zero and a fraction.

**número mixto** Número compuesto por un número cabal distinto de cero y una fracción.

$5\frac{1}{8}$

---

**mode** The number or numbers that occur most frequently in a set of data; when all numbers occur with the same frequency, we say there is no mode.

**moda** Número o números más frecuentes en un conjunto de datos; si todos los números aparecen con la misma frecuencia, no hay moda.

Data set: 3, 5, 8, 8, 10
Mode: 8

---

**multiple** The product of a number and any nonzero whole number.

**múltiplo** El producto de un número y cualquier número cabal distinto de cero es un múltiplo de ese número.

---

**Multiplication Property of Zero** The property that states that the product of any number and 0 is 0.

**Propiedad de multiplicación del cero** Propiedad que establece que el producto de cualquier número y 0 es 0.

$6 \times 0 = 0$
$-5 \times 0 = 0$

---

**multiplicative inverse** One of two numbers whose product is 1.

**inverso multiplicativo** Uno de dos números cuyo producto es igual a 1.

The multiplicative inverse of $\frac{3}{4}$ is $\frac{4}{3}$.

---

**negative number** A number less than zero.

**número negativo** Número menor que cero.

$-2$ is a negative number.

$\leftarrow$ | | | | | | | | $\rightarrow$
$-4\ -3\ -2\ -1\ \ 0\ \ 1\ \ 2\ \ 3\ \ 4$

---

**net** An arrangement of two-dimensional figures that can be folded to form a polyhedron.

**plantilla** Arreglo de figuras bidimensionales que se doblan para formar un poliedro.

10 m    10 m
6 m    6 m

---

**numerator** The top number of a fraction that tells how many parts of a whole are being considered.

**numerador** El número de arriba de una fracción; indica cuántas partes de un entero se consideran.

$\frac{3}{4}$ $\longleftarrow$ numerator

---

**numerical expression** An expression that contains only numbers and operations.

**expresión numérica** Expresión que incluye sólo números y operaciones.

$(2 \cdot 3) + 1$

**0**

**obtuse angle** An angle whose measure is greater than 90° but less than 180°.

**ángulo obtuso** Ángulo que mide más de 90° y menos de 180°.

**obtuse triangle** A triangle containing one obtuse angle.

**triángulo obtusángulo** Triángulo que tiene un ángulo obtuso.

**odd number** A whole number that is not divisible by two.

**número impar** Un número cabal que no es divisible entre dos.

**opposites** Two numbers that are an equal distance from zero on a number line.

**opuestos** Dos números que están a la misma distancia de cero en una recta numérica.

5 and −5 are opposites.

**order of operations** A rule for evaluating expressions: first perform the operations in parentheses, then compute powers and roots, then perform all multiplication and division from left to right, and then perform all addition and subtraction from left to right.

**orden de las operaciones** Regla para evaluar expresiones: primero se resuelven las operaciones entre paréntesis, luego se hallan las potencias y raíces, después todas las multiplicaciones y divisiones de izquierda a derecha y, por último, todas las sumas y restas de izquierda a derecha.

| $3^2 - 12 \div 4$ | Evaluate the power. |
| $9 - 12 \div 4$ | Divide. |
| $9 - 3$ | Subtract. |
| $6$ | |

**ordered pair** A pair of numbers that can be used to locate a point on a coordinate plane.

**par ordenado** Par de números que sirven para ubicar un punto en un plano cartesiano.

The coordinates of $B$ are $(-2, 3)$.

**origin** The point where the x-axis and y-axis intersect on the coordinate plane; (0, 0).

**origen** Punto de intersección entre el eje x y el eje y en un plano cartesiano: (0, 0).

**outcome** A possible result of a probability experiment.

**resultado** Posible resultado de un experimento de probabilidad.

When rolling a number cube, the possible outcomes are 1, 2, 3, 4, 5, and 6.

**outlier** A value much greater or much less than the others in a data set.

**valor atípico** Un valor mucho mayor o menor que los demás valores de un conjunto de datos.

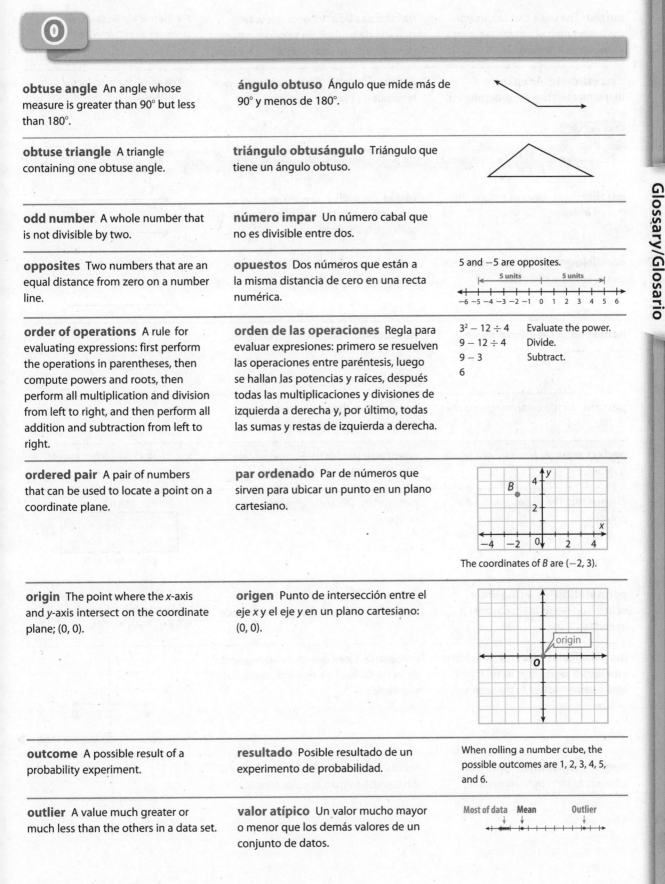

Glossary/Glosario

**output** The value that results from the substitution of a given input into an expression or function. | **valor de salida** Valor que resulta después de sustituir un valor de entrada determinado en una expresión o función. | For the rule $y = 6x$, the input 4 produces an output of 24.

**overestimate** An estimate that is greater than the exact answer. | **estimación alta** Estimación mayor que la respuesta exacta. | 100 is an overestimate for the sum $23 + 24 + 21 + 22$.

# P

**parallel lines** Lines in a plane that do not intersect. | **rectas paralelas** Líneas que se encuentran en el mismo plano pero que nunca se intersecan. | 

**parallelogram** A quadrilateral with two pairs of parallel sides. | **paralelogramo** Cuadrilátero con dos pares de lados paralelos. |

**pentagon** A five-sided polygon. | **pentágono** Polígono de cinco lados. |

**percent** A ratio comparing a number to 100. | **porcentaje** Razón que compara un número con el número 100. | $45\% = \frac{45}{100}$

**perfect square** A square of a whole number. | **cuadrado perfecto** El cuadrado de un número cabal. | $5^2 = 25$, so 25 is a perfect square.

**perimeter** The distance around a polygon. | **perímetro** Distancia alrededor de un polígono. |

18 ft
6 ft
perimeter = 48 ft

**permutation** An arrangement of items or events in which order is important. | **permutación** Arreglo de objetos o sucesos en el que el orden es importante. | For objects A, B, and C, there are 6 different permutations: ABC, ACB, BAC, BCA, CAB, CBA.

**perpendicular bisector** A line that intersects a segment at its midpoint and is perpendicular to the segment. | **mediatriz** Línea que cruza un segmento en su punto medio y es perpendicular al segmento. |

$\ell$ is the perpendicular bisector of $\overline{AB}$.

**perpendicular lines** Lines that intersect to form right angles. | **rectas perpendiculares** Líneas que al intersecarse forman ángulos rectos. |

Glossary/Glosario

| ENGLISH | SPANISH | EXAMPLES |
|---|---|---|
| **pi ($\pi$)** The ratio of the circumference of a circle to the length of its diameter; $\pi \approx 3.14$ or $\frac{22}{7}$. | **pi ($\pi$)** Razón de la circunferencia de un círculo a la longitud de su diámetro; $\pi < 3.14$ ó $\frac{22}{7}$. | |
| **plane** A flat surface that has no thickness and extends forever. | **plano** Superficie plana que no tiene ningún grueso y que se extiende por siempre. | plane *R* or plane *ABC* |
| **point** An exact location that has no size. | **punto** Ubicación exacta que no tiene ningún tamaño. | *P* • point *P* |
| **polygon** A closed plane figure formed by three or more line segments that intersect only at their endpoints. | **polígono** Figura plana cerrada, formada por tres o más segmentos de recta que se intersecan sólo en sus extremos. | |
| **polyhedron** A three-dimensional figure in which all the surfaces or faces are polygons. | **poliedro** Figura tridimensional cuyas superficies o caras tienen forma de polígonos. | |
| **population** The whole group being surveyed. | **población** El grupo completo que es objeto de estudio. | In a survey about eating habits of middle school students, the population is all middle school students. |
| **positive number** A number greater than zero. | **número positivo** Número mayor que cero. | 2 is a positive number. |
| **power** A number produced by raising a base to an exponent. | **potencia** Número que resulta al elevar una base a un exponente. | $2^3 = 8$, so 2 to the 3rd power is 8. |
| **prediction** A guess about something that will happen in the future. | **predicción** Pronóstico sobre algo que puede ocurrir en el futuro. | |
| **prime factorization** A number written as the product of its prime factors. | **descomposición en factores primos** Un número escrito como el producto de sus factores primos. | $10 = 2 \cdot 5$ $24 = 2^3 \cdot 3$ |
| **prime number** A whole number greater than 1 that has exactly two factors, itself and 1. | **número primo** Número cabal mayor que 1 que sólo es divisible entre 1 y él mismo. | 5 is prime because its only factors are 5 and 1. |
| **principal** The initial amount of money borrowed or saved. | **capital** Cantidad inicial de dinero depositada o recibida en préstamo. | |
| **prism** A polyhedron that has two congruent, polygon-shaped bases and other faces that are all rectangles. | **prisma** Poliedro con dos bases congruentes con forma de polígono y caras con forma de rectángulos. | |

| ENGLISH | SPANISH | EXAMPLES |
|---|---|---|
| **probability** A number from 0 to 1 (or 0% to 100%) that describes how likely an event is to occur. | **probabilidad** Un número entre 0 y 1 (ó 0% y 100%) que describe qué tan probable es un suceso. | A bag contains 3 red marbles and 4 blue marbles. The probability of randomly choosing a red marble is $\frac{3}{7}$. |
| **product** The result when two or more numbers are multiplied. | **producto** Resultado de multiplicar dos o más números. | The product of 4 and 8 is 32. |
| **proper fraction** A fraction in which the numerator is less than the denominator. | **fracción propia** Fracción en la que el numerador es menor que el denominador. | $\frac{3}{4}, \frac{1}{13}, \frac{7}{8}$ |
| **proportion** An equation that states that two ratios are equivalent. | **proporción** Ecuación que establece que dos razones son equivalentes. | $\frac{2}{3} = \frac{4}{6}$ |
| **protractor** A tool for measuring angles. | **transportador** Instrumento para medir ángulos. | |
| **pyramid** A polyhedron with a polygon base and triangular sides that all meet at a common vertex. | **pirámide** Poliedro cuya base es un polígono; tiene caras triangulares que se juntan en un vértice común. |  |

# Q

| | | |
|---|---|---|
| **quadrant** The *x*- and *y*-axes divide the coordinate plane into four regions. Each region is called a quadrant. | **cuadrante** El eje *x* y el eje *y* dividen el plano cartesiano en cuatro regiones. Cada región recibe el nombre de cuadrante. | Quadrant II, Quadrant I, Quadrant III, Quadrant IV |
| **quartile** Three values, one of which is the median, that divide a data set into fourths. | **cuartil** Cada uno de tres valores, uno de los cuales es la mediana, que dividen en cuartos un conjunto de datos. | First quartile least value, Third quartile Median greatest value 2 4 6 8 10 12 14 |
| **quotient** The result when one number is divided by another. | **cociente** Resultado de dividir un número entre otro. | In $8 \div 4 = 2$, 2 is the quotient. |

# R

| | | |
|---|---|---|
| **radius** A line segment with one endpoint at the center of a circle and the other endpoint on the circle, or the length of that segment. | **radio** Segmento de recta con un extremo en el centro de un círculo y el otro en la circunferencia, o bien la longitud de ese segmento. |  |

**range** In statistics, the difference between the greatest and least values in a data set.

**rango (en estadística)** Diferencia entre los valores máximo y mínimo de un conjunto de datos.

---

**rate** A ratio that compares two quantities measured in different units.

**tasa** Una razón que compara dos cantidades medidas en diferentes unidades.

---

**rate of change** A ratio that compares the difference between two output values to the difference between the corresponding input values.

**tasa de cambio** Razón que compara la diferencia entre dos salidas con la diferencia entre dos entrados.

The cost of mailing a letter increased from 22 cents in 1985 to 25 cents in 1988. The rate of change was
$$\frac{25 - 22}{1988 - 1985} = \frac{3}{3}$$
$$= 1 \text{ cent per year.}$$

---

**rate of interest** The percent charged or earned on an amount of money; see *simple interest*.

**tasa de interés** Porcentaje que se cobra por una cantidad de dinero prestada o que se gana por una cantidad de dinero ahorrada; ver *interés simple*.

---

**ratio** A comparison of two quantities by division.

**razón** Comparación de dos cantidades mediante una división.

12 to 25, 12:25, $\frac{12}{25}$

---

**rational number** A number that can be written in the form $\frac{a}{b}$, where $a$ and $b$ are integers and $b \neq 0$.

**número racional** Número que se puede expresar como $\frac{a}{b}$, donde $a$ y $b$ son números enteros y $b \neq 0$.

3, 1.75, $0.\overline{3}$, $-\frac{2}{3}$, 0

---

**ray** A part of a line that starts at one endpoint and extends forever in one direction.

**rayo** Parte de una línea que comienza en un extremo y se extiende siempre en una dirección.

---

**reciprocal** One of two numbers whose product is 1.

**recíproco** Uno de dos números cuyo producto es igual a 1.

The reciprocal of $\frac{2}{3}$ is $\frac{3}{2}$.

---

**rectangle** A parallelogram with four right angles.

**rectángulo** Paralelogramo con cuatro ángulos rectos.

---

**rectangular prism** A polyhedron whose bases are rectangles and whose other faces are rectangles.

**prisma rectangular** Poliedro cuyas bases son rectángulos y cuyas caras tienen forma de rectángulos.

---

**reflection** A transformation of a figure that flips the figure across a line.

**reflexión** Transformación que ocurre cuando se invierte una figura sobre una línea.

---

**regular polygon** A polygon with congruent sides and angles.

**polígono regular** Polígono con lados y ángulos congruentes.

Glossary/Glosario

| ENGLISH | SPANISH | EXAMPLES |
|---------|---------|----------|
| **relative frequency** The ratio of the number of times an event or data value occurs and the total number of events or data values. | **frecuencia relativa** La razón del número de veces que ocurre un evento o dato (frecuencia) al total del número de eventos o datos. | |
| **repeating decimal** A decimal in which one or more digits repeat infinitely. | **decimal periódico** Decimal en el que uno o más dígitos se repiten infinitamente. | $0.75757575\ldots = 0.\overline{75}$ |
| **rhombus** A parallelogram with all sides congruent. | **rombo** Paralelogramo en el que todos los lados son congruentes. | |
| **right angle** An angle that measures 90°. | **ángulo recto** Ángulo que mide exactamente 90°. | |
| **right triangle** A triangle containing a right angle. | **triángulo rectángulo** Triángulo que tiene un ángulo recto. | |
| **rotation** A transformation in which a figure is turned around a point. | **rotación** Transformación que ocurre cuando una figura gira alrededor de un punto. | |
| **rotational symmetry** A figure that can be rotated about a point by an angle less than 360° so that the image coincides with the preimage has rotational symmetry. | **simetría de rotación** Una figura que puede rotarse alrededor de un punto en un ángulo menor de 360° de forma tal que la imagen coincide con la imagen original que tenga simetría de rotación. | 90° 90° 90° 90° |
| **rounding** Replacing a number with an estimate of that number to a given place value. | **redondear** Sustituir un número por una estimación de ese número hasta cierto valor posicional. | 2,354 rounded to the nearest thousand is 2,000; 2,354 rounded to the nearest 100 is 2,400. |

## S

| ENGLISH | SPANISH | EXAMPLES |
|---------|---------|----------|
| **sales tax** A percent of the cost of an item, which is charged by governments to raise money. | **impuesto sobre la venta** Porcentaje del costo de un artículo que los gobiernos cobran para recaudar fondos. | |
| **sample** A part of a group being surveyed. | **muestra** Parte de un grupo que es objeto de estudio. | In a survey about eating habits of middle school math students, a sample is a survey of 100 randomly chosen students. |

| ENGLISH | SPANISH | EXAMPLES |
|---|---|---|
| **sample space** All possible outcomes of an experiment. | **espacio muestral** Conjunto de todos los resultados posibles de un experimento. | When rolling a number cube, the sample space is 1, 2, 3, 4, 5, 6. |
| **scale** The ratio between two sets of measurements. | **escala** La razón entre dos conjuntos de medidas. | 1 cm: 5 mi |
| **scale drawing** A drawing that uses a scale to make an object proportionally smaller than or larger than the real object. | **dibujo a escala** Dibujo en el que se usa una escala para que un objeto se vea proporcionalmente mayor o menor que el objeto real al que representa. | A blueprint is an example of a scale drawing. |
| **scale model** A proportional model of a three-dimensional object. | **modelo a escala** Modelo proporcional de un objeto tridimensional. | |
| **scalene triangle** A triangle with no congruent sides. | **triángulo escaleno** Triángulo que no tiene lados congruentes. | |
| **scholarship** A monetary award to a student to support their education. | **becas** Dinero que se otorga a los estudiantes en base a logros. | |
| **scientific notation** A method of writing very large or very small numbers by using powers of 10. | **notación científica** Método que se usa para escribir números muy grandes o muy pequeños mediante potencias de 10. | $12{,}560{,}000{,}000{,}000 = 1.256 \times 10^{13}$ |
| **segment** A part of a line made of two endpoints and all points between them. | **segmento** Parte de una línea que consiste en dos extremos y todos los puntos entre éstos. | |
| **sequence** An ordered list of numbers. | **secuencia** Lista ordenada de números. | 2, 4, 6, 8, 10, . . . |
| **set** A group of items. | **conjunto** Un grupo de elementos. | |
| **side** A line bounding a geometric figure; one of the faces forming the outside of an object. | **lado** Línea que delimita las figuras geométricas; una de las caras que forman la parte exterior de un objeto. | |
| **significant figures** The figures used to express the precision of a measurement. | **dígitos significativos** Dígitos usados para expresar la precisión de una medida. | |
| **similar** Figures with the same shape but not necessarily the same size are similar. | **semejantes** Figuras que tienen la misma forma, pero no necesariamente el mismo tamaño. | |

**simple event** An event consisting of only one outcome.

**suceso simple** Suceso que tiene sólo un resultado.

In the experiment of rolling a number cube, the event consisting of the outcome 3 is a simple event.

---

**simple interest** A fixed percent of the principal. It is found using the formula $I = Prt$, where $P$ represents the principal, $r$ the rate of interest, and $t$ the time.

**interés simple** Un porcentaje fijo del capital. Se calcula con la fórmula $I = Cit$, donde $C$ representa el capital, $i$, la tasa de interés y $t$, el tiempo.

---

**simplest form (of a fraction)** A fraction is in simplest form when the numerator and denominator have no common factors other than 1.

**mínima expresión (de una fracción)** Una fracción está en su mínima expresión cuando el numerador y el denominador no tienen más factor común que 1.

Fraction: $\frac{8}{12}$
Simplest form: $\frac{2}{3}$

---

**simplify** To write a fraction or expression in simplest form.

**simplificar** Escribir una fracción o expresión numérica en su mínima expresión.

---

**simulation** A model of an experiment, often one that would be too difficult or too time-consuming to actually perform.

**simulación** Representación de un experimento, por lo regular de uno cuya realización sería demasiado difícil o llevaría mucho tiempo.

---

**skew lines** Lines that lie in different planes that are neither parallel nor intersecting.

**líneas oblicuas** Líneas que se encuentran en planos distintos, por eso no se intersecan ni son paralelas.

---

**slope** The constant rate of change of a line.

**pendiente** La tasa de cambio constante de una línea.

---

**solid figure** A three-dimensional figure.

**cuerpo geométrico** Figura tridimensional.

---

**solution of an equation** A value or values that make an equation true.

**solución de una ecuación** Valor o valores que hacen verdadera una ecuación.

Equation: $x + 2 = 6$
Solution: $x = 4$

---

**solution of an inequality** A value or values that make an inequality true.

**solución de una desigualdad** Valor o valores que hacen verdadera una desigualdad.

Inequality: $x + 3 \geq 10$
Solution set: $x \geq 7$

---

| ENGLISH | SPANISH | EXAMPLES |
|---|---|---|

**solution set** The set of values that make a statement true.

**conjunto solución** Conjunto de valores que hacen verdadero un enunciado.

Inequality: $x + 3 \geq 5$
Solution set: $x \geq 2$

$$-4 \; -3 \; -2 \; -1 \;\; 0 \;\; 1 \;\; 2 \;\; 3 \;\; 4 \;\; 5 \;\; 6$$

---

**solve** To find an answer or a solution.

**resolver** Hallar una respuesta o solución.

---

**square (geometry)** A rectangle with four congruent sides.

**cuadrado (en geometría)** Rectángulo con cuatro lados congruentes.

---

**square (numeration)** A number raised to the second power.

**cuadrado (en numeración)** Número elevado a la segunda potencia.

In $5^2$, the number 5 is squared.

---

**square number** A number that is the product of a whole number and itself.

**cuadrado de un número** El producto de un número cabal multiplicado por sí mismo.

25 is a square number since $5^2 = 25$.

---

**square root** A number that is multiplied by itself to form a product is called a square root of that product.

**raíz cuadrada** El número que se multiplica por sí mismo para formar un producto se denomina la raíz cuadrada de ese producto.

$16 = 4 \cdot 4$ and $16 = -4 \cdot -4$, so 4 and $-4$ are square roots of 16.

---

**standard form (in numeration)** A number written using digits.

**forma estándar** Una forma de escribir números por medio de dígitos.

Five thousand, two hundred ten in standard form is 5,210.

---

**statistical question** A question that has many different, or variable, answers.

**pregunta estadística** Pregunta con muchas respuestas o variables diferentes.

---

**stem-and-leaf plot** A graph used to organize and display data so that the frequencies can be compared.

**diagrama de tallo y hojas** Gráfica que muestra y ordena los datos, y que sirve para comparar las frecuencias.

| Stem | Leaves |
|---|---|
| 3 | 2 3 4 4 7 9 |
| 4 | 0 1 5 7 7 7 8 |
| 5 | 1 2 2 3 |

Key: 3|2 means 3.2

---

**straight angle** An angle that measures 180°.

**ángulo llano** Ángulo que mide exactamente 180°.

---

**subset** A set contained within another set.

**subconjunto** Conjunto que pertenece a otro conjunto.

---

**substitute** To replace a variable with a number or another expression in an algebraic expression.

**sustituir** Reemplazar una variable por un número u otra expresión en una expresión algebraica.

---

**sum** The result when two or more numbers are added.

**suma** Resultado de sumar dos o más números.

**supplementary angles** Two angles whose measures have a sum of 180°.

**ángulos suplementarios** Dos ángulos cuyas medidas suman 180°.

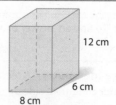

30°  150°

**surface area** The sum of the areas of the faces, or surfaces, of a three-dimensional figure.

**área total** Suma de las áreas de las caras, o superficies, de una figura tridimensional.

12 cm

6 cm

8 cm

Surface area = 2(8)(12) + 2(8)(6) + 2(12)(6) = 432cm²

## T

**term (in an expression)** The parts of an expression that are added or subtracted.

**término (en una expresión)** Las partes de una expresión que se suman o se restan.

$3x^2 +$    $6x -$    $8$
↑          ↑        ↑
Term      Term     Term

**terminating decimal** A decimal number that ends, or terminates.

**decimal finito** Decimal con un número determinado de posiciones decimales.

6.75

**tessellation** A repeating pattern of plane figures that completely cover a plane with no gaps or overlaps.

**teselado** Patrón repetido de figuras planas que cubren totalmente un plano sin superponerse ni dejar huecos.

**theoretical probability** The ratio of the number of ways an event can occur to the total number of equally likely outcomes.

**probabilidad teórica** Razón del numero de las maneras que puede ocurrir un suceso al numero total de resultados igualmente probables.

When rolling a number cube, the theoretical probability of rolling a 4 is $\frac{1}{6}$.

**tip** The amount of money added to a bill for service; usually a percent of the bill.

**propina** Cantidad que se agrega al total de una factura por servicios. Por lo general, es un porcentaje del total de la factura.

**transformation** A change in the size or position of a figure.

**transformación** Cambio en el tamaño o la posición de una figura.

**translation** A movement (slide) of a figure along a straight line.

**traslación** Desplazamiento de una figura a lo largo de una línea recta.

**trapezoid** A quadrilateral with exactly one pair of parallel sides.

**trapecio** Cuadrilátero con un par de lados paralelos.

B ——→ C

A ——→ D

| ENGLISH | SPANISH | EXAMPLES |
|---|---|---|
| **tree diagram** A branching diagram that shows all possible combinations or outcomes of an event. | **diagrama de árbol** Diagrama ramificado que muestra todas las posibles combinaciones o resultados de un suceso. | |
| **trial** Each repetition or observation of an experiment. | **prueba** Cada repetición u observación de un experimento. | In the experiment of rolling a number cube, each roll is one trial. |
| **triangle** A three-sided polygon. | **triángulo** Polígono de tres lados. | |
| **Triangle Sum Theorem** The theorem that states that the measures of the angles in a triangle add to 180°. | **Teorema de la suma del triángulo** Teorema que establece que las medidas de los ángulos de un triángulo suman 180°. | |
| **triangular prism** A polyhedron whose bases are triangles and whose other faces are rectangles. | **prisma triangular** Poliedro cuyas bases son triángulos y cuyas demás caras tienen forma de rectángulos. | |

# U

| ENGLISH | SPANISH | EXAMPLES |
|---|---|---|
| **underestimate** An estimate that is less than the exact answer. | **estimación baja** Estimación menor que la respuesta exacta. | 100 is an underestimate for the sum $26 + 29 + 31 + 27$. |
| **union** The set of all elements that belong to two or more sets. | **unión** El conjunto de todos los elementos que pertenecen a dos o más conjuntos. | |
| **unit conversion** The process of changing one unit of measure to another. | **conversión de unidades** Proceso que consiste en cambiar una unidad de medida por otra. | |
| **unit rate** A rate in which the second quantity in the comparison is one unit. | **tasa unitaria** Una tasa en la que la segunda cantidad de la comparación es una unidad. | 10 cm per minute |
| **unlike fractions** Fractions with different denominators. | **fracciones distintas** Fracciones con distinto denominador. | $\frac{3}{4}$ and $\frac{1}{2}$ are unlike fractions. |

**Glossary/Glosario**

## V

**variable** A symbol used to represent a quantity that can change.

**variable** Símbolo que representa una cantidad que puede cambiar.

In the expression $2x + 3$, $x$ is the variable.

---

**variation (variability)** The spread of values in a set of data.

**variación (variabilidad)** Amplitud de los valores de un conjunto de datos.

The data set {1, 5, 7, 10, 25} has greater variation than the data set {8, 8, 9, 9, 9}.

---

**Venn diagram** A diagram that is used to show relationships between sets.

**diagrama de Venn** Diagrama que muestra las relaciones entre conjuntos.

---

**vertical angles** A pair of opposite congruent angles formed by intersecting lines.

**ángulos opuestos por el vértice** Par de ángulos opuestos congruentes formados por líneas secantes.

∠1 and ∠3 are vertical angles.
∠2 and ∠4 are vertical angles.

---

**volume** The number of cubic units needed to fill a given space.

**volumen** Número de unidades cúbicas que se necesitan para llenar un espacio.

Volume = $3 \cdot 4 \cdot 12 = 144 \text{ ft}^3$

## W

**work-study program** Program in which students are able to work at jobs on campus to make money to pay their college tuition.

**programas de trabajo y estudio** Programas que permiten a los estudiantes universitarios trabajar a medio tiempo y así ganar dinero para las matrículas universitarias y los gastos.

## X

**x-axis** The horizontal axis on a coordinate plane.

**eje x** El eje horizontal del plano cartesiano.

| ENGLISH | SPANISH | EXAMPLES |
|---|---|---|

**x-coordinate**  The first number in an ordered pair; it tells the distance to move right or left from the origin, (0, 0).

**coordenada x**  El primer número en un par ordenado; indica la distancia que debes avanzar hacia la izquierda o hacia la derecha desde el origen, (0, 0).

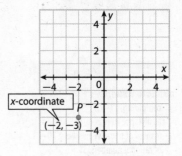

## Y

**y-axis**  The vertical axis on a coordinate plane.

**eje y**  El eje vertical del plano cartesiano.

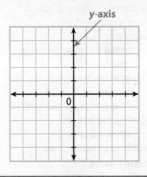

**y-coordinate**  The second number in an ordered pair; it tells the distance to move up or down from the origin, (0, 0).

**coordenada y**  El segundo número en un par ordenado; indica la distancia que debes avanzar hacia arriba o hacia abajo desde el origen, (0, 0).

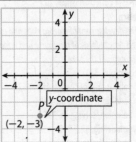

## Z

**zero pair**  A number and its opposite, which add to 0.

**par nulo**  Un número y su opuesto, que sumados dan 0.

18 and −18

# Index

Index

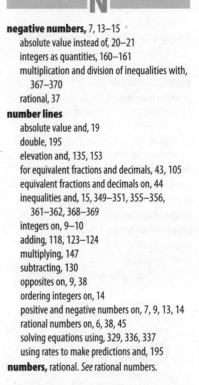

Index

representing rates with, 213
writing equations from, 393–395
**ten-by-ten grids,** 235, 242
**terms,** 182, 311
**test prep.** *See* Texas Test Prep.
**test-taking tips.** *See* Hot Tip.
**Texas Test Prep,** 26, 50, 55–56, 88, 112, 142, 166, 173–174, 200, 230, 256, 261–262, 288, 316, 344, 374, 406, 415–416, 442, 472, 477–478, 518, 521–522, 554, 559–560
**three-dimensional figures,** 465–468
**three-panel flip charts,** 267
**trapezoids,** 448–449, 460
**triangle inequality relationship,** 424
**triangles**
area of, 453–456, 459
determining when three lengths form, 422, 423–426
problem solving using area of, 459
relationship between sides and angles in, 435–437
sum of angle measures in, 422, 429–431
**tri-folds,** 29, 203, 527
**two-panel flip charts,** 179, 347

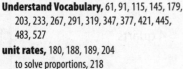

**Understand Vocabulary,** 61, 91, 115, 145, 179, 203, 233, 267, 291, 319, 347, 377, 421, 445, 483, 527
**unit rates,** 180, 188, 189, 204
to solve proportions, 218
using to convert units, 224–225
**units**
converting using conversion factors, 225–226
using models to convert, 223
using proportions and unit rates to convert, 204, 224–225
**Unpacking the TEKS,** 6, 30, 62, 92, 116, 146, 180, 204, 234, 268, 292, 320, 348, 378, 422, 446, 484, 528
**upper quartile,** 491

**variable data,** statistical questions and, 497
**variables,** 294
independent and dependent in tables and graphs, 385–389
writing equations from tables and, 394–395
**Venn diagrams,** 30, 33
**veterinarian,** 547
**Video Tutor.** *See* Math on the Spot.
**vocabulary,** 22, 35, 325, 382, 397, 432, 438, 514
Understand Vocabulary, 61, 91, 115, 145, 179, 203, 233, 267, 291, 319, 347, 377, 421, 445, 483, 527
Visualize Vocabulary, 5, 29, 61, 91, 115, 145, 179, 203, 233, 267, 291, 319, 347, 377, 421, 445, 483, 527
Vocabulary Preview, 2, 58, 176, 264, 418, 480, 524
**volume equations,** 465–468

**wages,** salaries, careers and, 547–550
**water,** weight and size of, 467
**websites,** paying for college and, 542
**weight,** measurements of, 224
**What If?** 12, 81, 110, 133, 152, 160, 191, 209, 215, 276, 293, 314, 331, 393, 458, 487, 503, 504, 516, 533, 534
**whole numbers**
classifying, 30
dividing decimals by, 100
multiplying with fractions, 65–66
Venn diagram of, 33
**work-study programs,** 528, 541

**x-axis,** 379
**x-coordinate,** 379

**y-axis,** 379
**y-coordinate,** 379

**zero**
absolute value and, 6
division by, 154
as exponent, 270
points on axes and, 380
properties of operations and, 309
**zero pairs,** 124

Index

# TABLE OF MEASURES

| METRIC | CUSTOMARY |
|---|---|

## Length

| | |
|---|---|
| 1,000 millimeters (mm) = 1 meter (m) | 1 foot (ft) = 12 inches (in.) |
| 100 centimeters (cm) = 1 meter | 1 yard (yd) = 3 feet |
| 10 millimeters = 1 centimeter | 1 yard = 36 inches |
| 10 decimeters (dm) = 1 meter | 1 mile (mi) = 5,280 feet |
| 1 kilometer (km) = 1000 meters | 1 mile = 1,760 yards |

## Capacity

| | |
|---|---|
| 1,000 milliliters (mL) = 1 liter (L) | 1 cup (c) = 8 fluid ounces (fl oz) |
| 100 centiliters (cL) = 1 liter | 1 pint (pt) = 2 cups |
| 10 deciliters (dL) = 1 liter | 1 quart (qt) = 2 pints |
| 1 kiloliter (kL) = 1,000 liters | 1 quart = 4 cups |
| | 1 gallon (gal) = 4 quarts |

## Mass / Weight

| Mass | Weight |
|---|---|
| 1,000 milligrams (mg) = 1 gram (g) | 1 pound (lb) = 16 ounces (oz) |
| 100 centigrams (cg) = 1 gram | 1 ton (T) = 2,000 pounds |
| 10 decigrams (dg) = 1 gram | |
| 1 kilogram (kg) = 1,000 grams | |

| TIME | |
|---|---|
| 1 minute (min) = 60 seconds (s) | 1 year (yr) = 12 months (mo) |
| 1 hour (hr) = 60 minutes | 1 year = 52 weeks |
| 1 day = 24 hours | 1 year = 365 days |
| 1 week (wk) = 7 days | 1 leap year = 366 days |

# FORMULAS

## Perimeter

| | |
|---|---|
| Rectangle | $P = 2\ell + 2w$ or $P = 2(\ell + w)$ |
| Square | $P = 4s$ |

## Circumference

| | |
|---|---|
| Circle | $C = 2\pi r$ or $C = \pi d$ |

## Area

| | |
|---|---|
| Circle | $A = \pi r^2$ |
| Parallelogram | $A = bh$ |
| Rectangular | $A = \ell w$ or $A = bh$ |
| Square | $A = s^2$ |
| Rhombus | $A = \frac{1}{2} d_1 d_2$ or $A = \frac{d_1 d_2}{2}$ |
| Trapezoid | $A = \frac{1}{2}(b_1 + b_2)h$ or $A = \frac{(b_1 + b_2)h}{2}$ |
| Triangle | $A = \frac{1}{2} bh$ or $A = \frac{bh}{2}$ |

## Volume

| | |
|---|---|
| Cylinder | $V = Bh$ or $V = \pi r^2 h$ |
| Cube | $V = s^3$ |
| Rectangle prism | $V = Bh$ or $V = \ell wh$ |
| Triangular prism | $V = Bh$ |
| Cone | $V = \frac{1}{3} Bh$ or $V = \frac{1}{3} \pi r^2 h$ |
| Pyramid | $V = \frac{1}{3} Bh$ |
| Sphere | $V = \frac{4}{3} \pi r^3$ |

## Surface Area

**Cylinder:**

| | |
|---|---|
| Lateral | $L = Ch$ or $L = 2\pi rh$ |
| Total | $S = 2B + L$ or $S = 2\pi r^2 + 2\pi rh$ |

**Prism:**

| | |
|---|---|
| Lateral | $L = Ph$ |
| Total | $S = 2B + L$ or $S = 2B + Ph$ |

## Other

| | |
|---|---|
| Distance traveled | $d = 2r$ |
| Interest (simple) | $I = Prt$ |
| Pythagorean Theorem | $a^2 + b^2 = c^2$ |

# SYMBOLS

| | | | |
|---|---|---|---|
| $\neq$ | is not equal to | $\pi$ | pi: (about 3.14) |
| $\approx$ | is approximately equal to | $\perp$ | is perpendicular to |
| $10^2$ | ten squared; ten to the second power | $\parallel$ | is parallel to |
| | | $\overleftrightarrow{AB}$ | line $AB$ |
| $2.\overline{6}$ | repeating decimal 2.66666... | $\overrightarrow{AB}$ | ray $AB$ |
| $\lvert -4 \rvert$ | the absolute value of negative 4 | $\overline{AB}$ | line segment $AB$ |
| $\sqrt{\phantom{x}}$ | square root | $m\angle A$ | measure of $\angle A$ |